Augustine and Nicene Theology

Augustine and Nicene Theology

Essays on Augustine and the Latin Argument for Nicaea

Michel René Barnes

CASCADE *Books* · Eugene, Oregon

AUGUSTINE AND NICENE THEOLOGY
Essays on Augustine and the Latin Argument for Nicaea

Cascade Books
An Imprint of Wipf and Stock Publishers
199 W. 8th Ave., Suite 3
Eugene, OR 97401

www.wipfandstock.com

PAPERBACK ISBN: 978-1-7252-9215-4
HARDCOVER ISBN: 978-1-7252-9216-1
EBOOK ISBN: 978-1-7252-9217-8

Cataloguing-in-Publication data:

Names: Barnes, Michel R., author.

Title: Augustine and nicene theology : essays on Augustine and the latin argument for Nicaea / Michel René Barnes.

Description: Eugene, OR : Cascade Books, 2023 | Includes bibliographical references and index.

Identifiers: ISBN 978-1-7252-9215-4 (paperback) | ISBN 978-1-7252-9216-1 (hardcover) | ISBN 978-1-7252-9217-8 (ebook)

Subjects: LCSH: Augustine, of Hippo, Saint, 354–430. | Theology—History—Early church, ca. 30–600.

Classification: BR65.A9 B37 2023 (print) | BR65.A9 B37 (ebook)

01/31/23

for my mother,
Renée Denise Ponchin Barnes
and
for my father,
Lewis Barnes (who once was poor)

With love, their sons

Contents

Contents

Preface

I FIRST PUBLISHED ON Augustine in 1992. All my Augustine articles since have followed the question of Augustine as a Latin Nicene. Although many of these chapters were first published as articles, published together they can be read beneficially in the sequence they have here as a book and not simply a collection. This book would never have seen the light of day without the generous indulgences of the editors at Wipf and Stock Publishers. This book would not exist if it were not for bottomless well of energy of Lewis Ayres: Lewis motivated me, guided me, goaded me, and he served as the editor of this volume, in all its bits and pieces. I am also grateful for the decades we have had as friends and research partners. Four other scholar friends also each played an essential part in stimulating the "Augustine Ressourcement" to which this volume bears witness: The Right Rev. Rowan Williams; Rev. Gilles Emery OP; James Wetzel; John Cavadini. Finally, but first in the realm of patience, support, and care, I must thank my beautiful and loving wife, Julia, who endured many (many) days of the loss of me to my work. Julia must rank as a co-conspirator with Lewis as agent of this publication.

Through God's grace I have whatever merits sharing.

Michel René Barnes

Abbreviations

AugStud	*Augustinian Studies*
CCSL	*Corpus Christianorum Series Latina*
CPL	*Clavis Patrum Latinorum*
FotC	*Fathers of the Church*
JECS	*Journal of Early Christian Studies*
JThS	*Journal of Theological Studies*
ANF	*Ante-Nicene Fathers*
NPNF	*Nicene and Post Nicene Fathers*
PG	*Patrologia Graeca*
PL	*Patrologia Latina*
RecAug	*Recherches Augustiniennes*
SC	*Sources Chrétiennes*
SP	*Studia Patristica*
TS	*Theological Studies*

Introduction

THIS BOOK PRESENTS A series of essays on Augustine and Latin Nicene Trinitarian theology. Many of the essays have been published before; three of them are foundational for contemporary scholarship on Augustine; two of those essays take the ground out from under contemporary Trinitarian systematics, and as such, since 1995 they have been boycotted by systematicians where there is no outright ban on reading them. The shock that continues is shared by Catholic and Protestant systematicians alike. This new appearance of them, together for the first time (!), reiterates what, some think, should never have been spoken in the first place. The suffocated will not stay dead, oxygen or no oxygen, because the accuracy of these two articles cannot be disputed—cannot be disputed, at least, without reading a shelf-full of books equally defiling to the twentieth-century myth of self-definition among systematic theologians (those, at least, who still can read Latin—or French).[1] Nonetheless, garlic in hand, read on! The collection begins with those articles "theologically unsuited in part for all." All the articles in this collection were written with the aim of re-narrating accepted accounts of Augustine's Trinitarian theology and the character of Latin Nicene theology in general. False narratives of Latin Nicene theology supported an equally fictional account of Augustine's Trinitarian theology; Augustine's theology thus established retroactively supported the narratives regarding the character of Latin theology generally. However, once the ideological circle had been severed, accounts of Latin patristic Trinitarian theology were relieved of the burden of preparing for and supporting the ideologically constructed genealogy of "Augustine and Western Trinitarian theology";

---

1. After such a build-up, the young who read the essays for the first time here should be prepared for a sense of anti-climax—some of which is justified, and some of which lies in the fact that you do not know how it is, as Freud taught us, that when one mask falls to the floor, the others slip, and you become aware of the performance nature of the whole.

the subject could be explored for its own sake. "Augustine's Trinitarian theology" and "Latin, Nicene, pre-Augustinian Trinitarian theology" were both in need of Rereadings by fresh eyes of scholars who knew the utilities the books had previously served and were driven now by the desire to read these texts in the world of texts they had once lived in. There were no other desires that could provide the necessary blend of excitement and patience, the intransigence and the verve.

The historical Augustine was rejected at both ends of the doctrinal spectrum. Moderns were outraged to see that what they regarded as a law of gravity—the ahistorical, monist Augustine—was revealed to be a creation of late-nineteenth-century scholasticism. But living scholastics, Thomists, were irritated by the distance between Trinitarian theology of the historical Augustine and "their" Augustine with his proto-scholastic Trinitarian theology. Scholastics and moderns had investments in the ahistorical, monist Augustine: the first because he was their creature, but they could not allow that to be admitted; the Augustine the moderns hated was the scholastic Augustine. The scholastics defended their creature against modern-day critics; the moderns attacked the Augustine created by the scholastics because he was successfully the necessary "other"—and because they did not want to admit that their "dialectical" Augustine had no purchase in history. (How could he create medieval scholasticism when he was its creature? And *a fortiori*, scholasticism had to pre-exist sufficiently to create and fill out this "Augustine" that, after all, had survived five- to seven-hundred years of scrutiny, hostile and otherwise). The scholastics wanted no part in the historical Augustine and did not like him being "recovered"—thus, my technical Augustine writings that seemed innocuous to moderns were, in each historical reconstruction, a desecration. What the scholastics had feared in 1940 would happen to Thomas's credibility as an exegete was happening now from—of all places—a ressourcement of Augustine!

The first two articles in this collection are two sides of a single coin: they are both fruits of my research as a doctoral student in Toronto at the St. Michael's Library of the Pontifical Institute of Medieval Studies. The library houses the best collection of nineteenth- and twentieth-century French Catholic scholarship available in North America. It was there I read Régnon. There are only seven sets of this three-volume work in North America—none of them west of the Mississippi: two sets are in Ontario, Canada, four sets are in American University libraries, and, lately, I own the seventh (after it was "discarded" by a major Catholic University on the East Coast).[2] My original research was for a paper in a systematics course on the Trinity.[3] It later

2. As a search on WorldCat will reveal, the "lore" was not accurate: there are several other sets available in North America, though the catalogue does not list the sets in Toronto and Ottawa.

3. The reader will notice that neither article ever quotes Augustine, or any other patristic author. The final version was a hermeneutical study of the "reception" of Augustine's Trinitarian theology. David Brown's *The Divine Trinity* had the most influence on me because he recognized and labeled the two dominant Trinitarian hermeneutics current in the West: the "unity model" and the "plurality model" (UM and PM, respectively).

won an award from the Canadian Patristic Society, and later still was presented as a session paper at CTSA. The original paper was too long to be an article, so I split it in two and added to each half. The session version of "Régnon Reconsidered" was first read publicly at NAPS, where it was warmly received. The other half, with references to contemporary French- and English-language references, was published as an article in *Theological Studies*. The two articles make this case: what has been accepted by the vast majority of theologians as a self-evident fact or truism that "Western theology began with unity, while Eastern theology began with plurality" is actually a hermeneutical *construct* by the late-nineteenth-century French Catholic scholastic Théodore de Régnon, SJ.[4] What I called "Régnon's paradigm" became a kind of theological virus that had infected most Catholic, Protestant, and Orthodox theologians. An antinomic articulation of "Western unity" versus "Eastern plurality" became a theorem foundational in most modern Trinitarian theologies.[5] This simplistic (or Ideal) antinomy of Greek and Latin Trinitarian theologies has been regarded by modern systematicians as "too big to fail," i.e., too foundational to be given up.[6]

What ultimately gave force to the charge that the reading "Augustine's Trinitarian theology starts with Unity" was a modern construct were the articles by myself and Lewis Ayres that revealed that there was indeed an "Augustine outside the caricature," and thus reading his theology relieved of the antinomic hermeneutic provides what had hitherto been so difficult to render: it put Augustine *into history*.[7] Alongside the attempts to peel away both the *scholastic Augustine* and the *Neoplatonist Augustine*,[8] Ayres and I successfully revealed Augustine the *early fifth-century*

4. Régnon himself never accepted such simplistic characterizations as historically the case, and, in particular, his understanding of Western and Eastern theologies denied any antinomic relationship between Latin and Greek theology.

5. I never intended to "name names" because then the critique could be buried in ceaseless arguments over whether Prof. X's theology used Régnon's paradigm or not. The articles provide historical criteria for critiquing contemporary theologians. More importantly, they supported any student who read Gregory of Nyssa and Augustine and did not find the polarity in Trinitarian theologies between them that the reader had been taught was there.

6. At an academic conference, an established East Coast Catholic systematician greeted me by saying, "You took my Augustine away from me!" It was a melancholic statement, tinged with umbrage.

7. I had the privilege of being seated next to Prof. Peter Brown at a banquet at Villanova. He offered kind remarks about the paper I had given that day (here, chapter 11). Brown said that if he were to write another biography of Augustine, it would be an entirely different book, one built upon the letters and sermons recovered since he had written the first biography, as well as taking advantage of the historical context papers like mine provided. His intention in the first book had been to put Augustine into history, to take him out of the netherworld of scholasticism and make Augustine real. The only means available to him was to set Augustine within the Neoplatonic milieu, since Neoplatonists were historical figures and developing their philosophies in response to new challenges. Unfortunately, "Augustine as Neoplatonist" ultimately had a different effect: it moved Augustine from one ahistorical narrative to another. (I thought this happened as it did because, ironically, Neoplatonism became a fealty of scholasticism).

8. Both these groups of Augustine readers have proved to be as resistant to the "historical" Augustine reading as most modern theologians. My suspicion is that both scholastics and systematicians

Latin theologian.[9] However, I must be clear that my first two articles do not situate or read Augustine as a fifth-century Latin Nicene theologian; that is the underlying purpose of all the other essays. The first two readings simply reveal the late-nineteenth-century origins of the separation of Latin theology from Greek theology as "starting" with the unity of God verses "starting" with the plurality in God—and thus they deconstruct most of contemporary Trinitarian theology. The deconstruction and demythologization of most modern ideological readings is to uncover their origins and previous history.[10]

When I began to write on the Trinitarian theology of *De Trinitate* (c. 1990), I made a methodological judgment: I would read Augustine as a fifth-century Latin "Nicene" theologian. This was a radical judgment at the time, for hardly any scholars had thought to place the book within the context of Latin Nicene Trinitarian theology. He was considered as a fifth-century Aristotelian, a fifth-century Neoplatonist, and, most recently, as a fifth-century Stoic. Even the research on Augustine and the Pelagian controversy, which seemed intrinsically to invoke historical context, was written within a very small world. The most obvious way to read his Trinitarian theology, it seemed to me, was to read it as a fourth- and fifth-century Latin Nicene work of polemic—a perspective that had hardly, if ever, been taken before. Thousands of articles have been written on *De Trinitate* (*On the Trinity*) without locating it within fourth-century Latin Nicene theology: no words spoken.[11]

Before I first read the *De Trinitate*, I was already familiar with the writings of fourth-century Latin "Nicene" theologians such as Hilary of Poitiers and Ambrose

---

work from the same "Augustine": the Augustinian Trinitarian theology that is the product of scholastic synthesis of the fragmentary pieces of *Trin.* provided by Lombard. Exempt from all these, and any other, criticisms of scholastic treatment is Fr. Roland Teske, SJ, deceased. Fr. Teske's scholarship stood above the barriers and moved freely wherever his search led him. He was unique as a scholar and as a person. I wish I had better used the short opportunity I had at Marquette University to learn from him.

9. As Ayres's book, *Augustine and the Trinity* (2010), later made clear, there was actually quite a lot to be said about Augustine as a Latin Nicene theologian.

10. The following references document the scholastic character of Régnon's paradigm. His earliest readers wrote from within the Thomist school, and their references ante-date Orthodox and English-reading theologians by years, if not decades. These references also testify to the scholastic "in-house" nature of Régnon's work, given that these French scholars are all but unknown in English-speaking Augustine scholarship. However, we need to note that by the mid-forties, Régnon's book was indeed known among French ressourcement and the Paris-based "neo-patristic movement" among the Orthodox; we know this through Lossky's citations of the book in his own Paris-based writings. These references are cited chronologically: Legrand, *La Notion philosophique de la Trinite chez Saint Augustin*; Chevalier. *Augustin et la Pensee Grecque*; Boyer, "L'image de la Trinite synthese de la pensee augustinienne"; Paissac, *Theologie du Verbe*; Malet, *Personne et Amour dans la theologie trinitaire de saint Thomas d'Aquin.*

11. The same year I wrote my paper on *Trin.* V, Brian Daley, SJ, wrote his essay, "The Giant's Twin Substances." By coincidence, we each "premiered" our papers at the Augustine conference at Marquette University, 1991. The piece is subtle and sensitive, and I was grateful to hear a scholar like Brian Daley raising the question of the anti-Arian context.

of Milan, as well as those of their anti-Nicene opponents. As I read *De Trinitate*, I recognized the presence of the same polemical tropes that I had seen in these late-fourth-century Latin Trinitarian "anti-Arians." My task then was to identify such passages in *De Trinitate* and other Trinitarian writings by Augustine, draw those passages out so that the "Arian" controversy could be recognized, and then to give an account of how Augustine's arguments were a "Nicene" response. Augustine's Trinitarian writings were, each to different degrees, written to counter the teachings of anti-Nicene Christians (who were enjoying some success in North Africa and Spain).

The next four chapters in the book treat, in this order, early Latin Trinitarian theology, varieties of Nicene theologies, varieties of Latin Nicene Trinitarian theologies, and Marius Victorinus' articulation of a non-Athanasian *homoousios*-Trinitarian theology. Some of the key concepts in Latin Trinitarian theologies, especially Latin Nicene theologies, may not be familiar to readers. Patristic Latin Trinitarian theologies, much less Latin Nicene theologies, have not been treated in depth or with finesse in many recent works on patristic theology—and it is important that the reader have an accurate understanding of this Trinitarian theology. A false understanding of the relevant Latin theology will lead to a false account of the motivation for and content of Augustine's Trinitarian theology.[12] If the four background chapters are read carefully, then it will become clear that, after Tertullian, Latin Trinitarian theology follows a fourfold logic: first, the most fundamental account of the unity of the Trinity is based upon the one power common to the Three; second, distinctions among the Three are explained in terms of inner-Trinitarian causal relationships;[13] third, each of the Three is himself and not the other Two; and fourth, what is Three in God we call "person" (*persona*). The argument from common power is tied to an argument that the Three Persons of the Trinity do the same works, and must therefore share the same nature. The argument from inner-Trinitarian causal relations means that the status of the Father as cause and the status of the Son (and Holy Spirit) as caused are eternal relations *within the Trinity*. (This approach to the identity of the Three also occurs in Greek theology. The emphasis on "The Father is the Father and not the Son; the Son is the Son and not the Father," etc., is a deeply embedded result of the anti-monarchian origins of Latin Trinitarian theology.) In Augustine's writings, the four propositions of this logic are sometimes taken as points that need to be proved, but more often, as

12. Each of these chapters stand on its own and can be read simply as treatments on each of the four subjects.

13. A good example of theology following this axiom may be found in Tertullian's *Treatise Against Praxeas* 2, where Tertullian contrasts his beliefs with those of Praxeas and the monarchians: "[We believe] that the only God has also a Son, the Word who proceedeth from himself." The origin of the Son is not tied to creation, nor is "Son" used only of the Incarnated Word. The Son and Word exist before being sent, not as part of God's creating act. In *Trin.* II:7–11, Augustine elaborates (at length) on how the Son/Word sends/is sent on his mission. Moreover, just as Tertullian goes from "the Son proceeds from God" to "the Son is sent" (as well as how the Holy Spirit is sent), Augustine goes on in *Trin.* from his "pre-existing" to his "being sent," and indeed the Son as divine sends himself as he shares the same power as the Father.

in *De Trinitate*, Augustine takes these four as axioms inherited from previous authors writing on the Trinity. Any reader familiar with classical logic or geometry will understand how axioms are the basis for the logic that allows the theo*logician* to adduce a large set of doctrines or propositions. Perhaps a more useful analogy is to compare these four points to four stars in the sky by which to navigate oceans filled with destinations. Augustine often starts his argument with a statement to the effect that "We know such and such to be true, so from this we can see . . ."

The chapter devoted solely to Victorinus deserves special attention. My first purpose for that chapter was to place Victorinus squarely within the mainstream trajectory of Latin Nicene polemical discourse in the writings of his contemporaries, Phoebadius of Agens and Gregory of Elvira; in the end, I found more common ground with Phoebadius than with Gregory.[14] Pierre Hadot has already argued that Victorinus writes in reaction to the proclamations of the Synod of Sirmium (357); I placed Victorinus within the same exegetical constellation of texts as "undoubtedly" Nicene authors. On the other hand, I wanted to recognize the unique character of a true Neoplatonic psychological analogy of the Trinity—which Victorinus explicitly offers, and which many scholastics and moderns falsely accuse Augustine's theology of teaching.[15] However, in the process of demonstrating this, I uncovered two new theses that have not, to my knowledge, ever been expressed before—and which, in retrospect, are perhaps more important judgments to share than those which initially motivated me (and which I accomplished). The first discovery is recognizing a "Victorine hermeneutic" at work in Augustine's *De Trinitate*—one which I had no idea came from Victorinus' polemics. This hermeneutic may be summarized as the decisive factor in any particular choice about where to engage the various layers of anti-Nicene theology: always engage the most contemporary and most fulsome articulation of anti-Nicene theology in preference to the old and/or simplistic articulation, whether in person or in writing.[16]

The second unexpected discovery is not unrelated to the first. As I just said, Victorinus engages contemporary substantial expressions of anti-Nicene theology. Victorinus is emphatically a believer in *homoousios* theology; indeed, in 357 he believes

14. Only the first four books of Hilary's *Trin.*, more properly called *De Fide*, are possibly contemporary to the writings I consider here. (Perhaps.) Only Hilary's pre-exilic writings are synchronous with my subject here, which is the first two books of Victorinus' *Against Arius*.

15. This judgment—that Augustine's theology does not use a psychological analogy of the Trinity—is a good example of what the "new" historical reading of Augustine says that fractures scholastic and modern Trinitarian construction alike.

16. This is true of all Augustine's public debates not only in Trinitarian matters: only the best. Recall the public debate between Augustine and the anti-Nicene Count Pascentius recounted in *Epistle 238*, or his reply to "the Arian Sermon," and his debate with Maximinus, Latin Homoianism's brightest star in the new century, showed this Victorine rhetorical hermeneutic firmly in place. Maximinus' theological roots lay with the Council of Rimini (359), and that seventy-year-old creed is what Maximus wanted to be recited as his creed at the beginning of the debate. Augustine refused to have the old creed read, and Maximinus recited a doctrinal summary which showed its character as the theology of Palladius (381) as well as the theologies of late-fourth- and early fifth-century Homoian documents, and the well-known anti-Nicene bishop, Ufilas.

that the Father, the Son and the Holy Spirit are all *homoousios*. He regards the Holy Spirit as feminine. He is completely at home in *ousia*-based Trinitarian theology, and argues against those theologies using points that derive from neo-Aristotelian logic provided by Porphyry. He has a strong one-power theology. He makes little use of the Father-Son relationship and does not appeal to it in his argument for *homoousios*. He does not understand *homoousios* to be a term originating with Nicaea, and he is uncertain about the reason it was emphasized by the council of three-hundred bishops at Nicaea in 318 or 325 or sometime around then—except as a decisive rejection of homoiousian theology (which was already in use in the late-third century). His arguments are consistently against contemporaries, and he makes little use of disproving the beliefs of Arius or of Arian writings thirty to forty years old. In 357 he condemns Marcellus and Eunomius, by name and in full knowledge of their doctrines. He regards *homoousios* as a treasure of the Great Church. He never mentions the name Athanasius and apparently has no knowledge of him or sense of him as significant. None of the statements here describing Victorinus account of *homoousios*—whether the affirmations or the denunciations—can be applied to Athanasius' own *homoousios* theology in 357–58; some, *or ever*. In short, we have in Victorinus' writings beginning in 357 a theology of *homoousios* which is not congruent with Athanasius.' Victorinus represents a Western *homoousios* theology that owes nothing to Athanasius (and in some ways, runs counter to that of his Greek contemporary). We should not hold Augustine to the emphases and language of what we can now recognize as the Athanasian hermeneutics for *homoousios* theology.

Each of the articles on Latin Trinitarian theology, the Latin Nicenes, Marius Victorinus, and those on Augustine have their own specific questions or topics to explore. I hope that all these chapters, taken together, will give the reader a sufficient fluency with the forms and contents of Latin Nicene theology, and not only support a synchronic hermeneutic for reading Augustine's Trinitarian theology.[17] More than all this, I think that when these chapters are read as a whole, a new judgment will arise that is beyond the scope of any one or two of the articles: a new judgment about "Augustine's Trinitarian theology"—namely that Augustine's Trinitarian theology did not survive the Middle Ages.[18] There were, undoubtedly, some years after Augustine's

17. As should become clear by the end of this book, Augustine's Trinitarian theology is not contained exclusively (or perhaps even most substantially) in the *Trin*. Moreover one should gain a sense of the dynamic at work diachronically in Latin Nicene Trinitarian theology generally. Lewis Ayres's monograph is indispensable as a means to understand the diachronic character of Augustine's Trinitarian theology: *Augustine and the Trinity*.

18. What first made me suspicious of the platitude of a "radical [conceptual] discontinuity" between scholastic articulations of Augustine's theology and modern articulations of his theology was the ease with which modern theologians "interrogated" Augustine's theology. This "ease of interrogation" is often found in the works of good theologians (e.g., Rahner). Moderns took scholastic lists of Augustine's Trinitarian doctrines, recognized enough of the logic and content of the doctrines on that list to enable them to articulate "an inverted Augustine": intra-Trinitarian versus extra-Trinitarian, primacy of the Word in the Incarnation, person as a rational substance, "grace" as a necessary concept

death during which theologians worked with the same intellectual concepts at hand; for approximately two centuries after Augustine's death there were Homoian (Arian) bishops in North Africa; sea lanes to southern Europe remained open; and whoever the Western "emperor" was that held jurisdiction over North Africa, he would claim to be "Roman." Over time, each of these would fall away until none were left. The complete text of *De Trinitate* was replaced by piecemeal quotation—which for centuries was the only way the text was known. New philosophies and conceptual idioms dominated reading, and a form of exegesis and commentary designed to "read" fragmented texts developed: scholasticism. Through this hermeneutic, "fragmentation" was lost as the disparate remains of previous books were woven into new unities by the emerging European culture of scholasticism, but the sense that something important might be missing was covered over by the intellectual seams that grew stronger as the independent vigor of post-Roman, neo-Latin cultures grew. Thomas and others developed sophisticated and dense literature based upon individual tropes originally found in the textual fragments. Somewhere in all this benign reception the logic and doctrine of Augustine's Trinitarian theology as expressed in his writings was denatured and reinvented as a hermeneutical bridge connecting islands of Augustinian thought otherwise lost or submerged. It is impressive to note that this "Augustinian Trinitarian theology"—even though a construct—was in itself strong enough and profound enough to last half a millennium—and counting.[19]

Each of these articles on *De Trinitate* directly is concerned with the interaction of exegesis and the development of doctrine in a polemical context. There is a longstanding debate about Augustine's motives for writing the book. He tells us that his friends implored him to write his thoughts out—but that does not answer the motive question: Why were Augustine's friends so keen on his writing a book that explained the Trinity? The motive which scholarship passed over was the one that seemed so

in salvation history, elevation of Trinitarian doctrine over Christological doctrine, Ideal discourse about God (flipped as discourse about the "idea" God and as a "God in history"), etc. There is lack of agreement with the doctrines of Augustine as presented, but there is nothing so indecipherable about those doctrines, nothing so alien that it interrupted a judgment on "useful" or "not useful." By contrast, when the theology of the "historical Augustine" is articulated by me or others, there is bafflement about where and how such a theology, or means of doing theology, "fits." How can one develop Nicene theology by following out, "The Son sees the Father perfectly"? Compare how easily "Augustine" can fit into a modern model of Trinitarians (right next to Thomas) without the difficulty there would be with Marius Victorinus or Hilary of Poitiers—neither of whom warranted a scholastic assimilation.

19. The Trinitarian theology expressed by Augustine in his books (376–429) was received by a theological culture unable to read them intelligently. A coherent body of thought emerged through the isogenesis of brilliant minds in the Middle Ages; but this coherent body did not derive in any substantial way from the patristic texts. The received theology was projected onto the historical texts as they emerged. Differences between what Augustine "said" in 412 and what he was perceived to have "said" in any text existing in 1412 (or 1912) that were accounted for were glossed over ("existent relations"?) by the scholastics. The theology of scholastic Augustine was received by all sides as the theology of the historical Augustine, and still is today. "Scholastic Augustine" who taught, e.g., a Neoplatonic triad of Father, Son, and Holy Spirit, etc., became one of the most enduring straw man in history since, e.g., *The Testimony of the Twelve Patriarchs.*

obvious to me: polemic. Augustine was offering a comprehensive discourse of counter readings of the Scripture passages that anti-Nicenes were preaching—with some success. But Augustine brought to this project an overriding concern that had driven his theology of God to that point, especially any theology regarding the being of the divine or the Trinity: our material minds remain so boxed in by our material imagination— our understanding of all reality is as though it were all material. Nothing was more important than that our minds should learn to think of God in an immaterial manner: to free our thoughts from the constraints imposed by thinking of material existence. Only if we were free to think immaterially could we form proper thoughts about God. Thus in *De Trinitate*, questions of material, immaterial, the habits of thought, and the purification of heart all figured in addressing the human being's seeking to understand the Trinity in such a way that gave greater confidence in love for him—or confidence that the God we hoped to love was indeed the God who made us, saved us, and brought us back to him. However, suggesting that *De Trinitate* belong to the genre of polemic was (and still is) a shocking idea to many of the book's readers!

Reading the Gospels makes it obvious that "inseparable operations" cannot mean "doing the exact same thing." The narratives contain distinct actors or agents— Jesus, John the Baptist, Mary, etc.—who do things. As I have remarked before, at Jesus' baptism at the river Jordan, Jesus steps into the river, the Father speaks, and the Holy Spirit (in the form of a dove) descends to rest over Jesus. An exegesis sensitive to Trinitarian "inseparable operations" does not overturn the narrative so as to claim—as if in a sidebar or footnote—that the Father and the Spirit stepped into the river too. In the New Testament it is clearly one of the three who is acting in the material world at any given point. The distinctness of each of the Three Persons of the Trinity is revealed by individual action in the created world—Judea, approximately two-thousand years ago, in this case. It is not a material coincidence of action that constitutes inseparable activity: it is a perfect unity of divine Will or Intention resulting in an action some aspect of which occurs in the material world, but other aspects of that commonly willed action occur outside the material world. Only awareness of the immaterial aspect of a specific act gives the reader an understanding of the complete action. This "outside the material world" can be the spiritual world, or it can mean the specific agreement or "assent" of the Three in a perfect union which therefore follows or occurs as an action of or by the Three. Speaking specifically of the Gospels, one can say that the understanding of any described action—in the conventional sense—is not understood unless and until the spiritual content of the action is recognized. The willingness of Christian exegetes to seemingly construct an entire world from one small material piece of the story is the consequence of recognizing the spiritual content of a story's detail. (How much, after all, can you say about a story with flowers in a field or a barren fruit tree?) The literal and the spiritual senses of a Gospel passage are not at odds with each other, nor are they even "alternative" readings: they are the different senses that together give the complete meaning of a passage (or word).[20] After all this, we should be able to recognize that however loaded with technicalities Book V may be, it nonetheless begins (V:9) with the overall exegetical concern of "How do we understand materially derived characteristics—attributions or predications—when they are used of God in Scripture?" While Augustine's way of answering this question may suggest that his book was intended for circulation among readers with similar educations to his own, the fact remains that the question he is addressing in this book is one that Scripture readers of whatever education can and do ask of a scriptural passage: How do we understand that word when it is said of God? In Augustine's time, such a simple question could be a lead-in to an argument that the Son has a different nature or essence than the Father does: indeed, at the Council of Sirmium (357) the strongest opponents of Nicaea met to reject and condemn the use of the word "essence" (*ousia*) applied to God. The argument became a key one in anti-Nicene polemics, East and West, and engaged the brilliant mind of Marius Victorinus, to whom I have dedicated a chapter. In 357–61, Victorinus wrote against anti-Nicenes, those who in different ways promoted a doctrine of the two different natures of God the Father, on the one hand, and "God," Christ, the "Son of God," on the other. Victorinus has not received the credit he deserves for establishing a truly Latin Nicene theology, rather than simply a translation of Greek theology. I have reasons for doubting that Augustine read much Victorinus, but in at least one way Augustine was deeply indebted to the older Roman African, for Victorinus was able to make clear which of the anti-Nicene criticisms carried weight, and equally for revealing which pro-Nicene theology was an advance and which were rear-guard actions. With all this, we have basic backgrounds to my first two articles on the book *De Trinitate* in itself.

Chapter 7 brings to light three early works by Augustine that are often ignored by scholars, not to mention by theologians skimming over Augustine's many writings. This chapter should give you a sense not only of my own methodology, but also of Augustine's early and unsophisticated way of talking about Scripture before he was given the time to study it carefully after he was ordained.

Chapter 8 concerns the first two books of *De Trinitate*. The books are often simply characterized as dealing with Old Testament theophanies, with no explanation for why Augustine thought it important to exegete the specific texts he does. These two books are an excellent place to begin to learn Augustine's Trinitarian theology because they reveal to us how Augustine theologizes: how he brings his exegesis of Scripture together with prior authoritative commentaries on the passage, other relevant passages in Scripture (why are they relevant?), and the sense of the church. One sees immediately that Augustine is not reading Scripture alone, but in a community of readers that goes back hundreds of years. Read correctly, this chapter prepares you for the next, for it too is part of understanding how, in a fully Nicene Trinitarian theology, Christ reveals the Trinity. The foundational Latin interpretations of the theophanies had been developed

---

20. Compare the literary project of the *The Alexandria Quartet* by Lawrence Durrell.

against the monarchians—what we now call modalists: the Trinitarian response to the monarchians is to stress how the "visible" aspects of the Son reveal the invisible God, the Father. Intrinsic to this logic—which continues well into the fourth century—is a certain subordination of the Son. A new post-Nicene interpretation of the theophanies has to be offered to strip away the old inherent subordinationism.[21]

Chapter 10 concerns a number of Augustine's important doctrines. In Books I–IV, Augustine discussed the theophanies in order to discuss the "great theophany", the Incarnation. The anti-Nicenes say that because the Son became incarnate he cannot truly be God since God is invisible and immaterial. What do we "see" in Christ who is fully human and fully divine? The pure of heart, who believe in Christ's invisible divinity, will see that divinity as the full Trinity; those who lack faith and imagine Christ's visible humanity exhausts the content of his person will never see God, they will only see the humanity that they saw or believed Christ to be. Nothing more (or less) than what they believed about Christ will ever be revealed to them. Whatever else this chapter accomplishes, there is at least this: Augustine makes clear the Christocentrism of his anthropology and his epistemology. It could be considered a retelling of the story of Christ and fallen humanity based almost solely on understanding how, in a fully Nicene Trinitarian theology, Christ reveals the Trinity. Many of the old accounts of this revelation had developed in pre-Nicene theology, when monarchianism was the great threat Western theology faced. After Nicaea, however, the vision of God through Christ had to be re-thought in terms of "the Father is in me, and I am in the Father."

Chapter 9 shows that in *De Trinitate* V, Augustine is arguing against Latin anti-Nicene theology and not against the Greek theology of Arius. See Augustine's *Epistle 238* for a transcript of a public debate between Augustine and the Latin anti-Nicene, Pascentius. In this letter, Augustine explicitly defends the Greek word *homoousios* as the sense expressed in John 10:30 in the Latin New Testament. The date of this transcript is thought to be between 400 and 405, which is also the common window of time given by scholars for when Augustine began to write *De Trinitate*. My article provides a theological context for Book V as well as a commentary on the "Arian" fragments cited by Augustine. Book V is regularly treated by scholars as Augustine's contribution to the ongoing philosophical debate on the place of Aristotle's *Categories*, but my article shows its polemical character in Augustine's argument against the anti-Nicenes. The argument in *De Trinitate* V can be tedious and technical, but I believe that my article makes some sense of what the argument is about—as well as preparing the reader for Books VI and VII.

De Trinitate Books VI and VII are extended commentaries by Augustine on the scriptural passage, "Christ the Power and Wisdom of God" (1 Cor 1:24).[22] It was the

---

21. D. Williams, "Monarchianism and Photinus of Sirmium."

22. The most common reading of *Trin.* V–VII is to mine them for their use of substance and predication, a question made relevant by the fact that Augustine does indeed have a sophisticated—if idiosyncratic—understanding of Aristotle's *Categories* and some parts of the *Metaphysics*. Such research

problems that Augustine faced in these two books that led me to write on the types of Nicenes (ch. 3) as well as to write this article (ch. 10). Books VI and VII of *De Trinitate* continue what was begun in Book V: How is it that we say God is simple and yet we use multiple titles for him? The argument goes further: How do we say God is one and yet we attribute some divine titles to the Son or Holy Spirit? As a Christian "problem" or mystery, these questions are two centuries old, but the anti-Nicenes have used them against Nicene theology. Chapter 11 is the last of my articles on the book *De Trinitate*, but not the last on Augustine's Trinitarian theology.

Chapter 12 is on Augustine's pneumatology expressed in writings from late in his career—two of them after he had finished *De Trinitate*. The last two writings by him are in the same form as the early *Epistle 238*—transcripts of his public debates with Latin anti-Nicenes. One could expect Augustine's pneumatology to involve the famous triad of memory, intelligence, and love—but as you will see, that triadic way of speaking about the Trinity is not the only way he speaks about the Trinity. I would not call "triad" logic fundamental to his Trinitarian theology, though he does appeal regularly to metaphors of three-in-one. As this chapter shows, in this most mature theology of the Holy Spirit, Augustine follows what he takes to be the Lucan practice of calling the Holy Spirit "the Power of God."

The final chapter, gnomically entitled "Ebion at the Barricades," is an Augustinian articulation of a modern, post-Vatican II, Catholic *personalism*—the original being one of those spirits that flew and fell with ressourcement. This is a neo-personalism born from a neo-ressourcement that accepts Augustine as a Church Father: neo-ressourcement implicitly tests the exegesis of Augustinian texts by scholastic and modern theology. It does with Augustine what the scholastics of 1940 were afraid that the Sources Chrétiennes series would enable with Thomistic exegesis of the Greek fathers.[23] Twentieth-century *ressourcement* theology did not turn to Augustine—in large part because for them he was intrinsic to Thomas and scholasticism, and to a degree, they were right—"right" in the sense that this "Augustine" was scholasticism in another form, and "right" in that both sides agreed to recognize this "Augustine" as the one and only, he who spoke with the voice and from the life of late-fourth century Latin Christianity. Ressourcement accepted the scholastic creature of "Augustine" as the historical Augustine, which left a veil over Augustine's writings. Moreover, ressourcement theologians were as complete a set of victims to Régnon's paradigm as any of their theological peers. One can, I think, rationally hazard the thesis that Ressourcement theology (a French reality distinct from nouvelle theologie) depended upon Régnon's paradigm for its character and content. The paradigm provided the rationale for reading East separate from West and the attendant conviction that Eastern

---

has either given us a sense of the influence of the neo-Aristotelian movement in the third through fifth centuries, or it has returned Augustine to the world of medieval scholasticism.

23. And regards the Régnon paradigm as a heuristic ideology made on the basis of a poor reading of Théodore de Régnon.

Christianity had, somehow, preserved the vitality and community of the early church that Latin theology had locked down.[24] With the paradigm, one need not wait until Augustine to find the beginning of Western monism: it was incipient, indigenous, to Latin Christianity. Augustine was the genius of the spirit of Latin Christianity, and through self-critique and confession Western Christian theology had liberated itself from "Augustine" and all that flowed from "him" conceptually. It is a biting irony that the very confidence theologians placed in the almost materially determined difference between Latin and Greek theologies kept most of Western Christian theology at less than six degrees of separation from scholasticism.

Thus, this last chapter is not a piece *on* Augustine's Trinitarian theology *per se*, but it is an essay which strongly represents a kind of thinking that arises out of reading his Trinitarian writings (especially *De Trinitate*) and his works on moral psychology. It arose out of these for me, at least. Many of Augustine's critics would agree with me that in his Trinitarian theology, we see the bare structure of all of Augustine's theology, and the Trinitarian expression of that structure ought not be set aside as "pure or speculative theology," monastically secluded, as a form without matter, a geist without a mechanism. In what follows, I do not set aside what I have learned from the study of Augustine's Trinitarian theology, nor the anthropology consistent with his Christology. This is the knowledge and experience within which I see, recognize, and express what follows.

In this essay, Augustine explicitly provides the substructure for the argument: we cannot know the efficient cause for acts of evil. This provides the logic for my critique of what I recognize as "a post-Christian Catholicism".[25] Augustine's lifelong theological focus on the individual as the true place for the rise of moral consciousness, the source of moral action, and the real battleground of moral conflict fits well with the twentieth-century turn (especially in France) to the individual for theological and philosophical insight and experience. The emphasis on memory as the principle site for moral consciousness scattered across many French theologians, artists, and philosophers of the time owes, in some decisive way, to Augustine—even if only as "mediated" through Descartes or Pascal.[26]

---

24. Even a well-trained practitioner of German biblical criticism cannot detect the weight of the modern longing for the vitality (action!) and community that was alternately placed either in Jesus or on the "Primitive Church" by such critics between 1840 and 1970.

25. The theology of the Roman Catholic Church has no monopoly on denominations continuing their church's name, sans any distinctly Christian content, or any worship of Christ the Son of God. (After slightly more than forty years of academic study, one of the few singular claims I can make is to be a specialist in fourth-century Trinitarian theology, as well as the Greek and Latin epitomic theologians of the Trinity of the time, Gregory of Nyssa and Augustine of Hippo. Even if I were an atheist I could claim the scholarly credentials enabling me to recognize the presence or absence of the distinguishing features of Christian worship of, and belief in, the Trinity according to what is commonly called the "faith of Nicaea" as symbolized in the creed of Constantinople, 381.)

26. If Augustine had been a filmmaker during the 1930s or 40s, his thought would have undoubtedly been called, "Theologie noir".

I began by speaking of an Augustinian articulation of a modern, post-Vatican II, Catholic *personalism*. The original personalism grew out of the existential and social crises of the early twentieth century. Like most social philosophies developed between 1840 and 2001, personalism criticized modern culture for its destructive effect upon "community" and it promoted "action for the community." This prescription was shared across the political spectrum, left to right. The presence of this longing in European personalism left it in a poor position to do what was needed: to critique the nostalgia for community, the return to Paradise.[27] One "advantage" our twenty-first-century perspective has on the widely shared twentieth-century longing and nostalgia for community is that we can see how the greatest horrors of the past century arose directly out of longing for and nostalgia for a lost, once-upon-a-time, ideal community that was no longer present, if indeed it had ever existed. In this article, the reader will find critiques of ideologies of community of the right or the left, but, all the time, in the church. Given the unprecedented (and one hopes, unique) evidence of the twentieth century, a twenty-first-century personalism must be critical of any romanticized "nostalgia for the eschaton" preached in the City of Man. The purpose here of historical theology is to undercut any nostalgia for past communities and to uproot any (Romantic) longing or nostalgia for future communities.

One of the truths that became apparent to me over many years of teaching graduate students is that current generations of scholars have a tendency to read only that which was published in the previous hour. I believe the pieces offered here made a significant contribution to the emergence of more historically sensitive accounts of Latin Trinitarian theology than were prevalent before them. Hearing them again can, I hope, play a role in reminding scholars how that view was developed and the important work that remains to be done.

I have taught many graduate seminars on Augustine Latin Trinitarian theology. Many of my students went on to dissertate on subjects in Latin theology. Over the years, my research has benefitted from the unpublished translations of Phoebadius (by Mark Weedman), Gregory of Elvira (Rebecca Hylander), and Isaac the Jew (Alexander Huggard). More recently, I have benefitted from a draft of Mark DelCogliano's translation of Phoebadius.[28]

---

27. Nineteenth-century German liberal Christianity was confident in the scientific judgment that there never had been a Eden. But that same confidence was given to the scientific judgments that a Garden of Paradise had existed in the pre-Christian Aryan tribes in central Europe, north and west of Hell, the Slavs. A science of culture bemoaned the loss of the Grecian Eden. Another science could map the material layers and generations to when once there had been no property.

28. All translations of other primary texts are based on the translations provided in the bibliography. Minor variations are not noted.

Chapter 1

Augustine in Contemporary Trinitarian Theology

ALTHOUGH IT HAS BEEN some time since Augustine's Trinitarian theology was studied in depth,[1] the last decade has seen a significant and widely expressed interest on the part of systematic theologians in the implications of Augustine's theology for the development of Trinitarian doctrine. For example, a consensus among systematicians on the existence and character of an early "economic" understanding of God has led, among other things, to the not uncommon judgment that Augustine's Trinitarian theology sacrificed this sense of *oeconomia*, with unfortunate consequences for later theology. This sacrifice is frequently contrasted not only with primitive Christianity's experience of God but with the emphasis on relationship in the Trinitarian theologies of the Cappadocians.[2] My purpose in this article is to examine many of these recent theological works for what they reveal about the methodological presuppositions operative, more or less, in most systematic treatments of Augustine today, and to critique those presuppositions from the point of view of a historical theologian whose speciality is patristic Trinitarian theology. After thus providing what could be called a general phenomenology of contemporary systematic appropriations of Augustine's Trinitarian theology, it will be possible to show how these presuppositions have figured in

1. One exception is Johannes Arnold's "Begriff und heilsökonomische Bedeutung der göttlichen Sendungen in Augustinus De Trinitate," *Recherches Augustiniennes* 25 (1991): 3–69. Arnold's work is of particular interest because he analyzes Augustine's Trinitarian theology specifically from the perspective of testing out its economic content.

2. An influential account of the opposition between Cappadocian and Augustinian Trinitarian theologies precisely in terms of a relational and economic theology versus a theology lacking both these dimensions is given in T. R. Martland, "A Study of Cappadocian and Augustinian Trinitarian Methodology," *Anglican Theological Review* 47 (1965): 252–63.

readings of Augustine by systematic theologians, in their methods, and, particularly, in their conclusions.[3]

Most accounts of patristic Trinitarian doctrine divide this theology into two fundamental categories: Greek and Latin. By this account, Greek theology begins with the reality of the distinct persons, while Latin theology begins with the reality of the unity of the divine nature. That this schema is true cannot be assumed; as I will show, the effect of assuming this schema has been to conceal as least as much as it revealed. But setting aside whether the schema is true, that is to say, whether it accurately describes the doctrines it purports to describe, what is certain is that only theologians of the last one-hundred years have ever thought that it was true. A belief in the existence of this Greek–Latin paradigm is a unique property of modern Trinitarian theology. This belief, and the associated diagrams that one finds in Margerie[4] and LaCugna,[5] or the "plurality-model–unity-model" jargon that one finds in Brown,[6] all derive from a book written about a hundred years ago, namely Théodore de Régnon's studies on the Trinity.[7] For it is Régnon who invented the Greek–Latin paradigm, geometrical diagrams and all.[8] Régnon's paradigm has become the *sine qua non* for framing the contemporary understanding of Augustine's theology. To this extent, works as otherwise diverse as LaCugna's and Brown's both exhibit a scholastic modernism, since they both take as an obvious given a point of view that is coextensive with the twentieth century. So do Mackey[9] and O'Donnell.[10]

All of these works organize patristic Trinitarian theology according to Régnon's paradigm. None of them shows any awareness that the paradigm needs to be demonstrated, or that it has a history. LaCugna and Brown need the paradigm to ground the specific problem they diagnose; although both Mackey and O'Donnell are frustrated by the strictures of the paradigm, neither of them notes that it is a creature of late-nineteenth-century scholarship, an observation that would have given them a way out of their frustrations. At times Moltmann seems to avoid Régnon's paradigm,[11] but in fact he only transforms it into its mirror image, namely that Augustine's unity paradigm may be distinguished from the Greek social paradigm through his use of a psychological

3. The scope of this article is limited to a critical analysis of works in contemporary systematics, and so my own proposal for a substantial alternative account of the economy and Augustine's Trinitarian theology will have to wait.

4. Bertrand de Margerie, *La Trinité chrétienne dans l'histoire* (Paris: Beauchesne, 1975) 227.

5. Catherine Mowry LaCugna, *God for Us* (San Francisco: Harper, 1991) 96.

6. David Brown, *The Divine Trinity* (La Salle: Open Court, 1985).

7. Theodore de Régnon, SJ, *Études de théologie positive sur la Sainte Trinité*, four volumes bound as three (Paris: Victor Retaux, 1892/1898).

8. Régnon, *Études*, 1.339.

9. James P. Mackey, *The Christian Experience of God as Trinity*, (London: SCM, 1983) 142–63.

10. John J. O'Donnell, *Trinity and Temporality: The Christian Doctrine of God in the Light of Process Theology and the Theology of Hope* (Oxford: Oxford University, 1983) 40–52.

11. Jürgen Moltmann, *History and the Triune God* (London: SCM, 1991).

analogy—an argument which has been popular among French Augustinians for some time. Moltmann is wrong, however, for the psychological analogy of the Trinity based on the idea, as he puts it, of a "soul that controls the body,"[12] can be found in Eusebius of Caesarea and Gregory of Nyssa, both Greeks.[13] All the above works thus illustrate in vivid fashion the degree to which modern reconstructions are captive to modern interpretative categories. To be fair, however, nothing is more common in contemporary systematics than the inability to read Augustine outside of Régnon's paradigm.[14]

Such modern appropriations of Augustine thus depend upon broad, general characterizations of Augustine's theology; these broad general characterizations themselves depend upon turn-of-the-century continental histories of dogma, of which, as I will show, Régnon's paradigm is but the most obvious.[15] Similarly, these contemporary appropriations share the same two presuppositions: the first is that characterizations based on polar contrasts are borne out in the details that are revealed clearly and distinctly through the contrasts; and the second is that the same process of presenting doctrines in terms of opposition yields a synthesizing account of the development of doctrine.[16] In short, there is a penchant among systematic theologians for categories of polar opposition, grounded in the belief that ideas "out there" in the past really existed in polarities, and that polar oppositions accurately describe the contents and relationships of these ideas. Why these categories would be so valued by late-nineteenth- and twentieth-century readers of dogma is a question I leave for specialists in those eras, although, as will become clear, I believe that this penchant for polar categories reveals something about methodological choices systematicians have made in this century. Whatever the origins of this emphasis on polar categories may be,

12. Moltmann, *History and the Triune God*, 60–62.

13. See Eusebius of Caesarea's *Demonstration of the Gospel* 4:5, edited by Ivar Heikel, GCS 6. 156.18–26. A similar argument to this effect, written for polemical purposes, may also be found in Gregory of Nyssa's *On the Making of Man* (PG 44.137d–140c).

14. Some time ago, Edmund Hill criticized Rahner's implicit dependence on Régnon; see his "Karl Rahner's 'Remarks on the Dogmatic Treatise De Trinitate and St. Augustine" *Augustinian Studies* 2 (1971): 67–80.

15. Such as the oppositions between "Greek" and "Latin," or between "economic" and "immanent," or, in more general applications, "Jewish" versus "Hellenistic."

16. Although all the oppositions noted in the preceding note could, theoretically, be used to describe static relationships, in practice these oppositions have been used to describe movement from one doctrinal form to another, whether it is a progressive or regressive movement. The typical use of such an opposition to describe doctrinal progression can be found, e.g., in Margerie, *La Trinité chrétienne dans l'histoire*, 223, 226, and in Crowe, *Doctrine of the Holy Trinity*, (Willowdale: Regis College, 1965/66) 110. I quote Margerie to illustrate: "[L]es Grecs et les Latins ont constitué deux branches différentes au sein de l'unique grande tradition chrétienne. On n'a peut être pas assez remarqué que la spéculation grecque représente un premier stade d'élaboration et d'évolution du dogme trinitaire, auquel la réflexion latine succède comme un stade postérieur" (Margerie, *La Trinité*, 223). By contrast, although Greek thought from pre-Socratic through to Hellenistic remained consistently dependent upon categories of polar opposition, such categories were often used to describe static or even eternal relationships. I suggest that it is the exclusive use of polar opposites to characterize development that constitutes an "idealistic" use of categories of polar opposition.

there are severe limitations in the histories produced by this polarizing hermeneutic of doctrine, and contemporary systematic theologians seem to have accepted these limitations as foundational.[17]

To take just one of these limitations, the standard division of Trinitarian theologies into the Greek tradition, paradigmatically expressed by the Cappadocians, and its opposite, the Latin tradition, paradigmatically expressed by Augustine, ignores the close affiliation that flourished between Alexandrian ("Greek") and Roman ("Latin") theologies a generation earlier. The more one tends to speak of a real division between Greek and Latin Trinitarian theologies in the late-fourth and early-fifth centuries, the more one must acknowledge and explain a fundamental shift away from the mid-fourth-century synthetic theology of Alexandria and Rome. The more one postulates a turn-of-the-century opposition between Greek and Latin theologies, the more one implicitly claims the loss of the prior consensus, and a dominant consensus at that, found in the theologies of Rome and Alexandria, a consensus that was above all "Nicene."[18]

A few historians of dogma have bravely followed their own logic and admitted the loss of a Rome–Alexandria consensus. Harnack did so. The era we recognize, through Régnon, as the era of the paradigmatic expression of Greek and Latin theologies was, in Harnack's account, the era in which the Rome–Alexandria Trinitarian consensus was betrayed. Harnack was so critical of the new theology of the Cappadocians and Constantinople, in 381, that he described it as "semi-Arian" and a subversion of Nicaea.[19] On the other hand, we have a very different opinion from French Augustinians like Paissac and Malet,[20] who are of particular significance for Catholic theology since they have provided so much of the conceptual idiom which is the repertory of modern Catholic systematic theologians. French scholastic Augustinians have rejoiced that, as they saw it, Augustine left behind the inhibiting concepts of Nicaea, in particular the constraints imposed by the watchword *homoousia*. For these scholars, the development of the doctrinal era described by Régnon in his Latin, i.e., his Augustinian and proto-scholastic paradigm is the development of a happy separation from the earlier

---

17. An article similar to this one could be written analyzing the debt that contemporary reflections on *oeconomia* owe to the emphasis laid on this category of theology by nineteenth-century theologians at Tübingen and by John Henry Newman in his *The Arians of the Fourth Century* (1.1.3). Practically speaking, such scholars as these discovered the division between "economy" and "theology" and invented its modern significance. One might explore for ways in which contemporary systematic theology needs this division.

18. We may note that in 380 (leading up to the Council of Constantinople in 381) the normative expression of the imperially approved doctrine of the Trinity was the pro-Nicene doctrine(s) of Rome and Alexandria, as article 16.2 of the *Theodosian Code* makes clear.

19. Adolph Harnack, *History of Dogma*, trans. Neil Buchanan, repr. as 7 books in 4 vols. (New York: Dover, 1960) 4.84–88.

20. Henri Paissac, *Théologie du Verbe: Saint Augustin et Saint Thomas* (Paris: Cerf, 1951); Andre Malet, *Personne et Amour dans la théologie trinitaire de saint Thomas d'Aquin* (Paris: Vrin, 1956); also Le Guillou, "Réflexions sur la thélogie trinitaire," *Istina* 17 (1972) 457–64.

orthodox consensus.[21] Their frank separation of Augustine from Nicene theology well dramatizes the issues a Cappadocian–Augustinian opposition presupposes. Of the texts under discussion here, only LaCugna brings the French positioning of Augustine over against a Nicene consensus into the body of her discussion, though without any illumination; Congar refers to it in his notes.[22]

The overwhelming presence in systematic discussions of Augustine of a watered-down version of Régnon's paradigm, coupled with an ignorance of the origin of the paradigm, reveals the systematic penchant for using grand, broad-stroked narrative forms. Like turn-of-the-century historians, contemporary systematicians seem to be distinguished by the confidence with which they will deploy such grand, architectonic narrative forms. This confidence springs, I think, from two attitudes. First, the confidence reflects a positive sense of all the new things that we have learned as moderns through the mechanism of "paradigm shifts"; not the least of what we have learned is the existence of such paradigms themselves. Secondly, the confidence to speak in architectonic narrative forms reflects a general sense that details matter less than perspective, that historical facts are only epiphenomena of an architectonic paradigm or hermeneutic, so that a sufficient knowledge of "facts" can be acquired solely through the practice of a hermeneutical or an ideological critique in itself, since any "fact" can itself be reduced to an expression or the symptom of a hermeneutic or ideology. One can imagine that either or both of these attitudes would make historical judgments or characterizations more tentative and rare, but I think it is fair to conclude that this has not been the case.

The idea that historical facts are only epiphenomena of a hermeneutic is now implicit in left-wing histories of doctrine just as it has been implicit in right-wing histories of doctrine. It will be remembered that many of the accomplishments in Catholic historical theology (and Catholic theology generally) in the first half of this century were driven by a desire to escape the tendency of the right to regard the actual reading of historical sources as superfluous if not subversive in virtue of official interpretations (such as those of Thomas Aquinas). A striking illustration of a similar tendency on the left may be seen in a recent article by Thistlethwaite,[23] who is able to characterize the

---

21. See Paissac, *Théologie du Verbe*, 30–31; Malet, *Personne et Amour*, 21; Guillou, "Réflexions sur la thélogie trinitaire," 459; also Louis Legrand, *La Notion philosophique de la Trinité chez Saint Augustin* (París: Oeuvre d'auteuil, 1931) 133.

22. Congar, *I Believe in the Holy Spirit* vol. 3 (New York: Seabury, 1983). Congar shows an awareness of the French scholastics Malet, Le Guillou, and Lafont (92n16). He also makes the influence of Régnon explicit (83; for more on Régnon, see 92nn10–11).

23. Thistlethwaite, "On the Trinity," *Interpretation* 45 (1991) 159–71. Thistlethwaite's readings are produced by, and in support of, a feminist hermeneutic, but her specific purpose in recounting early Christian Trinitarian theologies follows from a larger hermeneutical project which is neither limited to, nor intrinsically a feature of, feminist theology, namely, the reduction of early Christian Trinitarian theologies to episodes in a *Logos* theology. (Here the rise of an imperialistic *Logos* theology is the architectonic narrative.) My position remains, however, that the more tightly controlled a reading is by an ideological end the more damaged is the historical sensitivity. Such ideologies limit systematic

sense of Trinitarian language in all the apostolic fathers, the Apologists, and Tertullian without ever citing a single specific text or even a mediating secondary source.[24] Her argument pivots on a characterization of Gregory of Nyssa's Trinitarian theology that appears all but manufactured to support her own position.[25] The idiosyncratic nature of Thistlethwaite's judgment that Gregory held a *Logos*-centered theology is telegraphed by the fact that she cannot provide a single primary source in support of this position and that she can only draw upon a secondary source that is a hundred years old to get as far as impugning Gregory by association with Origen.[26] Thistlethwaite thus provides a painful illustration of a grand narrative which is based upon something other than a knowledge of the texts being narrated, indeed a narrative which is positively based on conceptually bypassing the need, simply put, to read the texts being narrated. The texts have no content(s) apart from the grand narrative, and thus no integrity that would demand a direct encounter.

The preferred narrative form among systematic theologians is, as I have already called it, the architectonic, by which I mean two things: first, an account that is open-endedly comprehensive; and second, a description of the development of doctrine in terms of the internal logic of an idea. What seems to me to be distinctive about the systematicians' quest for comprehensiveness is the way in which it is tied to understanding change in a cultural form, that is to say, in a doctrine, in terms of the logic of an idea. Yannaras's recent account of the influence of Augustine on Western civilization provides a conspicuous example of this kind of idealizing account of doctrine.[27] Yannaras argues that the rise of "logocentrism" in the culture of Western Christendom

---

theology's appropriation of the subject of historical theology (i.e., the Christian tradition) to an exploitation of this subject through the usual mechanism of cultural exploitation, namely a transformation of the material for the sake of consumption.

24. Ibid., 163.

25. Thistlethwaite is attempting to refute the position that "Father, Son, and Holy Spirit" are the proper names of God. To do that, she contests the significance of Gregory as an authoritative witness of an early "proper name" theology. In particular, Gregory's authority is questioned: "[Nyssa] is not widely regarded to be the theologian his teacher and master, Basil of Caesarea, was" (Thistlethwaite, "On the Trinity," 166). There is no indication by Thistlethwaite of specifically who it is that widely lacks this regard for Gregory, a point which is not moot, given that the normal scholarly evaluation of Gregory is precisely that he was *more* a theologian than Basil was. E.g., Johannes Quasten says, "If we compare Gregory of Nyssa as a theologian with the two other Cappadocians, we recognize his superiority immediately" (Quasten, *Patrology*, 3:283). More recently, R. P. C. Hanson offered that "Gregory of Nyssa is to be sharply distinguished from the other two Cappadocian theologians in that he devised a doctrinal, indeed a philosophical, system more coherent and more elaborate than any the other two ever produced" (*Search for the Christian Doctrine*, 719). Such evaluations of Gregory's eminence could be multiplied indefinitely (this side of Harnack). Moreover, the question of Basil's preeminence is relevant only if Basil and Gregory disagreed on the issue of the character of divine names (which they do not).

26. Thistlethwaite, "On the Trinity," 166. Thistlethwaite's authority for Gregory's relationship to the theology of his day (given in her nn17–18) is the introduction to the *Nicene and Post-Nicene Fathers* volume on Gregory (1892).

27. Christos Yannaras, *Philosophie sans rupture* (Geneva: Labor et Fides, 1986).

(as opposed to the culture of Eastern Christendom) is due to Augustine's influence as the theological paradigm of the West. Yannaras takes the same description of Augustine as the theologian of the *logos* par excellence that one finds in the French Augustinians mentioned earlier and applies the logic of idealism to Augustine's influence: each historical epoch is defined by Yannaras by the way it purifies and enlarges as an idea the scope of what was originally a doctrinal insight by Augustine. This method of describing the development of doctrine in terms of conceptual purification and expansion appears in a number of treatments of doctrine in general and Augustine's doctrine in particular; LaCugna's and Jenson's works, especially, follow this pattern.[28]

Yannaras's own work with Martin Heidegger makes it impossible to deny his debt to German idealism, and he would not want to deny it. Let me offer the thesis that (1) the fascination with conceptual categories of polar opposition, (2) the use of the logic of ideas to describe cultural forms, and (3) the claim to comprehensiveness on the basis of polar categories and ideal logic all suggest that the influence of German idealism among systematic theologians is not limited to Yannaras. There has been a decision by systematicians to prefer an architectonic and idealistic style of writing; this decision has been objectified, for no one can remember making it. Aside from amnesia, the problem with the influence of idealism in systematic appropriations of patristic theology is not that philosophy in general has no place in theology, or even that idealism in particular has no place in theology. Rather the problem is that, unacknowledged, idealism draws to itself bad history: the integrity of the discipline of historical studies is ruptured by the need to find a "historical" account which is already cast in idealistic terms.[29] History is then treated as the material enstructuring of those themes which are constitutive of contemporary systematics. The dialogue between systematic theology and historical theology is transformed into a conversation between a ventriloquist and her or his prop.

The way in which systematic appropriations of Augustine are based upon "historical" accounts pre-selected for mirroring the idealizing methods of systematic theology can be seen in two specific properties of such appropriations. First, there is the ubiquitous presence of the work of Olivier du Roy as a mediating authority in the reading of Augustine's theology.[30] To discover this presence, one sometimes has to pay attention to footnote references, as in the case of Muller,[31] but LaCugna brings her debt to Du Roy into the body of the text, so that what was originally a methodological

28. Robert W. Jenson, *The Triune Identity* (Philadelphia: Fortress, 1982).

29. I note that making sense of theological history through German idealism is not limited to Christian theology: see Richard Taylor's review of Ian Newton's *Allah Transcendent* in *The Middle East Journal* 44 (1990): 521–22. Taylor criticizes Newton's depiction of Islamic philosophers as an "almost Hegelian view of the advance of Islamic" thought, in which they are "controlled by their chosen mythologies" and their thoughts are organized as "historical phenomena in an unfolding drama."

30. Olivier du Roy, *L'intelligence de la foi en la trinité selon saint Augustin* (Paris: Études Augustiniennes, 1966).

31. Earl C. Muller, SJ, *Trinity and Marriage in Paul* (New York: Peter Lang, 1990), 468nn167–69.

presupposition in Du Roy becomes a theological conclusion in LaCugna. Congar is a rare example of a theologian who has noticed just how "radical" Du Roy's perspective is, and how Du Roy is driven to it in reaction to the French Augustinians that I mentioned earlier.[32]

Du Roy's description of Augustine's Trinitarian theology shows significant methodological idiosyncrasies. One important idiosyncrasy is Du Roy's description of Augustine's doctrine of the Trinity in terms of a fundamental relationship with philosophy, not in terms of a fundamental relationship with doctrine.[33] In this, Du Roy fits in with dominant twentieth-century systematic presentations of Augustine's Trinitarian theology. While there are a number of monographs on Augustine's Trinitarian debt to philosophy, sustained discussions of a similar debt to his immediate Christian Latin predecessors are few and far between. Such discussions as there are reduce Augustine to Tertullian, or position this debt in terms of Régnon's paradigm: e.g., How does Augustine's theory of relations differ from that of Gregory of Nazianzus'? We are brought to the odd position that, according to many systematic theologians, the influence of philosophy in religious doctrine is fundamental, while the influence of prior expositions of religious doctrines is not.

Another distinctive feature of Du Roy's methodology is that Augustine's Trinitarian theology is presented statically or thematically. Although Du Roy's apparent perspective is developmental, his operating principle is that Augustine's Trinitarian theology consistently reduces to a triadology, although Augustine's preferred terms for the triad change over time, from text to text, or from chapter to chapter (for which one consults Du Roy's appendix).[34] Such a description leaves no room for the observation that in *De Symbolo ad Catechumenos*, Augustine's argument for the unity of the Trinity is indistinguishable from that of his Greek contemporary, Evagrius.[35] They both argue, "against the Arians," that John 5:19, "the Son can do nothing without the Father," is a declaration of the Son's natural relationship with the Father, since common activities require a common nature and only a common nature can produce common activities. In the form of Régnon's paradigm typical of the contemporary works discussed in this article, this argument and this language are thought to be "Cappadocian," but in any case exclusively Greek.

32. Congar speaks of Du Roy's description of Augustine's debt to Neoplatonism as "radical," and knows that Du Roy is reacting to authors such as Malet, Le Guillou, and Lafont (*I Believe in the Holy Spirit*, 3:92n16).

33. Rowan Williams recently characterized Du Roy's work as one which presents "Augustine's Trinitarian thought as monist and essentialist, a scheme in which the economy of salvation plays relatively little part" ("Sapientia and the Trinity," *Collectanea Augustiniana: Mélanges T. J. van Bavel* [Leuven: University Press, 1990] 317–332, at 319 n. 6).

34. It goes almost without saying that Du Roy's emphasis on the triadology in Augustine's Trinitarian theology is related to the hermeneutical privileging of philosophy as Augustine's "source."

35. See "Basil's" (i.e., Evagrius') *Letter* 8:9.

Du Roy's account of Augustine's Trinitarian theology in which the fundamental source of doctrine is philosophy, articulated in categories that are static or thematic, brings us to a second way in which systematic appropriations of Augustine are based upon "historical" accounts that mirror the idealizing methods of systematic theology. Most systematic treatments of patristic Trinitarian theology generally and of Augustine's theology specifically are characterized by an avoidance of texts in the genre of Trinitarian polemic, and a failure to take the polemical context of such writing seriously. There is a decided preference among systematicians for patristic Trinitarian texts that are not polemical in genre, and a tendency to "read out" polemics when such intentions are likely.[36] For example, the most commonly used statement of Gregory of Nyssa's Trinitarian theology is his work *On Not Three Gods*; I have not yet found a collection of selected primary sources on early Christian Trinitarian doctrine that does not showcase this work, although no one can claim that it was, before this century, influential in any way. It is, of course, a very short work, and one which has the obvious appeal to Westerners of showing a Greek worrying about possibly being tritheistic.

Régnon focused on this work because, as he saw it, it shared the same "nature–operations" language that was so important for scholastic commentaries on Aquinas's Trinitarian theology, such as Cajetan's.[37] The passages Régnon emphasized for this reason are the same passages that show up later in Severino González's article on exterior operations in Gregory's theology, in Quasten's summary of Gregory's Trinitarian theology, and in Bettenson's selection of extracts from Gregory.[38] Moreover, Régnon's idiosyncratic abstraction of the nature–operations language of Gregory's *Ad Eustathium* continues in the assumption of essence–energy language evident in a host

---

36. A nascent sensitivity to Gregory's polemical context may be due to the new role Hanson's *The Search for the Christian Doctrine* is beginning to play as a resource for systematicians. Continued dependence on the utility of Lebon and Prestige, on the other hand, is puzzling.

37. Régnon, *Etudes sur la Sainte Trinité*, 1.391, 394. Régnon emphasizes nature and operations language in his account of Cappadocian theology as part of his argument that the difference between patristic and scholastic Trinitarian theologies is a difference of organizing paradigms rather than a difference of substance. Régnon will argue that the appearance of nature and operations language in both patristic and scholastic Trinitarian theologies is evidence of the common doctrinal substance, while the different senses attached to the terms is evidence of the different theological paradigms within which the language is interpreted.

38. Namely, Nyssa, "Ad Eustathium," the pseudo-Basilian *Ep.* 189.6 (Yves Courtonne, ed. trans. and comm., *Saint Basile Lettres,* 3 vols. [Paris: Société d'Éditions "Les Belles Lettres, 1957, 1961, 1966] 2.138.12—139.26), treated at *Études* 1.391, and *Ep.* 189.7 (Courtonne 2.140.29-33) treated at *Études* 1.392; *On "Not Three Gods,"* Greg. Nyss. opera (GNO) 46.20—48.8 treated at *Études* 1.396-97; and 48.20—51.5 treated at *Études* 1.397-98. For the treatment of these passages by the authors cited, see González, "La identidad de operacion en las obras exteriores y la unidad de la naturaleza divina en la teologia trinitaria de S. Gregoria de Nisa," *Gregorianum* 19 (1938): 280-301, where González cites the same passages from *On the Holy Trinity* as Régnon; Quasten, *Patrology*, 3:286-88, where, following Régnon, he cites *On "Not Three Gods,"* GNO IIIa 47.17—48.2 and 48.20—49.7; and Bettenson, *Later Christian Fathers* (London: Oxford University Press, 1970), 154, who cites GNO IIIa 46.16-18, as Régnon did at *Études* 1.396-97.

of theologians and scholars.[39] In practice, the observation that *On Not Three Gods* is not a polemical work supports the understanding that the description Gregory develops in this text functions as a conceptually generalized form of his theology, once his terminology has been related to the universal translator of Aristotelianism. The apparent lack in *On Not Three Gods* of a specific doctrinal opponent, and the fact that Gregory's language there is susceptible to an Aristotelian reading, allows the text to be read simply for its thematic emphasis. Yet it is interpretations of Augustine's Trinitarian theology that show even more the systematic avoidance of polemical readings and a widespread failure to consider Augustine's Trinitarian theology in a polemical context. Trinitarian works by Augustine that are incontrovertably polemical are no longer read, and works that can bear a polemical reading are consistently not read that way.[40] If the judgment that the *De Trinitate* lacks polemical intention were not so automatic, it would be infamous; the ideological need for *De Trinitate* to be free of polemical intent means that the well is poisoned on that judgment, even if it is true we cannot say that we know it to be so. I can illustrate the significance of this point with an example.

Augustine's treatment of Trinitarian economy in *De Trinitate* occurs primarily in books II to IV; it is book II particularly which has served as a scholar's laboratory, as it were, of Augustine's economic theology of the Trinity.[41] Formally, there are three noteworthy features to Augustine's argument in this book. First and foremost, it is a polemically charged argument, designed to combat a false "economy of the Trinity": various clues (e.g., the debate over the exegesis of John 5:19) as well as the evidence of *Collatio cum Maximino 26* and *Contra Maximinum 2* identify the proponents of this

---

39. See, for example, LaCugna, *God for Us*, 72. Typically, the idea that the Cappadocians used essence–energy language generally to speak of the Trinity comes through some neo-Palamite mediation, as is the case with Christopher Stead's statement that "[Cappadocian] theology therefore uses the term *energeia*, to stand for operations which are distinct from, and even contrasted with, the substance or essential nature from which they proceed . . . the divine energies are regarded as eternal and unvariant manifestations of God's power . . . This distinction between the intelligible divine energies and the inexpressible substance from which they proceed became an authoritative position of later Eastern orthodoxy" (Stead, *Divine Substance*, 279), a statement which shows a massive debt to neo-Palamite scholarship. That the neo-Palamite emphasis on an "essence–energy" distinction owes heavily to Régnon is clear from a careful reading of Lossky's *Essai sur la théologie mystique de l'église d'orient* (Paris: Aubier, 1944), 43–64, although the signs of Régnon's influence have been taken out of the English translation of *The Mystical Theology of the Eastern Church* repr. (Cambridge and London: James Clark, 1973). See my article "De Régnon Reconsidered," forthcoming in *Augustinian Studies*.

40. Congar surveys the influence of Latin pro-Nicenes on Augustine and acknowledges an attenuated polemical context for *Trin.* (*I Believe in the Holy Spirit*, 3:80); on the same page, he declines to describe Augustine "over against" the Greeks. Congar also knows and utilizes Augustine's late polemical works (see 3:91n3).

41. See Régnon's work in *Études*, 1.258–62, on Augustine's interpretation of theophanies in book II of *Trin.* Régnon claimed that Augustine's exegesis is polemically inspired. See also Lebreton, "Saint Augustin theologien de la trinité," *Studi Agostiniani* 2 (1931) 821–36, 821–36, and Pelikan, "Canonica Regula: The Trinitarian Hermeneutics of Augustine," *Proceedings of the PMR Conference* 12/13 (1987–88) 17–3. Most recently, J. Arnold has emphasized the soteriological content of Augustine's working through of the theophanies ("Begriff und heilsökonomische Bedeutung," 8–12).

false economy as Latin Homoians (Arians).[42] Anti-Nicenes excluded the Father from Old Testament theophanies so as to argue from these appearances the Son's changeability and materiality, and so Augustine must counter this argument. Another interesting feature of book II is that it is cast as a series of exegeses of Scripture (primarily passages from the Old Testament). Probably Augustine's choice of scriptural texts to exegete, and thus to dispute interpretations, is governed by Old Testament passages Homoians have chosen in support of their arguments (as is the case for New Testament passages in books V and VI). Nonetheless, the book remains structured around scriptural exegesis. The final noteworthy aspect of the argument in book II is that while the specific passages disputed are determined in response to Homoian polemic, some scriptural passages cited in support of Augustine's position are used because these have an older history, authority, and role in an economic theology of the Trinity. I am thinking, in particular, of the pivotal appeal to John 1:1–3 at *De Trinitate* II.2.9, which resembles Tertullian's (and Hippolytus') use of the Johannine prologue (but especially John 1:1) as the paradigmatic expression of the economy of the Trinity.[43]

Any substantial interpretation of Augustine's argument in book II, like any credible characterization of Augustine's argument in *De Trinitate* as a whole, would have to interpret the text in light of these three aspects, for otherwise Augustine's argument would be represented in a false context and thus misunderstood. However, I have not found that readings of *De Trinitate* in light of aspects such as the three just enumerated are common among contemporary theologians. Moreover, given the importance of book II for most modern patristics' accounts of Augustine's economical theology of the Trinity (especially Catholic accounts), it is surpising to find this subject skipped over in, e.g., LaCugna's treatment.[44]

If one compares the number of Augustinian texts consulted in contemporary accounts of his Trinitarian theology to the number of Augustinian texts consulted in accounts from a hundred years ago, what one finds is that the number has shrunk drastically. Hardly anyone refers to the last Trinitarian writings by Augustine anymore,

42. Edmund Hill suggests that Augustine's opponents in book II included Tertullian (in Augustine, *The Trinity* [Brooklyn: New City Press, 1991], 122n7). I cannot agree with that; see my next footnote.

43. The mention of Tertullian allows us to raise the question of the influence of Tertullian's distinctive understanding of the "economy" on Augustine. Unlike the tradition exemplified by Irenaeus and the Cappadocians, Tertullian uses *dispensatio* or *oikonomia* to refer to the reality of the relations in the Trinity (although not in a way which sets the relations over against their manifestations). See especially Robert A. Markus, 'Trinitarian Theology and the Economy," *Journal of Theological Studies* n.s. 9 (1958) 89–102. Markus' article is well known to LaCugna, but she shows no interest in developing the potential point contained in it, namely, that there is another "economic Trinity" tradition available in the early church, i.e., Tertullian's. Moreover, one must at least acknowledge the question of whether Tertullian's idiosyncratic use of economy influenced Augustine's treatment. If there is this specific influence from Tertullian, then Augustine's treatment of the economy will look very different than, e.g., the Cappadocian's treatment.

44. Given that LaCugna accepts so much of the scholastic analysis of Augustine (i.e., Régnon), it is likewise surprising that she should pass over this Catholic idiom in silence.

those against Maximinus.[45] The fact that these texts are not translated from Latin into a modern language means that, practically speaking, they are not being read by systematicians, a limitation that was not in place a hundred years ago.[46] Given that systematic reconstructions of Augustine's Trinitarian theology are now made on the basis of the single text, *De Trinitate,* or, not uncommonly, a canon of selections from this single text,[47] we can conclude that the actual reading of Augustine has been made functionally superfluous. The rhetorical voice of such reconstructive narratives is one of comprehensiveness, but the "historical method" supporting the narrative is in fact reductive. Stories of increasing scope are told on the basis of diminishing experience and evidence.

Given the preference in systematics for accounts framed in conceptual oppositions, the lack of interest in Trinitarian polemics is noteworthy and initially even puzzling. If one's rhetoric favors a presentation of one theology as over against another, then why avoid texts in which a doctrine is developed explicitly in opposition to another? The influence of Du Roy provides an initial clue: polemics are, explicitly at least, arguments over doctrines, and doctrines are not intrinsically significant or even integral to an idealistic history; ideas are. The project of an idealizing history is to restate doctrines (and all cultural forms) in terms of architectonic ideas, since the history of doctrine is truly understood only as the developing relationship among such ideas. The contemporary lack of attention to the polemical genre results from the need to present a thematic or universalized understanding of the theology at hand; polemical intention continues to be understood as a limit on the thematic application of a theology. For most of this century, such an approach has been characteristic of authoritative accounts of both Gregory's and Augustine's theologies.

It will be remembered that for the generation of scholars in the first half of this century who rediscovered Gregory of Nyssa, the initial appeal was the significance of his theology for twentieth-century Christianity, particularly for the possibility of a post-scholastic Catholicism. The distinctiveness of Gregory's debate with Eunomius was given short shrift by Daniélou (initially) and Balthasar.[48] Rather, their accounts of Eunomius' theology served only to introduce issues they eventually found better dramatized in the theology of Arius, who was himself only a transparent mask for the real protagonist, Origen. There is a similar universalizing tendency behind the lack of consideration of the polemical context of Augustine's theology. Any explanation

45. While I do not agree with much of his analysis, some use can be found for William A. Sumruld's *Augustine and the Arians* (Selinsgrove: Susquehanna University, 1994).

46. This omission will find a potential remedy in the forthcoming publication of Roland Teske's English translation of these later polemical works.

47. Pelikan, "Canonica Regula," 17, gives examples of the influence and authority of such selections of *Trin.* passages.

48. Hans Urs von Balthasar, *Présence et pensée: Essai sur la philosophie religieuse de Grégoire de Nysse* (Paris: Beauchesne, 1942) xvii; Jean Daniélou, *Platonisme et théologie mystique* (Paris: Aubier, 1944) 7.

of Augustine's Trinitarian theology as a polemical reaction to a problem distinctive to the late-fourth and early fifth centuries would diminish the claim (such as by those French Augustinians mentioned earlier) that Augustine's Trinitarian theology had an intrinsic authority that superseded that of his predecessors (including Nicaea) and that was not simply local (even if "local" is taken to mean "Western").[49]

The elimination of a polemical context to Augustine's Trinitarian doctrines has been further supported by a thematic (if not fictive) account of the stability of the West in terms of Trinitarian theology over against the instability of the East. Such an account implies that Latin Trinitarian theology, paradigmatically expressed by Augustine, possesses a generalized form that developed in a polemic-free context, as well as the prerequisite orthodoxy needed to supersede doctrines with more ambivalent ("heterodox") genealogies (such as a *homoousios*-based theology). It should be noted, however, that it is not just Augustine's sympathizers who feel the need for his Trinitarian theology to be free of polemical origins so that it might have an ideal application throughout the history of Catholicism (or Western civilization). As I have tried to show, critics of Augustine's Trinitarian theology have just as great an investment in conceiving his theology in an ideal, context-free (except for philosophy) fashion, and for the same reason: namely, for the sake of arguing for its universal application in later Western theology.

In conclusion, I have argued that contemporary systematic appropriations of Augustine are based upon methods and accounts that are pre-selected for mirroring a widely held hermeneutic or ideology of systematic theology. These methods and accounts typically include an unconscious dependence on Régnon, a tendency towards a logic of ideas, including a lust (operative even when unfulfilled) for encyclopedic comprehensiveness at the conceptual level coupled with a reductive use of primary sources, a retreat from the polemical genre, with an emphasis on the philosophical content of doctrine. The popular judgment that Augustine's Trinitarian theology sacrificed the *oeconomia* is presently too burdened by the unreflective use of such hermeneutical presuppositions to be regarded as established or even likely.

49. For more on the French Augustinian understanding of the relationship between Augustine's authority and his lack of polemical motivation see my 'The Arians of Book V and the Genre of *de Trinitate*,' *JThS* ns 44 (1993): 185–95.

Chapter 2

De Régnon Reconsidered

SLIGHTLY MORE THAN ONE-HUNDRED years ago, Théodore de Régnon, SJ, published the first volume of his *Études de théologie positive sur la sainté Trinité.*[1] This anniversary requires some observance because the publication of this work in 1892 made Régnon the most influential and yet least known of Catholic historians of doctrine. His influence comes from the widespread acceptance of his account of the character of Augustinian and Cappadocian Trinitarian theologies. His anonymity is due to the fact that in English language scholarship especially, his account of these theologies has been promulgated and used without credit. The two most important of Régnon's conclusions are, first, that the core of Cappadocian theology is that it argued the unity of nature from the unity of activities; and second, that patristic Trinitarian theology, as represented by the Cappadocians, proceeds from the diversity of persons, while scholastic Trinitarian theology, as represented by Augustine, proceeds from the unity of nature. This latter conclusion contrasting patristic and scholastic Trinitarian theologies will be referred to as Régnon's paradigm. The related descriptions of Augustinian and Cappadocian Trinitarian theologies appear regularly in scholarly discussions, and—with equal regularity—without any recognition of their origin. My purpose in this article is to recognize Régnon's influence and to offer a critical account of the debate that his work initiated among French Augustinians, a debate which has remained largely unobserved among English-language scholars.[2]

Régnon's study of the theology of the Trinity is a massive four-volume work, typical of the etude style of scholarship later exhibited in Festugière's treatment of *Corpus*

---

1. *Études de théologie positive sur la sainté Trinité* (Paris: Victor Retaux, 1892/1898).

2. Since my purpose involves introducing the reader to the contours of an argument carried on primarily in French, I will translate all the representative texts I offer (except in the few cases where translations are already available).

Hermeticum,[3] or Larcher's work on the Wisdom tradition,[4] meaning, among other things, that the material is organized thematically rather than historically. Volumes 3 and 4 were published in 1896, posthumously, after Régnon died in his study on December 26, 1893, surrounded by the manuscript. Régnon's two earliest works are on the then-topical controversy between Banes and Molina,[5] which may have led him to his other major work of scholarship, a treatment of the understanding of causality in the thought of Thomas Aquinas and Albert the Great.[6] These works altogether reveal Régnon's background in Thomism and scholasticism. In this article, I will speak only of the first volume of his *Etude* since it contains Régnon's paradigm regarding the character of Augustinian and Cappadocian Trinitarian theologies, his most enduring legacy.

This work begins with a forty-page review of theories of epistemology, in which Régnon gives an historical summary of realism, idealism, nominalism and Kantianism. Régnon describes each epistemology according to its account of the relationship between the external object to be known and the noetic object: the thing and the idea of the thing. Only after offering these descriptions does he reveal the need for such a review: a theory of knowledge is the prerequisite foundation for the act of reading, and Régnon's purpose in the study is to provide an occasion for the reading of patristic texts on the Trinity. The fact that this is his purpose leads Régnon to use the innovative technique of quoting long sections from important authors, a departure from the old style of citing just authoritative phrases or paraphrases. Indeed, the very quotations selected by Régnon will leave their mark on later scholarship as signs of his influence, a point I will return to later.

Régnon's own epistemology is, not surprisingly, of the realist school as developed by Thomas Aquinas: he believes that the object to be known exists in the mind according to the nature of the mind, or to use the well-known aphorism, something is known according to the capacity of the knower. In this epistemology there is a positive relationship between the existent that is known and the idea of that existent, but because of the difference in the kind of existence of the object known and the object of knowledge, that relationship is that of an analogy.

In the theological application of this epistemology, Régnon judges that the Trinity cannot be known in itself, but that the key to knowledge of the Trinity lies in acknowledging the reality of the manifold expressions of its existence, which, in terms of doctrine, means acknowledging the authority or authenticity of the different (orthodox) accounts or doctrines of the Trinity. This understanding of the relationship between

3. R. P. Festugiere, *La révélation d'Hermès Trismégiste*, 4 vols. (Paris: Société d'Éditions des Belles Lettres, 1944–45).

4. Chrysostome Larcher, *Études sur Ie Livre de La Sagesse* (Paris: J. Gabalda, 1969).

5. *Banes et Molina: Histoire, Doctrines, Critique métaphysique* (Paris: V. Retaux, 1883). Régnon also wrote several articles on Banes and Molina during his career.

6. *Métaphysique des causes d'après saint Thomas et Albert Ie Grand* (Paris: Retaux-Bray, 1886). Gaston Sortais gives a pleasant and useful posthumous summary of Régnon's career in the second edition (1906) of this work.

the nature of God's existence and the propriety of doctrines about God should be familiar to most readers: it resembles, for example, Basil of Caesarea's doctrine of *epinoia*, or, more pointedly, the *energeia* language used by Basil or his brother, Gregory. This latter resemblance is not a coincidence, as I will show shortly. Régnon explicitly links the fact that God's nature is known only in manifold expressions to the necessity of true theological knowledge having manifold expressions; he offers the charming analogy (borrowed from Irenaeus) of the process of reconstructing a marble floor mosaic which was originally of one grand design, although now its facets appear to us as unrelated pieces.[7] This indeed is Régnon's "hermeneutic" of doctrine (Régnon himself uses the word *hermeneutique*), that is to say, it is the epistemological ground for Régnon's scholarly mission to present different accounts of the Trinity without requiring or forcing the reader to choose among them, since they are all necessary to understand God and since, as we shall see, there exists among them all a kind of unity.

Régnon's idea of this multifaceted understanding of the Trinity is developed explicitly from Ginoulhiac,[8] who believed that dogmatic history may be divided into epochs or eras, each of which is distinguished by a theological insight or problematic that determines the doctrinal parameters of that era. For example, Ginoulhiac argued that underlying all pre-Nicene Trinitarian theology is a concern for the order and dignity of the Three Persons, while underlying Nicene and post-Nicene theology is a concern for the equality of the Three Persons.[9] Such underlying concerns that shape the doctrines of an era I call doctrinal paradigms. Régnon's own doctrinal paradigms are responses to Ginoulhiac's project of organizing the history of dogma as a succession of doctrinal paradigms. Régnon development of Ginoulhiac's judgment can be seen in three distinctive ways: the first is to subsume the pre-Nicene and Nicene eras of theology that Ginoulhiac postulates into one over-arching epoch with one over-arching paradigm of Trinitarian doctrine, i.e., the "patristic"; the second is to show how the "patristic" doctrinal paradigm of the Trinity differed from its successor, the scholastic doctrinal paradigm; and third, to demonstrate at the same time the patristic roots of scholastic doctrine in Augustine and thereby to show how each successive stage of Trinitarian theology contains its predecessor.[10]

---

7. *Études de théologie positive*, 1:43.

8. Jacques Marie Ginoulhiac, *Histoire du dogme catholique*, in three vols., 2nd ed. (Paris: Auguste Durand Librarie, 1866.)

9. Régnon cites Ginoulhiac's *Histoire du dogme catholique* VIII.I at *Etudes* I.335–36, and again at I.358. Ginoulhiac summarizes his overall divisions of the epochs of doctrine at *Histoire du dogme catholique*, I.lxxxviii. Régnon's other references to Ginoulhiac are scattered throughout the text (e.g., I.117).

10. As one would suspect, behind Régnon's understanding that each "successive stage of Trinitarian theology contains its predecessor" lies the Aristotelian understanding that each stage of soul contains its predecessors. Régnon makes extensive recourse to the soul as a paradigm object of knowledge in the introduction to *Études* (I.26–28).

Régnon agreed with Ginoulhiac that dogmatic history could be distinguished by eras with their particular doctrinal paradigms, but he disagreed with Ginoulhiac that there were the two distinct epochs and doctrinal paradigms of pre-Nicene and Nicene. Régnon recognized in the first four hundred years or so of Christianity a single epoch and a single corresponding doctrinal paradigm. The single dogmatic epoch, with its corresponding single theological paradigm, is what Régnon means by the word patristic. The content of the patristic paradigm is that the divine is always encountered in or as a person.[11] Régnon found this paradigm consistently expressed in, e.g., the writings of Irenaeus, Athanasius, Cyril of Jersusalem, Hilary, the Cappadocians, and John Damascene. Régnon does maintain that the patristic doctrinal paradigm of the Trinity finds its most developed expression in Cappadocian theology, but he never limits the emphasis on person over nature to Greek theology. Although later scholars often identify this doctrinal paradigm with Cappadocian or Greek theology, Régnon himself never made this identification, and indeed this kind of identification contradicts his overall point. Régnon never reads pre-Augustinian Latins out of this patristic emphasis on the individual persons. Nonetheless, the popular understanding of the categories that Régnon called patristic and scholastic has identified them with Greek and Latin theologies respectively, which leads us to Régnon's third development of Ginoulhiac.

Régnon's last development of Ginoulhiac's description of the history of doctrine as a series of dogmatic epochs lies in his understanding that in Augustine's theology the patristic paradigm is transformed into the scholastic; in particular, the end of the patristic epoch meets the beginning of the scholastic in the doctrine of inner-Trinitarian relations. The scholastic paradigm is, of course, that divinity is always understood in or as a nature. The "raw insight," as it were, in patristic theology of understanding the Three Persons of God through their relations—i.e., Father, Son, and Spirit—remains intact in scholastic theology, but it is reconfigured by a new paradigm. The difference between the patristic paradigm and the scholastic paradigm is illustrated in the difference between Gregory of Nazianzus' doctrine of internal relations and Augustine's doctrine of internal relations. What Régnon described as the Augustinian and proto-scholastic doctrinal paradigm has been "discovered" by modern scholars in pre-Augustinian Latin theology, including Tertullian, various bishops of Rome, and Ambrose. However, Régnon never made this case, and his belief that the scholastic paradigm began only with Augustine may be illustrated by two examples: first, he regularly uses Hilary to illustrate the doctrinal paradigm today usually said to be "Greek";[12] and second, when Régnon turns to examining the philosophical

---

11. "La premier concept de la divinite tombe sur une personne, concrete, reelle, individuelle, incommunicable" (Régnon, *Études,* I.336).

12. Régnon, *Études,* I.104–5, 372–76, and 395.

background of the "scholastic" paradigm, none of the sources pre-date Augustine. The earliest is Boethius.[13]

The continuing importance of Régnon's paradigm can easily be seen in modern works on the Trinity, as, for example, Frederick Crowe's 1966 *Doctrine of the Holy Trinity*,[14] James Mackey's 1983 *The Christian Experience of God as Trinity*,[15] John O'Donnell's 1985 *Trinity and Temporality*,[16] David Brown's 1985 *The Divine Trinity*,[17] and Catherine LaCugna's 1991 *God for Us*.[18] In each of these works, patristic Trinitarian theology is organized according to Régnon's paradigm. There is no acknowledgment of the scholastic origins of the paradigm by any of the authors, or any sense that the paradigm is something other than self-evident. The limitations of the paradigm are a source of frustration to Mackey and O'Donnell, yet their own assumption that the paradigm is self-evident prevents them from escaping the very limitations they chafe against. Similarly, Brown and LaCugna embrace the paradigm and develop it fruitfully in order to critique the Augustinian component, but both scholars seem unaware that the paradigm is not embedded in the original texts.

French scholarship, on the other hand, has had a lively running argument over whether Régnon was right about his paradigm, as one sees in Henri Paissac's 1951 *Theologie du Verbe*,[19] Andre Malet's 1956 *Personne et amour dans la théologie trinitaire*,[20] Guy Lafont's 1969 *Peuton connaitre Dieu?*,[21] M.J. Le Guillou's 1972 "Reflexions sur la théologie trinitaire,"[22] and Bertrand de Margerie's 1975 *La trinite chretienne*.[23] What is common to all these works is the criticism that Greek Trinitarian theology is not only nature-based but improperly nature-based because of the Greek attachment to the term *homoousios*. According to these same scholars, Latin Trinitarian theology, by which they mean Augustine's Trinitarian theology, is person-oriented, and not nature-oriented as Régnon would have it, because Augustine's theology is based on psychology and not physics. In the opinion of Paissac, Malet, and Le Guillou, Augustine

13. Régnon's interest in Boethius springs, of course, from Boethius' importance for the scholastic understanding of person. See Régnon, *Études*, I.130–131, 227–32.

14. *Doctrine of the Holy Trinity* (Willowdale: Regis College, 1965/66).

15. *The Christian Experience of God as Trinity* (London: SCM Press, 1983).

16. *Trinity and Temporality: The Christian Doctrine of God in the Light of Process Theology and the Theology of Hope* (Oxford: Oxford University Press, 1983).

17. *The Divine Trinity* (La Salle: Open Court Publishing Company, 1985).

18. *God For Us* (San Francisco: Harper, 1991).

19. Paissac does not cast his book explicitly as an argument with Régnon's position, but there are many reasons for recognizing that this position is his target, not the least of which is his overall silence regarding Régnon, which provokes the same question as the silence of the watchdog in the Sherlocks Holmes story, "The Adventure of Silver Blaze": Why doesn't he bark?

20. Malet, *Personne et Amour*, 11.

21. G. Lafont, *Peut-on connaitre Dieu en Jesus-Christ?*, (coll. Cogitatio fidei, 44, Paris, 1969), 458–462.

22. Le Guillou, "Reflexions sur la theologie trinitaire," 457–64. Esp. 458.

23. Le Guillou, "Reflexions sur la theologie trinitaire," 222–25.

escaped the inhibiting polemical context that made the Greeks avoid a *logos*-centered Christology and substitute in its place a materialistic understanding of divine nature based on *homoousios*. This critique is not only meant to show that Greek Trinitarian theology was inhibited by its polemical context, but also to deny completely the force of that inhibition upon Augustine, and, in particular, to reject Régnon's understanding that Augustine's interpretation of the theophanies in book II of *De Trinitate* is a polemical rejoinder to Maximinus.[24]

Now, there are many problems with the French Augustinian critique of Régnon, although I will name only three. First is the assumption that Greek pro-Nicene theology is centered on *homoousios,* a distorting assumption that unfortunately is widely shared in most modern traditions of scholarship. Second, the French Augustinians exhibit an ignorance of the fact that Latin pro-Nicene theology in the figures of Hilary, Victorinus, and Ambrose is much more centered on *homoousios* than any comparable Greek pro-Nicene theology (excepting only Athanasius), though yet again this misunderstanding is by no means limited to French Augustinians. Third, the French Augustinians have a hard time distinguishing what Augustine thought from what Aquinas thought. In their favor, however, these scholars do know that the patristic–scholastic Trinitarian paradigm in question came from Régnon's pen. For more than sixty years, they have been arguing over whether he was right, just as for most of this century much of English and German language scholarship has been arguing over whether or not Harnack was right. Most importantly, the French Augustinians understand that, from the hermeneutical point of view, Régnon's paradigm represents a moment in Catholic scholastic Trinitarian theology, an understanding that is largely lost among English-language scholars, and even English-language scholastics such as Crowe. Thus, while most scholarly accounts of Trinitarian theology in the early church assume Régnon's paradigm, English-language scholarship has largely taken this paradigm as an axiom while, by contrast, French-language scholarship makes it clear that this is Régnon's own paradigm, and that he may be wrong.[25]

One particular episode in modern scholarship dramatizes well both the peculiar feature of Régnon's influence and the unacknowledged role of scholasticism in his account of doctrine. In Régnon's view, the paradigmatic expression of Cappadocian Trinitarian theology is found in the writings *De Trinitate* and *On Not Three Gods*, two works now attributed to Gregory of Nyssa, although Régnon thought that *De Trinitate* was

24. Régnon refers first to Maximinus' argument, given in the *Collatio cum Maximino* (26), that OT theophanies are appearances of the Son; then to Augustine's rebuttal of that thesis in *Contra Maximinum* (II.c.xxvi, 10ff). The arguments in *Trin.* II interpreting the OT theophanies as appearances of God are thought—by Régnon—to develop (and follow chronologically) those in *Contra Maximinum.* See Régnon, *Études,* I.258–62.

25. I do not know when exactly the paradigm crossed the channel from French to British scholarship, but I suspect that it was either when Lampe invited Krivocheine over from Belgium to help finish the Patristic Lexicon, or through the research of Prestige, one of the few British authors of the first half of this century to cite French scholarship. (The French, of course, returned the compliment, so that Prestige is one of the few English scholars cited by French Augustinians.)

by Basil. Régnon found in these works the fundamentals of Cappadocian Trinitarian theology.[26] Although Régnon does not say why he chose these two works, two reasons reveal themselves. First, by treating the divinity of the Spirit, and therefore recognizing the complete Trinity, these texts give the impression (falsely, I would maintain) that the arguments for full divinity contained in these works are equally applicable for each Person of the Trinity. A corollary to this is the lack of any obvious polemical context to these two works. This lack is taken to imply a more "universal" significance.

The second reason for Régnon's treating *De Trinitate* and *On Not Three Gods* as paradigmatic expressions of Cappadocian Trinitarian theology is a familiar one today. The arguments in these two works build upon the relationship between *physis* and *energeia*. According to Régnon, the fundamental doctrine of Cappadocian Trinitarian theology, indeed of patristic Trinitarian theology, is that the unity of activities among the Persons proves the unity of nature.[27] Régnon's argument for the importance of *energeia* and *physis* language in Cappadocian theology is based on passages from *De Trinitate* and *On Not Three Gods*. This characterization has become a scholarly commonplace on Greek Trinitarian theology, but if one reads Régnon's original argument, one learns that he fixed upon *physis* and *energeia* because he considered the Cappadocian use of nature and operations to be analogous to the use of nature and operations in scholastic Trinitarian theology (specifically Cajetan). What appealed to Régnon in this analogy was not that the senses of nature and operations were the same in both Cappadocian and scholastic Trinitarian theologies, but that the same concepts were given such different applications or interpretations in these two theologies.[28] Like the doctrine of divine relations that I referred to earlier, Régnon sees in the common patristic and scholastic use of nature and operations evidence of common doctrines being shaped by different theological paradigms. Régnon therefore chose not only *De Trinitate*[29] and *On Not Three Gods*,[30] but specific passages in these two

---

26. Régnon, *Études*, I.391–98.

27. "Tous les Pères ont suivi cette même voie pour etablir la consubstantialite des trois personnes. Tous se sont appuyes sur l'unite d'operation exterieure pour demontrer l'unite de la nature divine" (Régnon, *Études*, I.392).

28. "Comparez ce concept d'une operation qui est une, parce qu'elle circule a travers les trois personnes qui la produisent; comparez-le, dis-je, avec le concept thomiste d'une operation qui est une, parce qu'elle sort d'une nature subsistante en elle-même avant d'être completée par les subsistences relatives. Sans vous contraindre a choisir entre saint Basilée et Cajetan, ne puis-je vous demander d'avouer que leurs manieres de concevoir l'unite de operation divine sont absolument differentes?" (Régnon, *Études*, I.391). Régnon's point here may indeed be how absolutely different the Greek understanding of divine operation is from the Thomistic understanding of the "same" terms, but it is the Thomistic precedent that leads him to focus upon *energeia* language in the first place. See also Régnon, *Études*, I.394.

29. Régnon, as was typical of his day, attributes *Ad Eustathium* to Basil: at Régnon, *Études*, I.391, he cites *Ep.* 189.6 (Courtonne II.138.12—139.26); and at I.392 he cites *Ep.* 189.7 (Courtonne II.140.29–33). Régnon does not refer to a Greek edition of the letter.

30. *On Not Three Gods*, GNO IIIa 46.20–48.8 at I.396–97; and 48.20—51.5 at 397–98. Régnon's references are to the Migne and not to the GNO.

works as normative of Cappadocian theology because of the conceptual relationship to scholastic categories evident in their use of *physis* and *energeia*. The same passages, without the conceptual flying buttresses, are selected by González in his article on the identity of the exterior works and the divine operations;[31] they are the same passages that Quasten uses to give his description of *physis* and *energeia* in Cappadocian theology;[32] and they are the same passages that Bettenson extracts in his selection of representative Cappadocian Trinitarian theology.[33] In short, *physis* and *energeia* are now normally understood as the fundamental categories of Cappadocian Trinitarian theology, and the passages Régnon emphasized from *De Trinitate* and *On Not Three Gods* have functioned as a "canon" of Cappadocian Trinitarian theology.[34]

It could be suggested that the description of Cappadocian Trinitarian theology in terms of *physis* and *energeia* is supported by the analysis of neo-Palamite scholars such as Vladimir Lossky. Such a description of Cappadocian theology can be found, for example, in chapter 3 of Lossky's book *The Mystical Theology of the Eastern Church*, where he treats Cappadocian Trinitarian theology precisely in terms of *physis* and *energeia*.[35] This description may seem to provide independent substantiation of Régnon's account, and it certainly has been taken that way. However, if one turns to the original French edition of Lossky's work, *Éssai sur la théologie mystique de l'église d'orient*,[36] one finds that in the chapter 3 account of Greek Trinitarian theology, Lossky cites Régnon repeatedly: out of the forty-three footnotes in that chapter, twelve refer to Régnon. Yet in the 1957 English translation of the original French work, all the citations to Régnon are missing except two direct quotations, and his name does not appear in the book's index of authors cited. What, in the original, were Lossky's footnote references to passages in Régnon's *Études* become in the English translation footnote references to the Cappadocian texts originally discussed by Régnon. There is more at work here than

31. See Severino Gonzalez's "La identidad de operacion en las obras exteriores y la unidad de la naturaleza divina en la teologia trinitaria de S. Gregoria de N isa," Gregorianum, XIX (1938), 280–301. González cites the same passages from *On the Holy Trinity* as Régnon: *Ad. Eustathium, Ep.* 189.6 (Courtonne II.138.12–139.26) and 189.7 (Courtonne II.140.29–33). González's references predate Courtonne's critical edition.

32. See Johannes Quasten's *Patrology: The Golden Age of Greek Patristic Literature*, 4th ed. (Utrecht/ Antwerp: Spectrum Publishers, 1975) III:286 ff., where, following Régnon, he cites *On Not Three Gods*, GNO IIIa 47.17–48.2 and 48.20–49.7. Quasten gives no references to a Greek text.

33. Bettenson, *Later Christian Fathers*, 154, cites GNO IIIa 46.16 ff., as does Régnon at I.396–97. Bettenson gives no references to Greek language texts.

34. One can contrast typical accounts of Gregory's theology based on Régnon's canon of concepts and texts with Hanson's account in *The Search for the Christian Doctrine of God: The Arian Controversy 318–381* (Edinburgh: T. &. T. Clark, 1988), 723–30. That account shows no substantial debt to Régnon's canon, but rather builds upon texts which Hanson selects with an eye on the historical context. In particular, Hanson explains Gregory's Trinitarian theology with greater emphasis on those works against Eunomius than is typical of accounts that follow Régnon.

35. Lossky, *Mystical Theology of the Eastern Church*, rpt. (Cambridge and London: James Clark & Co., Ltd., 1973), 44–66.

36. Lossky, *Éssai sur la théologie mystique de l'église d'orient*, (Paris: Aubier, 1944), 43–64.

a slip of the translator's pen: there is in fact the appropriation of Régnon's paradigm by modern neo-Palamite theology, coupled with a hesitation, if not embarrassment, at acknowledging its Roman Catholic (indeed, Jesuit) origins. If this appropriation is recognized, however, the neo-Palamite fascination with Thomism begins to make sense. I am not the first to suggest this appropriation. André de Halleux has already said as much,[37] but I am able to offer the specific evidence of Lossky's Régnon footnotes in support.[38]

The mention of Halleux provides the opportunity to enlarge the discussion of Régnon and French Augustinian scholarship. In 1984 and in 1986, Halleux published articles which treated directly the influence and standing of Régnon's "Greek–Latin" thesis among scholars writing primarily in French.[39] I offer a lengthy quotation from Halleux to provide a clear overview of the state of the debate in French scholarship over Régnon's paradigm.

> The opposition between Greek personalism and Latin essentialism has been systematized by Régnon in the fourth, fifth, and sixth volumes of his distinguished *Études*. Today, Régnon's formula is reversed by French Thomist theologians such as Malet, Lafont, or Le Guillou. The last two give less importance to geographical differences between the Trinitarian theologies of the East and West than to the chronological rupture that the council of Nicaea introduced in Christian theology, that is, between an "immanent trinity" with its eternal processions, and "the economic trinity," with its temporal missions.[40]

Here Halleux raises the economic-immanent dichotomy; he makes it clear that this dichotomy was conceived as a competing paradigm to Régnon's. Indeed, all the French theologians I will discuss recall Régnon's model for the sake of rebutting it with an alternate model of their own. Halleux refers to A. Malet, G. Lafont, and M.-J. Le Guillou in particular; Paissac and Margerie can be added to this list, as well. Margerie is worth noting for two other reasons: first, in his own work he groups together Malet, Lafont, and Le Guillou in a judgment similar to Halleux's, though with more sympathy to

37. "Personnalisme ou essentialisme trinitaire chez les Pères cappadociens?" *Revue theologique de Louvain* 17 (1986), 129–55, 265–92. I note with sadness and a sense of loss Halleux's recent death.

38. My suspicion is that Lossky's very choice of Cappadocian theology as the summarizing expression of Greek theology is owed to Régnon.

39. In 1984, Halleux, "Hypostase et personnedans la formation du dogme trinitaire (ca. 375–381)," *Revue d'histoire ecclesiastique* 79 (1984), 313–69, 625–70; and in 1986, the already cited Halleux, "Personnalisme."

40. [L]'opposition du personnalisme grec et de l'essentialisme latin a eté systematisée par le P. Régnon dans les IVe, Ve et Vie de ses celebres Études. Le schema du P. Régnon se trouve aujourd'hui inverse par des theologiens thomistes francais tel que Malet, G. Lafont ou M.-J. Le Guillou. Le deux derniers accordent d'ailleurs moins d'importance a la divergence 'géographie' entre les théologies trinitaires de l'Orient et de l'Occident qu'a la rupture 'chronologique' que le concile de Nicée introduit, dans la théologie chretienne tout entiere, entre la 'trinité immanente', avec ses processions eternelles, et la 'trinité economique', avec ses missions temporelles (Halleux, "Hypostase et personne," 669n1).

their project(s);[41] and second, Margerie's work is a clear example of an account of patristic Trinitarian theology built upon offering an alternate paradigm to Régnon's.[42]

Margerie, Malet, Lafont, and Le Guillou all share and reveal a feature characteristic of their scholarly opposition to Régnon: they treat Régnon's "diversity–unity" paradigm as a given, a commonplace, which while explicitly linked to Régnon in origin, is nonetheless treated with great generality. For example, while Le Guillou begins his article, "Reflexions sur la theologie trinitaire apropos de quelques livres anciens et recents," with a section entitled "The Simplistic Scheme of Régnon," he does not actually quote, cite, or treat Régnon in this section or anywhere else in his article.[43] Instead, he quotes (extensively) an article by Malet to make this point:

> In effect, it has been, seventy years since Régnon established the simplistic formula of two irreducible forms of Trinitarian theology, one which was founded on the priority of the persons, and which would be closer to the scriptural approach—namely, the approach of the Greek fathers; the other founded on the priority of the nature, which was more distant from the Scriptures, more philosophical and more abstract, and which would become the approach of Latin fathers ever since Augustine.[44]

Guillou gives no citations from Régnon in support of any of his conclusions. More importantly, neither does Malet or Lafont, both of whom Guillou quotes to make his argument that Régnon's scheme is fundamentally simplistic and wrong.[45] Margerie (writing after Guillou) treats Régnon the same way. He says, "More generally, we have to be suspicious of cliches about the Latin and Greek traditions that have been made more or less sacrosanct, particularly those of Régnon."[46]

Margerie offers no references to Régnon's own work, but instead cites Malet. Further examples of similar "arguments" against Régnon could be provided, but the quote from Margerie makes the point clearly, if somewhat ironically: Régnon's paradigm is such a "cliche" that its refutation does not require citing its original authentic

---

41. Bertrand de Margerie, *La Trinité chrétienne dans l'histoire* (Paris: Edition Beauchesne, 1975), 225, for example.

42. See Margerie, *La Trinité chrétienne*, 225–27.

43. Margerie, *La Trinité chrétienne*, 225–27.

44. "Voilà soixante-quinze ans, en effet, que le P. Régnon a accrédité la schéma simpliste de deux formes irréductibles de théologie trinitaire, l'une fondée sur la primauté des Personnes, qui serait plus proche de l'Ecriture—ce serait celle des Pères grecs,—l'autre, fondée sur la primauté de la Nature, qui serait plus éloignée des Ecritures, plus philosophique et plus abstraite—ce serait celle des Pères latins depuis Augustin" (Margerie, *La Trinité chrétienne*, 457).

45. Malet and the others do cite specific passages from Régnon, at times; but none of these citations are to the *Études* in the premiere series where Régnon offers his Greek versus scholastic (meaning Augustinian) paradigm. The references to this theory of Régnon's are consistently in general terms, even when other parts of Régnon's work is referred to specifically. There will be examples of such citations of Régnon throughout this essay.

46. "D'une façon plus générale, ii faut se méfier des 'clichés' plus ou moins consacrés, notamment à la suit du P. Régnon, sur ces deux traditions latine et grecque" (Margerie, *La Trinité chrétienne*, 225).

expression. I can only say that while Régnon may indeed be wrong, nothing these scholars say against him proves it. However, aside from their vague attacks on Régnon, Margerie and Guillou do both bring forward their own alternate paradigms of patristic Trinitarian theology.

Margerie, for example, lists three differences between Greek and Latin Trinitarian theology. First is the linguistic difference between the two languages. Second, Margerie notes that the Greeks "divide" the Trinity after the Father; the Latins "divide" the Trinity after the Son.[47] This characterization seems to be, first, an attempt to reclaim the diagram usually associated with Régnon; and second, a restatement of traditional material such as the understanding that Greek theology begins with the "Father as cause,"[48] and the general fascination with the *filioque* problem. Margerie's comments on the different causalities inherent in the Greek use of *ek,* as opposed to the Latin use of *ab,* combines both these characterizations.[49] I think the third "difference" Margerie offers is the most telling of the three: namely, that the two traditions represent two different moments in history.

> Greeks and Latins have constituted two different branches at the root of a single grand Christian tradition . . . Perhaps we have not noted sufficiently that Greek speculation represented a first stage of the elaboration and evolution of Trinitarian dogma, which Latin reflection followed as a later stage.[50]

> The Greeks never arrived at the point of examining the mystery of the Trinty with the help of the psychological analogy; they stopped before they got there.[51]

For Margerie, as already for Crowe,[52] the difference between the Greeks and the Latins is a question of development: the Greeks just never got as far as the Latins did, and the sum total of this further development is the psychological analogy. I have

---

47. Margerie, *La Trinité chrétienne,* 225–26.

48. This characterization seems to be borrowed from Prestige, even if it does not originate with him, since several of these authors—English and French—speak of this feature of Greek theology, namely, that the Father is understood as the originating cause and source of the divinity. Malet (*Personne et Amour,* 14) argues that despite this understanding, the Greeks did not totally identify the Father with the divine, and points to the use of the "Wisdom from Wisdom" (Sagesse de Sagesse), etc., type model—i.e., a non-personal model—to describe divine production and unity as an indication of an essence-based Trinitarian theology. See Halleux, "Personalisme," 266.

49. Margerie, *La Trinité chrétienne,* 224.

50. "[L]es Grecs et les Latins ont constitué deux branches differentes au sein de l'unique grande tradition chrétienne. On n'a peut-être pas assez remarqué que la spéculation grecque represente un premier stade d'élaboration et d'évolution du dogme trinitaire, auquel la réflexion latine succede comme un stade posterieur" (Margerie, *La Trinité chrétienne,* 223).

51. "[L]es Grecs non sont pas parvenus à approfondir le mystère a l' aide de l'analogie psychologique, ils se sont arrêtés avant. Ce qui n' empêches pas leur scheme trinitaire d'avoir certains avantages que nous verrons" (Margerie, *La Trinité chrétienne,* 226).

52. Crowe, *Doctrine of the Most Holy Trinity,* 110.

already noted authors for whom the Augustinian model means the psychological analogy, and I shall have more to say about this identification later in this article.

Guillou's characterization of differences between Greek and Latin theologies is slightly different from Margerie's; Guillou's alternate paradigm is more powerful, I think, than Margerie's, though it is not truly Guillou's, for it had been percolating up in French Augustinian scholarship for years.[53]

> From the study of patristic texts, one arrives at a certain conclusion: the separation between *theologia* and *oeconomia* is an indirect consequence of the council of Nicaea. Required to think in terms of consubstantiality, to place the *hypostasis* in relation to the essence, the fathers of the fourth and fifth centuries were forced to reverse the order of theological considerations of the Trinity, a way of thinking which had not been contemplated by ante-Nicene theologians, all of whom started with the Father and concentrated on the economy.[54]

Guillou makes this point, as is his fashion, by quoting extensively from Malet and Lafont.[55] The most succinct statement of Guillou's point is offered by him in his quotation from Lafont:

> It would be, undoubtedly, more exact to see a separation in the time, not in the space, between anti-Nicene and post-Nicene fathers. Between these two categories, there is a difference of theologies; between Greeks and Latins of the same period, there is only a difference of doctrines.[56]

As is clear in this set of distinctions, "pre-Nicene" stands in for "economic," and "post-Nicene" stands in for "immanent." The point of the claim that the real distinction among patristic Trinitarian theologies is the one between pre- and post-Nicene is that the Cappadocian and Augustinian theologies are in the same category, i.e., post-Nicene, and that appearances and Régnon to the contrary, the Cappadocians have as much an "immanent" theology as Augustine. Both theological traditions operate under the burden of the doctrine of *homoousios* or consubstantiality. The effect of this burden is that henceforth all Trinitarian theology, even that of the Cappadocians, is no

---

53. Halleux draws attention to this judgment in Ghislain Lafont's writing. See Halleux, "Personalisme," 276.

54. "L' etude des textes patristiques impose une certitude: la rupture entre la 'théologie' et 'l'économie' est une conséquence indirecte du Concile de Nicée. Constraints de penser le 'consubstantiel', de situer Jes hypostases par rapport à l'essence, les Pères des IV–V siecles ont dû renverser l'orde de la consideration théologique de la Trinité, qui n'avait été contemplée jusqu'alors par les théologiens anténicéens qu'à partir du Père et toute tournée vers l'économie" (Le Guillou, "Reflexions sur la theologie trinitaire," 457).

55. Le Guillou, "Reflexions sur la theologie trinitaire," 458–62.

56. "II serait sans doute plus exact de voir un clivage dans le temps, non dans l' espace, entre Pères anté-nicéens et Peres post-nicéens. Entre ces derniers, ii y a une différence de théologies; entre Grecs et Latins d'une même époque, ii y a seulement une différence d'écoles" (Original text in Lafont, *Peut-on connaitre Dieu en Jesus-Christ?*, 69–70; cited in Guillou, "Reflexions sur la theologie trinitaire," 459–60).

more than an attempt to save the appearances of the economic Trinity. An argument such as Martland's,[57] Brown's, or even LaCugna's, namely that Cappadocian theology is somehow more true to the traditional economic Trinity of revelation, is pre-empted. Given this common ground between Cappadocian and Augustinian theology, the superiority of the Augustinian model is evident, these scholars argue, because Augustine faced the "immanence" model more squarely and offered a better account of that immanence, namely, the psychological analogy. It should also be noted that the Guillou-Lafont thesis is another quiet criticism of Régnon, who explicitly taught that post-Nicene "patristic" theology continued pre-Nicene "economic" theology.[58]

The understanding that post-Nicene Greeks laboured within the immanent context of *homoousios*–consubstantiality as much as did post-Nicene Latins has led French scholars to critique the *homoousios* model they understand to have been offered by the Greeks, in particular by the Cappadocians.[59] For these scholars, the best critique of the Greek model is also the best exemplar of Augustine's model, namely, in Augustine's *On the Trinity*, books VI and VII,[60] where Augustine prepares the way for his own doctrine of interior relations and the psychological analogy by offering his exegesis of 1 Corinthians 1:24, "Christ the Power and Wisdom of God." These scholars understand the attributions or titles Wisdom and Power to be essence-based models of unity, like (the comparison is made explicitly by the French) Light, Life, etc., and the sense of 1 Corinthians 1:24 is expanded to include these other models of unity. These titles are then compared to Augustine's direct use of essence and his own essence-based model of interior relations and the psychological analogy. The psychological analogy is then identified with the attribution of the title Word, which again forms the basis for criticizing the other titles. Word really names the second Person, and the ground of the Divine Unity, in ways which Wisdom, Power, etc., do not. The rest of this article will be devoted to a critical response to this argument by the French Augustinians.

The French interpretation of Augustine focuses on the description of the relationship between (in particular) the First and Second Persons as the causal relationship of Like from Like, e.g., Wisdom from Wisdom, Power from Power, Light from Light, or generally put, *X from X*. This model is found wanting when compared to a strict essence-based relational model, i.e., Augustine's model of interior relations. This emphasis on a critique of the Greek *X from X* causal model may begin with Denys Petau, who is cited by early modern scholars such as Legrand (in 1931).[61] The emphasis continues through the French Augustinian Thomists: e.g., Paissac and Malet each offer detailed arguments on the doctrine of Sagesse de Sagesse, etc., in the Greek

57. T. R. Martland, "A Study in Cappadocian and Augustinian Trinitarian Metholodology," *Anglican Theological Review*, 252–63.

58. Régnon, *Études*, VI.335ff.

59. See Halleux's detailed defense of the Cappadocians in "Personalisme," 278–86.

60. In Paissac, *Théologie du Verbe*, 38ff.; in Legrand, *La Notion philosophique*, 93ff.; for Malet's argument on the "Sagesse de Sagesse" model, see 14ff.

61. Legrand, *La Notion philosophique*, 56–57, 132.

fathers. While their arguments are not repeated by authors such as Margerie or Guillou, the conclusion derived from the arguments of Legrand, Paissac, and Malet is retained: specifically, that the Greeks had a faulty sense of both person and consubstantiality. As will be seen, attention to the *X from X* causal model also appears in some English authors who are concerned with contrasting Augustine's Trinitarian theology with "Greek" Trinitarian theology, e.g., Paul Henry and T.R. Martland.[62] However, among the French scholars, the characterization of *X from X* causality as "Greek" and its attendant "rebuttal" at the hands of Augustine et al. serves to discredit Régnon's paradigm and establish some distance between Régnon and Petau. The shape of the argument can be given quickly from Legrand.

Legrand begins with the details of Augustine's argument; namely, the Arian context: "The opponents of Arius, in order to refute him and conclude the eternity of the Word [argued that] the Father was wise solely because He was the source of Wisdom."[63] The "Arian" position seems to be that either God is Wisdom (Power, etc.,) itself, or he is not, and the Son is.[64] The inevitable conclusion of such "Arian" logic must then be:

> "There was a time when the Father was not wise!" As St. Augustine noted, this reasoning by Arians requires one to say that God the Father was not wise until he had generated his Wisdom; in other words, he is not Wisdom itself. If this is true, and we still say that the Son is God of God and Light of Light, then we must ask if we would say equally of him that he is Wisdom of Wisdom, if indeed God was not Wisdom itself, but was only the Father of Wisdom.[65]

Legrand sets the *X from X* causality and the exegesis of 1 Corinthians 1:24 (from *On the Trinity*, bks. 6–7) in the context of person and *hypostases*: "Logically, the concept of consubstantiality precedes the notion of *hypostasis*, and this is the way that the author of *De Trinitate* understands the Pauline text, 'Christ is the Power and the Wisdom of God.'"[66] Legrand remarks that even Augustine was not, in his early work, free from the faults of the Greek *X from X* Trinitarian theology:

62. Paul Henry, "The *Adversus Arium* of Marius Victorinus, the First Systematic Exposition of the Doctrine of the Trinity," *JThS* n.s. 1 (1950), 42–55. The Martland reference has been given above.

63. "Les adversaires d' Arius, pour le réfuter, et conclure à l'éternité du Verbe, s'étaient rangés à la première alternative. Ainsi le Père était sage uniquement parce qu'il était la Source de la Sagesse" (Legrand, *La Notion philosophique*, 92). Paissac also refers to the Arian context but misunderstands 1 Cor 1:24 as an Arian prooftext; see his *Théologie du Verbe*, 38.

64. Legrand, *La Notion philosophique*, 91–93.

65. "'Il fût donc un temps où le Père n'était point sage!' Car, ce raisonnement [chez Ariens], remarque saint Augustin, amenait forcément à dire que Dieu le Père n'est sage qu' ii a sa Sagesse engendrée, non parce qu'il est la Sagesse même. Ensuit, s'il en est et ainsi, comme on dit du Fils qu'il est Dieu de Dieu, Lumière de Lumière, il faut voir si on pourrait dire également de lui qu'il est Sagesse de Sagesse, supposé que Dieu ne fût pas la Sagesse même, mais fût seuelement le Père de la Sagesse" (Legrand, *La Notion philosophique*, 92).

66. "C'est que, logiquement, le concept de consubstantialité précède la notion d'Hypostase, et c'est en ce sens que l'auteur du Traité de la Trinité entend ce texte paulinien: 'Le Christ est la Vertu et la Sagesse de Dieu'" (Legrand, *La Notion philosophique*, 93).

It is true that the earlier treatises incline noticeably towards conceptions typical of Greek theology: undoubtedly the reason for this is St. Augustine's marked predisposition for Neoplatonism, which had already provided the context for his first efforts towards the intellectualization of the Trinitarian faith.[67]

The conceptual error Legrand sees in *X from X* causality, which is the same error to be found in the Neoplatonism of Augustine's youth, is participation: *X from X* is obviously a participatory model of causality. On the other hand, if interior relations owes any philosophical debt, it is to Aristotle. Here Legrand cites Régnon:

> Nonetheless, we should not conclude that the absoluteness of the essence must be confused with the absolute of the relation. St. Augustine, who understood the Aristotelian "categories" [Legrand refers to *Confessions*] could only recognize, following Aristotle, a kind of logical anteriority of the first in comparison to the second. In the same way that Régnon observed in his *Etudes de Theologie positive sur la Sainte Trinité,* that the personal relationships appear from that moment as terminating in a substance already endowed, by itself, of its absolute perfection. So do we conceive that the Father, in being God, is being wise by his substantial wisdom before conceiving that the paternal act of this wisdom had a personal term. Regarding this term, we give it the name Wisdom to recall that it proceeds from the fruitful Wisdom of the Father.[68]

The critique of a Trinitarian theology based on a *X from X* causality is established. The initial question the causal model raises is whether the Second Person (who is identified by the X property) is identical to that property in the Godhead or identical to that property in the First Person. In other words, is the Second Person the Wisdom of the Godhead, or is he the Wisdom of the First Person? The danger in a "yes" answer to either question is the conclusion that God or the First Person is then "not wise" (not X) without the Second Person, as Augustine pointed out.[69] To a careful reader, the French argue, these kinds of questions and the kinds of answers they require, alert us to the conceptual limitations of a causal, specifically *X from X*, way of identifying

67. "Les traités antérieurs, il est vrai, inclinent visiblement vers la conception des Grecs: la raison en est, sans doubt, dans une prédilection marquee de saint Augustin pour le néoplatonisme, qui avait orienté ses premières recherces vers l' 'intellectualisation' de Foi trinitaire" (Legrand, *La Notion philosophique,* 93).

68. "II ne faudrait pas en conclure, toutefois, que l'absolu de l'Essence doive se confondre, pour autant, avec l'absolu de la Relation. Saint Augustin, qui avait compris les 'catégories' aristoteliciennes [Legrand cites *Confessions,* IV, XVI] ne pouvait que reconnaître, avec le Stagyrite, une sorte d' antériorité logique du premier par rapport au second. Ainsi que l'observe Régnon, dans ses *Études de Théologie positive sur la Sainte Trinité* [third series, Etude XVI] *les relations personelles apparaissent, dès lors, comme 'terminant' une Substance déjà douée, parelle-même, de ses Perfections absolues. Aussi, concevons-nous que le Père, en tant que Dieu, est sage par sa Sagesse substantielle, avant concevoir que l'Acte paternel de cette Sagesse ait un Terme personnel. Quant a ce terme, on lui attribue le nom Sagesse, pour rappeler qu'il procède de la Sagesse féconde du Père*" (Legrand, *La Notion philosophique,* 132; italics indicate the citation from Régnon).

69. Augustine, *Trin.* VI.1.2.

the individual Persons of the Trinity. Malet thinks that the Greeks were insensitive to such limitations because of their poor notion of *hypostasis:*

> For the Greeks there is no contradiction in saying that the Son proceeds from the Father or that an essence proceeds from essence, or that light proceeds from light, or wisdom proceeds from wisdom. Their theology of the *hypostasis* was not precise enough for them to see the impossibility of placing on the same plane the person and the nature in the act of generation.[70]

> Already among the Greeks, the importance given to consubstantiality could not help but to affect the way they understood the *hypostasis* . . . Thus, among the Greeks themselves, under the influence of the theology of consubstantiality, the significance of person is in some way made smaller, reduced to the most fluid of categories.[71]

Whatever the possibility of an Arian-like conclusion inherent in an *X from X* Trinitarian model, it is clear, as one reads the French scholars, that the real fault in the causal model is the lack of univocal naming, which then fails to support a relational model. The dangerous conclusion I noted above is possible, the Augustinians argue, because titles such as Wisdom, Power, Light, Life, etc., do not designate one Person of the Trinity in an unequivocal fashion. In some contexts, the First Person may be so-called, in others the Second or Third Persons. Indeed, such titles do not even necessarily name any Person, but may refer to the common existence (to defer the term essence for the time being). The term Word, on the other hand, seems unequivocally to name the Second Person (aside from its other virtues, such as suggesting a mental relationship and carrying philosophical associations of mediation).

> For the Son alone receives the name of Word, and not the Father and the Son together. One could not say: the two persons are at the same time Son, just as one cannot say that they are both Word or Image. These names exclusively express the fact that one person exists relative to the other.[72]

The French will argue that the real weakness in the Greek *homoouosios* model is that it is, in fact, not an account of unity based on a common essence, but simply another

---

70. "Pour les Grecs, il n'y a pas de contradiction a dire que le Fils vient du Pere ou que l'Essence vient de l'Essence, la Lumiere de la Lumiere, la Sagesse de la Sagesse. Leur theologie de l'hypostase n'etait pas assez precise pour qu'ils voient l'impossibilite de mettre sur le meme plan la personne et la nature dans l'acte de la generation" (Malet, *Personne et Amour,* 14).

71. "Déjà chez les Grecs, l'importance prise par la consubstantialité ne pouvait manquer d' avoir des répercussions sur la manière de concevoir les hypostases. Ainsi, chez les Grecs eux-mêmes, sous l'influence de la théologie de la consubstantialité, la personne est en quelque sorte amenuisée, réduite qu'elle est a la plus fluide de toutes les catégories" (Malet, *Personne et Amour,* 21).

72. "Car le nom de Verbe, le Fils est seul à le recevoir, et non pas le Père et le Fils ensemble. On ne peut dire en effet: les deux Personnes sont en même temps Fils, on ne peut dire davantage: elle sont Verbe ou Image; ces noms expriment exclusivement le fait pour une Personne d'être relative à telle autre" (Paissac, *Théologie du Verbe,* 39).

example of *X from X* causality: Light from Light, Essence from Essence, God from God.[73] The Greeks failed to recognize the difference between arguing that the First and Second (and Third) Persons are equally God because they are Power from Power, Light from Light, *X from X*, and arguing that they are equally God because they are of the same essence.

> The Father, in reality, is not uniquely Father, the Son is not only the Son. Their wisdom does not result from their union. For this reason the orthodox catholic notion of consubstantialty [*homoousia*] must be considered separately, for it could not follow from the concept of *hypostasis* as the Greek theory of procession claims. Clearly, this theory was never the foundation of Greek theology, yet nonetheless one has to acknowledge that there are limitations in the Greek language itself.[74]

The Latin solution to the Greek problem of *X from X* causality is to interpret all titles as referring to the essence, despite occasional apparent references to one specific Person in Scripture and tradition.

> [A]s the whole undivided essence is in each person so an action via a particular mode is in reality via the three. For Augustine this means even the traditionally associated characteristics of source, wisdom, and love fall to the doctrine. Whereas he might boldly assert in one place that God the Son is the source of knowledge and that "He is wisdom by that whereby He is essence," (*Trin.* VII.ii.3) he elsewhere effectively nullifies its ontological power by asserting that although the Son may have the special attribute of wisdom it is also possible to apply such title to the Father.[75]

What is a problem of equivocal titles in Greek theology is no longer one in Latin: all such titles describe the essence, excluding Word and Son (though the emphasis for many of these scholars, English and French, has been on Word). Indeed, for these

---

73. "Celle-ci s' est, en effet, formée a partir de la personnification, deja amorcée dans les livres sapientiaux de la Bible, de certainns des attributs divins. Pourquoi les scholastiques, qui on retenu comme personnels ceux de Verbe et d'Esprit, ont-ils range ceux de Sagesse et de Puissance, ou de Verite et de Vie, parmi les absolus, malgré le temoignage du Nouveau Testament et des Pères? Leur théorie des appropriations rend-elle compte de témoignages pauliniens et johanniques tels que 1 Co 1, 24 ou Jn 14, 10 d' une manière théologiquement et logiquement plus satisfaisante que l' argumentation antiarienne par laquelle Gregoire de Nysse défendait la génération eternelle du Fils? Et d'ailleurs, les noms de Verbe et d'Esprit ne conservent-ils pas, eux aussi, une dimension 'naturelle', commune aux trois personnes divines?" (Halleux, "Personnalisme," 215).

74. "[L]e Père, en effet, n' est pas uniquement Père, le Fils n' est pas que le Fils. Leur Sagesse ne résulte pas, non plus, du fait de leur union. La nótion de consubstantialité, l' "ομοουσια" [*homoousia*] de l'orthodoxie catholique, qui, pour la raison, doit être consideréé à part, ne saurait être, cependent, consécutive au concept d 'hypostase, ainsi que le prétendent les théories grecques de la Procession A la vérité, tel n'était point le fond de la pensée grecque, mais il y avait, toutefois, quelque imperfection dans la langage" (Legrand, *La Notion philosophique*, 93).

75. Martland, "Study of Cappadocian and Augustinian Trinitarian Methodology," 258.

scholars the Western emphasis on the title Word is justified by the judgment that this term escapes the confusion of attribution since it can refer only to the Second Person.[76]

For the French, this criticism of Greek Trinitarian theology (with its *X from X* causality) functions as a criticism of Régnon's original paradigm, as well. In the first place, whatever flaws the *X from X* causal model may show, the issue remains that it is fundamentally an essentialist model and not a personal model. To the extent that *X from X* causality accurately summarizes fundamental Greek Trinitarian thought, this thought is not "personalist," as Régnon's claimed. In a development of this critique of Greek theology and Régnon's claims for this theology, Malet tries to "save" Greek Trinitarian doctrine by pointing out that the Greeks had two types of titles for God: examples of the first sort would be unbegotten, begotten, processional; examples of the second would be Light, Power, Wisdom, etc.[77] These two types of titles were understood as different types of names or descriptions of Divine Persons.

> When the fathers describe the first procession by the formulae, the Son from Father, Begotten from Unbegotten, Generate from Ingenerate, these formulae are rigorously personal. When they use expressions such as God from God, Light from Light, Life from Life, Source from Source, and Highest from Highest, and even Essence from Essence, these formulae, while having a personal reference, also have an essential reference.[78]

The final criticism directed immediately at the Greeks, and through them at Régnon, takes the form of an axiom that the concept "person" necessarily presupposes psychological relations—a person can only be defined in terms of a psychological relation—and the primary title invoking relation is Word. If Word is not present, then a developed notion of person cannot be present either, with the attendant limiting effects on a developed doctrine of Trinitarian Persons. Régnon's critics make this point by emphasizing the Arian (and "Sabellian") context of Greek (meaning Cappadocian)

76. Jean Daniélou, *Gospel Message and Hellenistic Culture*, trans. 1. A. Baker, A History of Early Christian Doctrine, vol. II (London: Darton, Longman and Todd, 1973), 350.

77. "Ainsi, on relève chez les Pères grecs une double série de termes. Ceux de la première série sont les suivants: le ternaire Père-Fils-Esprit, à quoi correspond le ternaire Paternité-Filiation-Procession. Ensuite le ternaire Inengendré-Engendré-Procedant, à quoi correspond le ternaire InnascibilitéNiscibilité-Procession. Les termes qui constituent la deuxième série sont: Dieu, Lumière, Vie, Source, trés-Haut, Nature. Que ces termes désignent les personnes, c'est certain. Sont-ils pour autant, et aux yeux mêmes de Grecs [*sic*], interchangeables avec ceux de première série? C' est impossible. En effet, les termes de la deuxième série, tout personnels qu'ils soient, sont, au dire des Peres eux- memes, également communs [*sic*] aux Trois, alors que ceux de la première série ne le sont pas. Et puisque les termes de la deuxième série sont aussi communs, c'est la preuve qu'ils conservent quelque chose d'essentiel, car seule l'essence en Dieu peut fonder la communauté. S'ils n'avaient rien d'essentiel, ils ne pourraient s'appliquer aux Trois en quoi que ce soit [*sic*]" (Malet, *Personne et Amour*, 16).

78. "Lorsque les Pères expriment la première procession par Jes formules: 'le Fils du Père,' 'le Nascible de l'Innascible,' 'l'Engendré de l'Inengendré,' ces formules sont rigoureusement [*sic*] personnelles. Lorsqu'ils utilizent les expressions: 'Dieu de Dieu,' 'Lumière de Lumière,' 'Vie de Vie,' 'Source de Source,' 'Trés-Haut de Trés-Haut,' et parfois 'Essence d'Essence,' ces formules, tout en ayant un caractère personnel, ont aussi [*sic*] un caractère essentiel" (Malet, *Personne et Amour*, 16).

theology. Paissac, for example, begins his discussion of the patristic doctrine of the Word with an explanation of the Eusebian (i.e., "semi-Arian") associations of the title, and how Nicaea preferred "Son" instead for this very reason.[79] Anti-Arian sentiment drove the pro-Nicenes to the essentialism of *homoousios* and prevented them from exploiting relational language—in particular, Word. Malet makes a similar point to show the links among anti-Arian polemic, *homoousios,* and the *X from X* causality.

> Elsewhere, Athanasius criticizes those Arians who not do believe that "the Source has generated Wisdom" . . . He affirms that the Word and the Wisdom are that which have been generated by the Father. He equates God with the essence . . . and he concludes that the Son comes from the essence of God. In his argument to the Arians proving that the *homoousios* of Nicaea is the only acceptable expression, he emphasizes that "the true and eternal essence generated the Word."[80]

Augustine knows Arianism too, as books V and VI of *De Trinitate* make clear,[81] but, the French argue, he does not let it drive him away from a relational understanding of the Trinity and a proper emphasis on Word. The only doctrine Augustine actually attributes to Arius is "There was when he was not." For the French Augustinians, the eternal existence which must be defended is the eternal existence of the Word, and this Augustine does through his exegesis of 1 Corinthians 1:24, as Legrand shows: "In order to refute Arius and to prove the eternity of the Word his adversaries side with . . . [the position that] the Father was wise solely because He was the source of the Wisdom [as shown in 1 Cor 1:24]."[82]

The French argue that it is Augustine's strength, and thus the strength of Latin Trinitarian theology, that he is able to transform both a rebuttal of the Arians and an exegesis of 1 Corinthians 1:24 into a statement of the primacy of Word as the title of

---

79. Paissac, *Théologie du Verbe*, 30. As I have already remarked, Paissac's ambiguous attitude towards the proffered titles of Wisdom and Power in 1 Cor 1:24 is made clear by his assumption that the passage is an Arian prooftext, an assumption that lacks credibility.

80. "Ailleurs, Athanasius reproche aux Ariens de ne pas confesser que 'la Source a engendré la Sagesse.' Il affirme que le Verbe et la Sagesse sont ce qui. a été engendré par le Père. Il assimile Dieu à l'Essence. et conclut que le Fil vient de l'Essence de Dieu [*ek tēs ousias tou theo*]. Pour demontrer aux Ariens que le [*homoousios*] de Nicée est tout à fait admissible, il souligne que 'la vrai et éternelle Essence a engendré le Verbe'" (Malet, *Personne et Amour*, 14). This remark follows from Petau, but Malet continues on his own: "Saint Grégoire de Nysse, dans un long passage trés caractéristique de sa polémique contre Eunome où il s'efforce de prouver à l'hérétique que le Fils et le Père ont la même essence, part de ce fait que !'Essence est engendrée [*gennesin tēs ousias*] et se réjouit de ce que son adversaire l'admette aussi" (Malet, *Personne et Amour*, 15).

81. See my "Arians of Book V."

82. "Les adversaires d' Arius, pour le réfuter, et conclure a l'éternité du Verbe, s'étaient rangés à la prèmiere alternative. Ainsi le Pere était sage uniquement parce qu'il était la Source de la Sagesse [chez 1 Cor 1:24]" (Legrand, *La Notion philosophique*, 92).

the Second Person because of its relational character.[83] One need hardly add that this transformation is something the Greeks could never accomplish.

As suggested by my quotations and descriptions, the apparent favorite of equivocal titles to contrast with Word is Wisdom (Sagesse). In this preference modern scholars are, indeed, following Augustine's apparent preference as well: Wisdom receives considerable explicit treatment in Augustine's exegesis of 1 Corinthians 1:24, while the title Power is not treated directly. It is common to find scholars referring to 1 Corinthians 1:24 as though the text reads only "Christ, the Wisdom of God." For example, Paissac quotes the Pauline text, mentions Power (puissance) once, and then collapses the concept into Wisdom, which thereafter is all he treats.[84] Malet refers, as I noted above, to the series of titles used among the Greek in *X from X* causality: God, Light, Life, Source, Highest (Tres-Haut), Nature, with no mention of Power.[85] Similarly, Crowe refers to 1 Corinthians 1:24 in his discussion of the Old Testament sense of Word: "So with the word of God: it goes forth from his mouth with a potency, it accomplishes what he intends; it is operative in creation." Despite a description built on "potency" and "operative," his own reference to 1 Corinthians 1:24 is only to wisdom (*sophia/sapientia*).[86]

The reason for this preference for Wisdom is clear: Wisdom suggests a rational analogy similar to that of Word (Reason, etc). Augustine speaks of Wisdom producing Word, for example, suggesting the essential ground upon which personal relations stand. Nonetheless, while Wisdom may have seemed to Augustine himself to be a concept similar to Word, modern Augustinians do not hesitate to redeem Wisdom from any possible participatory connotations in the literature by giving it a rational or psychological status:

> Must we then accept for the Wisdom what we accept for the Word?
>
> . . . or rather the Father has Wisdom in the same way He says Word, saying the Word or having the Wisdom not by himself but also by the fact that he generated the Wisdom and the Word . . . if so then the Father is the One who has the Wisdom, in the same way that He is the One who says the Word, for the Wisdom must be understood to be included in the same way as the Word.[87]

The interpretation of 1 Corinthians 1:24 in terms of an opposition between an account using *X from X* participatory causality and an account based on psychological

83. Ironically, it is the very strength of the relational content of Word that contemporary authors such as R. Haight, SJ, find unacceptable.

84. Paissac, *Théologie du Verbe*, 43ff.

85. Malet, *Personne et Amour*, 16.

86. Crowe, *Doctrine of the Most Holy Trinity*, 127.

87. "Faut-il donc accepter pour la sagesse ce qu' on accepte pour le Verbe? [O]u bien le Père, il a la Sagesse comme ii dit le Verbe, disant le Verbe ou ayant la sagesse non par soi seul mais par le fait qu'il engendre Sagesse et Verbe. Si donc le Père est Celui qui a la Sagesse de la même façon qu'il est Celui qui dit le Verbe, la Sagesse devra être comprise comme le Verbe" (Paissac, *Théologie du Verbe*, 39).

relations must be suspect, however, if only for a simple exegetical reason: Where is power—puissance, *dynamis, virtus*—in the account(s)? It is the presence of power in 1 Corinthians 1:24 which indeed suggests a third option between an account based on *X from X* participatory causality on the one hand, and an account based on psychological relations on the other. Brown has already pointed to the alternative power exegesis, with its corresponding alternative Trinitarian theology, although he does not fully explore the possibility.

> The point [in Augustine] is that, just as there are three faculties in man which are not ultimately totally separate entities, so there can be three "persons" in one God, each of whom roughly corresponds to these three faculties.[88]

Henry makes a similar point in comparing Augustine's theology to Victorinus':

> The essential fact is that Victorinus explicitly compares the Life of the Blessed Trinity to the inner Life of the Soul. Is that not the real origin of the "psychological doctrine"? He even says that the soul is *bipotens* (I.32), although he defines these two "faculties" as Life and Intellect.[89]

Both scholars thus draw attention to a major problem in the reading of Augustine typical of the French scholars already discussed; namely, their implicit, unexamined decision as to the meaning of power. Brown's own emphasis on the term "faculty" is helpful here, since this is a legitimate translation of *virtus/dynamis,* and indeed historically the more typical sense of the term, as Henry's comment suggests.[90]

These quotations are important evidence of Brown's and Henry's insight; namely, that there is an implicit use of a power or faculty psychology in Augustine (and Victorinus). One could argue, for example, that books VI and VII of *De Trinitate* treat 1 Corinthians 1:24's wisdom in an explicit fashion, while treating power or faculty in an implicit fashion: e.g., faculty is the psychological category the reader would recognize in Augustine's discussion of memory, emotion, etc., in book VI.6.8. One intriguing example of an implicit reference to power–faculty is at the end of book VI: Augustine explicitly quotes a portion of Romans 1:20—the portion left unquoted is to the title power.[91]

---

88. Brown, *Divine Trinity,* 272; emphasis added.

89. Henry, "Adversus Arium of Marius Victorinus," 54.

90. What I mean by faculty may usefully be suggested by referring to Simplicius, who said that the Stoics defined a power or faculty as a "sort of disposition of the soul which can produce and regulate a set of activities as discreet events." This and other references from the era can be found in Brad Inwood's *Ethics and Human Action in Early Stoicism* (Oxford: Claredon Press, 1985),chs. 1–2. The Simplicius texts is from his *Commentary on the Categories,* quoted in Inwood, *Ethics and Human Action,* 31. See also F. E. Peters, *Greek Philosophical Terms* (New York: New York University Press, 1967), pp. 42–45; and Jean Souilhe, *Etudes sur la terme* Δύναμις (Paris: Librairie Felix Alcan, 1919).

91. Augustine, *Trin.* VI.x.11. Augustine begins this chapter by referring to Hilary of Poitiers, and if one looks at Hilary's discussion in his *Trin.* VIII.56, one sees that he also uses the Romans 1:20 quote, but as an explicit reference to divine power.

A serious treatment of the role of power in Trinitarian exegesis of 1 Corinthians 1:24 would provide a doctrinal option that would be situated between Trinitarian doctrines based upon *X from X* participatory causality and Trinitarian doctrines based upon psychological relations, because the concept of power is in fact common to both models of doctrine. A power-based Trinitarian model would resemble the *X from X* causality, since a power is precisely that causal capacity which produces something which has its own nature, e.g., fire from fire, *X from X*.[92] A power-based Trinitarian model would resemble the psychology of interior relations because those relations are derived—abstracted—from the action of psychological powers (faculties).

CONCLUSION

In this article, I have tried to show how Régnon's understanding of patristic and scholastic Trinitarian theologies has been developed by later scholars into a characterization of Greek and Latin Trinitarian theologies. The widespread appropriation among English-language scholars of this development of Régnon's paradigm has occurred largely in ignorance of its original stage. In contrast, French-language scholarship has recognized Régnon's origination of the paradigm, while some such scholars have rejected the content of that paradigm. A tradition of French Augustinians have argued that Greek Trinitarian theology, as developed by the Cappadocians, does not begin with the presupposition of individual persons, but rather with the presupposition of a material causality. It is, such scholars argue, Augustian-influenced Latin Trinitarian theology that makes the presupposition of the individual divine Persons fundamental to Trinitarian theology.

Régnon's French critics have chosen to argue against his characterization of Greek versus Latin Trinitarian theology on the basis of Augustine's exegesis of "Christ, the Wisdom and Power of God." They have developed this exegesis into a critique of the *X from X* Trinitarian doctrine they find to be typical of Greek theology. Both French- and English-language scholars also use forms of this critique to support their emphasis on the title Word over against other titles such as Wisdom and Power. I have sought to show that their consideration of Augustine's exegesis is limited, since the full sense of power is never explored, and unreflective, since they mirror the conceptual dependence of word upon faculty without realizing it.

Given that the larger project under discussion here and in the works described is the attempt by Régnon and others to characterize Greek and Latin Trinitarian theologies, one particularly puzzling omission of the French critics is their failure to ask the question: Why does Augustine turn to the 1 Corinthians 1:24 passage? It is a fruitful

---

92. Indeed, in Greek medicine and physics, the original term for an elemental caused by reproducing its own nature was power—*dynamis*. The hot, the wet, etc., considered as pure reified qualities were powers. See, for example, A. L. Peck, "Anaxagoras: Predication as a Problem in Physics." *Classical Quarterly* XXV (1931), 27–37,112–120.

question to ask in this context of characterizing theologies, because clearly one answer would be that it is a text which figures largely in Augustine's Latin predecessors: Hilary, Victorinus, and Ambrose. Furthermore, the text is important to several Greek theologians: Origen, Athanasius, and Gregory of Nyssa.[93] The First Corinthians passage is probably important to the Latins because it was first important to the Greeks as they began the struggle against "Arianism." There is thus a common ground between East and West, which is not to destroy in advance any differences of interpretation that there may be: Augustine's exegesis of the passage is clearly not Origen's or Hilary's. Again, this is an unexamined aspect of the Arian background of Trinitarian doctrine which the French scholars acknowledge in a general form but do not explore with any insight.

Finally, I note in closing that Régnon's constellation of themes remains recognizable in recent Augustinian scholarship, such as Edmund Hill's introduction to his translation of *De Trinitate*.[94] Hill's emphasis on Augustine's interpretation of the Old Testament theophanies;[95] his comparison of Gregory Nazianzen's relational theology with Augustine's;[96] and his insistence on the theological continuity between early Greek and Latin theologies (cast in opposition to a hard-line division of these two traditions ironically attributed to Prestige),[97] all these features reveal to the reader a scholarly world still circumscribed by Régnon's insights a hundred years later.

I am indebted to Jean-Marc Laporte for his comments on an earlier draft of this essay.

---

93. The exegesis of 1 Cor 1:24 by Origen and Athanasius is documented by William McFadden, SJ, in his dissertation, "Exegesis of 1 Cor. 1:24." The title is ambiguous, since it does not make clear that McFadden's treatment includes only the early "Arian" controversy, e.g., Athanasius. He does not treat the later controversy.

94. Augustine, *Trinity* (Brooklyn: New City Press, 1991).

95. Augustine, *Trinity*, 38–39.

96. Augustine, *Trinity*, 45, 50, and 57n6.

97. Augustine, *Trinity*, 41–42.

Chapter 3

Early Latin Trinitarian Theology

MANY READERS OF THESE essays may already have in mind some kind of "history of Latin patristic Trinitarian theology." Such a history could range from a distillation enlivened by exemplary anecdotes (contributing to a mythic quality) to that of an epic drama in which each of the many significant characters and events have a role to play whose significance reaches far beyond the discrete scenes in which they enter, act, and pass away. Almost all such histories have a "job to do" in the larger theologies into which they fit. The job of this chapter is to give the reader some idea of the notions and exegeses that were important for Latin Trinitarian theology and which gave Latin theologians of the era their vocabulary and their logic. These notions (or tropes) are a list of those subjects Latin theologians either spoke about directly or else to which other conversations were anchored. They are doctrinal vocabulary which carried with them—through use—their own grammar. I do not expect this approach, or the "list" of key notions (tropes), to be familiar to (or to settle easily into) every established "history of Latin Trinitarian theology." In some cases, the very act of identifying a given notion as key to Latin Trinitarian theology will be seen as outside some modern historical narratives or of very limited utility. I can live with that: the task of this brief "history" is to enable the modern reader to better understand the vocabulary, logic, and discourse of Augustine's Trinitarian theology.[1]

1. This chapter is written with two parts, each of which has its own perspective; distinctive but complementary. The first part is an overview of the fundamental themes or topics which characterize Latin Trinitarian theology since its beginning with Tertullian. The second part is intended to set those themes within their doctrinal milieu and with the exegetical thinking that is the expression and origin of these themes open to view. The first part is roughly a thematic summary of Latin Trinitarian theology, while the second part is a revelation of Latin Trinitarian theology as it develops into Nicene theology. The common thread between the two parts is the hypothesis of Latin Trinitarian theology is, at its core, anti-monarchian (or anti-modalist). At no time did I write with Régnon's paradigm or axiom in mind; neither did I set out to "prove" or "disprove" what is, after all, an axiom.

One example that I think will help illustrate what this chapter does as a whole is to begin by reflecting on "Scripture" for Augustine and earlier Latin theologians. One important consequence of the late-second-century beginnings of Latin Trinitarian theology is that Latins begin their theologizing with a New Testament that is already largely determined and canonical. Latin Christian authors never work from only the Old Testament, for example. Latin Trinitarian theology is particularly indebted to the Gospel of John, which looms not simply as a background influence (as it would have been a generation or two earlier), but as a sacred text that is itself the subject of the kind of exegesis previously reserved for the books of the Septuagint. As we shall see, historically, the first great exegetical task of Latin Trinitarian theology centered upon the polemical interpretation of select passages from John. This emphasis on John is never lost, and the greater part of later Latin Trinitarian theology is consistently "Johannine" to the extent that it expresses and authenticates itself through a close exegesis of the Fourth Gospel. John's Gospel—the words of this Gospel, many of them seemingly direct from Jesus—provide the working idioms of Latin Trinitarian theology to a degree that no other Gospel approximates.

Latin-language Trinitarian theology is born in the tumult of the fight against monarchianism (also known as patripassianism or modalism). In the late-second century, eloquent Christians with Eastern origins who resided in Rome and Carthage taught that the divinity in Jesus was the "Father," the one God,[2] otherwise known as Spirit. The scriptural proofs that the divine in Jesus was the Father came from Jesus' own words in the Gospel of John: "The Father and I are one" (John 10:30), "He who has seen me has seen the Father" (John 14:9), and especially, "Do you not believe that I am in the Father and the Father is in me? The words I say to you I do not speak on my own authority; but the Father who dwells in me does his works" (John 14:10). These teachers differed amongst themselves as to what or who the name "Son" referred to, but they agreed with the equivalence of Father, Spirit, and divinity, and that the divinity *in* Jesus was the Father-*Spirit*. Those who spoke this way also rejected the *Logos* theology of the Apologists (principally, Justin and Theophilus): the "uttered" Word was not a separate being, but only words, as when God "spoke" in Genesis 1.[3] The necessity of rebutting this predominantly Greek-language theology provides the setting for the beginning of Latin-language Trinitarian theology.[4]

2. The key names are Noetus, Theodotus, Praxeus, Callistus, and Sabellius; later famous modalists include Paul of Samosata and Photinus. (Some would add Marcellus of Ancyra to a list of Greek "modalists," but Athanasius did not think so, and neither did most of the West.) It is not true that all monarchianism in the West comes from relocated Greeks: it just sometimes seems that way. The anonymous work *De Montibus Sina et Sion*, Cleomenes, and (in the fourth century) the Priscillianists represent monarchianism indigenous to the West.

3. I have already mentioned the role of Hippolytus, the author (?) of *Against Noetus* and *Against All Heresies*. See Tertullian, *Treatise Against Praxeas*, 5–9.

4. If *De Montibus Sina et Sion* is in fact a late-second-century work, then it is an exception to this scenario. Its origins are not in Greek monarchianism, but in Jewish-Christian theology that is still close to Hebrew-language sources. It nonetheless has in common with "Roman" monarchianism the equation

In developing their arguments against the monarchians, Tertullian and Novatian[5] first of all reaffirm two basic doctrines from the generation of the Apologists: that divinity is *from* the Father, but not identical *with* the Father; and that the Father's Word (identified in the prologue to John) has a real and distinct existence as a mediator (*the* Mediator).[6] Whereas the Apologists are concerned with the cosmological activity of the Word, however, the Latins focus attention on the Second Person's divine action within the context of the Incarnation: What divine works did Jesus do? Latin theology then sets out to refute the monarchians by reclaiming John 14:10 from their exegesis.

Tertullian, Novatian, and Latins thereafter articulate another basis for the unity of Father and Son, one that is based not upon the temporary "descent" of the Father "into" the Son, but upon a commonality of the two that is free of topological descriptions, even as it preserves the Johannine language of "in."[7] This basis of unity between Father and Son is "common power–common substance."[8] While these Latins strongly emphasize the Word as *the Spirit* or *divinity* who unites with flesh, "Word-Spirit" serves as the fulcrum not for demonstrating that Jesus and the Father were both divine, but for demonstrating that the divine Being joined with flesh was not the Father. Tertullian's expression of the anti-monarchian argument is a paradigm for Latin Trinitarian theology thereafter.

> Therefore the Father, abiding in the Son through works of power and words of doctrine, is seen through those things through which he abides, and through him in whom he abides: and from this very fact it is apparent that each Person is himself and none other, while he says, *I am in the Father and the Father in me.*[9]

For virtually every Latin theologian of the Trinity from Tertullian to Augustine, the logic follows this form: there is an explanation for how the Three are understood to be one—*unity of works and power*; there is an explanation for how the Three are distinct from one another—*causal relations*;[10] there is a statement that the Three are eternally

---

of divinity with the Spirit. "The Holy Spirit, who came down from heaven, was called by God Christ. The Holy Spirit mingled with flesh is Jesus Christ" (Danielou, *Origins of Latin Christianity*, 56).

5. An English translation of Novatian's *Trin.* can be found in the Fathers of the Church series, vol. 67.

6. Seemingly every stage of Israelite religion included a belief in a "mediator" between God (YHWH) and humans, as well as all creation. The identity, power, and role of such a mediator were understood differently over time (e.g., an angel, Moses, the high priest, or the prophet), but the existence of a mediator was a given.

7. In the fourth century, freeing the theology of the Holy Spirit from the topological implications of "descended" and "sent" will become the project of Hilary, Ambrose, and Augustine.

8. It is ironic that Tertullian, who had to refute and replace the monarchical understanding of the Spirit descending into Jesus, is commonly characterized by moderns as having too "materialistic" an understanding of divine substance.

9. Tertullian, *Treatise Against Praxeas*, 8.

10. It is the traditionally strong role of aetiological models in Latin Trinitarian theology that provides a basis for the Western understanding of the Creed of Nicaea's, "God from God, Light from Light, true God from true God" language.

irreducible and unconvertible—*they are each always themselves and not another*; and there is a word for what is Three in God—*person* (*persona*).[11] The content of "person" is not psychological, but ontological: "a substance [i.e., existent] which is himself," Tertullian says of "person," and, "Whatever therefore the substance [i.e., existent] of the Word was, that I call a Person, and for it [in this case] I claim the name of Son."[12] Person is something like Aristotle's first substance.[13] However, it is important to note the following: person is not used as a contrast to essence or substance, it is used to name the "whatness" of the Three in the Trinity. In Latin Trinitarian theology, the idea "person" does not provide the conceptual grounding for "real distinctions" in the Godhead: that grounding is provided by the second and third items in the "logic" listed just above. In short, the originating logic of Latin Trinitarian theology is anti-monarchian (i.e., anti-modalist), and in that logic the grounds for real distinctions in the Trinity is provided by causal relations and eternal irreducibility, not, as modern readers expect, by a logic built on the ontological difference between "person" and "essence" (or "nature.") Moderns expect Trinitarian theology to develop through a polar logic of "person" and "essence," but Latin Trinitarian theology develops instead through the logic of eternal causal relations and irreducibility.[14]

Another fundamental concern of Latin Trinitarian theology is articulated in Tertullian's counter-exegesis of John 14:10 (quoted above): our sight of the Father in the Son. The exegesis of John 14:9, which speaks of this sight, is linked to the exegesis of 14:10, and the meaning of the latter passage gives content to the former. (The point is also developed through exegesis of Philippians 2:5–7, 1 Colossians 1:15, and Hebrews 1:3.) The Father is seen in the Son, not, as the monarchians would argue, because the divine in the Incarnation is the Father and the "Son" is the union of Father with flesh, but because the works of the subsistent Son are also the works of the subsistent Father. From its beginning, Latin theology has an emphasis on "sight" in Trinitarian theology: our sight of the Son, of the Father in the Son, and the Son's sight of the Father. The most important case for the Latin emphasis on our sight of the Son is the

11. An excellent example of this "Latin Trinitarian logic" at work can be found in Hilary, *Trin.* VII.38–41, where all three of the arguments I list can be found. Hilary is an especially important example to acknowledge, because his Trinitarian theology is often presented by modern authors as discontinuous with previous Latin Trinitarian theology (e.g., Tertullian). However, careful attention to *Trin.* VII.39–40 reveals an account of the Trinity that reads like a glossing of the Tertullian passage I just quoted. All the key elements of Tertullian's theology are there: the use of John 14:9–10, the emphasis on the Father seen in the works of the Son, the fact that "each Person is himself and none other" (Hilary says, "Father is Father and Son is Son"), and the ontological understanding of "person."

12. Tertullian, *Treatise Against Praxeas* 7.

13. I am not claiming that the Latin sense of person *is* Aristotle's sense of first substance, but that an analogy may usefully be drawn between the two. We should, however, remember the argument raging in Greco-Roman philosophy at this time over whether and how Aristotle's *Categories* can be applied to immaterial or spiritual existents such as God, etc.

14. One sees this logic at work in books VIII–XII of Augustine's *Trin.*, where a variety of possible similitudes to the Trinity are rejected because they either fail to offer a similitude to inner-Trinitarian causality, or they do not maintain the irreducibility of each of the Three.

theophanies—where the theophanies support an anti-monarchian argument—but it should be remembered that much of Augustine's *De Trinitate*—not just books I to III—is concerned with our sight of the Son.

THEOPHANIES

Tertullian begins the Latin anti-monarchian emphasis on the theophanies as "proofs" for the separate existence of the Father and Son. Tertullian's argument that there are *two* of divine substance or Spirit (which is what he means by "God") and not just one appearing in various guises is that Scripture (LXX) teaches that God is invisible and yet speaks of the appearances of God. Against the monarchians, Tertullian argues that a God that makes appearances of any sort is clearly not a God that is invisible: instead, Scripture leads us to say that there is an invisible God and a visible God. The invisible is not the visible, and vice versa, therefore the Father and Son cannot be collapsed into one person. For Tertullian, a doctrine of two divine Persons, one invisible (the Father) and one visible (the Son–Word) is more true to Scripture and makes better sense exegetically than the monarchian reading. Tertullian's reading preserves the reality of the Father who sent the Son and the Son who was sent, that is, the teaching of the *regula* and Scripture on the *oikonomia*. The *movement* from "theophany" to "Trinity" is further illustrated by the arguments of Novatian (Rome, fl. 240–50?). In *De Trinitate* XVIII ("On the Rule of Truth"), Novatian cites, in quick succession, Exodus 3:20, "No one can see God and live"; John 1:18 (cf. 1 John 4:12), "No one has ever seen God"; and then Paul, "Whom no man has seen or can see" (1 Tim 6:16). These scriptural texts mean that the Father has never been seen, that it was the Son who was seen. The Son of God, Who is the Image of God, is thus the visible of the invisible God. The Son is not the Father, but the Son–Image is the one scripturally attested to as the "visible God."[15] In Latin theologies of the OT theophanies, the Son reveals himself (i.e., the fact of his existence) and prophetically reveals his future Incarnation; in Latin theologies of the NT theophany, i.e., the Incarnation, the Son is said to show the Father as well as to reveal his own divinity.

Tertullian develops this Trinitarian hermeneutic of the theophanies one step further when he asks: In what way is the Father seen in and through the visible Son–Word? There are multiple passages in which the Son is described in—indeed, identified with—visual language such as form and shape. The key passages are Philippians 2:5–7,[16] Colossians 1:15, Hebrews 1:3, and John 5:17–19 and 14:9–17. The Second

---

15. For the broader context of Novatian's theology of the theophanies, see Daniélou's treatment in his *Origins of Latin Christianity*, 329–39.

16. Most Latin texts of Phil 2:5–7 have *forma* for the Greek *morphe*, but Tertullian gives " . . . quod in *effigie dei* constitutus non parinam existimavit pariari deo sed exhausit semetipsum accepta *effigie servi . . .*"

Person is the perfect and true "form" of God.[17] This description can apply to the pre-incarnational Wisdom or Word of God, who contains all the thoughts and intentions of the Father within himself—especially those thoughts that are the forms of things yet to be created but according to which they will be patterned.[18] In other words, by containing in himself a copy of all that the Father thinks and wills, the Son is a perfect image of the Father. This is the first possible way in which the Father is "seen" in the Son—but it is a noetic sight of the pre-Incarnate Word.

The doctrine that the Son's unity with the Father is demonstrated in the fact that he "images" the Father can also support a "Nicene" Trinitarian theology whose logic is neither power-based nor substance-based, but *iconic*. Faustinus (Rome, c. 376–80)[19] opens his argument that scriptural descriptions of the Son's iconic or visual relationship to the Father establish the substantial unity between Father and Son[20] by citing John 1:14, "And we beheld his glory, the glory as it were of the only begotten of the Father." The visual glory that is seen is in itself the mark of the only-begotten Son: glory attests to Sonship.[21] Faustinus does sometimes describe the relationship of the Father and Son in terms of power or substance, but even these declarations of "one substance" and "one power" are tied to the visual-logic of his Trinitarian theology.

The third and last in my list of Latin understandings of the way in which "the Son is the visible of the invisible Father" is perhaps the most important. This understanding is based upon the visual or theophanic statements in John 5:17–19 and 14:9–17. The way in which the Son reveals the Father is the very same way in which the Son reveals his own divinity—by his works (*opera*).[22] This last sense will prove to be the most important in Latin patristic Trinitarian theology, for a distinctive feature of that theology is the early, and thereafter consistent, articulation of a doctrine of same power (and thus same substance) between the Son and the Father. The argument takes

17. The LXX itself may not supply the content of the Son's revelation, but the "clues" that the apostolic writings give to what is seen in and through the visible Son–Word point us to the world of non-canonical Jewish speculation on theophanies such as Ezek 1:26, "the likeness as the appearance of a Man . . . This was the appearance of the likeness of the Glory [*kabod*] of the Lord." The *kavod* or manifestation/glory of God is, in Ezek 1:26, 1 Enoch 46:1 and the reports of Jewish theology in Justin, *Dial Try*. 28, described or equated with the apocalyptic "Son of Man," the heavenly presence who has a human *form*. In short, Jewish apocalyptic theology speaks of a heavenly Son of Man who is the *kavod*–glory–manifestation of God (YHWH). Quispel summarizes the identification thus: "The extent, dimension, form or body of God is identical with his Glory. Form, Adam [as in "Son of *Man*"], Body, Glory are interchangeable and refer to the manifestation of God" (Quispel, "Ezekiel 1:26"). For a more specific treatment of "form" language in particular, see Fossum, "Image of the Invisible God."

18. A line of thought one finds in Philo and Irenaeus.

19. Faustinus' *De Fide Contra Arianos* may be found in CSEL 35.

20. Scripture's "iconic" descriptions of the Son here include principally the NT language of our sight of the Son, the Son's sight of the Father, and image descriptions of the Son's relationship to the Father.

21. Compare with Tertullian, *Treatise Against Praxeas* 15, "'And we beheld his glory, the glory as it were of the only begotten of the Father' . . . the "glory" of the the visible Son."

22. Evans says that "for Tertullian the Father is seen in the Son in consequence of the Son's acts of the divine power, and not in consequence of an actual manifestation of the person of the Father" (Evans, in Tertullian, *Treatise Against Praxeas*, 30).

this form: the works that Christ does are evidence of the kind of power that causes them; the works are the products of operations that are uniquely associated with a divine power.[23] Power is *substance as cause*, and the distinctive causality of a specific substance is contained in (or exists as) its power, for all works arise out of a power and indicate, by their acts, the identity of that power.[24] This account expresses in a technical way the almost common-sense judgment that actions are the manifestations and results of what a thing is: "Fire burns, wind blows," etc.[25]

ONE POWER, COMMON WORKS

Tertullian begins Latin Trinitarian theology's argument that the divinity of the Son and his unity with the Father is shown by the character of his works or actions, and Tertullian lays down the basic understanding that the Three individually manifest the same one power.[26] In the Son's workings we perceive the operation of his power, and in recognizing the power we also recognize the substance to which it belongs. That substance is the same as the Father's, and insofar as any one recognizes Christ to be God in the power of his substance, he would thus come to recognize the substance. This doctrine is not quite that of "inseparable operations," because the conceptual emphasis is on the *common power* that causes, and is manifested in, the operations or works. The doctrine does not describe a direct parallelism between what the Father and Son does so much as describe the common cause manifested in what each does. Augustine, for example, will later give extensive accounts of how the Father, Son, and Holy Spirit all *do the same thing*,[27] such as bring about the Incarnation or the Passion

23. For a full account of this causality, and its role in Trinitarian theology, see the Introduction and chs. 3 and 4 of my *Power of God*.

24. There is nothing distinctly Greek or Cappadocian about the causal sequence of power-operations-works, despite what neo-Palamite scholars say. See my "Background and Use of Eunomius' Causal Hierarchy."

25. Some fourth-century Latin definitions of "power" are: "For everything has a power, and moreover every action is an effect of a power. The work of the power and the power are not identical since that which effects can be distinguished from the effect" (Hilary, *In Matthaeum*); "For substance is called that which always is from itself: this is what exists within itself by its own power" (Phoebadius, *AA* VII. 2); and in *Trin.* IX.52, Hilary gives a definition of power which says, "power is the very reality of the nature, and the operation is the capability of the power." Potamius says, "But since the power of the Father is the Son, the power itself pertains to its substance, because substance cannot exist without power" (*Letter on the Substance*, X). A useful definition to keep in mind is that power is the capacity of an existent to affect insofar as it is what it is. In its original medical and philosophical use, power is inseparable from any existent, whether the existent in question is an individual or a nature. Among third- and fourth-century Latin theologians, an "existent" would be, in this instance, a *substantia*. (On "[an] existent as *substantia*" among third- and fourth-century Latins, see Tertullian, *Treatise Against Praxeas*, 41–42.)

26. We shall see that the great task Augustine takes upon himself is to imagine how this reality can be understood by the mind.

27. A succinct illustration of the doctrine of "inseparable operations" may be found in Rufinus' *De Fide* (405): " . . . the Holy Spirit also is of the same substance of God and . . . *those things which God the Father does, the same in an equal degree the Holy Spirit also does* . . ." (55; emphasis added).

(see his *Sermon* 52), but in the third and most of the fourth century, Trinitarian theology (Latin or Greek) is not at the point of a fully Trinitarian understanding of common or inseparable operations. As we shall see, the logic of the doctrine of inseparable operations is easily adaptable to describing the Holy Spirit—but only insofar as there is a sense from one's reading of Scripture (principally the OT LXX) that the Holy Spirit acts in divine ways.[28]

In third and early fourth centuries of Latin theology, the *common power* argument continues to be applied almost exclusively to proving Jesus' divinity and to establishing that the miraculous works that Jesus performed are of the same sort as the Father's works, and that if the Incarnate Son does them, he must have the same divine power (and substance) as the Father.[29] As I remarked earlier, this emphasis on the divine in the Incarnation specifically follows from the original anti-monarchian intent of the theology. When Tertullian and the Latins that followed him speak about the acts by the Son through which the Father is recognized, they are not speaking of cosmic acts by the Son;[30] they are speaking about the miracles performed by Jesus. The reality of those actions testifies to the presence of the divine power and substance; the reality also testifies to the integrity of the divine power and substance in the Incarnate Word, which is why Tertullian (and most Latins) emphasize the acts of the dual substances in Jesus. The divine substance is seen to be present in the works that only it could perform; the human substance is seen to be also present and intact in the works ("passions") typical of it. The flesh does not impede the operations or power of the spirit; the spirit does not expel or transmute the power and substance of the flesh. As Tertullian says: "And to such a degree did there remain unimpaired the proper being of each substance, that in him the Spirit [divine substance] carried out its own acts, that is, powers and works and signs, while the flesh accomplished its own passions . . ."[31] In the late-fourth century, the "works indicate power" argument shifts from the Incarnation to demonstrating the common works and power amongst the pre-existent Word, the Holy Spirit, and the Father. This transition occurs neither suddenly nor completely.

THE INCARNATION AND TWO SUBSTANCES

Tertullian's argument appears in Novatian (*Trin.* XI.4.9). "If Christ is only man," Novatian asks, "how is it that 'what the Father does, the Son also does in like manner'?"

28. See Hilary, *Trin.* VIII.

29. See Jason Gehrke, *From Power to Virtue. The Early Latin Theology of Lactantius* (Oxford: Oxford University Press, forthcoming).

30. Tertullian does say, at *Treatise Against Praxeas*, 15, that "all things were made by the Son" when he saw and accomplished what was in the Father's consciousness. But it is not the "all things made" that Tertullian points to when he offers that the Son is the visible of the invisible God.

31. Tertullian, *Treatise Against Praxeas* 27.

Lactantius gives the same argument in more technical language: "The power of God appeared in him from the works he performed; the weakness of man from the passions which he endured."[32] In the first Latin work written against anti-Nicenes, Phoebadius' *Against the Arians* (359), the argument appears in a new context: the divine in the Son performed "its own activities in Him: namely powers, works, and signs. And the flesh exercised its own passions." In 378, Niceta of Remesiana argued that "If he [Christ] is seen as a man in his sufferings, in his divine works he is recognized as God." In 405 (?), Pseudo-Rufinus offers the proposition that "the substance and the power of the Father, the Son, and the Holy Spirit are one and the same" and supports it by citing John 10:30 and John 14:9. The latter verse figures especially significantly for Rufinus because the purpose of the verse is, in his opinion, "to teach us to perceive from the miracles which he performed that the Father and he [the Son] are one and the same in power and likewise in substance . . ."[33] The common conceptual and exegetical ground in Latin theology between Trinitarian and incarnational doctrines is evident. The same kind of logic applies to understanding the real humanity of Christ as to understanding his common divinity with God the Father: "By their works you shall know them."

In the main, Latin Trinitarian theology of the fourth century does not pivot on the language of divine substance, but rather utilizes that language for polemical reasons (i.e., Nicaea used it; Sirmium tried to ban it). This is a startling thing to say, but it is true: other than Nicaea, not until 357 do any synodal creed-like statements refer to essence or substance, Latin or Greek: it is not a mainstream way for talking about the Trinity. The most common language for describing Trinitarian unity is "one *power*." In this regard, Latins of the fourth century continue the doctrinal habits of Latins from Tertullian to Lactantius.[34] In the fourth-century "Nicene" controversy, Latin Trinitarian theologians remain with the traditional Latin language. Phoebadius, for example, understands the Sirmium (357) attempt to suppress essence–substance language as meaning, "Let no one in the Church preach that there is one Power of the Father and Son." Whenever Zeno of Verona (c. 360 to late 370s)[35] speaks of the Two or Three as "one substance," he also says they are "one power";[36] and like Phoebadius, he will sometimes say "one power" without any mention of "one substance." Lucifer of Caligari, an "unreconstructed" Nicene, declares that the Father and Son have "one glory, one power and one majesty." Niceta of Remesiana (378) never says that the Three have one substance, but he does say that the Three have one power. Finally,

---

32. Lactantius, *Inst.* 4.13.

33. Cf. Novatian, *Trin.* 28 "His sole purpose in these words was to make it clear to us that every man should henceforth account it to be the same thing to see the image of God the Father through the Son, as if he had seen the Father." Fathers of the Church, 98

34. Novatian, for example, used substance language only to talk about the Incarnation, i.e., the two "substances" in Jesus.

35. Zeno's *Tractatus* may be found in CSEL 22.

36. See Zeno, *Tractatus* I.7.30, 37.11–12; II.5.84

typical among Damasus of Rome's formulae are the expressions, "the Trinity of one power, one majesty, one divinity, and substance so that their power is inseparable" and "[the] Father, Son and Holy Spirit are of one deity, one power, one figure and one substance."[37] Clearly, this is not a Trinitarian theology that pivots on the notion of substance, and in this Damasus is being consistent with the usual form of traditional Latin Trinitarian theology. We may wonder why the question of the "metaphysics" of fourth-century Trinitarian theology is approached solely through excluding the most common ontological language for the Trinity while myopically reading that doctrine for the singular essence or substance.[38]

There is a fourth-century Latin tradition that strongly emphasizes substance language in its description of Trinitarian unity: its primary representatives are Ossius of Cordoba, Marius Victorinus, and Potamius of Lisbon.[39] Potamius and Ossius may represent an Iberian school influenced by Ossius' deacon, the Platonic philosopher, Calcidius. Whenever Ossius attends a synod, substance language appears prominently in the bishops' proclamations (e.g., Nicaea, western Serdica, and Second Sirmium). Victorinus' focus on substance language owes to the strong influence *homoousios* excerted on his thought, as well as his own intimate familiarity with Porphyrian platonism.[40]

SPIRIT CHRISTOLOGY AND THE THEOLOGY OF THE HOLY SPIRIT

The common assumption is that the result of Tertullian's Montanism would be a strong pneumatology, but such is not the case. Montanism leads Tertullian to stress the continuing role of the Holy Spirit as the source of prophecy, inspiration, and ecstatic revelation. If we compare Tertullian's understanding of what the Holy Spirit *does* with, e.g., the comparable understandings of Athenagoras, Theophilus, and Irenaeus, we find that Tertullian gives a diminished account of the Holy Spirit's activities. Unlike Athenagoras, Theophilus, and Irenaeus, Tertullian does not describe the Holy Spirit as co-creator, which is a very important omission. A second omission, inherited from Irenaeus, is a weak account of the generation of the Holy Spirit;[41] from the late-second

37. Damasus, *Ea gratia*.

38. If any answer is to be hazarded, it may be that medieval Trinitarian theology started with the bare minimum of theological ontology (i.e., words in the creed) and developed that particular metaphysics beautifully, but without any sense of the range that had characterized patristic Trinitarian theology, East and West. Medievals had that word, and they ran with it. Here, again, modern Trinitarian theology has remained true to its scholastic heritage.

39. And, of course, Athanasius himself. In the fourth century, Alexandria was counted as distinct from East or West, or as simply Western. Athanasius spent some of his exiles in Europe.

40. Potamius' writings may be found in the CSEL 69. An English translation of Victorinus' *Against Arius* can be found in the Fathers of the Church series, vol. 9; two volumes of the Sources Chrétiennes are devoted to this work, vols. 68 and 69.

41. Tertullian's famous "shoot from the root, river from a spring, beam from the sun" analogy at *Adversus Praxeus*, 8, describes only the Father and Son; when Tertullian restates the analogy, he does so to show that the Holy Spirit is *third*, not to seriously offer an aetiological analogy of the Holy Spirit

century on, aetiological accounts play a fundamental role in Christian theology, and the lack of a causal model for describing the Spirit's origin translates into a weak sense of the Spirit's relationship to God the Father. (Conversely, the "high" pneumatologies of the late-fourth century all articulate specific accounts of the Spirit's origin.) A third reason for Tertullian's weak pneumatology is that in his account of the Incarnation, "Spirit" names the Second Person who joined human flesh in Mary's womb. The exegetical result of this judgment is that any Old Testament "high" description of God's Spirit is taken to refer to the Son, and not to the Third Person of the Trinity.[42]

Spirit Christology may be found in the writings of Tertullian, Hippolytus, Novatian, Cyprian, Lactantius, Western Serdica, Phoebadius, and Hilary (the pre-exile *In Matthaeum,* as well as the post-exile *De Trinitate*) The most self-conscious, developed, and exceedingly complicated, account of the relationship amongst common Spirit, the Spirit "in" a Person, and the Holy Spirit occurs in Hilary's *De Trinitate* VIII; Augustine attempts to untangle Hilary and reconceive this relationship in his *De Trinitate* XV. After Hilary, Spirit Christology fades from Latin writings: if Potamius' writings are indicative, the turn occurs in 360 or soon thereafter, when power-substance logic assumes the full burden of explaining one divinity existing in common among the Three.[43] Given that one important effect of Spirit Christology is a low pneumatology, the decline of Spirit Christology is an important part of the resurgence of a "high" pneumatology.[44] The remedy to the understandings that the Holy Spirit is not creator, and that he has an origin that is either unspecified or thinly conceived by Christians, comes exegetically when a Christocentric monopoly on Old Testament "spirit" references is overturned in late-fourth century exegesis of key Old Testament Spirit passages (most notably, Psalm 33/32) resembles the exegesis and conclusions of Athenagoras, Theophilus, and Irenaeus rather than Tertullian's and Novatian's. (I say "resembles" because I am not suggesting that this late-fourth century Latin exegesis is influenced by, or in any way depends upon, these earlier Greek-writing authors.)[45]

(e.g., "the irrigation canal from the river out of the spring"), and when he again returns to the original analogies at chs. 13 and 22, there is no discussion of the Holy Spirit.

42. I have already pointed out how the reason for Tertullian's strong Spirit Christology lay in his anti-monarchianism.

43. Later, Gregory of Elvira identifies the "in" theology of John 14:10 with the theology of Nicaea: "This is *homoousios,* it is of one substance with the Father, just as the Lord himself said: 'I in the Father and the Father in me,' and: 'I and the Father are one,' and: 'I have come from the Father,' and: 'Who sees me, sees also the Father.'" All the Johannine passages that Gregory cites are texts that were important in the old anti-monarchian polemics. Gregory's *De Fide* may be found in CSEL 69.

44. There is a similar diminishment of the Holy Spirit in Greek theology during roughly the same span of time. I cannot presently say whether Spirit Christology plays the same role in a low Greek pneumatology as it does in Latin Trinitarian theology.

45. The degree to which Irenaeus' writings circulated in the West is uncertain: specific evidence of his influence in Gaul or Rome is very difficult to establish. Recent scholarship leans towards a late date for the Latin translation of Irenaeus' writings (e.g., *Against the Heresies*), with a suggested range between AD 380 to 420.

None of this is to say that Latin formulations of the Trinity in the third and early fourth centuries omit mention of the Holy Spirit: he is indeed included in summary statements of the Trinity, including Tertullian's key statement of criteria for what is one and what is Three in God: there are the Father and Son and Spirit as three; three in sequence, aspect, and manifestation; one in substance, quality, and power. Aside from the problems with Latin pneumatology during this period that I outlined above, the functional binitarianism of Latin theology from 200–370 can be described most succinctly in the following way: the "logic" of God's internal or natural relations worked with dynamics that successfully described a two-personed God were unsuitable and ineffective as logics for a three-personed God.[46] For example, Father-Son language offers no application to the Holy Spirit, except in second-century semitic-based theologies, in which the Holy Spirit is added as *Mother*, or in gnostic-like models in which multiple "brothers" or "sisters" are countenanced. Or, a two-stage *Logos* theology works well to describe the original and causal relationships between God and His *Logos*, but there is nothing comparable for the Holy Spirit, even with a theologian like Irenaeus who identifies Wisdom with the Holy Spirit, for he declines to offer a second intellectual generation model. (This is not the case in Theophilus, who finds causal models based upon the Holy Spirit as Wisdom.) In any case, in Latin and Greek theologies of the third and early fourth centuries, the Word and Wisdom are identified as one. Again, if Old Testament "spirit" language is appropriated to the Son, then passages such as Lamentations 4:20 are understood to describe the origination of the Second and not the Third Person. Finally, "image–form" Trinitarian logic and the very strong and widespread role it plays in Latin theology means that there is a dominant type of Trinitarian logic in which the Holy Spirit simply has no possible place. There were no doctrines of a "visible" Holy Spirit who was the Image and Form of the Father (or Son); no key authoritative texts like Philippians 2:5–7 and Colossians 1:15 to establish visual–shape language for describing the Holy Spirit; no passages like John 14:9 in which it is said of the Holy Spirit that whoever sees him sees the Father (or the So).[47] Visual–shape logic is very strong in Latin Trinitarian theology, as, for example, the case of Faustinus illustrates: on the one hand, Faustinus applies Psalm 33 to the Son *and the* Holy Spirit, but, on the other hand, his understanding of Trinitarian unity articulates itself through a logic of image and figure, and that logic cannot in itself include or explain the co-divinity of the Holy Spirit.

46. By "internal or natural relations," I do *not* mean "internal to the divine substance," but "relations among the Three and not to creation." These relationships are causal, i.e., how is the Father the cause of the Son, how is the Father (and Son) the cause of the Holy Spirit. They have nothing whatsoever to do with "a relational three-ness within the substance," a perspective regularly attributed to Latin Trinitarian theology without any supporting documentation.

47. That the Holy Spirit is "visible" in at least the noetic sense is implied by Victorinus and assumed by Augustine. Victorinus says at *Against Arius* IA.11, "The Spirit of Truth whom the world cannot see because it does not see Him" (John 14:17), while Augustine begins his *Trin.* XV.27 discussion of the Holy Spirit with, "Now we must discuss the Holy Spirit as far as it is granted us with God's help to see him." This use illustrates how important the logic of "sight" was in Latin Trinitarian theology.

It is true that Latins speak of the Holy Spirit as being "one in substance" with the Father and Son before Greeks do. Potamius of Lisbon says (c. 360) that "the substance of the Father, the Son and the Holy Spirit is one" (*De subst.* 10). One cannot find a Greek who says in 360 (or anytime in that decade) that the Holy Spirit is *homoousios* with the Father and the Son—because, at least in significant part, of the particular understanding Greeks have of *homoousios* that has no parallel in the West. The advantage Latin theology has from its "ignorance" of Greek Nicene theology (as exemplified by, e.g., Athanasius) is that it was free to make statements about a one or single substance that would not have been possible with an Athanasian understanding of *homoousios*. For Athanasius and the Greeks he influenced, *homoousios* was a unique and one-way predicate statement: one could and should say "the Son is *homousios* with the Father" but one could not meaningfully or piously say "the Father is *homousios* with the Son." Ignorant of this technicality, Latins were free to say that the Father and the Son—and the Holy Spirit—were of one, single substance.

The first Latin descriptions of the Holy Spirit in terms of the interior life of the Trinity[48] occur in the writings of Marius Victorinus and Hilary of Poitiers, both of whom thus contribute significantly to Augustine's mature pneumatology. It is Hilary who offers a description of the Holy Spirit as interior or inner-Trinitarian "Gift." Ambrose of Milan is often treated as the first Latin theologian to articulate a theology of the full divinity of the Holy Spirit, and certainly his *On the Holy Spirit* is the first lengthy Latin treatise on the Third Person.[49] In fact, however, Ambrose's pneumatology follows in the footsteps of the earlier accomplishments of the Latin theologian, Niceta of Remesciana (as well as owing heavily to the Alexandrian, Didymus the Blind). It is Niceta who first articulates a Latin theology of the Holy Spirit that fully redresses the limitations of pneumatology since Tertullian.[50]

Niceta describes in detail the power and operations of the Holy Spirit: he says explicitly that it is only by the causal trail of power and operations that we know that the Father and the Son are divine, and the same hermeneutic holds in the case of the Holy Spirit. We cannot fully know the nature of the Holy Spirit unless we know his works. Niceta then argues strongly that Holy Spirit creates in common with the Father and Son: he cites both Psalms 33 and 104 as authorities for this judgment, restoring them as testimonies to the Holy Spirit's creative activity (and not only to the Son's). In short, like the Father and the Son, the Holy Spirit creates, gives life, foreknows, fills all things, judges all, and is good. These activities are works that the Holy Spirit performs

---

48. That is, the Holy Spirit existing or arising between the Father and the Son. Most accounts of the Holy Spirit's origin seem to fail the test of logical density, and the advantage of Augustine's *filioque* theology was, historically, that it was a stronger description of the Spirit's causal origins than alternative accounts.

49. Though heavily dependent upon Greek sources, such as Basil of Caesarea's writing.

50. See my "Beginning and End."

in common with the Father and the Son, exhibiting the one power that they all share in common, and which is the sign of their common divinity.

> [T]he Holy Spirit has worked and will ever work with the Father and the Son ... It would be easy to adduce more proofs from the Divine Scriptures to show a Trinity of single power and operation ... The Holy Spirit is not different in majesty[51] from the Father and the Son since He is not different from the Father and Son in the power of operation.

The traditional weakness in pneumatology since 200—a comparatively vague account of the Spirit's origins—is used into the second half of the fourth century, by some Latins and Greeks to press the point that either the Holy Spirit is a creature or he is not; and if not, then he is either unbegotten or a Son. Niceta replies by saying that the Holy Spirit is not a creature—as his works and power reveal—and we cannot limit the causal options in God to unbegotten or begotten. Scripture gives us a causality other than generation; namely, procession (John 15:26). This type of causality is not obvious to unaided reason, but once revealed by Scripture a meaningful and coherent account (logic) of God's natural productiveness can be developed. With this perspective, an exegetical pattern emerges from Scripture: "spirit" passages associated with God's "breathing" or "exhaling" are images of the Third Person's origin from the Father through "procession." Niceta explicitly criticizes Spirit Christology for the effect it has had through exegesis in undermining pneumatology. He is emphatic that it is the Holy Spirit who overshadowed Mary and not the Word himself.[52] However, the weakness of Niceta's pneumatology that results in the historical occlusion of his contribution to late-Nicene doctrines of the Holy Spirit is that it lacks any account of the internal (inner Trinitarian) relationship of the Spirit to the Father and Son. In this regard Niceta offers less than Victorinus and Hilary, and thus it is with the aid of these latter two authors that Augustine develops his doctrine of the Holy Spirit's procession from the Father and the Son. Augustine recognizes that of all the terms we use for God (e.g., spirit, good, wise, eternal, etc.), it is "spirit" alone that initially seems to be substance, but he declines to continue the Latin "common substance of God is spirit" approach.[53] Augustine does accept from previous Latins the judgment that the Spirit is the Spirit *of God* and *of the Son*, and restates it as the Holy Spirit is the

51. In most early Latin translations of Wisdom of Solomon 7:25, up to and including the Vulgate, *majestas* translates the Greek word *energeia*.

52. It is worth noting that Niceta's own creed, a variant of the Roman creed, contains the clause, "born of the Holy Spirit and the Virgin Mary," while the Creed of Nicaea contains no such clause and indeed does not mention Mary or anything remotely related to Luke 1:35–36 at all. The creed of Constantinople (381) says that the Son was "incarnate[d] from the Holy Spirit and the Virgin Mary ..." (The familiar Post-Vatican II "Nicene-Constantinpinopolian" liturgical creed contains the clause, "By the power of the Holy Spirit ..." which is a pleasant echo of Luke 1:35, seems to originate in some modern translation of Constantinople, 381, by some anonymous liturgical committee, because the clause is not in the original creed.)

53. Augustine, *Trin.* XV.8.

inner-Trinitarian love. Augustine's principal concern, however, is in articulating an aetiology of the Holy Spirit (i.e., procession) that is logically parallel to and as dense as the traditional aetiology of the Son's generation.[54]

The positive content and appeal of the monarchian exegesis of John 14:9–10 was that it remained true to the Johannine testimony that God "the Father" was united with the "Incarnate Son" and to the peculiarly Johannine emphasis on the experience (or doctrine) that the Father is "seen" in the Son. Any criticism of monarchian theology had to retain a positive belief in and interpretation of these two *prima facie* claims by the Gospel of the uniqueness of Jesus' relationship with God. Passages such as John 14:9–10 make claims of unity that could be called—perhaps anachronistically, but nonetheless—*ontological* on the one hand, and *epistemological* on the other. Ontologically God existed in, and existed united with, Jesus in an unprecedented way that called for a new understanding of prior language—Word, Son. Epistemologically, God was revealed in Jesus, his Son, in ways that reconfigured traditional titles like Lord, and re-interpreted categories like "obedience to the will of God," the "Power of God," "God's works," and even the presence of God (the Paraclete). In short, the apostolic testimony of John 14:9–10 could not be lost in any catholic anti-monarchian exegesis of the verses. The tension between the co-presence-but-real-distinction of the Father and Son had to be maintained; also necessary was the tension of the vision of Christ as the Son himself and the vision of Christ as the Image of the Father. No *interpretation of some part of the passages* could be allowed to overcome the tension of an *exegesis of the whole of passages' revelation.*[55] The borders on the exegeses of the two issues raised by John 14:9–10 remained intact in throughout the anti-monarchian controversy and carried over into Latin Nicene polemical exegesis.[56] Chapter 24 of Tertullian's *Against Praxeas* is devoted to reclaiming John 14:9–10 from the monarchians. Tertullian quotes John 14:9–12, and then glosses it in a way that takes the recurring word *opera* as its point of departure.

> Therefore the Father, *remaining* [*maneo*] in the Son through works of power [*opera virtutem*] and words of doctrine, is seen through those things through which he *remains*, and through him in whom he *remains*: and from this very fact it is apparent that each Person is himself and none other, while he says, *I am in the Father and the Father in me.*[57]

---

54. Augustine, *Trin.* XV.37, 47–48.

55. For some authors the tension was almost antinomic: Marcellus, Apollinarius.

56. In his substantial article, André de Halleux argues that the Latins' understanding of "person" was "manifestational"—each person almost defined by the sight or sound or "anointing" of a divine Person, but that in 381, in conversations that led up to the Council of Constantinople, the Greek reading of *persona* as *hypostasis* began a process of "metaphysicalizing" the Latin notion of person. (Boethius would be a good author to look at for this.) See Halleux, "Hypostase et personne."

57. "Si non facio *opera* Patris mei, nolite credere; si vero facio, et mihi credere non vultis, vel propter *opera* credite. Et scitote quod ego in Patre sim, et Pater in me."

The first point to make about this passage is that Tertullian is arguing that the Father "becomes visible in the Son, in consequence of acts of power, and not in consequence of actual manifestation of his person." The apostles did not look at the Son standing in the road and see the Father standing there, which is what the Spirit monarchians could claim. Thus, Tertullian says, the Father is visible "not to the eyes but to the mind."[58] Tertullian's statement that *each Person is himself and none other* is a conclusion he draws from the difference between the ways the Son and Father are visible: the Son is visible in the way we moderns use the word "personally," and the Father is visible in the actions of the Son. The actions—the *opera*—being described are those of the Incarnate Son; this argument has nothing whatsoever to do with a pre-Incarnate Word. This is an argument intended to show that the Father is seen in *Jesus'* works, and that the Father is not seen in the *body* of the one called Jesus.[59] The Father is indeed "*in* the Son continuously" but "*in* the Son" has its own specific connotation, one which has nothing to do with spirit. "By means of the works," Tertullian says, "the Father will be in the Son and the Son in the Father . . . *and* thus by means of the works [*opera*] we understand that the Father and Son are one . . . [thus] we should believe that there are two [Persons], but in one power."[60] I think that the anti-monarchian polemical exegesis of John 14:9–10 by Tertullian and Hippolytus is the first time in which a *common power, common works* theology is articulated in Christian Trinitarian theology, *ever.*[61]

Such attention to the exegesis of John 14:9–10 has a long life among Latins. For example, Novatian's *De Trinitate* (28) is devoted to an exegesis of 14:10, as is all of book III of Hilary's *De Trinitate*. Phobaedius regards the passage as providing a normative reading of Nicene *X from X* statements, and Victorinus treats John 14:10 and 11 as the best scriptural statement of *homoousios.*[62] Hilary's comments on the text at *De Trinitate* IX.52 are particularly worth noting:

> [the Son] had borne witness to the unity of His nature with the Father's: He that has seen Me, has seen the Father also (John 14:9): The Father is in Me, and I am in the Father . . . to behold the Son is the same as to behold the Father; that the One remains in [*maneo*] the One shows that They are inseparable.

58. Tertullian, *Treatise Against Praxeas* 24.

59. The central focus on the Incarnation will continue in Latin Trinitarian theology, and even when Trinitarian disputes require attention to the pre-existent Second Person, the old vocabulary of the Incarnation continues. For example, the "two nativities" model continues through at least to Leo; the related habit of using *substantia* primarily to speak about what is two in Jesus remains, if not quite as strong.

60. "By means of the works, the Father will be in the Son and the Son in the Father, and thus by means of the works we understand that the Father and Son are one . . . that we should believe that there are two [Persons], but in one power" (Tertullian, *Treatise Against Praxeas* 22).

61. Athenagoras speaks of "one power," but he does not connect it to "common works" (which is not discussed as such at all). Justin and Tatian identify the Son as the "Rational Power of God/the Father."

62. As Mary Clark has already pointed out in her FotC translation of Victorinus' Trinitarian writings (207n34). Clark's note is to AA II.6; see also AA 1A.11, 103.

> And, lest they should misunderstand Him, *as though when they beheld His*
> *body, they beheld the Father in Him,* He had added, "Believe Me, that I am in
> the Father and the Father in Me: or else believe Me for the works' sake." His
> power belonged to His nature, and His working was the exercise of that power;
> in the exercise of that power, then, they might recognize in Him the unity with
> the Father's nature.[63]

Hilary gathers together all the key scriptural texts from anti-monarchian polemic:
when he says that the Father *remains* in the Son, he uses the same verb Tertullian
did when he said, "the Father *remains* in the Son through works of power"; namely,
maneo; it is the exercise of his power (*virtus*) in works (*opera*) that shows the Father
in the Son and so to behold the Son is the same as to behold the Father; and last but
certainly not least, Hilary says that no one should believe that *by looking at the body of*
Jesus they are seeing the Father, an unusual point to make in the 360s.

It is John 14:10 that becomes the basis for subsequent Latin arguments for the
unity of power and the common operations between the Father and Son (and eventually, the Holy Spirit), and it is unity of power that becomes the dominant way of
describing the unity between the Father and the Son among Latins with sympathy
for Nicaea or with animus for anti-Nicenes. The language of unity of substance is
dominant for Ossius of Cordova, Potamius of Lisbon, and Marius Victorinus. It is
not dominant in the theologies of Phoebadeus of Agen, Zeno of Verona, Faustinus,
Niceta of Remesiana, Damasus of Rome and all the letters associated with him, and
Ps.-Rufinus of Syria, which thus takes us from 359 to approximately 405. All these Latins lead with the concept of divine power rather than the concept of divine substance:
Phoebadius, for example, understands the Sirmium (357) prohibition on essence language as meaning that he would not be allowed to preach the "one power." Hilary's
exilic work and Ambrose of Milan's major writings are difficult to categorize because
they represent *Latin* theologies confused with and by *Greek*.

The doctrine that the Son's unity with the Father is demonstrated in the fact that
he "images" the Father can also support a "Nicene" Trinitarian theology whose logic
is neither power-based nor substance-based, but *iconic*. Faustinus, writing in Rome
around 380, opens his argument that scriptural descriptions of the Son's iconic or visual relationship to the Father establish the substantial unity between Father and Son[64]
by citing John 1:14, "And we beheld his glory, the glory as it were of the only begotten
of the Father." The visual glory that is seen is in itself the mark of the only-begotten
Son: glory attests to Sonship.[65] The image terminology of Genesis 1:26, Philippians

---

63. NPNF IX, 173.

64. Scripture's "iconic" descriptions of the Son here include principally the New Testament language of our sight of the Son, the Son's sight of the Father, and image descriptions of the Son's relationship to the Father.

65. Compare with Tertullian: "'And we beheld his glory, the glory as it were of the only begotten of
the Father' . . . the 'glory' of the the visible Son" (Tertullian, *Treatise Against Praxeas* 15).

2:5–7, Colossians 1:15, and Hebrews 1:3 all figure in Faustinus' argument. As these prooftexts suggest, Faustinus is not focused upon the Incarnate Word as the Image of the Father. When Faustinus turns to exegete the passages in John 14 claimed by Nicenes, he starts with John 14:9, "Whoever sees me, sees the Father." He then moves to the usual Nicene prooftexts: Hebrews 1:3, John 10:30, John 14:9–10 (again), and John 5:19–21.

I turn now to the question of the Son's sight of the Father. While the doctrine that the acts of the Son are the acts of the power that he shares with the Father may not in itself lead to questions about the Son's sight of the Father, the Johannine texts supporting that doctrine do, for they link the Son's doing to his seeing of the Father. Novatian provides a good illustration:

> He [Christ] said [John 14:7] that whoever followed the Son would see the Father. He did not mean that the Son himself was the Father, now seen, but that whoever was willing to follow him and become his disciple would obtain the reward of being able to see the Father. He is also the image of the Father; therefore this truth can be added to the others: As the Father works, so does the Son also; and the Son is the imitator of all his Father's works. Accordingly, every man can feel that, in a sense, he has already seen the Father, inasmuch as he sees Him who always imitates the invisible Father in all his works.[66]

The anti-monarchian context is clearly audible in the quotation: the promised sight of the Father does not mean "that the Son himself was the Father, now seen"; the Son is "the image of the Father," "As the Father works, so does the Son also," and, finally, the statement that everyone can feel that they have, in a sense, already *seen the Father* because the works of the visible Son imitate the invisible Father in all his works.[67] Novatian's addition to the anti-monarchian mix is to say that when the Son does what the Father does, he *imitates* the Father's works. The Son does what the Father does because he sees what the Father does, and, since the Son has the same power as the Father, he then does what the Father is doing, for he possesses the capacity and his will follows the Father's perfectly. It is passages like this one that causes scholars like J.N.D. Kelly to judge that for Novatian the relationship between Father and Son is a moral unity.[68] There is a loose precedent for Novatian's imitation language in Tertullian, when he says, "The Father acts by consciousness, whereas the Son *sees* and accomplishes that which is in the Father's consciousness."[69] There are also conceptual parallels with Irenaeus' *Against Heresies* and with Philo. However, there is a difference

---

66. Novatian, *Trin.* XXVIII.15.

67. If someone says that Novatian was a monarchian then she or he needs to answer a "monarchian" like *who*?

68. Kelly, *Early Christian Doctrines* 5th edition (London: Longman, 1977), 125. Kelly continues: "This comes out strikingly in his avoidance, when expounding texts like 'The Father and I are one' and 'He who has seen me has seen the Father,' any suggestion of unity of essence."

69. See Tertullian, *Treatise Against Praxeas* 15.

between *watching the Father do something* and then doing it too, and *seeing the Father's intention* and putting it into action. The first dynamic inevitably suggests a temporal interval that the second one doesn't. One can also wonder if Novatian is drifting from the central anti-monarchian doctrine of the common power, since at one point he says that the Son imitates the *opera adque virtus* of the Father. Finally, Tertullian's description and Novatian's language beg questions that Philo and Irenaeus answered but which are now confused again. Philo and Irenaeus both spoke of this "seeing the Father's intention" in terms of *the Word seeing the intelligible architecture in the Mind*: that the *Logos* of the *Nous* knows the *Nous* is a relatively straightforward statement, given the meanings of *Logos* and *Nous*; but the concept of *Son* does not offer an explanation for how he is able to see the Father's mind or intention. I cannot find any fourth-century Latins who followed Novatian on the language of "imitation," but I can find one case of someone who seems to have "called out" Novatian on the subject; namely, Hilary.

> [The Son] displays the nature which is His by birth; *a nature which derives its power of action not from successive gifts of strength to do particular* deeds, *but from* knowledge. He shows that this knowledge is not imparted by the Father's performance of any bodily work, as a pattern, that the Son may imitate what the Father has previously done; but that, by the action of the Divine nature, He had come to share the subsistence of the Divine nature, or, in other words, had been born as Son from the Father.[70]

Hilary objects specifically to the notion that the Son *imitates* the Father's work: it is, at the least, too materialist an explanation. The Father's work is not a pattern for the Son to follow. The Son does what he does on the basis of his knowledge of the Father, and that knowledge is based upon Sonship, that is, the sharing of a common nature. "Son" is thus given some epistemological content. But Hilary's basic argument is simply that no one speaks of someone imitating his or her own nature.

Finally, there is a third Latin text to consider for its association of *the Son's doing what he sees the Father doing* with *the Son can see what the Father does because he is the Son*, and that is Augustine's argument in *Trin.* 2.1.3?

> [T]he life of the Son is as unchangeable as the Father's, and yet He is of the Father;
>> and the working of the Father and of the Son is indivisible,
>> and yet so to work is given to the Son from Him of whom He Himself is, that is, from the Father;
>> and the Son so sees the Father, as that He is the Son in the very seeing Him.
>> For to be of the Father, that is, to be born of the Father, is to Him nothing else than to see the Father;

70. *De Trin.* VII.17, NPNF IX, 125.

and to see Him working, is nothing else than to work with Him:
but not working from Himself, because He is not from Himself.
And, therefore, those things which "He sees the Father do, these also does
the Son likewise," because He is of the Father.

The principal common ground between Hilary and Augustine is that they both say that the Son's knowledge of the Father and the Son's ability to act as the Father does come from the Son's identity as the true Son of the Father. *Hilary* says: "The Son receives by his birth from the Father a nature which derives its power of action from knowledge, and this knowledge is imparted to the Son as He shares in the divine nature, that is, as He has been born from the Father." *Augustine* says, "To work with the Father is given to the Son from the Father in the same act as the Father gives the Son existence, that is, his birth, and to be born from the Father is nothing else than to see the Father." To line these two statements up side by side as it were ignores the baroque character of Augustine's thought on the subject, but my point is simply to show the enduring link in Latin theology between the Son's knowledge or sight of the Father and the Son's ability to work as the Father works.

CONCLUSION

To conclude, I return to the passage from *Against Praxeas* that I put forward earlier as Tertullian's response to Spirit monarchianism—and his "reclamation" of John 14:9–10. Not only the language, but the logic of the passage is important for Latin Trinitarian theology.

> Therefore the Father, *remaining* in the Son through works of power [*opera virtutis*] and words of doctrine, is seen through those things through which he *remains*, and through him in whom he *remains*: and from this very fact it is apparent that each Person is himself and none other, while he says, *I am in the Father and the Father in me.*

For virtually every Latin theologian of the Trinity from Tertullian to Augustine, their logic follows this form: the explanation for how the Three are understood to be One is the *unity of power and works*; the explanation for how the Three are distinct from one another is *causal relations*;[71] the explanation for a statement that the Three are eternally irreducible and unconvertible is that *they are each always themselves and not another*; and there is a word for what is Three in God—namely, "person" (*persona*).[72]

---

71. It is the traditionally strong role of aetiological models in Latin Trinitarian theology that provides a basis for the Western understanding of the Creed of Nicaea's "God from God, Light from Light, true God from true God" language.

72. An excellent example of this "Latin Trinitarian logic" at work can be found in Hilary of Poitiers' *Trin.* VII.38–41, where all three of the arguments I list can be found. Hilary is an especially important example to acknowledge, because his Trinitarian theology is often presented, by modern authors, as discontinuous with previous Latin Trinitarian theology (e.g., Tertullian). However, careful attention

The content of person is not psychological in the modern sense,[73] but ontological: "a substance [i.e., existent] which is himself," Tertullian says of "person," and, "Whatever therefore the substance [i.e., existent] of the Word was, that I call a Person, and for it [in this case] I claim the name of Son."[74] Person is not used as a contrast to essence or substance; it is used to name the "whatness" of the Three in the Trinity. Whatever work the idea "person" does in Latin Trinitarian theology, providing the conceptual grounding for "real distinctions" is not one of them: that grounding is provided by the preceding second and third items in the "logic" just listed. This logic is not complete in all Latins: in particular, Latins who argue primarily in terms of "substance" do not work with all these propositions. Nonetheless, I will say that the originating logic of Latin Trinitarian theology is anti-monarchian (i.e., anti-modalist), and in that logic the grounds for real distinctions in the Trinity is provided by causal relations and eternal irreducibility, and not, as modern readers have been taught to expect, by a logic built on the ontological difference between "person" and "essence" (or "nature.")

To summarize, the original formative context for Latin Trinitarian theology is anti-monarchianism: the polemic with the monarchians is foundational and obviously predates the controversy surround the reception of Nicaea (325). A key point of engagement with the monarchians is John 14:9–10, and how one understands the visibility of the Father *in* the Son.[75] The Latin argument is that the Father is seen in the works of the Son, for the Son does the work of the Father: the two do the same work; they have the same power. There are other arguments for the sight of the Father in the Son that are based on scriptural image language—e.g., by Faustinus. The fact that the Son does what the Father does leads to the question: How does the Son know what the Father does? Which is restated as the question: What is the basis of the Son's knowledge of the Father? The answer includes giving epistemological content to Sonship—indeed, to see the Father is to be the Son of the Father, and to be the Son of the Father is to see the Father.

---

to *Trin.* VII.39–40 reveals an account of the Trinity that reads like a glossing of the Tertullian passage I just quoted. All the key elements of Tertullian's theology are there: the use of John 14:9–10, the emphasis on the Father seen in the works of the Son, the fact that "each Person is himself and none other" (Hilary says, "Father is Father and Son is Son"), and the ontological understanding of "person."

73. If indeed there remains in modern thought any concept of "person" other than social "construct."

74. Tertullian, *Treatise Against Praxeas*, 138.

75. There is also the question of how the Father is *in* the Son, which I have not treated, but which has the same anti-monarchian answer as does the question of the "sight" of the Father in the Son.

Chapter 4

The Forms of Latin Theology

THIS ESSAY IS NOT *intended to provide an account, or even a summary, of the theologies involved in the "Arian controversy": the twenty-first century has already seen a plethora of such accounts, and adding something substantial to that work would require yet another monograph. What I am interested in here is intra-Nicene dynamics: What is "Nicene theology," when, and where? How do these "Nicene" theologies relate to one another? Most importantly for this collection is: what language, logic, and formulae would Augustine have received as "the Trinitarian theology of the fathers of Nicaea"? Clearly, Augustine did not regard the formulae, language, and logic of the council(s) to be the last necessary articulated orthodox doctrine of the Trinitarian faith in the Catholic Church. What is necessary for a pious understanding? What is there left to be said?*

Sometime early in the first decade of the fifth century—approximately seventy-five years after the Council of Nicaea—Augustine was challenged to a public debate on the word *homoousios* by Pascentius, an anti-Nicene member of the Imperial Court. This confrontation occurs in roughly the same time period as Augustine started to write *De Trinitate* (*On the Trinity*). The debate begins with the point by Pascentius that the word *homoousios* is nowhere found in Scripture. Augustine replies that *homoousios* is a Greek word and therefore we cannot expect it to occur in the Latin New Testament. Then what does this Greek word mean, given our Latin New Testament? Augustine knows that Pascentius is fishing for him to suggest and commit to some Latin equivalent—such as *euisdem substantia* or *una substantia*. Then the debate will shift onto the subject that is really at the heart of Pascentius' question; namely, how can we use a non-scriptural word to name in the creed that which both the Father and the Son are said to be? But Augustine does not do that. He asks: If we have in the Latin New Testament something with the same meaning as the Greek *homoousios*, will that suffice to say "We know the Latin for what the Greek word means"? We can say, "Of course the Greek word *homoousios* does not occur in our Latin New Testament, but something else, with the same meaning, does occur in the Latin, and so we know what *homoousios* means." Pascentius has to accept this as true, but he feels safe in his knowledge that *substantia* does not occur in the Latin just as *ousia* does not occur in the Greek. What is the Latin New Testament equivalent to *homoousios*? Augustine's answer is *Ego et pater unum sumus*, "The Father and I are one" (John 10:30).[1] That is the Latin for what the Greek word *means*. This is a pious and clever answer by Augustine, not least because it brings the conversation to what Augustine thinks is fundamentally at stake: that the Son is the true Son of God who is truly the Father of that Son.[2]

I rehearse Augustine's argument to make a simple point: approximately seventy-five years after the Council of Nicaea, and a few more than twenty years after Constantinople, the conflict between anti-Nicenes and those aligned with the theology of Nicaea was still going on. That conflict is not equally vigorous throughout Latin Christianity, nor is the same "balance of powers" between the two consistently in place throughout the Western empire.[3] Our own conviction that the Council of Nicaea completely defeated "Arianism" in 325 has only recently ceased to be a commonplace— even by scholars in the field. The full extent of the struggle to bring about a limited consensus at the Council of Constantinople (381) is still not yet widely recognized in the "consciousness" of contemporary theologians on the Trinity.[4]

In this chapter, I will give an account of "Nicene" theology as it was received in Western theology in the second half of the fourth century. I focus on Latin theology as much as possible and is prudent, but the earliest relevant texts are Greek: to state the obvious, the Creed of Nicaea was written in Greek, and the first signs of its reception are Greek, as well. The creed is not referred to in Western theology until approximately 355 or 357.[5] Practically speaking, this is the beginning of the Latin phase of the

---

1. Despite the convention of translations giving "The Father and I are one," both the Greek and the Latin begin with "I and the Father . . ."

2. Something very much like this way of exegeting *homoousios* can be found in Gregory of Elvira's *De Fide* (IV.53): "This is *homoousios*, it is of one substance with the Father, just as the Lord himself said: 'I in the Father and the Father in me,' and: 'I and the Father are one,' and: 'I have come from the Father,' and: 'Who sees me, sees also the Father.'" We know for certain that Augustine had read Gregory, but we do not know if it would have been this early in his episcopacy. "One substance" is read from John 14:9, 10:30, 16:27, and 14:10. Gregory provides the full Latin neo-Nicene constellation of New Testament prooftexts. From just this one passage by Gregory, Augustine would see the neo-Nicene scriptural "logic" supporting and giving meaning to *homoousios*.

3. Shortly after Augustine's death, a conquering army, Homoian (anti-Nicene) by self-definition, will defeat all the forces of the Western Roman empire in North Africa, and soon thereafter the bishop of Carthage will be an anti-Nicene.

4. The errant cliché runs strong: "Nicaea settled the 'problem' of the Son; Constantinople (381) settled the 'problem' of the Holy Spirit." See my essay, "Fourth Century as Trinitarian Canon," in *Christian Origins: Theology, Rhetoric and Community*, ed. Lewis Ayres and Gareth Jones (London: Routledge, 1998), 47–78.

5. Hilary says that he did not hear of the creed until 355. His publication of a translation in his *On the Synods* may have been the first time it appeared in Latin.

"Nicene controversy": this is the beginning of Latin knowledge of what the Greeks had been talking about.[6] The Creed of Sirmium II—the "Blasphemy"—was communicated and interpreted across Gaul by Hilary and Phoebadius of Agen. Lester Field sums up what Sirmium (357) did, and its substantial effects: "the *blasphemia* not only banned the homoousion and the homoiousian but also asserted '*duas personas esse Patris et Filii, maiorem Patrem, Filium subiectum com omni his quae ipsi Pater subiecit.*'"[7] It became clear that much more was at stake than whether Athanasius had been a good bishop or not. No previous creed had overturned (and not just ignored) Nicaea, its logic and language, and its clear doctrines.

If one thinks of 357 as the Latin "beginning" of the controversy, then it is clear that a number of earlier Greek texts—often thought pivotal in the controversy as a whole—are not directly relevant to Latin Trinitarian theology.[8] It has been argued that the Council of Serdica (342) was definitive to the creed's reception in the West and the beginning of Latin Nicene theology.[9] I do not think Serdica played such a role, but I have included Serdica in my chapter on "Other Latin Nicenes" because it testifies to Western theology within its own confines in 342. However, while the Nicene Creed may not have been the subject of Western episcopal concern before 357, soon after Sirmium there follows another *Western* council fundamental to the course of the "Nicene versus anti-Nicene" controversy for both Latins and Greeks: the Council of Rimini (359)—which resulted in imperially imposed subordinationist Trinitarian theology.[10]

My purpose in surveying Latin theology as I do is to support the thesis that "Nicene" theology developed over the course of its reception in the fourth century. There were various "Nicene" theologies. There is a consensus among those American scholars who still study fourth-century Trinitarian theology that we need to recognize and speak of Nicene *theologies*: plural![11] The principal reason for such a judgment is

6. I know very well that this "starting point" for the present review is controversial, even if my purposes for recalling this era of Latin theology are limited. Elsewhere I include the Council(s) of Sardica as an entry point. The simple truth is that I do not take Sardica to be the beginning of Latin engagement with the "Arian controversy."

7. I utilize this kind of quotation because Field happily supplies us with the Latin of the text which so shocked those hitherto on the fence about Nicaea by explicitly linking the rejection of *homoousios* to the acceptance of a clearly subordinationst theology (like Arius'). These anti-Nicenes made the controversy an either/or theological encounter, and gave name (and thus gave unity) to their opponents. "If you are not with us then you are a 'one-essence' person—like that Athanasius guy!" They drew the line in the sand. See Lester L. Field, *On the Communion of Damasus and Meletius: Fourth Century Synodal Formulae in the Codex Veronensis LX* (Toronto: Pontifical Institute of Medieval Studies, 2004).

8. Moreover—and this is significant—after 357, Hilary, among others, no longer had to expend time and energy defending Athanasius and could focus on the theological complexities covered over by the political and ethical charges brought against Athanasius.

9. There is a very broad range of scholarly opinions on the extent to which Nicaea, or the doctrines of Athanasius, were significant issues at Serdica; these opinions range from "No significance" to "The Subject of the Synod"(that is, from 0 to 10)!

10. A meaningful account of "the Western response to Nicaea" could be written focusing in detail on "the road from Sirmium II to Ariminum (359/360)."

11. In a short while, we will no longer have a quorum—until, perhaps, a few decades from now.

that the language and logic used in early polemical writings is not the same as later proponents who champion the name.[12] I propose that there were three principle genera of Nicene theology, and that we can separate generations of "Nicene" theology into one or more of these genera, and by doing so, use each genera to help us recognize the reasoning that formed different-but-related understandings of the faith of Nicaea—especially as Augustine received that faith. The first genus of Nicene theology is the creed itself as a document of 325: I reconstruct that theology as best I can, but of the three, this one may—strangely enough—be the least important for later, especially Latin "Nicenes." The second form I call neo-Nicene: we use the word "neo-" to signify a conscious attempt to replicate an earlier way of thinking (whether conceptually, musically, or fashion-wise). The last of the three I call pro-Nicene: we use the word "pro-" to designate a form of thinking that is in sympathy with an earlier way of thinking, but without trying to duplicate the exact shape of the original, "primitive" form. If there is anything radical or idiosyncratic about the divisions I propose here, it is my judgment that there were three and not two kinds or stages in the trajectory I trace out of Nicaea: neo-Nicene theology is different in its logic from pro-Nicene. Most scholars who recognize distinctions in Nicene theology use neo-Nicene as synonymous with pro-Nicene, but preferring one name over the other.[13] Finally, the reader should know that I am not seeking to obscure the fact that *homoousios* played a central role in serving as a litmus test for Nicene Trinitarian theology—one could not claim to be Nicene and reject *homoousios*. One could, however, be Nicene without recourse to an argument based on *ousia*.[14] Augustine's Trinitarian status cannot be determined by counting the number of times he uses *consubstantialis* or *homoousios*.

THE CREED OF THE EPISCOPAL COUNCIL SUMMONED IN NICAEA (325)[15]

The most distinctive feature of the Creed of Nicaea is its use of essence—*ousia*—language to describe the fundamental being of divinity—that is, the divinity of the Father.

12. Such a distinction has been recognized by modern scholars who use it as a value judgment: Harnack's antinomy of Athanasian versus Cappadocian "Nicene" is a well-known case. Usually the distinction is between "real" Nicene theology versus "fraudulent" or "destructive" Nicene theology. Unlike the divisions in or types of Nicene theology early twentieth-century scholars proposed, my distinctions have no modern denominational or ideological motives: I do not offer these distinctions in order to criticize intra- or extra-church identities or self-definitions.

13. Often "pro-Nicene" means something like "in favor of what 'Nicene' meant at the time." Without more lexical sophistication, this usage can result in conundrums like "pro-Nicene sympathies."

14. One regularly comes across puzzled scholars who recognize Nicene theology in a text "even though the word *homoousios* never appears." I am showing why a Nicene text need not have *homoousios* in its argument or declaration.

15. For the approach that I take in summarizing the Western parallax view of the "triumph" of Nicaea at Constantinople, I am particularly indebted to the following (alphabetically): Field, *On the Communion*; A.H.B. Logan, "Marcellus of Ancyra and the Councils of AD 325: Antioch, Ancyra,

At times, *ousia* seems to supersede Father language; it always refers to the divine what-ness of God (the Father). A few other traditional descriptions of the continuity of nature between Father and Son are taken up in the creed and restated briefly in terms of the *ousia*. Statements such as "Light from Light, true God from true God" are com-mon in pre-Nicene theology; I have named such statements *X from X* causality. Often in such statements, the originating *X* has some ontological priority or superiority over the originated *x*, but sometimes *x from X* names the production of an *x* which entirely equal to the original *X*. "Fire from fire" is a good example of such a causal statement, or "Light from light." There can be some cases where the originating *X* is different from, or at least superior to, the produced *x*. So although the *x from X* language of the creed is familiar as a context, it cannot in itself tell us anything decisive.

If one sees the Nicene Creed as written in a couplet-type form—such as one often finds in Scripture—in which the initial statement is glossed or unpacked by a second clause (AB AB AB), then the creed reads something like this:[16]

The phrase *the Son of God* means *born of the Father* (*Only-begotten*, means "uniquely," which in this case means "the only one to be begotten and not created"); to be *Son of God, born of the Father* and *Only-begotten* means to be *of the essence of the Father*. Nothing else is "from the essence."

God from God, Light from Light, true God from true God, mean roughly the same as *Son of God born of the Father*, while *begotten not made* revisits *only-begotten*. Fi-nally, *of one essence with the Father* brings us back to that same striking word, *essence*, already in *of the essence of the Father*. Looking at just the second set of clauses, we can also say that *x from X* statements like *God from God, Light from Light, true God from true God* mean the same thing as *of one essence with the Father*.[17] This is how the original proponents of the Nicene Creed understood all true *X from X* statements.[18]

In short, the claim of the creed is that any terms of what might be called "relation language," such as *born of the Father, Only-begotten*, and all *x from X* statements, are to be understood as having to do with the one divine *essence*. Whatever predicates we speak of, whatever verbs we use, these have to do with a divine essence that is acting within itself. No wording in this section of the creed refers to anything outside the divine essence: the essence is the real subject of all such language.[19] If a reader has the

---

and Nicaea," *JThS* ns 43 (1992): 428–46"; Daniel H. Williams, "Monarchianism and Phontinus of Sir-mium as the Persistent Heretical Face of the Fourth Century," *HTR* 99 (2006): 201–20." Unfortunately, Alistair Logan's substantial contribution to the recovery of "the road to (and from) Nicaea" has often been overlooked.

16. In each case, "means" is "to say the same as" or "is to be understood as."

17. *X from X* is the single most common way to express the origin of the Son from the Father, and/or the continuity between Father and Son.

18. Notice that in the original *X from X* statements, as well as in the essence-based understanding of the statements, there are no qualifiers for either *X*. In the late 350s, Eunomius will interpret *X from X* as inherently meaning "begotten *X* from unbegotten *X*," so that he will understand "Light from Light" to mean "begotten light from unbegotten Light."

19. One clause may be an exception—as in the case of Marcellus of Ancyra's reading of the clause: "begotten" may refer to the economy of the Incarnation (only) understood as the divine essence

entire text before them, the key clause(s) would be "Son of God . . . begotten from the essence of the Father."

If we hope to get some idea of the theological sensibilities of those whose theology was sympathetic to the content and motives behind the Creed of Nicaea, we can compare their vocabulary and logic to what we find in the creed of 325. For example, the writings of Bishop Alexander of Alexandria, the first hierarch to come into open conflict with Arius, express his theology of the unity between Father and Son largely in terms of unbegotten and begotten. The unbegotten what? The Father. The begotten what? The Son. Alexander does not use *ousia*: he refers to *hypostasis*—taking his cue from Hebrews 1:3.

Alexander stresses the perfection of the Son—that he has all that the Father has—and he concludes that if the Son is not, for any interval, the Word or Power or Wisdom or "any other things by which the Son is known," then that glory is not in the Father's nature, which is unthinkable.

> "Thus he took from his nature an impression of his likeness in all regards and is an unchangeable image of the Father can express the image of the Archetype."[20]

> "We believe that the Son always is from the Father. 'For he is the brightness of his glory and image of the Father's *hypostasis*.'"[21]

> "We confess him begotten from the unbegotten Father, God the Word, truth, light, righteousness, Jesus Christ, Lord and Savior of all. He is the image not of the will or any other thing but of *hypostasis* of the Father himself."[22]

> "[T]he Son alone is the form and image [of the Father] . . Our Redeemer is proclaimed [to be] the form of the Father."[23]

Having cited these passages from Alexander and the Synod of Antioch (325),[24] it is best to remind readers what I intend for you to appreciate in terms of "Nicene theology." First, as I have already said, the creed uses "from the essence [*ousia*]" as its fundamental description of the Son's origin (and thus his nature). As we see from

---

existing in the human Jesus without partition or duplication. Later texts in sympathy with Marcellus will say, for example, the divine "extended" into the creature. See Joseph T. Lienhard, *Contra Marcellum: Marcellus of Ancyra and Fourth-Century Theology* (Washington DC: CUA Press, 1999).

20. Alexander, "Letter to Alexander of Thessalonika," 40.

21. Alexander, "Letter to Alexander of Thessalonika," 42.

22. "Synodal Letter," 47.

23. "Synodal Letter," 47.

24. An Armenian council held in Eznik roughly contemporary to Antioch and Nicaea produced a creed that described the Son as "From the Father, and with him and close to him, the one offspring . . . equal in *power*" (Gabriele Winkler, "The Antiochene Synods, and the Early Armenian Creeds Including the 'Rezeptionsgeschichte' of the Synod of Antioch 341 in the Armenian Version of the Anaphora of Basil," *Bolletino della Badia Greca Grottaferrata* 3 (2006): 275–98. 293). I include the Armenian reconstruction of Antioch as an illustration, not as part of the proof.

Alexander and Antioch (325), the Nicene emphasis on "production *by the essence*" is striking in its ubiquity: no other kinds of production are considered. (Although *ousia* and *hypostasis* are regarded as synonyms, the creed uses *ousia* consistently.) For example, there is no appeal to "image" language despite the fact that it appears strongly in the letters of Alexander and in the Creed of Antioch (325).[25] At Nicaea there are variations on the basic clause—*from the essence* of the Father, *same in essence*, etc.—and "the Son is generated from the essence [*ex ousia*] of the Father" is a succinct and fair articulation of the creed's theology. In the Nicene Creed, *ousia* language sets the meaning for *the Christ is the "Son of God"*—a proclamation common across all articulations of the faith—as meaning "from the essence of the Father."[26] The second major point illustrated in the quotations is that those who can be reasonably presumed to be in sympathy with the creed—those bishops who in fact composed the creed to express a clear and distinct line in the sand that could not be crossed (and which Arius had crossed)—did not themselves use *ousia* language previously, though their writings show a concern for the question of the origin and generation of the "true Son" just as the Nicaea does.[27] Finally, we should note and not simply pass over the implicit but fundamental fact that there being no explicit doctrinal statement appeal to sequence other than Father-Son is very important: there is no explicit appeal to *taxis* or *ordo*.[28] For all Trinitarian theologies involved in the Nicene controversy, the Father is first because he is uncaused and first cause of Son and Holy Spirit. The argument can be reduced to: "What is revealed to us by the fact that the Father is first, uncaused, and the Son is 'second,' caused?" The spectrum of answers to that question runs from Marcellus to Eunomius.[29] From "first" and "second" enters the concepts of subordinationism, modalism, and even that of "mission."

25. We have a tenuous grasp of the Creed of Antioch: fragments of the text have traveled through Greek, into Syrian, and finally into Armenian. The word I have twice given as "form" is from Hebrews 1:3, the *xarakter* of *hypostasis*. Even if I had the Greek text before me, I would have trouble coming up with words that are not synonymous with the Greek for form, character, image, or impression.

26. Marcellus of Ancyra, bishop of the city where the council was planned to convene until an earthquake required a change of venue, an early advocate for the creed produced by the council, interprets the exclusive use of "from the essence" language to mean that there is a stage in God's action which locates the Word within the essence; "Son" refers only to the Incarnation.

27. Looking at other texts by the bishops instrumental in the writing of the creed, one can easily imagine that the Creed of Nicaea could have read along the lines of the Son being "born of the *hypostasis* of the Father, one in *hypostasis* or of the same *hypostasis* as the Father." The bishops declined a biblical term in favor of *ousia*!

28. This is not a feature unique to this creed, but even when there is no explicit reference to a Trinitarian order, that conceptuality is present and supplying a logic. In some creeds and the supporting logic the order, "first, second, third" are intrinsic to the faith; in others, the Son and Holy Spirit are simultaneously (as it were) from the Father. The order of persons is a basic concept in Tertullian's Trinitarian logic: the *taxis* of the Trinity is itself embedded in the revelation of the existence of a Trinitarian God. (Compare the logic of sequence or order in the Trinitarian theology of Marius Victorinus.)

29. Marcellus is said to have summarized his Trinitarian theology as, "No number in God! No two or three!"

As is clear from the quotations from the "Epistle of Alexander" and the Creed of Antioch, the bishops who wrote the creed did not use *ousia* in their own texts or creeds: they typically used "image" or "participating perfectly," following the precedent of Hebrews 1:3. I think the creed is purposely placed outside important scriptural terminology and testimony. We know the creed was written with a polemical or exclusionary intention: to judge the teachings attributed to Arius as heretical. The canons are explicit about that particular condemnation. I believe that the creed was intentionally placed outside the scriptural language or other "production" models in order to use it as a means to test or measure those traditional or commonplace doctrines. It is a hermeneutical device. The Son is from the essence of the Father, the Son is the Son of the Father's essence, the Son has the same essence as the Father. All other doctrines are measured against the "from the essence" standard. The Son is the Son of what? You have to say "essence." The Father generates the Son from his—what? Moreover, whatever ambiguity we now find in the creed was not there for its intended audience: they knew this "measure" excluded "from/of the will," and if pressed it would reject or at least radically reconfigure "image" and "radiance" language. The creed's perceived measure or canon shifted from "from the essence" or "of the essence of the Father" to "[of the] same essence [*homoousios*]" and to "from the Father."

The transition from image language (for example) to essence language that occurred at some moment in the council is unknown to us, and will remain unknown, and which, moreover, the authors of the creed took no opportunity to hint at, much less to explain.[30] The Son is fully divine (and truly Son) because he is "from the essence" or "from the essence of the Father" (whom all acknowledge implicitly is truly "God"). This is the theology of the Creed of Nicaea. All the writings that later follow in attempts to explain and to justify the creed as a whole (comparatively few), or as propositions or clauses of the creed (more), or simply as an individual phrase or single words (the goal of most polemical apologias) will have little more conceptual context to work from than that simple summary clause: "from the essence of the Father." Perhaps just as important to keep in mind is that those who attacked the creed or what it "stood for" had nothing more to sink their teeth into than a Trinitarian theology

30. I am not saying that *ousia* language or even *homoousia* appeared with no theological precedents or philosophical logic; I am concluding from the fact that there are several precedents, each of which could provide a logic or the reason why the council fathers used *ousia* language and even the term *homoousia*. The creed itself, as a text, offers no signs or clues as to which of these several trajectories "supplied" the language of the creed or the tradition of conceptualizing the tri-une God. Christopher Stead's still useful book, *Divine Substance,* provides evidence of, and insight into, different authors and texts, any of which could have been the decisive source for the language of the creed. Joseph Lienhard's article, "The Arian Controversy: Some Categories Reconsidered," *TS* 48 (1987): 415–36, gives us insight into why the creed was received by some as it was—it was the product of the "miahypostatic" school, as the council's first condemnation gives evidence. But the creed does not use "one" (*'en* or *mia*) and, moreover, there are precedents for *homoousias* among prior representative of the "dyohypostatic" trajectory. *Perhaps* homoousios *is most accurately parsed as "one in essence"*— except from the unfortunate Marcellan resonance this would have. Perhaps the council fathers used *homoousias* to decline Marcellus' direct statement "one-essence"?

whose content can be expressed in the propositions "from the essence" of or "same in essence" with the Father.[31] To a great extent, either side will work by building a conceptual context for essence-based clauses, phrases, or a single word (i.e., *homoousios*). Those who argue for essence-based logic for the union of "Father and Son" in order to defend what they think is "the faith of Nicaea" I call neo-Nicenes.[32] Those who argue against essence-based logic in order to attack and end what they think of as "the faith of Nicaea" I call anti-Nicenes.[33] Nicenes answer the question of "from what/who is the Son or the Word *out of*?" with "from the essence [of God the Father]." Second, Nicenes have an answer for the question of *how* he was produced or generated from the essence (of the Father). By what kind of "from" or "out of," specifically? "begotten." The decisive language is "from" and "out of" "the essence [of the Father]." In my opinion, *homoousios* is not the central, decisive expression of the theology of the council; rather, the word provides a name for the question: How do we relate the generated essence to the generating essence? We say that the generated essence is the *same in essence* with the generating essence.[34]

I am walking slowly over what is surely evident and hardly needs be said aloud, but what is not evident and needs to be said clearly—in light of events later—is that the council fathers were saying that a generated essence "out of" an ungenerated essence was still properly said to be *homoousios* with the ungenerated generating essence. "Always the Father, always the Son" was how Alexander had put it. But the council's assertion that a generated essence was one with its generating essence, even if that generating essence was ungenerated, was a weak use of essence logic, not its cornerstone. Christopher Stead concluded (in 1977) that

> the vast majority of the texts examined [in his book] above and elsewhere, including those from Athanasius' *de Decretis*, indicate that the phrase [from God's essence] was not designed to make the directly ontological statement

31. Repeating what I said above: all *X from X* statements are to be understood as "essence from the same essence," just as "[only-begotten] Son of the Father" is understood.

32. Why are these later authors not simply designated "Nicene"? For the same reason 357 anti-Nicenes are not "Arians": the chain of evidence is broken, and the logic of 357 (in either case) need not be the same as 318–25. See Eusebius of Caearea's justification to his parish in "Letter to His Church Concerning the Synod at Nicaea," in Rusch, *Trinitarian Controversy*, 57–60.

33. A significant number of synods and creeds took no interest in, or were ignorant of, Nicaea. During the 340s, synodal letters take care to reject Arius and his ilk, while at the same time condemning the theological of Marcellus—though the condemnations of Marcellus were more spirited than the rejections of Arius. "Arianism," as we define the term today, was thought, in the West during the 340s, to be dead letter. See Meslin, *Les ariens d'Occident 335–430* (Paris: Editions du Seuil, 1967).

34. See Kelly Spoerl, "Two Early Nicenes: Eustathius of Antioch and Marcellus of Ancyra," in Peter W Martens, ed., *In The Shadow of the Incarnation* (Notre Dame IN: Notre Dame University Press, 2008), 121–48. Kelly's purpose is to compare the theologies of two participants of the council to reveal their similarities and differences. Spoerl notes the lack of "any reference to the controversial Nicene watchword homoousion" in the writings of these two bishops who attended Nicaea and whose theology was represented in the creed (Spoerl, "Two Early Nicenes," 125). My thesis explains and indeed expects that "absence." For those at Nicaea, *homoousios* gave a title to the outcome of a logic.

about the Son, that he is "of" the *ousia* (i.e., rank, dignity, status) which is proper to the Father; but rather to show that he derives from the Father by a process comparable to natural generation, as opposed to some process of "making."[35]

I think that those other, later uses of "from God's essence" to which Stead refers were designed to make the directly ontological statements about the Son. Neo-Nicenes build upon "Father–Son"[36] and anti-Nicenes build (and attack from) "ungenerated-generated." Eunomius did not invent or discover the problems with "ungenerated essence producing a generated essence, one with itself."

The final point I want to make before moving on is that we should take note of what traditional Trinitarian language (pre-325) does not appear in the creed. There is no "image" language (e.g., perfect image) that, as I mentioned before, was a common way of speaking of the Son's congruency with the Father, nor is there any use of *hypostasis*.[37] (There are no intimations of the otherwise very influential Heb 1:3.) A corollary to this observation is that there is likewise no "participation" language (e.g., perfectly participates). We also note the conspicuous absence of *Logos* language. Origen had previously warned against any Christology that focused exclusively on the title *Logos*, and within five years of the council, Marcellus' theology bears out that warning with his strong "modalist" interpretation of the eternal, essential unity of the Word with the divine essence.[38] Bishops with a strong image or participation model of the Trinity could either re-interpret the creed's essence language into their own image theology—or continue with their traditional language after accepting the brief Nicene interruption.[39] Looking back from the perspective of the Cappadocians and Augustine, the one omission from the creeds of 325 and 381 with the greatest effect is their failure to conceptually link the universally accepted attribute of God as "simple" with "one in essence." But the fathers of Nicaea lacked that mandate (Arius never cast his arguments in terms of "divine simplicity"), and, more importantly, the only theology which had a Trinitarian logic at hand to talk about one in terms of the other was Marcellus (and the miahypostatic tradition). One of the major problems in Latin Trinitarian theology which Augustine faces is to develop a logic which brings

35. G. Christopher Stead, *Divine Substance* (Oxford: Oxford University Pres, 1977), 233.

36. There is one exception—or delayed response—to what I say about neo-Nicenes: in his *First Oration against Arius*, Athanasius tries to build from "from/of the essence" and leaves *homoousios* as a summary term that carries little of the weight of his argument. The text is a flashback, almost a déjà vu, to Nicaea, likely influenced by Marcellus' own strong preference for "one essence" and the "same essence" that Eusebius of Caesarea argues against in *Ecclesial Theology*.

37. "Light from Light" is not participatory causality: no ones says, "This candle's fire perfectly imitates the flame on the match from which I lit it."

38. The mention of Marcellus gives me the opportunity to make clear the non-controversial use of the word *ousia*, as both Eusebius and Marcellus use it freely to refer to the divine being. The distinction between "God" and "the divine being" is not kept strongly by either side.

39. Mark Delgogliano, "Eusebian Theologies of the Son as the Image of God before 341," *JECS* 14 (2006): 459–84.

together the divine attributes, the co-essential Trinity, and the absolute simplicity of God's essence.[40]

In the long "Nicene" controversy in which *ousia*-language played a major part—for and against—*homoousios* is the most well-known of the summaries by which the Son's divinity is related and compared to the Father's, but I do not take the logic implied in "[the two are] *homoousios*" to be the same as that of "from the *ousia* of the Father" as most scholars do.[41] If we use the distinctions Stead offered above, then I say that "from the essence of the Father" was intended "to show that he derives from the Father by a process comparable to natural generation, as opposed to some process of 'making,'" but that the term *homoousios* made "the directly ontological statement about the Son, that he is 'of' the *ousia* (i.e., rank, dignity, status) which is proper to the Father."[42] The "Father-Son" logic by itself would seem initially to be a scripturally derived and unambiguous basis for a definitive, unequivocal logic of unity and distinction. But it was not. "Son" could be understood as "a perfect creation" to whom the Father delegated his creative and judicial power.[43] The Son could be the name of the unity formed when divinity (God, Father) "extended into," as it were, the human Jesus. "Sonship" could refer to God the Father adopting a creature and investing him with those divine powers that a human could contain. Finally, "son" could refer to a temporary created "vehicle" or presence of God like the burning bush or the Angel of the Lord. Every use of the Christological title "Son" presumed a prior or contextualizing logic of unity—and that is what the Nicene "from the essence" *ousia*-logic

40. However, it is important to understand that Augustine knew none of the Greek theology I have offered as background to the Nicene controversy: after 325, no one wrote about Nicaea for nearly thirty years. Hilary of Poitiers says that he had never read it until his exile into the Eastern empire (c. 355). Athanasius did know, however, details of Arius' theology because, as Bardy has shown, several dossiers of "Arian documents" circulated in the West; moreover, a number of Arius' own writings were translated into Latin. See Bardy, "L'occident et les documents." The so-called "Second Letter of Candidus," preserved in Marius Victorinus' work *Theological Treatises on the Trinity*, is a Latin translation of Arius' "Letter to Eusebius of Nicomedia." Similarly, the proceedings of the Council of Aquilaea (381) to condemn second- and third-generation anti-Nicenes, as well as anti-Nicene works like the *Anonymous Commentary on Job*, were in circulation in North Africa, the Iberian peninsula, Gaul, and Italy. See Williams, *Ambrose of Milan*. After the turn of the century, Augustine has good access to a variety of translated Greek or originally Latin anti-Nicene documents, either because they are in "popular" circulation or because they have been sent to him (to refute) by worried correspondents. See, for example, Augustine's late work, *Answer to the Arian Sermon*.

41. We can imagine that, in the West after 357, any bishop who rejected another theology as subordinationist (making the Son less God than the Father) would find to his liking almost anything he may have heard about *homoousios*, particularly if linked to *una subtantia*.

42. Three points for the reader here. In his *First Oration*, Athanasius makes the precise argument that the honor, rank, etc., of the Father is due to the Son because the Son is proper to the Father. Secondly, whatever distinction the two conveyed was lost by the 350s, and *homoousios* became the sign or trademark of "What Nicene theology was." Thirdly, the distinction I am making here is a highly speculative or experimental one. If the reader finds this distinction between "from the essence of" and *homoousios* useless, an unnecessary burden, or just plain wrong as a reading, then they should lay the experiment off to the side and move on to the substance of my argument, rather than strain over a needle.

43. One should detect an echo of Philo in this usage.

statement provided when it goes on to say "the Son of God, begotten from the Father as only-begotten, from the *ousia* of the Father," etc.

To show that by the titles Nicene, neo-Nicene, and pro-Nicene I mean three different "logics" by which the theology of the 325 creed is understood, defended, and developed, and not simply three different time periods during which the creed is engaged against a subordinationist theology often associated with Arius, I begin with Athanasius, *First Oration Against the Arians*, as an example of Nicene theology. The theology of the *Oration* is not based upon a "one essence" or "from the essence" logic, although Athanasius is trying to relate and develop what "one essence" means. His logic is based upon the technical relationship between an essence and "what is proper to it"—*idios*.[44] Most of the *Oration* identifies the relationship between the Son and God the Father and argues, based upon *idios* logic, that the Son is "proper" to the Father's essence, and if "proper" then what truths can we conclude about the Son? The bulk of essence language in Nicaea 325 is the assertion of the Son being "of" or "from" the Father's essence—without there resulting any second essence, whether in kind or number or separation. The Son is of the essence and one with it. Athanasius' logic in *First Oration* runs: "peculiar offspring" means *homoousios* means "of the Father's essence." *Idios tēs ousia* means "the property of an essence" or "that which belongs to or is distinctive of a specific essence": its *own*. Athanasius used this same language in his work, *On the Incarnation*, where the union between the Son–Word and flesh was described in terms of "the body was *idios* to the Son"—the body was proper to Christ, it was *own*. The worth of Christ's own body was infinite. The soteriological significance of the Passion was that Christ's *own* body had suffered and his *own* body had been given in exchange for our salvation. In the *First Oration*, *idios* is used in a sense cognate to that in *On the Incarnation*. The Son is *proper to* the Father's essence: the Son is his own, proper Son—*monogenes*, "only-begotten." Being *idios* to the Father's essence, whatever is true of that essence is true of what is *idios* to that essence: the essence is eternal, so the *idios* of the essence is eternal. "Because the Father is everlasting, his Word and Wisdom would be everlasting." The Son "is by nature true Son and legitimate from the Father, peculiar [*idios*] to his substance, the only-begotten Wisdom and true and only Word of God. He is neither a creature nor a work, but an offspring *idios* to the Father's essence."[45] Athanasius then relates the *idios* language (or logic) to Nicaea's *ousia* language or logic: "Therefore he is true God, *homoousios* with the true Father." To be *idios* to something is to be of the same essence as it.[46] We can go

---

44. Athanasius develops this *idios tēs ousia* argument relying upon conceptual relationships he assumes the reader already knows.

45. I will return to the language of "peculiar [*idios*] to his substance, only-begotten Wisdom and true and only Word of God." *Or.* 1.9.

46. From one perspective, this statement is almost redundant: if something "is *idios* to . . . ," then it must be *idios* to an essence. There is no such thing as a free-floating, non-essential idiom: it must be an *idios* of some specific existing essence; in this case, God the Father's essence, to which the Son is *idios*. *Or.* 1.58.

further with this logic: in this case, what is *idios* to the Father's essence is not simply some divine property or attribute, but a Son—which means that what this *idios* logic also says is given that it is *idios* to the essence that there be a Son, this must mean that it is also *idios* to God that he is a Father (for no son exists without a father). In the late 350s, Hilary of Poitiers and Gregory of Elvira used "proprium" in arguments to the same effect.[47]

Athanasius' argument from the *idios* of God's *ousia* provides the opportunity (and obligation) to discuss another Trinitarian logic in wide use from the New Testament through to Augustine's time. From the Christian perspective, in all of Scripture the Son is referred to by a variety of titles, some of which describe the Son as God's own, the _____ of God. Word, Wisdom, and Power were the three most significant.[48] The relationships among these titles, how the different titles compliment one other, which titles are to be taken literally and others figuratively, and which provide the basis for Trinitarian logic, was an ongoing concern which could burst into controversy and schism. Making sense of seemingly contradictory attributes of God—Mercy, Justice— is a key exegetical task for the rabbis and Philo. The first hundred pages of Origen's *Commentary on the Gospel of John* is an argument against those who take "Word" as the singularly decisive title for the Son.[49] "Wisdom Christology" occurs in the Epistle to the Hebrews, Justin Martyr, Origen, and Eusebius of Caesarea. In Origen's *On First Principles* (I.ii), one can see the interweaving of Wisdom 7:25, Hebrews 1:3, and 1 Corinthians 1:24 as the logical "platform" from which he develops his theology of the Trinity.

I am not interested in contrasting the different "title" Trinitarian theologies—Wisdom versus Word versus Power (if there is any significance among them).[50] What I am interested in is making explicit the logic of participation(s) that make these titles of use for a participatory Trinitarian logic, and then distinguishing how the grammar of degrees of union figure in the different types of Nicene theology. What does "Christ is the Power and Wisdom of God" mean in speech about the identity and relationship of union(s) between the Son and God the Father? By arguing that the Son is "of one essence with the Father" because the Son is "*idios* to the Father," Athanasius introduces into our study the question of attribution—how does identifying the Son as an attribution of God demonstrate that the Son is of the same essence as God? Since the first

47. To help the reader better understand the relationship among these technical terms, I offer this definition from Galen of Pergamon's *De placitis* 7.5.15: "For peculiarities [*idios*] of substance [*ousia*] carry with them corresponding peculiarities [*idios*] of powers [*dunamis*]." Galen was a physician and philosopher in the court of Marcus Aurelius. He traveled extensively and established schools of medicine in Rome, Alexandria, and Antioch. He took a particular interest in the "philosophy" of Christianity.

48. Consider, for example, the elaborate set of relationships described in Proverbs 8 between God and "his Wisdom."

49. Word—"spoken Word," as in Gen 1:3—is the decisive title in Marcellus' Trinitarian logic.

50. Winkler gives a detailed account of the importance in the Syriac and Armenian traditions of the Christological title alone and in 1 Cor 1:24; see "Antiochene Synods and the Early Armenian Creeds," 282–86.

century, Christians identified the Second Person, and at the same time identified his relationship with God, through the logic of attribution and participation. For example:

> In the beginning was the Word, and the Word was with God, and the Word was God. He was in the beginning with God, all things were made through him, and without him was not anything made that was made. (John 1:1–3)

> [the Son] reflects the Glory of God and bears the very stamp of his nature, upholding the universe by the Word of his Power. (Heb 1:3)

> [for the Son is] a breath of the Power of God, and a pure emanation of the Glory of the Almighty. (Wis 7:25)

Years ago[51] the old school of Scripture studies balked at recognizing any personification or hypostasization in these titles (as particularly in the case of Wisdom). Now we can depend upon a rich body of scholarship that has recognized the "prepositional grammar," "possessive" attribution, and traditions of "personification" and "hypostization" that existed in different genres of Second Temple and early Christian texts and exegesis.[52] The passage from Clement of Alexandria that follows illustrates how scriptural exegesis informed early Trinitarian and Christological doctrine: "This is the highest excellence, which orders all things in accordance with the Father's will, and holds the helm of the universe in the best way, with unwearied and tireless *Power, working* all things in which it *operates*."[53] One immediately recognizes the commonality with Sirach and Wisdom of Solomon—except that in these cases, doctrine is articulated using terms constellated from power aetiology: power, works, operations.[54]

In the Trinitarian doctrines of the fourth century, we can recognize four different kinds of unity postulated between God and his "properties"; four different ways in which a title identifies the Second Person and specifies the type of union he has with God the Father. Three of these "kinds of unity postulated" appear in Nicene theologies. I use "power" as my principal example of a "property," but the distinctions offered can be for any divine property with which the Son is identified: e.g., Wisdom, Light or Glory, and Word.

The Second Person images a divine property (e.g., wisdom or power) from which it is derived;[55] the Second Person is a perfectly imaged property of God (with a sepa-

51. When I wrote my dissertation.

52. There is no longer need for hesitating to allow "hypostatization" in Second Temple Jewish theology. One may not agree with the reading, but it cannot be excluded *a priori* the way Margaret Barker's work was for so long, or Helmer Ringgren, *Word and Wisdom: Studies in the Hypostasization of Divine Qualities and Functions in the Ancient Middle East* (Lund: Hakan Ohlssons Boktryckeri, 1947).

53. Clement of Alexandria, *Stromateis* VII.2.

54. See my "Background and Use of Eunomius' Causal Language."

55. "The Wisdom of God made an image of itself, divine wisdom." See below the quotation from Arius.

rate or distinct existence); the Second Person is that very property of God which has coexisted in (or "beside") God; the Father and the Son share, or both equally participate in, or possess the same divine property as they possess the same divine essence.

Authors such as Clement of Alexandria, Tertullian, Hippolytus, and Origen commonly articulate two kinds of power-based Trinitarian theologies.[56] These two doctrines of divine power will play fundamental roles in the Trinitarian controversies of the fourth century. The first doctrine of divine power holds that in God there is only one power, a power that is co-extensive with his nature, such that to say "power" is to say "nature." Power and nature together make up the existence of divinity. Tertullian, for example, uses power (often *potestatis*, but also *virtus*) in doctrinal formulations in which the sense is "one power, one substance." This understanding and use of the term appears particularly in the *Against Praxeas*, when Tertullian, having insisted upon the distinctness of the Divine Persons, draws back to affirm their substantial unity: the three are "one substance, and one condition, and of one power."[57] Hippolytus similarly remarks that God "has a single Power; and that as far as Power is concerned, God is one."[58] Origen's *Dialogue with Heraclides* provides a well-known case of his use of this sense of "one power" as an expression of common nature.

Origen: *The Father is God?*

Heraclides: *Completely.*

Origen: *The Son is different from the Father?*

Heraclides: *How could the Son exist if he were the same as the Father?*

Origen: *Though the Son is distinct from the Father, he is also God?*

Heraclides: *He is also God.*

Origen: *And in their unity there are two Gods?*

Heraclides: *Yes.*

Origen: *We confess two Gods?*

Heraclides: *Yes. The power is one.*[59]

In the second doctrine of "divine power," the term is understood as a title of the Second Person specifically and exclusively. The Second Person, whether otherwise called the Son, the Word, or Wisdom, is *the* Power of God the Father.[60] This second

---

56. See Barnes, *Power of God*, ch. 3.

57. *Against Praxeus* (*Adversus Praxeus*) 2, CSEL vol 47 230.2–3. ANF 598.

58. *Hippolytus of Rome: Contra Noetum* 8.2, Butterworth, 64–65.

59. Origen, *Dialogue with Heraclides*, 2.15–27.

60. "Power" was once a central ontological and theological concept—but it has fallen out of use (or consciousness) in modern thought to the extent that its former importance cannot be recognized. Why? There are no clear answers, but one that has emerged is that because Hegel left Kraft out as

doctrinal sense of a "power" Trinitarian theology appears in Tertullian's writings, and in Hippolytus' *Against Noetus*, where the concept is understood as being descriptive of the Word, who is then identified by the title Power, which is to say *the* Power of the Father.[61] In this understanding, Power, Word, and Wisdom are all considered to be roughly synonomous as titles for the Second Person: "He was Word, he was Spirit, he was Power" is how Hippolytus puts it, but the thought is the same as Tertullian's. Origen can serve as an example of a proponent of this kind of power theology when he says, "[T]he will of God comes itself to be a power of God. There comes into existence, therefore, another power, subsisting in its own proper nature . . . a kind of breath of the first and unbegotten power of God."[62] What Origen here makes explicit is the connotation of a *second* power: the Son is identified as the "Power of God," but that power is not God's *own* power but a power from that power. Origen claims divinity for the Son by identifying him as the *Power of God*, but that power is not the very connatural power of God but a second power. We may see Origen's doctrine as a solution to the problems posed by the famous "two-stage" *Logos* theologies of Origen's predecessors, but it also serves as a precedent for one side in the controversies of the fourth century.

When we turn to the Trinitarian controversies of roughly the first half of the fourth century, we can analyze the two sides as opposed adherents of different understandings of what it means that the Son is, as 1 Corinthians 1:24 puts it, the "Power of God." Again I refer to Athanasius' recollections in *De Decretis* V.20 and *De Synodis* 18 that at Nicaea various titles were first proposed by his side as descriptions of the Son's unique union with God. The first of these titles was Power; the debate over this title is the only episode that Athanasius gives any details about. When the term Power was proposed, the "Eusebians" accepted the title because it was susceptible to an equivocal attribution: here we have the famous case of Asterius remarking that even the locusts of Moses's plague are called the "powers of God" by Scripture. That Asterius is the spokesman for

---

a Transcendental Concept power began to fall out of use. But this answer only makes sense if one understands why Kraft was not a viable concept in a post-Kantian world (Hegel being post-Kantian). But what does this answer mean? In the post-Kantian epistemology, and theology developed into philosophical agnosticism, we cannot know the Real because we can only know what our mind synthesizes for itself from the apparent external world. We reach Epiphenomena, not Being. "Power" (*dynamis, virtus*) is an ontology and epistemology that necessarily predicates real existence and a truth beyond it which is analogous to the bundle of phenomena before us, or power predicates a real world consistent with our analysis of the power *that we really know*. Finally, power is above all an aetiological concept, and if one takes all causality to be a construct—then the concept of power (being as cause) is deceptive and useless. Post-Enlightenment "ontology" and theology has been deeply, consistently, and deceptively "epistemologically agnostic." Recent "Power Analytics" has begun to gain some traction in this millennium because "Power theory" can be considered a systematic logic that explains (i.e., organizes) the recuring bundles of phenomena we "encounter."

61. William McFadden, "The Exegesis of 1 Cor. 1:24, 'Christ the Power of God and the Wisdom of God until the Arian Controversy," diss. Pontifical Gregorian University, 1963, 60, relates Hippolytus' identification of titles in *Against Noetus* to a similar statement in his *Commentary on the Canticle of Canticle*. The *Commentary* is the only time Hippolytus clearly cites 1 Cor 1:24.

62. Origen, *On First Principles* I.2.9.

this understanding of power returns as an echo when, in the *Discourse Against the Arians* and *On the Councils of Ariminum and Seleucia*,[63] Athanasius cites a fragment from Asterius' *Syntagmation*, which says, "[T]here are many powers; one of which is God's own by nature and eternal; but phrase the so-called powers."[64] Athanasius also gives a representative passage of Arius' theology of the production of "Wisdom":

> [T]here are two "Wisdoms," one which is proper to God and exists together with him, and [the other] the Son who has been brought into this Wisdom; only be participating in this Wisdom is the Son called Wisdom and Word. Wisdom came into existence though Wisdom, by the will of the God who is wise.[65]

In terms of a Trinitarian theology, we have what can be called a "two-powers" theology,[66] the first is God's own eternal and proper power, the second is a derived power which has its own existence.[67] Athanasius understands Arius' "two-wisdoms" doctrine as equivalent to Asterius' doctrine of "two (kinds of) powers," and he was right: both limit the Son's unity with the Father to "an image of the property God's

---

63. In the first *Discourse Against the Arians*, Athanasius combines passages from Arius with passages from Asterius: in the *Thalia*, Arius says that there are two Wisdoms and another Word in God besides the Son, and in other texts "of theirs they" teach that there are many powers (*Discourse* I.2.5). In *Discourse* II.18.37, Athanasius reports the same doctrine of power(s) and attributes it explicitly to Asterius. In the *Councils of Ariminum and Seleucia* (*De Synodis*) 17–18, Athanasius gives extensive quotations of this doctrine from Asterius' *Syntagmation*. Again, Spoerl's and Vinzent's *Eusebius of Caesarea: Against Marcellus and Ecclesiastical Theology* (FoTC 135) is invaluable.

64. *Discourse* I.2.5 NPNF IV.309. Here Asterius' use of "Powers" (*dynameis*), has more the sense of *works* than *source*, and is close to the use, in the Gospels, of *dynameis* to mean "miracles."

65. *Discourse* I.2.5. In Arius scholarship of the 1950s and early 1960s, the nature of Arius' doctrine of *wisdom from wisdom* was the object of some debate. G. Christopher Stead takes pains in "Platonism of Arius," 16–31, to distinguish his opinion that Arius held to a "two-level" theory from Wolfson's opinion of Arius' "two-stage" Logos. In Arius' system, Stead says, "terms such as *wisdom* and *logos* [*sic*] have two meanings." These homonyms are attributed to both Father and Son. "The Son's attributes are parallel to the Father's; but his wisdom is a *generated* wisdom. the true and *ingenerate* wisdom is an inalienable attribute which belongs to the Father alone" (Stead, "Platonism of Arius," 20; emphasis added). It is surprising how much like Eunomius Stead makes Arius sound, for Eunomius' own explanation of the common attribution of titles such as Light, Power, and Wisdom, etc., is precisely as Stead says: "Our response" to such titles, according to Eunomius, "is to say that the one 'light' is unbegotten and the other begotten. When spoken of the unbegotten, does 'light' signify an entity other than that signified by 'the unbegotten'?" (Eunomius, *Apology* 19:8–10, in *Eunomius of Cyzicus: The Extant Works*, ed. and trans. Richard P. Vaggione (Oxford: Clarendon Press, 1987), 57).

66. The phrase "two-power theology" does *not* here mean the kind of Temple-Apocalyptic "two powers" that is discussed in Alan Segal's *Two Powers in Heaven: Early Rabbinic Reports about Christianity and Gnosticism* (Leiden: Brill, 1977)—but I am not denying the existence of those power theologies. For pre-Nicene Latin use of power theology, see Roy Kearsley, *Tertullian's Theology of Divine Power* (Milton Keynes: Paternoster, 1977); Gehrke, "Lactantius' Power Theology," *Nova et Vetera* 17 (2019): 683–715. Gehrke's work reveals the widespread use of *virtus* for the concept of Power in Latin classical literature (e.g., Cicero) as well as among early Latin Christian apologists. Also see Hankinson, "Galen and the Ontology of Power."

67. "The first is God's own eternal and proper power, the second is a derived power which has its own existence" See the chapter: "Other Latin Nicenes" for numerous examples of either use.

own."[68] In each case, a distinction is made between the property as it exists as God's own, and the property as it exists as a derived or participated property: the Son as perfect Image. The existence of these two kinds of properties is taken as indication of two kinds of existence, or as Eusebius of Caesarea put it, "two essences, two things, two powers." This point reveals to us the further truth, applicable to all Image theologies whatever their relationship to Nicaea (if any): whenever one speaks of the Son as the Image, the question arises as to what kind of being does that Image reside? Created? Uncreated? Even the *mirror-image* of something resides in some kind of being—the being of the mirror! What "reflects"?

The alternative understanding of what it means that the Second Person is the "Power of God" is to identify the Son or Word with the very power of God's existence. The Second Person is the Power of God, the Father's *own* power, the power that the Father was never without. Such an identification can prove the full divinity of the Son in a variety of ways. Athanasius' argument is that if the Father was never without his power, then that power is *eternal*; and if eternal, then divine. Such an understanding does not fully exploit the conceptual unity of power and nature. Marcellus of Ancyra has a better grasp of the ontological link between whatever exists and its power, and understands that two *dynameis* means two *hypostases*. Against this doctrine, Marcellus asserts that the Second Person is "Power, he is Wisdom, he is God's own true Word . . . the inseparable power of God"; "I have learned," Marcellus says in his letter to Pope Julius, "that the Father's power, the Son, is inseparable and indivisible."[69] Nicene theology among its earliest defenders and proponents identified the single and only Power—or property—of God with the Son, and saw in this identification a way of describing the unity of the Father and the Son. The limitations of this identification was that it allowed for no distinct existence that of "property": Marcellus taught that at the proper time of the economy, God's own Word takes on a presence in the human Jesus, and at the proper time of the economy, the Word returns to the essence of God, resolving the triad into the perfect monad of the Divine Essence. The Incarnation is the only "episode" in the life of the Word: the rest is eternal existence in simple unity with God. For Marcellus and others, this is the proper understanding of "from the essence of the Father."[70]

68. Athanasius, *Discourse* I.2.5, quoted in Williams, *Arius*, 100.

69. *Apud* Eiphanius, *Haer.* 72.3.2.

70. The most significant use of "from the essence of the Father" is, obviously, in the Nicene Creed of 325. (It is "struck" from or absent in the Creed of Constantinople, but congruent phrases remain.) However, it is unlikely that the Nicene fathers invented the phrase—that bishops who used the phrase had no other source and must, therefore, be quoting the creed of 325.

THE CREED OF NICAEA RECEIVED

In the middle and late 350s, we begin to see another understanding of the doctrine of God's single power among those sympathetic to Nicaea. This doctrine may be found in the writings of Latin authors such as Phoebadius and Hilary.[71] Their development of Nicene theology can legitimately be distinguished from Athanasius' because *they teach a doctrine of God's single power which never appears in Athanasius and thus cannot owe to his influence.* Their theology argues that because the Father and the Son have the same power as one another, they have the same nature. Here we have the rise of *pro-Nicene theology*: same operations, same power, same essence.[72]

Phoebadius' statement of this "one power" doctrine is explicitly cast as an exegesis of 1 Corinthians 1:24: "We claim that both are one power. Concerning this the apostle says 'Christ is the power of God.' That power . . . is said [to be] substance."[73] So close is the conceptual unity between power and substance that Phoebadeus sometimes has trouble articulating the difference between the two. Phoebadius defines substance as that which "subsists by its own intrinsic [*intra se*] power [*virtus*]," and likewise he regards *virtus* as "a synonym for *substantia*."[74] Hilary's argument that the Son has the same power as the Father is couched in his rebuttal of a Homoian teaching which identifies God (the Father) as "true God" and so distinguishes him from the Son (who is not "true God").[75] Hilary argues that the Son is included in the determination "true God" because Scripture shows the Son to possess the same nature, power, and name as the Father. According to Hilary, to determine whether two things are truly named by the same name, one compares the "nature and power [*virtus*]" of a thing:[76] if these are

71. Phoebadius of Agen is second only to Hilary in importance of the early development of Latin Nicene theology and has not received the attention he deserves. Field makes clear Phoebadius' role as a foundational Latin Nicene theology as well as his importance for the historiography of the early years in the 350s. See *On the Communion,* 240 f. Lewis Ayres includes Phoebadius in his narrative of the rise of Latin Nicene theology, but Hanson treats him as a second-string player. See Ayres, *Nicaea and Its Legacy,* 178–83. Mark Weedman improves over Hanson on Phoebadius in his *The Trinitarian Theology of Hilary of Poitiers* (Leiden: Brill, 2007). If you want to get into the nitty-gritty of Latin theology after Nicaea, read Williams, "Monarchianism and Phontinus." I identify and discuss Phoebadius and "Other Latin Nicenes" in the next chapter.

72. Here something important needs to be recalled: in Ps.-Evagrius' translation of the Nicene Creed into Armenian, all occasions of the Greek word *ousia* are given the Armenian word for "power," and he translates *homoousia* into the Armenian expression for "one Power." See Winkler, "Antiochene Synods," 285.

73. "Et unam utriusque dicimus esse *uirtutem.* De qua idem Apostolus ait: Christus *uirtus* Dei est. [1 Cor 1:24] Quae quidem *uirtus,* quia nullius extraneae opis indiget, dicta substantia est, ut supra diximus: quidquid illud est sibi debens" (*Contra Arrianos* VIII.3, CCL 64.31.10–13). More context is provided in the next chapter.

74. Hanson, *Search,* 518; Weedman, *Hilary of Poitiers,* 51–63.

75. After book V of his *Trin.,* Hilary never explicitly identifies his opponents as "Arian," and there are reasons for judging that the opponents he has in mind are of a more contemporary variety: Latin Homians or Latin anti-Nicenes. See Weedman, *Hilary of Poitiers,* chp. 3.

76. Hilary, *Trin.* V.3, CCL LXII, 153:15, NPNF IX.86.

the same, the two existents have the same name in the same way, for "natural powers are evidence of the truth [of a name]; let us see, by this test, whether He [the Son] . . . is God."[77] The unity between the First and Second Persons is discovered and articulated in terms of common nature and common power; this is Hilary's phrasing repeatedly. "[He] Who possesses both the nature and the *virtus* of God . . . had at his disposal the *virtus* of the divine nature[s] to bring into being"; or, "that by a bodily similitude [of the Son's *hand*] you may learn the *virtus* of the one divine nature which is in both; for the nature and the *virtus* of the Father is in the Son."[78]

Hilary makes the neo-Nicene doctrine of "unity-in-generation" clearer in *De Trinitate* VII.11, where he aligns key Christological titles. He begins from the Christ's identity as "Word," and makes the point that the generation of the Father's Word brings forth an existent without leaving the Father "Word-less," so too Wisdom and Power are generated in the same way, to produce a separate existent without robbing the Father of Power and Wisdom.[79] Hilary continues, "And therefore the titles of those substantive properties are applied to God the only-begotten, for when he came into existence by birth it was they that constituted his perfection."

Hilary's *De Trinitate* is built up from layers of his writing from the time before he was exiled, to writings while exiled, and then materials added after he returned to the West from exile in 361.[80] As a consequence, the book contains strata of different kinds of thinking about what Nicaea meant and different models for arguing that meaning (a logic). Here I offer statements by Hilary which constitute a "theology of Nicaea" that I call neo-Nicene. These passages contain *ousia* or *substantia* "logic" language which made possible—and orthodox—the kind of statements that the creed itself (or its council supporters) never articulated. However, unlike Nicaea, this theology makes strong use of "image" language (derived especially from Heb 1:3). *Even while using image language that the creed never used, the next generation of "Nicenes" connect "from the ousia" with "emanating from God's hypostasis."* More characteristics could be offered. The source layers" in Hilary's book allow us to see in his theology the pivots from the Nicaea logic built upon "from the substance" to the "neo-Nicene" logic built upon "one substance—one essence" to yet a third Nicene logic different from either of these.

In pro-Nicene theology, a different kind of arguments than before is offered as obtaining the same meaning as Nicaea 325.[81] Among such theologians, there is a

77. Hilary, *Trin.* V.3.15, NPNF IX.86.

78. Hilary, *Trin.* V.4.7, CCL LXII, 154:, NPNF IX.86.

79. "[S]ince they are the elements of God's nature, they are all still immanent in him in an undiminished extent, although they were born from him to be his son" (Hilary, *Trin.* VII.11).

80. Weedman identifies the "new" (i.e., pro-Nicene) arguments in Hilary's exile writings in *Trinitarian Theology*, 93 f. Hilary's *Commentary on Matthew* predates 356.

81. The excerpt from Augustine's *Letters* shows us that, for the Latins especially, the theological project of "recovering Nicaea 325" meant arguing, "What did Nicaea 325 *mean*?" Augustine's answer also shows us that "Nicaea" did not simply boil down to "the Son is fully divine." "Nicaea"—or John

conscious exploitation of the technical philosophical understanding of the connatural union that exists between nature (or substance) and power.[82] An explicit invoking of the technical sense of power can be found not only in Phoebadius and Hilary, but in Ambrose, as well.[83] Phoebadius says, "There . . . signified by means of the word substance, or power, or divinity";[84] and, "That power, which is in need of no external aid, is said to be substance, just as we said above, that power is whatever it owes to itself."[85] Hilary says, "power is the very reality of the nature."[86] Ambrose says, "What is power, but the perfection of nature?"[87] The culmination of "same works, one essence" logic is expressed in the pro-Nicene doctrine of "common operations because of the same substance." Augustine will develop the logic one step further: the operations common to the Three who are one in substance are *inseparable*. This insight makes clear the *common work of the Trinity* in salvation.[88]

For example, we read the following from Hilary writing in the early 360s:

> There the Son is the perfect image of the Father: there under the qualities of an identical essence, the *Person* of the Son is not annihilated and confounded with the Father: there the Son is declared to be image of the Father in virtue of a real likeness, and does not differ in substance from the Father, whose image He is: there on account of the life which the Father has and the life which the Son has received, the Father can have nothing different in substance (this being implied in life) from that which the Son received to have: there the begotten Son is not a creature, but is a *Person* undistinguished from the Father's nature: there, just as an identical *power* [*virtus*] belongs to the Father and the Son, so their essence admits of no difference: there the Father by begetting the Son in no wise degenerates from Himself in Him through any difference of nature: there, though the likeness of nature is the same in each, the proper qualities which mark this likeness are repugnant to a confusion of Persons, so that there is not one subsisting *Person* who is called both Father and Son: there, though it is piously affirmed that there is both a Father who sends and a Son who is sent, yet no distinction in essence is drawn between the Father and the Son, the Sent and the Sender: there the truth of God's Fatherhood is not

---

10:30—contains the idea that "the Son's divinity is one with the Father's."

82. Or any analogous property, predicate, or homonym: e.g., wisdom, logos.

83. Ambrose's involvement in the struggle against the anti-Nicenes is told by Daniel H. Williams, *Ambrose of Milan and the End of the Nicene-Arian Conflicts* (Oxford: Clarendon Press, 1995). Augustine refers to it in *Confessions* VIII.

84. "Ibi enim per substantiae uocabulum aut *uirtutem* aut diuinitatem significari" (Phoebadius, *Contra Arrianos* VIII.1, CCL 64.31.5).

85. "Quae quidem *uirtus*, quia nullius extraneae opis indiget, dicta substantia est, ut supra diximus: quidquid illud est sibi debens" (Phoebadius, *Contra Arrianos* VIII.3, CCL 64.31.10–13).

86. "[C]um uirtus naturae res esset" (Hilary, *Trin.* IX.52.10–14).

87. "Quid est enim virtus nisi perfecta natura?" (Ambrose, *De Fide* I.5.39, CSCL 78.17).

88. See Lewis Ayres, "'Remember That You Are Catholic' (serm. 52.2): Augustine on the Unity of the Triune God," *JECS* 8 (2000): 39–82.

bound by limits of times: there the Son is not later in time: there beyond all time is a perfect birth which refutes the error that the Son could not be born.[89]

Elsewhere Hilary puts the argument more simply:

> Thus, He to whose nature it belongs to do the same things possesses the same nature. But, where all the same things are done by the Son in like manner, the similarity of the works excludes the solitude of the one who does the work, so that all things that the Father does the Son in like manner.[90]

The theology is recognizably Nicene, but Hilary's argument does not pivot on Nicene arguments; on the contrary, there is language that the creed avoided—for example, image, likeness, and more importantly for our present purposes, power: "just as an identical *power* [*virtus*] belongs to the Father and the Son, so their essence admits of no difference." The unity of their essence is a conclusion from their unity of power. The notion that the Father and the Son are one in essence is articulated as an inevitable conclusion from all the other characteristics shared by Father and Son. "Father" and "Son" terminology sometimes supports the assertion of a common nature, but there are other occasions where the terminology supports an argument for a real distinction between the Two. In pro-Nicene arguments, there is no generation "out of the essence" or "from the essence" of the Father as there is in the Nicene Creed: the Father himself generates the Son.[91] Hilary can thus offer a succinct logic of divine unity and distinction. In this understanding, the philosophical concept of Power—and the unity of Power between the Two—carries the logic of "the Two necessarily have the same": same power, same essence, same nature. I note in passing that the unity of the Two is *not* based upon the Son being identified as the "Power of God [the Father]." If Hilary had argued from that logic, he would have been in accord with many supporters of Nicaea (that I call neo-Nicenes);[92] indeed, if Athanasius' memory is correct, Hilary would have been in accord with the intentions of the authors of the creed.[93]

---

89. Hilary, *Trin*. NPNF IX.11; *Syn* XII.27.

90. Typically, I have not methodically given the Latin for each translated passage I have used, but this passage is so important that I feel an obligation to supply the reader the Latin: "In his enim quae et quaecumque et eadem sunt, nec diuersitas potest esse nec reliquum. Adque ita in natura est, cui eadem omnia posse naturae sit. Ubi uero similiter per Filium eadem omnia hunt, similitude operum solitudenem operantis exclusit, ut omnia quae Pater facit, eadem omnia similiter faciat et Filius. Haec est uerae natiuitatis intellegentia et fidei nostrae, quae ex naturae diuinae initate unius indifferentisque diuinitas ueritatem in Patre et Filio confitetur, absolutissimum sacramentum, ut eadem faciendo Filius similiter faciat, et similiter faciendo eadem sint ipsa facit: quia sub una hac significatione testentur et similiter facta natiuiatatem ea eadem facta naturam" (Hilary, *Trin*. VII.17.5–10).

91. No one looks at a newborn and glowingly says, "He has the eyes of his nature!" We recognize in the baby the "eyes of"—the genetic deposit—a parent, not of a nature. The essence or nature did not generate the Son, as it seems that Nicaea is saying; the Father generates the Son.

92. Elsewhere, Hilary does make that argument. My point is developed fully in the next chapter.

93. Athanasius claims the authors of this creed want to say "one power": see his *De Decret*. V.20.

Hilary does not use phrases that some supporters of 325 would have demanded: he is, for example, not strongly interested in defending *homoousios*.[94] In the reception of the Creed of Nicaea—this is an important fact to note—many other Nicaea supporters felt that essence language was necessary, and indeed there is a fixation upon essence language in the creed. This is what might be called the "essence wave" that some mid-fourth century Nicene theologians were caught up in: to a significant extent, this "being 'swept to essence'" is the product of the fact that the opponents of Nicaea—anti-Nicenes of almost any variety—made *homoousios* and *ousia* language the center of their attack.[95] (Augustine says in *Ep. 238* that the Homoians call on him "to defend *homoousios* almost as if it was a man.") Hilary's "power-based" argument marks him as a theologian slightly out of his time; within twenty years "orthodox Nicene theology" (pro-Nicene theology) will be articulated in power language without the need to privilege essence terminology. The Latin view of the "triumph" of Nicene Trinitarian theology at Constantinople can be told in an abbreviated form which emphasizes the "local" (i.e., Roman) role in reaching an East-West accord that was anti-"Arian," anti-Photinian; a restatement of the Nicene faith. All this had been accomplished before—except the "unity."[96] A short, Western summary would see the years 378–83 as decisive, and would highlight the following events.

In 378, the saintly but stubborn Basil of Caesarea dies. That same year the Eastern, anti-Nicene Emperor Valens dies, making travel by Nicenes of all varieties possible. In 379, in a useless attempt to heal the longstanding ecclesiastical breach in Antioch where two "Nicene" bishops each claimed the episcopacy of Antioch, a synod in Rome of ninety-three bishops led by Damasus sent a letter to churches of Antioch. The letter was received tepidly in Antioch; with equal enthusiasm 153 bishops returned the letter to Rome with their signatures, announcing that they believed in the Nicene faith, one *ousia*, three *hypostases*.[97] The letter failed to settle anything in Antioch, but the *Exemplum* of the letter became Roman law, and thus gives us documentary evidence of what Latins recognized as orthodox Trinitarian theology—which is why I refer to the letter here.[98] The Letter—or at least the *Exemplum*—starts with a list of nine bishops (headed by Damasus), and after the usual greetings, begins

94. The "Old Nicenes" who never wavered from *ousia* and *hypostasis* mean the same.

95. This fact has previously had the result that any reference by Augustine to an any argument over "essence" was judged by modern scholars to be Augustine "obviously" arguing with an Eunomian. See my chapter on genre and doctrine, "Arians of Book V."

96. Due to the Melitius question. See Field's well-executed, detailed, and exhaustive study of the effects on the "Melitian problem" on East-West-Alexandrian attempts at communion, *On the Communion.*

97. The numbers of bishops in attendance at each council are the numbers traditionally given; they are not assumed to be exact.

98. The letter may be said to have been a significant contributing cause for the calling of the Antioch Synod in 379. The death of the anti-Nicene emperor, Valens, made the Synod possible, for it meant that Nicene bishops were free to travel.

"Confidimus quidem "—by which name it is often called—though it is better known as the *Exemplum synodi*.[99]

The letter to Antioch compares the controversy in Antioch to the Arian "blasphemies" and goes on to say that the Council of Nicaea "established a wall against diabolical arms [the 'Arians']" and asserted that "it was proper to believe that the Father, Son, and Holy Spirit are of one Godhead, one power, one form, one substance [*substantia*]." The sense of Nicaea is summed up as "the Father, Son, and Holy Spirit are of one Godhead, one power [*virtus*], one form, one substance [*substantia*]." The emperor and the majority of Nicene bishops agreed to this, and it became law.[100] The "sense" of Nicaea to its believers in 379 was not *homoousios*, etc., pure and simple: it was "the Father, Son, and Holy Spirit are of one Godhead, one power, one form, one substance [*substantia*]." In 381, the Council of Aquileia produced a limited victory for Nicene theology in the West, and the emperor called for a single council to be held at the "center" of the empire, Constantinople, to produce a creed for the whole church.[101] The first law the emperor promulgated *before* the Council of Constantinople read:

> It is our will that all the peoples who are ruled by our administration shall practice that religion which the divine Peter transmitted to the Romans, as the religion which he introduced makes clear even to this day. It is evident that this is the religion followed by the Pontiff Damasus [of Rome] and by Peter, Bishop of Alexandria . . . that is, according to the apostolic doctrine and the evangelic doctrine, we believe in the single Deity of the Father, the Son, and the Holy Spirit, under the concept of equal power and of the Holy Trinity.[102]

The ecclesiastical form (i.e., the literal content) of Nicaea 325 is observed, and a creed using the vocabulary of the 325 creed is drawn up.[103] *After* the Council of Constantinople (381), imperial law was supplemented:

> We command that all churches shall immediately be surrendered to those bishops who confess that the Father, the Son, and the Holy Spirit are of one majesty and power, of the same glory, and of one splendor; to those bishops who produce no dissonance by unholy distinction, but who affirm the concept

99. See Field, *On the Communion,* 10–23. Field is a resource for the next paragraph, as well.

100. In each case the "one" in question—Godhead, power, form, substance—is the Latin word *unius*.

101. I grossly simplify complex political events in 381 because my purpose here is not a narrative, much less a history, but only to offer a frame for the documents I bring to the reader's attention. The fact that I am only interested in "the view from the West" further distorts the narrative.

102. Theodosian Code—Imperial Law, February 28, 380

103. For the East-West imperial roles of the emperors, especially after Theodotus became sole emperor, see Williams, *Ambrose of Milan.* See Kelly on the literary relationship between the creeds of Nicaea and Constantinople in *Early Christian Creeds,* 296–338.

of the Trinity by the assertion of three Persons and the unity of the Divinity
... in order that the priesthood of the true Nicene faith may remain pure.[104]

How the theology of the council's creeds relates to the theology of those "with boots
on the ground" (or "miters in hand") is a story that allows of no single, simultaneous,
universal (catholic), and synchronic historical "event" as cause.

CONCLUSION

I hope that I can usefully restate and elaborate upon the thesis that began my treatment
of the Latin appropriations of the theology of Nicaea in the fourth century—with an
eye towards, "This is Augustine's received orthodox Latin theology of the Trinity"
(insofar as he received anything at all, either as a catechumen or a bishop).

I began with a close reading of the text of Nicaea so that my understanding of the
theology of that text—context, content, and argument—developed from my reading
and not from any imported, established whole narrative of what the Nicene Creed
means. In this reading, I offered my exegesis of the text, placing the writing and reception of the creed within a rolling state of polemical doctrinal interests. I followed the
appearance of sympathetic readings in Latin Christianity of "the Creed of Nicaea,"
the "theology of Nicaea," and original vocabulary made technical or used as signs
for the doctrinal content of "Nicaea"—most significantly, *ousia*-related words such
as *homoousios*. My subject was the perception of the creed among those who found
their own Trinitarian concerns reflected in the symbol of Nicaea, as well as their articulations of a doctrinal logic by which they established the faithfulness of Nicaea
and the congruence of their own theologies with the conclusions of Nicene theology.
Different doctrinal logics demonstrated the meaning of "the faith of Nicaea" in the
midst of controversies over the meaning and authority of "Nicaea"—its theology, but
its authority, as well.

I have claimed that *we can identify three different kinds of unity postulated between
God and his "properties"; four different ways in which a title identifies the Second Person
and specifies the type of union he has with God the Father.* Each of these kinds is associated with a certain kind of "attribution logic," principally the ontology of "power"—or,
to put it just as well, a different exegetical tradition of understanding the Christological title, Power. First, the Second Person is that very property of God: if we allow Alexander, the 325 Creed of Antioch, and Athanasius to be representatives of the theology
of Nicaea, then we may say that this doctrine is "Nicene." Secondly, the Second Person
is that very property of God which has coexisted in or with God but has, in some
way, always had a distinct existence; this doctrine is expressed by anti-"Arians" from
at least the time of Athanasius. It is offered as "the faith affirmed at Nicaea" and what
the church has traditionally believed. There is no settled term for the kind of distinct

104. Theodosian Code—Imperial Law July 30, 381. The date of the Council is usually placed between these two imperial edicts.

existence the Son possessed in distinction from the Father. The relationship of "Father to Son" is used principally as an argument for continuity of essence, rather than as a means of distinction between Father and Son, using Son from Father in the "parental" relation. I call this kind of understanding of *homoousios* "neo-Nicene."[105] Thirdly, the Father and the Son share equally in the divine essence, evidenced by their common possession of divine Power.[106] All Three can possess the same divine power only if they possess the same divine essence. (For example, all Three are creator.) I call this theology "pro-Nicene": it recognizes Nicaea and *homoousios* as normative—in the sense that one must be "for Nicaea" insofar as it occurs in the theology at all—but its own theology is built upon other "logics" (e.g., "common operations" or Syriac "Spirit" Trinitarian theologies). Neo-Nicene and pro-Nicene theologies can exist side by side, or they can be held successively: they are not antithetical.[107] Both show a consistent concern for naming the distinct existence the Son has, but pro-Nicene theology hastens an explicit concern for developing a fully Trinitarian logic that includes the Holy Spirit.[108] It is not clear when or where the Nicene One-Power formula fell away, and it cannot be assumed that it was at that same moment that the formula Same Substance (*homoousios* or consubstantial) gained the privileged and exclusive role for articulating the "faith of Nicaea." I suspect that a widespread judgment that "the content of Nicaea is summarized by *homoousios* (and only *homoousios*)" was a development in the wake of the Christological controversies associated with the Council of Chalcedon (451)—although the word *homoousios* figures significantly already in the Apollinarian

105. One reason this theology is called *neo*-Nicene is that often no textual lineage can be traced back to the Creed of Nicaea, and indeed the only thing the author may know about the creed is that its Trinitarian theology was based on an *ousia* logic, that the essence-based logic used *homoousios* for its summary, and that it was anti-"Arian"—or "Arians" were anti-Nicene. (The enemy of my enemy . . .) This theology usually treats *homoousios* as a litmus-test—even when the exact meaning of *homoousia* is unknown.

106. This would include the Antiochene-Armenian Churches if Gabriele Winkler—see "Antiochene Synods and the Early Armenian Creeds"—is right.

107. Some authors in the late-fourth and fifth centuries will use a neo-Nicene argument for their Christology and a pro-Nicene argument for their Trinitarian theology. The Son as true divinity who took upon himself our humanity is referred to as "the Power of God," while the Son in his full divinity in the Trinity is clear from his common acts with God (e.g., creation, the economy of salvation, etc.). See Apollinaris, "Kata meros pistis," 11, 12.

108. Compare Gregory of Nazianzus' neo-Nicene argument for the Son's divinity in the *Third Theological Oration* to his pro-Nicene argument for the Son's and the Holy Spirit's divinity in the *Fifth Theological Oration*. Some scholars have asserted the influence of Gregory Nazianzus on Augustine—that the five orations were all translated into Latin and in equal circulation, or that Augustine himself translates some texts by Gregory. It would make a difference if Augustine had read only the early *Orations*, or if he had read the *Fifth* included with the others or alone. I see no reason to postulate Cappadocian influence—except whatever came through Ambrose. (While some scholars tend to look to Ambrose's *Sermons* as mediating sources for Cappadocian or Alexandrian influence, I believe that Augustine did not regard Ambrose as a "father" of the church (as Hilary was) until after the latter had been dead for some time.)

controversy of the 380s.[109] The underlying Christological concerns motivated Chalcedon to preserve the creeds of 381 as well as that of 325.

In his magisterial article of 1984, "'Hypostase' et 'Personne' dans la formulation of dogma trinitaire (c. 375–81)," Andre de Halleux argued that when Constantinople made *persona* equivalent to *hypostasis*, it "metaphysicalized" the West's Trinitarian theology, which up to that time was more "manifestation" oriented.[110] If anything like this was thought to have happened, then it became Augustine's task to "metaphysicalize" the Latin phenomenological Trinitarian theology, *or* to extend the "manifestation"-based Latin theology into new realms—e.g., metaphysical realms. (Victorinus had tried something like this, but had failed.) If one takes Halleux's insight seriously as one reads *De Trinitate*, then one could say that the work starts with a "manifestational" Trinitarian theology as the basis for extending traditional Latin Trinitarian theology into a more metaphysical discourse. The heart of that accomplishment was to understand the very existence and identity of the Son in his unique sight of the Father. The chapters from "Exegesis and Polemic" to "The Visible Christ and the Invisible Trinity" follow Augustine's initial treatment of the theophanies through to Augustine's reconceived theophany of the Trinity in Christ.

109. The majority of instances where Gregory of Nyssa uses *homoousios* is in polemical texts against Apollinarius—who used the word as the rallying term for his Christology. See my "Fourth Century as Trinitarian Canon," 59–60.

110. Halleux, "'Hypostase' et 'Personne.'" A glance at the two antinomic categories reveals the danger lurking in using any such thesis of a "single underlying logic of a diachronic hermeneutic in a body of literature" spread over centuries. Halleux uses the rhetorical antinomies, "metaphysical" and "manifestational," that have served for over a century to delineate kinds of Trinitarian theologies—used consciously and with moral connotations. Is Halleux trying to claim Augustine (and Latin Trinitarian theology) as being more phenomenological in nature (and less metaphysical) than he is usually judged to be? Does Augustine tie in with the epistemological concerns associated (pre-WWII) with Louvain? How do "metaphysical" and "manifestational" have meanings such that they can be placed side-by-side as antinomic options? In my article, "Régnon Reconsidered," lies lurking the usually uncommunicated-upon thesis that while modern Trinitarian theologies that think—with vigor!—that they have separated themselves from scholastic "givens" and hermeneutic, modern Trinitarian theology has done no such thing. At the center of the organizing logic of most modern Trinitarian theology lies a scholastic axiom—happily received as an axiom—which I called Régnon's paradigm. Most modern treatments and "speculations" on the doctrine of the Trinity, whatever the denomination, should begin with this clause: *In this text I intend to build upon Régnon's axiom and show . . .*

Chapter 5

Other Latin Nicenes

INTRODUCTION

THE SUBJECT OF THIS chapter is the great tradition of Latin Trinitarian theology as it appears in the second half of the fourth century. I say "great tradition" as a way of encompassing the variety of Latin Trinitarian traditions that coexisted within Christianity in the Western half of the Roman Empire. I am particularly interested in the theologies of those authors who were responding to the series of crises triggered in the aftermath of Nicaea (325), and of these I limit myself to those authors who either evidenced sympathy with a theology like that expressed at Nicaea, or to those authors who attacked critics of the language found in the Creed of Nicaea. Neither of these circumstances necessarily presupposes direct contact with the Nicene Creed, since much of the language in the creed had a prior and separate history in Latin Trinitarian theology. This fact is especially true, for example, of "one substance" language.

The phrase "other Latins" in my title is meant to signal that my intention is to approach my chosen era of Latin Trinitarian theology from some perspective other than the theologies of Hilary's *De Trinitate* and Ambrose's *De Fide* and *De Spiritu Sanctu*. It is typically the case in scholarship that the theologies of these two authors are used to provide a description of Latin Nicene Trinitarian theology generally, and to determine the context for other Latin Nicene authors.[1] Here I will begin instead

---

1. For example, R. P. C. Hanson uses the knowledge and use of Hilary's theology by a Latin Nicene as the standard for measuring the sophistication and significance of other "Nicene" Trinitarian theologies in the West. See his *Search for the Christian Doctrine*, 459ff. Hanson's use of Hilary of Poitiers as the standard for Latin pro-Nicene theology finds its most important (and peculiar) expression in his schematizing Hilary as "Western pro-Nicenes [stage] I," even though a number of those authors in the chapter "Western pro-Nicenes [stage] II" write before Hilary's "Nicene" works. (The subtitle of Hanson's work is both more descriptive and useful than the "before the colon" title. "The Search for the Christian Doctrine of God" is a majestic title that does no credit to the scholarship Hanson's book contains.)

with the *many* as the means to provide a doctrinal context that includes the *few*.[2] One result of excluding Hilary and Ambrose from my treatment of Latin Nicenes is the clear appearance of a methodological and historical question: Why exactly are the theologies of Hilary and Ambrose privileged in scholarly accounts of fourth-century Latin Nicene Trinitarian theologies? Because they wrote so much? Because they so neatly fit the dominant narrative that *Latin Trinitarian theology only develops when Greek Trinitarian theology pushes it*?

I will begin my study of Latin Nicenes—as I have just defined them—with the Council of Serdica (342).[3] My interest here is Western Trinitarian theology within the boundaries of Latin thought,[4] and for this purpose, Serdica has a special place because of what it reveals and embodies of Latin Trinitarian theology in the middle of the fourth century. I am not suggesting that the theology expressed in the creed of western Serdica is "Nicene" or that the intention of the council was to uphold and defend the creed of the Council of Nicaea. The utility of western Serdica is as a window onto the continuing presence of key tropes in Latin Trinitarian theology. Serdica gathers these theological idioms together into a crowded package, one which allows us to recognize easily the influence of these tropes or idioms in post-Serdican Latin Trinitarian theology. Serdica also has a special place because some scholars have suggested that the creed of western Serdica injected Greek theology into the living body of Latin Trinitarian theology.[5] I am not at all concerned with the question of whether

2. The name that is here missing from both the small list of paradigmatic Latin Nicenes (Hilary, Ambrose) and the longer list of "other Latin Nicenes" is Marius Victorinus. Frankly, despite the number of erudite publications on Victorinus, we still lack what I would regard as a credible and sophisticated account of the place of his theology in the Nicene controversy and the significance of his theology for Latin Nicene Trinitarian theology. There is no consensus whatsoever in scholarship as to whether Victorinus would ideally belong in the "Paradigmatic Latin Nicene" category, or the "Other Latin Nicenes" category, or a "Mutated Nicene" category, and nothing decisive can be constructed here within the limited scope of this essay.

3. Joe Lienhard has a helpful discussion of the "creed of Serdica" in *Contra Marcellum,* 148–52.

4. The most trustworthy and comprehensive account of the Trinitarian controversies of the fourth century is Ayres, *Nicaea and Its Legacy.* Ayres's treatment of Western theology is broken down into three blocks: Tertullian to Lactantius (70–76); the years 360–65 (Hilary principally, 177–86), and the years 365–400 (260–67). The "other Latin Nicenes" that I treat in this chapter are not discussed in Ayres's book. Hanson's treatment of Western Trinitarian theology is more extensive—most of the figures I discuss here are treated in *The Search*—but the Latins are brought forward principally to show how poorly their theology compares to Greek pro-Nicene theology. (Except for Hilary: Hanson likes Hilary.)

5. The "Greek" theology injected into Latin Trinitarian theology was, according to Jorg Ulrich, from Marcellus. In his "Nicaea and the West," Ulrich argues that from the time of 340 "the first official Western statement in the Trinitarian controversy [triggered by Nicaea] was an adoption of the ideas of Marcellus of Ancyra as the correct and orthodox doctrine of the Trinity" (17). Ulrich goes on to identify the theology of Serdica ("western creed") as "entirely subjected to Marcellan influences." The councils of Gaul, Carthage, Sicily, Sardinia, and Spain that met in the late 340s "concurred with the decisions and with the 'Western,' in fact Marcellan, creed of Serdica" (19). For a more recent as well as developed and detailed argument for the Marcellan character of the "western creed" of Serdica, see Sara Parvis, *Marcellus of Ancyra and the Lost Years of the Arian Controversy 325–345* (Oxford: Oxford University Press, 2006).

Serdica can be considered any kind of "Nicene" or not, nor will I engage the question of the general "Greekiness" of parts of western Serdica's theology. I will only identify those aspects of western Serdica's theology that provide me with a place to begin as I discuss, in sequence, the theologies of the Latins that constitute the proper subject of this essay. Thus, I will first identify key Latin doctrines in western Serdica, show their Latin precedents and sources, and then in the last four-fifths of this article, treat their presence in Latin writers explicitly sympathetic to Nicaea.[6]

LATIN NICENES OF THE SECOND HALF OF THE FOURTH CENTURY

The first of the Latin trajectories I will trace, and that appears in Serdica is the use of John 14:10, "Do you not believe that I am in the Father and the Father in me?" This Johannine passage, along with John 10:30, is cited to support to a doctrine of the co-eternity of the Father and Son. The Western pedigree of the passage as a Trinitarian prooftext goes back to Tertullian. In *Against Praxeas* 20, Tertullian identifies 14:10 and 10:30 as the two New Testament texts Praxeas's followers accept as authorities for their doctrine of God. In *Adversus Praxeas* 22, John 10:30 and 14:9–11 are co-exegeted by Tertullian, and at chapter 24 he treats John 14:10 in detail in a way that foreshadows Hilary of Poitiers's lengthy engagement with the passage in book III of his *De Fide* and *De Trinitate*. The passage also figures significantly for Hippolytus in the *Contra Noetum*.[7]

Tertullian's Trinitarian exegesis of John 14:10 is shaped by recurring references to the "works"—*opera*—found in John 14:10–12.[8] Tertullian reads 14:10 as meaning, "By means of the works, the Father will be in the Son and the Son will be in the Father, and thus by means of the works [*opera*] we understand that the Father and Son are one."[9] In short, the works reveal what the Father and Son have in common, which is the very capacity to produce those works. Tertullian concludes this discussion by saying, "we should believe that there are two [namely, the Father and Son], albeit in one power [*una virtute*]." Indeed, according to Tertullian, the Son's manifestation of the Father—referred to in John 14:9—is not of the sort in which the Son makes visible the person of the Father, but that the Father becomes visible as a "consequence of [the

---

6. My method uses a variation of Ockham's Razor, namely, "the influence of the *local* context has an inherent prior authority in interpretation," however "local" may be defined in a given context.

7. See Hippolytus, *Contra Noetum* XXX.

8. Tertullian's texts of John 14:10 read: "Si non facio *opera* Patris mei, nolite credere; si vero facio, et mihi credere non vultis, vel propter *opera* credite. Et scitote quod ego in Patre sim, et Pater in me."

9. Tertullian, *Treatise Against Praxeas* 22.

Son's] acts of power [*per opera virtutem*]."[10] This is what it means to believe "for the works' sake" (John 14:11).[11]

The second Latin trajectory I will trace is the language of the "Power of God" as a means of describing the unity in the Trinity. Serdica says, "We confess that the Son is the Power of the Father. We confess that the Word is [the] Word of God the Father, and that beside Him there is no other. We believe the Word to be the true God, and Wisdom and Power" (Theodoret *Eccl. Hist.* II.6). Power is the capacity of an existent to affect insofar as it is what it is. In its original medical and philosophical use, power is inseparable from any existent, whether the existent in question is an individual or a nature. Any two existents that possess the same power must possess the same nature, and vice versa. However, like the divine titles Wisdom, Word, Glory, and Spirit of the Lord, in Second Temple literature Power is understood to possess a kind of hypostatic existence. In early Christian literature, Power is hypostasized in First Corinthians, Romans, Hebrews, and Luke's Gospel. The old philosophical sense is not lost in the hypostasized usage; the older philosophical sense provides the basis for the understanding that the hypostatic Power remains connaturally united with its existent or nature of origin. However, in Trinitarian theology, any specific statement about God's Power can mean either the connatural or the hypostatic sense.

When Serdica calls the Son "the Power of God," it identifies him as the hypostatically existing Power. When Tertullian speaks of the Power of God, he means, at one point, the connatural sense of power, as when he says, famously, that the Father and Son and Spirit are Three, "three however not in manner of being [*status*] but in sequence [*gradus*], not in substance [*substantia*] but in aspect [*forma*], not in power [*potestas*] but in its manifestation [*species*], yet of one substance and one manner of being and one power" (*Prax.* 2). However, elsewhere in the *Adversus Praxeus*, Tertullian takes Power of God in its hypostatic sense, as when he says that in Proverbs the title "Wisdom" means the "Son" as the apostle says, "Christ the Wisdom and the Power of God" (1 Cor 1:18). Similarly, Psalm 32:6 says, "By his Word were the heavens established, and all their powers by his Spirit." Thus, Tertullian concludes, "the Word, the Power and the Wisdom, will himself be the Son of God."[12]

Both Greek- and Latin-language theologies had strong intellectual resources in power ontology or power aetiology for articulating Trinitarian theology and for lending a kind of logic to assertions made about the Father, the Son, the relationship between the Two, and their relationship to creation. However, neither Latin nor Greek "power"-articulated Trinitarian theology was simply the mirror image of the

---

10. Tertullian, *Treatise Against Praxeas* 22.

11. The key John passages in pre-Vulgate Latin are: "Nihil Filius facere potest a semetipso, nisi viderit Patrem facientem" (Joan. V.19); "*Ego et Pater unum sumus*" (Joan. X.30); "*Qui me videt, videt et Patrem*" (Joan. XIV.9); "*Ego in Patre, et Pater in me*" (Joan. XIV.10); "Pater autem in me ipse facit opera, non creditis quia ego in Patre et Pater in me est, alioquin propter opera ipsa credite" (Joan. XIV.10B-11).

12. *Sermone ejus coeli solidati sunt, et spiritu oris ejus omnis virtus eorum.*

other. Although there were significant common resources between the two languages, it must be emphasized that the conceptual history of power ontology in one language tradition varied significantly from the other.[13] My subject here is Latin Trinitarian theology; the conceptual and textual resources distinctive to Latin theology need to be emphasized, and the point needs to be made that Latin Christians were *not* simply borrowing concepts translated from Greek texts (Christian or pagan).[14] The most dense and the most influential Latin use of power ontology is by Cicero, in whose philosophy the concept already figures as an important theological term. The following provides an illustration of the Cicero-based use of power theology in Latin Trinitarian theology—it provides an illustration, not a full elaboration, of distinctively Latin power Trinitarian theology:

> The power of character and *virtus* [*vis ingenii atque virtutis*] was so great in [Romulus], that what had never before been believed [*credidissent*] about any mortal was believed [*crederetur*] concerning him and from [the report] of Julius Proclus, a rustic no less . . .[15]

> And so through the works [*opera*], we understand that the Father and Son are [*esse*] One. [John] kept pressing this point in order to bring us to see that two should be believed [*crederetur*] albeit in one power [*in una virtute*] because otherwise the Son could not possibly be believed [*crederi*] unless two is believed [*creditur*] . . .[16]

The third Latin doctrinal tradition expressed at western Serdica that I will trace is what Simonetti and Grillmeier have called "Spirit Christology," that is, the identification of the divine element in Jesus as Spirit and the human element as body or flesh.[17] One of the charges western Serdica levels against Valens and Ursacius is that these two teach that the "Word and the Spirit" (in Jesus, presumably) was pierced, wounded, died, and rose again.[18] "Word and the Spirit" name the divine in Jesus. From the time

13. This point has not been made previously in "power" scholarship, whether my own or that of others, and it needs to be stated clearly and with strong emphasis.

14. Latin power Trinitarian theology is a conspicuous and important contradiction to Danielou's thesis that Latin theology developed by borrowing Greek "sophisticated" thought translated for the illumination of Latin theology.

15. Cicero, *Republic,* 2.20, "Concerning Romulus."

16. Tertullian, *Adversus Praxeas,* 22.13.

17. In his treatment of Serdica in *Nicaea and Its Legacy* (125), Ayres remarks about the creed: "One of the oddities of this text is its seeming lack of any doctrine of the Spirit: although Father, Son, and Spirit are all named and said to share a *hypostasis,* elsewhere the statement speaks as if the Spirit were identical with the *Logos* and once describes the Son as '*Logos*-Spirit.'" There is a "Holy Spirit" whose soteriological significance is very limited, but where "Spirit" has any soteriological significance it refers to the divinity in Jesus. See my next footnote for the passage Ayres is referring to.

18. See Theodoret, *Eccl. Hist.* 2.6. Serdica says: "We believe in and we receive the Holy Spirit the Comforter, whom the Lord both promised and sent. We believe in It as sent. It was not the Holy Spirit who suffered, but the manhood with which He clothed Himself; which He took from the Virgin Mary . . ."

of Tertullian until sometime in the late 360s or early 370s a "Spirit Christology" is the normal anthropological model in the West for the Incarnation. As a corollary, one can say that scriptural passages that had previously supported a strong or "high" pneumatology were,[19] during this time, understood as referring to the pre-existent divine Spirit of the Son (e.g, Luke 1:35–36, Ps 33:6). Latin Trinitarian theology is functionally binitarian from Tertullian until sometime in the late 360s or early 370s: stated more directly, one can say that there is, during this time, a weak or "low" pneumatology.

The Latin authority for a Spirit Christology is, again, Tertullian. In *Against Praxeas* 26 and 27, Tertullian counter-exegetes the patripassianist glossing of Luke 1:35–36, in which Most High, Power, and Holy Spirit are all identified with God the Father. Tertullian replies with an understanding traditional since Justin: the one who overshadows Mary and fills her womb is the Word himself, who is also called the Spirit and the Power of God. The Lucan passage is linked to the Johannine "What is born of Spirit is Spirit" (John 3:6). Tertullian continues, and it is best to quote him, albeit in an edited fashion:

> This Spirit of God will be the same as the Word. For as, when John says "The Word was made flesh," we understand also Spirit at the mention of the Word, so also here we recognize also the Word under the name of the Spirit. For spirit is the substance of the Word, and word is an operation of the Spirit, and the two are one thing . . . Of these Jesus is composed, of flesh as Man and of Spirit as God . . .(*Prax.* 26).

Grillmeier's hypothesis for why Spirit Christology fell out of use—namely, that the encounter with Stoicism revealed its conceptual weaknesses—is strange and unconvincing, given that the great theoretician of Spirit Christology is the very Stoic Tertullian, and that with the passing of every century of the Common Era, the existence of a "Stoic" philosophy became more and more just a figure of speech, not at all comparable to, for example, the existence in the fourth century of Platonic or Aristotelian *philosophies*. In any case, the use of "Spirit" to name the divine person that enters Mary to be born in a human body occurs in Novatian, Cyprian, and Lactantius. There is nothing uniquely Latin about using Spirit to name either the pre-incarnational divine "person" or the divine element in the divine-human composite of Jesus: what is distinctive to the Latin tradition of Spirit Christology is its strong association with an exegesis of Luke 1:35–36, in which the Word-Spirit—to use Serdica's nomenclature—is identified as the "overshadower" of Mary.

---

19. In Theophilus and Irenaeus. Surprisingly, there is no sign of any presence of Irenaeus' theology in Gaul or Rome during the third and fourth centuries, this despite the popularity during this time of Irenaeus' burial site as a martyr's monument. (There is at least one case of a bishop from elsewhere in Gaul having his body taken to Lyons to be interred with Irenaeus.)

PHOEBADIUS OF AGEN

Between Serdica and Hilary's *De Trinitate* lay the writings of the young Hilary him-self, Phoebadius of Agen, Gregory of Elvira, and Potamius of Lisbon.[20] Phoebadius was probably the first bishop of Agen, a city about seventy-five miles southeast of Bordeaux, a fact which presents us perhaps with the opportunity to find a milieu for his theology.[21] Bordeaux was the home of Decimus Magnus Ausonius, who was born there early in the fourth century. He studied rhetoric and grammar there and in Toulouse, and then returned to Bordeaux, where he taught. From Bordeaux, Ausonius went to the court of Valentinian to become the tutor of the young Gratian. After-wards, he went on to become the governor of Gaul, then Italy, Illyria, and Africa. After the murder of Gratian in 383, he retired, but continued his correspondence with, for example, Symmachus, Paulinus of Nola, and the Emperor Theodosius.[22] In the mid-fourth century, the province of Aquitania II was not an isolated, cultureless wasteland, and we must be careful what we assume about Phoebadius' intellectual resources, a care we should extend to all Latin theologians of the fourth century.

As I turn now to the presence in Phoebadius' writing of the traditional Latin Trinitarian tropes in evidence at western Serdica, the first is the exegesis of John 14:10, "The Father is in me, and I am in the Father."[23] Tertullian's understanding of the sig-nificance of John 14:10 is not Phoebadius', who has two other readings of the passage. In the first, less important reading, Phoebadius sees the passage as expressing the fact that whatever the Father is or sends is in the Son. By this relationship, the "whatness" of the Father is found to be the "whatness" in the Son. The Father sends the Holy Spirit, for example, and the Holy Spirit is said to be the Son's; or, "eternal life was with the Father" and that life is in the Son. In the second, more important reading, Phoe-badius sees the predication "in the Father" or "in God" in contrast to the simple and potentially ambiguous use of *x from X* language. Sirmium (357) described the Son as being "God *from* God" and "Light *from* Light," expressions which, Phoebadius points out, "makes *from* God another God and *from* light another light [such] that the Son may be *from* the Father but not *in* the Father . . . from God but not the only-begotten in God." This is a clever and original move on Phoebadius' part: it represents his at-tempt to remove ambiguities from descriptions of divine causality.[24]

20. The Western theologians I discuss in this chapter are distributed geographically from Portugal, Spain, and France, through Italy, and into present-day Romania. Rufinus "the Syrian" is as Greek a theologian as Jerome.

21. For more on Phoebadius, see Field, *On the Communion*.

22. Rose, *Handbook of Latin Literature*, 527.

23. The most recent study of Phoebadius' theology—and indeed only the second dedicated study in the twentieth century—is Jorg Ulrich's introduction and commentary in his German translation of Phoebadius' *Contra Arianos*. Ulrich's unrelenting reading of *Against the Arians* is that it represents the theology of Marcellus as mediated by Serdica.

24. Phoebadius, *C. Ar.* 23.3. Elie Griffe's *La Gaule Chrétienne à l'époque Romaine, Vol 1. Des Origi-nes Chrétiennes à la fin du IVe siècle* (Paris: Picard, 1947), is, despite its title, almost exclusively about

As is well-known, the Creed of Sirmium says that no one should use the term "substance" when speaking of God.[25] On the basis of most scholarly accounts of Latin Nicene theology in the aftermath of Sirmium (and Serdica?), we should expect Phoebadius to give a strongly worded defense of "substance" in Trinitarian discourse. His response is, first, to give a list of scriptural passages that contain the word *substantia*,[26] proving that the word is known from the Bible.[27] Phoebadius' argument for the significance of "substance" language begins with: "They say, 'Let no one say *one substance*,' that is, let no one in the Church preach that there is one Power of the Father and Son" (*C. Ar.* 6.2). The second time Phoebadius quotes the Sirmium prohibition of "substance" language he says, "substance is called that which is always from itself: this is what exists within itself by its own power" (*C. Ar.* 7.2). The words of John 10:30 were spoken by Jesus, Phoebadius says, "so that the Two [Father and Son] may be believed to be one in Power" (*C. Ar.* 25.1). In short, Phoebadius has no discussion of the divine substance that is not restated as a question of the divine Power. Indeed, Phoebadius says that "they say that I claim that through the designation 'substance' either Power or divinity is signified." Phoebadius does not decline this characterization of his theology: instead he responds, "We, claiming one substance for the Father and Son, . . .

Hilary. One has to go to, e.g., Rose's *Handbook of Latin Literature* for a broader picture of the intellectual life of late-fourth century Gaul.

25. Although some scholars have declined to name Sirmium a "council" and its manifesto a "creed," most scholarship recognizes the meeting as an episcopal council, convened by Germinius (formerly bishop of Cyzicum, but translated to Sirmium). Sirmium (357) counts as the third council in Sirmium: the "first" being in 347, the second in 351. Confusingly, the creed or manifesto produced in 357 is, in older scholarship, referred to as "Second [Creed of] Sirmium." The city was the scene of such recurring activity because the Emperor Constantius had a residence there. Hilary refers to the creed the small council produced as "the Blashemy": see his *De Synodis* XI. A Greek translation is given by Athanasius in his *De Synodis* XXVIII. See Kelly, *Early Christian Creeds*, 284–87.

26. Hanson, *The Search*, 518n54, remarks strangely that Phoebadius gives a list of passages in the Bible which he (Phoebadius) "alleges" to contain the word *substantia*. Whether or not the scriptural passages Phoebadius provides contain the word *substantia* is something we can check from other sources, and we are not simply taking Phoebadius' at his word.

27. *Substantia* has a varied and wide-ranging use in the Vetus Latina: it translates ὑπόστασις in Psalms 68:2 and 38:5, 7, as well as in Jeremiah 23:22; ὕπαρξις in passages from Tobit; and even κτίσις in Proverbs. That one Latin word was translating a variety of Greek words would not be something Latin theologians recognized unless they were consulting the Greek scriptural texts, that is, unless they themselves knew Greek. Victorinus, arguing against the Blasphemy, gives a short list of Latin scriptural passages where the word *substantia* appears, acknowledges the variety of Greek words being translated by the one Latin word, and then explores each of the Greek words to discover how it relates to the concept of "substance." (We must be careful, however, about what we claim for Victorinus' knowledge of Greek texts. He knows the Greek Bible, Greek conciliar (broadly construed) documents, and Greek works of philosophy, but I have found no sign of his having read Greek works of Christian theology—by, e.g., Marcellus or Athanasius.) On the other hand, Phoebadius and the young Gregory of Elvira seem not to have known Greek, and who can presently say whether Zeno of Verona or Faustinus used the LXX? To my knowledge, the question of the languages of the scriptural texts used by each of my "other Latin Nicenes" has not been explored in modern scholarship, and unless we have positive evidence to the contrary, we must assume that they were working from the Vetus. See Henri Jeanotte, *Le Psautier de saint Hilaire* (Paris: Lecoffre, 1917).

say that the Power of each is one" (*C. Ar.* 18). I do not think that we can say that for Phoebadius "substance" language is in itself of decisive importance for his Trinitarian theology, although the polemical context has given a centrality to the term. Phoebadius' own habit is to speak in terms of one divine *power*.

Phoebadius' Spirit Christology is central to his understanding of the Incarnation and thus to his doctrine of the Trinity.[28] Spirit is Phoebadius' term both for the divine that pre-exists the Incarnation and for the divine component of the Incarnation. The human component of the Incarnation is called flesh. Phoebadius says that according to the Creed of Sirmium, the divine Spirit and the human flesh of Christ are united in a mixture, so that a third entity is produced. For the authors of Sirmium, we must conclude that Christ was constituted by this third stuff because Christ, having been born in flesh, could not be thought to be truly divine or spirit; and yet Christ could not be thought to be human because he is not only human. Phoebadius replies that in the Gospels, each of the two components is shown to retain its nature by the acts it performs: the divine works miracles, the human feels physical needs such as hunger and thirst, as well as human pasions such as grief and sorrow (*C. Ar.* 6).

This argument is taken from Tertullian's *Adversus Praxean* 27 in its logic, terminology, and scriptural supports. Phoebadius has redacted Tertullian's argument, shortened it, changed the order of statements, and of course given it an entirely new application. *Adversus Praxean* 27 was written against modalists who claimed that God the Father was joined to the human Jesus, and that this union, the *tertium quid*, is the Christ. By contrast, for Phoebadius the idea of a *third stuff* functions in the theology of Sirmium as the grounds for asserting that Christ suffered, and if he suffered then he is not divine. To the contrary, Phoebadius says, "We know that the the Spirit of God has not suffered, because God is incapable of passion, and God is Spirit . . . The Spirit of God [in the Son] is therefore incapable of passion, although he suffered in his human nature" (*C. Ar.* 22). Phoebadius' redaction of Tertullian's argument works well. However, there is one other important continuity that remains between Tertullian[29] and Phoebadius:[30] both authors ascribe Jesus' miracles to the work of the Spirit in him,

28. Hanson, *The Search*, 518, is confused by what Phoebadius says about "Spirit" because he does not recognize the fact of Phoebadius' Spirit Christology.

29. "And to such a degree did there remain unimpaired the proper being of each substance, that in him the Spirit carried out its own acts, that is powers and works and signs, while the flesh accomplished its own passions, hungering in company of the devil, thirsting in company of the Samaritan woman, weeping for Lazarus, sore troubled unto death—and at length it also died . . . But because both substances acted distinctively each in its own quality, therefore to them accrued both their own activities and their own destinies" (Tertullian, *Adversus Praxeus*, 27).

30. "For the Spirit also did (perform) its own activities in Him: namely powers, works, and signs. 'The eternal God will neither hunger nor thirst.' Besides, what about the strong emotion of a human being? He wept for Lazarus and Jerusalem. Finally, He was sorrowful unto death. But what He expressed with strong emotion, did He not bear witness with words? For He said to Nicodemus, 'What has been born from flesh is flesh, and what [has been born] from Spirit is spirit.' And He said, 'The flesh [is] weak; the spirit is willing'" (Phoebadius, *C. Ar.* V.1).

and Jesus' passions as the work of the flesh. In short, the epistemological significance of the two kinds of works is understood in terms of the incarnational anthropology they are thought to reveal: a Spirit-flesh Christology.

The Blasphemy's description of the Incarnation begins by speaking of the gestation of the Son in Mary's womb. The Blasphemy twice refers to the Son taking flesh in Mary's womb, and that through this flesh the Son suffers. Phoebadius glosses the Sirmium Creed by quoting from a letter of Potamius of Lisbon, allegedly one of the major architects of the synod. Potamius says, "God became capable of passion by Christ's flesh and spirit coagulated in the blood of Mary and reduced to one body" (apud. Phoebadius, *C. Ar.* 5.1). I have already sketched Phoebadius' response to this understanding of the Incarnation, and I refer now to the presence of the *topos* of the fertilization of Mary to note two features of Phoebadius' theology: first, he accepts that the point of departure for describing the composition of the Son in the Incarnation is the conception and gestation of Jesus in Mary's womb;[31] and second, he feels no need to correct the Blasphemy's list of *dramatis personae* present at the overshadowing: the Son, Mary, and the angel. Neither the Blasphemy nor Phoebadius mention the Holy Spirit in connection with the overshadowing of Mary at the Annunciation.

The understanding that the Word himself overshadowed Mary goes back at least to Justin, and from the beginning of the third century it became the standard exegesis of Luke 1:35–36. Sometimes the word "Spirit" is applied directly to the Word, as is the title "Power of the Most High," and indeed Phoebadius accumulates a variety of titles for the Son: Word, Wisdom, Spirit, Power, and Mind, for example. Each title, he says, names the Son in terms of a particular function: Wisdom, for example, names the Son as creator. Phoebadius cites Psalm 33:6 as testimony to the creative action of the Word-Wisdom-Spirit: "By his Word were the heavens established," the psalm says, "and by the breath of his mouth all their power." Phoebadius' exegesis of the psalm follows that of Tertullian and Hippolytus: both lines refer to the same "person," the Word. Thus, while Phoebadius may include the Holy Spirit as the "Third [divine] Person," his pneumatology is otherwise weak to the point of non-existent. The old Second Temple Jewish and the later second-century Christian understanding that in Psalm 33 the "Breath of his mouth" names the Holy Spirit as co-creator is gone; indeed, it is forgotten. Phoebadius speaks of the Holy Spirit as the second "paraclete" and as the agent of inspiration, but as nothing more.

---

31. This feature of Latin theology remains consistent. Hanson diagnoses certain errors in Hilary of Poitiers' Christology (in *Trin.*) as owing to the fact that Hilary "made the disasterous mistake of allowing the story of the Virgin Birth, which plays so insignificant a part in the New Testament, to control the whole of his Christology" (Hanson, *The Search*, 501). However "insignificant" the story of the Virgin Birth may be, Hilary is only being a good Latin theologian by focusing upon it. The same may probably be said later for Leo of Rome.

GREGORY OF ELVIRA

Gregory was a prolific (and long-lived) writer whose works have scarcely been translated. There are scholarly debates over which books are properly attributed to him, but minimally he wrote *De Fide*, *Tractates on the Song of Songs*, and *Homilies on Scripture*.[32] That such works remain largely unrecognized today is regretful, and brings to mind the all-but-recent abandonment suffered by Hilary of Poitiers's *Commentary on Matthew* and his *Tractates on the Psalms*. Gregory is important: Hanson judges him to have written "one of the earliest statements of the consubstantiality of the Holy Spirit."[33] Previously unremarked in scholarship is the emphasis in Gregory's Trinitarian theology on sight, vision, and light, which has later analogues in the theologies of Faustinus of Rome and Augustine of Hippo. Gregory and Faustinus are important early examples of a "visual" logic in Latin Nicene theology. Gregory may be the first Latin to incorporate the transfiguration into his account of Christ's divinity.[34] Augustine read Gregory thinking he was Gregory of Nazianzus, and the understanding of theophanies that Augustine articulates in the first four books of his *De Trinitate* owes to Gregory.[35]

Like Phoebadius' *Liber Contra Arianos*, Gregory's *De Fide* is written in response to the manifesto produced at Sirmium, which had excluded the use of any *ousia* or *substantia* language when speaking of God. Gregory offers an extended argument for the unity of essence between the Father and the Son (and the Holy Spirit). He seeks to refute the criticisms of "essence" conceptuality as used of God: he defends, in particular, the term *homoousios* (or *unius substantia*). Gregory works through in detail the logic of the creedal language of "God from God, Light from Light"[36]—language which is expressed by many councils other than Nicaea, and which had recently been

---

32. Manlio Simonetti concludes that as a result of manuscript research by Dom Morin, Dom Wilmart, and A.C. Vega, a variety of writings are now attributed "with absolute certainty to Gregory and have made him the most important and best-known Spanish author prior to Isidore of Seville" (Quasten, *Patrology*, IV.85).

33. "Towards the end of the *De Fide*, Gregory produces one of the earliest statements of the consubstantiality of the Holy Spirit. 'He sent the Holy Spirit to us' [Gregory says], 'from his own and his identical one substance . . .' And he concludes the work by setting out a Rule of Faith ending with the words 'three Persons of one substance'" (Hanson, *The Search*, 526). Hanson then goes on to remark that Gregory's derived-from-Tertullian materialist notion of divine substance sounds orthodox, but would have scandalized Greek Nicenes.

34. Halleux, "'Hypostase' et 'Personne,'" argued that the East's acceptance of *persona* as equivalent to *hypostasis* metaphysicalized Western Trinitarian theology, which hitherto had been more "manifestational" oriented.

35. On Gregory's understanding of the Son appearing in different forms, see Hanson, *The Search*, 524.

36. The argument Gregory faces is whether "God from God, Light from Light" represents *X from X* causality in the sense that "the same comes from the same" (i.e., X is in both cases the same), or in the sense that the product X is not identical in its "X-ness" with the cause X. I coined the expression *X from X*, and through its applications by Joe Lienhard and Lewis Ayres the expression became one logical tool for analyzing Trinitarian theologies in the fourth century.

interpreted to support a subordinationist doctrine of the Son.[37] Gregory's argument centers upon a causal logic: "they" say that the Son is from God not as begotten, but as made directly; it is generation that transmits nature and guarantees continuity of natures; Scripture attributes divine characteristic to the Son as if he were divine and describes his origins from God as though the originating process is generation or birth. We signify unity and continuity of nature with the *homoousios*, just as we describe the origins of that-which-is-one-in-nature with "God from God, Light from Light." No one would reject the claim that the child of a parent is of the same nature as the parent: the unity and continuity of nature is, in such cases, denoted by "same nature."

As I noted just above, Phoebadius recognizes that the anti-Nicenes themselves claim the traditional *X from X* formulations as expressions of their own Trinitarian aetiology. To counter their claims, Phoebadius emphasizes "*in* the Father" or "*in* God," in contrast to the simple and potentially ambiguous use of *X from X* language. Like Phoebadius, Gregory of Elvira recognizes that the anti-Nicene claims on such formulae must be refuted, and he devotes a significant part of *De Fide* to providing a "logic" for *X from X* statements in authoritative creeds, including (especially) Nicaea, since it is the relationship between that creed's *X from X* language and its *homousious* language that is at stake. Gregory initially cites *X from X* at *De Fide* II.20, but it is at III.38–41 and V.55–59 where he offers a dense account of what is meant by *X from X* creedal formulae; indeed, he offers two different logics to explain the proper understanding *X from X* creedal formulae. At *De Fide* III.38–41, Gregory uses Scriptural citations (all taken from Johannine literature) to show that Christ is identified as "Light" and that God the Father is identified as "Light." Gregory then reads the shared titles together with John 16:27 and a series of scriptural texts idenitfying the Son as light, concluding that, "if the Father is Light and the Son is Light, and the Son is from the Father, then we can say 'Light from Light.'"[38] Gregory's reasoning here is significant and does indeed advance his claims on *X from X* language: up to this point in time, the anti-Nicenes have failed to offer a logic to support their interpretation of *X from X* statements.[39]

Gregory's argument at *De Fide* V.55–59 again depends upon John 16:27—"I have come forth from the Father"—but it develops differently: the logic offered at V.55–59

37. "Subordinationist/ism" can be a loaded term, often used anachronistically, but Gregory's argument allows us to be specific about what the term means when we use it in his historical context: that the Son's nature or substance is other than, and therefore ontologically less than, the Father's. (The possibility that a nature or essence that is other than God's would be ontologically greater than God's is logically excluded in all cases.)

38. Gregory offers a compact but comprehensive statement of his understand of *X from X* statements at *De Fide* V.56: "[W]hether you say Light from Light or Word from Word or Spirit from Spirit or Lord from Lord, whatever you might say about God, you believe that the Father and the Son are of one essence, that is, you understand that the Son was born from the very thing which the Father is."

39. I suspect that Eunomius' exegesis of "Light from Light" (*X from X*) in his *Apology* is an attempt to offer the heretofore missing anti-Nicene "logic"; certainly his argument attempts to refute any explanation based on scriptural attributions to the Father and the Son

is aetiological and epistemological. Gregory initially appeals to the cases of a flame from a flame, or sunlight from the sun, to establish that in neither case would we say there are substantially *two*. The argument from "the brightness of the sun" is developed further—and Gregory moves beyond what was said by Justin or Tertullian when they used the same analogy. The light or brilliance of the sun reveals the sun; through the emitted radiance we know the sun—and only on this basis (no emitted brilliance, no knowledge of sun)—and the knowledge we gain is through a kind of image of the sun. The epistemological content of this image of the sun surpasses the content of any other image because this Image is the direct product of the Source:

> [T]he Son as the radiance of [the same] brightness, which concerning this the prophet has said, "In your presence is the fount of light and in your light we will see light" [Ps 35:10], or Solomon, when he says, "He is the brilliance of eternal light and the mirror without blemish of the majesty of God" [Wis 7:26] or the apostle in the place where he proclaimed that our Savior is the image of the invisible God [Col 1:15], inasmuch as the image of the sun is its light, which proceeds from the same sun . . . Inasmuch as the light exists, *what* God is cannot be measured, understood, or defined, nor indeed can anything from the things which are in this world be compared with the divine majesty, because none of the things which are seen or which can be spoken of can be considered a worthy similitude in accordance with that which God is, for He is greater than these thoughts and judgments.[40]

I turn now to the three themes (or *topoi*) that I am arguing are common to most Latin Nicene theology, and that are, from my perspective, already expressed as traditional at Serdica: first, an appeal to John 14:10, "Do you not believe that I am in the Father and the Father in me?"; second, an understanding of the language of "Power of God" as a description of the unity in the Trinity; and finally, "Spirit Christology." On the first point, it must be said that Gregory's use of John 14:10 alone is not extensive: rather, Gregory links the passage to a constellation of other Johannine passages that together link *the Son being from the Father* with *the Son revealing the Father*. Gregory identifies the content of *homoousios* with the content of John 14:10: "This will be *homoousios*, that is, of one substance with the Father, just as the Lord himself says: 'I am in the Father and the Father is in me.'"[41]

The second Latin Trinitarian theme—"*Power* of God," used as a means of describing divine unity—appears regularly in Gregory's arguments. There are two kinds of power-based arguments for the unity of Father and Son in theology sympathetic to Nicaea: the first argument identifies the Son or Word as the very Power of God (meaning, God the Father)—that Power that God has, just as he has a Word or Wisdom; the second argument demonstrates that the Son or Word has the distinctive Power(s)

---

40. Gregory, *De Fide* V.57–58; edited.

41. *De Fide* 53. See Hanson, *The Search*, 522, for his comments on this passage.

unique to the divine nature.[42] These are two related but distinct arguments: both share
the notion of the relationship of power to existent or nature, but in the first case the
unity of the Son with Father is the sort of unity a power has with the existent of which
it is a necessary property; in the second case, the concept of power, insofar as a given
power, is distinct and unique to a specific nature or essence. So neat a statement of
distinctions cannot, of course, survive reality. Sometimes the claim that the Son is
"*the* Power of God" is made on the basis of simply identifying the Son with the divine
Power (as 1 Cor 1:24 seems to do); sometimes the claim is made on the basis of an
X from X argument (i.e., the Son is the Power from God's own Power); or—another
potential source of confusion—the two kinds of arguments can be mixed together:
Christ is the Power of the Father and Christ possesses the Power of divinity just as the
Father does. The logic underlying both is the unity that obtains between some existent
and its power.

Gregory has a clear statement of the first kind of power-based argument that
identifies the Son with the Power of God: "He is called 'power' because he is truly from
God and is with God and all the power of the Father in is him; . . ."[43] Gregory also uses
the *X from X* variant argument: "For I who said that the Son of God was not begotten
from somewhere else than properly from the Father—the whole from the whole, the
complete from the complete, the perfect from the perfect and perfect power."[44] Finally,
one can find in Gregory's writing logic and language taken directly from Tertullian:
"We believe that the three names and three persons are of one essence, and of one
majesty and power. And this is why we confess one God, because the unity of majesty
prohibits that gods be named with the terminology of many."[45]

42. This argument is fundamentally epistemological, but is often expressed using the categories
of a causal sequence (*De fide* 28–9): "Therefore Wisdom has been created, or rather begotten, not
with respect to itself because it always existed but with respect to those things which ought to have
been made by it in order that, since how great or what sort it was could not be known, *its* strength
and power *should be known from the* effect *of its* works, so that, what we value from created things,
we might fear more, when we marvel at the deeds." The technical causal sequence is "non poterat,
de effectu operum suorum virtus eius et potentia nosceretur . . ." Francis J. Buckley singles out this
passage in his treatment of Gregory's doctrine of the "Procession of the Son": "Wisdom (the Son) is
born not for himself but for those that had to be made by him, in order that his power and strength
could be known from the effects of his works. [A]lthough the above passage is the only spot where this
[that the Son proceeds from the Father in order to create and to make God known to men] is stated
so explicitly, the same thought is implied in the explanation of various figures and titles to the Son"
(Francis J. Buckley, *Christ and the Church according to Gregory of Elvira* [Rome: Gregorian University
Press, 1964], 6–7). Buckley does not recognize the technical sequence *power-works-effects*. See my
"Background and Use."

43. *De fide* 64: "Virtus dicitur, quia uere de deo et semper cum deoest et omnis potestas patris in
ipso consistit . . ."

44. *De fide* 9: "Qui enim Filium Dei non aliunde natum dixeram, quam proprie de Patre, totum de
toto, integrum de integro, perfectum de perfecto, consummatamque virtutem." One could argue that
in Gregory's logic "*proprie de Patre*" is in fact *consummatamque virtutem*.

45. *De fide* 11: "Nec extensionem partis alicujus ex Patre (ut quidam putaverunt) Dei Filium dicimus, nec verbum sine re, ut velut sonum vocis accipimus: sed tria nomina, et *tres personas unius*

The third doctrine that Latin Nicenes such as Gregory take up from the Western tradition (expressed in part at western Serdica) is "Spirit Christology": the identification of the divine element in Jesus as "Spirit."[46]

> For indeed the Virgin conceived from the Spirit of God and gave birth to what she had conceived, that is, God joined to flesh and soul, that is, to a human being—as I have already said—by a unity of person, just as himself said, "What is born from spirit is spirit" [John 3:6] because "God is spirit" [John 4:24], and he was born from God. Just as the angel also said to the virgin Mary, "The Spirit of God will come upon you and the power of the Most High will overshadow you. And therefore what is born from you is holy and will be called the Son of God" [Luke 1:35].[47]

Gregory reports that the "Arians" argue against the true divinity of the Son because in the Incarnation the Son's nature was changed, and God's nature cannot be changed.[48] Gregory uses "Spirit" to name the divine that pre-exists the Incarnation, that joins with "flesh," and that constitutes the Spirit-and-flesh, divine-and-human entity, Jesus Christ. The union between Spirit and flesh does not constitute a transformation of divine nature (i.e., spirit):

> And likewise, when he deigned to put on a human being, he did not introduce a destruction of eternity, in such a way that the spirit transformed itself into flesh, but in order to grant the assumed human being the immortality and

---

esse essentiae, unius majestatis atque potentiae credimus. Et ideo unum Deum confitemur, quia *unitas majestatis* plurium vocabulo deos prohibet appellari." In Gregory's theology, the *majestas* is singular as well, where *majestas* is carrying the conceptual weight of the Scriptural notion of God's *Kabod.*

46. This is not the belief that the Son is the "Holy Spirit," but that "Spirit" is a term that names divinity generally, as in "God is spirit" where "God" is take as either the divine unity or nature. The theology arises exegetically: Who does this use of "spirit" in this scriptural passage refer to? As I remarked earlier, one key marker of a Spirit Christology is the understanding that the "Spirit" overshadowing Mary at Luke 1:35 is the Word rather than the Holy Spirit (i.e., the Third Person of the Trinity).

47. *De fide* 91: A look at the two versions (the original and the revised) of *De Fide* reveals noteworthy additions by Gregory. The original Latin runs thus: "Nempe enim de siritu dei uirgo concepit, et quod concepit, hoc peperit, id is, deum homini suo ut iam dixi sociatum," but in the revised version, Gregory inserts "carni et animae suae, id est homini ut iam dixi personae unitate sociatum" before he continues with what remains common to both versions: "sicut ipse dixit: 'Quod nascitur de carne, caro est: et quod nascitur de siritu, siritu est, quia [dues] spiritus est [et] de deo natus est', sicut et angelus ad Mariam uirginem dixit: 'Siritus dei ueniet in te uirtus Altissimi obumbrabit te. Proptera [et] quod nascetur ex te sanctum, uocabitur filius dei'" (CCL LXIX 245. 905–15). To remove the possibility of a monarchian interpretation Gregory adds, "God joined to flesh and soul, that is, to a human being, by a unity of person."

48. "[They say that the Son] having been transformed immediately by this alteration from God into a human being, from spirit into flesh; and indeed every transformation is also a destruction of the former state. And on account of this they say: If the Son were from the substance of the Father, the Father would also be seen [to be] inferior either by the transformation or limit of his substance. And therefore they prefer to believe that the Son is from another substance, which can be changed, transformed, and seen, because this is not permitted to be believed about the substance of the Father" (Gregory, *De Fide* VIII.75).

eternity of the heavenly life. For although the apostle says that "he emptied himself, by taking on the form of a slave" [Phil 2:7], we certainly do not accept that he was emptied in such a way that the same spirit became something other than what it was, but [rather] having withdrawn the honor of his majesty for the moment, he put on a human body, by which assumption the salvation of the Gentiles was accomplished.[49]

Sections 88–95 of *De Fide* VIII are devoted to refuting this Christology, and are thus the occasion for Gregory referring to the divinity as "spirit unchanged"—as opposed to the idea of spirit converted into, on the one hand, a lesser kind of being, or, on the other, matter or flesh. Two short extracts exemplify Gregory's use of spirit and the polemical context:[50]

> For although the apostle says that "he emptied himself, by taking on the form of a slave," we certainly do not accept that he was emptied in such a way that the same spirit became something other than what it was.[51]

> And when he put on a human being, he did not change his position (*status*) nor lose his rank (*ordo*), nor transform his substance.[52]

When Gregory seeks to deny that the Incarnation caused any change or transformation of the divinity of the Son (i.e., whether the Son's divinity is of a sort that can be transformed, unlike the Father's), he names the divinity in Christ the "Spirit" and the question is phrased as, "Has the Spirit changed [by undergoing the Incarnation]?" The question of whether or not the Incarnation caused a "transformation" of the divinity of the Son is a central concern in Latin theology, and the care with which an author deals with that issue locates him with the "great tradition" of Latin theology. Moreover, an author's treatment reveals the relative sophistication or depth of his theology.

The question in the West of whether the Spirit (divinity) undergoes a "transformation" by being joined to flesh is a controversy that goes back to the monarchianism that Tertullian engages in depth in *Against Praxeas* 27–29. Monarchians in Rome and North Africa offered a *reductio ad absurdum* argument in favor of their modalist theology of the Incarnation: if the divine substance is united with human substance, then divinity must undergo transformation,[53] for (1) it passes from "separate" to "joined," and (2) it changes from impassible to passable; to say that an existent

---

49. Gregory, *De Fide* VIII.88.

50. This short passage from *De Fide* VIII.93 also illustrates Gregory's use of Tertullian's technical language: position (*status*), rank (*ordo*), substance (*substantia*). "Human being" translates *hominem*. CCL LXIX. 245:937–39.

51. Gregory, *De Fide* VIII.88.

52. Gregory, *De Fide* VIII.93.

53. This Latin Trinitarian use of "substance" language owes to Tertullian; Gregory uses this terminology in his characterizations of his opponents' theology, and we cannot, on the basis of Gregory's report, say that his opponents—past or present—used such terms themselves.

goes from "immutable" to "mutable" is a contradiction, since by definition whatever is "immutable" cannot change. Either there is one God and one divine substance, and that substance changes as it joins with a body, or there are two Gods, one with divine immutability and one mutable. But if divine substance does not change, then it was the true God who was present in Jesus, and there are not "two Gods." Therefore, the divinity in Jesus was not in a union with Jesus' humanity, but remained separate, though joined "in place" with Jesus, untransformed.

Either the "Spirit transformed in the Incarnation" remained a live question in the West until past the middle of the fourth century, or it became, by that time, a necessary trope for orthodox discourse on the Incarnation.[54] The fact is undeniable that polemic against "transformed Spirit" had a strong representation in mid-fourth-century Latin theology. I make this point regarding Gregory of Elvira, an "other Nicene," but the traditional character of the polemic is established by its presence in Hilary of Poitier's *Commentary on Matthew*, written at a time before Hilary could be counted as a Nicene at all: as with Tertullian, so Hilary draws upon a traditional pre-Nicene Latin Christology.[55]

POTAMIUS OF LISBON[56]

Potamius had a strange theological career: the ancient sources (including Phoebadius) say that that he was at some time an Arian, but later treatises attributed to him are anti-Arian and sympathetic to Nicaea.[57] We do not know whether Potamius was first anti-Arian, then changed sides, and then changed again, or began as an Arian and then rejected that theology. Four short examples of his writing exist, plus a fragment provided by Phoebadius (see *JECS* 9 (2001): I quoted from before), who is our source for the charge against Potamius that he was amongst those responsible for the

54. Daniel H. Williams, "Defining Orthodoxy in Hilary of Poitiers' *Commentarium in Matthaeum*," 7–22.

55. See Hilary, *In Matthaeum*, 31, and Williams' comments in his Introduction to the *Commentary on Matthew*, FoTC 125 25–27. Another way of framing the question about anti-transformation polemic in Hilary and Gregory is this: At what point did the anti-transformation argument against monarchians develop into an anti-transformation argument against subordinationists? Did the development follow the adaptation of the transformation argument by presently unidentified Western subordinationists, or did a non-subordinationist articulation of the anti-transformation argument develop "logically" prior to, or independent from, any subordinationist adaptation?

56. Given that the judgment of the critical edition of the *Letters* later attributed to Potamius are indeed written by a "reformed" Nicene bishop of Lisbon, I will use the name "Potamius" as an avatar for the author of these works (much the same way "Posidonius" was used by classicists in the first half of the twentieth century). If the reader wants to mentally insert "unknown author" into this article wherever—after the first paragraph—I say "Potamius," I do not object. If, however, the reader wants to check the Latin, they will have to go to the volume with the name "Potamius of Lisbon" on the volume's spine.

57. See Introduction, text, translation, and commentary by Marco Conti, *The Life and Works of Potamius of Lisbon* (Steenburgis: Brepols, 1998).

Blasphamy of Sirmium. The first of his two extant Trinitarian writings takes the form
of a letter to Athanasius, written after the Council of Ariminum (359), in which Potamius rejects and attacks Arian theology and defends the theology of the *one substance
of the Father and the Son*.[58] Some of Potamius' arguments in this letter seem to be
directed against Sirmium. One passage in particular bears quoting:

> [W]hat did the blasphemers argue? *He who sent me*, they cite, *is greater than
> I*. The one from whom he was begotten is his Father, certainly: since he is ac-
> knowledged as Son. However the Father is greater than the Son because he is
> Father. The rank [ordo] is placed first, but the substance is not separated.[59]

The rest of the letter is given over to reciting scriptural passages that contain the word
substantia—e.g., Psalm 68:3, Jeremiah 9:10, and 23:22; Potamaius continues and
enlarges upon the list of prooftexts in his second extant Trinitarian writing, *On the
Substance of the Father and the Son and the Holy Spirit*. Other than the list of Old Testament passages using "substance," Potamius' recourse to Scripture is minimal: in each
letter, he cites John 10:30 once, and in the *Epistle on Substance* he cites 1 Corinthians
1:24 once. Virtually the only other Trinitarian prooftext he cites—and clearly his favorite—is 1 John 5:8, "And the three of them are one"; in total, this New Testament
text appears four times in the two epistles.

The very few scholars who have an opinion on the dates of Potamius' writings
place the *Epistle on Substance* soon after the *Epistle to Athanasius*, which means during
the early 360s.[60] More recent research supports the account of Potamius (re)convert-
ing to the cause of Athanasius, *homoousios*, and Nicaea in the year 359.[61] The first
two of the four tasks Potamius accomplishes in the *Epistle on Substance* can be easily
summarized: he provides an extensive list of scriptural passages in which *substantia*
appears, as Phoebadius had before him; and he provides a long and occasionally bu-
colic list of examples of the continuity and unity of substance from source to product.
Such examples include wool, wheat, flour, and fruits from trees. Potamius third task
in the *Epistle* is the most extensive and utilizes the results of the first two: Potamius
offers a lengthy account of the unity—and commonality—of substance between Father and Son. The logic of substance is deployed and applied to the Trinity. The logic
of substance, which is Potamius' main concern, turns upon the ontological continuity between substance and power, or more generally, on substance as causal source.

---

58. The review of Conti's book by D.H. Williams in the *Journal of Theological Studies* makes clear
that Conti left a number of significant issues unresolved when he gave the same judgment on Potamius
and the *Epistles* as his director, A. Montes Moreia, had previously. The identification of the author of
these letters with the person whom Phoebadius names and quotes is not widely accepted outside the
contemporary Italian school of patristic studies.

59. *Ad Athanasium*, line 32ff.

60. See, e.g., Hanson, *The Search*, 526–27; and Simonetti's judgments in Quasten, *Patrology*,
IV.80–83.

61. See Conti's summary of the debate, and his own conclusion, at *Potamius*, 24–26.

Substance itself, is described as "all that causes a thing to exist"[62] and moreover, "substance cannot exist without power."[63] With this ontology, Potamius can develop a logic of divine unity: "since the power of the Father is the Son, the power itself pertains to its substance, because substance cannot exist without power" (*De substantia*, 10). The unacknowledged scriptural "distributed middle" (as it were) is 1 Corinthians 1:24, "Christ the Power and Wisdom of God."

In this passage, substance seems to be identified with the Father, which is not an unusual move in "one substance" or even "one *ousia*" theology. However, at another place in the *Epistle*, Potamius seems to have a different understanding of the generative substance. Twice Potamius uses the similitude—familiar from the writings of Tertullian and Novatian—of the spring which "gushes and flows out," but for Potamius the spring which gushes is the "innermost nature of the substance,"[64] and not, as it is for the third-century Latins, the Father. I quote Potamius at length again:

> [T]he origin of all things is the beginning, but for all things substance is primary. Thus when the rays emitted by the dawn diminish in the twilight, they return to their sun, and the origin of rivers is the pouring out of a spring. The substance of a thing is all that causes a thing to exist . . . Therefore the substance of the Father, the Son and the Holy Spirit is one.[65]

This quotation brings us to the second argument from "substance as causal source" that Potamius advances in support of his doctrine of "God of a single substance" (*unius substantiae deum*).[66] One of Potamius' examples of a single substance across products is that of the figs of a fig-tree, in that, in Potamius words, "figs are made of the substance of the fig-tree . . . the substance of the figs is the tree by which the figs are produced."[67] Having offered this arborial illustration of a single substance, Potamius turns to the Trinity:

> Therefore *fig is from fig* in order that the power of its substance might be operative [*ut substantiae suae operaretur vis*], in order that its nature might begin to be one thing with its stock through the substance of the unity [unity of the substance?—*per substantiam unitatis*] [God has revealed this in trees] so that no one should doubt that there could exist *God from God, Light from Light*, a God of a single substance [*unius substantiae deum*].[68]

In other words, when *fig produces fig*, this is the operation of the power of its substance: a substance is that which causes a thing to be; a power is substance as cause.

62. Potamius, *On the Substance*, 282.

63. Potamius, *On the Substance*, 172–74.

64. Potamius, *On the Substance*, 162–63.

65. Potamius, *On the Substance*, 280–285.

66. Potamius, *On the Substance*, 218.

67. Potamius, *On the Substance*, 207–09.

68. Potamius, *On the Substance*, 214–18.

The most fundamental operation of the power of the substance is for substance to reproduce itself, not reproduction in the sense of making a second substance, but in the sense of a continuity of itself. This aetiology describes divine generation, as well; the differences among the Three Personas are distinctions in name and order (which is *ordo*, not *gradus*).

This is not the only occasion in the *Epistle* that Potamius defends the "God from God"—or *X from X*—aetiology of one substance Trinitarian theology, but it is not clear if he has in mind a defense of the language of Nicaea (325) or simply means to propose an alternate to the Sirmium (357) understanding of *X from X* causal language; Phoebadius had already argued against the Blasphemy's use of this language. Potamius may, however, have known the Creed of Nicaea either from Ossius or possibly Hilary's *De Synodis*.

The rest of the letter is given to offering similes to the Trinity: the three-part structure of a face, for example, or of the two eyes. Almost nothing is said about the nature of the Incarnation except to remark that it is through the "singleness of substance" that Christ works his miracles. Potamius' pneumatology is undeveloped and unarticulated, except for one interesting statement he makes that "The Father, the Son and the Holy Spirit are of one substance [*una substantia est*]."[69] Potamius' quietly radical statement hangs in mid-air, however, for although he says it, he does so only on the way to saying more about the Son. Nonetheless, something significant about Latin Nicene theology is revealed here: the advantage Latin theology has from its ignorance of Greek Nicene theology (as exemplified by, e.g., Athanasius) is that it was free to make statements about a one or single substance that would not have been possible with an Athanasian understanding of *homoousios*. For Athanasius and the Greeks he influenced, *homoousios* was a unique and one-way predicate statement: one could and should say "the Son is *homousios* with the Father," but one could not meaningfully or piously say "the Father is *homousios* with the Son." Ignorant of this technicality, Latins were free to say that the Father and the Son—and the Holy Spirit—were of one single substance.

I will close my comments on Potamius by turning to his fellow Iberian, Ossius of Cordova, who is the more famous and senior Iberian bishop associated with "substance" language for God. Ossius attended each of the three councils during his lifetime that expressed a strong interest in substance language: Nicaea (325), Serdica (342), and Sirmium (357). At Sirmium, Ossius, like Potamius, accepted the logic of its creed and thus turned away from the seeming touchstone of Nicaea and its *ousia* terminology. A fact only rarely noted is that Ossius' archdeacon in Cordova was none other than the famous Latin Platonist, Calcidius, best known for his very influential translation of Plato's *Timaeus*. On the basis of now outdated scholarship, Hanson rejected the identification of the Ossius whom Calcidius speaks of with the bishop

---

69. Potamius, *On the Substance*, 285.

Ossius,[70] but even so, Hanson allows that if it were true that Calcidius the Platonist were Ossius' Calcidius, then "that would make a considerable difference to our estimate of Ossius' contribution to the Council and Creed of Nicaea, because we could conclude with some confidence that the issues debated by Eastern theologians would not have been strange to Calcidius' Hossius."[71] Passing without comment Hanson's widely shared assumption that the Trinitarian issues debated by Eastern theologians were unknown to Westerners—as opposed to being unacceptable to Westerners—I make this proposal, then: there is an Iberian school of substance-logic Trinitarianism, probably drawing upon philosophical sources for its understanding of "substance," given that Potamius' intellectual apparatus for analysing "substance" is advanced, coherent, and even technical. Potamius and Ossius may have been willing to follow the logic of a substance-centered ontology even at the expense of the *ousia*-based language used in the Creed of Nicaea. If this last point is true, then it would explain the otherwise puzzling identification in the Western Serdican Creed of the use of *ousia* with heretical theology, and would indeed draw a line of thought connecting that clause in Serdica with the condemnation of *ousia*-based language at Sirmium.

ZENO OF VERONA

Zeno's *floruit* is the mid- to late-360s into the mid-370s. He was bishop of Verona, but there is a strong likelihood that he was North African. Ambrose of Milan, writing in 380, speaks of Zeno as "of holy memory," meaning, *dead*. The writings that survive are ninety-two sermons (or *tractates*) ranging in length in the CCL from two paragraphs to six pages. Given the genre of Zeno's writings as well as their general brevity, these writings may give us a window onto the "ordinary" Trinitarianism of non-Roman Italian theology piously devoted to one-substance and one-power formula.

Very few of the key scriptural passages in the contemporary Trinitarian controversy appear at all in Zeno's sermons: there are no citations of John 14:9–15, John 5:19, Luke 1:35, or Psalm 33:6. John 10:30 is cited twice, as is 1 Corinthians 1:24, with the Johannine text showing more of a polemical setting than the Pauline. I believe that Hanson misspoke when he said that Zeno was a "student"—in the sense of distance learning—of Hilary's.[72] Zeno's theological world is primarily that of Cyprian and Lactantius; indeed, Zeno is that unexpected oxymoron: a kind of *humble* Lactantius. His principal Christological concern is to affirm the traditional Latin doctrine of the Son's two "nativities"—the first nativity being his spiritual birth from the Father, the second

---

70. Hanson, *The Search*, 199. Hanson disparagingly refers to Declercq "assuming" that Calcidius was Hossius' Calcidius, and bases his own conclusion that Calcidius was *not* Hossius' Calcidius on Waszink. Since Waszink's time, both John Dillon and Stephen Gersh have argued *for* the identification, and the majority of recent scholarship now stands with that judgment.

71. Hanson, *The Search*, 199.

72. Hanson, *The Search*, 529. See Simonetti's comments on Zeno in Quasten, *Patrology*, IV.127–30.

being his physical birth from Mary. This basic explanation of the Trinity and the Incarnation is found in Cyprian and in Lactantius, the latter of whom places great emphasis upon it. Lactantius says, for example: "[W]e testify that He was born twice; first, in the spirit, later in the flesh . . . since He was from the beginning the Son of God, he was reborn according to the flesh."[73] Zeno says, "[T]he Christian people must know that there are two nativities of our Lord Jesus Christ, lest it fall into error: one, by which he was born, the other, by which he was reborn. Just as the first was spiritual, without a mother, so the second is carnal, without a father."[74] Lest this theology seem merely conventional, I will add that by the *first birth*, Zeno means the Son coming forth to create according to the Father's will and design. Before coming forth, the Son existed "in" the heart or bosum of God, and it is this interior existence that allows us to speak of the Son's *eternal* existence prior to his first nativity, for the Son existed in the Father by conception before he was "born." For Zeno, the life of the Son begins at his conception.

The fact that Zeno never uses Word (*Verbum*) to describe this gestating Second Person possibly indicates some sensitivity on his part to the Marcellan distinction between Word and Son. In general, however, Zeno goes lightly with the title Word—either because of its Marcellan connotations; or because it is not susceptible to an *X from X* formulation; or because Lactantius described creation as the act of *the Son* endowed with God's *power*;[75] or because the Apuleian form of Platonism known in Carthage[76] had little use for the concept of *verbum* to describe God creating, but relied heavily on *potestas* and *virtus*.[77] Thus while Zeno initially gives the impression of having a kind of two-stage *Logos* theology, he may actually have just as much in common with unreconstructed Origenism as with the Apologists or Tertullian: the Son existed eternally because the Father *conceived* him eternally. Zeno does not often articulate this aspect of his theology, nor does he preach it as the great central narrative of orthodoxy, as he does the two nativities.[78]

Zeno's engagements with contemporary controversies occur within the theological context of this doctrine of the Son's two nativities. For example, Stepanich suggests[79] that at one point, Zeno expresses his doctrine of the eternally existent Son in

73. Lactantius, *Divine Institutes* IV.8, FotC, 258–59.

74. *Tractatus* 2.7.1. Translation, Stepanich, *Christology of Zeno of Verona*, 45; slightly altered.

75. Lactantius, *Divine Institutes* IV.6, FotC, 255.

76. John Dillon, *The Middle Platonists : 80BC to 220 AD* (London: Duckworth, 1977), 306–11, for biographical overview; here specifically: "[H]e is found [after Tripoli], somewhat later (AD 161), back at Carthage, being held already in high honour as rhetorician, poet and Platonic philosopher" (307). Apuleius was born in Madaura, North Africa, around AD 123, and educated in Carthage and then Athens.

77. Stephen Gersh, *Middle Platonism and Neoplatonism: The Latin Tradition*, 2 vols (Notre Dame IN: Notre Dame University Press, 1986), 272–85.

78. Stepanich, *Christology of Zeno*, 44–45, observes that in his *In Matthaeum*, Hilary used similar language to Zeno's (at 31.3), but rejected it later in his *Trin.* (12.31). Stepanich also cites Gregory of Nazianzus' criticism of the idea that the Son existed before he was born (*Theo. Or.* 3.9).

79. Stepanich, *Christology of Zeno*, 43, Zeno's formula is *ante quam nasceretur* as opposed to Arius' *non erat anteqam nasceretur*, in his *Letter to Alexander* that Hilary includes in his *Trin.* (IV.13).

language chosen to contradict a specific formula by Arius that the Son is not eternally existent, and yet even in this confrontation with Arianism, Zeno reacts by defending the doctrine of two nativities that he considers orthodox. Or, again, when Zeno cites the Photinian doctrine that *Christ was not born God but was made God*, he treats it as a kind of Ebionism, and thus a direct challenge to the two-nativities theology.[80] Zeno may even be blind to the pre-Cyprianic radical monarchian crisis that is so central to the concerns of Hippolytus, Tertullian, and Novatian. I just remarked that Zeno cites very few of the key scriptural texts of the Nicene controversy. Similarly, he cites very few indeed of the key scriptural texts of the monarchian controversy, and the two passages he does cite are given no anti-modalist elaborations. Zeno does not cite, ever, Exodus 3:6, 20:3, or Isaiah 44:6; nor does he ever cite John 14:10 or Romans 9:5. The two "monarchian crisis" passages he does cite are Isaiah 45:14 and Baruch 3:36, but without—to repeat myself—any anti-modalist application. As Lofstedt, the CCL editor for the Zeno volume, recognized, both of these Scripture passages are included in section 6 of book II of Cyprian's *Testimonies*, and fit the broader pattern of Zeno's substantial appropriation of Cyprian's scriptural *testimonia* in his own writings. The older, anti-modalist purposes these texts had served seem not to have interested Cyprian, and they certainly did not interest Zeno.

A third, more contemporary controversy Zeno seems to know and respond to is the Apollinarian doctrine of the pre-existent human body of Jesus.[81] He summarizes the doctrine by commenting on the associated scriptural passages of the controversy: 1 Corinthians 15:47, John 3:13, and Ephesians 4:9. Again, Zeno perceives the problematic theology in terms of its compatibility with two-nativities theology—which is minimal—and he replies by re-affirming the traditional Latin doctrine: the Son is called "Son *of God*," Zeno says, according to his ineffable origin from the Father, and he is called "Son *of Man*," not because he always had a human body, but because he is human "ad sacramentum."[82]

Like Phoebadius, whenever Zeno speaks of the Two or Three as "one substance," he also says they are "one power";[83] again like Phoebadius, he will sometimes say "one power" without any mention of "one substance." Zeno uses one-power and one-substance language, but he uses the logic of neither power nor substance to describe how or what the Trinity is; his Trinitarian theology is filled out by the two-nativities Christology. In particular, it is not clear what Zeno means by the formula, "one power." That he uses it in parallel to "one substance" suggests that he means that in God there is a single power common to the Persons. However, when Zeno speaks of God creating, he invokes 1 Corinthians 1:24 and identifies the Son as the Power and Wisdom of

---

80. For a slightly different take on this passage, see Williams, "Monarchianism and Photinus of Sirmium," 204.

81. See Zeno, *Tractatus* I.12.

82. *Tractatus* 2.4: "Igitur Dei filius ad ineffabilem originem pertinet, hominis ad sacramentum."

83. See Zeno, *Tractatus* I.7.30; I.37.11–12; II.5.84.

God who accomplishes all the things the Father commands to be made.[84] In another sermon, Zeno identifies the terms of 1 Corinthians 1:24 as the Power and Wisdom within the Father that emits the Son: "omnipotence propogates omnipotence," he says, "God is born of God."[85] Thus, like Phoebadius and Potamius, Zeno singles out "God from God"—X from X-type statements—to explain, but it is not clear that he is, as they were, *defending* such formulae.[86] For Zeno, all X from X expressions restate some part of two-nativities doctrine, and it is in that context that Zeno will refer to such formulae. Finally, like Potamius, Zeno includes the Holy Spirit in his statements of "one substance [and] one power,"[87] and, as with Potamius, such formulae do not result in any advancement in his description of the identity, life, and work of the Holy Spirit. While Zeno's pneumatology is fulsome when compared to that of Lactantius, the logic of his "Trinitarian" theology is satisfied by a binitarian account of the diversity in God; indeed, the very passage that Hanson offers as evidence of Zeno's development also reveals his limitations,[88] for there Zeno says that in God we find "a double person, a double name, but there is one substance of original eternity and deity."[89]

NICETA OF REMESIANA

In previous scholarship, the major question surrounding Niceta of Remesiana was his *floruit*. In 1905, A.E. Burns argued that his writings should be dated in the mid- to late-370s because they showed no awareness of the Apollinarianian controversy; in 1909, W.A. Patin argued that Niceta's sophisticated Trinitarian theology, especially regarding the Holy Spirit, required that his writings date from after Constantinople, 381, perhaps well after 381. I side with Burns. There are three short Trinitarian writings by Niceta that I will discuss: *De Ratione Fidei*, *De Spiritus sancti potentia*, and *De Symbolo*. All the works belong to a catechetical genre and have been compared to Cyril of Jerusalem's *Catechetical Discourses*, a work which Niceta knew and cited in his own writings. Niceta is the only one of the Latin Nicenes that I discuss here who we can say certainly had contact with some Greek theology, such as Cyril's, but it is important not to assume that since Niceta knew *some* Greek theology, he must have *known it all*. There are, in particular, noticeable "Latinisms" in his use of texts: for

84. Stepanich, *Christology of Zeno*, 36.

85. Zeno, quoted in Stepanich, *Christology of Zeno*, 37.

86. Given that he is writing in the 370s, my judgment is that he speaks of X from X formulae because of the Nicene Creed directly, and not because of the Creed of Sirmium.

87. See, e.g., "Gladius enim spiritus sanctus est unum capulum habens, id est unam substantiam, virtutem, deitatem, majestatem voluntatem que patris et filii contestans . . ." (Zeno, *Tractatus* I.37).

88. Hanson, *The Search*, 529–30.

89. "Si enim verbum in deo est et deus est verbum et hoc est, in quo est, quod est ille, duplex persona, duplex vocabulum, sed originalis perpetuitatis ac deitatis est una substantia, domino ipso dicente: *ego et pater unum sumus* [John 10:30]. Quod non utique sic ait . . . sed ut duorum unam divinitastis potestatis que esse omnipotentiam nos doceret" (Zeno, *Tractatus* II.8).

example, Niceta's Latin translation of the Nicene Creed belongs to what nineteenth-century scholars classified as the Gallican group; and when he quotes in passing two lines from Gregory Thaumaturgus' creed, he is citing from a Latin translation and not rendering it himself.

Niceta's own description of the circumstances of his writing *De Fidei* is that while nearly every church had condemned Sabellianism and Photinianism, the threat of Arianism still remained and must be combatted. Arius' theology, according to Niceta, consisted in denying that the Father could beget a real son: the Son, Arius said, was not begotten, was of another origin, made out of nothing. Twice Niceta says that Arius denied that the Son was "of the substance" of the Father. Against such statements by Arius, Nicaea proclaimed that the Son was "born of the Father, that is of the substance of the Father [*de substantia patris*], God from God, Light from Light, true God of true God, begotten, not made, of one substance [*unius substantiae*] with the Father" (*De ratione fidei*, 3). The part of Niceta's argument that is a refutation of Arius makes repeated use of *substantia* phrases: he says, for example, that the Son is *eiusdem substantiae*, a different expression than he used to translate the creed's "of one substance with the Father." Burns says that Niceta did not shrink from using *homoousios*, but since that Greek term nowhere appears in Niceta's writings, Burns must mean by that remark that Niceta understands *unius substantiae* to have recognizably the same meaning as *homoousios*.

Niceta explains that what is meant by saying that the Son is *unius substantia* is that the Father begot—without any diminution of himself—a Son who was likewise perfect, and who has in himself all that the Father has; namely, power, potency, goodness, incorruption, glory, and eternity. This is the meaning of scriptural texts such as John 16:28, John 14:9–10, and John 10:30. Scriptural texts such as "The Father is greater than I" (John 14:24) or "I came not to do my will" (John 6:28) or "The Son can do nothing of himself" (John 5:19) do not lessen the Son, they serve simply to distinguish the Son from the Father.

What Niceta never says is that the Father and the Son are of the same or one or single substance, nor does he ever attribute one or the same substance to the Father, Son, and Holy Spirit. Niceta uses substance language because Nicaea did, and what he says about substance is largely limited to explaining what *unius substantia* means: it means that the Father generated from himself a Son who has all that he has. Niceta does *not* use formulae built upon "one substance [and] one power"—and he does *not* link the two terms or use them in parallel sequences. Niceta never says that the Three have one substance, but he does say that the Three have one power. By demonstrating the Spirit's common power with the Father and Son, Niceta demonstrates the Spirit's equal divinity.

Niceta's argument begins with the importance of the "works" (*opera*) in recognizing God; indeed, for recognizing the nature of any substance, divine or created, which takes us back to Tertullian and Phoebadius. The examples of the two different kinds of works are almost exactly the same. The miraculous works of Jesus revealed his divinity, and his passions revealed his humanity. The tears Christ shed for Lazarus reveal his humanity; his resurrecting of Lazarus reveals his divinity. Those who deny the divinity of Jesus fail to recognize and acknowledge his divine works: there was no difference *in power* between Father and Son. "If," Niceta says, "he is seen as a man in his sufferings, in his divine works he is recognized as God" (*De ratione fidei*, 6). I spoke at the beginning of this essay about the way in which Phoebadius, following Tertullian, attributed Jesus' miraculous works to the Spirit in him and the works of passion to his flesh; Niceta continues the Latin tradition of the two kinds of works identifying two kinds of "natures" in Jesus, but Niceta names them as "God" and "human"—not Spirit and flesh: "It is only by the works that we know the Father and the Son—[which is why] the Lord said, *Believe the works*. In the same way, we shall not full know the nature of the Holy Spirit unless we know how wonderful are his works" (*De spiritus*, 6). Like the Father and the Son, the Holy Spirit creates, gives life, foreknows, fills all things, judges, and is good.

> [T]he Holy Spirit has worked and will ever work with the Father and the Son . . . It would be easy to adduce more proofs from the Divine Scriptures to show a Trinity of single power and operation [*Trinitatem unius operationis ac potentiae*] . . . He [the Holy Spirit] is not different in majesty from the Father and the Son since He is not different from the Father and Son in the power of operation [*Non utique alienus est a Patris et Filii majestate, qui non est ab operum virtute alienus*]. (*De spiritus*, 18)

We can note that while Niceta's power-works formulations are Trinitarian in content, his substance formulations are not. The latter usage is possibly due to limitations imposed by the Creed of Nicaea, or by the inherent difficulties in Trinitarian theologies based upon a substance logic.

I turn now to what Burns called, with some excitement, Niceta's "free use" of the word *persona*, "from which S. Augustine was inclined to shrink."[90] *Persona* occurs three times in the work *De Spiritus sancti*, and never in *De Ratione Fidei* or *De Symbolo*. One of these three times *persona* is used in a grammatical sense, referring to the prophet Haggai speaking in the "person" of God. The first theologically significant time *persona* appears, Niceta is asserting that the Spirit is a *persona* in the proper and true sense of the word. I take this to be his reply to those who claim that the Holy Spirit is an operation or a thing (this latter claim can be found in Lactantius). However, the argument that follows to show that the Spirit is a person sounds more like a demonstration that the Spirit is divine: Niceta says the Spirit is the source of sanctification, he sanctifies and is not sanctified, the Spirit is the light of souls who illumines and is not illumined.

---

90. Burns, *Nicetas*, 152.

Whatever the proper and true sense of *persona* might be in Niceta's understanding, the term does not occur where it seems it might. I cannot summarize the passage I have in mind any more briefly than simply to quote it for you:

> Some people have been rash enough to say that the Word by which the heavens were made was nothing but the voice of God commanding and that the Spirit was nothing but a passing breath of air. This position leads inevitably to Judaism, since, just like Photinus the Jews deny that anything was made by a subsistent Word [*verbum substantiuum*] or by the Spirit. (*De spiritus*, 7)

Given what Niceta has just said that the Spirit was to be considered a *persona*, it seems as though the same term might have also been used here to say that the Word was not just a temporary thing. Instead, Niceta speaks of *Verbum substantiuum*. I think that this is Niceta's rendition of *hypostasis*—that he means a hypostatic Word. Why the Word is not called a *persona*, and the Holy Spirit is not said to exist *substantiuum*, I do not know. I can say that Niceta never uses the Trinitarian formula of Two or Three *Personae* (in God). You will remember that I previously pointed out that Niceta's explanation for the scriptural testimonies that seem to imply the Son's inferiority to the Father was that such texts serve *to distinguish* the Son from the Father. Niceta did not have the terminology to express in a formula: *one something and three something elses*—or perhaps he simply never saw the merit in speaking like that.

We now arrive at the point at which something needs to be said about the developments in Niceta's Trinitarian theology. These developments take the form, by and large, of changes in exegesis which support new doctrinal statements. There are strengths in his Trinitarian theology which are not bound up in changing exegesis, such as his use of the "one power–common works" argument—an argument he articulates without recourse to the scriptural texts that other late Nicenes use, such as 1 Corinthians 1:24 and John 5:19. But the striking developments in Niceta's Trinitarian theology compared to those of his Latin predecessors occur as changes in exegesis.

Several remarkable exegetical developments occur in the early chapters of *De Spiritus sancti potentia*: in chapter 7, Niceta turns to establishing the truth of his claim in the previous chapter that the work of the Holy Spirit is the same as that of the Father and the Son. Here Niceta quotes Psalm 33:6[91] and identifies the "Word of the Lord" as the Second Person, and the "Spirit of His mouth" as the Holy Spirit, as Faustinus did before him, and Rufinus of Syria will after him. "Thus, in one text, you have the Lord, the Word of the Lord and the Holy Spirit making the full mystery of the Trinity" (*De spiritus*, 7). Niceta then quotes Job 33:4 and Psalm 104:30 as Old Testament descriptions of the Holy Spirit creating. In chapter 8, he turns to those who evade the truth about the Holy Spirit

---

91. For the sake of comparison, I know that in the works of Athanasius prior to *Ad Serapion*, Ps 33:6 appears only in references to the Word. Basil of Caesarea cites 33:6 in his *Spir.* 19:49 in his argument that the Spirit is creator, too. Gregory of Nazianus does not quote the psalm in his *Theological Oration* on the Holy Spirit, but he does quote it in his *Discourse on Pentecost* 15 to support the statement that the Spirit creates, which is why Gregory of Nyssa quotes it in his *Refutation of Eunomius' Creed of 383*, 9.

by saying that "whenever there is mention of the Spirit as creator, the name and person of Spirit belong to the Son. The Son is a Spirit, they say, just as the Father is a Spirit."[92] (This is the third occurrence of *persona* in Niceta's writings.) By such an exegesis, Niceta says, the Holy Spirit is robbed and the glory of the Father is diminished. In short, if I may paraphrase, a proper understanding of the full divinity of the Holy Spirit, particularly the Holy Spirit as creator, is hindered by a Spirit Christology and the scriptural exegeses that supports it. To seal his point, Niceta soon refers to the synoptic prohibition of sinning against the Spirit and takes it as referring to sins against the Holy Spirit—just as Rufinus later will in his *De Fide*. "Terrible judgment!" Niceta says, "The sin of one who blasphemes against the Holy Spirit is unpardonable."[93]

Before I turn to Faustinus, I need to pause over the appearance of the word majesty (*majestas*), a term that is also important for Lucifer and Faustinus. The word *majestas* can suggest to a modern reader nothing more than associations of royalty and court, but this is an anachronistic understanding. In all the early Latin translations of Wisdom of Solomon 7:25, up to and including the Vulgate, *majestas* translates the Greek word *energeia*. The philosopher Apuleius gives as the two aspects of divinity *majestas* and *potentia*,[94] and Lactantius, who knows the writings of Apuleius, Hermes Trismegestes, and the *Sybilline Oracles*, says that the First-begotten Son possesses the power and majesty of the Father.[95] We can wonder whether for Latin theology (pagan or Christian), *potentia* and *majestas* have an analogous senses to *dunamis* and *energeia*. We must not, in any case, fail to appreciate the kind of discourse in which the word has traditionally stood.

FAUSTINUS

Faustinus writes his *De Fide* in 380, in Rome, as a priest among the Luciferian sect.[96] Although his book is principally a polemical work on the Trinity attacking the Arians, Faustinus treats other subjects—for example, moral anthropology—and he may have set the standard for a Roman *De Fide* genre such as one finds in Ps.-Rufinus' *De Fide*. Faustinus accepts recent developments in Nicene theology (such as a more vigorous pneumatology), but he handles these doctrines in a brittle fashion—perhaps due to the conservative attitude Luciferians had to the Nicene Creed.

Faustinus' preferred title for the Second Person is the Wisdom of God, which he equates with Word. He uses *Sapientia* Scripture passages to support his Christological

---

92. *De spiritus, 8.*

93. *De spiritus, 17.* Niceta then cites 1 Kgs 2:25.

94. Apuleius, *De Mundo* 24, 341–27, 352; Gersh, *Middle Platonism and Neoplatonism*, 277.

95. Lactantius, D.I. IV.6, FotC, 255.

96. Hanson provides an extensive and useful introduction to Lucifer in his *The Search*, 508–16; his comments on the "Luciferians" are less extensive and helpful, but at least the reader learns who they were.

exegesis of *Verbum* passages, and vice versa. The most interesting feature of Faustinus' argument for the unity of Father and Son is the central role he gives to visual language in scriptural descriptions of the Son's relationship to the Father; "visual language" here includes the language of our sight of the Son, the Son's sight of the Father, and image descriptions of the Son's relationship to the Father. John 1:14, "and we saw his glory, the glory as it were of the only begotten of the Father [*et vidimus gloriam ejus, gloriam quasi unigeniti a patre*]," opens Faustinus' argument that scriptural descriptions of the Son's iconic relationship to the Father show the unity between Father and Son. The image terminology of Genesis 1:26, Philippians 2:5–7, Hebrews 1:3, and Colossians 1:15 all figure in Faustinus' argument. When Faustinus begins to exegete the important passages in John 14, he begins—as no other Nicene that I know of begins—with John 14:9, "Whoever sees me, sees me and the Father [*Qui me videt, videt et patrem*]."[97] Then he moves to the usual Nicene prooftexts:

> Certainly, according to Moses, there is one image [*imago*] which pertains both to [the Son] and to the Father [Gen 1:25–26], and there is the same likeness [*forma*] according to the apostle Paul [Col 1:5], who also taught me that [the Son is] "the splendor of his glory and the character of his substance" [Heb 1:3]. But [the Son himself has] taught (this), saying: "He who has seen me, has seen the Father," and "I am in the Father and the Father is in me. I and the Father are one." And whatever the Father does, [the Son] also do likewise: for [his] words are: "For whatever he does, these things the Son does also: the Son vivifies those whom he wishes, and just as they honor the Father, so also may they honor the Son."[98]

Faustinus does describe the relationship of the Father and Son in terms of "one substance," just as he also uses power language for the same reason, though to a lesser degree: not only does substance language take precedent, but his interest in 1 Corinthians 1:24 centers on the Wisdom identity. However, even his declarations of "one substance" and "one power" are tied to the visual-logic of his Trinitarian theology.

> For just as the Son has in immutable and unchangeable substance with the Father, so also the Son has an immutable and unchangeable will with the Father. And therefore there is one will of the Father and the Son, just as there is one power and one image, or rather I should have said that the Son himself

97. However, see Gregory of Elvira, *De Fide*, discussed earlier. As I remarked earlier, Gregory and Faustinus share a Nicene "visual logic" even if their use of visual models for unity are not exactly the same.

98. *De Trin.* 4.2: "Certe una tibi et patri imago est secundum Moysen, eademque forma secundum apostolum Paulum, qui me etiam docuit, quod sis splendor gloriae et character substantiae ejus [Heb 1:3]. Sed et tu ipse docuisti dicens: Qui me vidit, vidit patrem; et ego in patre et pater in me [Johon 14:9, 10]. Ego et pater unum sumus [John 10:30]. Sed et quaecumque facit pater, facis et tu similiter: tua enim verba sunt: Quaecumque enim ille facit, haec et filius similiter facit: et sicut pater suscitat mortuos et vivificat, sic et filius, quos vult, vivificat, et ut honorificent filium, sicut honorificant patrem [John 10:19–21]."

is the will of the Father. For just as although there is one image of the Father and the Son according to Moses, nevertheless the Son himself is described as the image of the invisible God [Col 1:15] by the apostle, and thus because there is one will of the Father and the Son, this will is defined by the faith to be of the Father and the Son. *Just as he is the image of the invisible God, so you should understand concerning power.* For the Catholic faith says that there is one power of the Father and the Son; *and nevertheless the apostle says that Christ is the Power and Wisdom of God* [1 Cor 1:24]. Therefore it is said by the faith [or piously] that the Son is the will of the Father, just as *he is the wisdom of God.* And nevertheless if this sense is still moving you pay attention to those things which we are saying: certainly Christ is the Wisdom of God . . . Whence Christ is both the existent Wisdom of God and the will of God; because in God the will is not one thing and wisdom another.[99]

If one compares what Faustinus says about the Son as the Power of God to Lucifer's statements on the one divine power, one sees how Faustinus has subordinated power Trinitarian logic to a Trinitarian logic of image and resemblance. The illustrations of Lucifer's theology that Hanson provides include two declarations that the Father and Son have "one glory, one power and one majesty." A grammatical examination of John 10:30 shows, Lucifer says, that there are "two Persons and one Power of these two Persons."[100] (It goes without saying that Hanson was not searching for "power" Trinitarian passages in Lucifer or any other fourth-century author.) Hanson goes on to provide a passage in which Lucifer speaks of the single substance, majesty, and power in the Father, Son, and Holy Spirit.[101] (Note the "majesty" language.)

Simonetti remarks that Faustinus' *De Fide* ends with a "brief but exhaustive treatise on the Holy Spirit"[102]—and indeed it is true that Faustinus says explicitly that the Holy Spirit has the same substance as the Father and Son. Moreover, Faustinus quotes Psalm 33 and applies it to the Son *and* the Holy Spirit. These are two very important statements for Faustinus to make. I am conscious, however, of the danger of claiming too much for Faustinus—and the danger owes to this: his understanding of Trinitarian unity articulates itself through a logic of image and figure, and that logic does not in itself include or explain the co-divinity of the Holy Spirit, for the Spirit cannot be described as the image or likeness of God (since he has no image or likeness). Faustinus' spirit is willing, but his logic is weak.

---

99. *De trin.* 1.14.

100. Hanson, *The Search*, 508–16; here, 512.

101. Hanson, *The Search*, 513.

102. Quasten, *Patrology*, IV.90.

DAMASUS OF ROME

It was Damasus of Rome who represented the Western point of view to the coalition of Eastern bishops coalescing behind the language of one *ousia* and three *hypostases*. In this meeting of minds, Damasus is often portrayed as less capable than his Eastern correspondents, but there is little evidence to support this caricature. Nothing that Damasus says about one substance and Three Persons, on the one hand, and one essence and three *hypostases*, on the other, is stupid.

The letters I am presently concerned with are those Damasus sent to Eastern bishops between 376 and 378. One set of letters consists of those sent to the coalition of Greek bishops led by Basil of Casarea; the other letter I cite from is the one Damasus sent to Paulinus of Antioch, criticizing the Apollinarianism of his former emissary, Vitalis. Damasus recognizes three basic kinds of heretics: Arius and Eunomius, who say that the Son and Holy Spirit are creatures; the Macedonians, about whom Damasas can say nothing more than that they are "Arius redux"; and Photinus, who has revived the error of Ebion, saying the Christ was born only of Mary. In his letters to Basil, Damasus is vehement that a Trinitarian formula of one *ousia*, three *hypostases* is unacceptable to Westerners. It is, however, Damasus' positive statements that are my concern here, although he articulates only two of the basic themes I have been following. The first is his use of power language to identify and describe the basis of unity in the Trinity. Typical of his formulae are, "the Trinity of one power, one majesty, one divinity, and substance so that their power is inseparable" and "[the] Father, Son and Holy Spirit are of one deity, one power, one figure and one substance." Note the relative lack of emphasis on "one substance"—that the conclusion of Damasus' first list is a statement that the power among the Three is inseparable. This is not a Trinitarian theology that pivots on the notion of substance.

The triumph of Damasus' person-centered, power logic Trinitarian theology occurs, of course, before and after the Council of Constantinople (381), when the Emperor Theodosius issues a proclamation from the Roman vicarate of Thessalonica, normalizing the council's decisions:

> We command that all churches shall immediately be surrendered to those bishops who confess that the Father, the Son, and the Holy Spirit are of one majesty and power [*qui unius maiestatis adque virtutis Patrem, et Filium et Spiritum sanctum confitentur*], of the same glory, and of one splendor; to those bishops . . . who affirm the concept of the Trinity by the assertion of three Persons and the unity of the Divinity.[103]

Neither *substantia* nor the Greek *ousia* are given as required norms; "one majesty and power . . . [and] three Persons" are.

---

103. Theodosian Code, July 30, 381

The second basic theme Damasus expresses lies in his pneumatology: in 368 and repeatedly thereafter Damasus speaks of the Holy Spirit being "one in power and substance" (*unius potestatis atque substantiae*)[104] with the Father and Son, and and that the Holy Spirit is "uncreated and of one majesty, one usia, and one power" (*unius majestatis, unius usiae, [atque] unius virtuti*) with the Father and the Son.[105] Damasus also explicitly speaks of the Holy Spirit as co-creator, as I would expect him to, given his otherwise well-formed, "strong" pneumatology. Related to Damasus' pneumatology is, if my theories are right, what might be called the "second-and-a-half" basic theme in Latin Nicene theology: in his letter to Paulinus attacking the improper Christology of Vitalis, Damasus sets out a number of statements about Christological anthropology. Spirit Christology is entirely absent from Damasus' articulations.[106]

RUFINUS OF SYRIA

The last text I will treat is the *De Fide*, traditionally attributed to a Rufinus who worked with Jerome in Bethlehem, who translated most of the Pauline epistles for the Vulgate, and who was entrusted by Jerome to carry his translation of *On First Principles* and some letters to Rome.[107] The first two-thirds of the work is concerned with Trinitarian theology, but a third of the work attacks Origen and an anthropology suspiciously like Augustine's in *Confessions*. Some scholars have called this Rufinus the Syrian the "father of Pelagianism."[108] Recently, however, the very existence of this Rufinus has been questioned, and the thesis has been offered that the *De Fide* was originally a Greek work, from Antioch or Palestine, that was translated, redacted, and supplemented by the author otherwise known as Ps.-Jerome.[109] I am persuaded that the recent questions require us to make judgments cautiously, but even those who hypothesized Rufinus the Syrian's influence on Pelagius' theology never claimed to be able to say anything

---

104. Damasus, *Epistle 56*, ln. 5.

105. Damasus, *Epistle 51*, lns. 19–20. See also, "perfect in power, honor, majesty and deity," as the Father and Son are (*Epistle 55*, 319).

106. Apollinarius himself occasionally used a kind of Spirit Christology: "God dwelling in a man is not a man. But spirit united to flesh is a man. Now Christ is a man, as it is said, in a special sense. Therefore he is divine Spirit united to flesh" (Apollinarius, *Recapitulation* 16 [Leitzmann, 244 lines 2–5]; and "For man is flesh and spirit according to the apostle. And this is what came about in the case of his flesh, the Word having been united to flesh in the same way as the human spirit is. For he calls us man according to the flesh. But the Lord on behalf of us is man, and therefore heavenly on account of having received the heavenly spirit as his own (1 Cor 15:47) . . ." *Tomos Synodikos* [Lietzmann, 262 lines 1–10].

107. See Jean Gribomont's overview of "Rufinus the Syrian" in Quasten, *Patrology*, for the accepted identification and description of the author of *De Fide*.

108. See, e.g., Eugene TeSelle, "Rufinus the Syrian, Caelestius, and Pelagius," *AugStud* 3 (1972): 61–65.

109. Walter Dunphy, the editor of the not-yet-published critical edition of *De Fide*, offered this opinion in a communication at the Oxford International Patristics Conference, August 2007, and repeated his thesis to this author in private conversation.

significant about his person. Perhaps (Ps.-)Rufinus *is* Ps.-Jerome: this changes nothing for my reading. However, I can say that I do not find the claim that the *De Fide* began as a Greek text originating in Antioch or Palestine convincing: the Trinitarian theology of the work is Latin in its idioms, and not Greek.[110] (For example, the author of *De Fide* argues for "common operations" on the basis of John 14:9–12 and not John 5:19.) If, after all, *De Fide* is a Greek text translated into Latin, then it is a Greek Trinitarian text that argues for a filioque-type of Trinitarian theology, which makes it a very remarkable "Greek" text, indeed! However, I do agree with a "redactional" or source account of *De Fide* to this extent: I think that chapters 52–61 (i.e., the end of the work) have a different origin than chapters 1–51. Chapters 52–61 reflect a different context of articulating Trinitarian theology than chapters 1–51, one very similar to book V of Augustine's *De Trinitate*.

One other aspect of the theology of the *De Fide* requires comment. A minor argument for the Antiocene or Palestinian provenance of the work is the fact that some features of its Trinitarian theology are like those of Theophilus of Antioch or Irenaeus. (Perhaps this resemblance was seen as a support for naming the author Rufinus *of Syria*.) The most significant point of resemblance is that (Ps.-)Rufinus identifies the Holy Spirit with the Wisdom of God, an identification that is found in Theophilus and Irenaeus (not to mention Wisdom 7). The weight of the argument is thus that the work comes out of a milieu with a tradition of identifying the Holy Spirit with Wisdom, i.e., Antioch or Palestine. The problem with this argument is, first, there is no continuous presence of Wisdom Pneumatology in Antiochene Trinitarian theology: when everyone else loses the identification, so does Antioch. Secondly, Greek authors (e.g., Origen and Athanasius) who quote Irenaeus do not pick up on his Wisdom pneumatology or his robust pneumatology generally. Thirdly, the argument requires that we can say something about the disappearance of Irenaeus' influence in the West (and we presently cannot). Finally, and after the first point the most important, how do we explain historically what happens when a theology has been unexpressed and in practice denied for a century and a half "returns"? How is it that the robust pneumatology of some authors of the late-second century "disappeared," and then something very much like their theology is discovered, rediscovered, or received? My judgment, then, is to speak of the author as (Ps.-)Rufinus (but not to write this out each time, as this would become tedious for the reader), who may or may not be the person described by scholars as Rufinus the Syrian, and that *De Fide* is a work of the first decade of the fifth century (a dating that is not denied), originally written in Latin, with no clear provenance, but resembling Latin polemical works on the Trinity in a number of ways (specified below).

Rufinus begins the *De Fide* by declaring that the "substantial Word" and "substantial Wisdom"—the Son and Holy Spirit, respectively—are "equal to God [the Father]

---

110. A similar argument that the point of origin for the *De Fide* is Antioch may be found in H. Rondet, "Rufin le Syrien et le Liber de Fide," *Augustiniana* 22 (1972): 531–9.

in all things." There is, Rufinus says, one substance and one power of the Father, Son, and Holy Spirit. The formula of "One substance and power" (*una substantia atque virtus*) appears repeatedly in the *De Fide*; it is Rufinus' usual way for describing the unity amongst the Father, Son, and Holy Spirit.[111] When he speaks of the divinity of a single Person—e.g., the Son or the Holy Spirit—Rufinus tends to refer to the "one substance" without also mentioning the "one power." (Thus Rufinus will say that "the Holy Spirit also is of the substance of God.")[112] Rufinus will also say, on at least one occasion, that the "power of the Father, Son and Holy Spirit is one and the same"[113] without also using substance language. The one time that he speaks of "three Persons" (*tres personas*),[114] Rufinus balances this description with the statement "their *nature* [*natura*] is one and the same and their divinity undivided."[115] While it is not possible to make any conclusive judgment about the role of "nature" language in Rufinus' Trinitarian theology, we can say that Rufinus never uses a formula of "three persons and one nature" or—more significant in its absence—"three persons and one substance." The language of divine unity is the formula: "one substance and power." I will have more to say below about the way Rufinus speaks of the real distinctions among the Three.

Rufinus grounds his treatment of the proposition that "the substance and the power of the Father, the Son, and the Holy Spirit are one and the same" by citing John 10:30 and John 14:9 (*De Fide*, 3). The latter verse figures especially significantly for Rufinus because the purpose of the verse is, in his opinion, "to teach us to perceive from the miracles which he performed that the Father and He [the Son] are one and the same in power and likewise in substance . . . For, in accordance with their will, their works are the same; their substance is also the same." Speaking specifically of the divinity of the Holy Spirit, Rufinus argues, "[T]he Holy Spirit also is of the same substance of God and . . . those things which God the Father does [*facit*], the same in an equal degree the Holy Spirit also does [*facit*]."[116]

Thus Rufinus restates the old Latin (i.e., going back to Tertullian) argument that the works (*opera*) that the Son performs are the same as the works the Father performs, and the identity of works reveals the identity of power and thus the identity of substance. Given the invisibility of God, Rufinus says, there is no other way to recognize divinity except through God's visible works, i.e., creation. Rufinus then cites

---

111. Something of the sense of the phrase "substance and power" is conveyed later in *De Fide* when Rufinus speaks of the creation of the angels: the angels, he says, were numerous and different from one another in their "substance and power" (Rufinus, *De Fide*, 75).

112. Rufinus, *De Fide*, 55.

113. Rufinus, *De Fide*, 61.

114. Rufinus, *De Fide*, 61.

115. Rufinus, *De Fide*, 61; emphasis added.

116. Rufinus, *De Fide*, 55.

Wisdom 13:5 and Romans 1:20,[117] the latter being a *virtus* passage that will figure strongly in Augustine's Trinitarian writings.

The principal common "work" that the Father, the Son, and the Holy Spirit perform in common is the act of creating. The key example of this common work is the creation of mankind (Gen 1:26–27). For Rufinus, the passage is manifestly one that testifies to God as Trinity because of the plural first-person in the statement by God, "Let *us* make mankind to *our* image and likeness." This is a familiar Christian reading of the Genesis 1 creation account which, once again, has a history of Latin Trinitarian application that goes back to Tertullian.

The Son's role in creating the universe is testified to at John 1:3, "All things were made through Him" (*Omnia per ipsum facta sunt*): "For if all things were made through him and if in respect to all things there is also a beginning, the Word himself is the source and cause both of beginning itself and then of everything after the beginning of time" (*De fide*, 9). The scriptural passages that Rufinus brings forward as testimonies to the Holy Spirit's creative activity are predominently Wisdom passages; as already noted, Rufinus identifies Wisdom with the Holy Spirit. One testimony that Rufinus quotes is Psalm 103:24, "How manifold are your works [*opera*], oh Lord! In wisdom you have wrought them all."[118] This quotation from the psalm brings together key Trinitarian doctrines of Rufinus'—that Wisdom (i.e., the Holy Spirit) creates, and that the *creation* of the cosmos is a kind of *work* (*opera*). "Therefore," Rufinus summarizes,

> we are taught not to speak of three distinct substances: the Father, the Son, and the Holy Spirit, nor to speak of *powers and activities* distinct in turn from one another [*Ideo autem docemur non tres dicere substantias segregatas: Patrem et Filium et Spiritum Sanctum, neque potestates atque virtutes a semet invicem separatas*], because God, who creates all things through His Word and Wisdom, is one.[119]

The declaration in John 14:10 that the Father was *in* the Son and the Son was *in* the Father gave Phoebadius the opportunity to provide for the correct understanding of "from the Father" *X from X* language. Rufinus likewise puts a great deal of emphasis on the Johannine testimony that the Son is *in* the Father (and the testimony of 1 Cor 2:10–11 that the Spirit is *in* the Father). The Son "is *in* the Father, not as in a place, for his substance is not encompassed by limits, but as the word [is] in the mind [*sensum*]."[120] Thus begins Rufinus' extended attempt to offer a way of thinking of how the Son and Holy Spirit are *in* God the Father. The initial titling (at the first line of *De Fide*) of the Son as Word and the Holy Spirit as Wisdom provides Rufinus with his

---

117. "For from the greatness and the beauty of created things their original author is clearly seen"; and, "For since the creation of the world his invisible attributes are clearly seen—his everlasting power and divinity—being clearly understood through the things that are made," respectively.

118. Rufinus, *De Fide*, 63.

119. Rufinus, *De Fide*, 63.

120. Rufinus, *De Fide*, 5; emphasis added.

point of departure: "I call the Father the 'mind' so that we may comprehend how the Father is in the Son and the Son in the Father."[121] If the Father is understood as "mind," and the Son as "word" or "reason," and the Holy Spirit as "wisdom," both of which exist *in* the mind, then we have a way of understanding what "existing *in* the Father" means. Rufinus concludes:

> [We say that] the Holy Spirit is of the same substance and power as in the Father and the Son, just as we say that the wisdom [*sapientia*] is at the same time in the word [*verbum*]. Furthermore, we say that the Father and the Son are of the same substance and same power as in the Spirit and that, just as the mind and the word, these are not distinct from wisdom.[122]

We thus have two related but distinct arguments from Rufinus, each one emphasizing a different part of the Johannine statement that the Son and Holy Spirit are in the Father. First, the Father, Son, and Holy Spirit perform the same works because they have the same power and substance; and second, to be the same "in power and substance" is to coexist in a manner similar to the way in which word/reason and wisdom coexist in the mind.

At this point in his argument, Rufinus introduces his description of the real distinctions among the Three. This first description happens *en passant*, and is offered by Rufinus as an elaboration of his psychological exemplum of the Trinity: from mind and word/reason arises wisdom, and although the three coexist they are distinct as cause and effect(s); mind and reason beget wisdom: "Therefore, the Holy Spirit is of the Father and the Son, because he is neither the Father nor the Son."[123] The Holy Spirit proceeds from the Father and the Son. If the Holy Spirit lacked a causal relationship with either the Father or the Son (i.e., if the Holy Spirit was not caused by either the Father or the Son) his distinction from either would be lost. In the simplicity of God, non-identity is due to the relationship of cause and effect, source and product. In the simplicity of the mind, non-identity is due to the relationship of cause and effect. (As I said earlier, if *De Fide* is a Greek text translated into Latin, then it is a Greek Trinitarian writing with a filioque theology.)

Later in *De Fide*, Rufinus restates his doctrine of the eternal irreducibility of the Three in language more reminiscent of the monarchian controversies: "For the Father, not ceasing to be the Father, always is; the Son, continuing uninterruptedly to be the Son, always is; and the Holy Spirit, who never becomes the Father or the Son, always is."[124] Whether "uninterrupted and irreducible identity" constitutes the definition of "person" is an open and probably useless question to ask of Rufinus: he certainly never goes so far explicitly, nor does he seem to feel any need to do so. Rufinus has a word for

121. Rufinus, *De Fide*, 5.
122. Rufinus, *De Fide*, 61.
123. Rufinus, *De Fide*, 61.
124. Rufinus, *De Fide*, 61.

what is Three in God: person. He has an idea of how the Three are distinct from one another: causal relation. And he has a clear statement that the Three are eternally ir-reducible and unconvertible: they are each always themselves and not another. Whatever work the idea "person" is thought by Rufinus to do in his Trinitarian theology, providing the conceptual grounding for "real distinctions" is not one of them.

My treatment of Rufinus' theology of the Holy Spirit can be relatively brief because it is already clear that he has a "high" pneumatology:[125] Rufinus says repeatedly that the Holy Spirit has one and the same substance and power as the Father and Son; the Holy Spirit performs the same *opera* as the Father and Son; and the Holy Spirit is creator just as the Father and Son are. Some of Rufinus' scriptural evidence that the Holy Spirit is creator turns upon his identification of the Spirit with Wisdom, the Wisdom spoken of and who speaks in books such as Proverbs and Wisdom of Solomon. However, not all of Rufinus' scriptural evidence that the Holy Spirit is creator draws upon Wisdom literature. The key prooftext that I have followed throughout this account of Latin Nicenes of the late-fourth century is Psalm 33: following the exegesis of this psalm provides the means to recognize Spirit Christology in an author,[126] and to determine whether the author regards the Holy Spirit as co-creator with the Word–Son. Rufinus' statement on the full divinity of the Holy Spirit and his role as co-creator is clear and vigorous:

> The prophet David also teaches that the power [*virtus*] of the Father, the Son, and the Holy Spirit is one and the same when he says: "By the Word of the Lord the heavens were made; by the Spirit of his mouth all their hosts."[127]

It is worth noting one last distinctive doctrine in Rufinus' pneumatology. Rufinus cites the Lucan (11:20) passage in which Jesus says that he casts out demons by the "*finger* of God"—and compares it to the Matthean (12:28) passage which has it that Jesus casts out demons by the "*Spirit* of God." From these two analogous passages, Rufinus sees that the *Finger* of God is the *Spirit* of God. He concludes:

> When our Lord said this, he clearly taught us to believe that the substance of the Father and the Holy Spirit is one and the same [*unam eandemque*

---

125. The fact that the *De Fide* nevers refers to "Macedonians" or Pneumatomachoi has led previous scholars (e.g., Garnier) to wonder if it ought to be dated prior to that set of arguments (i.e., 362), but other internal evidence strongly indicates a date near or after the turn of the century. We are left simply to puzzle over Rufinus' silence. See Rondet's discussion of this question in "Rufin le Syrien et le Liber de Fide," 537.

126. The other distinctive indicator of whether a Spirit Christology is present in a work is the author's understanding of who the "Spirit" is in Luke 1:35–36. Rufinus says (*De fide* 1), "And that the Word, the one and only God, was born at the end of ages of the Holy Spirit and of Mary"—which suggests that he understands the Holy Spirit not to be the Word himself, although by itself this lone remark would not provide a decisive judgment one way or another.

127. *De Fide*, 8; slightly altered.

substantia], since the finger is also of the same substance [*euisdem substantia*] as he whose finger it is.[128]

Rufinus' pneumatology is perfectly in line those of Faustinus and Niceta; just as important is the fact that Rufinus clearly felt the need to elaborate on the full divinity of the Holy Spirit and to offer what we will call a "pneumatological logic."

CONCLUSION

Latin Nicenes made statements about the Holy Spirit being one in substance with the Father and Son out of their own resources, and earlier than Greek Nicenes were able to say the same thing. However, development or change in doctrine was not dependent upon simply one new insight or articulation (viz., "the Holy Spirit is one in substance . . ."), it is dependent upon a constellation of changes, some of which may not seem directly related initially (e.g., Spirit Christology related to Pneumatology?). Such constellated changes included shifts in exegesis of key Scripture passages (or passages that don't seem key but turn out to be).

The fact that Latin Nicenes in the 360s could say "the Holy Spirit is one in substance with the Father and Son" is noteworthy, and an interesting new statement by them—but it did not in itself result in a new and stronger pneumatology until other changes occurred, as well. I have pointed to Spirit Christology and the exegetical questions that accompany it as being decisive. There may be other "sympathetic dynamics" at work as well that I did not observe. Just as importantly, there is a partially different set of constellated issues at work in Greek theology that does not figure in Latin Nicene doctrinal awareness and development. The East, for example, faced Eunomius, and countering Eunomius shaped Greek Trinitarian theology, while the West did not: it faced Sirmium, a history of strong monarchianism read as Christological problems, and a vigorous Spirit Christology. The West did acknowledge the full divinity of the Holy Spirit via its own resources, but its own "resources"—i.e., the Latin tradition—contained a strong low Pneumatology element in Lactantius and even in Novatian. The West simply had different problems than the East, both in the deposit of its doctrinal tradition(s) and in the crises it faced.

---

128. *De Fide*, 4. Pieter W. van der Horst makes the interesting observation that while key targumim—Neofiti, Ps.-Jonathan, and Onkelos—all replace the words "finger of God" in Exod 8:15—Moses's and Aaron's confrontation with the court magicians resulting in the plague of "gnats"—these same targumim keep the expression "finger of God" at Exod 31:18—God writing the law upon the tablets of stone—and at Deuty 9:10—Moses relating the same event. (It should be noted that while the ancient targumim and the MT/JPS English translation of Deut 9:10 keep the wording "the finger of God," the RSV drops it.) Horst also provides a very helpful but admittedly not exhaustive list of patristic authors besides Rufinus who cite Exod 31:18 or Deut 9:10 or who identified "finger of God" with the Holy Spirit. See Horst, "Finger of God"; for the targumim discussion, 94; for the patristic authors, 103n47. The JPS/RSV comparison is my own.

I have identified certain elements, tropes, or idioms in Latin Trinitarian discourse, most of which are typical of fourth-century Latin Nicene Trinitarian theology. In this category, I place the inverse relationship between Spirit Christology and Pneumatology, the interest in *X from X* doctrinal formulae, two-nativities theology, and the argument that "works reveals nature." If these elements are mapped out chronologically, then two groups or stages of fourth-century Latin Nicene theology appear. In the first group, we see an association of doctrines of Spirit Christology, a low pneumatology, and a strong interest in *X from X*-type Trinitarian statements, due to both Nicaea and the Second Creed of Sirmium. Western Nicene theology with these traits I call "Latin neo-Nicene" Trinitarian theology. In the second group or stage of doctrines, there is no Spirit Christology, there is a high Pneumatology, and there is no particular interest in *X from X*-type Trinitarian statements. Western Nicene theology with these traits I call "Latin pro-Nicene" Trinitarian theology. Two-nativities theology appears predominately, but not exclusively, in neo-Nicene Trinitarian theology, and the "works reveal nature" argument is consistent all along the Latin tradition, though at different times it stands in different relationships with substance or power logics. It is also true that in neo-Nicene theology, it tends to be the Son who is identified as God's own "Power," while in pro-Nicene theology, God's own Power tends to be the power shared amongst the Three. Phoebadius, Gregory of Elvira, and Potamius are neo-Nicene; Niceta, Damasus, and Rufinus the Syrian are pro-Nicene.

I do not think that on the whole Westerners who knew Greek theology were guilty of failing to appreciate its subtleties: I think that those few who knew of it understood it reasonably well, and many just didn't like it. (The exception to this feeling would be the writings of Cyril of Jerusalem.)[129] Latin theologians such as Damasus had a reasonable case when they said that claiming that "*hypostasis* was different from *ousia*" was nonsense philosophically. What happened in the East around distinguishing and contrasting *ousia* and *hypostasis* was never really driven by the pressures of philosophical consistency: it was hatched out of convention, out of the meeting and eventual merging of two theological traditions of God-talk. You really had to be there to get it, and even then the conjoining of these two traditions never found canonical expression in the fourth century. Greek theology never endorsed in an ecumenical creed the distinction between *ousia* and *hypostasis*: it is not there in Constantinople (381), and on these grounds Constantinople was no different from Nicaea, and Nicaea was filled with expressions Latins could work with. The Western articulation of the resolution in 380–382 is both more consistent with contemporary Latin Trinitarian theology and more expressive of the new insights than the Creed of Constantinople is consistent with contemporary Greek theology and expressive of the new insights. When the proclamation *Episcopis tradi* specified that the Catholic faith believed in "one power . . . and three persons," Damasus could look at Theodosius' decree and

---

129. See the theologies of Zeno, Niceta, and Rufinus of Aquileia.

say, "This is exactly what I believe," which is something that Gregory Nazianzus, for example, could never say about the Creed of Constantinople.

It is said that the letter from the Council in Constantinople in 382 written to Damasus and Western bishops was "intended to be compatible with Western statements."[130] The doctrinal summary begins with: "according to . . . [our] faith there is one Godhead [*theotes*], Power [*dunamis*], and essence [*ousia*] of the Father, and of the Son and of the Holy Spirit; the dignity being equal, and the majesty being equal in three perfect *hypostases*, i.e., three perfect *prosopa*."[131] Notice that power is mentioned before essence. All Western Nicenes used a Latin word similar in meaning to *theotēs* to speak about the unity of the Trinity (e.g., *deitas*, *divinitas*), but there is little that they could argue from it. Most Western Nicenes used the Latin equivalents of *dunamis* to speak about the unity of the Trinity and to argue for it. Many Western Nicenes used *substantia* to speak about divine unity, and some used it to argue for the unity of the Trinity. The letter equates *hypostases* with *prosopa*, implicitly allowing that either could be used. If the letters of Damasus to Basil and the Eastern bishops are accurate, then that Greek party's refusal to allow any word but *hypostasis* for the formula "three what?" ended with either Basil's death or the council in 381. Damasus and Latin theologies of "one power, three persons" won.

---

130. Ayres, *Nicaea and Its Legacy*, 258; slightly modified.
131. Theodoret, *Eccl. hist.* 5.9.

Chapter 6

Marius Victorinus

A Non-Athanasian Latin Trinitarian Logic

INTRODUCTION

THE INSEPARABILITY OF THE doctrinal content of the Council of Nicaea (325) and the doctrinal content of the term *homoousios*, is a well-established fact for virtually all accounts of "The development in the fourth century of the Creed of Nicaea, 325, as a doctrinal norm or canon for Trinitarian theology."[1] It is clear for most scholarship that Athanasius was the driving force behind equating the doctrinal content of the Creed of Nicaea with the doctrinal content of the term *homoousios*. The period during which theologians of Nicene sympathies regarded *homoousios* as a kind of doctrinal litmus test were largely the years of Athanasius' greatest authority in the West.[2] But it is also clear that not every theologian during the late-fourth century thought *homoousios* was a necessary marker of a "Nicene" theology; this is true especially in the last quarter of the century. One important but unrecognized consequence of these axiomatic judgments is the presumption that the origin and content of any Latin *homoousios* theology between 357 and 376—the years Western Nicene theology, for all intents and purposes, may be said to have been born (again)—is assumed to be "Athanasian."[3]

1. Barnes, "Fourth Century as Trinitarian Canon," 47–67.

2. If the story of Potamius' "conversion" (back) to Nicene theology is true, then the "Western" Potamius writes to Athanasius to learn what *homoousios* means. However, the story of Potamius' conversion has, until recently, been received by scholars with strong skepticism. The anti-*homoousios* Potamius, nominally bishop of Lisbon (his signature appears on the lists of most of the synodal creeds produced during 357–60, so he spent little time in far-away Lisbon). In my chapter on "Other Latin Nicenes," I include the letters to Athanasius attributed to him, but if his conversion to *homoousios* theology is true, and those letters are by Potamius of Lisbon, then they were written after 361, and Victorinus would know him only as what he then was, an architect of Sirmium (357) and an opponent of *ousia*-based Trinitarian doctrine.

3. For an excellent overview of the alliances and animosities in the Trinitarian theologies of Marius Victorinus, Phoebadius, Hilary of Poitiers, Sirmium (357), and Basil of Ancyra (358), see Weedman,

It is, therefore, not easy, much less conventional, to postulate the existence of any *homoousios* theology of that era with a source other than the "Athanasian" trajectory.[4]

If one followed this axiom, then one would expect Latin Nicene theology to follow a certain form. Such a form would lead to a set of expectations beyond a simple declaration that the original and continuing meaning of the creed (and especially of the term homoousios) was opposition to Arius and "Arianism." Such Western Nicenes would also think, conversely, that contemporary anti-*homoousios* theology is anti-Nicene and "Arian" in its character. It would be their understanding that documents relating to Arianism between 318 and 333 have a defining place in anti-*homoousios* theology of 357 and later, and what Arians believed before the council they would continue to believe more than twenty-five years later. Some such Nicenes might go so far as to regard as Arian and anti-Nicene (anti-*homoousios*) every council in the previous thirty years that failed to speak of *homoousios*. For these Nicenes, the genealogical continuity between the Arianism of 318–25 and the 357–60 debates is so strong that the crises c. 357–61 are unintelligible without reference to the Arianism of 318–325. Many scholars have argued that Athanasius is the architect of a set of judgments such as these, that these judgments constitute Nicene theology, and that, twenty to thirty years later, Nicene theology existed only as Athanasius presented it.[5] I do not recognize the accuracy or precision of this axiom. My central claim in this article is that Victorinus provides us a strong *homoousios* Trinitarian theology that is entirely independent of Athanasius' promotion of a Nicaea theology shaped by anti-Arianism.[6] My argument is divided into two main sections. The first shows that the temporal location of Victorinus' *Trinitarian doctrine* in the period between 357 and 361, and that it owes nothing to Athanasius, or to Athanasius' genealogical approach to the controversy. The second section expounds Victorinus' *Trinitarian logic*, showing it to depend on Porphyry.

PART 1

Victorinus entered the church in either 355 or 357, baptized in Rome by the same Simplicianus who would figure so prominently in Augustine's *Confessions*.[7] His own

---

Trinitarian Theology, 63–73. What Weedman misses is the Porphyrian background of Victorinus emphasizing "Life" as a title for the Second Person, but otherwise Victorinus is nicely placed within the context of Latin Nicenes and the homoiousians.

4. I include Marcellus of Ancyra within what I here call the Athanasian trajectory of *homoousios* theology. If the subject of this chapter were Western theology of the 330s and 340s, the opposite would be applicable: for that era, it would be more accurate to say that Athanasius' theology belonged to a broad Marcellan trajectory. See Parvis, *Marcellus of Ancyra*.

5. The proper expression would be "only within the intellectual structures and boundaries in doctrine only as Athanasius re-presented it and presented it (in himself)."

6. See Henry, "'Adversus Arium' of Marius Victorinus," 42–55.

7. Luise Abramowski, "Marius Victorinus, Porphyrius und die römischcen Gnostiker," *ZNTW* 74 (1983): 108–28.

understanding of the Trinity, articulated as early as 357, is that the Father, Son, and Holy Spirit were each fully divine, a *homoousios* Trinity. He recognized the alternative conceptions of the Trinity offered by those who condemned *ousia*-based theology. Victorinus had access to the dossier of documents circulating from the earliest stages of the controversy leading up to Nicaea, but more importantly, he had the "live" spectacle of a controversy being played in front of him in the Synod of Sirmium (357) and the Synod of Ancyra (358). Most scholars tend to trace the beginning of a new sympathy for Nicaea to the Councils of Seleucia and Arimini of 359 and Ariminium of 359 (culminating in Constantinople, 360); but Victorinus argues for *homoousios* in 357 and 358 simply on the basis of Sirmium. Victorinus exemplifies a Latin Nicene theology that is already turning to *homoousios* and Nicaea before the councils of 359 and 360.

When Victorinus enters the controversy c. 356/7, he regards the controversy of 318–25 as a foreshadowing (with the emphasis on "shadow"); the real confrontation, present now, is with those who reject essence-based Trinitarian theology altogether, and those who use but distort *ousia*-based theology, and finally, those who prefer other forms of Trinitarian discourse (e.g., Second Antioch).[8] For Victorinus, the theology of *homoousios* was formulated (or resurrected?) specifically against homoiousian, heterousian, and homoian theologies. He acknowledges that approximately one hundred and fifty years earlier, the church had allowed the use of homoiousian Trinitarian theology,[9] but he held that Nicaea had signaled that that leniency could no longer be indulged because of the errors to which it led. In short, for Victorinus the fight in 357–361 is between homoousians, homoiousians, and those who disallow *ousia*

8. Gabrielle Winkler has argued, on the basis of the creeds produced by the Synods of Antioch in 341 and 345, as well as by Sirmium (351), that the Antiochene Church stretching north towards Armenia had in place a "one *dunamis*" Trinitarian theology that taught the equivalent of a "one *ousia*" Trinitarian doctrine. Each of these creeds has the phrase *una dunamis* in the list of terms common to Father and Son. Each creed contains echoes of 1 Cor 1:24 and Heb 1:3, two of the texts regularly "constellated" in Nicene New Testament polemical exegesis. (Note that the list does not include First Antioch 341, which lacks the terminology of the others.) That the "equivalent" of *homoousios* would exist in other ecclesiastical languages—such as Syriac—is a rational proposition. What pre-empts the possibility is the fact that Athanasius insisted on a *homoousios* creed; scholars have never, to my knowledge, followed out the concept of language "equivalent" to *homoousios* functioning at this time in the churches. Athanasian Nicene theology did not admit of conceptual and verbal equivalents (although the truly catholic phrase "one power" could not be repressed; after Sirmium, "one power" became a widely recognized equivalent of *una substantia*. For Winkler, see "Antiochene Synods"; here, 282–85.

9. Victorinus may be thinking of a synod in Antioch (268) which made use of *ousia*, and which the Homoiosians invoked in 359 as the authority for their own use of *homoiousios*. Victorinus' judgment on the term can be inconsistent: at one point he can regard "*homoiousios* as defined over-against *homoousios*, but at another he can speak of *homoousios* of Nicaea as intended to ban the use of *ho-moiousios*. In any case, he regards Nicaea's use of homo*ousios*, Sirmium's banning of *ousia*-laguage, Basil's use of homoi*ousios*, and Eunomius' use of heter*ousios* as four confrontations over the use of *ousia* language amongst theological "parties" who all recognize *ousia* as a *bona fide* theological term.

ontology altogether or except when related to a dominant logic of the "will" (this is Candidus).[10]

It is vital to understand the very tenuous links that tie Victorinus directly to Nicaea.[11] He refers to Nicaea only four times: none of these give us any evidence that is crucial. He also never mentions Athanasius, and thus can show no signs of an alliance with him.[12] He does know something of the years between 325 and 357: he explicitly condemns the doctrines of Marcellus, Photinus, and patripassianism. He also knows exegetical arguments offered by different parties from 343 to 358. Victorinus regards *homoousios* as the key term for Trinitarian orthodoxy,[13] but the Father-Son relationship is not invoked by Victorinus as decisive (or even central) for the transmission of divine nature. Victorinus' *homoousios* doctrine of Trinitarian unity is a logic of "triadic mutual co-inherence."[14] He consistently includes the Holy Spirit as *homoousios*,[15] and

10. Edwards's recent characterization of the conceptual idioms of the fourth century is very important. "When Christians of the fourth century undertook to defend the Nicene Creed by philosophical reasoning, the terms of greatest moment to them were *ousia* and *dunamis* ('*being*' and '*power*' or *potentiality*), both of which occur only sporadically in Plato. To Christians, they [the terms] were scriptural, but the meaning grafted onto them by all parties to theological controversy in this epoch, are derived, by way of Plotinus and Porphyry, from the Aristotelian lexicon" (Mark Edwards, *Aristotle and Early Christian Thought* [London: Routledge, 2020], 78).

11. At *Adv. Ar.* 2.12 (SC 68.430; Clark 216), Victorinus gives us his account of the Nicene faith: "We believe in God the Father almighty and in his Son the only begotten Jesus Christ our Lord, God from God, light from Light, *homoousios* . . . This is the faith of Nicaea, this is the faith of the apostles, this is the Catholic faith. In this way the Arians, all the heretics, are vanquished."

12. There are two names who are conspicuously absent from the *Adv. Ar.* and, given the timing, this absence needs to be acknowledged: Athanasius and Aetius. That these two important players in the controversy at the time should both be ignored (or unknown!) is startling. When scholars say that Victorinus is unaware of the controversy as a whole, they are referring—at the least—to Victorinus' apparent lack of knowledge of Athanasius' *De Decretis* (350), and to his ignorance of the recent origin of term *anomoios* (356/7). Victorinus seems unaware that Basil's Council of 358 was directed at Aetius' in-circulation brand of "two essences."

13. See his densely-packed statement of the unity of substance and power between Father and Son at *Adv. Ar.* 1.9. There is not a single page in the *Adv. Ar.* which does not include at least one "Therefore they are *homoousios*."

14. See *Adv. Ar.* 1.13–14. The fundamental principle of Victorinus' Trinitarian logic is what is called the "triadic analogy"—although it would be just as accurate to say that the fundamental logic of Victorinus' Trinitarian logic is John 10:30 and John 14:9–10. We have difficulty with the straightforward assertion that a constellation of Scripture passages could constitute a "fundamental logic," but that is our hermeneutical problem, not a patristic immaturity. In any case, a "Trinitarian logic of [a noetic] triadic analogy" is a statement using a technical vocabulary that requires some context for us to understand its meaning. For our purposes, the best introduction to the idea of a "noetic triad" may be found in Peter Manchester, "The Noetic Triad in Plotinus, Marius Victorinus, and Augustine," in R. Wallis and J. Bregman, eds., *Neoplatonism and Gnosticism* (Albany: SNUY Press, 1992), 207–22." Manchester begins by remarking upon the scholarly habit of "a degree of complicity between the progressive 'metaphysicalizing' of the doctrine [of the Trinity] and the emergence of triadic conceptual schemes in the new Platonism of Plotinus and his successors." Manchester's utility is immediately apparent.

15. It is easy to find passages where Victorinus says that the Holy Spirit is *homoousios* with the Father and the Son. See, for example, *Adv. Ar.* 1.8 (SC 68.206; Clark 100): "[F]or just as the Son is from

he has a positive understanding of the Holy Spirit as feminine.[16] Holding to these positions distinguishes him from Athanasius, and from his Latin predecessors. Although he seemingly has no knowledge of pre-357 conciliar controversies over *homoousios*, he is well-versed in the controversies of 357–60 East and West; he knows the three most important synods of these years (Sirmium, 357; Rimini, 359; Constantinople, 360). He knows about many of the key personalities "flourishing" during those dates, as well as the theological parties beginning to form by aligning themselves with one of the three councils against the other two.

There is much more than can be said about the distinction between Victorinus' account of the controversy and that of Athanasius'. According to Athanasius, a council in Nicaea of 318 bishops was called by the emperor in 325 to produce a creed that would put a halt to the theology of Arius and all Arians (for example, Eusebius of Nicomedia). The creed contained an unprecedented term, *homoousios*, which was intended to convey the doctrine that the Son was not a creature, but that he was begotten (not created) from the Father, and thus the same in essence of the Father. By contrast, Victorinus speaks of *three hundred* bishops meeting in Nicaea "forty years before" 357, in order to (re-)establish the normative place *homoousios* had had in Trinitarian theology until some began to champion the term *homoiousios* (a term which had some small circulation in the late-second or third centuries). Victorinus never mentions Athanasius or any of his writings, in any context at all: there is no physical evidence that he knew of Athanasius or associated the Trinitarian use of *homoousios* with any one theologian in particular. It was the heritage of the Great Church.[17] Unlike Athanasius, Victorinus does not regard the term *homoousios* as unusual or as needing special defense; his judgment is that the creed of 325 normalized *ousia*-based Trinitarian theological speculation, and as such it remained in place until 357, when bishops meeting at Sirmium rejected all *ousia*-based Trinitarian theology; *homoousios*, in particular. While rejecting *ousia*-based theology, the effect of Sirmium was nonetheless to bring into the debate a doctrine of the two separate *ousia* of the Father and of the Son. This was the teaching represented by Eunomius—but Victorinus saw the homoiousians (Basil of Ancyra) as little else than Anomians (Eunomius).

The threats to Nicene Trinitarian theology that Victorinus perceive come, first, from the attack on *homoousios* theology in the Synod of Sirmium (357), and secondly,

---

the bosom of the Father and 'in the bosom' of the Father, so the Spirit is from within the Son. The three are therefore *homoousioi* and on that account in all three there is one God." However, Victorinus' pneumatology is not, for all that, an easy doctrine to follow or give an account of, and his doctrine deserves careful examination.

16. See Manchester, "Noetic Triad in Plotinus," 217. A doctrine of a "feminine Holy Spirit" is often brought forth by scholars as arguing for the influence of the *Chaldean Oracles*. See Ruth Majercik, *The Chaldean Oracles, Text, Translation and Commentary* (Leiden: Brill, 1989). For the significance of the *Oracles* for fourth century Trinitarian theology, see Dillon, "Logos and Trinity." Such examples also make it clear that a "feminine Holy Spirit" is not *by itself* proof of the influence of Syriac theology.

17. See Victorinus, *Adv. Ar.* IA.28.

from the "homoiousian" theology promulgated by Basil of Ancyra's council in 358.[18] Victorinus' argument for *homoousios* begins by recognizing an obvious propriety of the term for the subject rather than any perceived need to argue defensively from the unusual, even problematic, status of the term (the second seems more typical in the East and is thought to have been carried West by Athanasius and Marcellus).[19] For Victorinus, the "present" nature of the crisis of anti-*homoousios* that he faces is expressed in contemporary documents, including two letters from Candidas, a contemporary Neoplatonic Christian who was anti-Nicene and anti-*homoousios* (although neither *homoousios* nor Nicaea are referred to).[20]

Against this background, it is no surprise that while Victorinus' book is entitled *Against the Arians*, Arius' theology does not dominate, but appears only as quotations from Arius' "Letter to Eusebius." *Against the Arians*, book I, arises out of Victorinus' response to Eusebius' letter, yet as Victorinus' writing in the text progresses, one can see the genre of his writing shifting from a polemically motivated response to the dossier's letters to an independent "exposition of *homoousios*" theology. The doctrines that he specifically attacks in this case are those of "first generation," pre-Nicaea Arians.[21] But, as has been pointed out many times, Candidus' theology in his *First Letter*

18. I am comparing Victorinus' Trinitarian theology to other "early" Latin Nicenes—e.g., Phoebadius, Gregory of Elvira—who wrote against the Blasphemy of 357 or Rimini (359). I limit my description of Victorinus' theology to the pre-360 part of his *Against Arius*. "Dating" the four books of the *Adv. Ar.* is a judgment identifying which anti-*homoousios* text he is writing against—not a difficult task given that his early works regularly cite the texts to which he objects. We can add to the evidence provided by "explicitly opposed text" to changes in the kinds of arguments he makes in a book, each with varying preferred terminology, which mark out *Adv. Ar.* 3 and 4 from the earlier books and from each other. In this study, I consider almost entirely *Adv. Ar.* 1 and 2.

19. Logan, "Marcellus of Ancyra."

20. See Thomas A. Kopecek, *A History of Neo-Arianism*, 2 vols. (Cambridge MA: Philadelphia Patristic Foundation, 1979), 176–88, for the character of Homoiousian, Eunomian, and Homoian theology in 358–60. The Council of Sirmium of 357 was decisively important for the course of the *ousia* controversy: it was in the wake of the 357 controversy that theological "parties" began to define themselves in relation to the same "technical" term, *ousia*, and to distinguish one faction from another through the use of the spectrum of *ousia*-modifying adjectives—such as *same*, *like*, *different*, *like in will*, etc. This terminology served for the purpose of theological "load bearing" by providing a loose logic and a set of terms which characterized (not quite defined, but more than described) Trinitarian theologies considered as a "whole" rather than as simply competing exegeses of sets of constellated scriptural texts, aligned repetitiously to "signify" a theology as a whole. I believe that this is a significant development not just in Christian self-definition, but in Christian "development of doctrine." It was un- or post-rabbinic. The Christian way of exegeting controversial scriptural passages was to offer alternate "logics"—not necessarily found in Scripture—which produced different interpretations. This was not the way the rabbis were beginning to organize Jewish doctrine in the *Talmud*. Leading up and into the summer and fall of 359, Easterners (principally) defined their theologies by positioning themselves vis-à-vis the word *ousia* and relations between existents (the Son, the Father) cast in terms of comparisons of the *ousia*, and to a lesser extent, in terms of aetiological relations to God's will (e.g., "the Son is the effect of God's will").

21. I imagine (and it is no more than such) that the letters Victorinus translated were part of the aforementioned dossiers on Arius (and Arianism) held by the bishop of Rome, and originally obtained from either Marcellus or Athanasius (probably Marcellus) in 341, when they both were in the city during their exile. We cannot speculate whether twenty years after the fact, "oral histories" of the

to Victorinus contains little that resembles the early Arian language with which we are familiar, and for that reason it is regarded by many scholars as a piece written by Victorinus himself in an Arian voice. Regardless of its source, Candidus' first letter to Victorinus is a good representative statement of anti-Nicene theology articulated in the language of the late 350s (I avoid taking a view on the question of whether or not it is a construct by Victorinus; the question is unanswerable and makes no difference to my argument).[22] The *Second Letter to Victorinus* by Candidus consists almost entirely of extracts from genuinely Arian documents (including a letter by Arius) of the first generation. And yet, through the vast majority of this book, Victorinus condemns Basil of Ancyra and the council of 358 as Eunomian, and in 360 he refers to Homoians "showing themselves" as Arian because their common beliefs with the Eunomians are revealed (no ontological relationships between the essences).[23] Victorinus thus knows of Eunomius by name and that he has a theology of "different essences." Victorinus regards homoiousians (Basil of Ancyra) as functionally Eunomians. (Victorinus refers to this theology as the product of Eunomius.) He connects Basil of Ancyra to Eunomius, which seems reductionist (inverted) to us,[24] but from the perspective of evaluating competing *ousia*-based Trinitarian theologies it makes perfect sense: if the Son's essence was "like" the Father's essence, then it was not the same essence as the Father's: it was a different essence. Even if we were to describe the Son's essence as *like* the Father's except for *one* feature, then (restated) if the Father's essence is called "N," then the Son's was N-1, that is: possessing the same properties as the Father's "N" essence except for one feature, then the Son's essence was "N-1," which means it is a different

---

visits in Rome of Marcellus and Athanasius were still in the church's common memory in Italy, but in the case of Athanasius, it is likely that the memory of his visit(s) were still alive, given that Athanasius himself had not yet died and was still busily writing treatises against the Arians. At the end of the 350s, Athanasius and Hilary independently wrote their *On the Council* (*De Synodis*), in which each give an account of the important episcopal councils of the preceding decades convened to deal with continuing controversies after Nicaea. See Gustave Bardy, "L'Occident et les documents de la controverse arienne," *Revue des sciences religieuses* 20 (1940): 28–63.

22. The most important point is that God is unbegotten, which means the essence of God cannot reproduce itself. Candidus' logic is self-contained in its own porphyrian way. Otherwise, Candidus sounds very much like Eunomius in his *Apology*, although he knows about a *tonos* model of Trinity production, something which doesn't show up in any Anomian works; and finally, of all the models of "God generating" the one most criticized by Candidus is "ray" or "emission" imagery, such as based on Heb 1:3. Such an "emission"-model or a "ray"-model coincidentally happens to be Athanasius' strongest argument in his nearly contemporary *Third Oration*.

23. For a study of anti-Nicene theology in the West, I emphasize the importance of Michel Meslin, *Les Ariens d'Occident 335–430* (Paris Editions du Seuil, 1967). Meslin allows one to escape thinking of Western anti-Nicene theologians as "Arians after Arius who did their theology in Latin" (as it sometimes seems Bishop Hanson regarded them). As will become clear in the following Augustine-related chapters, there were many important doctrinal features of Latin anti-Nicenes (more properly known as Homoians).

24. Victorinus' mention of Eunomius in 357/8 is not only the *first* report of Eunomius—it is most likely the first accurate description of his theology to emerge (and disappear).

essence.[25] If Eunomius' *ousia*-centered theology temporarily fell victim to 357, that would be nothing more than a case of being hoisted by your own petard (from which Aetius would suffer directly). Basil of Ancyra attacks Eunomius before 360; Basil of Caesarea attacks Eunomius shortly after 360. Basil of Caesarea's star begins to rise as Basil of Ancyra's declines.[26]

As I will show in the second half of this essay, Victorinus' own *homoousios*-based Trinitarian theology is based upon a Porphyrian understanding of a triadic Trinitarian theology, the logic of which itself centered upon *homoousios*. He supports and develops his theology with New Testament prooftexts that are, in the 350s, used by his contemporary Nicene theologians. However, as a genre his writing is more of an exposition of *homoousios* theology than a polemic defending *homoousios*. The point of his "polemic" is to insist that *homoousios* gives us a strong understanding of the mutual indwelling of the Three. It is necessary to speak of God in terms of *ousia* because otherwise we would understate the full divinity of the Three (as the heresies Victorinus catalogues illustrates). The conclusions of his arguments or demonstrations are to "Q.E.D. *homoousios*" not to "Q.E.D. Nicaea." In short, all that he understands from the New Testament he understands because

> If the Three are *homoousios* then the following must be true: a given passage, properly understood, tells us of the common life of the Trinity . . . In this way we confess that these Three are together, in this way we confess that they are one and one God, *homoousios*, and always together, Father and Son and Holy Spirit, and that Jesus Christ is the Son of God by an ineffable power and inexpressible begetting, being Logos with God, image and form and character and reflection of the Father and the power and wisdom of God, through which God appears and is made known[*Et isto huius modi modo et simul confitemur esse haec tria et isto quod unium et unum deumet homoousia ista et semper simul et patrem et filium et spiritum sanctum, ineffabili potentia et ineloquilbili generatione filium dei Iesum Christum, Logos qui sit ad deum, et imaginem et formam et characterem et refulgentiam patris et virtutem et et sapientiam dei, per quae appareat et declaratur deus in potentia omnium et existens et manens et agens omnia . . .*].[27]

Victorinus' *homoousios* triadic theology has a logic because he already knows what a word like *homoousios* means; that is, he knows what the phrase "same in essence" means because he has a pre-understanding of what "essence" means. As I will show, statements about the identity of, differences within, and differences between essence(s) is a way of knowing and speaking that Victorinus is familiar with from the content of Porphyrian Neoplatonism. There is no gainsaying that Victorinus came to

25. In this light, Athanasius' coolness to Basil of Ancyra and *homoiousios* makes some sense, but seen in this light, the fierce theological contest between the two Basils and Eunomius does not.

26. See Kopecek, *History of Neo-Arianism*, ch. 6.

27. *Adv. Ar.* 1.48 (SC 68. 330; Clark 166).

Christianity as a formed Platonist—more deeply formed than Augustine was when he recognized in the Christian *Logos* the doctrines of the Platonists. Comparing the two at the time of their conversions, one can easily say that Augustine was a dabbling enthusiast while Victorinus was a senior scholar (perhaps *the* senior scholar of Platonism).[28] For Augustine, his experience of Platonism prepared his mind for seeing points of contacts between the two transcendental philosophies with doctrines of the Christian Trinity and doctrines of the Platonic Triad; for Victorinus, his Platonism was congruous with the Christian theology of the transcendental triad, and vice versa.[29] Leaving contexts and schooling to the side, Augustine's understanding of Platonism was never near to Victorinus', and Platonism "revealed" less to Augustine than it seemed to do to Victorinus.[30] Indeed, I will hazard the following—that there came a time when Augustine ceased to learn more *of* or *from* Platonism than he would have otherwise if his highly contextualized private reading had allowed it. That time folds out, I think, within the first ten books of *City of God*. Victorinus, however, continued to learn as much as there was to learn from "transcendental Platonism"—this is not a criticism of Victorinus or Augustine, but it might allow us to say about ourselves that Victorinus *was* that Platonic Trinitarian theologian that some moderns have for so long feared (or celebrated!) Augustine was.

There is one more important point that Victorinus brings to our attention that must be recognized and alluded to, however briefly. Victorinus' theology was one of the few Western Nicene writings that was not an anachronism before the text was even "published." It was often a feature of Latin anti-Arian theology that its arguments did not meet the Trinitarian threat *immediately at hand*. The very fact that Latin Nicene theology was usually *anti-Arian* (i.e., against Arius and his theology) identifies a common, deep flaw in the Western theologies that "began" in the 350s. Latin Nicene literature was anti-Arian—but the threat to a Nicene theology had not been Arian for at least one, perhaps two, decades. In the 350s, no one against the Nicene Creed believed that the Son was made from nothing—not even Eunomius! Yet some Latins still wrote against such believers. Latins engaged an anti-Nicene theology that had been dead for twenty years, at the minimum. The first books Ambrose of Milan wrote (377–78) to give the emperor an exposition of the Nicene faith and a fatal blow against

28. Whenever I use the word Platonism in this chapter, I am speaking as inclusively (or vaguely) as the occasion allows: sometimes I am thinking of Plotinian Neoplatonism, sometimes Porphyrian Neoplatonism, sometimes neo-Aristotelian Neoplatonism. The word takes its meaning from the time it lives—just like, if anyone cared to quibble, when I say "*homoousios* Trinitarian theology" I am being as inclusive as I can be given the differences over times both in Victorinus' and Augustine's lives and that of the doctrine.

29. Any suspicion that I have squashed together these two "transcendental philosophies" under a generic term is correct. Augustine, at least, would not have recognized this category. See further in the chapter for clarifications.

30. After the explosion of the discovery that Augustine was a Neoplatonist there has gradually developed among scholars an awareness of Augustine's limited knowledge of, debt to, and understanding of Neoplatonism. See, for example, Manchester, "Noetic Triad in Plotinus," 217ff.

Arians wrote, as Dan Williams showed long ago, who did not exist.[31] It took some years for Ambrose to learn what living anti-Nicene, anti-*homoousios*, theology was—what the contemporary anti-*homoousios* theologian Palladius believed, not what dead-for-forty-years-Arius believed.[32] I believe that this was a theological hermeneutic that some Latin Nicenes inherited along with their Athanasian understanding of Nicaea, *homoousios*, and the Arian crisis. This was a deep flaw that Victorinus' avoided: he wrote against *living* contemporary heretics. I believe it is meaningful for reading Augustine to suppose that it was Victorinus' Nicene theology that he received—even if only the form of the argument (i.e., not tied to a refutation of Arianism, but based on finding a positive ground for understanding the Three-in-One God). That Augustine writes against anti-*homoousios* literature of Latin origin, written after 381, is a major hermeneutical accomplishment of Victorinus'.

PART 2

In the second half of this chapter, I will set out the conceptual milieu of Victorinus' doctrine of the Trinity so that we are prepared to ask this question:[33] If our triadic soul is in the image and likeness of the triadic God, then what do we learn about the divine Trinity from its analogue, the human soul? How does the analogy work, and what are the conclusions?

In 359, no Latin Nicene author had a pneumatology more developed or "higher" than Victorinus'. The West still struggled with the exegetical confusion caused by the long Latin commitment to Spirit Christology, as Hilary's *In Matthaeum* and *De Fide* (the first four books of *De Trinitate*), as well as the works by Phoebadius and Gregory of Elvia treated in the previous chapters, make clear. Moreover, in 360 neither Latin nor Greek Nicene Christianity had a Trinitarian logic—one that made the Spirit's generation as intrinsic to God as was the generation of the Son—except what was suggested by Victorinus in the earliest book (IA) of his *Adversus Arium*. In 359, Victorinus' *homoousios* pneumatology was as good as it got in all of Christianity.[34]

My treatment of Victorinus' polemical exegesis draws exclusively from the "Candidus correspondence," and the first and second books of *Against the Arians*.[35] I agree

31. Williams, *Ambrose of Milan*.

32. See Gryson, in SC 267.

33. The bane of historical accounts of theology—indeed, any account of any defined, protracted, intellectual endeavor with claims of diachronic unity—is the sacrificing of accuracy for the sake of precision. The dialectical partner of such historical accounts is the sacrificing of precision for the sake of an enforced unity or continuity.

34. Some authorities think that *Adv. Ar.* 3 and 4 were written after the Alexandrian Council of 362, and that Victorinus is in possession of the two epistles associated with that synod, e.g., Hadot in SC 68, 54.

35. There are two or three references which come from Books III or IV (e.g., the last quote of this part of the chapter), but these passages illustrate, they are not load-bearing quotations upon which I build my argument.

with Clark and others that we can redactionally separate book I into two parts, according to its two functions as a whole document: it constitutes, first, Victorinus' response to the *Second Letter of Candidus* (which was itself a work made up of extracts from various anti-*homoousios* texts), and, second, Victorinus' responses to the condemnations issued at Sirmium (357) and to Basil's council in 358 (which Victorinus took to be sympathetic elaborations or dissimulations of Arianism). Beyond Victorinus' reactive polemics against the Sirmium Creed and the condemnations formulated at Basil's Council of 358, Victorinus offered a significant argument for his own *homoousios*-based doctrine of the Trinity, including a "Confession of Faith." The Sirmium Synod of 357 and the Decrees of Basil's Council of 358 (decisive for dating), mean that Victorinus' *Against Arius*, book IA, is not later or earlier than 359.[36]

But, before we move directly into Victorinus' psychological analogy for the triadic Trinity, I must explain as best I can the reasons for what seems to most readers, including many of those with some background in late-antique philosophy, Victorinus' idiosyncratic way of speaking ontologically. Concepts such as existence, life, and intellect are usually named as nouns, as I just have here; the gerund form—existing, living, and thinking/reasoning—is a familiar form of naming the concept considered in its state of activity. We name the concept *qua* itself through the infinitive, "to be" (or "not to be") living and thinking. Victorinus speaks differently, and seemingly adds an unnecessary qualifier. This passage below has the dual virtues of illustrating some of the difficulties in reading Victorinus:

> For every being has an inseparable species, or rather the species itself is the substance itself, not that species itself is prior to *"to be,"* but because the species defines *"to be."* Indeed *"to be" is the cause of the "to be" of the species,* insofar as the *"to be"* of the species is *"to be"* [*Omne enim esse inseparabilem speciem habet, magis autem ipsa species, ipsa substantia est, non quo prius sit ab eo* **quod est esse**, *species, sed quod definitum facit species illud* **quod est esse** *etenim* **quod est esse** *causa est specie esse in eo* **quod est esse**].[37]

For Mary Clark, the English translator, "to be" consistently translates the phrase *quod est esse*, for she (following Hadot) correctly regards it as a technical term in Victorinus' ontology, and the reader can be thankful that every time they read "to be," they know that Clark is rendering the Latin, *quod est esse*—but that only leaves us with the original problem: What does *quod est esse* mean? If we take counsel from the French translation, then we see that Hadot translates *quod est esse* as *l'espèce*, which most dictionaries render as "in this case" or "in the case at hand." If Hadot's French is a

---

36. Immediately after Victorinus has finished refuting Candidus' *Second Letter*, he briefly sums up Arianism, i.e., the theology of Arius and Eusebius of Nicomedia, which is the cue that he has turned to begin his [*First*] *Book Against Arius*. At *Adv. Ar.* 1. *pro.* 3, Victorinus announces the scope of his book, which is, as he puts it, to refute Eusebius' demonstrations (by scriptural exegesis) that "the Son is made, not born; and that the Son is substantially Son."

37. *Adv. Ar.* 1.19 (SC 68. 234; Clark 116).

guide, then *quod est esse* means "existing as what it is." Read this sentence (from the quotation above), which I have rewritten with my small tweaking:

> Something existing as what it is, is the cause of the species existing as what it is. The existence of particular(s) as what they are is the cause of species exist-ing as what it is (i.e., a particular species).

I will attempt to sum up the key presupposition(s) which distinguishes Victorinus' Neoplatonism. It is a commonplace to think of Being as unmoving or motionless because it "goes" nowhere, nor changes for it has no parts. For Neoplatonists, Being brings being(s) into existence. For the interested but not specialist reader, what must be kept in mind is that the goal or logic of Neoplatonism is, for our purposes here, to explain the origin(s) and kind(s) of being. Plotinus has the famous "dual-motions" of higher being: the inward motion which results in identity, the outward motion which results in (a) new being. Each level of "generation and return" produces a new being (*hypostasis*?) whose being-ness is derived and lesser than the level of origin. Hence the famous hierarchy of being which is known as a "vertical causality."[38] I have character-ized this dual-motion as "Stoic *tonos* stripped of it materiality," and I have made no claims to originality by this linking of Neoplatonic hierarchy of being to the Stoic no-tion of the inward and outward motion (*tonos*) of the *pneuma*. If the conceptual ori-gins of Neoplatonic aetiology may be found in Stoic origins, then to that philosophy we add Aristotelian concepts of potentiality and actuality to being, but understanding "potentiality and actuality" not in a strict Aristotelian sense, in which actuality brings into being what was there potentiality, but as power and act. "Power" is not an un-completed act; it is that which makes an act possible, and which determines what that act "will be." The existence of the act does not diminish it; indeed, what a thing is—its *ousia*—may be its power(s) existing in the unity of whatever the "it is." Or as Plato so succinctly put it: "I am proposing as a mark to distinguish real things that they are nothing other than power."[39]

Given that Neoplatonism is a philosophy which seeks to provide the explanation of the origin and kinds of being (as I said above), here I provide the reader with a provisional definition of Being which should be kept in mind, as word-for-word as possible, for understanding any characteristic Victorinus attributes to Being. Thus:

> Being (in the sense of "God is Being, from whom all creation takes its be-ing") is an auto-kenetic crystalline active power unfolding within itself un-ceasingly. The key concept is that of intrinsic cyclic motion, power to act.

---

38. See Manchester, "Noetic Triad in Plotinus," for a good summary of the reasoning supporting the "analogical" approach, especially, 213–15. Manchester's opening remark, 208, is worth noting: "The Plotinian hypostatic series never made a plausible model for the Christian trinity even when it held the field more or less alone." That "field . . . alone" would have not been more than twenty-five years.

39. Plato, *Soph.* 247e.

Existence is a verb, an action, a doing. "Action springs forth" (from "to be") as the "Word leapt."[40]

THE SOUL IN THE IMAGE AND LIKENESS OF THE TRINITY

Marius Victorinus begins his Trinitarian theology by reflecting upon the meaning of Genesis 1:25, where it is recorded that God said, "Let us make man in our image and likeness." An image reveals something of the Original (the "Us," in this case), and therefore whatever or wherever we identify as that image will tell us something about the Maker. The passage is relevant as well because of the plural: "Let *us* make." From an early time, patristic exegesis of the passage has engaged the plural noun and verb—as did rabbinic exegesis: it was a troublesome text for Jewish "radical monotheism" even without the Christian claims. Patristic exegesis of the "image and likeness" did not always use it as a basis for theological speculation; sometimes the "image and likeness" was understood on the order of "virtue" or as doxological. It was a universal given that the image was spiritual or intellectual in character. Often the "like to God" was reduced to "rational" or "having a mind," since God certainly was rational, and it was reason that set us apart from other living things.[41] When Christians did exegete

40. I remind you of the sense of "crystalline" in modern molecular physics: "Crystalline is an adjective that describes the periodic translational [triadic] ordering of atoms or molecules within a solid. The atoms or molecules form a three-dimensional arrangement within a single repeating unit called a unit cell." It means "triadic." Remove the materialist terms "periodic" and ordering of "atoms or molecules within a solid." "Unit cell" could be "one essence," but so could "solid"; "dimension" is "relational." Crystalline is by definition triadic (https://www.corrosionpedia.com/definition/6436/crystalline).

41. It verges on the phenomenological to note that for the first three hundred years of Christian literature, there is abroad in the culture an axiomatic construction in which "being human" means negotiating an antinomic tension between rational or spiritual on the one hand, and irrational or material on the other. This axiomatic construction is strongly present in Johannine-Pauline anthropology as it is in Pythagorian-Platonic anthropology. Life is mapped by these latitudes and longitudes; indeed, life is *experienced* as the confluence of these two "forces." No small wonder that what is given in anthropologies as the *human* distinction is the rational or spiritual. No small wonder that in the previous centuries, the same would over time be increasingly understood as a property—and further, clearly *the* essence—of God. The theo-pology of Sabaoth was replaced by the theo-pology of Father or Wisdom or—most interestingly—the "externalization" as powers of goodness/wisdom, on the one hand, and judgment on the other. I suggest that it is in Victorinus' anthropology where the soul is no longer part of the axiomatic antinomies, but is "simply" life just as God becomes, in a fully analogous way, "simply Life." The existential experience of a *true* (i.e., ontological) *antinomy* of death to life, matter to spirit, irrational to rational is collapsed by Augustine: all the antinomies may still be seen as "antinomies," but they are not, and the *Psyche*-logical definition of "being human"—i.e., the soul of man—is no longer mapped by the axiomatic construction described in the first sentence (for that description is and remains axiomatically antinomic, and it can experience nothing more), but the soul is discovered and experienced as what it is, a simple triad. "Search in yourself in yourself—perhaps the image of the Trinity [Gen 1:25] may hold some trace of the Trinity . . . I will search in me, you search with me; not I in you and you in me, but you in you and I in me. Let us search in common, and in common study our common nature and substance [*ousia*] . . . What has your soul got inside? Take a look at yourself" (Augustine, *Serm.* 52.18). Memory, understanding, and will—an (axiomatic?)

"image and likeness" in a theological way, it was often Christologically—to identify the Son as the true Image in contrast to humans as "images of the Image." On those occasions when Christians did read the passage as a theistic simile—"We are *like* God in this way . . ."—the God imaged was, as a rule, either the Father speaking to the implied audience or God speaking as One. The first exegesis of a threefold image of a Trinitarian God linked three rational parts or faculties in humans to three known rational traits, circumlocutions, or powers of God as testified to in Scripture. All "rational"—what we call "psychological"—analogies between the triadic God and our nature were organized as ratios with "rational" as the common unit.[42] For example, "God has a *Logos* which means he is rational" because we define "rational" as having a *logos*. If God is rational, with a *Logos*, he also possesses a Will, just as we are rational, with a *logos*, and also "possess a will."[43]

Victorinus' understanding that "Let us make in our image" meant that *the image in us was a triadic image of God* qua *Trinity* was extremely rare—most scholars say unprecedented. Like nearly all of his Nicene contemporaries, he understood (perhaps silently but certainly) that all Trinitarian analogies were only as useful as the presumed unity (its degree or kind) they were selected and constructed to illuminate. Knowing the unity beforehand—prior to the analogy—determines the analogy to be pursued for what the analogue itself can further reveal about the analogous. At the very time when Victorinus entered the controversy the polarity of unbegotten versus begotten was proposed as defining the antinomy at stake in Trinitarian theology (unlike the previous categories of Father and Son).[44] What put Victorinus' theology in a

---

phenomenology of self—without antinomy. If Victorinus' conceptual moment in the "movement out" of antinomies is consistently applied, then his Pauline commentaries will not play well with others, i.e., those contemporary commentaries still built on the axiomatic antinomies (including, at the time, Augustine's).

42. I use the term "analogy" to mean a sort of ratio between two ratios, in which the relationship between the two members ("magnitudes"?) of the first ratio have the same relationship as between the two members ("magnitudes"?) of the second ratio. Thus: "As A is to B, so is C to D." *Voila*, an A:B::C:D!

43. Origen is well-known as a theologian who used tripartite or trichotomous anthropology to develop not just his Trinitarian theology, but also his Christology as well as his rules of exegesis.

44. We should note that neither text, 357 or 358, makes use of the distinction between "unbegotten" and "begotten." That antinomy plays no role in the arguments circumscribed by Sirmium, Victorinus, Basil of Ancyra, or any of the councils in 358–59 leading up to Constantinople (360). The antinomies are fundamental only in Eunomius' in *Apologia* (361–63?), which cannot be used to backtrack to Constantinople. In Kopecek's careful study of the terms' appearance in the debate with the Anomians, he comes to the conclusion that there is a clear tradition of referring to God as unbegotten to distinguish between God and creation, and a few to distinguish Father as Son (See Ignatius' *Letter to the Ephesians* 7), and a few in which the term is applied to the Son (Irenaeus, *AH* III.8.3). Kopecek concludes there was a "dominant tradition to reserve the term for the Father" (*AH* II.266). I believe that outside Alexandrian circles, pre-350, the term was virtually unregarded except by those who read Parmenides' *Proem* 8. In any case, it was Athanasius who introduced the antithesis into the controversy in *De Synodis* 47, which was re-enforced by Aetius' rejoinder in the *Syntagmation*, in a drama not unlike that between Alexander and Arius where a term previously (it was thought by some) reserved for the Father is now given to the Son. See Kopecek's *History of Neo-Arianism*, II.249–66.

category beyond his peers was that he realized that (A) while the logic of production was central, it needed to be a *Trinitarian* logic intrinsically and not a binitarian logic (Father-Son) with an add-on or "Father and Son, plus one" (the Holy Spirit); and (B) centerpiecing the antithetical concepts of unbegotten and begotten was not a fruitful way to develop Trinitarian theology—even if that centerpiecing consisted of a Nicene theology as defined by arguing against the antinomies.[45] Victorinus' Trinitarian theology was truly a "logic of Three," and while he recognized that the ungenerated-versus-generated had to be dealt with, it was not a major *topos* in his doctrinal logic.[46]

Victorinus understands our identity as "*image*" to refer to our soul, and the identity "of *God*"—of which we are the *image*—as God "the Trinity." Victorinus uses the fact that the soul is made in the image and likeness to the triadic God as his beginning point for articulating a Nicene Trinitarian theology.[47] Various accounts of the soul—all derived by reason—tell us that the soul is triadic: three-in-one. Previous Christian attempts developed by understanding the "Image of God" in us as mind or reason. Victorinus, however, finds the "image" in the *soul*—and he is the first Christian to do so.[48] To develop this knowledge of *God-Who-Is-a-Trinity* through the divine *image-which-is-the-soul* requires significant knowledge of the image, that is, the soul, upon which we can draw to clarify our understanding of the Original. (In modern parlance, this would be known as "reverse engineering.") In Victorinus' time, there

45. Victorinus knew that the anti-Nicenes emphasized the identification of God with unbegotten, and that they distinguish God and the Second Person through the opposition between ἀγέννητος and γέννητος: the so-called Candidus' *Second Letter to Victorinus* consists of Arius' letter to Eusebius of Nicomedia and a fragment of Eusebius' letter to Paulinus, both of which emphasize the unbegotten–begotten distinction. The first of Arius' doctrine Victorinus cites in book I of *Against Arius* is that he taught that *the Son was not* ἀγέννητος (an emphasis which is not there in the original). By his own subordinating the ἀγέννητος-γέννητος distinction to the Porphyric doctrine of dual motions, Victorinus avoids the problems posed by his Greek contemporaries, Aetius and Eunomius, who built their theology on the ἀγέννητος-γέννητος distinction, and who forced later pro-Nicene theologians to fight the dogmatic battle on ground chosen by the Heterousions (i.e., Aetius and Eunomius).

46. It is important to recognize that Augustine's Trinitarian theology incorporates these Victorine "axioms" ("A" and "B"). Manchester, "Noetic Triad," 216, makes this point strongly: "It can be shown that Victorinus achieved a dialectical analogue for the later Latin orthodox distinction between proper predication of such terms as 'principle,' 'logos,' 'wisdom,' 'nous,' and 'spirit,' which all denote substance, and the 'appropriation' of such terms to one another of the relational threesome. It is even possible to show that his handling of the reciprocities among the moments of the noetic triad amount to a functional precursor of the Augustinian doctrine of predication by relation." On the other hand, Manchester helpfully remarks "that Augustine may not even know, and in any case does not understand Marius Victorinus' Trinitarian metaphysics" (209).

47. David Bell puts it this way: "More precisely, [for Victorinus] it is in the soul that we are *ad imaginem* . . . The soul is therefore a *trinitas unalis secunda*, a reflection, a shadow, and image of the consubstantial Trinity, and it follows from this, just as for the Neoplatonists, that by an examination of its own nature the soul may come to some awareness of the nature of its Creator." See his "Esse, Vivere, Intelligere: The Noetic Triad and The Image of God," *Recherches de Théologie ancienne et Médiévale* 50 (1985): 5–43," here 17–18.

48. Manchester, "Noetic Triads," makes a very strong statement to this effect on the basis of John O'Sullivan's conclusions in his *The Image of God: The Doctrine of Saint Augustine and Its. Influence* (St Louis: Priory Press, 1963), ch. 5.

were a number of strong accounts of the soul, types of soul, and the mind. The culture-wide (Latin and Greek) presence of these substantial and detailed accounts of the soul provide a wealth of details by which to guide and fill out a dense exegesis of scriptural references, as well as being a second source of a web of connections among words and images through which it may communicate.[49] Knowledge of "physics" and psychology provides sources of the web of connections through which the web communicates—in exegetical manners similar to the ways Scripture is read.[50]

That is, what the soul consists of, and what are the interior relations of the soul's constituents. The understanding of soul operative here may presently be described as "Aristotle-like," rather than "Plato-like." Aristotle speaks of the three "souls" which, held together as a unit ("form"), make up the living being—the self-moving and the rational human. By Victorinus' time, Aristotle's understanding has been modified by the Stoic perception that prior to any such "soul" is existence, and that nutrition and movement have been telescoped into "life." For the Stoics, the soul is, among the living, the principle of unity and life; the principle of unity among the non-living is maintained by the *hexis*. Interactions of Stoic and Aristotelian conceptions produce an understanding of soul in which it is one, it exists,[51] it is alive, and it is rational. Each kind of soul has its distinctive powers. Victorinus' exegesis draws upon his thoughts about existence ("Let us make"), soul, image-ness, unity, and the Three-in-One God. The reader is thus advised not to borrow in a rigid way from contemporary "official" Aristotelian definitions of "soul."[52]

---

49. See the later judgments of a near-contemporary rhetor to Victorinus on the importance on "broadening one's fields of references as much as possible" for Christian exegesis: Augustine, *Doc.* III. xxv–xxxviii.

50. This is important for us to recognize: within each "exegeting" culture there are any number of webs or networks which supply the reader with content for each, tagged by a word or symbol. (In the exegetical process the probability that an interpretation of a symbol is correct is often discovered by finding that the given symbol is presented in the midst of symbols tagged by or related to symbols with related meanings.) These webs or networks are distinguished by kind and subject, and they are made present by the memory of the reader. (They are "associations.")

51. It is not always clear which of these two is articulated first, or whether they are really separable outside abstraction.

52. The best resource for the reader, and likely an important part of Victorinus' own education on the soul, is Alexander of Aphrodisias' translation with commentary of Aristotle's *De Anima*. At *De Anima* I.15–16, Alexander says that the first power of the soul is to give a thing its form, that is, its identity as such and such (the "to be"?) and that all living things have life because of soul. In the "to be" (we might say "identity"; there is form) there are present powers so that the "thing" may act according to its nature, and these powers are said to pre-exist activities, since only a power can give the capacity for the thing "to do" its proper activities. "Powers" here are the source of activity, not the "potential to do/be" that we might understand that for Aristotle understood "power"—potential—to be. See also, Iamblichus, *Commentary on De Anima* IV.17–24.

VICTORINUS AND THE PLOTINIAN SOUL

Most Latin Nicene theology contemporary to Victorinus falls into the category I call "neo-Nicene." Among these Nicenes there is frequent reference to *substantia* language, but arguments are rarely conducted by beginning with, or working through, the logic of substance. The arguments typically link substance to power, and by arguing for the common power among the Two (or Three), the conclusion is then offered as "if one power then one substance," or something of this sort. "What is substance (*ousia*) in its own right [i.e., *qua* substance]?"; or, "How are one common substance with two or three substance-produced existents necessarily equal?" are not lines of argument that are brought forward in defense of the key term of the Nicene Creed *homoousios* (*eius substantia*). Marius Victorinus, by contrast, argues from a logic based on what substance is and what it "does"; he argues on the basis of how *substantia* or *ousia* exist. He begins with the question of unity of substance among a plurality. He argues for *homoousias* based upon a pre-standing philosophical logic which he can employ on the basis of the image and likeness of the Trinitarian God in us, the soul.[53] He argues based upon the scripturally-attested image of God in the soul.[54] The specific aetiology that Victorinus finds so helpful will be discussed in more detail below, but the logic of his exegesis and doctrine-making can be laid out here in a straightforward way. My treatment of the psychological "ratio" in the Trinitarian analogy follows this order: Victorinus' use of Plotinus' definition of soul to provide himself with the fundamental psychology he needs; his re-articulation of the Plotinian soul into a more explicitly "Porphyrian" triadic description of the three powers in the soul;[55] and having thus

53. Manchester, "Noetic Triads," 211, summarizes that logic as that of "*the noetic triad, Being, Life, Nous. This triad is horizontal in the sense that. in each of its various developments, it interprets the interior integrity of the Second Hypothesis itself. Even when relations of priority and consequences are seen among them, when Porphyry for example makes the first moment the 'father' or Iamblicus construes them in the dialectical sequence hyparxis, dunamis, nous, they remain moments within the Second Hypothesis and components of its integrity.*"

54. Mark Edwards puts it succinctly in his recent book, *Aristotle and Early Christian Thought*: "When Christians of the fourth century under-took to defend the Nicene Creed by philosophical reasoning, the terms of greatest moment to them were *ousia* and *dunamis* ('*being*' and '*power*' or *potentiality*), both of which occur only sporadically in Plato. To Christians, they [the terms] were scriptural, but the meaning grafted onto them by all parties to theological controversy in this epoch . . . [were philosophical]" (78). See Edwards' treatment of Victorinus and Porphyry, 81–83.

55. The reader is more likely to be familiar with the triad of transcendental Kinds elaborated by Plotinus, that is *One–Mind–Soul*, and know that this triad is a descending causal hierarchy. By contrast, Porphyry's triadic transcendentals are *Being–Life–Mind*. The logic of the elaboration is similar to Aristotle's analysis of *ousia*, such that "If there is reason there must be life, and if there is life there must be being." For Porphyry the progression of Life and Mind is an elaboration "horizontally" from Being: in *ousia* (e.g., soul) there are the triadic powers of existence, and they act internally each upon the others so that each of the Three participates in the other Two. The fundamental triadic structure is set by Plato's *Sophist* 248e–249a, albeit with Porphyry the dynamic (du-na-me-tic?) principle of Dunamis (see *Sophist* 247d) is intrinsic to each of the Three as powers of *ousia*. (The dynamic character of this Triad forces upon me the inelegant term crystalline, which is the closest analogy that we find in nature to what is, after all, a kinetic triangle.) See Mark Edwards, "Porphyry and the Intelligible Triad,"

articulated the triadic content of the soul, he offers the doctrine of the Trinity as the Christian ratio in the analogy. The analogy gives him the basis for developing the doctrine of the Trinity as a triad of one substance, *homoousios*. "*Just as* the *ousia* of the soul *is to* its powers *so is* the *ousia* of God *to* the Three." The important work of the analogy is carried within the judgments, "just as . . . so is . . . is to . . ."—as it is in all such analogies.[56]

Victorinus uses the fact that the *soul* is *made* in the *image and likeness* to the triadic God as his beginning point for articulating a Nicene Trinitarian theology of a common *ousia*.[57] Victorinus' "triadic psychological analogy" is grounded in what could almost be called a common-sense logic for reading Genesis 1:25: Scripture says we are in the image of God; exegetically, we understand that image to be the soul; we understand "soul" to be such-and-such; and we understand "to be the image" to mean "analogously." How do we understand "made" in the context of God and soul? Among the analogous terms—God, image, soul—we understand being in the same ontological language, applied analogously: triad being. The ontology which the exegete supplies is "triadic being," or as I defined it above, the soul is made in the image through the triadic God's auto-kenetic crystalline active power unfolding within itself unceasingly action that presents itself to the "created" soul that God calls forth. So, what is our soul, or what do we know and say about that *ousia*, soul?

Victorinus' account of soul begins by asking the "state of the art" psycho-ontologous question of how do we speak of soul as one and yet a plurality—a problematic he takes straight from Plotinus' *Ennead* VI.2. My judgment is that Victorinus uses Plotinus' treatment of the soul as the blue-print of his own understanding of *the triadic*

Journal of Hellenic Studies 110 (1990): 14–25. The fact that Plotinus uses the triad of Being–Life–Mind about soul at *Ennead* VI.2 gives Victorinus the opportunity to set "soul" as the "image of God" in us (Gen 1:25) in the Porphyrian ontology within which he thinks.

56. Any ratio involves the perception or postulating of a relationship between the two members of the ratio: a ratio necessarily presumes "a sort of relationship between" A and B which is compacted into the expression "is to." That "sort of relationship" is then predicated of the two members of another ratio: "just as . . . is to." This clear in an analogy like, "The divine is to Jesus just as . . ." which requires me to have in mind a specific relationship in this ratio before I can offer a second ratio which has the same specific relationship. Analogies are never proofs.

57. Anca Vasiliu, "L'argument de l'image dans la défense de la consubstantielité par Marius Victorinus," *Les Etudes Philosophiques* 101 (2012): 191–216. And thus the famous "one essence, three *hypostasis*" phrase used four times by Victorinus is not spoken to formulize the Trinity or Trinitarian doctrine, rather it expresses the Porphyrian axiom of "out of one essence there arises three upostasis [or powers]. *Adv. Ar.* 3.4 is Victorinus' articulation of the Porphyrian ontology of the triadic character of everything that exists: it has no particular "register" for the Trinity. *Adv. Ar.* 3.9 is a statement of the triadic coexistence of all being, including the Holy Spirit. The Three are One, but that is true for the soul, for all that is. Many attempts over several decades have been made to explain its foreshadowing of the "one essence, three *hypostasis*" of later, post-Cappadocian Nicene theology (Lienhard, "'Ousia' and 'Hypostasis.'"). Also see John Voelker, "An Anomalous Trinitarian Formula, in Marius Victorinus' Against Arius," *Studia Patristica* 43 (2006): 517–22" which contains a good summary of the debate in German scholarship which is not easily accessible in American theological libraries.

essence of the soul:[58] that is, he restates Plotinus' minimalist argument found in VI.2 into a richer argument—probably articulated from Porphyry—and then compares what is said about the plurality of a simple, single soul to the Nicene doctrine of triad God as *homoousios*. My treatment of Plotinus focuses entirely on his description of the soul in terms of how we can speak of the unity and yet compoundedness of the soul.[59] The problematic of an unquestionably simple essence—an essence which is by definition simple—being many, and the language Plotinus uses, is key to Victorinus' "psychological analogy." The language by which Plotinus articulates the problematic allows Victorinus to move from describing soul as *homoousios* to describing the Trinity as *homoousios*:

> If someone takes one soul, without spatial separation of parts, without magnitude, supremely simple, as it will seem at the first application of the mind to it, how would one expect to find that it was after all many? For one would have thought that one could stop at this, when one had divided the living being the soul and body, and found the body multiform and composite and various but was confident that one had found that the soul was simple and could rest from one's journey since one had come to the principle?[60]

THE *OUSIA* OF SOUL AND ITS "CONSTITUENTS"

In the thought experiment, Plotinus moves from the original assumption of the soul's unity—that is to say, it is one *ousia*—to the discovery that the soul is composite, for from one soul comes radically different actions: "What then are the constituents seen in soul and how many are there? Since we find in soul *substance* [*ousia*] and *life* together and *substance* is common to all soul, and *life* also common, and *life* is also *Intellect*."[61] The fact of Being and Life are presumed by the "to be" of Intellect is a familiar conclusion drawn from exegesis of Plato's *Parmenides*, and the production of such triads is a *topos* of the era.[62] What connects the Plotinus passage to Victorinus is:

58. For the transmission and earliest appropriation of Plotinus in the Latin-speaking world, see Paul Henry, *Plotin et l'Occident* (Louvain: Spicilegium Sacrum Lovaniense, 1934), 44–62. Henry finds in *Adv. Ar.* Plotinian material from *Enneads* V.2, two citations from VI.3, and a citation from II.5.

59. *Ennead* VI.2 was one of the few Plotinian *Enneads* to be widely known, in whole, among Christians of the mid-fourth century.

60. Plotinus, *Ennead* VI.2.22 Loeb.

61. Plotinus, *Ennead* VI.2.7 Loeb. The existence of this passage in Plotinus' writings is significant. Manchester remarks that "The juxtaposition of Plotinus and Marius Victorinus immediately makes this a puzzlement. In the first place, Plotinus very rarely cites the threesome [Being–Life–Intelligence] in any kind of tightly schematic way, and in discussions where the three can be recognized by implication it is not necessarily clear whether they should be listed in that order" (Manchester, "Noetic Triad," 211). See Pierre Hadot, "Etre, Vie, Pensée chez Plotin et avant Plotin," in *Les Sources de Plotin*, Entretiens sur l'Antiquité classique V (Geneva: Fondation Hardt, 1960), 107–57.

62. See the very helpful article by Steven K. Strange, "Plotinus on the Articulation of Being," *Society for Ancient Greek Philosophy Newsletter* (1989): 155.

(1) the articulation of the unity of the essence of the soul despite its several produc-tions—in particular, that the vocabulary of the articulation is in terms of the unity of *ousia*;[63] (2) this passage from *Ennead* VI.2 is one of the few in Plotinus' writings where the triad generated are *Being–Life–Intellect*; the most common Plotinian version of the triad is One–Mind–Soul;[64] and (3) the subject of Plotinus' analysis in VI.2 is the *ousia of the triadic soul*—which Victorinus is pursuing for what it can reveal, as an image, about the *ousia* of the triadic God.[65]

In the system(s) of Plotinus, Porphyry, and Victorinus, the productive charac-teristic of the divine Life or essence is not a movement across distance (whether in a linear or circular fashion), though it is a kind of internal movement or expression.[66] The best conceptual analogy is that of a string pulled tight, then plucked, producing a note. The analogy is not perfect, but in Plotinus' thought it carries the foundational logic of the Stoic notion of *tonos*, in which everything that exists, exists as a vibration.[67] The stone is not moving, but its existence is specific vibration in a universally-present *pneuma*, which serves as both "that which is vibrating" and the uniting "container" of everything we judge to be existing, from "a thing" to "the accidents of the thing." The rock vibrates at a certain frequency to be a rock, and minor vibrations constitute its properties (heavy, hard) and accidents (color). The fundamental principle of exis-tence, from which comes being, etc., is this *tonos*. The essence of the soul moves in three fundamental or self-constituting (auto-genesis) ways or *tonoi* or frequencies—however we take the analogy to be best conceived: the motion of being, the motion of

63. Edwards, "Porphyry and the Intelligible Triad," 14–25.

64. Any search for "triad" will inevitably lead the scholar to the works of Pierre Hadot, who is indeed the foundation of twentieth-century scholarship on Neoplatonic triads generally, and in Vic-torinus' thought specifically. I do not know that I would recommend that an interested reader (or one that would "falsify" my scholarship) *begin* with Hadot. Instead, I recommend these two as a primer on the subject, insofar as it is relevant to this chapter: the aforementioned Manchester, "Noetic Triads"; and Bell, "Noetic Triad and the Image of God."

65. However, it is important to note, *Ennead* VI is not Plotinus' exposition of his doctrines re-garding the soul; it is not his *De Anima*. *Ennead* VI is, as the book makes abundantly clear, Plotinus' attempt to solve the Parmenidean problem of how many kinds of "being" there are. Aside from the short treatment of the soul in VI.2.4–8, the topic of the soul does not arise again in chs. 9–21. And yet, with some eloquence, Plotinus returns to soul in his very last chapter, 22. In lines 22–35, he restates the problem he first set out by the example of soul: How is the one many and yet still one? The prob-lematique is recast: "[W]hat we call its underparts is an image of it, but not cut off, but like images in mirrors . . . So then the image of the intelligible is not of its maker but of the things contained in the maker, which include man and every other living being: this here is a living being and so is that which made it, each in a different sense and both in the intelligible."

66. Cf. Plato, *Sophist* 248A12: "But since movement appears in the sphere of being, not just chang-ing the nature of being, but rather in being as if making it perfect, if one does not introduce rest as well one would be even more perverse than one who did not grant that there was movement; for the notion, and intellectual perception, of rest comes readier to hand where being is concerned than that of movement, for 'existing in the same state and in the same way' and having a single definition are there in being."

67. Laurent Lavaud, "Substance et movement,: Marius Victorinus et l'héritage Plotinien," *Les Etudes Philosophiques* 101 (2012):" 163–80; here, 170, 173.

life, the motion of intellection.[68] This motion is often called "horizonal" to distinguish it from the "descending" notion of being "spilling over" or flowing down. In vertical causation, the previous source is prior to (at least notionally) and superior to its product: the cause must always be prior to its effect, greater than its effect, and contain that effect. Without giving away any secrets or spoilers, I can say that this particular axiom of causality is central to much of the philosophy and physics west of the Himalayas: its lingering conceptual logic is a major problematique in Western (Greek-based) thought throughout that culture's existence. Most scholars place Plotinus' aetiology within this genera of causalities (vertical causation, source greater than its effects, etc). The key to understanding Victorinus' Trinitarian theology is to understand that his aetiology does not wholly (or principally) owe to this, Plotinian genera of noetic triad, but to the genera of another "Neoplatonism," one often attributed to Porphyry, or at least called after him.

VICTORINUS ON THE PRODUCTIVE MOVEMENT OF THE SOUL

If the soul is like God, we expect that the constitutive elements of the soul to be like that of God's being. In what way is the soul in the image and likeness of God? What are the fundamental attributes or titles we use of the soul? First, most fundamentally, we understand that the soul has existence or being. We understand the soul to exist according to the aetiological relationships in the terms of definition. First there is being—"to be"; from being is Life; and from Life and Being arises knowing or intelligence, for intelligence cannot exist without being and life.

> For the soul is simultaneously substance and movement; insofar as it is subject the soul is identical with that which lives and vivifies, with that which knows and is understanding, with one motion which is its species, since it itself is also one. For the soul is defined by movement and exists as one *on* [existent], with a double power, existing in one movement of life and understanding. And it itself is without passion; but in action they are two in one movement.[69]

For Victorinus, the *ousia* of the soul, insofar as the soul is one in itself—is substance— it is an intrinsically productive *kinesis*. *Ousia* (essence) is both the definition and the existence of the thing itself. *Ousia* is the existing identity of whatever it is the *ousia* of. For complex reasons (many from Aristotle), we intuit that a "dead soul" is both *a*

68. This is the triad associated with Porphyry and Victorinus, but not typically with Plotinus, or, indeed the majority of those in the late patristic and early Medieval who have recourse to a noetic triad. (Augustine being regarded as a conspicuous example of a late Latin theologian who makes no use of the "noetic triad" traditions.) The different triads are treated as marks of the triad's genealogy or "school" of origin.

69. *Adv. Ar.* 1.32 (SC 68. 282; Clark 142). At this stage of the controversy, with Nicene emphasis shifting to "Father" as the productive source of the same nature in the Son, the Eunomians in particular will criticize the use of "Father" as implying passion in God as well as materiality. Nicene arguments begin to emphasis God's "passionless" fatherhood, as Victorinus does here.

contradiction in terms (a false definition) and *impossible to be*. ("What it is" equals "is not").[70] Soul, if it is to be *soul*, if it is *to be what it is*, must exist. It "has" *to be*. *To be* is the defining moment, since without it, no thing is, and no thing is not another thing. Whatever something is, it must "is"; to *be* anything, a thing must *be*.[71]

But the *to be* of the soul is not like the *to be* or being of a rock;[72] for a soul to be an existent-soul, it must have *life*; the *to be* of soul includes *life* as its "to be"[73] (or to be what it is). It must be alive; it must have the *dunamis* of Life.[74]

> And the first power accompanying the soul's *to be* is life. Through its very "to be" the soul is life. For this very "to be" which is proper [*quod est*] to it, which is its substance, is at once life and above life. For it [the soul] does not receive life from another as something other than it. For that which is the "to be" of the soul is for it both to move itself and to be movement, and that which is movement, that is life.[75]

TO BE, TO LIVE, TO THINK

Soul must be intelligent: its being is to be rational: for the soul "is not one thing to live, another, to understand," at least as far as *ousia* goes. And indeed *it is proper* to the living to understand and to the understanding, to live:[76]

> For that which is the "to be" of the soul is for it both to move itself and to be movement, and that which is movement, that is life, and that which is life, that is understanding. But these things are substantial, I say: movement, life, understanding . . . Therefore, these two, life and understanding, are *homoousia*

---

70. It is also necessary to remember that we are talking about the definition of the soul, not the definition of a rock, or anything other thing at all: this is not a generic exercise in defining; this is the particular work of defining *soul*. Finally, Hadot remarks on the explicit emphasis by Plotinus on the difference between "Being" (alone) and a cadaver. See Hadot, "Etre, Vie, Pensee," 108–10.

71. A rock qua rock is one, or unified: *a unit*. It is part of the "to be" of a rock that if it is broken, each piece is univocally a rock, and neither piece has lost its rock-identity by being broken. Beyond the fascinating example of "rock" we may say that anything that *is*, possesses unity; unity is taken as a condition of existence. If one says "the being of rock is" the *to be* of rock must include unity (form?). The Stoics had thought about "different principles of unity" or "different kinds of unity," and Plotinus, Porphyry, and Victorinus took over the Stoic principles.

72. Example taken from Plotinus, *Ennead* VI.2.5–6.

73. A colloquial rendering of the "to be" of its being: "be what it is."

74. Alexander, *Commentary* I.17–18, I.23, lays out a kind of management chart of how a given set of activities require the power by which they are possible.

75. *Adv. Ar.* 1.32 (SC 68. 284; Clark 142).

76. *Adv. Ar.* 4.16 (SC 68. 546; Clark 274–75). On the basis of Alexander's *Commentary on De Anima*, I would speculate that Victorinus is translating *to noein*, and that the probable content of the concept "to know" is much of what the Greek *to noein* signifies.

[consubstantial] with "to be," that is, the "to be" of the soul. These two are one motion.[77]

The triadic *ousia* of soul is laid out.[78] From the *ousia* of soul there arises the to-be-ness of the soul, for it must have being; and from its being as a soul it must have life; and from the living being of soul there must be intellect, or, in Victorinus' terms, if the *ousia* of soul is what we describe—existing, alive, thinking—then being, life, and intelligence are its *ousia* of soul. So far, this sounds like a kinetic version of Aristotle's definition of the soul, one which not only stipulates but also generates. With the passage just quoted, we come to the true "triad of the Porphyrian' aetiology," the triadic character which makes this, analogously, an aetiology of the triadic God:[79] "For them it is not one thing 'to live,' another 'to understand,' at least as far as substance goes. And indeed it is proper to the living to understand and to the understanding, to live."[80]

A TRINITARIAN ANALOGY TO THE SOUL: ABOVE ALL, IT IS TO GIVE LIFE

All that has been said here is a description of the identity and aetiology of the soul—what the soul is, and how it is what it is: to be, to live, to understand. For soul to be, each of the three—being, life, and intellect—are necessary for the to-be-ness of the essence of soul. If we ask about the essence of soul and say first, "Life," the to-be of Life will reveal the priority (the necessary essential existence) of the to-be-ness of soul.[81] This mutual dependence reveals itself in the *kinesis* of the essence of soul; the *ousia* of soul reveals itself only in the production of all three, without which the other two would fail to be the essence of soul. Moreover, since this *kinesis* of interdependence is found equally in the three, for the "to be" of soul has no other essence than the "to live"

---

77. *Adv. Ar.* 1.32 (SC 68. 284; Clark 142–43).

78. *"For the soul is defined by movement and exists as one on (existent), with a double power, existing in one movement of life and understanding."* I said "laid out" above in the text the phrase is a happy idiom of English, which well suggests the specific character of the aetiology at work. The reader must become sensitive to the geometry inherent in any metaphor of movement. The English idiom "laid out" is especially appropriate for Porphyrian aetiology in a way in which "flows from," "pours," or "runs," etc., are not. (Remember Gregory of Nazianzen, *Oration* 29.2, refusing the metaphors of "overflowing" and "pouring out" as suitable for the Trinity.) As an idiom for production, the idiom "laid out" invokes all activity across the same horizonal plane; "pours"—to the contrary—suggests an activity generating new horizonal planes as it "overflows."

79. "[This] triad emerges from reflection on the relative self-constituted-ness of each *hypostasis*, that inner economy of power which belongs to its own proper truth and unity . . . Again I emphasize that a derived level in the Plotinian system is not an organized defectiveness or a pure dependency, but a self-gathered life and power, and in precisely *that* way an epiphenomenon of its source. The canonical example of such a triad is the noetic triad, Being, Life, Nous" (Manchester, "Noetic Triads," 210).

80. *Adv. Ar.* 1.33 (SC 68. 284; Clark 143).

81. Alain Petit, "Existence et Manifestation. Le johannisme platonicien de Marius Victorinus," *Les Etudes Philosophiques* 101 (2012): 152–62.

of soul has another *ousia*, and the rationality of soul has no other essence than these three, then the three have the essence of soul together. If the three each have the same essence, then each has, insofar as it has the same essence, the triadic structure, so that each of the three produce with the other two:

> And the first power is life. For form by its "to be" is life. For the first power of movement defines which is infinite "to be." But the second power is the notion itself since that which is defined is also grasped by understanding, not born by life, being itself a substance insofar as it is subsistent knowledge, having drawn itself forth through itself from substance of life.[82]

Any analogy to the Trinity must have two outcomes if it is to succeed as an analogy. First, it must identify what in the soul's triadic powers or moments stand as analogues to the Triadic God; second, it must say how the activity that characterizes the soul's identity (specifically) is reflected analogically in the relationship among the Three in the Triadic God. I have identified the correspondence: for Victorinus, of the triadic-ontology between soul and God articulated in terms of the question of the unity of the *ousia* (in each case). The soul's triadic powers are being, life, and thought, and these three correspond to Father, Son, and Holy Spirit. In the soul being, life, and thought are of the same essence, *homoousios*; in God, Being, Life, and Thought—Father, Son, and Holy Spirit—are of the same essence, *homoousios*. The dynamics that Victorinus identifies in the *ousia* of the soul have corresponding dynamics in the divine *ousia*: "[T]his is one God because that which is 'to live,' and 'to understand' is the same as that which is 'to be,' and for these two, that which is 'to live' and 'to understand' comes forth from that which is 'to be.'"[83] Or more effusively:

> God is tri-*dunamos* [tri-powered], that is, one having three powers, to be, to live, to understand, so that in each one power there are three powers, and anyone of the three is three powers, receiving its name by the power wherein it predominates . . . For nothing may be called "to be" unless it understands. Triple therefore in each individual, their individuality and triple also their unity in trinity.[84]

CONCLUSION

For most Latin Nicenes the content of *homoousios* is the same as "one in substance, one in power."[85] The two expressions refer to the same reality. There is no need to further unpack the sense of the phrase "unity of substance, unity of power"—the ontology is

82. *Adv. Ar.* 1.33 (SC 68. 284; Clark 143).

83. *Adv. Ar.* 3.7 (SC 68. 456; Clark 230–31).

84. *Adv. Ar.* 4.21 (SC 68. 564; Clark 284).

85. Simply put by Phoebadius, "Ibi enim per substantiae uocabulum aut *uirtutem* aut diuinitatem significari" (Phoebadius, *Contra Arrianos* VIII.1, CCL 64.31.5).

recognized and the content of the ontological statement is recognized. Victorinus, for example, can argue for the propriety of calling the Father and Son (and Holy Spirit) *homoousios*, but he does not engage the question: What does *homoousios* mean? If *ousia* is under a ban, then the church's doctrine is expressed by "one power." This is exactly how Victorinus and Phoebadius respond to the ban on *ousia* language: we know that *homoousios* means "one in substance, one in power," or simply, "one in power."[86] They regard the Sirmium ban as an insult to Nicaea, and an attempt to confuse the issue as though the theology of the non-scriptural *homoousios* was unknown or unexpressible—but the ban cannot circumvent a pious expression of the full unity of the Father, Son, and Holy Spirit in Latin. Whether the same ontological option is available or not for Greek Nicenes is unclear; whether or not the same ontological option existed for Greek Nicenes, did they (generally, partially) declined to acknowledge the ontological equivalence of *mia dunamis* with *homoousios*? From all this I speculate that the effect of Sirmium (357) is felt with greater force by the Greek-speaking Nicenes than by Latin Nicenes. Given that the ban in 357 is intended primarily against Basil of Ancyra and the homoiousians, the question to ask is whether the homoiousians were as emmeshed in *ousia* language as the Nicenes, Latin or Greek. Does homoiousian theology lack an expression comparable to "one power" not simply in content, but in authority, as well? Are they so exclusively Greek that no Latin "equivalent" appears? Is there a Latin equivalent which merely render homoiousias into Latin, retaining the *ousia* terminology? Was this the cause of their particular vulnerability to Sirmium and Constantinople (361)?

According to Athanasius' account of the long Trinitarian crisis, a council in Nicaea of 318 bishops was called by the emperor in 325 to produce a creed that would put a halt to the theology of Arius and all Arians (for example, Eusebius of Nicomedia). The creed contained an unprecedented term, *homoousios*, which was intended to convey the doctrine that the Son was not a creature, but that he was begotten (not created) from the Father and thus the same in essence of the Father. By contrast, Victorinus speaks of three hundred bishops meeting in Nicaea "forty years before" 357, in order

---

86. Three observations to make here: this "*homoousios* equals one power" understanding is in Victorinus and Phoebadius; it is not in Gregory of Elvira. Gregory uses the fully neo-Nicene argument that the Son, being born of the substance of God, has everything the Father does. Secondly, Gregory rarely refers to 1 Cor 1:24 or the other traditional "Power-constellated" New Testament texts. To these I will add the point that Gregory's argument involves refuting Arius' teachings—a lot. Comparing Victorinus to Gregory, we see Victorinus' references to Arius—more importantly, the need to refute specific passages by Arius—to be a predominant feature of Gregory's work, while in Victorinus' writings, he does it briefly at the beginning and then moves on. In Gregory of Elvira, we find a straightforward case of Athanasius' influence on Latin Nicenes. From these observations—which only supplement the distinctions I have made in the chapter—I believe we can identify two different Latin Nicene trajectories: the first represented by Victorinus and Phoebadius (who are close contemporaries); the second by Gregory of Elvira. The first uses "one power" language; the second does not. The first is not constrained by Arius' teaching as the reach of "Arianism"; the second is. Finally, while the first is concerned to defend *homoousios*, the theology is understood to be expressed using an alternate ontology; the second has no such understanding.

to (re-)establish the normative place it had had in Trinitarian theology until some began to champion the term *homoiousios* (a term which had had some small circulation
in the late second or third centuries). Unlike Athanasius, Victorinus does not regard
the term *homoousias* as unusual terminology: his judgment is that the creed of 325
normalized *ousia*-based Trinitarian theological speculation, and as such it remained
in place until 357, when bishops meeting at Sirmium rejected all *ousia*-based Trinitarian theology. While rejecting *ousia*-based theology, the effect of Sirmium was to bring
into the debate a doctrine of the two separate *ousia* of the Father and of the Son. This
was the teaching represented by Eunomius—although Victorinus saw the homoiousians (Basil of Ancyra) as little more than the Anomians (Eunomius).

Victorinus knows Basil of Ancyra's homoiousian theology directly. Basil never
links his party's use of *homoiousios* to rejecting or replacing *homoousios*; none of his
writings mention Athanasius or Nicaea. Basil refers to Antioch (268) as the source of
their use of *homoiousios*. It is their belief that the Synod of Sirmini (357) was a reaction to Basil et al. using *homoiousios* in a document in 356—and in this he is probably
right. Decades of pro-*homoousios* advocacy never provoked anything like Sirmium.
When the Anomians (alternately, "from the will") have to face another *ousia*-based
theology, they decide to act pre-emptively, with a lot of collateral damage. The threat
to Nicene *homoousios* Trinitarian theology that Victorinus perceives comes, first, from
the attack upon *ousia* theology in the Synod of Sirmium (what kind of theologian or
philosopher refuses to talk about God's *ousia*?) and, secondly, from the homoiousian
theology promulgated by Basil of Ancyra's council in 358 against Eunomius. These
threats are answered using the same conceptual idioms that they use. Victorinus' theology is founded on a deep knowledge of Porphyrian, post-Plotinian speculation on
the character of *ousia* and of the soul. Victorinus is positive evidence that a *homoousios* theologian could, during those years, live through and participate in the Nicene
controversy with no knowledge of Athanasius.

Chapter 7

Rereading Augustine's Trinitarian Theology

IT IS IMPOSSIBLE TO do contemporary Trinitarian theology and not have a judgment on Augustine; unfortunately, this is *not* the same thing as saying that it is impossible to do contemporary Trinitarian theology and not have *read* Augustine.[1] Strangely, it is not just possible but quite common to have a "reading" of Augustine without ever having read Augustine. My purpose in this essay to offer a report of or a reading of Augustine's Trinitarian theology which attempts to stand free (in the sense of not being dependent upon or repeating as if by rote) of the account or reading of Augustine's Trinitarian theology which is widely circulated in treatments of that theology by systematicians and some historians of doctrine. Briefly put, that reading identifies the root conceptual idiom of Augustine's Trinitarian theology as Neoplatonic. The substantial influence of Neoplatonism upon Augustine's Trinitarian theology is said to result in (or to express itself in) an overly metaphysical portrait of God, one which diminishes the reality of the Trinity to the point of being functionally modalist, and which divorces the God-who-is-Trinity from our experience in revelation. While I think this account of Augustine's Trinitarian theology is, frankly, dead wrong, it is not my purpose in this essay to engage directly in the various expressions of this account. What I hope to do is to offer a careful, informed reading of a few early writings by Augustine on the Trinity, and in so doing, draw out what I consider to be a more accurate and honest representation of Augustine's theology. Such an account is not as comprehensive as it might be, and in

---

1. There is a remark by Gerald Bonner which is quite apt here: "More than most authors Augustine has been the object of unjustified denunciation by those who have not read him." This remark is quoted as the very first line on the first page of John M. Rist's *Augustine* (Cambridge: Cambridge University Press, 1994).

particular I will not approach the issue of Neoplatonism directly, e.g., parsing passages in *De Trinitate* for what they do or do not owe to Neoplatonism. I would rather use this opportunity to offer something more constructive.

Moreover, it is important not to lend too great a credibility to the proof-like quality of characterizations of the monist or Neoplatonic nature of Augustine's Trinitarian theology. Such characterizations are rarely offered with the requisite apparatus to be considered proofs; they are, rather, episodes in an overall narrative which begins with the presupposition of a fundamental monism or Neoplatonism. Since such characterizations are in fact not proofs, any offering of refutations or counter-proofs ("facts") will not dislocate the "monist Augustine" narrative. What I am offering instead is a counternarrative, a relatively new set of categories within which Augustine's Trinitarian theology may be understood. I am in fact offering only the first chapter, the first act, of such a counternarrative, but I believe that the fundamental categories of the re-narrating can be established and communicated by working through two early texts by Augustine and by illustrating their trajectories in representative later writings. I had originally intended to treat Augustine's Trinitarian theology in three stages: *early* (e.g., from *Epistle* 11 to *De Trinitate* I–V), *middle* (*De Trinitate* VI–XV, various sermons and *Tractates*, etc.), and *late* (*Twentieth Tractate on John*, *Against the Arian Sermon*, the writing against Maximinus, and *De Fide ad Catechumenos*). Two developments changed all that, one negative development, one positive development. The negative development was the simple reality that there wasn't space enough to wholly construct a new narrative within the page limitations for our pre-circulated essays. The positive development was that I saw that in working from only the early texts, I was able to identify the key features of Augustine's theology of the Trinity. Doubtless there is further development in Augustine's Trinitarian theology and new things to uncover, but what I consider to be the fundamental concerns of that theology were substantially present in the the early writings I have been able to consider here. Just as importantly—for my purpose of providing a rereading of Augustine's theology of the Trinity—is the fact that if I could find in the early writings the presence of a Trinitarian theology which owed not to Neoplatonism, but to Nicene theology, which was polemical in its structure, and with an intense focus on the Incarnation—if I can show all these in Augustine's early writings, then I will have found all these under those conditions widely regarded to be least hospitable to my rereading.

READING AUGUSTINE ON THE TRINITY

One burden that has fallen upon the reading of Augustine's Trinitarian theology is the existence of a tradition or habit of reading the texts of that theology in a dismembered form. Augustine has been read in bits and pieces. Indeed, in bits and pieces sometimes seems to be the only way that Augustine's Trinitarian theology has been read. The medievals who read him read him that way. The moderns who read him have continued the practice. Undoubtedly all of Augustine's Trinitarian writings have been physically read together (i.e., by one person), yet within the discipline of theology the texts have not been "read together" in the sense of setting the theology from each text in: (a) the context of all of Augustine's Trinitarian writings; (b) the context of other late-fourth and early fifth century Latin Trinitarian writings; (c) the context of fourth-century Latin polemical literature; and (d) the context of authoritative Latin Trinitarian theology from the second and third centuries. Augustine's Trinitarian writings *have* been read in the context of late-fourth and early fifth-century Latin Neoplatonism—or, more frequently, in the context of an idealized understanding of what Neoplatonism then was. Where there has been a comparative reading of Augustine and other doctrinal authors, that comparative reading has been functionally a reading of two decontextualized and fragmented authors or texts, e.g., a dismembered Augustine and a dismembered Ambrose. It is ironic that while today there is some formal pressure towards doing readings which decontextualize, in point of fact there may have never been a "contextualized" reading of Augustine. What is today being held up as a new hermeneutical goal is rather a restatement of what has been unconscious (and conscious) practice. Let me suggest as an alternative that now is the time to do something radically new and excitingly different: to read Augustine's Trinitarian theology as a whole and in its context. For a change. In this essay, I am certainly not going to produce all of what could be produced from a single reading of Augustine in such a new manner, but whatever I have to say about Augustine's Trinitarian theology in this essay will follow from an attempt at a reading mindful of all that Augustine wrote of the Trinity[2] and the variety of contexts he wrote in. My intention in this essay is that my rereading of Augustine's Trinitarian theology will constitute a kind of re-membering of the texts of that theology.[3]

2. Presently, the best study available of Augustine's doctrine of God is Basil Studer's *The Grace of Christ and the Grace of God in Augustine of Hippo: Christocentrism or Theocentrism?* (Collegevilee MN: Liturgical Press, 1977). Despite some limitations, the book does an excellent job of articulating Augustine's theology in Augustine's own terms, that is, following Augustine's theology out via its own logic. See also: Johannes Arnold, "Begriff und heilsökonomische Bedeutung der göttlichen Sendungen in Augustinus *De Trinitate*" *Recherches Augustiniennes* XXV (1991): 3–69 and Studer's "History and Faith in Augustine's de Trinitate," *Augustinian Studies* 28 (1997): 7–50.

3. Since 1995, my work on Augustine has been conducted in continuous conversation with Lewis Ayres regarding his work on parallel and overlapping themes. Our daily exchange of research and texts via email means that it is difficult to acknowledge all the points at which this detailed conversation has influenced both our accounts. My own understanding of Augustine has been influenced particularly by Ayres's work on what he calls the "anthropological" component in Augustine's Trinitarian thought, especially the epistemological significance of the Second Person. See "Discipline of Self-Knowledge in Augustine's *De Trinitate* Book X," in L. Ayres, ed., *Passionate Intellect: Essays on the Transformation of Classical traditions Presented to Professor Ian Kidd*, RUSCH VII (Brunswick NJ: Transaction, 1995), 261–96; and "Christology and Faith," as well as "The Grammar of Augustine's Trinitarian Theology," in Robert Dodaro and George Lawless, eds., *Augustine and His Critics* (London: Routledge, 1999), 56–71. Ayres is presently writing a book entitled *Augustine's Trinitarian Theology*. I have also benefited substantially from two articles by Rowan Williams, "'Sapientia' and the Trinity: Reflections on *de Trinitate*," B. Bruning, ed., *Collectanea Augustiniana* (Leuven: Leuven university Press, 1990), 317–32;

One illustrative and important example of a decontextualized, dismembered reading of Augustine's Trinitarian theology may serve as an indication of how such readings have been significant in Western Trinitarian theology. We can take the case of the Trinitarian controversy involving Joachim of Fiore, Peter Lombard, and the Fourth Lateran Council, where, as Fiona Robb has recently noted, both Lombard and the Fourth Lateran Council emphasized the category of *quaedam summa res* as the fundamental category for describing the divine unity. Robbs remarks that Peter's "concept of the divine essence as a *quaedam summa res*, [was] attacked by Joachim but enshrined in the [Fourth] Lateran decree. The *quaedam summa res* represented both an abstract concept and a view of divine unity quite at odds with Joachim's own."[4] Robb then goes on to note that the category of *quaedam summa res* owed much to Augustine, and here she refers to book I.5 of *On Christian Doctrine*, which contains a credal formula by Augustine which reads, in part, "pater et filius et spiritus sanctus eademque trinitas, una *quaedam summa res* . . . unus deus, et singulus quisque horum *plena substantia* et simul omnes una substantia."[5] Robb makes the point that it is Augustine's *plena substantia* as well as the *quaedam summa res* which supports Lombard's own language of *quaedam summa res*.

The Trinitarian debate between Joachim and Peter Lombard is frequently treated in modern Trinitarian theologies as an exemplary case of an encounter between a Trinitarian theology with a strong emphasis on reality of the different divine Persons (Joachim's) versus a Trinitarian theology with a strong emphasis on reality of the unity of the divinity (Lombard's), and it may in fact have been just that. I would not want to dispute the judgment that Lombard may have either been given doctrinal insight or found a convenient authority in Augustine's *On Christian Doctrine*. I would want to suggest, however, that Lombard's reading of Augustine's Trinitarian theology cannot be given much weight in terms of his reproducing an Augustinian insight for development in his own Trinitarian theology. The reason why I say this is simple: the one and only time that Augustine ever uses either the phrase *plena substantia* or *summa res* is at *On Christian Doctrine* I.5; neither phrase ever again occurs in any of Augustine's writings.[6] The uniqueness of Augustine's Trinitarian language in *On Christian Doctrine* I.5 poses a question for Augustine scholars to try to answer, but most importantly, whatever significance *plena substantia* (following Robb) or *summa res* (simply following Lombard) had for later theologians, that significance can only stand apart from Augustine's own Trinitarian theology. Lombard's reading of Augustine is a clear—and influential—example of the decontextualized and dismembered

and "The Paradoxes of Self-Knowledge in the *De Trinitate*, in Joseph Lienhard et al., eds., *Collectanea Augustiniana. Augustine: Presbyter Factus Sum* (New York" Peter Lang, 1993), 121–34.

4. Fiona Robb, "The Fourth Lateran Council's Definition, of Trinitarian Orthodoxy" *Journal of Ecclesiastical History* 48 (1997): 22–43; here, 25.

5. CCL 32, I.V.6.9–10, emphasis added.

6. I make this claim on the basis of CETEDOC searches for both phrases.

way Augustine's Trinitarian theology has been read. Modern Trinitarian theologies which accept at face value Lombard's reading of Augustine—with whatever sympathy for either of the two sides in the debate—are in fact simply reproducing that dismembered reading.

Let me offer, then, a few methodological observations which I believe reflect necessary prerequisites for any credible reading of Augustine. I cannot claim that these comments are earth-shaking; indeed, I provide (and require) such prerequisites of work by my graduate students, so they can hardly be new to present readers. Nonetheless, it is the question of what a historically credible reading of Augustine's Trinitarian theology might be that is at the heart of my essay here, and my methodological presuppositions (and expectations) are best made explicit. These criteria may also, I hope, make more clear what I intend to do in this essay (or at least *how* I intend to do it).

There are, I propose, seven different criteria by which one judges a historical reading (or interpretation) of a text. A given reading is more credible as a work of scholarship in direct proportion to its degree of success in fulfilling these criteria. First, the reading must locate the text (or topic) in its contemporary context, and use that context to unpack the meaning or sense in the text. Second, the reading must identify the presence (or effect) of tradition in the text (or topic), and use that presence to identify the meaning or sense in the text. Third, the reading must identify and place the content of the text in a larger external narrative which supports the reading(s) derived from the previous steps by making such a content possible (or even, happy day, *likely*). Fourth, the reading must utilize a knowledge of scholarship on the author, text, and topic; the broader and more detailed the engagement with scholarship, the more sophisticated the reading. Fifth, there must be close reading or exegesis of the text which uncovers the key steps in the author's logic or expression. Sixth, the reading must identify, and show a fluency with, those conceptual idioms that are the key building blocks of the author's logic or expression. Seventh and finally, judgments on the sense of any part (a sentence, a phrase) of the text must relate that sense against the text as a whole (and test out that proposed out against the whole text). Such a relating of the part to the whole is necessary to avoid the danger of a "historical fundamentalism" (akin to "biblical fundamentalism") in which sentences or phrases are interpreted apart from the text within which the words stand. Steps such as these (and there is nothing definitive about this list or the order) are, I would argue, necessary for a credible reading of *any* theological (or philosphical) text, but it is enough for now to identify with such criteria the credibility of the reading of a text which falls under the rubric of historical theology.

One would imagine that there have been a variety of studies of Augustine's Trinitarian theology which place that theology and the key texts (e.g., *De Trinitate, Tractates on John*) in their contemporary context, either in terms of the late-fourth and early fifth centuries context within which Augustine developed his doctrines of the Trinity, or in terms of the context of Augustine's writings on the Trinity considered as a whole.

However, there is no variety of such studies; indeed, studies of this sort can hardly be found at all. The key scholarly works on Augustine's Trinitarian theology—e.g., Schmaus's or Schindler's[7]—either make only the most superficial historical placing of the theology or are wrong about the details of that setting (or both). The most detailed contextual study of Augustine's Trinitarian theology does not even have that theology as its proper subject: Olivier du Roy's detailed and very influential work, *L'Intelligence de la Foi en la Trinité selon saint Augustin*,[8] is about, as its title indicates, understanding and faith. Moreover, Du Roy's study limits itself to works written before 391, and most importantly, by design limits itself almost exclusively to the philosophical background of the ideas.

Likewise, scholarly treatments which identify the presence (or effect) of tradition in the texts (or topics) and which use that presence to recover the meaning or sense in the text are very few. As I noted earlier, there are no serious studies of Augustine's debt to second- and third-century Latin Trinitarian theology, nor are there monographs on Augustine's relationship to Latin Nicene polemical works of the fourth century (such as those by Phobaedius of Agen, Gregory of Elvira, Hilary of Poitiers, Eusebius of Vercelli, and Ambrose of Milan).[9] There are a few comments on this relationship made *en passant*, and there are comments in articles and books which presume this or that relationship, but there are no serious studies.[10] Scholarship identifying the role of tradition is largely limited to the study of the genre of *De Trinitate*, particularly its relationship to the ascent motif in Neoplatonism.[11] Obviously, it is true that historical theology, especially scholarship on the development of Trinitarian doctrine during the patristic period, has not been as productive or responsible as one would think it should have been. On the other hand, this lack of productivity (resulting in a lack of trustworthy insight or facts) has not visibly stopped anyone in the field of systematics from saying whatever they wanted to say about Augustine's Trinitarian theology.

Two of the criteria for judging the historical quality of a reading have collapsed into one another: it is often now the case that the placing of the text in a larger narrative

7. Michel Schmaus, *Die psychologische Trinitätslehre des heiligen Augustinus* (Münster: Aschendorff, 1927); Schindler, *Wort und Analogie in Augustins Trinitätslehre* (Tübingen: Mohr, 1965).

8. *L'intelligence de la foi en la Trinité selon saint Augustine* (Paris: Études Augustiennnes, 1966).

9. Although one should now see the very recent article by Christoph Markschies, "Was ist lateinischer 'Neunizanismus'?," *Zeitschrift für Antikes Christentum* 1 (1997): 73–95, which argues for a body of Latin neo-Nicene theology stretching from the second half of the fourth century in continuity through to Augustine.

10. There is one well-known account of Augustine's relationship to Greek theology, Irenée Chevalier, *S. Augustin et la Pensée Grecque: Les relations Trinitaires* (Fribourg en Suisse: Librarire de l'Université, 1940), but it is impossible now to credit the argument of that work. There are, however, a number of treatments of Augustine's Trinitarian theology written during the 1950s, in the first blush of Chevalier's publication, which take his conclusions as authoritative.

11. As I pointed out in "Arians of Book V," in older scholarship the emphasis on genre has served functionally as a way of removing *Trin.*, and the Trinitarian theology it expresses, from any historical context.

is functionally equivalent to reproducing (sometimes unconsciously) specific scholarly judgments. For many theologians writing about Augustine's Trinitarian theology, the larger external narrative is simply Régnon's grand scheme of Western Trinitarian theology *begins with* (in the sense of "presumes" and "is ultimately concerned with") divine unity (i.e., the essence), while Eastern Trinitarian theology *begins with* divine diversity (i.e., the persons). The narrative provided by Régnon's paradigm is filled in, as it were, with Du Roy's work to provide the following "historical context": *the emphasis in Augustine's Trinitarian theology on divine unity owes to the influence of Neoplatonism.* I have elsewhere argued the hidden character of the origins of this judgment, and I will not repeat that argument here.[12] What I will suggest now is that the judgment of the Neoplatonic character of Augustine's Trinitarian theology may have once had the function of placing that Trinitarian theology within a historical context and within a narrative of the development of doctrine (namely, placing that Trinitarian theology within the historical context of late-fourth- and early fifth-century Latin Neoplatonism). But if such a judgment on the Neoplatonic character of Augustine's emphasis on unity ever had the function of locating that theology within a historical context, the judgment does not, can not, continue to do so credibly any longer. There are several reasons why reading Augustine's Trinitarian theology as an event in Latin Neoplatonism can no longer credibly serve to locate that theology historically, of which I shall only three name. The first reason is that the understanding of Neoplatonism as a historical phenomenon which was presumed for that narrative is itself no longer viable from a scholarly point of view.[13] The second reason is that the secondary work which supposedly supports such a judgment (e.g., Du Roy's) in fact does not.[14] The third reason why reading Augustine's Trinitarian theology as an event in Latin Neoplatonism can no longer credibly serve to locate that theology historically is the point of departure of this essay: such a location fails to reflect the doctrinal content of the texts it is supposed to explain, depending as it does upon an *a*historical, decontextualized or dismembered reading of the texts.

12. I have argued that the narrative presupposed by many modern accounts of Augustine's Trinitarian theology is that of Théodore de Régnon—or rather, a greatly simplified version of Régnon's study. See my "Use of Augustine in Contemporary Trinitarian Theology"; and "Régnon Reconsidered."

13. Let me offer an obvious example: the last chapter of A.H. Armstrong's *The Architecture of the Intelligible Universe in the Philosophy of Plotinus* (1940; rpt. Amsterdam: Adolf M. Hakkert, 1967) is on Plotinus doctrine of the logos. In this work Armstrong argues that Plotinus had a 'subordinationist' understanding of logos, and he suggests that this Plotinian understanding had been absorbed into any Christian trinitarian theology influenced by Plotinus. Late, however, Armstrong recanted of this position, having recognized that the logos doctrine he had attributed to Plotinus was in fact Philo's. Thus, Armstrong's treatment of Plotinus in *The Cambridge History of Later Greek and Early Medieval Philosophy* (Cambridge: Cambridge University Press, 1967) makes no mention of the logos critique so prominent in *The Architecture of the Intelligible Universe.*

14. It is too frequently assumed that a triadic analysis of existence is Neoplatonic, but there is no historical reason for such an asumption. The authority for many observations on triadic language in Augustine's Trinitarian theology, Olivier du Roy, does not identify the triad as Neoplatonic since he is well aware of the alternative sources.

This brings us to the last three criteria: an identification of and fluency with conceptual idioms that are the building blocks of the author's logic or expression; a close reading or exegesis of the text which uncovers the key steps in the author's logic or expression; and reading the parts of the text in relation to the whole. This essay will utilize these three techniques especially (or most explicitly) in order to develop an alternative account of Augustine's Trinitarian theology. I will focus on three theological motifs in Augustine's Trinitarian theology. First, the doctrine of inseparable activity as the fundamental expression of divine unity; second, the epistemic character of the Incarnation as the decisive revelation of divine unity, that is, of the Trinity, especially as the decisive revelation of their inseparable activity; and third, the hermeneutical circle of faith by which true doctrine leads to the process of personal imaging (of the Trinity), which leads to greater doctrinal insight which leads to greater imaging of the Trinity, etc. This essay is principally a series of text-studies (what else can we read, must less *reread*?), but the reader should find these three motifs recurring amidst my underlying thesis that with these three motifs (or trajectories), we find the basis for a rereading of Augustine, one which better represents Augustine's Trinitarian theology by better fulfilling the seven criteria just articulated. The narrative of that rereading may be summarized: as one would expect of a late-fourth- and early fifth-century Latin writing on the Trinity, Augustine's basic frame of reference for understanding the Trinity is the appropriation of Nicaea. That appropriation takes place with a polemical context, and, moreover, involves rearticulating the Creed of Nicaea in terms which were not originally part of that text. In Augustine's time, the most important of such articulations is that "the unity of the Trinity is found in its Its inseparable activities or operations."

THE THEOLOGY OF *EPISTLE* 11

The earliest written engagement by Augustine with the doctrine of the Trinity is in his *Epistle* 11,[15] a letter to Nebridius, a friend and fellow North African who shared the experience in Italy.[16] Augustine clearly functioned as a mentor to the community of serious-minded young Christians he moved within in Italy and in Africa. In a series

15. I use the English translation of Sister Wilfred Parsons in the Fathers of the Church series, vol. 12.

16. *Epistle* 11, written in 389, is not simply the first time Augustine uses the term *trinitas* in his extant writings but—according to James J. O'Donnell—the only time the word is used by Augustine before his ordination in 391. See O'Donnell's commentary *Augustine—The Confessions*, 3 vols. (Oxford: Clarendon Press, 1992), III.309, which is his note on *Confessions* 12.7.7. Despite the seemingly obvious significance of *Ep.* 11 as an occasion to perceive Augustine's earliest Trinitarian theology, the recent substantial article by Nello Cipriani, "La Fonti Christiane della Dottrina Trinitaria nei primi Dialoghi di S. Agostino," *Augustinianum* 34 (1994), 253–312 contains no treatment whatsoever of the letter. See, however, Ayres's treatment of *Ep.* 11 in his "The Grammar of Augustine's Trinitarian Theology." Presently, the most extensive study of *Ep.* 11 remains Du Roy's in his *L'Intelligence de la Foi en la Trinité selon saint Augustin*, 391–401.

of letters which constitute the occasion for the earliest of Augustine's preserved correspondence, Nebridius asks Augustine to explain *how is it that if the Trinity do all things
together in unity, then why is the Son alone said to be Incarnate and not the Father and
the Holy Spirit as well*? Answering this question leads Augustine first into Trinity and
then—seamlessly—into Christology, a fact which will deserve some attention. But
first, Nebridius' question itself requires comment.

The point of departure for Nebridius' question is Nicene theology as it had been
developed—in both East and West—by the 380s. By the 380s, Nicene Trinitarian theology has developed substantially beyond the doctrine first articulated in the Creed of
Nicaea (325). There had developed, for example, a sensitivity to the need for language
which positively identifies the separate existence of the Father, Son, and—with somewhat lesser emphasis—the Holy Spirit. Such a sensitivity is nowhere to be found in the
original theology of Nicaea. However, a very important development in the "Nicene
Trinitarian theology of the 380s is the way in which the unity among the Three is
conceived and articulated. Obviously, the language of "Father" and "Son," and the
continuity of nature presupposed in any "fatherly" generation of a "son," articulates
a notion of a kind of unity within the Trinity. But the understanding that the very
language of "Father" and "Son" applied to God is to be understood as identifying the
kind of continuity of nature presupposed in any "fatherly" generation of a "son" is
precisely what is to be proved in the Trinitarian controversies (since the opposition
will argue that these titles are to be understood adoptively). It is the conclusion anti-
Arians strive for, not the demonstration of the unity.[17] I would suggest, rather, that
the most fundamental conception and articulation in Nicene Trinitarian theology of
the 380s of the unity among the Three is the understanding that *any action of any
member of the Trinity is actually an action of the three inseparably*. This development in
Nicene Trinitarian theology, which begins in the late 350s, becomes the most distinctive feature of pro-Nicene polemic, and—by the 380s—is identified as the substance
of Nicene theology.[18] Hilary of Poitier's use of such an argument is probably the most

17. Which is not to deny the fact that in anti-Arian polemics attempts are made to "save" Father
and Son terminology from any conceptual weakness (e.g., the idea that calling God "father" is implicitly to attribute passionate generation to him). Moreover, arguments are made, e.g., by Basil of
Ancyra and the homoiousians, which explicitly advance the Father–Son model as the paradigm of
descriptions of the Trinity in conscious opposition to anti-Nicene theology.

18. The terms "neo-Nicene" and "pro-Nicene" are technical, if still somewhat fluid, names for two
kinds of Trinitarian theology based on Nicaea. To a certain extent, it is appropriate to understand
these two theologies as two understandings of Nicaea, and one can also understand the difference
between the two to be that of sequence: pro-Nicene is later (although pro-Nicene theology does not
wholly replace neo-Nicene theology). The two terms correspond approximately to the difference between Athanasius' Trinitarian theology and the Trinitarian theology of, e.g., Gregory of Nyssa. Distinguishing features of the two forms of Nicene theology would include: (1) neo-Nicene theology is not
engaged in the debate over John 5:19, while pro-Nicene is, and (2) neo-Nicene theology identifies the
Son as the single proper "Power" of God, while pro-Nicene theology understands both the Father and
Son to share the "Power" of God, and thus to share the same nature. See my "One Nature, One Power:
Consensus Doctrine in Pro-Nicene polemic," *Studia Patristica*, XXIX (1997): 205–23.

appropriate to specify here, since his book will be read later by Augustine. In his *De Trinitate* VII.17–18, Hilary says that "the whole mystery of our faith [*omne sacramentum fidei nostrae*]"[19] is contained in the teaching that the Son does the same work as the Father and that "the same things the Father does are all done likewise by the Son [*ut omnia quae Pater facit, eadem omnia similiter faciat et Filius*]."[20] This truth Hilary calls "our confession of Father and Son [*et ut maneret salutaris in Patre et Filio confessionis nostrae ordo*]."[21]

The question which Augustine answers in *Epistle* 11 reflects Nebridius' attempt at understanding the Nicene faith which he wants to hold properly. Nebridius understands that catholic Trinitarian theology holds that all actions performed by the Father, Son, and Holy Spirit are performed in common. Augustine himself recognizes the source—and, if you will, the "canonical" context—of Nebridius' question when he begins his answer by making explicit that source or context: "According to the Catholic faith, the Trinity is proposed to our belief and believed . . . as so inseparable that whatever action is performed by It [the Trinity] must be thought to be performed at the same time by the Father and by the Son and by the Holy Spirit."

One last comment on the context of Nebridius' question: it is almost the same question that Augustine will refer to at the beginning of *De Trinitate*. At *De Trinitate* I.8, immediately after the work's original beginning (at I.7), and just after repeating the same summary of catholic faith found earlier in *Epistle* 11, Augustine says: "Yet this faith worries some people, when they hear that the Father is God and the Son is God and the Holy Spirit is God, and yet this threesome is not three gods but one God. They wonder how they are to understand this, especially when it is said that the trinity works inseparably in everything that God works . . ." Augustine finishes up this observation with the remark, "People ask us these questions to the point of weariness." When at the beginning of the fifth century Augustine wrote these words, Nebridius had been dead for nearly ten years, so it was not the persistant requests of his old friend which so wearied Augustine the bishop; it was the problem of understanding a Trinitarian theology which one wanted to believe—even as that theology was, as *De Trinitate* I.9 makes clear, still facing criticism and competition from an alternative theology (namely, the theology of the Homoians).[22] The inherently difficult task of

19. CCSL 62.279

20. CCSL 62.278

21. Hilary, *Trin.*, CCSL 62.278.

22. The standard account of Latin Homoianism is Meslin, *Les ariens d'Occident 335–430*. A substantial description of Latin Homoianism can be found in the two-hundred-page introduction by Roger Gryson for his translation, *Scolies Ariennes sur le Concile d'Aquilée*. A very good recent account of the growth of western Homoianism can be found in Williams, *Ambrose of Milan*. In *The Search for the Christian Doctrine of God*, R.P.C. Hanson has a chapter describing Homoianism which purports to describe both Greek and Latin Homoian theology, but in fact the chapter contains a significant treatment only of *Latin* Homoian theology (as though there are no differences between it and Greek Homoianism).

attempting to understand catholic or Nicene Trinitarian theology is a task Augustine admits he shares, must share, with Nebridius. Augustine's reply to Nebridius begins by admitting the difficulty of the issue and the tentativeness of his answer. That tentativeness is something to which we shall return.

Augustine's answer to Nebridius starts with the thesis that any nature may be analyzed in or through three characteristics: that the nature *is* (or exists); that such a nature *is this or that* (i.e., something specific, or has identity); and that it *continues to be* what it is (its identity endures). Such an analysis *suggests* an analogy to the Trinity because Augustine understands that the first characteristic of a nature—that it is— "shows us the very cause of nature from which all things come," while the second characteristic of a nature—that a nature is this or that "shows us the appearance in which all things are fashioned and in a certain sense formed." That a characteristic should indicate "the cause from which all things come" seems analogous to the distinctive characteristic of the Father, while "appearance" and "form" seem Christological in character—at least retrospectively, given what Augustine says in *Epistle* 14 and develops further in his later writings.

The rest of Augustine's argument is peculiarly cast: if we could observe any existing nature or substance which failed to possess one (or two) of these characteristics, then one of the Trinity could possibly act without the other two, but we never observe any existing nature or substance to lack one of the three characteristics, so the Trinity does indeed act in unity. Augustine adds that if one understands the logical necessity that mandates each of the three characteristics of being, then one can similarly understand that the Trinity must act in unity. Augustine introduces the triad not because it is a Trinitarian analogy in the sense that each of the three characteristics stands for one of the Three Persons. The point of the triadic analysis of substance or nature is to provide an example of a common operation which serves as an analogue to the point that Augustine is ultimately working through—namely, that the Three share common operations, and that such common operations indicate (and are caused by) their common nature.

There are many comments to make about this argument by Augustine. Whether or not the argument is quite so spectacularly subtle as Augustine claims it is, the argument is not very convincing: it is, perhaps, too subtle by half. Having said that, some slightly more constructive observations can be offered. First, the argument is an argument for the unity of action among the Three and not an argument that the Three are One. The description of unity among the Three in terms of the unity of action is very much a traditional Nicene way of speaking about Trinitarian unity. A second observation, which goes to the heart of Augustine's argument, is that the ontological analysis Augustine offers of *the kinds of action* that we are talking about in Trinitarian theology *as unified* is similar to other pro-Nicene polemics, like that of Gregory of Nyssa's, in its probable debt to a technical philosophical analysis of being. Gregory's debt is to Plotinius' notion of power;[23] Augustine, of course, has a *triadic* analysis of being—which is unlike Hilary of Poitiers and Gregory of Nyssa, but like Marius Victorinus. We cannot, however, say *where* that triadic analysis is coming from or what philosophical influence it represents. Cicero? Quintillian? Plotinus? Porphyry? Marius Victorinus?[24] The most important thing, which needs emphasizing, is that recourse in Trinitarian doctrine to a philosophical analysis of being is typical of Nicene and pro-Nicene argument or reasoning, and such recourse is not in itself distinctive to Augustine, nor, obviously, is it an innovation.

The underlying question of the pro-Nicene doctrine that unity of nature is demonstrated in the unity of action surfaces again in *Epistle* 14, another letter written to Nebridius which continues the conversation already begun in *Epistle* 11. Nebridius remarks upon the fact that although he (Nebridius) and Augustine are separate persons, they do many of the same things as the other (e.g., they both walk).[25] Nebridius then refers to the sun and the other stars: the sun does not do the same things the other stars do. The point of such remarks for Trinitarian theology is fairly straightforward: catholic Trinitarian theology argues that whatever shares the same nature performs the same actions, and what performs the same actions must have the same nature; the Father and the Son perform the same actions, so they must have the same nature, and sharing the same nature, they act in unity. But, Nebridius observes, Nebridius and Augustine share the same nature (i.e., humanity) and perform many of the same actions: Is that the kind of unity the persons of the Trinity have? Moreover, the sun and the stars, seemingly possessed of the same nature, do not do the same actions (the sun heats us, stars do not, etc.). How does this affect the logic of the argument that whatever shares the same nature performs the same actions?

23. See my "Eunomius of Cyzicus and Gregory of Nyssa.": Two Traditions of Transcendent Causality," *Vigiliae Christianae* 52 (1998): 59–87.

24. Du Roy's treatment of the triadic language in *Ep.* 11 is substantial, and his identification of the different possible sources for the language remains as the authoritative account. However, while in his treatment of *Ep.* 11, Du Roy is circumspect about attributing a specific source for the language, in his lengthy "Conclusion" he is less circumspect, and it is this part of the study which supports characterizations of Augustine's Trinitarian theology as constituted fundamentally by Neoplatonic triads.

25. Although this is not the place for a full treatment of this fact, it is nonetheless worth noting that Nebridius' reference to 'walking' as the activity shared by Augustine and himself indicates the Stoic provenance of the topoi employed in the discussion. Stoics regularly use walking as an exemplary example of continuity between intention (or impulse) and doing. Moreover, walking features in Stoic arguing points for the reality of individual acts over against Platonic and Aristotelian over-evaluation of the universal. In short, in these early epistles we have evidence of the influence of philosophical authorities other than neoplatonism, and, to push this point, insofar as we can recognize the continuity between what Augustine speaks of in his letter and the philosophical discussion he is drawing upon, then it seems as though Augustine is employing arguments used by Stoics to argue against the very sort of reification of universals Augustine is often accused of maintaining. See Seneca, *Epistle* 113. 18–24; John M. Rist, *Stoic Philosophy* (rpt. 1980; Cambridge: Cambridge University Press, 1969), 33–4; and Brad Inwood, *Ethics and Human Action in Early Stoicism* (Oxford: Clarendon Press, 1985), 52, 156.

Augustine's reply is informative for what it reveals about his logic. In the same way as he had already in *Epistle* 11, Augustine begins by transposing the question. In *Epistle* 11, Augustine argues for the necessity of the unity of the triadic characteristics of being and the presence of all three of the characteristics in the Trinity by simply saying that having the proper understanding of being, we see that each occasion of being demonstrates the presence of the three characteristics, and those three characteristics—with their attendant unity—must therefore obtain in the Trinity. In *Epistle* 14, Augustine begins his reply with the same kind of transposition: if it is true that you and I—we humans—do the same actions, then whatever else has the same nature must also do the same actions. If we move, Augustine tells Nebridius (and we do, both of us walking), then the sun and the stars also move. Just as we both awaken, the sun and the stars all shine. The reality of *common nature–common action* that we know serves as the basis for knowing that other cases of common nature result in common action. The provocative character for us of this argument by Augustine is due, to a degree not to be underestimated, to our not recognizing, these ignorant centuries later, the rhetorical or logical school of discourse Augustine is implicitly casting his argument in terms of for Nebridius. But the provocative character for us of Augustine's argument is also due to discursive moves within the text (and thus within Augustine's logic or rhetorical form) which begin to reveal themselves after a close reading. I shall return to this remark momentarily.

If, in *Epistle* 14, Augustine argues that our experience that identical activities must follow from natures which are in fact identical provides a basis for our knowing that the sun and the stars must share common activities since they share common natures, there must be, nonetheless (Augustine asserts), a significant qualification to all such comparisons. No two physical existents, no two bodies, ever really perform the same operation, since no two bodies can occupy the same space at the same time.[26] And if two bodies never really perform the same operation, so much more is there an intrinsic incommensurability in comparisons between intellectual operations and the actions of bodies: the unity in a common act of contemplation exceeds comparison with the unity in a common physical act. In other words, in terms of the argument overall, what Augustine really wants Nebridius to consider is what might be called the formal character of his arguments. Comparisons between physical and intellectual realities are always bound by intrinsic limitations or incommensurateness. Despite the limitations, there is, however, a certain utility to the comparisons. Articulating that utility brings us back to *Epistle* 11 and the initially provocative character of Augustine's argument noted above.

In *Epistle* 11, after Augustine has articulated his three-characteristics-of-nature argument, he turns to the topic of the Incarnation. Nebridius' original question was, after all, a question focused upon the Incarnation: if the Three act as One, then why do

---

26. This observation by Augustine also echoes the Stoic *topos* associated with walking: namely, that the same class of action (e.g. walking) varies in each actual case of doing.

we attribute Incarnation only to the Son and not to the Father and Holy Spirit, as well? Augustine describes the Son in terms of a distinguishing characteristic such as those already introduced. But the distinguishing characteristic is not immediately one of the original three which the reader might have suspected were Trinitarian analogues (especially a twentieth-century reader primed to look for Trinitarian analogues). The distinguishing characteristic of the Son is expressed in rather idiosyncratic terms by Augustine: a "system of life" and a "sort of art" and the understanding which forms a mind in its thoughts. Such titles suggest the unique role the Son plays—particularly in the Incarnation—in revealing the content and practice of knowledge and a way of life which are necessary in order for us to understand God the Trinity. This act of revelation is distinct to the Son and is properly understood as his distinctive characteristic or activity.

Having said this, Augustine then introduces a new set of questions which further the previous ontological analysis. The original triadic characteristics Augustine earlier invoked all followed the pattern of "All nature or substance [must] . . ." The first such characteristic was "All nature or substance exists." The second set of analysis introduced at *Epistle* 11.4 constitutes a further development of the question: Does this exist? The question of whether something exists implies the question: What is it? The question "What is it?" leads to the question of its value. Augustine remarks that "all these arguments are inseparably joined together." This inseparability is the reason why Augustine introduces the new analytic categories to illustrate an important case in which the three "moments" which occur in understanding existence are necessarily implied or joined to one another, even if we move through each question one at a time and may have to discover or be taught the existence of the "next" question and its connection to the previous question. Indeed, it is not the individual criterion of being which are of decisive interest, but the fact that they are inseparably joined and that each leads discursively one to the other.

The discovery, as it were, of the three "inseparably joined" arguments or characteristics provide the occasion—the necessary or prerequiste occasion—for Augustine (at last) to offer a triad that is in fact analogously descriptive of the Trinity. Understanding proceeds from the Father, through the Son (the character of that understanding in the Son has already been described by Augustine), and the Holy Spirit produces in the knower a delight in that knowledge. The distinctive characteristics of each person of the Trinity are not articulated through an ontological analysis, but through an analysis of the epistemological or soteriological prerequisite for human knowledge of the reality of the unity of the joint operations of the Trinity. All operations of the Trinity occur in perfect union, but due to our weakness we have to be brought to an understanding of this fact. The unity of action in the Trinity can only be understood (without meaning to be technical about that word) by a human mind that has been properly trained in right reason, a way of reasoning which, Augustine says, can best be understood as a way of life.[27] That way of life, revealed in the Son generally and in the Incarnation in a special way, is necessary for the unity of action among the Three to be understood by us in what we might call an organic way: although the operations of the Three "occur with the most complete union and inseparability, they nonetheless have to be proved separately, by reason of our weakness." Augustine's first triadic account of God is one which describes the joint action of the Trinity in providing humanity with the knowledge necessary in order to understand that life-in-Trinity properly. The common work of the Trinity in providing that knowledge finds its effect in the Incarnation. Augustine has thereby answered Nebridius' question: the Three are all acting in the Incarnation, but the Incarnation must be understood within the context of the Trinity's self-communication. "First we propose to know on what we may construct an argument and on what ground we may stand. That is why a certain rule and standard of reasoning had first to be proved. This has been accomplished by that dispensation of the Incarnation." Although *Epistle* 11 predates the beginnings of *De Trinitate* by more than a decade, it would be hard to find another summary which better captures the dynamic and motivation of that later work.

I have reviewed *Epistle* 11 in such detail not simply because the letter offers us a revealing, and underappreciated, view of Augustine's early Trinitarian theology, but more to the overall point of this essay, many of the key doctrinal points which Augustine articulated at this ealy period remained active throughout his writings on the Trinity. The most obvious (though not necessarily the most significant) example of such a doctrinal point would be Augustine's habit of seeking analogies to the unity of the Trinity. More significant, I think, is the aid *Epistle* 11 can serve in sensitizing the reader to the question of exactly what "unity" is it that Augustine is trying to explain. In *Epistle* 11, Augustine is seeking to provide an insight into the doctrine of the unity of action among the Three Persons of the Trinity.[28] The notion that the Three Persons act inseparably is, for Augustine, the fundamental doctrine of catholic (which is to say Nicene or pro-Nicene) Trinitarian theology. What I do not mean to suggest is that already in *Epistle* 11 Augustine's Trinitarian theology is mature and well-conceived. It is not. Augustine knows that the Three Persons act inseparably, but his sense of the

27. This insight of Augustine's will develop and continue to undergird his Trinitarian theology, thereby proving the practical import for the psychological analogies he will offer in *Trin.* and other works. The type of mental life—mapped out within the analogies and elsewhere—that we are to lead is one which purifies the heart and reflects the love which is the root dynamic of the Trinity. Precedents for such a link between "faith and right conduct" may be observed, for example, in Gregory of Nyssa's *Life of Moses* and in Evagrius' ("Basil of Caesarea") *Ep.* VIII, where the goal of a purified contemplation (identified with the "kingdom") is intellectual sight of the Lord and the Trinity.

28. When in *Sermon* 52.17 and 18 Augustine introduces the psychological analogy to the Trinity, he is clear that he is searching for an analogy to the inseparable activity. Thus he says: "Let us see, then, if I can't find something in creation, by which to show that there are three somethings whch can both be separatedly presented and also operate inseparably" (*Sermon* 52.17). And: "So turn your eyes to the person within. That is where some kind of likeness is rather to be looked for of *three somethings that can be indicated separately but operate inseparably*" (*Sermon* 52.18; emphasis added).

logic of that doctrine is not strong, and there is a certain artificiality in his explanation to Nebridius of the doctrine. One can say either that Augustine does not yet really understand the doctrine, or alternately, one can say that Augustine is, at the time of *Epistle* 11, ignorant of the polemical argument developed (by, e.g., Hilary or Ambrose) in support of the doctrine that the Three Persons act inseparably. The traditional polemical argument is sophisticated in its use of Scripture and philosophical notions of aetiology, and in the linking of those two resources. Augustine's argument in *Epistle* 11 lacks the sophistication attained nearly forty years earlier by Hilary in *De Trinitate* VII. Augustine knows what he must believe; he has some interesting ideas in support of those catholic beliefs, but there is much of catholic theology which has not yet begun to play in his thought.

There is one last point to make (again) about *Epistle* 11. As an early (389) work by Augustine, it dates precisely from that period in Augustine's life when he was most engaged with Neoplatonism, and during which, some scholars have suggested, his thought was largely dominated by Neoplatonic categories (to the extent, according to a few influential scholars, he is better understood as a "convert" to Neoplatonism, rather than a convert to Christianity).[29] Over against this vision of rampant Neoplatonism, we find in *Epistle* 11 a treatment of the Incarnation and the unity among the Three expressed in language clearly informed by Nicene or pro-Nicene doctrine. (Not a mature treatment, to be sure, but nonetheless . . .) Moreover, the philosophical categories that are clearly and undeniably in Augustine's account of the unity of the Trinity are not of any clear Neoplatonic provenance; in fact, they are most likely draw from Stoic sources. The very authority—Du Roy—which is often held to have proved the Neoplatonic character of Augustine's Trinitarian theology is rather the source for our glimpsing that the triadic language in *Epistle* 11 may come from a wide variety of sources.

THE THEOLOGY OF *EIGHTY-THREE DIFFERENT QUESTIONS, NO.* 69

The Christological focus articulated in *Epistle* 11 can be found again in no. 69 of the collection *Eighty-Three Different Questions* (or *Div. Quaest.*). These notes by Augustine on various topics that arise in his theological reflection (sometimes privately, sometimes in response to a question posed by someone) date from 388 to 395/6. *Div. Quaest.* 69 is usually dated to 394–96, which means about five years after *Epistle* 11, in that time when Augustine has settled into his life as a cleric, but before he had been consectrated bishop and before he had begun to write the *Confessions*. *Div. Quaest.* 69 either slightly predates Augustine's turn to scriptural investigation (particularly the works of Paul), or marks one of our earliest expressions of that well-known turn.[30]

29. Whatever the later articulations of these judgments, the modern source is probably Otto Scheel, *Die Anschauung Augustins über Christi Person und Werk* (Tübingen: Verlag von J. C. B. Mohr, 1901).

30. E.g., Augustine wrote *De libero arbitrio* from 391–95; the *Usefulness of Belief* was written soon

The note is, in fact, an exegetical reflection on 1 Corinthians 15:28, with recurring attention to John 14:18 and Philippians 2:5–7. The cause of Augustine's reflection on 1 Corinthians 15:28 is, as he tells us explicitly (indeed, in the first line of the text), the heretical exegesis some lay upon the passage. These heretics are commonly identified as Arians,[31] but the more accurate term is Homoians. The term Arian pushes not simply the origin but the identifying features of such a theology back too far in time, so that a modern reader imagines the distinctive traits of the theology Augustine opposes to be the specific doctrines expressed by Arius.[32] This is a misleading conclusion, for Augustine's opponents espouse doctrines beyond whatever Arius himself believed. This fact is especially significant—indeed, decisive—if one is to understand Augustine's exegetical strategies, and thus to understand the role of exegesis in the development of Augustine's Trinitarian theology.

First Corinthians 15:28 is a good example of a scriptural text under polemical pressure.[33] We know that in the second half of the fourth century, one way that Latin Homoians articulated their opposition to the Trinitarian faith, by then associated with Nicaea, was through an exegesis of 1 Corinthians 15:28.[34] In their eyes, this text says that at the end of time the Son will be subject or subordinated to the Father. The fact that we use "subordination(ism)" as a generic category for a kind of Trinitarian or Christological doctrine should not desensitize us to the fact that in Latin Homoian

---

after Augustine became a priest (in 391); and the *Letter to Simplicianus* dates from 397.

31. Mosher, the English-language translator of *Eighty-Three Different Questions*, so identifies Augustine's opponents as Arians in his Fathers of the Church translation (vol 70. 167n2). Similarly, G. Bardy, J.-A. Beckaert, and J. Boutet, the editors of the Bibliothèque Augustinienne, *Oeuvres de Saint Augustine*, vol. 10, likewise identify Augustine's opponents as Arians (83n82).

32. Augustine's reasons for using the title Arian have to do with the polemical strategy adopted by Latin Nicene polemicists and those Greek Nicene polemicists who followed Athanasius. Opponents to a theology identified with Nicaea were reduced to, or identified as, followers of Arius and holders of his theology. See my "Fourth Century as Trinitarian Canon." Augustine himself understood the difference between doctrines and exegeses which originate directly from Arius, and those which originate with later anti-Nicenes: in *Trin.*, for example, he is quite specific in what he attributes to "Arius," "Arians," and "Eunomians," respectively. Modern confusions of the three should not be projected back on to Augustine, whatever rhetorical identifications he may sometimes have employed in his polemics.

33. In Greek theology of the first half of the fourth century, 1 Cor 15:28 figured prominently in the hyper-Nicene (modalist) theology of Marcellus of Ancyra. Augustine seems unaware of the association of the Scripture passage with Marcellus. Evagrius' *Ep.* 8 provides an example of a Greek anti-Homoian (though Evagrius argues against the Greek variety of Homoians) argument for 1 Cor 15:28 which focuses exclusively on the Homoian claims on the passage and shows no indication of anti-Marcellan sensitivity. (I cite this letter, erroneously attributed to Basil, because Evagrius is Augustine's almost exact contemporary. Like Augustine, Evagrius was born in the 350s, and in the 380s witnessed close-up, but not as one directly engaged, the confrontation with anti-Nicenes. *Ep.* 8 could have been written anytime from the early 380s to the early 390s (i.e., it is approximately contemporary to Augustine's *Ep.* 11 and *Div. Quaest.* 69).

34. In the *Acts of the Council of Aquilaea* 39, the homoian Palladius evidently cites 1 Cor 15:28 when he says that the Son is subject to the Father. See Gryson, *Scolies Ariennes sur le Concile d'Aquilée*, 359. Some scholars think that this Palladius is the author the *Arian Sermon* Augustine writes a rebuttal of in 419.

theology there is, literally, the attribution of a subordinate status to the Son, based, in part, upon exegesis of scriptural texts like 1 Corinthians 15:28. Other scriptural passages under polemical pressure from the Homoians included John 14:28, a text Augustine invoked at the end of his first paragraph of *Div. Quaest.* 69 as one which is associated by some with what he considers to be a problematic interpretation of 1 Corinthians 15:28.

Augustine's refutation of Homoian exegesis begins with the standard Nicene exegetical rule: wherever Scripture speaks of the Son as less than the Father, Scripture is there speaking of the Son's humanity; wherever Scripture speaks of the Son as equal to the Father, Scripture is there speaking of the Son's divinity. This rule provides the basis for a correct understanding of scriptural passages such as John 10:30; John 1:1, 14; and Philippians 2:5–7. However, Augustine recognizes that the Homoians are not arguing for the Son's inferior and different nature simply on the basis of incarnational passages; the Homoians are arguing that some of the scriptural passages which distinguish the persons of the Trinity indicate the Son's inferiority (in short, these passages have nothing to do with Jesus' human weakness). Augustine himself recognizes two kinds of statements in Scripture about the Second Person: those which distinguish the persons of the Trinity, and those which apply to the assumption of humanity in the Incarnation.

The Homoians read 1 Corinthians 15:28 to mean either that some things are not now subject to the Son, or that the Son is not now subject to God. The anti-Nicene impetus to saying that "some thing are not now subject to the Son" is fairly obvious, but the polemical weight of suggesting that the Son is not now subject to God is less clear. Interestingly, though, it is this second reading that Augustine treats as the most significant to refute. Augustine is most concerned to reject the suggestion that the status of the Son vis-à-vis the Father will change intrinsically at the end times (i.e., that the Son will become subject to God, although he is not now). He is concerned to reject such a suggestion not because Augustine thinks that nothing changes at the end-time, but because he has his own very significant and substantial understanding of what "happens" at the end-times, an eschatological dynamic Augustine does not want derailed or confused in our understanding.

Augustine's argument follows this form: the passage "when he [the Son] will hand the kingdom over to God and the Father" is to be understood following the model of "Hallowed be thy name." The line from the Lord's prayer does not mean that God's name is not now holy; rather, the prayer asks that God's name be recognized as holy. Similarly (Augustine argues), "when he [the Son] will hand the kingdom over" does not mean that the kingdom is not now under the dominion of God; rather, Paul speaks of the time when God's kingdom will be recognized in and through the Son. Or, as Augustine puts it, "when he [the Son] will show that the Father reigns." At the end-time the Son will "show" or reveal that the Father reigns as he has always reigned. That dominion has not always been, indeed has never been, *shown*: it has, rather, been believed. What happens at the end-times is that Son will show that the Father reigns, so that what believers have known through belief will be made manifest to them. "Therefore Christ will hand the kingdom over to God and the Father when through him the Father will be known by sight, for his kingdom consists of those in whom he now reigns through faith." The meaning of "the Son will hand the kingdom over" is that "then the Father will be known by sight as he—and the Trinity ('God')—is known now by faith."

The purpose of this "handing over of the kingdom," that is, the revealing of the kingdom's existence, is both Christological and Trinitarian, if we can still use such clumsy categories which are already beginning to crumble under a pressure they cannot bear.[35] The Christological and Trinitarian *telos* of the "handing over of the kingdom" is the Incarnate Son's leading "those nourished by faith in his Incarnation to the actual seeing of his equality with the Father."[36] At some future point in time the humanity of Christ, which is now the occasion of our faith, will become perfectly transparent to the divinity of the Son: the vision of that divinity will itself open up into a vision of Trinity. The Son will "through himself, the only-begotten, cause the Father to be seen by sight . . . by leading those who now believe in him through faith in his Incarnation to the vision of divinity."[37] That vision is our blessedness, our happiness; of this Augustine is both certain and explicit.[38] In Augustine's theology there is an analogy between the *seen* and *unseen forms* or *natures in Christ*, and the *seen* (*form* or *nature*) *of Christ* and the *unseen of the Trinity* (an analogy offered with polemical—anti-Homoian—purpose). As the analogy would suggest,[39] the proportionality expresses the equality of the *unseen* of Christ and the *unseen* of the Trinity: in each case the *unseen* is the divine nature. The proportion thus expresses the unity of divinity in Christ with the divinity of the Trinity. Moreover, in different ways over time (beginning with the Incarnation), but nonetheless, what is *seen of Christ* resolves into (or is the basis for discerning) the *unseen of Christ* and the *unseen of the Trinity*. In all cases, the *unseen* is divinity; in all cases the *unseen* is the *same* divinity. The dynamic resolution of the unseen in Christ is itself the

35. We have come now to a key insight into Augustine's Trinitarian and Christological theology. If the Trinitarian axis around which Augustine's theology is structured is the common activity of the Trinity, then the Christological axis which equally structures his theology is the Son as revealer of God the Trinity. These two, particularly at the point of intersection of the two axis, map out Augustine's theology; indeed, the intersection of the two is very important in that his theology is one which radically resists the distinctly modern categories of "Trinitarian" and "Christological." It may indeed be that the widespread modern misreading of Augustine is due, in some substantial way, to an inability to escape the theological violence of the presumed dichotomy between Trinitarian and Christological.

36. FotC, 175.

37. FotC, 175–76. Here again we find an echo of the old question from Nebridius, for Augustine remarks that the decisive faith which recognizes the Son-humbled-as-a-servant properly has the Son as its object, for it is the Son indeed who has undergone this descent "for one cannot say that the Father either became flesh or was judged or crucified" (FotC, 176).

38. "For our blessedness is in direct proportion to our enjoyment of God in contemplation" (FotC, 170).

39. An analogy is, after all, a proportion, which in this case can be expressed: the seen of Christ : unseen of Christ :: the seen of Christ : the unseen of the Trinity.

dynamic resolution of the unseen of the Trinity, and in each case the resolution appears through what will be seen, the *seen* of Christ.[40]

Augustine's treatment of the Trinitarian significance of 1 Corinthians 15: 28 has its climax in book I of *De Trinitate*. In that work, Augustine continues the problematic of *Div. Quaest.* 69 and makes wholly explicit what was waiting in his earlier argument. The already-present kingdom and the drama (within that kingdom) of the Son "bringing to God" all humanity[41] is stated precisely in terms of the epistemic role of the Son as the occasion, the just means,[42] for the revelation of the Trinity (especially in that final revelation), and in terms of the inseparable work of the Trinity. This revelation of the Trinity through the Incarnation Augustine understands both as dependent upon and as the fruition of the real unity that exists between Son and Father. Augustine's description of the epistemic drama of the Incarnation is literally contained, as if by bookends, by assertions of the unity between Father and Son.

We can, in fact, read *De Trinitate* I.15–18 as a virtual check list of references back to issues articulated in the earlier texts. *De Trinitate* I.15 begins with Augustine invoking 1 Corinthians 15:28, and he then cites John 14:28, the same Scripture passage invoked in *Div. Quaest.* 69 in conjunction with 1 Corinthians 15:28, as examples of texts that are being subjected to Homoian claims. The Homoian claim on John 14:28 is deflected by the use of Philippians 2:5–7, the same citation used in the same role it had in *Div. Quaest.* 69. As Augustine returns to 1 Corinthians 15:27–28 and the question of how the "handing over [of the kingdom]" is to be interpreted, he says that *the Father's and the Son's working are inseparable*, the technical and quasi-credal expression of Nicene orthodoxy which again serves to pivot the discussion into the "handing over" issue, this time tied to an exegesis of 1 Corinthians 15:24. The anti-homoian impetus to this discussion is flagged at the beginning of *De Trinitate* I.16 with the reference to (as Hill puts it) the "cranks" who believe that when the Son "hands over the kingdom" he deprives himself of it. At this point in his argument, Augustine is at a position within which he can direct our attention to the basic question, "What then does it really mean, 'When he hands over the kingdom to God and the Father'?" The answer to this question brings us directly into an articulation by Augustine of the epistemic quality of the drama of the Incarnation, the developing revelation of the Trinity accomplished by and through the Incarnation over time:

40. A good illustration of this point may be found in Augustine's *Forty-third Tractate on John* (written sometime between 416 and 420). In section 12, in an explicitly anti-Homoian argument, Augustine asserts that the Son, invisible and equal to the Father, made himself visible when he assumed the form of a servant. The Son will show himself again, in the future, when God will be revealed not through a created image (as in the Old Testament), but through the Son.

41. "Humanity" here means both the humanity of human nature *per se* and the humanity of all of us ever alive.

42. One can indeed recognize in Augustine a foreshadowing of Thomas's understanding of the Incarnation as "beautiful" and the paradigmatic work of fine art.

The fact is that the man Christ Jesus, mediator of God and men [1 Tim 2:5], now reigning for all the just who live by faith [Heb 2:4], is going to bring them to direct sight of God, to the face to face vision . . . that is what is meant by "When he hands over the kingdom to God and the Father," as though to say When he brings believers to a direct contemplation of God and the Father."

Augustine next returns to the Trinitarian issue of the "inseparable nature in the inseparable works" by citing John 10:30, a preferred Nicene prooftext (since before Nicaea! Since Alexander of Alexandria). Augustine then links this revealed unity to one of his favorite narratives of divine unity, the discourse to Thomas in John 14:8–25. "In a word, because of this inseparability, it makes no difference whether sometimes the Father alone or sometimes the Son alone is mentioned as the one who is to fill us with delight at his countenance."[43] This connecting of the Trinitarian content of the epistemic event of the Incarnation with a traditional prooftext (John 10:30) for the fundamental unity that exists between Father and Son is repeated again later on in *De Trinitate* I.18: "The actual truth is that 'I and the Father are one,' and therefore when the Father is shown, the Son who is in him is shown also, and when the Son is shown, the Father who is in him is shown too."[44]

Augustine's understanding of the soteriological role of the Son locates the Son's mission precisely in the way in which he functions as a kind of epistemic event. Such an epistemological (or revelatory) function is not so much that of revealing what a good human, or even what a good Christian, looks like (although he reveals that, as well), but rather that the Son, as humbled servant, is the *proper occasion for* and *proper object of* faith. Already in *Div. Quaest.* 69, Augustine uses words which suggest his later argument in *De Trinitate* XIII that the Son saves not through the "power game" but through "the humility game," Augustine says that "those believing in him are saved, not through his glory, but through his humility."[45] The movement from *form of God*—in which the Son's equality with the Father is evident—to *form of servant*—in which the Son's equality with the Father is masked (but available in faith)—makes possible a decisive or substantial revelation of God's love and the unity of that love in action among the Three. The drama of the Incarnation reveals the Three acting in unison in expressing their love; the content of the revelation of the Incarnation is the joint action of love.[46] Stating Augustine's theology in this way makes clear the way Nicene and

43. Augustine, *Trinity*, 77.

44. Augustine, *Trinity*, 79.

45. FotC, 175.

46. The editor of the critical edition of *Trin.*, W.J. Mountain, sees in Augustine's articulation of a doctrine of divine inseparability (e.g., *Trin.* I.8) signs of Ambrose's doctrine of divine inseparability from *De Fide* (IV.6.68; see CCSL L, 36, ln. 22/24). The parallel is not a precise one, but what may be found there in the Ambrose is a doctrine of the inseparability of divine action articulated in terms of the inseparability of divine love. This aspect of Ambrose's treatment comes closest to Augustine's understanding of what is at stake in any Trinitarian theology of inseparable or common activity. The NPNF give the Ambrose as: "Furthermore, to prove to you that it comes of Love, that the Son can

pro-Nicene theology "control" his theology of the Incarnation, as well as providing an insight into why Nebridius' question[47] continues to echo throughout Augustine's Trinitarian writings long after Augustine has moved on from that friendship.[48] The depth of divine love is flattened, with a corresponding vitiation of the revelatory character of the Trinity in the unity of their love, if there is no true, full Incarnation, that is, if Philippians 2:5–11 does not describe the drama of someOne who is fully divine.[49] This fact alone is sufficent to set Augustine on the road to a full engagement with the subordinationist theology of anti-Nicenes. But, more to the point of Augustine's specific understanding of the Son as decisive revelation, Augustine must make it clear—must make it certain and secure—that the very act of revelation-in-humiliation is not understood as proof of the impossibility of real union between Father and Son.[50] I am not talking simply of Augustine dealing with—and refuting—a challenge of "the Son suffers, therefore he is not (really) God." The debate has widened beyond that point; it was widened when Homoians found in the Old Testament theophanies grounds for doubting the Son's divinity.[51] The Homoians have set the epistemic or revelatory character of the Son against his unity with the Father; Augustine would add that they set the epistemic character of the Son against the unity of divine love in action.

---

do nothing of himself save what he has seen the Father doing, the apostle has added to the words, 'Whatsoever the Father has done, the same thing does the Son also, in like manner,' this reason: 'For the Father loves the Son' and thus Scripture refers the Son's inability to do, whereof it testifies, to unity in Love that suffers no separation or disagreement" (NPNF, 2nd series, X, 270).

47. Is the Son acting alone, or if not, why do we not say that the Father and Spirit as well were incarnated?

48. For just one of many more possible examples, see *Sermon* 213.7 (Hill, the English editor/translator, will say only that it was delivered "before 410"), a sermon on the creed in which Augustine says "the Son, the Word, became flesh; not the Father, not the Holy Spirit. But the whole Trinity made the flesh of the Son; the Trinity, you see, works inseparably" (*Augustine's Sermons*, The Works of St. Augustine III/6, 144).

49. Augustine draws upon Phil 2:5–7 in virtually every one of his treatments of the Trinity, although the basis for his understanding of the special authority of the scriptural passage is not clear. That a text like *De Fide et Symbolo* (393), which otherwise reveals almost nothing distinctively Augustinian in its theology, still contains frequent appeals to Phil 2:5–7 suggests that Augustine's linking of the Philippians passage to a normative understanding of the Trinity may not have been his idea alone, and his claim in *Trin.* II that Phil 2:5–7 has a "canonical" function may not be just Augustine's own idea about the significance of that passage. Both Marius Victorinus and Hilary of Poitiers (see especially Hilary, *Trin.* IX.14–15) give special attention to Phil 2:5–7. An initial suggestion of how Phil 2:5–7 functions in Augustine's Trinitarian theology may be found in Pelikan, "Canonica regula."

50. My judgment that with *Eighty-Three Different Questions* 69 Augustine's Trinitarian concern is for the Son as visible revealer of the Father and of the Trinity itself is, I think, supported by the subject of *Div. Quaest.* 74 (written shortly after no. 69). In *Div. Quaest.* 74, Augustine's interest turns to Col. 1:14–15, "In Whom we have redemption and remission of sins, *who is the image of the invisible God*" (emphasis added). As one would expect from the account I have given, it is precisely the character of the Son as perfect Image that concerns Augustine in the later *Question*.

51. I have mapped out developments in Latin Homoianism criticism of Nicene theology in "Exegesis and Polemic in de Trinitate I," *Augustinian Studies* 30 (1999): 43–59. A portion of that article was presented as the communication, "Augustine's 'De Trinitate' in its Polemical Context: Book I," at the North American Patristics Society 1997 annual meeting.

In Augustine's judgment, Homoians misunderstand the revelation of the Incarnation (that is, the way in which the Incarnation functions as revelation); in fact, they misunderstand it twice. The first misunderstanding constitutes their own theology of the Incarnation: the Son's life and death reveals the true God through his obedience to the will of the Father; this obedience is the obedience of a subordinate following the commands of a superior.[52] The second Homoian misunderstanding of the revelation in the Incarnation lies in their understanding of what is the Nicene doctrine of divine revelation in the Incarnation. The Homoians think that Nicenes identify it with the obedience of the Son's body to the divine in the Son. However, this reading is close enough to the truth that Augustine can (as his theological sophistication grows) feel the sting of its criticism.[53] The Nicene "everything weak to the human body, everything glorious to the divine Word" can, improperly nuanced, leave one with a sense that the divine is impervious to the trauma (the "humiliation") of the Incarnation.[54] Eventually, Augustine will take steps to correct false tendencies in standard Nicene accounts of the Incarnation, just as he will rework the Nicene understanding of the Trinitarian significance of 1 Corinthians 1:24, in both cases developing more and more a pro-Nicene understanding of each doctrine.[55]

CONCLUSION

In modern theology, when works of Augustine's theology of the Trinity are read, they tend to be read with the presumed context of 'neoplatonism'. It is this 'neoplatonic' context which serves to makes sense of that theology of the Trinity, which provides the basis for identifying the key terms or concepts, the underlying logic, and then even the 'historical' milieu of this theology of the Trinity. By contrast, I have offered a reading of Augustine's theology of the Trinity which locates that theology within a more likely and more credible historical context, namely Latin 'catholic' theology of the late

---

52. For example, the so-called *Arian Sermon* contains repeated assertions that the Son acted "at the will and command" of the Father. One such assertion appropriate to quote here reads, "At the will and command of the Father, he [the Son] came down from heaven and came into this world" (Translated by Roland Teske, SJ, in his select collection of Augustine's writings, *Arianism and Other Heresies*, The Works of St. Augustine I/18, 133).

53. One does not have to believe that Hilary's Christology was actually docetist to see that it—like Athanasius'—kept any suffering from the divine element in the Incarnate Son. On the other hand, some of what Augustine was interested in articulating would have been expressed in the *kenosis* categories of theology in the second half of the fourth century.

54. Augustine says regularly that "it was the Lord of glory who was crucified"—as at *Trin.* I.28.

55. After the early books of *de Trinitate,* Augustine no longer uses 1 Cor. 15: 28 as an occasion to discuss the epistemic character of the Incarnation, rather he treats the passage in line with the questions raised at the beginning of *de Trinitate*, I. 15: does the Son's human nature pass away by being absorbed into divinity at the end time? The fact that Augustine relates 1 Cor. 15: 28 to the same trinitarian/christological issues in *Div. Quaest.* no. 69 and *de Trinitate*, I and II, but ceases thereafter, is one reason why I included *de Trinitate*, I–V in the same chronological set of writings (i.e. 'early') as *Ep.* 12 and *Div. Quaest.* no. 69.

fourth and early fifth centuries ('catholic' meaning Latin theology which looked to the reception of Nicaea as normative). In his earliest writing on the Trinity Augustine invokes the doctrines and terminology associated with Nicene theology. I have shown that the fundamental shape and development of Augustine's theology may be found in his attempts to understand or make sense of the key doctrines and terminology of that theology within the polemical context of the end of the fourth century. I have proposed that Augustine's theology of the Trinity is centred on divine unity conceived in terms of the inseparable activity of the Three (the traditional Nicene understanding of divine unity), the epistemic character of the Incarnation as the decisive revelation of the Trinity, and the role of faith in leading forward our reflection of the Trinity. These three 'Nicene' features can be documented in Augustine's earliest writing on the Trinity through a reading of those texts which is more credible than the 'neo-platonic' reading in terms of criteria of a bona fide 'historical' reading. Once identified, these three 'Nicene' features can be found in various stages of development throughout Augustine's writings, although admittedly the demonstration (or revelation) of this fact lies outside the scope of this essay. The purpose or use of what I have offered here is not to explain example by example how something which looks 'neoplatonic' is not, but to provide an alternative narrative with which to make sense of Augustine's theology of the Trinity, which provides the basis for identifying the key terms or concepts, the underlying logic, and the 'historical' milieu of this theology of the Trinity

While many in systematics today would describe their work as postmodern and thereby marking off a separation from the theological issues and forms of discourse arising out of Enlightenment agendas and sensibilities, the fact remains that the judgments of such theologians of the key moments, figures, and dynamics in the history of Christian theology are still firmly imbedded in the perceptions of Enlightenment Christianity. One can easily name several givens in the modern understanding of doctrinal history which still function as foundational presuppositions in contemporary—even postmodern—theology: the existence of the "Cappadocians" and a Cappadocian theology;[56] the presumed integrity of the concept of "Christology"; the portability of *oeconomia* language; the accuracy of Régnon's paradigm; and the fundamental character of Neoplatonic Trinitarianism in Augustine's theology. Each of these thoroughly modern categories for understanding patristic theology is, in fact, an act of self-definition on the part of *modern* systematic theology, and needs to be acknowledged (and studied) as such. Conceptual or "systematic" claims to the contrary, contemporary efforts at fresh beginnings are really articulated and conceived largely in ecclesiological terms—how do I believe and articulate something "new" that my communion (predominantly) does not?—but the terms of reference remain deeply old-fashioned

---

56. A search for the appearance of the category of "Cappadocians"—such as recently conducted by Lewis Ayres—reveals the late-nineteenth century origins of the grouping. If there were any doubts about the decidedly "modern" character of the enthusiasm for such a category, one would need only to read Jaroslav Pelikan's book on the Cappadocians.

and unquestioned.[57] My own desire would be that contemporary theology investigates each of these historical characterizations for what each reveals about the needs of modern and contemporary theology. The least I would expect from contemporary theology is that it recognize that its claims to postmodernity are cheaply won, for its conceptual tender remains that of the Enlightenment confederacy.

57. Many contemporary systematicians like to think—and will say—that they are doing something new. My phrase "[in] ecclesiological terms" is an attempt to identify and localize that "newness": a position sounds new because it has a "new" judgment on familiar terms (e.g., the "Cappadocians," Augustine's Neoplatonic Trinitarian theology, etc.), but in fact the "new" is just a re-arranging of old, worn, and very familiar presuppositions (e.g., Does the Augustine of Régnon's paradigm and Du Roy's "triads" violate the *oeconomia* of Cullman and Newman?). The "edge" to the newness is all ecclessiastical: a new doctrinal fashion statement within the same old garment district of historical fabrication.

Chapter 8

Exegesis and Polemic in *De Trinitate* I[1]

FOR MUCH OF MODERN scholarship, Augustine's first substantial encounter with "Arian"—that is to say, *Homoian*—theology is associated with his receipt of the so-called *Arian Sermon* and his response to that document in 419, by which time virtually all of the *De Trinitate* had been written. It has been said authoritatively and repeatedly that prior to receiving the *Arian Sermon*, Augustine's knowledge of Homoian theology was unsubstantial, formal, or secondhand in character: Berrouard, for example, has called Augustine's knowledge of Arian theology "theoretical" and "manualist" in nature,[2] an opinion recently repeated at face value by Rettig in his otherwise useful translation of *Tractates on John*. What I intend to do in this article is to argue that already in book I of *De Trinitate*, which is regarded as the earliest stratum of that work by virtually everyone, Augustine is demonstrably engaged with refuting Homoian theology, and that even at this very early stage, Augustine's knowledge of Homoian theology cannot legitimately be characterized as limited or formal. Indeed, there is a certain irony in such scholarly judgments since Augustine is being judged to have had only a "manualist" understanding of Homoianism by modern scholars who themselves have

1. I want to thank Lewis Ayres, Mark E. Weedman, and Daniel H. Williams for their comments and suggestions in the writing of this article.

2. Marie-François Berrouard, "La date des *Tractatus I-LIV in Iohannis Evangelium* de sain Augustin," *Recherches Augustiniennes* 7 (1971): 105–168; here 144, "L'Arianisme contre lequel Augustin met en garde les fidèles apparait comme un Arianisme de manuel de théologie." Starting at 141 and continuing to 146, Berrouard offers his judgments on the status of Arianism and the character of Augustine's engagement with Arianism; I cannot agree with *any* of his judgments offered in those pages. On the other hand, Berrouard's account of the change in Augustine's exegesis of John 5:19 (148ff) is insightful and nuanced.

possessed no more than a "manualist" understanding of anti-Nicene theology. In all three types of theology that I will examine—Latin anti-Nicene theology, Latin Nicene theology, and Augustine's own reception and application of Latin Nicene polemic—we will find development over time of doctrine and exegesis of specific scriptural tests. Neither Nicene nor anti-Nicene theology remained static through the second half of the fourth century and the beginning of the fifth. I hope to show some of the ways in which Augustine's theology is polemically engaged in a substantial and detailed manner with Homoian theology; that is to say, the ways in which Augustine's theology develops in response to Homoian theology. I will make my argument through a close reading of *De Trinitate* I.7–18, especially 8–14, paying careful attention to the the Scripture passages Augustine feels are burdened by anti-Nicene claims as well as those passages which Augustine brings forward in support of his own doctrine.[3]

Let me begin with the suggestion that the CCL editor has misread the signs of polemics in the beginning section of *De Trinitate*. In section 9, Augustine refers to those "who have affirmed that our Lord Jesus Christ is not God, or is not true God, or is not with the Father the one and only, or is not truly immortal because he is subject to change."[4] Mountain identifies this summary with the anathemas of Nicaea on the basis alone, so far as I can see, of the presence of the word "mutabilem" in both documents.[5] The presence of this single term is not enough to justify Mountain's identification; the language of the two texts is overall quite different and articulates different theological emphases.[6] There is a more proximate source than Nicaea for Augustine's summary and the doctrines he lists; indeed, the list of errors at section 9 announces the later provenance of the theology Augustine is engaged with, for the doctrines are fairly clearly Homoian in framing.

The doctrine *that the Son is not true God* (*non esse uerum deum*) may be found in the *Commentary on the Acts of Aquiliae*, where Palladius is accused of believing this by Ambrose: "Et in hoc damna eum qui negat Filium *Deum uerum*,"[7] and at Palladius' reply to Ambrose in which Palladius will say that the Son is the *true Son* of God, but

---

3. It goes almost without saying that by beginning my reading of *Trin.* at section 7, I am starting at that point of the work which La Bonnardière thinks constitutes the original beginning of book I.

4. Augustine, *Trinity,* 71. The Latin reads: "Qui dixerunt dominum nostrum Jesum Christum non esse deum, aut non esse uerum deum, aut non cum patre unum et solum deum, aut non uere immortalem quia mutabilem."

5. Hilary's translation reads for the anathamas reads: "Eos autem, qui dicunt 'erat, quando non erat' et 'priusquam nasceretur, non erat' et quia 'ex nullis extantibus factus est,' quod Graeci 'ex uc onton' dicunt, uel alia substantia dicentes 'mutabilem et conuertibilem filium dei' hos anathematizat catholica et apostolica ecclesia" (*Collectanea Antiariana Parisina* 10.2, CSEL, 65.150).

6. A major difficulty in identifying a Latin translation of Nicaea as the source for language in a late-fourth-century Latin author is the fact that we are ignorant of any Latin translations prior to Hilary's in 360–61. Certainly, Latin translations of Nicaea circulated in the West before Hilary's, but none of these are extant. There are reasons to believe that these translations varied significantly from each other.

7. *Com. Max. Aquil.* 303v 34

not that he is the *true God*. The doctrine that *the Son is not the one and only God* (*non . . . unum et solum deum*) may be found in the *Letter of Ulfilas*, which begins "*Unum solum uerum Deum . . .*"[8] The doctrine that *the Son is not truly immortal* because he is *subject to change* (*non uere immortalem quia mutabilem*) may be found in Maximinus' *Commentary on the Acts of Aquileia*[9] and the fragments of Palladius.[10] Exactly what is at stake when Augustine argues over the terminology of "true God" has not always been recognized by scholars. The question of whether the Son is "true God" is a polemical argument with the Homoians, for it is they who make this category central to Trinitarian theology. The technical aspect of the phrase "true God" is recognized by Teske in his recent translation of Augustine's *Reply to the Arian Sermon*,[11] but Hill, in his translation of *De Trinitate*, does not recognize the specific and technical nature of the phrase; instead, he finds the significance of the phrase "true God" in the general problem of the ambiguity of the term "God" in the Greco-Roman world.[12] The three doctrines that Augustine cites at *De Trinitate* I.9 as representative of his opponents are each attested to in Latin Homoian literature and fit within the overall Latin Homoian emphasis on the Father as "true God" due to his unique or exclusive status as *ingenerate*—a theology which has too often been misrecognized as Eunomian.[13]

This summary at *De Trinitate* I.9 by Augustine of his opponents' beliefs resembles a large body of polemical literature which contains similar summaries of both Arian and Homoian doctrines. The oldest such summary, and the most widely distributed one among Latin Nicenes, is Arius' *Letter to Alexander*, which from the late 350s on was well known in the West. Arius begins that letter with a creed based, as Gregg and Groh have demonstrated,[14] on 1 Timothy 6:15–16: "We confess one God, alone unbegotten, alone eternal, alone unbegun, alone true, alone having immortality, alone wise, alone good, alone sovereign . . ."[15] In 1940, Bardy identified four separate appearances of the *Letter to Alexander* in Latin literature with Nicene sympathies.[16] First and most importantly, Hilary twice reproduces the entirety of this letter by Arius in his *De Trinitate*, a fact that I will return to shortly. Fragments

8. See Maximinus' *Commentary on the Acts of Aquiliae* 304v, which includes the "Letter of Auxentius" within which appears Ufilias' creed in Gryson, *Scolies Ariennes sur le Concile d'Aquilée*, 236.

9. Maximus, *Comm. Max. Aquil.* 303r 33.

10. Palladius, *Scolia* 340 v 107

11. See fn 1, p. 168 in Roland Teske's translation and commentary of *Answer to an Arian Sermon* in his volume *Arianism and Other Heresies, The Works of Saint Augustine*, I/18.

12. Hill, in Augustine, *Trinity*, 92n24.

13. See my "Arians of Book V."

14. Robert C. Gregg and Dennis E. Groh, *Early Arianism: A View of Salvation* (Philadelphia: Fortress Press, 1981), 88–90.

15. Or as it reads in Hilary's Latin translation: "Nouimus unum Deum solum infectum solum sempiternum solum sine initio solum uerum solum immortalitatem habentem solum optimum solum potentem" (Hilary, *Trin.* IV.12, 1–3, CCL LXII, 112).

16. Gustave Bardy, "L'occident et les documents de la controverse arienne," *Revue des sciences religieuses* 20 (1940): 28–63.

from the letter to Alexander also appear in Phobaedeus' *Contra Arianus*, which was written shortly before Hilary's *De Trinitate*. Thirdly, the letter is referred to by Ambrose in the proceedings of the Council of Aquileia, and in his *Epistle* 10. Fourth and finally, the *Index of Heresies* attributed to Ps.-Jerome alludes to the epistle, as well. These four citations represent at least two and quite possibly four independent Latin translations of Arius' *Letter* circulating among Nicenes and pro-Nicenes. The *Letter* is also cited in the Homoian *Sermonum arianorum fragmenta antiquissima*, as Bardy points out, and probably lies behind the creed of the *Letter of Ulfila s*, which begins "Unum solum uerum Deum . . . solum esse ingenitum, sine principio, sine fine," etc.[17]

When Hilary begins a summary of his opponents' beliefs in book IV of his *De Trinitate*, he invokes the Creed of Nicaea and its language of *homoousios*, saying that just as that creed replied to the heretics of that day, he is obliged now to reply to the misbelief of contemporary heretics. Starting at *De Trinitate* IV.8, Hilary identifies his opponents' key beliefs and the Scripture passages they use as prooftexts. Hilary's opponents assert that God (the Father) alone is true God, that He alone is good, that in God there is no change or turning, that He is without body, and that He is immortal and invisible. In support of this last assertion that the *Father only is immortal and invisible* Hilary's opponents evidently offer 1 Timothy 6:16 as a prooftext. It is at this point that Hilary introduces Arius' *Letter to Alexander*, focusing particularly on the initial credal material.

In other words, Hilary introduces Arius' *Letter to Alexander* in order to establish the continuity between the beliefs of the heretics of old, namely Arius, and the new heretics, and thus to tar his opponents with the brush of Arius. Both groups are concerned to limit true divinity to God the Father, and they both do so by identifying traits which are distinctly divine and then limiting these traits to the Father. Both old and new heretics anchor such a description to 1 Timothy 6:16–17. But there are differences between the two groups: only the new heretics make a point of distinguishing true divinity from the Son on the basis of *invisibility* and *immateriality*. In short, Hilary's "new" heretics find in the Son's visibility and materiality indications of the fact that he is not, and cannot be, truly *God*. This focus on the *visibility* and *materiality* of the Son marks off a definite difference from the theology of Arius, a fact which Gryson has already observed in passing.[18] Distinguishing the Son's nature from God's nature on the basis of the former's visibility and materiality brings us to the kind of doctrinal concerns found in Augustine's *De Trinitate* I–IV, but it does *not* bring us back to the theology of Arius. Moreover, *Hilary's* opponents discover *in the*

17. Gryson, *Scolia*, 304v, 236.

18. Gryson observes this in *Scolies Ariennes sur le Concile d'Aquilée*, 291fn2, where Ambrose is questioning Palladius about precisely such a belief. Ambrose first asks Palladius about doctrines clearly drawn from the *Letter to Alexander*, but then asks about materiality and visibility, doctrines— Gryson points out—which have no basis in Arius' *Letter*.

Incarnation exclusively that visible and material existence of the Son which leads them to deny the Son's full divinity.[19] But for *Augustine's* opponents, the visible and material existence of the Son which requires them to deny his full divinity is discovered not so much in the Incarnation but, as is well known, *in the theophanies of the Old Testament.* Augustine himself refers to these two thrusts in Homoian theology at *De Trinitate* II.15.[20] The Homoian theology Augustine describes in the first books of *De Trinitate* cannot be reduced simply to the theology opposed by Hilary, much less to the theology of Arius. Augustine's opponents represent a change, indeed perhaps a development, in anti-Nicene theology from the theology of Hilary's opponents, and a major development from the theology of Arius. In book I of Augustine's *De Trinitate*, we are dealing with a third generation of anti-Nicene theology and a second generation of Latin Homoian theology. These theologies do have in common the use of 1 Timothy 6:16 to provide key language with which to identify what is distinctive to true divinity—and thereby to exclude the Son from that divinity.

After Augustine has recited the three representative doctrines of his Homoian opponents, he begins immediately to refute their assertion that the Son is not "true God." Augustine understands from John 1:1–2 that the Son is not a creature, and if not a creature then he is of the *same substance* with the Father—a deduction offered in language reminiscent of Nicaea, but not in the exact technical language Hill's translation might lead an unwary reader to assume Augustine says *eiusdem substantiae*, not *consubstantialis* or even *una natura*.[21] It is, in any case, important to note that Augustine does not simply cite Nicaea: he makes an argument in language which seems

19. Manlio Simonetti documents this Homoian understanding of the Incarnation in the *Fragmenta Arriana* 4, 603. Simonetti says "The Arians [*sic*] bring forward even the Incarnation of the Son as proof of his radical inferiority, inasmuch as it admitted of visibility, passibility and mortality" (Simonetti, quoted in Quasten, *Patrology*, IV.109).

20. "For he [the Son] is he, they say, who showed himself to the fathers [of the OT]. In that case, suppose you answer them, just as the Son is visible in himself, so he must also be mortal in himself, to suit your [Homoian] view of the text, which you maintain applies only to the Father, who alone has immortality [1 Tim 6:16]. Or if you agree that what made the Son mortal was the flesh he took, then you must allow that was also what made him visible" (Augustine, *Trinity*, 107).

21. I believe that we can observe Augustine's development over time of *eiusdem substantia* as a technical Trinitarian term. The phrase occurs in Rufinus' translation of the Nicene Creed, but Rufinus also uses the phrase to translate from *Peri Archon* Origen's doctrine that souls are of the *same substance* as God—an application Rufinus would seem unlikely to use if in fact the phrase is recognized as fully technical, that is, fully Nicene. Also noteworthy are two facts: the phrase occurs with regularity in Marius Victorinus' discussion of Trinity, while it is not used at any time by Hilary (most notably, not in his translation of the Nicene Creed). Regarding Augustine's use of the phrase, I would argue that we see over time the development of a fully Nicene application of the phrase. That development has begun in *Trin.* I, continues in a number of texts—especially *En. Ps.* 68—and culminates in the late anti-"Arian" works. The significance of *Trin.* V for understanding Augustine's use of *eiusdem substantiae* has been pointed out by Roland Teske in his article "Augustine's Use of 'Substantia' in Speaking About God," *Modern Schoolman*, 62 (1985): 147–163. I would emphasize only two theological points: Augustine's understanding of Nicene theology deepened over time, and so did his use of language associated (by Victorinus? Rufinus?) with Nicaea.

to belong within Nicene circles, but there is no invocation of Nicaea.[22] Augustine's conclusion that the Son is of the "same substance" with the Father allows him to assert that therefore the Son is "not only God, but also true God"—categories contested by the Homoians as expressed in their preferred language. Augustine turns, at this point of his argument, to 1 John 5:20, a passage rich in "true" language, but frankly a passage objectively no less ambiguous theologically than the First Timothy material. What Augustine here gains from the Johannine epistle is the identification of the Second Person with "Life"; and if the Son is "Life," then—as Augustine puts it—he "can scarcely be mortal and subject to change."[23] Augustine then concludes that the words of 1 Timothy 6:16 "do not apply to the Father alone, but to the one and only God which the Trinity is." Not the best argument in the world, frankly, but a pretty good first shot, which is all that we can reasonably expect of Augustine at this early stage of his engagement with Homoianism.

Augustine's argument at *De Trinitate* I.9–10 is worth pausing over further, for its elements, however primitively utilized when Augustine first wrote the work, will form the basis for his later arguments with Homoians when he again turns in a substantial way to refuting their doctrine that the Son is not "true God." *De Trinitate* I.9 is the only place in all of the *De Trinitate* where Augustine cites 1 John 5:20, a fact which places the First John text in the forefront of Augustine's encounter with Homoianism. As one would expect of a passage invoked for its utility against Homoian theology, 1 John 5:20 appears in every one of Augustine's later anti-Homoian works—*Against the Arian Sermon,* the *Debate with Maximinus,* and his *Answer to Maximinus.* The Johannine text is clearly one which Augustine regards as foundational for refuting Homoian theology, although there is no precedent for Augustine's use of the passage either in any of the Nicene literature which would have been authoritative for him, or even in any extant Homoian writings which could have prompted a counter-exegesis.[24] The lack of precedent for Augustine's polemical use of 1 John 5:20 and the fact that the passage appears in his writings only in the most explicit points of engagement

22. It is my judgment that the very strong unity language at *Trin.* I.viii.6–9, CCL 50:47, complete with Nicene technicalities, is not an expression of Augustine's own theology, but rather a rehearsal of Marcellus' and Photinus' theology: "[S]ed est unitas trinitatis incorporea et incommutabilis, et sibimet consubstantialis et coaeterna natura."

23. This attention to "Life" as an important title for the Second Person may owe to Marius Victorinus, who puts great emphasis on this title in *Against Arius.* I say this on the basis of a computer search run by Mark E. Weedman for all forms of *filius* and *vita* in proximity in the writings of Latins from Tertullian to Hilary. Of 120 total appearances of the terms, 82 were in writings by Marius Victorinus. Likewise, for *Christ* and *vita,* 102 of 169 total appearances were in Victorinus. Hilary and Gregory of Elvira were second and third. Moreover, when the other theologians talked about Son and Life together, it was often in a different context. Most of Hilary's references to "Christ" and "life," for example, were to citations of John 17:3, where he is not talking about the Son as Life.

24. 1 John 5:20 is not cited at all in the Trinitarian writings by Novation, Gregory of Elvira, or Phobaedeus of Agenn. First John 5:20 appears once in Hilary's *Trin.* and the NPNF translator for Ambrose provides the Johannine epistle as the supposed authority for Ambrose's use of "Life" as a title for the Son. The scriptural text does not appear at all in the Homoian material collected in SC 267.

with Homoian theology suggests that the polemical utility of the scriptural passage is Augustine's own discovery. Probably Augustine first saw the utility of the passage in the appearance of "true" or *uerum* language, for in Latin, 1 John 5:20 reads: "Scimus quod filius dei uenerit et dederit nobis intellectum et cognoscamus *uerum* et simus in *uero*, filio eius Iesu Christo. Hic est *uerus* deus et unita aeterna."[25] If indeed I am right that Augustine's use of 1 John 5:20 marks his own development of an anti-Homoian exegetical strategy, what I find most interesting about his use of this passage is the *different* doctrinal role it plays in those later polemical works when compared to its appearance in the early polemical writting, *De Trinitate* I.

When one compares how 1 John 5:20 is used in *De Trinitate* I to its use in the later anti-Homoian works, one immediately notices a number of changes. The first shift is in what Augustine is using 1 John 5:20 to prove. In *De Trinitate* I, 1 John 5:20 is invoked as the scriptural prooftext in the argument that if the Son is not a creature, then he must be God, "true God." This argument is related, as I have already observed, to Augustine's assertion that if the Son is "Life," he is not mortal, and on these grounds again the Son is "true God." This is not the way Augustine uses 1 John 5:20 in those polemical works written twenty and twenty-five years later. In the three later works the earlier descriptions of the Son as creator and not creature and as "Life" have dropped away. Instead, the Johannine epistle supports an argument based upon the fact that 1 John 5:20 calls the Second Person "Son." If the Son is really a Son, the Son of God, then he is what the term "son" describes: a product out of the nature of the producer, God *the Father*. This is Augustine's argument. The argument from "Sonship" is classically pro-Nicene—one finds it in Gregory of Nyssa, for example.

The sense we might obtain from the "Sonship" argument that Augustine was—in those later writings—working with a more fully developed appreciation of pro-Nicene theology is supported by the second development in Augustine's use of 1 John 5:20. As I have already remarked, in *De Trinitate* I.9 Augustine argues that the Father and Son have the same substance, but that argument is not couched in the specific "substance" and "nature" terminology technically associated with Nicaea. Augustine's earlier use of a "one substance" argument in *De Trinitate* I.9 can be compared with arguments of "one or same in substance" in the three later anti-Homoian writings, where the use of "substance" and "nature" terminology is significantly more technical than in *De Trinitate* I.9. The argument in the *Against the Arian Sermon* and the *Answer to Maximinus* is in fact explicitly more Nicene: the term *homoousios* is invoked expressly, as is the Council of Nicaea, whereas in *De Trinitate* I.9 there is no invocation of Nicaea nor any utilization of its technical terminology. If there is anything about Augustine's Trinitarian theology in *De Trinitate* I that might fairly be called "manualist," then it may be his early grasp of Nicene Trinitarian theology.

If we return to following Augustine's argument as it develops, at *De Trinitate* I.15, Augustine next refers to the heretics' claim on John 14:28b, "I go to the Father; for the

---

25. Augustine, *Trin.* I.9.24–26, CCSL L.38; italics added.

Father is greater than I." This is, as I hope to make clear, a very important moment in Augustine's engagement with Homoian theology, and a careful contextual reading of Augustine's working through of the Trinitarian significance of John 14:28 can provide the opportunity to observe the polemical character of the theology of *De Trinitate* I. Augustine's treatment of John 14:28 reveals the polemical features already discovered: predecents among late-fourth-century Latin polemicists with Nicene sympathies, as well as evidence of Homoian use of either the specific language or the specific scriptural passage in question. I have already once made the observation that there is a development within the Homoian account of the Son's materiality; now we can find evidence of development in the way in which Homoian doctrine is linked to a polemically motivated exegesis. The fact of development in Homoian doctrine and exegesis is very important for two reasons. First, we see that Homoian theology was not a static, monolithic body of doctrine frozen in its expression, and if frozen then open to refutation by recourse, as it were, to a "manual."[26] The second reason why the issue of development in anti-Nicene doctrine is important is because the particular development occuring within Homoian theology constitutes a particular challenge to what is distinctive to Augustine's own Trinitarian theology. In other words, Augustine's engagement with Homoian theology can be seen to be a moment in which the heart of Augustine's own Trinitarian theology is at stake. Augustine's Trinitarian theology is at its most distinctive and fundamental level a response to the specific challenge posed by developing Homoian theology.

In *De Trinitate* I.14, Augustine's anti-Arian exegesis of John 14:28 begins by linking it with Philippians 2:5–7. This is a very telling linking of scriptural passages. Augustine had previously used Philippians 2:5–7 to support an anti-Homoian exegesis of John 14:28 in his *Div. Quaest.* 69, and Augustine is clear in *De Trinitate* I.14 that Philippians 2:5–7 has a sort of "canonical" function in Trinitarian (or Christological) theology.[27] But how or why Philippians has this function is not made clear, and Augustine never explains the source of the authority of Philippians 2:5–7 to the reader. The introduction of Philippians 2:5–7 to support a proper Nicene exegesis of John 14:28 provides a clue, I suggest, to the basis of Augustine's regard for the Philippians passage, for both Marius Victorinus and Hilary of Poitiers exegete John 14:28 in a Nicene way by linking its sense to that of Philippians 2:5–7. A review of the arguments by both Victorinus and Hilary can help us to recognize the "traditional" polemical character of Augustine's exegesis of John 14:28 *via* Philippians 2:5–7 in *De Trinitate* I.14.

26. Daniel H. Williams has shown that books I and II of Ambrose's *De Fide* utilizes arguments against his Homoian opponents which reduce them to followers of Arius, and that this stylized form of argument did not work, so that in the later books of *De Fide* Ambrose argues very specificly and concretely against his contemporary opponents, disputing their actual beliefs and not simply Arius.' See Williams' "Polemics and Politicsin Ambrose of Milan's *De Fide*," *Journal of Theological Studies* ns 46 (1995): 519–531.

27. See, of course, Pelikan, "Canonica regula."

In *Against Arius* 1A.13, Victorinus asserts that "the *Logos*, that is, Jesus or Christ is both equal and inferior to the Father" on the basis of John 14:28, "I go to the Father because the Father is greater than I." Victorinus immediately adds Philippians 2:6: "He did not consider it robbery to be equal to God." It seems as though, for Victorinus, John 14:28 is a prooftext for the *Logos* . . . Jesus or Christ as inferior to the Father, and Philippians 2:6 is a prooftext for the equality of the Son with the Father.[28] The passage in *Against Arius* is overall concerned with articulating the combined facts of: (1) the Son's equality with the Father,[29] and (2) the Son's inferiority with the Father.[30] But Victorinus is not altogether clear or, rather, not altogether profound: equality is based upon common genetic nature, while inferiority is based on the priority of Father as cause (or more technically, the Father as "unacting cause" and the Son as "acting cause"). Despite the references to Jesus and Christ, neither the Johannine nor the Philippian passage is understood Christologically, in the sense that neither is understood to speak to or about the Incarnation or the duality of natures in the Incarnate Son. Despite the philosophical buttresses supplied by Victorinus from Porphyry, the theology Victorinus articulates is not very sophisticated or insightful. For example, Victorinus seems wholly unaware of anti-Nicene claims on John 14:28. We do see an association of the two Scripture texts in question—John 14:28 and Philippians 2:6—but they are used in service of primitive (or at least classical) Trinitarian sensibilities: subordination texts are used to indicate distinction of persons, equality texts to indicate unity of nature. However, one important aspect of Victorinus' use of the Scripture texts in question needs to be noted: Victorinus' equation of the *Logos* with Jesus or the Christ (in the quotation at the beginning of this paragraph) is, as Hadot has already observed, anti-Marcellan in character. The echoes of Nicaea in this paragraph at section 13—"Light from Light"—reinforce the anti-Marcellan intent of the argument since Marcellus, although strongly Nicene, was against the use of such *X from X* productive language to describe the relationship between Father and Son (or rather, between the Father and the *Logos*). This underlying anti-modalist application of John 14:28 is not isolated to Victorinus, as we shall see.

When we turn to Hilary, we see that in his *De Trinitate* IX.51, Hilary explicitly introduces John 14:28 as a scriptural text disputed and claimed by "heretics" as their basis for denying the unity of nature between Father and Son. Unlike Victorinus, Hilary reads John 14:28 as a Christological reference: "Can you [heretics] be ignorant

---

28. That Phil 2:6 is considered by Victorinus to be proof of the equality between the Son and the Father can be seen at *Against Arius* 1A.9, where Victorinus brings forward both John 10:30 and Phil 2:6, and then concludes, "These texts therefore signify both that they [Father and Son] are one substance and one power" (Clark, FoC, 100–101).

29. "If he [the *Logos*] is the whole from the whole as a light from a light, if the Father has given to the Son all that he has—but all includes substance and power and dignity—the Son is equal to the Father" (Clark, FotC, 105).

30. "But the Father is greater because he gave all to the Son and is cause of the Son's being and mode of being. But he is also greater because he is inactive action" (Clark, FotC, 105).

that the Incarnation for your salvation was an emptying of the form of God . . . ?" The way Hilary blends the Johannine passage into the Philipians passage is obvious. Once more unlike Victorinus, Hilary sees the Philippians passage as a statement parallel in sense to John 14:28. By the Incarnation, the Son gave up his simple equality with the Father and took an inferior form: "Christ possessed all that was proper to His nature: but the form of God had departed from Him, for by emptying Himself of it, He had taken the form of a servant. The divine nature had not ceased to be, but still abiding in Him, it had taken upon itself the humility of earthly birth." Like Augustine, Hilary finds a guarentee of the equality of nature between Father and Son in the transperant sight of the Father through the Son testified to at John 14:9: "He who has seen me has seen the Father also." Indeed, *De Trinitate* IX.51, where the invocation of John 14:28 and Philippians 2:5–7 occurs, functions as the lead-in to Hilary's argument in the very next section, *De Trinitate* IX.52, that the Son's visibility does not mean he is unequal to the Father. The Son's visibility, Hilary argues, is a visibility that reveals the invisible Father, the Son's material actions reveal the common immaterial nature he shares with the Father.[31] In short, *De Trinitate* IX.52 is Hilary's treatment of the topic that Latin anti-Nicenes have made the locus of their subordinationist argument; namely, the Son's material or visible existence. For these anti-Nicenes, however, the visible and material existence in question is, as I noted earlier, the Incarnation, and it is the fact of the Son's common nature (with the Father) even in the Incarnation that Hilary is concerned to defend.[32]

Hilary's acquaintance with anti-Nicenes who distinguish the full or true divinity of the Father ("God") from the divinity of the Son is certain, for his writing is a source for us of a document which articulates precisely such a doctrine; namely, the creed of Sirmium (357), which Hilary labels "the Blasphemy." In his *De Synodis* 10–11, Hilary gives the text of the creed produced by that meeting of bishops. From the point of view of a history of the Trinitarian controversies, the "Blasphemy of Sirmium" is an important document, for the theology articulated in it marks, for the first time, a clear rejection of the distinctly Nicene language of *homoousios*, as well as *homoiousios*. For our more limited purposes here, the Blasphemy is important for two reasons. The first reason why the Blasphemy is important for this study is because it articulates

31. For a statement that one might call "Augustinian-before-Augustine," see Hilary, *Trin.* VIII.47–49. The argument there that the Son cannot be the *visible* image of the Father and still trully be an image of God is especially noteworthy.

32. One of the more interesting features of Hilary's argument in *Trin.* IX.51 is the fact that the section begins with an argument directed against a Homoian-type subordinationist theology, but then is developed as an anti-modalist argument, as when Hilary says, "We confess that the only-begotten of God, while He abode in the form of God, abode in the nature of God, but we do not at once reabsorb into the substance of the divine unity his unity bearing the form of a servant. Nor do we teach that the Father is in the Son, as if He entered into bodily" (NPNF IX, 173). After this comment, the argument shifts once again back against subordinationist theology. The point of Hilary's argument here is that the fact of the (conditions of the) Incarnation does not preclude the Son's real divinity. But Hilary is careful to exclude false (i.e., modalist) understandings of how real or true divinity is in the Incarnate Son.

the exclusive divinity of God (the Father) in terms of him alone being "unbegotten, invisible, immortal, and impassible"—categories which were discussed at the beginning of this article. The second reason why the Blasphemy is important is because its subordinationist theology of the Son is built upon the invocation of John 14:28: "No one can doubt that the Father is greater than the Son . . . the Son Himself testifying, 'He that sent Me is greater than I.' And no one is ignorant that it is Catholic doctrine that . . . the Father is the greater and that the Son is subordinated to the Father." It is at this point that the creed attributes to the Father the terms "unbegotten, invisible, immortal and impassible" as an explanation for why the Father is greater and the Son is subordinated.[33] By contrast, the Son "took flesh, that is, a body, that is man of the womb of the Virgin Mary . . . through whom He suffered." The begotten, visible, mortal, and passible existence that characterizes the Son's different kind of existence from the Father's is the Son's Incarnation. This is the specific anti-Nicene theology that Hilary opposed. As we have noted before in this article, at this point in time we do not yet see the stage of development in Homoian theology that is so characteristic of the theology Augustine opposes, although we do see a sort of family resemblance—a predecessor, as it were. We can note as well that we do not yet see precisely the specific forms of Nicene doctrines distinctive to Augustine's Trinitarian theology, although we can see the geneology of his exegetical and polemical strategies.

John 14:28 appears three times in the late fourth century Latin Homoian material collected in the *Scolia*: once in Maximinus' summary of Ufilas' theology; once in a fragment from Palladius; and once in the proceedings from the Council of Aquileia, where Palladius invokes John 14:28 in response to Ambrose's question of where in Scripture it says that the Son is inferior to the Father. John 14:28 is invoked in all three of these texts to support a chacterization of the Son as inferior to the Father who is "greater," but the reference by Palladius in the Council of Aquileia is particularly noteworthy.[34] Palladius invokes the Johannine passage to support his understanding that the Son is inferior to the Father (and inferior precisely in his divinity). Ambrose replies that the passage in John refers to the body (of Jesus). Palladius' response to

---

33. The Latin reads, "Patrem initium non habere, invisibilem esse, immorialem esse, impassibitem esse" (PL 10 489A, line 466). The Latin makes clear that the expressions of Sirmium are not the same as later, typically Homoian expressions: the lack of *ingenitus* and *solus* language is especially noteworthy. This difference of expression may support the judgment of some scholars that "Homoian" theology did not come into existence until 360 (or the fall/winter of 359, at the earliest).

34. Although we have no explicit proof that Augustine knew of the *Acta* of Aquilaea and had read them, there is a strong *a priori* argument for precisely this. By the mid-fourth century, conciliar *acta* were preserved, as Jerome once noted of Arian activities (*Dial c. Lucf.* 18). Besides, the decisions of any major council, presumably along with the *acta*, would have been circulated throughout the Western sees—standard practice since Constantius. By the 380s, Gratian was enforcing conciliar decrees with imperial force, which would further the publicity of the Council of Aquiliaea since it entailed depositions. Finally, one cannot imagine Ambrose missing the opportunity to utilize the success of the event he had orchestrated to galvanize Western sees in support of a Nicene platform of faith. I thank Daniel H. Williams for this observation.

Ambrose is brutally effective: "Well, then, was only the body sent and not the Son as well?" In other words, Palladius makes the point that the usual Nicene argument that New Testament passages attributing weakness or inferiority to the Son are properly understood as speaking of Christ's human nature (functionally, his body) logically leads to the conclusion that what is sent—according to Nicenes—must then be only the human nature. This is a telling criticism of Nicene theology up to the 380s: we can note, in passing, that such an argument by Homoians contributes to the development, by those of Nicene sympathies such as Ambrose and Augustine, of a theology of the unity in the Son, that is, a theology that provides a way of articulating the unity of the the "one who is sent."[35]

The Homoian development in Christological exegesis here expressed by Palladius has the effect of precluding Augustine from using a straightforward Nicene or Athanasian exegetical rule of "'glory' passages in the Scriptures refer to the divinity of the Son, 'suffering' passages refer to the humanity of the Son." By so doing, Palladius' expression of the Homoian development in Christological exegesis puts an engine in Augustine's development of "two forms" (Phil 2:5–7) exegesis to describe the same two kinds of Gospel passages that Athanasius' earlier (and fundamentally logos-sarx) model exegeted from a Nicene perspective. Finally and most importantly, Palladius' rebuttal of Ambrose's Nicene reading of John 14:28 would pose a real problem for Augustine since the Homoian exegesis is framed precisely in a category much favored by Augustine for his Trinitarian and Christological reflection; namely, that of *mission*. Palladius asks: What or who is sent in the Incarnation? Nothing about Augustine could countenance a reply of "Just the body." Augustine's polemically motivated exegesis of John 14:28 becomes the occasion for him to explore ways of articulating what it is precisely in Jesus that is "inferior" to the Father.[36] In *De Trinitate* I, he offers that distinctive insight that from the perspective of divinity the Son is even inferior to himself, that is, the humanity ("form of servant") in Jesus is inferior to the divinity ("form of God") in Jesus. Philippians 2:5–7 functions as a way of describing precisely what is inferior and superior.

35. See, for example, Daley, "Giant's Twin Substance: Ambrose and the Christology of Augustine's *Contra Sermonem Arianorum*," in *Collectanea Augustiniana*, Joseph Lienhard, Earl Muller, Roland Teske, eds. (New York: Peter Lang, 1993), pp. 477–495.

36. In the *Answer to the Arian Sermon*, Augustine offers the "twin substanced giant" characterization of the Incarnate Son precisely in the context of explaining that Phil 2:5–7 refers to the Incarnation, John 14:28 refers to the humanity of the Son, and John 10:30 refers to his divinity. A wholly satisfying way of describing what is it that is "human" or "divine" in Jesus is still being working out: thus the invocation of "twin substanced giant" language. Moreover, as one would expect, the engagement with John 14:28 in terms of who (or what) in the Son is sent or is inferior to God (the Father) appears again in the late writings against Maximinus. At one point in the *Answer to Maximinus* (I.xv), Augustine says that the Son speaks the words in John 14:28 because of the visibility he took on in the Incarnation. Elsewhere, Augustine makes it clear that God the Father is not "greater than" just the *body* of the Son, but of the human mind, as well (II.xxv). We can also note that without the Homoian exegesis of John 14:28 supplied by Palladius in the *Acta*, Augustine's remark that the Father is not simply greater than the flesh makes no sense, since Maximinus has said (in the *Debate* 13) that John 14:28 shows that the Son is inferior to the Father *in the Son's divinity* (not in the Son's humanity).

Indeed, the Homoian understanding of John 14:28 articulated by Palladius is a major problem for Augustine's theology of the Incarnation, quite specifically, because Augustine's understanding of the Son being "sent" is tied up immediately in the question of material revelation; in general, Augustine's understanding of Trinitarian mission is understood in terms of divine intersections with material revelation. In the case of the Son, the material revelation is the Incarnation, but even in the case of the Holy Spirit, there are the various assumed material manifestations (fire, dove, etc.). Augustine is very emphatic that "sent" means "moving into material expression." Why? Because only a material existence can perform the epistemological (or anthropological) function of leading us to the vision of God. Even if the material existence has to be removed from sight (e.g., at the Ascension), that material existence is still necessary for its "sensible" content and as the occasion for faith. This understanding by Augustine of the function of the Incarnation may be presumed for *De Trinitate* I since it has already been articulated in *Eighty-Three Different Questions* 69. In that earlier work, Augustine says that at some future time the humanity of Christ, which is now the occasion of our faith, will become the means through which we see the divinity of the Son; and the vision of that divinity will itself open up into a vision of Trinity.[37] The Son will "through himself, the only begotten, cause the Father to be seen by sight . . . by leading those who now believe in him through faith in his Incarnation to the vision of divinity."[38] That vision is our blessedness, our happiness, the point of our existence, and—in a slightly different sense—the "point" of the Incarnation. The Son has to be(come) *really material* if he is to perform the "mission" of bringing us to the beatific vision. Augustine has put the material nature of the Son decisively at the heart of his redemptive act, his being sent. Augustine thus has to understand such materiality in a way that it does not detract from the possibility of the Son's true divinity. If the Homoians carry the day in this "material" critique, then his "'sent' when material, material for the sake of achieving the goal" Christology is challenged at a fundamental level. The Homoians claim "If material, then not divine," while Augustine wants to assert "Material, in order to bring us to the divine."[39] This theme is central to Augustine's Trinitarian theology from *Epistle* 11 to the end of *De Trinitate* itself. Here in *De Trinitate*, book I, that central theme undergoes development in the context of Augustine's engagement with Homoian theology. Not only is *De Trinitate* a polemical work, but

37. It is only slightly an overstatement to say that much of book I is best understood as a continuation and completion of an exegetically centered anti-Homoian polemic begun in *Eighty-Three Different Questions* 69; *Trin.* I.14–15, like the earlier work, is most concerned with 1 Cor 15:28, but the later work offers the defense or re-appropriation of John 14:28 lacking in *Eighty-Three Different Questions* 69. I analyze the theology of 83 *Div. Quaest.* 69 in Barnes, "Rereading Augustine's Theology of the Trinity." Another analysis of 83 *Div. Quaest.* 69, with similiar conclusions, may be found in Ayres, "'Remember That You Are Catholic.'"

38. Augustine, *Eighty-Three Different Questions*, 175–76.

39. In a recent article, Lewis Ayres has shown that this link between Christology and materiality governs the theology of books VIII–XV, as well. See Ayres, "Christological Context of Augustine's 'De trinitate' XIII: Toward Relocating Books VIII-XV," *Augustinian Studies* 29 (1998): 111–139.

many of its central themes—regularly described by some scholars as non-polemical "speculation"—are in fact shaped within and by that polemical engagement.

CONCLUSION

I began this article by suggesting that it is normal and even authoritative to understand Augustine's *De Trinitate* as being non-polemical in character. Basil Studer, for example, has remarked that "Dogmatic works, which simply explain the teaching of the Church without combating views judged to be heretical, are rather rare [in the patristic era]. A few may be named: above all . . . [Augustine's] *The Trinity*."[40] Obviously, I disagree with this characterization of *De Trinitate*. I will admit that limiting this brief study of the polemical context of *De Trinitate* to just book I (or rather, to a portion of book I) is a somewhat artificial or at least an arbitrary limitation on my part. However, my intention has been to work exclusively from that text which is commonly understood by scholars to be the very earliest part of *De Trinitate* and to show, thereby, that even at this relatively early point Augustine is already *knowledgeable of* and *engaged with* Homoian theology.[41] It will be obvious by now that the ultimate goal of the kind of reading I am offering in this article is to place all of *De Trinitate* and Augustine's Trinitarian theology in its historical context. The process of achieving that goal will, I think, give a new and different value to the reading of not simply book I of *De Trinitate*, but of the whole work.

40. A. Di Berardino and B. Studer, eds., *History of Theology I: The Patristic Period*, trans. M. J. O'Connell (Collegeville: Liturgical Press, 1997), 8. In more recent writings, Studer has seemed to describe *de Trinitate* more as polemic, and it may be that he has changed his mind since writing the first volume of the *History*. See Studer's "History and Faith in Augustine's *de Trinitate*," *Augustinian Studies* 28 (1997): 7–50; and *Grace of Christ*.

41. The hardest argument to make is the argument with a position with which you largely agree, but not entirely. The judgments of the editors of the BA volume 15 on *Trin.* I–VII fall into this category for me. The editors—Mellet and Camelot—understand much about the dynamic driving Augustine's thought in the early books of *Trin.*: they see the significance of the confrontation with Arianism in the development of the doctrine that the Trinity operate inseparably; they understand that the confrontation with Arianism transformed traditional doctrine on the theophanies. Moreover, the editors decline the division of the work into theological and philosophical halves, while still they see a unity in the first seven books. There is much in all this by Mellet and Camelot to support. Yet there must be hesitation and caution. For example, the editors remain with the old "the West starts with the unity" chestnut. The most significant problem, however, is that they do not carry their legitimate insights to the conclusion one might expect. Their treatment of book I hovers above the text, declining to engage with the book at the level of detail.

Chapter 9

The Arians of Book V and the Genre of *De Trinitate*

In judgments about the nature or origins of the Arian doctrines that Augustine rebuts in book V of *De Trinitate*,[1] we find one widespread and recurring opinion; namely, that these fragments reproduce the theology of Eunomius.[2] In this article, I will argue that the commonly accepted opinion is wrong, that it is based on assumptions that are unfounded and prejudicial to determining who the "Arians" of book V are. I will show, through a variety of considerations, that the anti-Nicene doctrines Augustine reports in book V have their origins in Latin Homoian theology, and not in Eunomian theology. What I shall say will emphasize the traditional character of Augustine's response to the Arians' of books V–VII. I make this last point plainly because scholarly treatments of *De Trinitate* have tended to emphasize its innovative qualities at the expense of its traditional ones.

In books V and VI, Augustine cites specific Arian' doctrines which he is concerned to refute. The doctrines Augustine attributes to Arius in book VI are all doctrines to be found in the three Western anti-Arian texts that I assume Augustine knew: Hilary's *De Trinitate*, Victorinus' *Adversus Arianum,* and Ambrose's *De Fide.* Any one of these works, if not Ambrose personally, could have served as Augustine's source for the examples of Arius' doctrines found in book VI. The Eunomian-like fragments offered in book V, on the other hand, are not to be found in any other extant source. They are not in the three Latin pro-Nicene texts just mentioned, nor are they in any

---

1. I am referring to the doctrines that Augustine cites at v. 3. 4: 6–11, v. 6. 7: 1–12 and 25–30 in *De Trinitate Libri XV,* W.J. Mountain (ed.), CCSL, 50.208, 211, and 212.

2. A recent expression of this judgment may be found in Edmund Hill's introduction to his new translation of *Trin.*; see Augustine, *Trinity,* 49.

Greek apologetic work of the era, including all of the Cappadocians. Furthermore, the fragments of book V are not found in Augustine's other anti-Arian works in *PL* 42, or in the *Scholia Arrianum*[3] or *Scripta Arriana Latina*.[4] These fragments are not in any extant text by Arius, Aetius, or Eunomius, nor are they to be found in any later reports of their doctrines, such as those by Epiphanius,[5] Rufinus,[6] Jerome,[7] or Nemesius of Emesa.[8] The debate over whether Augustine read Basil's *Contra Eunomium* is irrelevant to the question of textual sources, since the Eunomian theology in that work dates from the early 360s, i.e., from Eunomius' *Apologia*,[9] and as such stylistically does not resemble the fragments Augustine offers. Indeed, as I will show, the assumption that Augustine knew the theology of Eunomius contained in Basil's *Contra Eunomium* only makes the character of Augustine's arguments in book V more confusing. In short, while the fragments of Arianism cited in book VI are found in a number of Latin (and Greek) works, Augustine is the unique witness to the expressions of anti-Nicene theology he cites in book V. Yet it is extremely unlikely that Augustine would prove to be the exclusive witness to Greek anti-Nicene texts unless we make major assumptions about the communication of Eunomius' theology westward.

There has been a tendency in modern scholarship on Latin anti-Arian/pro-Nicene polemic to assume that Eunomian theology was available to the West very quickly. However, we have no explicit evidence that the theology of Aetius and Eunomius was known to the West before Jerome learned of it in Constantinople (380), when he claims to have heard Gregory of Nyssa read book I of his *Contra Eunomium* to Gregory of Nazianzus. This firsthand experience of the debate with Eunomius seems not to have survived Jerome's notorious theological tone-deafness, for his later characterizations of Eunomius' theology can cause one to renounce the testimony of eyewitnesses forever. Indeed, the very sketchy characterizations of Eunomius offered by Jerome and Rufinus

---

3. *Scolies Ariennes sur le Concile d'Aquilée,* Roger Gryson, SC, vol. 267.

4. *Scripta Arriana Latina,* Roger Gryson (ed.), CCSL 82

5. *Panarion* 76.1.1–54.37, Karl Holl (ed.), GCS, *Epiphanius (Ancoratus und Panarion),* Zweiter Band, reports on the doctrines of Aetius and Eunomius.

6. Rufinus mentions Eunomius in one fragment of his own *Apologia* preserved by Jerome in the latter's *Apologia,* bk. II.

7. Jerome has several references to Eunomius. In his *Lives of Illustrious Men,* cxxviii, where he says that he heard Gregory of Nyssa read his *Contra Eunomium* while with Gregory of Nazianzus in Constantinople. Jerome also refers to Eunomius in the *Lives,* cxx, but has nothing to say about Eunomius' theology. Other descriptions of Eunomius' theology by Jerome tend to reduce Eunomius' theology to that of Origen or Arius, or both, as in the *Apologia,* ii.19.

8. Nemesius refers to Eunomius at several points in *On the Nature of Man.* See, for example, Telfer's translation, *Cyril of Jerusalem and Nemesius of Emesa,* Library of Christian Classics, vol. IV (London: SCM Press, 1955), 281–82, where Nemesius refers to Eunomius' psychology, or pp. 301–2, where he refers to Eunomian Christology.

9. Eunomius' *Apologia* was originally delivered as an oral address in Constantinople in either Dec. 359 or Jan. 360. What we have as the *Apologia* includes material added at a later date (such as ch. 28). Therefore, I refer to the publication date of the *Apologia* rather than the earlier "delivery" date.

seem only to have served as handy sticks with which to beat Origen.[10] Likewise, Basil's *Contra Eunomium* has been suggested by some scholars as a source of knowledge about Eunomius for Latins, either directly by Augustine reading it late in his career, or indirectly in the supposition that Ambrose had read it. In either case, the possibility of Basil's work being a source is not only very unlikely but irrelevant.

The fact that scholars have assumed that an acquaintance with Eunomius' early work, the *Apologia,* was sufficient to communicate what was distinct about the character and content of Eunomius' theology is telling, for this assumption is evidence of a major presupposition about the distinguishing characteristics and contents of late anti-Nicene theology generally, and of late Latin anti-Nicene theology especially. Modern scholarship on late anti-Nicene theology is strangely marked by two opposing tendencies: the first collapses all anti-Nicene theologies into one body of doctrine; while the second treats Eunomius' theology as somehow radically different from that of his fellow anti-Nicenes.[11] Against both these readings, I would suggest that the real similarities between Eunomius' theology and other anti-Nicene (particularly Homoian) theologies are not signs of Eunomian influence, but of similar theological interests. A knowledge of the *Apologia* alone does not give a reader knowledge of the fundamental character of Eunomianism because very little of the theology expressed by Eunomius in his *Apologia* of 362 is uniquely his own even in 362, much less twenty or forty years later, except his technical theory of negative language. The description that Augustine offers of Eunomius' theology in book XV of *De Trinitate* does indeed resemble Gregory Nazianzus' description of Eunomian doctrine in his *Second Theological Oration,* as the editor of the *CCL* volume notes,[12] but the doctrine cited is expressed in Eunomius' *Apologia* of 362 and not in Eunomius' *Apologia Apologiae* of 379. Indeed, Augustine's description of Eunomius in *De Trinitate* XV makes him appear as much *Homoian* as *Anomoian* since Eunomius' doctrines are described in terms of "similarity to the will." In fact, Augustine's mention of Eunomius in *De Trinitate* XV, and the doctrine Augustine attributes to him there, shows that Augustine did indeed know of Eunomius, but declined to attribute the "Arian" theology of book V to him. Most importantly, nothing in the book XV account of Eunomius' doctrines suggests an association between his theology and an emphasis on *unbegotten.*

Although there are references to "Anomoians" to be found in Western authors, as at the end of Victorinus' *The Necessity of Accepting the Homoousion,*[13] there is nothing in Hilary, Victorinus, or Ambrose to indicate that they knew much more of Eunomius

---

10. Jerome links Eunomius with Origen in his *Apologia* ii.1.

11. Meslin, *Let Ariens d'Occident,* 300–305, and Gryson, *Scolics Ariennes,* 173–75, are good examples of this first tendency; Hanson, *The Search,* 598 and 636, is a good example of the second.

12. *De Trinitate Libri XV,* Mountain, 515nn4 and 6.

13. *De Homoousio Recipiendo* 4:32–33, 'Nam de illis non loquendum qui dissimilem dicunt . ' in *Traités Théologiques sur la Trinité,* Paul Henry and Pierre Hadot (eds. and trans.), SC 68.616.

than that some such anti-Nicene existed.[14] It is undeniable that they do occasionally describe doctrines which some modern scholars have thought were specifically Ano-moian, but the attempt by some scholars to find the theology of Aetius and Eunomius in the doctrine that the natures of the Father and Son are dissimilar depends upon the assumption that these two Greeks owned a monopoly on such a doctrine. André Rocher, for example, offers such a case of circular reasoning when he argues for the common ground between Acacius' and Eunomius' theologies by quoting Victorinus as a witness to Eunomian theology, thereby assuming that the doctrines Victorinus opposes are what we call *Eunomian* and not what we call *Homoian*.[15] Overall, we have no reason to believe that Eunomian theology was ever a real problem in the Latin West, or that anything beyond Eunomius' name and some crude caricatures of his theology was known by Latin theologians in the fourth and early fifth centuries. Rufi-nus and Jerome knew as much about Eunomius as any Westerner did, and they either knew or understood precious little.

While there is little evidence of direct knowledge of Eunomius in the West, there is definite evidence that Augustine had encountered a living, proximate, even power-ful Homoianism early in his life during his time in Milan, for it was then that Ambrose faced the anti-Nicene threat from Latin Homoians, such as Palladius. The special char-acter of Milan in the 380s may be said to have been that it was the last political strong-hold of Latin Homoian theology: in 385, Justina and the pro-Homoian court of Milan made the faith of Rimini and Constantinople (360) legal in their city, and threatened death to anyone who interfered with these re-enfranchised Homoians. In 386, the Emperor Valentinian proclaimed freedom of worship for all those in Italy subscribing to Rimini and Constantinople.[16] Augustine's time in Milan thus corresponded with

14. One apparent exception to this statement is Hilary's account in *In Constantium* 12 of his con-versation with a bishop at the Council of Seleucia. Hilary is inquiring into the doctrine that the Son does not resemble God, but does resemble the Father, a doctrine that certainly sounds Anomoian to modern ears. There have been conspicuous differences of opinion in recent interpretations of this conversation, however. Thomas Kopecek is certain that Hilary spoke to a "neo-Arian" (i.e., Anomoian or Heterousian) bishop, as he says in *History of Neo-Arianism*, 209. Hanson, on the other hand, identi-fies the bishop as Homoian; see Hanson, *The Search*, 574. Hilary's subtle insight in *In Constantium* 12 is not only difficult for modern scholars to recapture, but (more importantly) it seems to have had no influence or import for Latins engaged in pro-Nicene polemic. This last point is important: whatever Hilary may have heard from Anomoians did not translate into a clear sense of their identity, for him or his readers.

15. See Rocher's translation of and commentary on Hilary's *In Constantium* in *Contre Constance*, SC 334.81. The same kind of error of identification occurs regularly in Mary T. Clark's comments throughout FotC vol. 69; for example, 212n50. Simply put, Victorinus knows *nothing* of the theology of Eunomius or of pure Anomoianism; what he knows of Anomoianism he has gathered through Basil of Ancyra's *Epistle* (now to be found in Epiphanius' *Panarion* 73.2.1–11.11), which never mentions Aetius or Eunomius by name. Victorinus' testimony proves only the ambiguous state of anti-Nicene theology in the late 350s; more grandiose claims are the product of contemporary scholars who read his work with an anachronistic expectation of the same clarity in beliefs (and parties) in the late 350s as began to appear in the post-360 era.

16. I am indebted to Daniel Williams for this information. See his "Nicene Christianity and Its Opponents in Northern Italy," (diss., University of Toronto, 1990), 350, 361.

the peak of Homoian strength, for upon his return to Milan he witnessed the siege of the Portican Basilica by Auxentius (of Durostorum) and his followers.[17] The scholarly emphasis on Augustine's encounter with Arians late in his career in North Africa overlooks this very important early encounter with the most significant form of Latin anti-Nicene theology.[18] Book V replies to the theology of Latin Homoianism and not, initial impressions to the contrary, to Eunomianism.

The syllogistic form of the Arian citations, as preserved by Augustine, can suggest that these doctrines are Eunomian in origin, since Eunomius' theology, like that of his mentor Aetius, was often expressed in a syllogistic form. It was the claim of Epiphanius, for example, that this syllogistic form was an essential property of Aetius' theology, as much content as form.[19] Another feature of the theology of these three fragments which seems Eunomian is their use of essence or substance language. However, it is not the syllogistic form or the essence language which scholars have cited as proof of the Eunomian identity of the doctrines in the fragments, but the emphasis on *unbegotten* as the primary characteristic of divinity. This emphasis on unbegotten, i.e., ἀγέννητος or *ingenitus,* is consistently cited as evidence that Augustine is reproducing Eunomian theology in the fragments. For example, both Michael Schmaus[20] and Alfred Schindler[21] are reminded of Eunomius by the references in book V to *ingenitus,* while Olivier du Roy describes the argument *in toto* of books V–VII as anti-*Eunomian* in nature.[22] In each case, the unspoken assumption is that it was uniquely Eunomian to identify divinity with unbegottenness. But this assumption is incorrect.

The Latin Homoian theologies of Palladius and Maximinus, as well as the theology of the *Sermo Arianorum,* emphasized unbegottenness as the distinguishing feature of the one true God, i.e., the Father. This emphasis is found repeatedly in Maximinus' *Commentary on the Acts of Aquileia,* as when Maximinus remarks approvingly on Palladius' claim that God the Father is the only ingenerate and interprets Arius' confession of *one true God, alone ingenerate, alone eternal* as meaning that God is *ingenerately eternal, ingenerately good, ingenerately immortal,* and *ingenerately invisible.*[23] Or again in the *Letter of Auxentius* on the Creed of Ulfilas, where Maximinus notes that Ulfilas knew that "the one true God is the one ingenerate."[24] Arguments for

17. In *Confessions* IX.7, Augustine records the scene of this confrontation in terms of Monica's solidarity with Ambrose.

18. The *Fourtieth Tractate on the Gospel of John* has Augustine remarking on the possible presence of Arians in the audience. Augustine passes these Arians off as outside agitators (or words to that effect). The date of the tractate is contested, but it does show, at least, that there was a (foreign?) Arian presence in North Africa before that of the late 420s.

19. Epiphanius' opinion to this effect will be found in *Panarion,* 75.8.2.

20. Schmaus, *Die Psychologische Trinitätslehre des Hl. Augustinus,* 143.

21. Schindler, *Wort und Analogie in Augustine Trinitätslehre,* 151–53.

22. Du Roy, *L' Intelligence de la Foi en la Trinité selon Saint Augustin,* 458.

23. Gryson, *Scolies Ariennes,* 304r.38.

24. Gryson, *Scolies Ariennes,* 304r.42, 237.

the fundamental character of the *ingenitus–genitus* distinction in the theologies of Palladius and Maximinus are found in both Meslin[25] and Gryson.[26]

The Latin Homoian identity of the Arians of book V is further supported by examining Augustine's references to Arian exegesis of biblical texts. Augustine reports in book VI that the Arians use John 17:3 to support their belief that the Father alone is truly God.[27] John 17:3 was a popular prooftext among all the anti-Nicene groups,[28] and although it is used by the Greek Anomoians Aetius and Eunomius, as well as by Latin Homoians such as Palladius and Maximinus, it is the Homoian exegesis of the text that most closely resembles Augustine's report. Aetius has an implied reference to John 17:3 in his *Syntagmation*, where he says ὁ ὢν αὐτὸ ἀγέννητος θεός ὁ καὶ μόνος.[29] Aetius says this in the context of emphasizing the importance of the knowledge of God in providing eternal life. Eunomius' citation of John 17:3 occurs in his *Creed* of 383, and is closer to the exegesis that Augustine reports: Eunomius says that he believes in the "one and only true God" (τὸν ἕνα καὶ μόνον ἀληθινὸν θεόν), reverencing God as he really is, "one God" (θεόν ἕνα).[30] Eunomius' emphasis is on the *one* God rather than the *only* or the *true* God. In any case, no one has ever suggested that Augustine knew this *Creed* of Eunomius. John 17:3 is, however, a favorite among Latin Homoians, as both Hanson[31] and Gryson[32] have pointed out, and the specific exegesis of this text by these Arians is very close to the one Augustine reports. Augustine says that the Arians believe that John 17:3 shows that the Son is not *uerum Deum*. This is Maximinus' exegesis of John 17:3 in his *Commentary on the Acts of Aquileia,* where his citing of the Johannine passage is an opportunity for Maximinus to repeat the phrase *uerum Deum* three times within the space of two successive sentences.[33] Augustine is reporting on *Homoian* use of John 17:3, and not on its use by Aetius or Eunomius, and these Homoians are of the late Latin variety typified by Palladius and Maximinus.

Another aspect of book V that figures in any attempt to identify the source of the Arian doctrines that Augustine rebuts is his use of relational language, generally thought to derive from Aristotle's *Categories*. The appearance of "Aristotelian" logic in

25. Meslin, *Les Ariens,* 117, 205, 308–09.

26. Gryson, *Scolies Ariennes,* 181.

27. Augustine, *Trin.* VI.9.10, 10–12, Mountain, p. 239.

28. See Hanson's summary in *The Search,* 836–37.

29. Proposition 37, 544, in L. R. Wickham's edition and translation of "The *Syntagmation* of Aetius the Anomean," *JThS* ns 19 (1968): 532–69. Kopecek remarks in *History of Neo-Arianism,* 296, that this reference to John 17:3 is "the only absolutely identifiable quotation from scripture in the entire *Syntagmation*." Kopecek speculates (296–97) that Aetius found this text so authoritative because of its use in fourth-century Eastern liturgies, particularly the eucharistic anaphoras of Serapion's *Euchologium* and the *Apostolic Constitutions*.

30. Eunomius, *Creed* 2:1, in Vaggione, *Extant Works,* 150.

31. Hanson, *The Search,* 560, 567, 606, 836–37.

32. Gryson, *Scolies Ariennes,* 180–81, and 217n4.

33. Gryson, *Scolies Ariennes,* 300v.

book V is significant for the opinion that the Arian fragments are Eunomian because Eunomius was commonly condemned for the injection of Aristotelian terminology into theology. If Augustine had known anything at all about Eunomius beyond the name, he would have known this, since the most consistently reported summary account of Aetius' and Eunomius' theology was precisely that their heresy was the result of the use of Aristotle in explaining the Trinity. According to the hypothesis of Eunomian fragments proposed by most scholars, Augustine introduces examples of a theology which was, by Augustine's time, understood to have been condemned precisely for the use of Aristotle's *Categories*. While I do not think that the fragments Augustine produces are Eunomian, those scholars who have thought otherwise need to ask what Eunomian authorship of these fragments means for the context and content of Augustine's use of Aristotelian categories in book V. Thus far, however, the subject of Augustine's use of Aristotelian language in book V has been treated separately from the subject of his citing Eunomian theology in that same book.[34]

One could propose that Augustine chose Eunomian fragments precisely because of their perceived Aristotelian content, and that he is thereby wresting Aristotle from the heretics and providing an orthodox Aristotelian account of the Trinity as opposed to Eunomius' heretical Aristotelian account. The problem with this proposal is that Augustine betrays no sensitivity about his use of Aristotelian language: he simply proceeds in deploying his own case without any apparent hesitation or self-consciousness about either using language previously tainted by heretics or the possibility of his theological language resembling that of heretics. Augustine's attitude towards Aristotle's *Categories* is the same as Jerome's, and not that of the Cappadocians. The more one claims Augustine knew of Eunomius' theology, the more troublesome Augustine's Aristotelian language in book V becomes: and the tripwire for this troublesomeness is automatically crossed if one claims that Augustine knew Basil's *Contra Eunomium*. Indeed, everything Augustine could have learned about Eunomius' theology in Basil's *Contra Eunomium* would militate against the theology he develops in book V: namely, Basil's blanket condemnation of the use of Aristotle's *Categories*,[35] and his condemnation of identifying God's essence with one property.[36]

Finally, we should note that statements about the doctrinal content of *De Trinitate* are regularly tied to judgments on its literary form. For example, both the studies by Edmund Hill[37] and Joseph O'Leary[38] share the assumption that Augustine's theo-

---

34. A rare exception to the separate treatment of these two subjects is Chevalier's *S. Augustin et la Pensée Grecque*, 133–35. The problem of the prior Eunomian use of Aristotelian language was not felt by Chevalier, since he erroneously attributed the initial use of Aristotle to Basil, and ignored Basil's pointed rejections of Aristotle's *Categories*.

35. Basil, *Contra Eunomium*, 1.9, in *Contre Eunome*, Bernard Sesboüé, Georges-Matthieu de Durand and Louis Doutreleau (ed. and trans.), SC 299.201.

36. Basil, *Contra Eunomium*, 1.11 (SC 299.209–11).

37. Hill, "St. Augustine's De Trinitate," 277–86.

38. O'Leary, "Dieu-esprit et Dieu-Substance Chez Saint Augustin," *Recherches de Science Religieuse*,

logical development is mirrored in the literary distance between his work and the writings of his predecessors. These scholars express the common judgment that while Augustine's literary expression of his new Trinitarian paradigm of internal relations clearly incorporates previous texts, such as Hilary's and Ambrose's, it is distinct from these traditional texts in form. In this interpretation of *De Trinitate,* the nature and identity of the Arians of book V is linked to a description of the genre of *De Trinitate:* namely, that *De Trinitate* is an exposition free from the pressure of controversy because the Arians of book V are of only formal interest to Augustine.

The most elaborate and emphatic statement of the hypothesis of the theological and literary distance between Augustine and his immediate predecessors is offered by French Augustinians such as Paissac,[39] Malet,[40] and Guillou.[41] These scholars argue that Augustine's accomplishments in *De Trinitate* are possible precisely because of his intellectual distance from the Arian controversy.[42] Again according to these authors, because Augustine worked outside the pressures of the Arian controversy, he escaped the two tragic flaws of earlier orthodox theology: first, a hesitancy about using *Logos* as a title for the Second Person because of its semi-Arian heritage;[43] and second, a burdensome and conceptually limiting loyalty to the language of *homoousios,* a term which was excessively ontological if not materialist in its connotations.[44] Both these constraints are found in anti-Arian literature of the earlier generation of pro-Nicene authors, including (these scholars claim) the Trinitarian theology of the Cappadocians. *De Trinitate,* on the other hand, is not an apologetic work and because of this Augustine writes free from the two conceptual constraints.

---

69 (1981), 357–90.

39. Paissac, *Théologie du Verbe.*

40. Malet, *Personne et Amour.*

41. Le Guillou, "Réflexions sur la théologie trinitaire."

42. The argument of these French Augustinians is part of a controversy over the influence of Théodore de Régnon, who claimed in his *Études de Théologie positive sur la Sainte Trinité* that Augustine's interpretation of Old Testament theophanies in book II of *Trin.* is polemically inspired. According to Régnon, Augustine's line of thought moves from Maximinus' argument, given in the *Collatio cum Maximno* (26), that Old Testament theophanies are appearances of the Son; then to a rebuttal of that thesis in *Contra Maximinum* (ii, c. xxvi, 10ff); and finally to a more developed statement of that rebuttal in *Trin.* II. See Régnon, *Études sur la Trinité,* i:258–62. (Unlike most modern scholars, Régnon thinks that *Trin.* was written after *Contra Maximinum.*)

43. Paissac, *Théologie du Verbe,* 30–31.

44. "Ainsi, chez les Grecs eux-mêmes, sous l'influence de la théologie de la conaubatantialité, la personne est en quelque sorte amenuisée, réduite qu'elle est à la plus fluide de toutes les categories . . . Le danger de sabellianisme que peut comporter une insistance trop unilatérale sur la nature n'a pas eu le temps de se manifester dans la pensée trinitaire grecque et le homoousios y est maintenu au service de la théologie des hypoatases. Mais saint Augustin déjà du seul fait qu'il prenait comme point de depart le point d'arrivée des Grecs, risquait de minimiser l'aspect personnel du mystère trinitaire" (Malet, *Personne et Amour,* 21). See also Guillou, "Reflexions," 459, and Legrand, *La Notion philosophique,* 133.

In other words, the judgment that this "Arian" theology was Eunomian has meant for scholars that Augustine was dealing with a threat distant both in space and time, with the Eunomian identity of the fragments underlining the spent and alien, and as such abstract, nature of the problem Augustine faced in these books. Naming these fragments *Eunomian* carries the freight of presuppositions about the relative Trinitarian peace not only of Augustine himself but of the Latin church—excluding the Goths—in the face of the theological ravages found in the Greek church, while also lending a certain universality to Augustine's own doctrines (since he is a Latin refuting Greek errors).

The alternative conclusion that the Arians of book V are not Eunomians but Latin Homoians does not necessarily presuppose that "Arians" still offered real opposition as Augustine wrote, but it does leave open that possibility. I have already suggested that Augustine's early experience in Milan of vigorous Latin Homoian theology has been largely overlooked by scholars. Yet in terms of the literary character of books V–VII (as parts of the whole), the native Western identity of these Arians rather throws into relief Augustine's debt to received Latin pro-Nicene polemics. Hilary, Victorinus, and Ambrose were, after all, polemicists, writing against adversaries that they considered real threats to the true faith.

The most obvious example of the influence of Latin pro-Nicene polemics is Augustine's casting of his own Trinitarian doctrine in opposition to the theology of Arius and "Arians." Athanasius' personal emphasis on Arius has obscured the fact that the rhetorical strategy of identifying anti- (or non-)Nicene theologies with "Arianism" became largely a Latin—rather than a Greek—polemical device. Hilary, Victorinus, and Ambrose make such an identification; the Cappadocians do not. Outside of Athanasius (and those Greeks who are otherwise clearly indebted to him theologically), it is Latins, including Augustine, who find it useful to quote Arius. The use of "Arian" doctrines in book V and Arius' doctrines in book VI as springboards to pro-Nicene Trinitarian doctrine places these books clearly in the traditional literary style of pro-Nicene polemics. The formal character of the polemic against Arius in book VI continues, rather than departs from, the technique of Hilary, Victorinus, and Ambrose. The identification in book V of Latin Homoianism with Arianism borrows in particular from Ambrose's *De Fide* I and II, while the distinction between the "Arians" of book V and the "Eunomians" of book XV seems likely to correspond to Ambrose's distinction in *De Fide* I between the anti-Nicene theology of Palladius, Maximinus, and Auxentius, and the anti-Nicene theology of Eunomius and Aetius.[45] Scholars like the French Augustinians mentioned above have operated with too literal an understanding of the role of Arius in pro-Nicene polemics, as though Hilary, Victorinus, and Ambrose really were arguing with latterday proponents of Arius' doctrines. Such a misunderstanding has allowed a false opposition to be drawn between "real" Arians and the Arians Augustine deals with in books V and VI.

45. At Ambrose, *De Fide* I.vi.45.

I believe that I have shown that there are real problems with the judgment that the fragments of book V are Eunomian, and that there are legitimate reasons for judging the theology of the fragments to be Homoian, in the tradition of Palladius, Auxentius, and Maximinus. Although the identification of the fragments of book V as Eunomian has achieved a sort of commonplace status in scholarship, there are, in fact, no substantial reasons for making such a judgment. The supposed conceptual link between the Eunomian character of Augustine's opponents and the abstract nature of his response is severed. Like his polemical predecessors, Augustine found that the refutation of Latin Homoianism provided the perfect opportunity to develop his own account of the Nicene faith.[46]

46. A shorter version of this essay won the Canadian Society of Patristic Studies 1991 prize. An earlier draft of this essay was given as a communication at the Marquette University Conference on St. Augustine, November 1990.

Chapter 10

The Visible Christ and
the Invisible Trinity

Matthew 5:8 in Augustine's Trinitarian Theology of 400[1]

Nothing must mute the fact that all truth lies right before the eyes, and that its appropriation is a natural consequence of the facts. There is no need for any additional perfection of man as though he could not focus on the "supernatural" truth with his normal equipment for knowing.

—WOLFHART PANNENBERG, *REVELATION AS HISTORY*

Thus from every point of view our theological wisdom is bound up with the incarnate, personal wisdom of God, is conformed to him, and receives from him its characteristic divine-human signature.

—MATTHIAS JOSEPH SCHEEBEN, *THE MYSTERIES OF CHRISTIANITY*

INTRODUCTION

THE SUBJECT OF AUGUSTINE's understanding of the vision of God has been described in modern scholarship primarily in terms of the problematic of a Neoplatonic ascent to God, which was, it clearly seems, so much a part of Augustine's early aspirations. At the same time, Augustine's Trinitarian theology has recently seemed to some to possess too static a doctrine of God, with a diminished sense of the significance of

1. I would like to thank (alphabetically) Lewis Ayres and Basil Studer for their responses to an earlier draft of this essay. I would also like to acknowledge the influence of Ronald Heine's *Perfection in the Virtuous Life* Patristic Monograph Series, no. 2 (Cambridge: Philadelphia Patristic Foundation, 1975) as a precedent for the approach I take here to Augustine's Trinitarian theology.

Christology as the foundation of any theology of God, that is, of the Trinity. Yet to speak about "the vision of *God*" can itself lead inquiry away from the Trinitarian problematic that Augustine encountered so substantially towards the end of the fourth century, in which questions are cast in terms of our vision of the individual Persons of the Trinity—and the difference in the "visions" of each Person possible for us.

Books I–IV of *De Trinitate* are concerned with the question of the appearances of the Son in the theophanies of the Old Testament. According to Augustine's opponents, the Homoians, the appearance of the Son in these theophanies serves as proof that the Son is not true God; only the invisible—and non-appearing—Father is the true or real God. The same argument is applied to the Incarnation. The very appearance of the Son, his visibility, the vision or sight of him, constitutes sufficient evidence that the Son is not, cannot be, God. If we restate this critique more precisely in terms of the economy of the Trinity, then what is being argued by the Homoians is that the Son's role as revealer of the Father means that the Son cannot be God as the Father is God. The very attributes which constitute, as it were, the Son's capacity to reveal are judged as decisive indications of the Son's inferior status to the Father who is revealed by the Son—the Father who is the "one true God." Augustine's engagement with this argument begins immediately at the beginning of *De Trinitate*, for book I is concerned directly with the Homoian argument that the Son's character as revealer—or the Son's "noetic visibility"—constitutes the Son's inferiority to the Father. Indeed, the Homoian argument for an anti-Nicene Trinitarian theology based on the Son's character as revealer places that very character at the center of any account by Augustine of the Trinity; by the year 400, one of Augustine's primary tasks in *De Trinitate* (and in his Trinitarian writings generally) is to articulate an understanding of the Son's revelatory role which supports a theology of the Son's equal divinity with the Father. The "vision of God" has become a Trinitarian problem.

In the early books of *De Trinitate*, Augustine develops his understanding of the Trinitarian and Christological issues contained in the dispute over the content of the theophanies. As he makes this development, Augustine uncovers *links* between Trinitarian doctrines and the experience of faith, between the question of what of God is seen in the theophanies (when is functionally equivalent to the question, When does one see God?) and the question, How does faith bring the Christian to his or her proper end, namely, delight in the vision of God the Trinity? These two questions are brought together in the judgment by Augustine that Matthew 5:8 is significant for both questions. The exegetical connection of Matthew 5:8 to the question of how faith brings the Christian to the vision of God is obvious, but as we will see, there was a trajectory of Latin theology which also connected the beatitude—with its invocation of a vision of God—to a theology of the Trinity and Incarnation. This connection is based in part on the decisive role visibility and invisibility played in traditional arguments against the modalists for the separate existences of the Father and the Son, as well as the role visibility and invisibility play in then-contemporary anti-Nicene doctrines of the different natures of Father and Son. There is thus a Latin tradition which gives Matthew 5:8 a real Trinitarian–Christological significance, and Augustine incorporates that significance into his own Trinitarian and Christological doctrines.

The Trinitarian controversy as Augustine encountered it is argued in terms of whether God can be seen at all, has the Son been seen, and if yes, when and how? Aside from the historical question of when was the Son seen (e.g., in the OT theophanies, the Incarnation, etc.), there is an epistemological question at play, because for Augustine "to see" means "to know." Augustine finds the answers to these questions in Philippians 2:5–7, the root narrative of the Trinity, the very language of which Augustine understands to describe visual or epistemological categories (i.e., *Form* of God, *Form* of Servant). Augustine's judgment is that all the Persons of the Trinity can be seen only at the resolution of history—the end-time—and he describes the object(s) of this vision very specifically: what will be seen is either the Form of Man or the Form of God. Given the visual content of the Christological drama described in Philippians 2:5–7 and the visual resolution of that drama at the final judgment, the statement Matthew 5:8 makes about the sight of God is of profound significance, for it is the promise of the very vision of which Augustine has spoken. As a promise, Matthew 5:8 carries both the tension of the delay in the vision Christians hope to have and the means to resolve that tension; namely, purity of heart. The meaning of purity of heart lies in the possession of faith, and faith "proves" the reality of that final vision through the reality of what is gained now through faith.

Augustine invokes Matthew 5:8 immediately in his polemical engagement with the anti-Nicene Homoians, and the passage appears repeatedly in book I of *De Trinitate*.[2] Augustine treats Matthew 5:8 explicitly in book I because it is a foundation for what follows. The question of "the pure of heart will see God" is not a question specific to, or localized in, just book I of *De Trinitate*—it is not even specific just to books I–IV, although these books are indeed about one key kind of "seeing God": the theophanies. The exegesis of Matthew 5:8 provides the means by which Augustine "clears the ground" for a proper understanding of the sight of God.[3] Above all, Augustine starts with what Matthew 5:8 means "now," that is, what it means for those Latin-speaking Christians who know their own tradition and who are aware of the state of doctrine in or around the year 400.

---

2. *Beati mundo corde, quoniam ispi deum uidebunt.* Of the five citations of Matt 5:8 in *Trin.*, four of these are in book I of the work; the one other is in book VIII. lib.1, cap. 8, line 117; lib. 1, cap. 13, line 28; lib. 1, cap. 13, line 108; lib. 1, cap. 13, line 167; lib. 8, cap. 4, line 12 (according to CETEDOC).

3. The clearest example of the continuing presence of the Matt 5:8-supported theology of *Trin.* I–IV is to be found in *Ep.* 147 (dated to 413), which contains all the key points I am identifying in *Trin.*; the polemical Trinitarian provenance for Augustine of the question of our vision of God is especially clear in that epistle. (I will return to this work below.) Basil Studer shows the relationship between *Ep.* 147 and fourth-century Latin readings of the theophanies in his *Zur Theophanie-Exegese Augustins* Studia Anselmiana LIX (Roman: Liberia Herder, 1971).

I will argue in this article that Augustine's doctrine of the vision through Christ of the Trinity at the end-time should be understood as Augustine's solution to the Homoian subordinationist understanding of the Son's visibility. This specific thesis presupposes that Augustine's doctrine of the eschatological vision of God should be understood as a polemical issue since the significance of the Son's role as revealer of the Father was at that time a point of controversy in Trinitarian theology. The historical context meant that any doctrine of the vision or knowledge of God was set within theologies of the Trinity and the Incarnation. This polemical setting of Augustine's doctrine of the vision of God is manifested in his exegesis of Matthew 5:8 in *De Trinitate* I, and it remains as the backdrop for his other treatments of the Trinity. In *De Trinitate* I, the vision of the Trinity at the end-time is promised by God in Mattew 5:8; the Christological character of this vision is structured by Augustine's polemically motivated exegesis of 1 Corinthians 15:24–28, while Philippians 2:5–7 specifies the alternate objects of knowledge or sight.[4] The constellation of these three Scripture texts supports Augustine's account of how the Son is revelatory. Augustine offers what could be called a sophisticated account of what *exactly* is revealed by the Son in the Incarnation (and *when*). The real revelation is to a certain extent *ex post facto*, since faith—which is not a kind of *sight*—is that which recognizes what is being revealed. Thus, having the *right* faith is important, since until the end-time what knowledge of the Trinity that we have is through faith.[5]

4. This article has points of contact with the thoughts of at least two contemporary theologians, Colin Gunton and Jean Luc Marion. Gunton has argued that Augustine's Trinitarian theology is "un-economic" because it is anti-material, and one important sign of this anti-material, anti-economic bent is Augustine's rejection of OT theophanies as being appearances of God. See Gunton's "Augustine, the Trinity and the Theological Crisis of the West", *Scottish Journal of Theology* 43 (1990): 33–58 My article will show that such an account of Augustine's understanding of the significance of the theophanies misreads Augustine and renders his theology more simplistic than it is. On the other hand, Jean Luc Marion has, in a variety of writings, argued that Christians do not presently understand the event (the Incarnation) that they "know," that Christian faith entails accepting this present lack of understanding, and that understanding will come only eschatologically. In thoughts like this, Marion has much in common with Augustine. Where Marion and Augustine certainly differ is in their evaluation of the words which describe that event, the regula and creeds; with Augustine, the creeds must be treated very seriously because they provide the intermediate step in the purification of the heart. Creeds are the matter which works the discipline of faith upon us, enlightening our understanding. Without the creeds, Marion would not know that the event of two thousand years ago was the unequivocal and unique event it was, the event that is both fully real and wholly unintelligible in this lifetime.

5. If I were to propose a definition of faith in technical language reasonably cognate to Augustine's thought, I would say that *Faith is a (affective) consent or assent through which one interprets events.* Through faith we are able to interpret the events (or words) of Jesus' life—those things materially perceived—and recognize the truth about God that such events communicate or affirm.

I. THE TRINITARIAN CONTENT OF
MATT 5:8; *DE TRINITATE* I.16-20

Augustine's understanding of the Trinitarian significance of Matthew 5:8 appears in his earliest sermons on the creed, *Sermon* 214 (391) and *De Fide et Symbolo* (393). In *Sermon* 214, Augustine says that the credal affirmation that Christ will come to judge the living and the dead is to be understood with the sense that in the end-time "Christ will judge in the same form as that in which he was judged." In this sermon, Augustine casts the distinguishing features of the saved and the damned in visual categories: some believed in who and what they saw, and these are saved; others despised who and what they saw, and these are damned. Augustine then closes his discussion of the creed's theology of the Son by quoting Matthew 5:8. In *De Fide et Symbolo*, Matthew 5:8 again ends Augustine's summary of the faith: the beatitude supports Augustine's point that the truth of the Trinity is "seen" only by those with a pure heart—and seen by those only in proportion to the degree of their purity of heart. The "sight" that Augustine speaks of is not a beatific sight, but the intellectual sight (or knowledge) of propositions about God, as, for example, that there can be no accidents in God. In short, the knowledge arising from the "sight" of propositions of the faith—i.e., the creed—is conditioned by the relative purity of heart of the believer.

The first two appearances of the Beatitude in *De Trinitate* I occur within a tightly argued passage which runs from sections 16 to 19: this portion of the book consists of Augustine's explanation of 1 Corinthians 15:24–28, a scriptural passage which anti-Nicenes claimed supported their belief that the Son is not true God.[6] *De Trinitate* I.16 begins with Augustine's assertion that "The Son will not be deprived of the kingdom when he hands it over." The idea that the Son *would* be deprived of the kingdom when he hands it over is not simply a thought experiment on Augustine's part. In the second half of the fourth century, Latin Homoians articulated their opposition to the Trinitarian faith, by then associated with Nicaea, through just such an exegesis of 1 Corinthians 15:28.[7] For example, in the *Acts of the Council of Aquilaea* 39, the Homoian Palladius evidently cites 1 Corinthians 15:28 when he says that the Son is subject to the Father.[8] In anti-Nicene eyes, this scriptural passage says that at the end of time the Son

6. In Greek theology of the first half of the fourth century, 1 Cor 15:28 figured prominently in the hyper-Nicene (modalist) theology of Marcellus of Ancyra. Augustine seems unaware of the association of the Scripture passage with Marcellus.

7. On Latin Homoianism, see (chronologically): Meslin, *Les ariens d'Occident 335–430*; the Introduction by Roger Gryson to *Scolies Ariennes*; and Williams, *Ambrose of Milan*. The old judgment that Latin Homoianism owes *tout cour* to Ufilias and, through him, to Eunomius, is twice a canard. The most widely available survey of Homoian theology is that by R.P.C. Hanson in his *The Search*; Hanson, however, collapses the differences between Greek and Latin Homoianism and, as well, assumes *a priori* that all Homoians are devoid ("free") of any significant literacy in philosophy.

8. See Gryson, *Scolies Ariennes*, 359. Some scholars think that this Palladius is the author of the *Arian Sermon* that Augustine later writes against.

will be subject or subordinated to the Father.[9] Augustine, then, must offer a rebuttal of the Homoian exegesis of the First Corinthians passage. It is important to remember that by the time Augustine wrote *De Trinitate* I, he had already devoted his attention to challenging the Homoian exegesis of this passage: *Eighty-Three Diverse Questions* 69 (usually dated to 394–96) is, in fact, an exegetical reflection upon 1 Corinthians 15:28 (with recurring attention to John 14:18 and Philippians 2:5–7).[10] The cause of Augustine's reflection upon 1 Corinthians 15:28 is, as he tells us in the first line of the work, the heretical exegesis some give to the passage. Section 16 of *De Trinitate* I thus begins with a problem already once engaged: "The Son will not be deprived of the kingdom when he hands it over."

Augustine's own exegetical argument then follows: "The fact is that the man Christ Jesus, mediator of God and man, now reigning for all the just who live by faith, is going to bring them to direct sight of God, to a face-to-face vision . . . that is what is meant by 'when he hands the kingdom over to God and the Father,' as though to say 'When he brings believers to a direct contemplation of God and the Father.'"[11] Using the discourse to Philip in John 14, Augustine then makes the point that the vision of the Son *is* the vision of the Father, and vice versa. But Augustine has one very important qualification to add to this vision: not for the last time Augustine will cite 2 Corinthians 5:6, "[A]s long as we are in the body we are abroad from the Lord. For we walk by faith, not by sight."[12]

The eschatological location of the turning over of the Kingdom is a consistent part of Augustine's reading of the pauline text; eschatological, but *not* wholly unrealized. In *Diverse Questions* 69, Augustine had argued that the "coming-to-be" aspect of the verse "Hallowed by thy name" in the Lord's Prayer does not mean that God's name is not now holy; rather, the prayer asks that God's name be recognized as holy. Similarly (Augustine argued), "when he [the Son] will hand the kingdom over" does not mean that the kingdom is not now under the dominion of God; rather, Paul speaks of the time when God's kingdom will be recognized in and through the Son. Or, as Augustine puts it, "when he [the Son] will show that the Father reigns." At the end-time, the Son will "show" or reveal that the Father reigns as he has always reigned. In *Diverse Questions* 69, Augustine argued that God's dominion has not always been, indeed has never been, *shown*: it has, rather, been *believed*. What will happen at the end-time is that the Son will *show* that the Father reigns, so that what believers have known through belief will

9. The fact that we use the word "subordination(ism)" as a generic category for a kind of Trinitarian doctrine should not desensitize us to the fact that in Latin Homoian theology there is, literally, the attribution of a "subordinate" status to the Son, based upon exegesis of scriptural texts such as 1 Cor 15:28.

10. I have dealt extensively with *Eighty-Three Diverse Questions* 69 in my "Rereading Augustine's Theology of the Trinity," 145–76. See also Ayres, "'Remember That You Are Catholic.'"

11. All English translations of *Trin.* are taken from Edmund Hill's translation: here 76. (Further citations from this translation will be referred to simply as Augustine, *Trinity*.)

12. Augustine, *Trinity*, 76. See *Sermon* 21.1–4 and *Trin.* XIV.4 for developments of this idea.

be made manifest to them. Augustine says, "Therefore Christ will hand the kingdom over to God and the Father when through him the Father will be known by sight, for his kingdom consists of those in whom he now reigns through faith."[13] For Augustine, the meaning of "the Son will hand the kingdom over" is that *then the Father will be known by sight as he—and the Trinity ("God")—are known now by faith.*

Augustine then concludes this part of his argument by invoking Matthew 5:8: "Contemplation in fact is the reward of faith, a reward for which hearts are cleansed through faith . . . Proof that it is this contemplation for which hearts are cleansed comes from the key text, 'Blessed are the pure of heart, for they shall see God.'"[14] In this the first appearance of Mattew 5:8 in *De Trinitate*, Augustine's understanding of the role of Matthew 5:8 is that it is proof that the vision of God is indeed to happen.[15] Christ promised that God can be seen; but that vision, we should understand, will occur in the future, at the end-time. Matthew 5:8 refers to an eschatological event;[16] next Augustine identifies the object of that future vision.

Augustine then introduces Philippians 2:5–7 to explain what will be seen by the pure of heart when Christ reveals the kingdom—when the "King" is also revealed. Philippians 2:5–7 has already come into *De Trinitate* I as the *regula fidei* which provides a guide by which scriptural passages are to be understood.[17] Now Augustine uses the two-form distinction to describe the content(s) of the final vision; to be more precise, he uses Philippians 2:5–7 to distinguish the different visions believers and non-believers will experience. We need to note that Philippians 2:5–7 is cast in the language of sight: the Son moves from the "form" of God to the "form" of the servant.

13. Augustine, *Eighty-Three Diverse Questions*, 175.

14. Augustine, *Trinity*, 77. Augustine adds that because of the inseparability of the Father and the Son, "it makes no difference whether sometimes the Father alone or the Son alone is mentioned as the one who is to fill us with delight at his countenance."

15. The "Trinitarian application" of Matt 5:8 is also to be found in Augustine's *Third Tractate on John*, a work roughly contemporary to the early books of *Trin.* (perhaps exactly contemporary). At 18.1 of the *Third Tractate*, Augustine refers to the problem posed by the Homoians and answers: anything seen in an OT theophany was created and was not the substance of God, for those things were seen by the eyes of the flesh. "How is the substance of God seen? Ask the gospel. 'Blessed are the clean of heart, for they shall see God.'" Those who do not understand the necessarily spiritual character of the vision of God—i.e., the Homoians—think that something uncreated can be seen through the sense of sight; or, Augustine dangles, do they imply that *the Son is best understood as created?*—a doctrine anti-Nicenes have otherwise tried to wash their hands of for decades due to its scandalous association with the early Arius. (Note, also, that by this logic, Augustine excludes the introduction of a possible third category, i.e., *not God but not created.*) Thus, in the *Third Tractate*, Augustine links Matt 5:8 with a correct understanding of what of God is visible (and how), and contrasts this understanding with the idea that the Son was visible in the OT theophanies. See FotC 78, 89.

16. An explicit identification of that promised vision as an eschatological event is found in *Sermon 214*. When Augustine quotes Matt 5:8 at *Trin.* I.28 and in I.30 (and echoes its language at I.31), the vision is identified with the end-time judgment, and the object of that vision is Christ as Form of God (from Phil 2:5–7).

17. My own expectation is that the "normative" function of Phil 2:5–7, as well as the great significance of "form" terminology specifically, are the products of the Apollinarian controversy.

The Greek is *morphe*, the Latin is *forma*.[18] The visual character of this description may not have any continuing significance in the Philippians' hymn, but for Augustine the visual component of *forma* is decisive: it names the proper object of sight—which is also the proper object of knowledge. The Son's "two forms" thus correspond to two alternative epistemological acts and objects: *form of servant* or *of man* corresponds to the material object of perception of both believers and non-believers; *form of God* corresponds to the spiritual and immaterial object of perception at the end-time of those who have believed.[19] While under the *form of servant*, the Son does not reveal God or divinity as direct knowledge:[20] while incarnated, the Son reveals God or divinity only through the instrumentality of faith, which not being a kind of seeing is not "knowledge" in the sense that Augustine normally uses that word.[21]

At the end-time those who have responded to Jesus as *form of man* with faith will "see" God—that is, they will contemplate him. Those who did not respond with faith to Jesus as *form of man* will have their final vision limited to the human form of the Son that their faithlessness limited him to. Augustine's own words are worth quoting here:

> Both bad and good, of course, are going to look upon the judge of the living and the dead, but the bad, we may be sure, will only be able to see him in the form by which he is the Son of man, though in the proud splendor that will be his as judge, not in the mean guise he once presented as prisoner in the dock. The form of God, however, in which he is equal to the Father, this the wicked will undoubtedly not see. They are not pure of heart, and *Blessed are the pure of heart, because they shall see God*. This is to be a *face to face seeing*, and it is promised to the just as their supreme reward and it will happen *when he hands over the kingdom to God and the Father* (in which we understand the seeing of his own divine form).[22]

18. Most Latin patristic citations of Phil 2:5–7 agree with the use of *forma* (as the Vulgate later will), but Tertullian uses *effigie* instead in *Adversus Marcionem* V.20: "[Q]uod in effigie dei constitutus non parinam existimavit pariari deo . . . sed exhausit semetipsum accepta effigie servi."

19. This specific understanding of the two forms as objects of knowledge seems not to predate Augustine, and is likely his own development. As I will show in the next section, the "eschatological" and Trinitarian exegesis of Matt 5:8 is found in Hilary of Poitiers.

20. None of this is understood by Augustine to diminish the revelatory character of the Son as Form of God; indeed, as I point out, as Form of God the Son is transparent to the Trinity.

21. Faith is not knowledge because it is not a "seeing," either sensible or intellectual, and knowing is understood to be a kind of sight. Augustine's understanding of the relationship between faith and knowledge is treated more fully in the last section of this article.

22. Augustine, *Trinity*, I.28 (p. 87). The decisive nature of the promise of Matt 5:8 is referred to again in Augustine's later writing, *Ep.* 147: "Since, therefore, we do not see God in this life either with bodily eyes, as we see heavenly or earthly bodies, or with the gaze of the mind, as we see some of the things which I have mentioned and which you most certainly behold within yourself, *why do we believe that he is seen*, except for 'Blessed are the pure of heart, for they shall see God'?" (Augustine, *Ep.* 147.3, in *Letters*, 172; emphasis added).

If the resolution of the drama whose beginning is described in Philippians 2:5–7 is one of sight, then Matthew 5:8 is the description of that resolution from the perspective of the saved, the pure of heart. If, at the end-time, the Form of God will be revealed, the pure of heart are those who will see it.[23] It is clear that Augustine thinks of this vision of the Form of God as a Trinitarian event. The testimony of Christ's words to Philip in John 14 about the sight of the Son being the sight of the Father, and vice versa, as well as the credal-type testimony regarding the common substance and unity of operations shared by the Father, Son, and Holy Spirit provide the basis for Augustine to assert that the vision of the Son as Form of God will itself become a vision of the Father and of the Trinity. The Son—as the vision of the "Form of God"—will become transparent to the vision of the Trinity.[24]

Is the Son a revelation of the divine in any direct, available-to-the-senses way? Is the Son divinity-insofar-as-it-may-be-perceived? The question can be pushed even further: Is the Son, as divine, the occasion of human faith? Augustine's answer to all of these questions is *no*: the Son *is not* a revelation of the divine in any direct, available-to-the-senses way; the Son *is not* divinity-insofar-as-it-may-be-perceived; the Son, as divine, *is not* the occasion of human faith (the Son, as human, is). The divinity of the Son is, until the eschaton, unseen and unseeable, although it can be symbolized or signified by some created artifact, just as the divinity of the Father and Holy Spirit can be, and is.[25] If the Homoians have defined divinity as necessarily invisible, then Augustine can be unflinching because one could hardly have a firmer or more emphatic doctrine of the necessarily invisible character of divinity than Augustine does—which is why Augustine says, as he must say, that the divinity of the Son is invisible. This invisibility must describe the Son's divinity whenever or however he exists: whether as pre-Incarnate Word, as Incarnate, or as ascended but not yet glorified. All that is visible in the Son is his humanity, or more aptly identified, all that is visible in the Son is the *"form of servant"* or the *"form of man"*; before taking on the *"form of servant"* and taking on a human existence, the Son was invisible, since he was only in the *"form of God."* In short, Augustine does not dispute the identification of divinity as invisible,

23. In her studies on the theme of "purity of heart" in early Christianity (especially monasticism) published in *Studia Monastica* VIII (1966), X (1968), XI (1969) and 12 (1970), Juana Raasch does not treat Augustine's exegesis of the Beatitude, and in general shows little interest in the Latin patristic use of the concept. Recently reflecting upon Raasch's work and developing it further, Gertrude Gillette makes no comments on the presence of the exegesis of Matt 5:8 in Augustine's articulations of his Trinitarian theology. See her "Purity of Heart in St. Augustine," in *Purity of Heart in Early Ascetic and Monastic Literature*, Harriet A. Luckman and Linda Kulzer, eds. (Collegeville, MN: The Liturgical Press, 1999), pp. 161–195.

24. It is worth noting that when speaking of this eschatological vision, Augustine does not employ union, participation, or assimilation language in any significant way; the object of our vision—the Trinity—remains "out there," not something we are assimilated into by that vision. In this regard at least, Augustine's position corresponds more to Plato's understanding than to Plotinus'.

25. In the Incarnation, the divine Word reveals his presence through the signification of a created human nature. See Mark D. Jordan, "Words and Word: Incarnation and Signification in Augustine's *De Doctrina Christiana*", *Augustinian Studies* 11 (1980): 177–196.

just as he does not dispute that any of the other attributes enumerated or implied by, e.g., 1 Timothy 6:16–17—such as "immortal," "only," or simple—applies to divinity.[26] He merely argues that such attributes must be applied equally to and univocally of the Son (or to the Holy Spirit) as they are applied to the Father.[27]

The last point I want to make in this section of the article is to note that the use of 1 Corinthians 15:24–28 in constellation with Matthew 5:8 and Philippians 2:5–7 to ground a doctrine of the eschatological vision and its Christological locus is a feature exclusive to *De Trinitate*, book I.[28] After *De Trinitate* I, the Corinthians passage drops out of Augustine's description of the doctrine of the character and type of the final vision. Just as I remarked at the beginning of this essay that all but one of the references to Matthew 5:8 in *De Trinitate* occur in the first book, so too is it true that all but one of the references to 1 Corinthians 15:24–28 in *De Trinitate* occur in the same book; the one other occurs in book II.[29] Only in the *Reply to the Arian Sermon*, usually dated to 419, and his *Debate with Maximinus*, usually dated to 428, is 1 Corinthians 15:24–28 once again invoked, but not as a witness to the delivery of the kingdom to the vision of God. Between *De Trinitate* I and the *Reply to the Arian Sermon*, 1 Corinthians 15:24–28 makes no appearance whatsoever in Augustine's writing on the Trinity. I believe that this change in Augustine's understanding of scriptural testimony on the final vision alerts us to the fact of specific influences at work as he writes *De Trinitate* I. These influences, which I will describe momentarily, are the theological environment in which Augustine developed his doctrine of the eschatological drama by which God is seen by the faithful. This doctrine, once developed, remained in Augustine's thoughts about how and what the Son reveals of God. The doctrine, as I have described it here, is repeated frequently by Augustine in his writings after *De Trinitate* I. However, in the writings after *De Trinitate* I, it is Matthew 5:8 that provides the scriptural witness to the fact of vision occuring at the end-time.[30] I would hazard to say that the over-all

26. Another Latin of Nicene sympathies who identifies divinity with invisibility is Niceta of Remensiana. Like Augustine, Niceta speaks of the Incarnation using the categories of "unseen divinity, seen humanity," but Niceta uses these categories as part of his argument for the reality of the Incarnation. See his *De Fide* 4, written sometime between 375 and 385.

27. For example, the invisibility of the divinity—the *Form of God*—in Jesus is why Augustine argues so strongly for the importance of John the Baptist, John's recognition of Christ, and his announcement of Jesus' identity. As Jesus walked in the darkness that recognized him not, his divinity was hidden except for the light that John the Baptist shone upon him, so Augustine says in the *Second Tractate on John*, another work that is roughly contemporary to the first four books of *Trin*.

28. It should be observed that these three scriptural passages, like many other key passages in books I–IV, also figure in the Anthropomorphite controversy. It is hard to say to what degree this controversy carries over into Augustine's engagement with anti-Nicene theology at this time, except to note that both the Anthropomorphite and Homoian movements cite many of the same scriptural passages in order to prove the Son's intrinsic visibility, although the Anthropomorphites are orthodox in the Trinitarian theology (as Augustine remarks in *Ep.* 148). See Golitzin, "Demons Suggest an Illusion."

29. In other words, either Augustine's polemical engagement with 1 Cor 15:24–28 ends, or his exegetical rehabilitation of that scriptural text is transformed into another kind of argument.

30. Explicit recourse to Matt 5:8, alone or in constellation with 1 Cor 15:24–28 or Phil 2:5–7, does not occur again in *Trin.*, but it does occur in writings parallel in time to that work, and there are what

eschatological character or logic of Augustine's theology as a whole later became so pronounced and structured that a specific witness to the eschatological timing of the vision enjoyed by the pure of heart was unnecessary. As we will see, the eschatological placement of the fulfillment of Matthew 5:8 is something that Augustine shares with Hilary; I will show, moreover, that the doctrinal circumstances in which Augustine invokes the Beatitude are identical to the circumstances in which Hilary invokes the Scripture passage in his work on the Trinity; namely, in order to refute a doctrine of the Son's intrinsically *visible* and therefore *subordinate* status.[31] I turn now to the Latin context for Augustine's Trinitarian understanding of Matthew 5:8.

II. THE POLEMICAL CONTEXT FOR LATIN EXEGESIS OF MATTHEW 5:8

According to Latin Homoians in the second half of the fourth century, the appearance of the Son in the theophanies and the Incarnation serve as proof that the Son is not true God; only the invisible—and non-appearing—Father is the true or real God. These appearances by the Son, his visibility, constitute sufficient evidence that the Son is not God. A succinct articulation of this Homoian doctrine can be found in the fragments from Palladius collected in the *Scolia Arriana*. Palladius says:

> There is the question of whether the Son is the invisible God. It is written of the Father: "No man has ever seen, nor can see" [1 Tim 6:16] him; and similarly, "The invisible, immortal, only God" [1 Tim 6:17]; and "No one has seen God and lived" [Exod 33:20]; and again "No one has ever seen God, the only-begotten who is in the bosom of the Father, he has made him known" [John 1:18]. But about the Son it is said, "We have seen his glory, glory as of the only begotten from the Father" [John 1:14]; and "God appeared to Abraham by the oaks of Mamre" [Gen 18:1]; and then there is the episode with the blind man, who said, "Where is the Son of God, that I may believe in him?" and the

---

I would identify as implicit references to Matt 5:8 in books XIV and XV of *Trin.* in descriptions of the significance the Incarnation: In Augustine, *Trinity,* XIV.4 (p. 429): "We do not see now, but because we believe, we shall deserve to see, and shall rejoice at having been brought through to sight by faith"; in Augustine, *Trinity,* XV.44: "Faith unfeigned would be purifying the [believers'] heart in order that what is now seen in a mirror might one day be seen face to face." This doctrine, introduced in *Trin.* I, becomes fundamental in Augustine's theology, and finds substantial and moving expressions in his other works (such as *En. Ps. 86*).

31. However, I do not want to leave the impression that an eschatological and Trinitarian understanding of Matt 5:8 such as Augustine offers is the only possible orthodox understanding of that Beatitude. Gregory of Nyssa, for example, in his sermon on this passage, concludes that the promised vision of God is an interior vision of the restored image of God in us, insofar as we are the "image and likeness of God." Here the Matthew passage is not an end-time or eschatological promise, nor is the object of that promise—i.e., the sight of God—externalized, or as Augustine would put it, a "face-to-face" vision. A Greek position more like Augustine's can be found in Clement of Alexandria (a statement that is true for many subjects) at *Stromata* V.1.

Son of God himself said in reply, "He whom you would see, and to whom you would speak, I am that one" [John 9:36–37].[32]

There are several features to note about the theology articulated here. First, a key distinguishing feature of the true God is understood to be his invisibility. Second, the Son's distinguishing feature is his visibility. Third, theophanies of the OT—such as the appearance to Abraham at Mamre—are understood to be appearances of the Son. We can note in passing that such an understanding is traditional in both Latin and Greek theology—a point I will return to below. Note also that Old Testament titles for God's presence—specifically, the "Glory"—are appropriated to the Son. Fourth, as one might expect from point 3, the Son's visibility is found equally in the New Testament and the Old Testament—Palladius moves seamlessly from appearances in the Old Testament to appearances in the New Testament. The fifth feature to note about the theology of the *Scolia* fragment—even if of a slightly different order than the first four—is that Palladius expresses this theology as exegesis. First Timothy 6:16–17 figures prominently, as does Exodus 33:20 and John 1:18. The First Timothy passage is an important one for every generation of what we will call "anti-Nicenes," beginning with Arius' own theology.[33] The fact that 1 Timothy 6:16–17 is the key text by which all the other appearance texts are understood is of fundamental importance for an appreciation of the sight of God as a point of Trinitarian and Christological controversy in the late-fourth and early fifth centuries.

The Palladius fragment I have quoted does not include any reference to Matthew 5:8, and there are no references to that Beatitude in all of the material collected in the *Scolia*. The partially surviving Homoian text known as the *Opus imperfectum In Matthaeum* is lacking what exegesis of 5:8 there might have been originally.[34] There are, however, two citations of Matthew 5:8 in the fragments of Latin anti-Nicene writings edited by Gryson. These fragments date from the late-fourth or the fifth centuries. The first comes from a *Commentary on the Gospel of Luke*:

> In a beautiful way does the Gospel describe the arrangement and description of events because instruction is commended, and spiritual issues: piety and justice, holiness and truth, frugality and moderation. [A]nd if anything is called a *virtus* from the virtues [it is that] which is not seen with the eye and is contemplated with a *pure heart*; not regarded by sight but embraced by the mind: "Blessed are the *pure in heart* for they will see God."[35]

---

32. *Fragments of Palladius*, #106. Gryson, *Scolies Ariennes*, 290–91.

33. See my "Exegesis and Polemic in *De Trinitate* I," 43–59; here 47.

34. See Franz Mali, Das *"Opus imperfectum in Matthaeum" und sein Verhaltnis zu den Matthaus-kommentaren von Origenes und Hieronymus*, Innsbrucker theologische Studien, Band 34 (Insbruck: Tyrolia-Verlag, 1991), p. 359; and *Opus imperfectum in Matthaeum*, J. van Banning, S. J., ed., CCSL 87B (Turnholt, 1988).

35. Palladius, *Expositio euangeli secundum Lucam*, 1.1, in Gryson, CCSL 87.199.

This passage offers two interesting points. First, it begins by attributing a conventional or traditional set of moral virtues to the Christian life, and then links the possession of these virtues to "purity of heart." Second, the fragment specifies that what is to be seen is not seen with the eye but with the mind. This is a commonplace judgment that will be typical of Augustine's theology as well, although he will not be using such a conclusion to use visions of the visible Son as a means of excluding him from true divinity as the Homoian author probably was doing here.

The second fragment comes from an *Exposition of Psalm 15*:

> With this knowledge, therefore, of the Father and the Son and of the Holy Spirit, it is proper that we seek eagerly this which is promised in the present Psalm, namely a dwelling in the tabernacle of the Lord and rest in his holy mountain because such a soul is without sin, and that soul, led up to the heights, is able to walk the way, concerning which we related earlier. With clear and undistracted eye, and able to attend that journey and always to look upon these good things which are prepared accordingly, it is said, "Where your treasure is there will be your heart also"; it [the soul] also sees God as the giver of good things, as it is said, "Blessed are the pure in heart for they shall see God." This is why it is said "he who walks without sin and acts in justice."[36]

Again Matthew 5:8 is connected to a fundamentally moral or ethical reading, which is to be expected given that the Psalm is a moral exhortation. Indeed, what these two Homoian fragments have in common is precisely a moral or ethical exegesis of this Scripture passage. However traditional such a reading of Matthew 5:8 may have been in Latin Christianity, we will see a change among some Latins Nicenes, as I will show shortly; for the moment, there is more to say about the moral reading of the Matthew passage.

The same kind of moral understanding of the Matthew passage is found in Hilary's *Commentary on the Gospel of Matthew*.

> *Blessed are the pure in heart for they shall see God.* To those who are pure in heart—for they follow after nothing polluted or filthy, [nothing] contrary to divine splendor nor, seeking for a vision of God, do they allow their acuity to be dulled by a defiled conscience—he [the Lord] promises the vision of God. In other words, those who endure for the sight and encounter with God through the brightness of the soul and purity of life become capable of beholding Him. Not until we are perfected in spirit and changed into immortality [1 Cor 15:53] will we discern what has been prepared only for those who are pure in heart, which is in the immortal God.[37]

---

36. *Fragmenta theologica arriana e codice Bobiensi rescripto*, Frag. 16, Roger Gryson, ed., CCSL 87, p. 252.

37. *In Matt.*, IV.7., Sur Matthieu, Jean Doignon, ed. and trans., Sources Chrétiennes 254 (Paris: Editions du Cerf, 1978), pp. 126–127.

This is a passage that Doignon has worked through carefully and fruitfully—both in his notes to the Sources Chrétiennes edition of Hilary's *In Mattheum* and in separate articles.[38] In particular, Doignon has identified Hilary's description of what it means to be "pure in heart"—specifically, where Hilary says, "for they follow after nothing polluted or filthy, [nothing] contrary to divine splendor nor, seeking for a vision of God, do they allow their acuity to be dulled by a defiled conscience"—as a citation of material from Cicero.[39] This passage makes it clear that the moral reading of Matthew 5:8 is conventional among a variety of Latin Christians of the mid-fourth century—although we do not find this passage appearing in Augustine's writing. There is another exegesis of Matthew 5:8 by Hilary that is more directly significant for Augustine, namely *De Trinitate* XI.39, which is the only time that Hilary cites Matthew 5:8 in his *De Trinitate*. The development in Hilary's theology that we find in *De Trinitate* XI is profound and deserves substantial attention on just those terms, but now I turn to Hilary's *De Trinitate* XI for how it figures as a precedent for Augustine.

In *De Trinitate* XI, Hilary is arguing against Homoians who take certain New Testament passages as proof that the Incarnation disqualifies the Son from being true God as the Father is true God. These Homoians regard 1 Timothy 6:16–17 as a definition of the Father's divinity which excludes the Son (just as has been seen to be the case for Palladius). The key Scripture passages which Hilary is concerned to rehabilitate or re-interpret are Philippians 2:5–7 and 1 Corinthians 15:27–28. The Homoians evidently understand both the "form" language and the talk of a transition from divine to servant in Philippians 2:5–7 as indications of the Son's subordinate status. First Corinthians 15:27–28 is the passage that speaks of the Son "handing over" the kingdom to the Father at the end of time—a description which again indicates the Son's subordinate status. Hilary's use of Matthew 5:8 occurs in his explanation of 1 Corinthians 15:27–28:

> He [the Son] shall deliver the Kingdom to God the Father, not in the sense that He resigns His power by the delivering, but that we, being conformed to the glory of His body, shall form the Kingdom of God. It is not said, *He shall deliver up His Kingdom*, but, *He shall deliver up the Kingdom*, that is, deliver up to God those of us who have been made the Kingdom by the glorifying of His body . . . The just shall shine like the sun in the Kingdom of their Father, and the Son shall deliver to the Father, as His Kingdom, those whom He has called into His Kingdom, to whom also He has promised the blessedness of this Mystery, *Blessed are the pure in heart, for they shall see God.*

38. Jean Doignon, "Une exégèse d'Hilaire de Poitiers sur le désir de voir la face de Dieu (Hil., In Psalm 118, 8, 7/8)," *Freiburge Zeitschrift fur Philosophie und Theologie*, Vol. 41 (1994), pp. 542–545.

39. In "Une exégèse d'Hilaire de Poitiers" Doignon identifies "nihil enim pollutum et sordidum ad occursum diuinae claritatis insistit et ad conspectum Dei acies obsoletae mentis hebetatur" as being from Cicero, *Tusculan Disputations* I.73, and the *Hortensius* fragment 97 (Muller).

This passage from Hilary is significant for several reasons. Hilary is offering a polemically motivated counter-exegesis of 1 Corinthians15:27–28 to refute a subordinationist reading of that Scripture text by Homoians. Hilary's argument assumes that
the "handing over of the kingdom" by the Son to the Father is a way of articulating
the eventual realization of human salvation. This salvation occurs through our being
joined to the glorified or transfigured "body" of the Son. According to Hilary, Matthew
5:8 is the promise of our eschatological vision of God, the Father, through the activity
of the Son. Such a logic, sketched here in its bare essentials, forms the basis of Hilary's
argument not simply to the effect that the Son's giving of the kingdom to the Father is
by no means an act of subservience or subordination, but also that the handing over
of the kingdom is in fact a Trinitarian or Christological event (as we might say that
the transfiguration was a "Christological" event), for it is the transformation of the
"body" of Christ that is (as we can call it) the material, efficent, and formal cause of
our salvation. The end or resolution of that salvation is the enjoyment of God, which
is what—according to Hilary—Matthew 5:8 promises: the final contemplation of God.
The pure of heart are otherwise known as members of the kingdom united in Christ's
"body"; *the sight of God* is the Son presenting that kingdom—in that "Body"—to the
Father. If the "handing over of the kingdom" can legitimately be described as a Trinitarian event, then so is the "vision of God" as the climax of that event. At this point in
Hilary's theology, it need hardly be remarked, Matthew 5:8 is no longer simply about
being a good person. What *can* be usefully remarked is that much of Augustine's argument about the vision of God through the Son is to be found in Hilary: the exegesis of
the Beatitude as the promise of an eschatological vision, the link between this exegesis
with that of the "handing over of the Kingdom," and the anti-Homoian application of
this argument to refute a subordinationist understanding of the Son's visibility.

There is one last example that we need to mention of a Latin author using
Matthew 5:8 in a Trinitarian context: Novatian. This author is the earliest of all the
pre-Augustinian authors I cite here, and he obviously predates the Trinitarian controversies of the late-fourth and early fifth centuries. Yet it is worth remarking that
Novatian stands as one of the last representatives of the Trinitarian controversies of
the late-second and early third centuries, controversies primarily (but not exclusively)
involving modalism.[40] Matthew 5:8 figures explicitly in Novatian's anti-modalist argument at *De Fide* 28 (26–28). There Novatian says:

> [I]f Christ had been the Father himself, why did he promise, as though it were
> a future reward, what he had already bestowed and granted? When he says
> "Blessed are the clean of heart, for they shall see God," we find him promising
> the contemplation and vision of the Father. Therefore, he had not yet granted

---

40. Other figures in these controversies would be Tertullian, Hippolytus, and Origen, as well as
"Praxeus," Noetus, Paul of Samosata, and Sabellius. A very insightful account of second- and third-
century Lain Trinitarian theology which should not go forgotten is that by Ernest Evans in the Introduction to his edition, with translation, of Tertullian's *Treatise Against Praxeas*.

it; for why would he promise it, if he had already granted it? He would have given it, were he the Father; for he was being seen and had been touched. When Christ himself is seen and touched by the crowd and yet promises and declares that the clean of heart shall see God, he proves by this very fact that he, who was then present, was not the Father because he promised, while actually present to their gaze, that whoever was clean of heart would see the Father . . . However, because he was the Son and not the Father, it was fitting that the Son, inasmuch as he is the Image of the Father, should be seen; and the Father, because he is invisible, is deservedly promised and designated as the one who would be seen by the clean of heart.[41]

In short, because Matthew 5:8 is a promise of the vision of God, and Christ himself—in plain view, as it were—offers this promise, Christ cannot be the object of this vision. Novatian uses this argument to show that the Son cannot be the Father, and thus the modalists are wrong. But, as Novatian says explicitly here and elsewhere in *De Fide*, the Son is to be understood as intrinsically visible in contrast to the Father's intrinsic invisibility. This is a common anti-modalist argument at this early time: we distinguish the Son from the Father—and we are thus certain of their separate identities—on the basis of the Son's visibility and the Father's invisibility.[42] This way of distinguishing Father from Son is the bedrock of Latin Trinitarian theology: the Son is distinguished from the Father as the visible Image of the invisible Father. This is the theological function, in early Latin Trinitarian theology, of the identification of the Son as the one who appears in the Old Testament theophanies. Origen is the occasion of a tectonic shift in *Greek* Trinitarian theology when he describes the Son as the "invisible" Image of the Father, but it is not until Hilary—one hundred and thirty years later—that a Latin will argue that the Son, too, is invisible, and that the Son must be invisible if he is truly the Image.

I have lingered over Novatian in this way not simply because he is a striking example of an early Latin use of Matthew 5:8 in a Trinitarian context—though I do think that this is indeed true of Novatian. I have lingered over Novatian's use of Matthew 5:8 because I think that he is a source—albeit not the exclusive source—of a tension in the

---

41. Novatian, *Writings*, FotC 67, 98–99.

42. In *Against Praxeas* 14–15, Tertullian argues that a real distinction between Father and Son is proved by the scriptural understanding that God the Father is invisible but the Son is visible, God that has been seen. Tertullian says, for example, "Here one of our adversaries will wish to contend that the Son also is invisible as Word and as Spirit, and, maintaining that the Father and Son are in like case, to affirm rather that Father and Son are one and the same. But we have deposed that the Scripture, by its distinguishing of visible and invisible, advocates a difference" (Tertullian, *Treatise Against Praxeas*, 149). The same reasoning is found later in Novatian: in *On the Faith* 31 Novatian lists the different categories of existence that distinguish Son from Father; along with born–unborn, begotten–unbegotten and comprehensible–incomprehensible, there is visible–invisible. The Trinitarian significance of the difference between visible and invisible was treated in full earlier at *On the Faith* 18. I think that A. D'Ales misrepresents the significance of Novatian's doctrine of the Son's visibility by resolving the antinomy (between invisible Father and visible Son) via an anachronistic reading. See his *Etude sur la théologie romaine au milieu de IIIe siècle* (Paris: Gabriel Beauchesne, 1925), 126.

Trinitarian theologies of Hilary and Augustine.[43] There is a mainstream, authoritative tradition in Latin Trinitarian theology which allows for a subordinationist Christology for the sake of combating modalism, and this subordinationist Christology centers directly upon the role—the identity—of the Son as the revealed presence of God. This, I think, is why fourth- and fifth-century Latin Trinitarian theologies found the theophanies such a difficulty for Nicene orthodoxy: not simply because there were spokesmen articulating a problematic, subordinationist doctrine of the theophanies, but because such subordinationist interpretations of the theophanies were traditional. This fact was the foundation for Latin Homoian theology, and it presented those with Nicene sympathies with what I think can most accurately be described as a "double-bind"; namely, that the doctrine of the Son's visibility supports the understanding that he has a real, separate existence (he is not the Father), but the doctrine of the Son's visibility also supports the understanding that the Son's divinity is not the same as the Father's.[44] Moreover, it is not simply anti-Nicene Homoians who understand the Son to be visible while the Father is invisible, it is the tradition. Hilary and especially Augustine have to deal with this fact; their theology must face this double-bind.[45]

III. AUGUSTINE IN 400, OR: LA NON SIMPLICITÉ DU REGARD

Thus far I have spoken of the relationship between vision and faith in Augustine's early Trinitarian theology as that theology is developed in the first books of *De Trinitate*. I have, in particular, looked at the ways in which Augustine's understanding of the relationship between vision and faith is shaped by the then-contemporary polemical Trinitarian debates and by the determinations of traditional Latin theology on the Trinity. Yet at the same time—c. 400—that Augustine is developing an understanding of faith and how divinity is "seen" in its historical manifestations (i.e., the theophanies

43. I am not here specifically claiming that Augustine read Novatian, but that Novation, like Tertullian before him and Lactantius after him, taught the received orthodox Latin Trinitarian theology: *the Son is distinguished from the Father by the Son's visible nature*. This doctrine is a Latin Trinitarian commonplace. However, that Augustine did indeed read Novatian—despite the latter's schismatic status—is more possible than is perhaps first imagined: some of Novatian's writings travel under Cyprian's name; and Gregory of Elvira uses him freely in his writings of the 360s and again in 404, indicating that Novatian's writings were not without authority and currency. (Gregory is an important precedent to note, because we know that Augustine had read him. See *Ep.* 148, as well as Studer's discussion of Gregory in *Zur Theophanie-Exegese Augustins*, 17–27.) Besides, if it were true that a problematic ecclesiastical standing excludes a Latin author from being appropriated by later, more Catholic authors, then the tradition of Latin Trinitarian theology begins in the mid-fourth century, since no earlier Latin theologians of the Trinity remained in good Catholic standing.

44. The Son's visibility likewise served as the basis for describing the soteriological role or economic mission of the Son.

45. "Double-bind" is admittedly an American idiomatic expression, which nonetheless is most apt for describing Augustine's theological position on the issue of the Son's visibility. Other expressions with roughly the same meaning would include "Between Scylla and Charybdis," "Etre pris entre deux feux," or "Zwischen dem Teufel und dem See."

and the Incarnation), he is also coming to an understanding of the relationship be-tween faith and the vision of divinity as epistemological events in the immediate life of the believer. It is Augustine's general understanding of faith and the vision of divinity that I turn to now. The most important point to be made is this: there is a connec-tion between Augustine's development of a doctrine of the primacy of faith as the discipline of virtue and as the basis for "knowledge" about God and his development of the doctrine that the divinity of the Son is made manifest only at the end-time and that there are, properly speaking, no theophanies of the Son (or of any other Person of the Trinity).

By the year 400, Augustine had come to understand that in this life we were incapable of a vision of God—that we were now incapable of direct knowledge of the truth. This discovery is, of course, dramatized in *Confessions*, and we would expect two works from the same few years in Augustine's life to offer the same conclusion.[46] Augustine had also come to understand something else about such visions: funda-mentally, there was no virtue to them; there was no salvation through them.[47] In short, Augustine had a new understanding not simply of the (im)possibility of a vision of God in this life, but of the significance of any such vision, whether complete or in-complete: whatever joy might be experienced from the sight (or even the near-sight), there was, nonetheless, no salvation in or from that vision.[48] Salvation came from

46. At *Trin.* IV.20, Augustine criticizes those who pridefully claim to be able to rise to the sight of God through their own efforts. Some scholars have thought that this comment referred to Pelagius and was thus a later insertion by Augustine into *Trin.* But that conclusion seems to me to be unneces-sarily complicated: the most obvious candidate for someone who would make such vain claims is the younger Augustine himself. "[T]here are some people," Augustine says, "who think that they can purify themselves for contemplating God and [for] cleaving to him by their own power and strength of character, which means in fact that they are thoroughly defiled by pride ... Their reason for assur-ing themselves of do-it-yourself purification is that some of them have been able to direct the keen gaze of their intellects beyond everything created and to attain, in however small a measure, the light of unchanging truth; and they ridicule those many Christians who have been unable to do this and who *live* meanwhile *out of faith* [Rom 1:17; italics Hill's] alone" (Augustine, *Trinity*, 167).

47. One can say that Augustine saw that philosophy, like the Law, required what it could not en-able: the ability to be virtuous. Only a sage, purified from his passions, could expect to see the Good, but—Augustine discovered—philosophical training could not provide the very purification it held up as the natural state for humans. John Dillon is a hostile witness to Augustine's critical judgment of hel-lenistic soteriology in in pages 324–25 of his " 'A Kind of Warmth': Some Reflections on the Concept of 'Grace' in the Neoplatonic Tradition" in *The Passionate Intellect: The Transformation of Classical Traditions*, Lewis Ayres, ed., Rutgers University Studies in Classical Humanities, Vol. 7 (Piscataway, NJ: Transaction Publishers, 1995), pp. 323–332.

48. The most accurate description of Augustine's judgment about the possibility of a vision of God in this life is that it cannot happen, but it sometimes does anyway. (Something similar is documented by Roland Teske in his article, "St. Augustine and the Vision of God" in *Augustine: Mystic and Mysta-gogue*, F. Van Fleteren, J. C. Schnaubelt and J. Reino, eds. [New York: Peter Lang, 1994], 287–308.) Such exceptions are due to God's sovereign initiative. It is possible, however, to attain to visions of the intelligible realm or even to something like the "region" of God. Yet these intellectual visions have a limited character to them: they are not visions of God as Trinity, which is what is promised to us at the end-time. The visions of *Confessions* VII mark the limits of the ascent of reason unaided by grace, although even the vision bounded by that limit is more than a modern might think would be available

faith—this is faith's "utility."[49] Such a judgment is not merely one about discipline, as though the virtue of faith was primarily the act of obedience. The utility of faith for salvation lies in the fact that it marries an epistemology with a moral anthropology, and then grounds them both in Christology: "Everything that has taken place in time . . . has been designed to elicit the faith we must be purified by in order to contemplate the truth, [and] has either been testimony to this mission or has been the actual mission of the Son of God."[50]

One of the distinctive features of Augustine's thought is the emphasis he places on the understanding that "knowing" is a "seeing," for while this understanding was certainly a philosophical commonplace, Augustine makes it the foundation for much of his thought.[51] To know is to see, either with the eyes of our corporeal senses or with the eyes of mind in interior vision.[52] One consequence of such an equation is to put knowledge—true knowledge—very much in the realm of direct experience.[53] In such a line of reasoning, there is a kind of parallelism between sensation and intellection: as in sight we know what is "right before our eyes," so too in thought we truly know only what is "right before our mind's eye."[54] (I will return to this parallelism shortly.) Augustine himself subsumes these two kinds of vision under the limit he finds

_____

to "reason alone," i.e., philosophy. Nonetheless, we need to be clear about the limits of the vision compared to what Augustine had come to expect of philosophy, not simply in terms of duration, but in terms of content. It may indeed be that a pagan philosopher can rise to the vision of the World-Soul or the Forms—or, for that matter, that a Christian philosopher can as well. But such a vision is well short of God, and guarantees nothing for the eternal state of that mind.

49. Wetzel is right to speak of the "discipline of virtue," but he does not take the further step of making clear that Augustine identifies this discipline with *faith*, i.e., the *disciplina fidei*, as at *de Lib Arb* III.60. See James Wetzel, *Augustine and the Limits of Virtue* (Cambridge: Cambridge University Press, 1992), pp. 45 ff.

50. Augustine, *Trinity* IV.25 (p. 171).

51. A succinct description of this aspect of Augustine's thought is provided by Markus, "Marius Victorinus and Augustine," 348–50. Markus and I differ, however, in our respective emphasis on the difference for Augustine between faith and knowledge. See also, e.g., John J. O'Meara, "St. Augustine's View of Authority and Reason in A. D. 386", *Irish Theological Quarterly* 18 (1951): 338–346.

52. Something like this is remarked by Ambrose in the previously cited passage from his *Commentary on Luke* (as quoted by Augustine in *Ep.* 147): "no one has experienced it [God's full divinity] with mind or eyes, for the word 'seen' is to be referred to both."

53. The origins of this understanding are Platonic, as John M. Rist makes clear in *Augustine—Ancient Thought Baptized* (Cambridge: Cambridge University Press, 1994), 45: "For the most basic principle of Platonic epistemology is not the distinction between 'intelligibles' and 'sensibles' (important though that is), but the distinction between the first-hand experience which gives 'knowledge' (*episteme*) and second- (or other-)hand experience which gives various sorts of more or less justified 'belief' (*doxa*)." There were, as well, Jewish exegetical traditions which linked vision with knowledge; such traditions may be of interest given that they speak of the knowledge gained in terms *of measure, weight and number* (following *Wisdom* XI.20): see Gruenwald, "Knowledge and Vision," *Israel Oriental Studies* 3 (1973): 63–107.

54. "Is me autem aliquid docet, qui uel oculis uel ulli corporis sensui uel ipsi etiam menti praebet ea quae cognoscere uolo" (Augustine, *De Magistro* XI.36). A contrasting understanding of "knowledge" would be to find it most purely and certainly in deduction.

expressed in Romans 1:20, namely, that created things can themselves be known and in this way they reveal their creator, but the knowledge extends no further than of the created things.[55]

This notion of "knowledge" involves elements of both Platonic and Stoic thought. That true knowledge is best understood as a kind of seeing is, as already noted, a Platonic commonplace. The Stoic component lies in the understanding that this "seeing" is really not itself knowledge, but the basis of knowledge, that is to say, it is the basis for our assent to propositions that are manifestly true. For example, the data from our senses is understood as the proposition, "Here is a journal made of paper." The mind assents to that proposition, but the key question is: "Why?" What is the basis for my assent? I assent because I see (and feel) the paper. "Here is a journal made of paper" is knowledge properly speaking because it is known directly; "2 + 2 = 4" is another proposition which gains my assent because its truth is known directly—in this case, to my mind's eye. By contrast, propositions of the faith, e.g., *regula*, are assented to because of the disposition of our will.

The Incarnation does not bring salvation in such a way that allows knowledge (direct sight) to be the basis for our assent to propositions which are in fact true, and to which we must assent if we are to be both virtuous and saved.[56] The most important fact about the identity of Jesus of Nazareth cannot be known, for it is not available to any kind of sight, material or noetic.[57] Obviously, this is true for those who live "now" (an era which includes both Augustine and ourselves), since Jesus the Son of God is not available to be seen.[58] More importantly, this was true for those who lived when

55. As, for example, at *Confessions* VII.xvii (23). The two paragraphs of section 23 are written in parallel to each other, the second elaborating upon the first but describing the same sequence of events, each paragraph climaxing with the invocation of Rom 1:20, by which the tension or drama described in that paragraph is resolved.

56. Augustine's favorite parallel to this, used in *de Util. Cred.* and appearing more than once in *Confessions*, is our assent to the proposition, "That man is my father"—an assent which is made entirely on the basis of the disposition of our will, i.e., love, and the trust that follows from it. Augustine's other preferred example of a case of faith being necessary for virtue is that of friendship, in which we believe in the existence of a love we cannot prove: "Ecce ex cordo tuo, credis cordi non tuo; et quo nec carnis nec mentis dirigis aciem, accommodas fidem" (Augustine, *De fide rerum quae non videntur* II; written in 400 or shortly thereafter).

57. The connection between this doctrine and a two-natures Christology can already be discerned: in Christ there really is a something that can be seen, and there really is a something that cannot be seen; these "somethings" exist in two different epistemological fields, but they both exist with full integrity as what they are. See *Trin.* I.22 and IV.6. In *Trin.* IV.26, Augustine remarks, apropos of John 14:9, "Does this [John 14:9] not mean that he both could and could not be seen?"—a comment which is as much a rejoinder to Novatian's exegesis of Matt 5:8 as it is to Homoian "visible Son" theology. (See also *Third Tractate on John* 4.1 for an example of Augustine's polemical application of the "seen–not seen" distinction in Christ.)

58. Following this line of thought, Augustine says that the reason for Christ's ascension into heaven was to remove the resurrected Jesus from sight, so that faith would be both necessary and possible. See *Trin.* I.18. ("Now" in this context means "After the ascension and before the eschaton"; i.e., the "Sixth Age.")

Jesus was available to be seen: all that could be seen was the human, Jesus of Nazareth. But for the purposes of refuting the Homoian argument, the most important statement Augustine can make about visibility is that it was always true that the true existence or being of God could not be known, for it has never been available to any kind of sight, material or noetic: the theophanies did not make God available to be seen. Since the fall, at least, divinity has never been self-evident. In Old Testament times, as in all periods of salvation history, neither the Son of God nor the Father could be seen; only a created mark or instrument of their presence could be seen (e.g., the angels of Mamre, the burning bush, the pillars of fire, etc.).[59] The Incarnation likewise employed a created mark or instrument of his presence; namely, human nature.[60] In sum, we must note that the soteriological limits of our knowledge make an act of faith[61] fundamental to our salvation. We must also note that material sensation—e.g., sight—with its limited access to truths is nonetheless made completely fundamental to our salvation: in all cases, a created mark or instrument of God's presence is the occasion for us either to assent to the unseen signified, or to decline to assent, thereby denying the unseen. As Augustine put it, "we could only be purified for adaptation to eternal things by temporal means like those we were already bound to in a servile adaptation . . . Now just as the rational mind is meant, once purified, to contemplate eternal things, so it is meant while still needing purification to give faith to temporal things."[62]

If even noetic knowledge is most properly understood as a kind of sight, and faith is not sight but the assurance of things hoped for and the conviction of things *not seen* (Heb 11:1), then clearly faith is not knowledge, but something else—Augustine is emphatic on this point. Yet if faith is not really spiritual knowledge,[63] faith nonetheless is that which is now most like spiritual knowledge: charitable in its necessary dependence

---

59. Again it must be noted that in his criticism of Homoianism, Augustine does not dispute their fundamental presupposition; namely, that divinity is invisible and anything visible is not divine. (The Anthropomorphites did not make this presupposition; rather, they taught that there was visible divinity.) Augustine's argument is that precisely because the Son is divine he was invisible apart from created marks of his presence.

60. Albeit, in the case of the Son, a created instrument peculiarly appropriate to or commensurate with the mission of the Presence it signified, which is not the case for the Father or the Holy Spirit. Augustine occasionally seems to treat the miracles as evidence of Jesus' divinity, but even so, the miracles are not decisive for our assent, just as mystical visions of ascent are not decisive.

61. That is, an assent on the basis of the disposition of our will and not by sight.

62. Augustine, *Trinity* IV.24 (p. 169). Compare with *de Lib. Arb.* III.30: "But the human soul is rational . . . And was brought so low that by surmising from visible things it might strive to understand invisible things. The Food of the rational creature became visible, not by changing his own nature but by adapting it to ours, in order that he might recall those who follow visible things to embrace him who is invisible. So the soul, which in its inward pride had forsaken him, finds him again in humble guise in the outward world. By imitating his visible humility it will return to its invisible position of superiority" (*Augustine: Earlier Writings*, John S. Burleigh, trans., Library of Christian Classics (Philadelphia, PA: Westminster Press, 1953), p. 190).

63. What I mean exactly by "spiritual knowledge" will become clear shortly, namely, knowing which does not have sensation as its underlying form.

on others and its reception of a common experience; wise in its ability to take the proper measure of material objects and to know the real significance of those objects; certain in its judgment; and imaging the kenotic life of the Trinity in its assent to humility. Assent by faith to propositions gives us "sight" of (knowledge of) those propositions as signifiers. The limitations of language (signs) are important to remember here.[64] The proposition "The cow is brown" is understood only if we have seen a cow and the color brown; for anyone who has not seen either (much less both), the proposition fails to communicate since we only understand what is meant by "cow" and "brown" from our previous direct knowledge of these. The proposition "God is a Trinity" is unlike the proposition "The cow is brown" in that we cannot ever have seen God or the Trinity. The proposition "God is a Trinity" becomes meaningful through faith, in which we know that the proposition is true even if we really don't know what "God" or "Trinity" is, having seen neither. Our mind rushes to build images to see, the way it rushes to build "Alexandria" from mental images of cities we have seen.[65] Some of these images may be correct, many are not, but our constructed idea of Alexandria becomes tied to the word "Alexandria" and allows us to recognize what the word refers to from our mental montage: a montage built upon reasonable similarities, but a montage nonetheless.[66] Our montages of "God" tend to be misleading and need correction, even if the correction amounts to a prohibition of using certain mental images in our montages.[67]

If we know that "God is a Trinity" is a true proposition, then we know that certain propositions must follow (many of these propositions are revealed), and must be assented to: if "God is a Trinity" then, for example, we know that other words about this truth must refer to some unity and some triad. "God is three Persons" is assented to, even though we do not really know what a "person" is, because it has been revealed (through the church) that "person" is a suitable word for the kind of "Three" we are

64. Augustine's understanding of the limitations of signs is fully developed well before 400; see his discussion of this point in *De Magistro* X.33–34; see also Rist's comments at *Augustine,* 23ff. Is the insistence that language is dependent upon sensation from Porphyry? See his *In Categorias* 91.8.20.

65. The importance of this process for Trinitarian theology is later the subject of substantial study by Augustine in, e.g., *Trin.* VIII.9, but the interior construction of "Alexandria" from "Carthage" is already discussed by Augustine in *Against Fortunatus* XX.7.

66. At *De Doctrina Christiana* II.vi.8, Augustine discusses similitude as a way of language signifying and having content; he is concerned in particular with the affect of pleasure produced in a reader by signification-through-similitude. This kind of signification, then, has a particular pedagogic function (not unlike the Incarnation).

67. Augustine, *Ep.* 147 (from 413), is in many ways the mirror image of *Trin.* I–IV, as the same Trinitarian issues are treated, though with the vision–faith distinction in the fore: in this epistle, Augustine works hard to relate knowledge (things seen by the eyes or the mind) to faith (things unseen). L.J. van der Lof invokes *Ep.* 147 when he speaks of Augustine's distinction between *videre* and *comprehendere*, a text he then connects to *Sermon* 117. In the sermon, Augustine is responding to Ambrose's *Commentary on Luke* I.25, as the Latin for the Lucan passage juxtaposes the key terms. "Tout en," van der Lof concludes, "se basant sur Matthieu 5,8." See "L'exégèse exacte et objective des théophanies de l'Ancien Testament dans le 'De Trinitate'", *Augustiniana* 14 (1984): 485–99; here 488. For the present, however, the significance of *Ep.* 147 is that it shows that the conclusions Augustine reached in 400 continue in his later thoughts.

talking about (a suitable component of our mental montage), but as Augustine later says in *De Trinitate*, the real utility of "Three *Persons*" lies in the fact that we must say three *somethings* and in a consistent manner. The humility of the faithful, the discipline of faith, then, lies in what can be called, albeit anachronistically, a submission to intellectual *rebuke*, in which we must reject and cast out those inappropriate components of our montage for "God in Trinity" (or perhaps our entire "picture").[68] Together, these elements constitute what can be called (with only minimal violence to the terminology) "an epistemology of faith."[69] The epistemological implications of faith and purification are set out in already in *Eighty-Three Diverse Questions* 68:

> Therefore sinners are commanded to believe in order that they might be purged of sins through believing, for sinners do not have a knowledge of what they will see by living rightly. For this reason, since they cannot see except they live rightly, nor are they capable of living rightly except that they believe, it is clear that they must start from faith, so that *the commandments by which believers are turned from this world might produce a pure heart capable of seeing God*. For, "Blessed are the pure in heart, because they will see God."[70]

The mind's "servile adaptation" to sense knowledge does not lie only in its need to know through sense, but also (and more importantly) in the mind's adoption of the dynamic structure and limitations of sense knowledge as its own. Sight is itself one kind of sense knowledge, and any "vision"—physical or mental—follows the material form of sensation: the mind thinks in a material way or form, even when it thinks about immaterial realities (i.e., the Trinity, goodness, the nature of evil, etc.).[71] This

---

68. See, e.g., Augustine, *De Doctrina Christiana* I.vii.7–ix.9 for an example of Augustine building up a correct conceptual "montage" of God, and the end of II.vii.10 for a description of the success of this process in developing love for the Trinity. My use of the word "rebuke" is especially appropriate if one remembers Augustine's statements on the will's role in the production of an improper or erroneous inner montage. Examples of intellectual "rebuke" may be found in, e.g., *Sermon* 53, a later sermon by Augustine on the Beatitudes; there the exegesis of Matt 5:8 leads to an extended discussion of the kinds of mental images of God that must be rejected. Something similar, again clearly connected to Matt 5:8, but with a less extended "rebuke," can be found in *Sermon* 4.5; some of the "pictures" of God rebuked in this sermon apply as much to the error of the Anthropomorphites as they do to that of the Homoians. Finally, it should not be forgotten that Augustine spent most of the first half of his life in intellectual self-rebuke, trying to lose the material component of his own montage of God.

69. The so-called "psychological analogy" (which appears at the end of *Trin.* IV) is better understood as a correction to our inevitable noetic montage for "God the Trinity": intellectual images like those of the "analogy" should replace our material images of the Trinity, knowing, as we do, that material signs cannot signify the unity of common operations (see *Trin.* IV.30). These replacements are not properly called analogies and indeed Augustine declines to call them such. See Ayres, "Remember That You Are Catholic," 58–62.

70. Augustine, *Eighty-Three Diverse Questions*, No. 68, Mosher, trans., 161; emphasis added.

71. The limits of language also show the material form of our knowing: unless we already have seen (materially) what the words refer to, the words are meaningless. Words can tell us nothing that is truly new since language depends upon the repetition of a previous, non-linguistic, learning-event—a "sight." This is Augustine's explicit conclusion at *De Magistro* X.33.

material "form" of even intellectual vision shapes knowledge in the way the mind regards matter as the paradigm for existence, for example, or through the presupposition that knowledge is an individual or private act the way sense knowledge is individual or private.[72] The alternative "epistemology of faith" is articulated by Augustine not only in the first four books of *De Trinitate*, but also in a range of works written by and around the turn of the fifth century, and we must keep them in mind as we read the first four books of *De Trinitate* (and vice versa).[73] The task of *De Natura Boni*, for example, is to help the mind think of existence not in terms of matter, but in terms of being,[74] while *De Doctrina Christiana* I teaches us how to value existents properly.[75] Similarly, *De Libero Arbitrio* III offers a description of what the act of assent is like when freed of material habits. And what non-individuated, "common" seeing might be like is provided in the experience Augustine shared with his mother in their vision at Ostia, described in *Confessions* IX.x.

CONCLUSION

For Augustine there were no direct appearances of the Son recorded in the Old Testament, just as there were no direct appearances of the Father or Holy Spirit. What appeared in the Old Testament theophanies was created matter being used as an instrument of communication by the Trinity. What was seen was not God; it was an instrument of God's presence. An encounter with such an instrument, such as

72. All human sensations occur in an individual, and cannot be known as a shared experience: I see, without need for anyone else, and that very sight cannot be shared with anyone else. For fallen humanity, with our atomized mode of perception, "common" perception (e.g., "common" sight) is defined according to there being a common object of sensation (e.g., we all see the same tree), which is a very weak sense of a "common" perception. What if not simply the external object, but the very act of seeing was performed in common? If one can abandon the presumption that knowing is "necessarily individuated"—a presumption that derives from projecting a material and unspiritual character upon the act of knowing—then one can gain an insight into the spiritual knowing shared within the Trinity. The very best example of knowledge bound by a material form may be the character of our very self-consciousness; in particular, our inability to know our knowing or the knower as such, which mimics our inability to "see seeing" or to see that by which we see.

73. In later works, Augustine uses the contrast between *scientia* and *sapientia* to address the overcoming of the limited and problematic form of "knowledge," but this terminology (used in a linked way) does not appear in the writings under consideration here.

74. One of the more conspicuous problems faced by a mind that is thinking in too materialist a manner is that it cannot conceive of the coexistence the Trinity shares; Arian theology manifests this formal weakness which results in its doctrinal error (See, e.g., *Trin.* II.25 [p. 175]). Yet the epistemological weakness of materialist thinking mirrors the ontological weakness of material objects themselves as marks or signs of the Trinity: the Three, one in substance and acting inseparably, "cannot be manifested inseparably by creatures which are so unlike them, especially material ones" (*De Trinitate* IV.30, Hill, 175). Augustine then refers to that great trap the material world sets for our thoughts about God: as our words exist in intervals, separated from one another, so, too, do we imagine that the Three exist in intervals, separated from one another.

75. See Augustine, *De Doctrina Christiana* I.xxviii.28, where Augustine says that the Christian who lives justly will have a correct judgment of the true worth of things.

experienced by the patriarchs and prophets, was an occasion for assent to be given to that which remained unseen and only symbolized: in short, an occasion for faith in God. Similarly, Jesus' divinity was not visible while he lived in Israel. What appeared in events such as the theophany atop Mt. Tabor was created matter being used as an instrument of communication by the Trinity. What was seen was not Jesus' divinity; the light was a created sign of the unseen divine presence.[76] The vision of that light was an opportunity to assent to the reality of what remained unseen. The Son never possessed a kind of visible divinity, whether one understands such a divinity to be less than or equal to, different from or the same as, the divinity of the Father. What was hidden in the Father was hidden in the Son, and the same is true of the Holy Spirit.

For Augustine there are no visions of the divine in the life of the Christian. What appears to the Christian are created instruments of God's presence. What is seen is not God; it is a sign or symbol of God's presence. The list of such signs runs, on the one hand, from all of history to, on the other, the church and the Eucharist. Especially important are the propositions given to us about God, the *regula* and *doctrina*. Each created instrument (including words) is an occasion for a Christian to assent to the existence of what remains unseen. The discipline of faith causes our understanding of the sign set before us to grow: Lot knew his visitors were angels, though the citizens of Sodom and Gomorrah, who saw what Lot saw, knew them only as young men. Many looked upon Jesus and saw only a young man, but a few knew what was unseen—because they believed in what Jesus said.

The Trinitarian controversy, as Augustine encounters it, is about whether God can be seen at all, has the Son been seen, and if yes, when and how? Aside from the historical question of when was the Son seen (e.g., in the Old Testament theophanies, the Incarnation, etc.), there is an epistemological question at play, because for Augustine "to see" means "to know." Augustine finds the answers to these questions in Philippians 2:5–7, a root narrative of the Trinity, the very language of which Augustine understands to describe visual or epistemological categories (i.e., *Form* of God, *Form* of Servant). Augustine's judgment is that all the Persons of the Trinity can be seen only at the resolution of history—the end-time—and he describes the object(s)

---

76. As the centuries go by, Byzantine theology will emphasize a very different judgment; namely, that the "light" the apostles saw atop Mt. Tabor was in fact a Divine Light, i.e., an uncreated Light. The Greek theologians now regarded by the Byzantine church as especially definitive of the character of its theology are those who emphasize the visible-through-the-senses nature of that uncreated Light: e.g., Simeon the New Theologian and Gregory Palamas. The theology of Basil the Great has been recast in the mold of an "essence-energy" neo-Palamite theology so that he too might stand as one such definitive theologian. The Augustinian point of view represents a completely different theological judgment from that of the uncreated Light tradition in Byzantine theology, and this difference has figured significantly in acts of self-definition by the East and the West. (This is not to say that there is no overlap between the Augustinian and Palamite theologies on other subjects. It is now clear that Gregory Palamas read Augustine's *Trin.* in translation and made substantial use of the latter books. It is also clear that Gregory had no use for the theology expressed by Augustine in the early books of *Trin.*, i.e., the theology which is the subject of this essay. Not unlike some modern Western theologians, Gregory Palamas read the second half of *Trin.* severed from the first.)

of this vision very specifically: what will be seen is either the Form of Man or the Form of God. Given the visual content of the Christological drama described in Philippians 2:5–7 and the visual resolution of that drama at the final judgment, the statement Matthew 5:8 makes about the sight of God is of profound significance, for it is the promise of the very vision Augustine has spoken of. As a promise, Matthew 5:8 carries both the tension of the delay in the vision Christians hope to have and the means of the resolution of that tension; namely, purity of heart. The meaning of purity of heart lies in the possession of faith, and faith "proves" the reality of that final vision through the reality of what is gained now through faith.

How is Augustine's doctrine of the eschatological vision through Christ of the Trinity a solution to the Homoian subordinationist understanding of the Son's visibility? The Son is not visible before the Incarnation. The Son is visible only as an object of faith in the Incarnation. Jesus could be seen as any human can be seen, but *understanding* who and what Jesus was (and remains) is a matter of faith, not of simple sight.[77] Even in the Incarnation there is not a direct revelation via the Son's material existence (or "via matter"). One can "see" Christ and not recognize who and what he is. This is why Augustine refers repeatedly—thus emphasizing—to the fact of those who saw only the human and failed to recognize who Christ was, and the condemnation of these. If it is possible for us to say that Augustine reserves the vision of God to the end-time, then we can also say that Augustine reserves the direct revelatory content of the Son's incarnated existence to the end-time[78]—which is why the Transfiguration does not figure significantly in Augustine's Trinitarian theology (as it does in Hilary's). Those who recognize the Transfiguration as theologically significant recognize it as a "before the end-time" occasion of the direct revelatory content of the Son's incarnated existence. For Augustine, such events (which may indeed occur) are not definitive for an account of the revelation in Christ.

Earlier, I suggested that the problem of the epistemological status of faith—what is the kind of knowledge that is gained through it?—arises out of Augustine's firm denial of any simple, direct knowledge of God through the Son. If the divinity of the Son is invisible, if God is not seen directly in the Son—both assertions which must be true or else the Homoians are right—then Augustine is left with the task of describing what

77. It is through revelation and not through reason that we understand the fact of the Trinity—but we must we must use our reason in order to understand the revelation. Revelation does not come to us like a diamond piercing our skull; it comes to us through sensation, and it is the character of our understanding, our nature, that our sensations are not simply physiological events only insofar as we make mental judgments upon and from these sensations. The mental judgments we make upon and from these sensations is a necessary part of what we call understanding. Ultimately, because of what we are—i.e., the character of our way of knowing—revelation does not yet appear *to us* until it appears in our understanding. Thoughts such as these guide Augustine in the epistemological concerns treated in the second half of *Trin.*

78. For an example of how this doctrine of Augustine's figures in an individual's faithlife, see the Second Reading for the thirty-third Wednesday in Ordinary Time in the *Liturgy of the Hours according to the Roman Rite* (which quotes from Augustine's *Sermon* 21.1–4).

is given to us positively in faith. One might also offer the converse, namely that after book I of *De Trinitate* Augustine must eventually follow through and offer an account of how what is known directly—through the vision of sight or mind—is related to the assent of faith. Such a concern is, I take it, a significant part of Augustine's subject in the latter books of that work.

Chapter 11

De Trinitate VI and VII
Augustine and the Limits of Nicene Orthodoxy

THERE IS A SIGNIFICANT body of scholarship that regards books six and seven of *de Trinitate* as the "heart" of Augustine's Trinitarian theology: Eugene TeSelle uses these very words when he says, "The heart of Augustine's doctrine of the Trinity is found in books V through VII of *de Trinitate*."[1] TeSelle's opinion, like others to this effect, is based upon the fact that in these books Augustine treats the notion of what has come to be called the "interior" and "subsistent" relations of the Trinity. Doctrines of divine interior and subsistent relations figure prominently in medieval scholastic Trinitarian theology, and much scholarship on Augustine's Trinitarian theology has been in the form of "looking back" at Augustine as the wellspring of medieval, particularly Thomist, Trinitarian theology. The most dramatic example of understanding Augustine's Trinitarian theology in this way may be found in Edmund Hill's *The Mystery of the Trinity*. A substantial portion of that work is given over to an almost book-by-book exposition by Hill of Augustine's *de Trinitate*. When Hill comes to books V–VII and the subject of Augustine's understanding of subsistent relations in the Trinity, he says:

> This whole section of Augustine's work, books V–VII [of *de Trinitate*], is the most thoroughly appreciated and developed in the subsequent Latin scholastic tradition. So here I will not confine myself to considering what Augustine had to say about these matters, but will try to present the fruits of the developed tradition in their most mature form, which means in effect as formulated by Thomas Aquinas.[2]

The "account" of the doctrine of subsistent relations is thereafter discussed by Hill entirely in terms of Thomas' theology: nothing in books V–VII of *de Trinitate* is

---

1. Eugene TeSelle, *Augustine the Theologian* (New York: Herder & Herder, 1970), 294.
2. Edmund Hill, *Mystery of the Trinity* (London: Geoffrey Chapman, 1985), 93.

cited or glossed. My own response to finding no satisfactory exposition of a doctrine of subsistent relations in *de Trinitate* books V–VII would have been to entertain the suspicion that perhaps there is no doctrine of subsistent relations in *de Trinitate* V–VII worthy of the name, and thus perhaps some other account ought to be found for the theology of Augustine in those books.

One of the undeniable features of *de Trinitate* VI and VII is that in those two books Augustine offers his most extended engagement with a scriptural text in all of that work. Books VI and VII are an extended exegesis of 1 Cor 1:24, "Christ the Power and Wisdom of God," an exegetical project that is without any parallel in the rest of *de Trinitate*. The considerable attention Augustine pays to the exegesis of 1 Cor 1:24 indicates the importance he attached to arriving at a proper understanding of the text. However, despite the seemingly obvious significance of the role of 1 Cor 1:24 for the development of Augustine's own Trinitarian theology, there have been no accounts of books VI and VII that take the Scripture text as their proper subject and point of departure, nor have there been any treatments, substantial or otherwise, of why, exactly, Augustine would analyze this particular scriptural passage in such detail. I have already hinted at what I take to be the reason for this strange omission or failure in the scholarly reading of Augustine. In this essay I intend to do three things: (1) to identify the anti-Homoian context of Augustine's exegesis of 1 Cor 1:24 in *de Trinitate* VI and VII; (2) to identify the context of the exegesis of 1 Cor 1:24 among those sympathetic with Nicaea; and (3) on the basis of tasks one and two then to suggest how we should read Augustine's exegesis of 1 Cor 1:24 in books VI and VII of *de Trinitate*, in its own setting.

Augustine first encountered 1 Cor 1:24 used in a Trinitarian context in the writings of the Manichees, the occasion of his first encounter with Paul's writings generally. We have a report of the Manichaean Trinitarian application of the passage from Augustine himself; in *Reply to Faustus the Manichaean* (392) Faustus is recorded as saying:

> We worship, then, one deity under the threefold appellation of the Almighty God the Father, and his son Christ, and the Holy Spirit. While these are one and the same, we believe also that the Father properly dwells in the highest or principal light, which Paul calls "light inaccessible," and the Son in his second or visible light. And as the Son is himself twofold, according to the apostle, who speaks of Christ as *the Power of God and the Wisdom of God*, we believe that His Power dwells in the sun, and His Wisdom in the moon. We also believe that the Holy Spirit, the third majesty, has His seat and His home in the whole circle of the atmosphere.[3]

Augustine replies:

> It is difficult to understand how you have been taken with the absurd idea of placing the power of the Son in the sun, and His wisdom in the moon. For, as

---

3. *Reply to Faustus the Manichaean*, Book XX.2, NPNF I/4, 253.

the Son remains inseparably in the Father, *His Wisdom and Power* cannot be separated from one another, so that one should be in the sun and the other in the moon. Only material things can be thus assigned to separate places. If you only understood this, it would have prevented you from taking the productions of a diseased fancy as the material for so many fictions.[4]

Besides faulting the Manichees for their materialist understanding of God, Augustine criticizes Faustus for making wisdom inferior to power, as the moon's light is inferior to that of the sun's. Moreover, while the Manichees "separate Christ from Himself, [they] do not distinguish between Christ and the Holy Spirit; whereas Christ is one, the *Power of God, and the Wisdom of God*, and the Spirit is a distinct person." Finally, Augustine deploys an astronomical argument regarding the moon's movement and waning to contrast such with the unchangeable and immaterial nature of the Power and Wisdom of God: he says, "If, as is certainly true, the *Wisdom of God* is unchangeable in power, and the *Power of God* unchangeable in wisdom, how can you separate them so as to assign them to different places? And how can the place be different when the substance is the same?"

There are a number of recognizably Augustinian tropes already present in this early book: that material concepts are wholly inadequate for describing God; that the Son remains inseparably in the Father; that the divine is unchangeable; that the substance is the same among the Three; and that wisdom is a key term for describing the Son. With this glimpse at Augustine's first recorded encounter with 1 Cor 1:24 as a scriptural passage read for its significance in Trinitarian theology, I turn now to the proper subject of this essay.

THE POLEMICAL CONTEXT

Book VI of *de Trinitate* begins with Augustine saying:

> Some people find it difficult to accept the equality of Father and Son and Holy Spirit because of the text, "Christ the Power of God and the Wisdom of God." Equality seems to be lacking here, since the Father is not himself, according to this text, power and wisdom but the begetter of power and wisdom. And indeed the question how God can be called the Father of Power and Wisdom calls for and commonly receives very careful attention: there it is, in the Apostle's own words, "Christ the Power of God and the Wisdom of God."[5]

I take Augustine at his word here. First he presents 1 Cor 1:24 both as a text under claim by subordinationists whom he later identifies, with some subtlety, as two or three distinct generations of "Arians." Augustine then says that 1 Cor 1:24 has called for and commonly received very careful attention from those with whom Augustine's

4. *Reply to Faustus the Manichaean*, Book XX.8, (p. 255).
5. Augustine, *Trinity*, 205.

sympathies lay, and who have opposed the so-called Arians. I think it is important to begin by properly identifying Augustine's opponents. If we are content simply with the vague or general category of "Arians" we miss the distinctive features of the theology Augustine is opposing. Moreover, we are as scholars simply repeating the polemically charged language that Augustine used without fully appreciating why he used such polemical categories. Furthermore, we need to recognize that from the 360s onward, anti-Nicene theology in the West is different from anti-Nicene theology in the East. Both Latin and Greek anti-Nicene theology fasten upon the notions that the Son's generation from the Father can be described as a generation only by or from God's will and cannot be described as a generation by or from God's essence. The Son's nature is like the Father's but is not the same as the Father's. In the East the anti-Nicene consensus on this language broke at a Synod in Antioch in 361, with the emergence of a theology that insisted on the doctrinal priority of the difference between the essences or natures of the Father and the Son: thus was born anomoian theology, known more popularly as "Eunomian" theology, after its most visible and prolific proponent, Eunomius of Cyzicus. However, "Latin Homoians managed to contain some of the distinctions that resulted in distinct groupings in the east";[6] in particular, Eunomian theology has no play in the West.[7]

Augustine understood the difference between doctrines and exegeses that originate directly from Arius, and those that originate with later anti-Nicenes: in *de Trinitate*, for example, he is quite specific in what he attributes to "Arius," "Arians," and "Eunomians" respectively. Whenever Augustine attributes a belief to Arius, this is always followed by a quotation from Arius that we can recognize as coming from one of Arius' letters—letters that are well known to have had a wide circulation in the West.[8] When Augustine attributes a belief to the "Arians" such beliefs are *not* doctrines we can recognize as Arius'; rather these beliefs belong to Latin anti-Nicenes who are properly called "Homoians." Augustine is careful about distinguishing among the beliefs of Arius, and different groups of "Arians." Here at *de Trin.* VI.1, for example, he notes that Arius himself believed that the Son is not eternal, while later "Arians" do not believe this. Moreover, I can add that I have never seen Augustine use the adjective "Arian" for a doctrine which belonged specifically to Eunomius: all Eunomian doctrines are explicitly attributed to Eunomius by Augustine. If we misidentify his opponents completely and label them "Eunomians" then we supply the wrong context for Augustine's arguments, and in ignorance again miss the distinctive features of the theology Augustine is opposing.

6. Ayres, *Nicaea and Its Legacy*, 139.

7. Previous generations of Augustine scholars have made a habit of identifying Augustine's opponent in *de Trinitate* as Eunomius, but those identifications depend upon a lack of familiarity with Latin anti-Nicene literature. I think that Sumrold assumes rather than proves Eunomius's influence, but in this he follows Simonetti: see Sumruld, *Augustine and the Arians*. On the scholarly misidentification of Augustine's opponents as Eunomians, see my "Arians of Book V," 185–95.

8. Bardy, "L'occident et les documents," 28–63.

First Corinthians 1:24 has significant play within anti-Nicene theology. It is at the center of one of the fundamental beliefs of anti-Nicenes, namely that the title "Power"[9]—like other titles applied to the Son—is attributed only equivocally. When Scripture says that the Son is the "power of God," Scripture does not mean that the Son is the very power that God has as an existent, God's own power, but that the Son is one of many instrumental powers that serve as God's agents. Asterius, writing in the 330s, makes this argument quite notoriously:

> there are many powers; one of which is God's own by nature and eternal; but Christ, on the other hand, is not the true power of God; but, like others, one of the so-called powers.[10]

In the 381 confrontation between Ambrose and the Homoian Palladius recorded in the *Acts of Aquileia,* Palladius is asked whether the *Son is God,* to which he replies that the Son is the "power of God."[11] The so-called *Arian Sermon,* sometimes attributed to Palladius by modern scholars, exegetes 1 Cor 1:24 as follows:

> The Son is the living and true, proper and worthy, image of the whole goodness and wisdom and power of God; the Spirit is the manifestation of the whole wisdom and power.[12]

The *Arian Fragments* collected by Gryson in CCL 60 include two specific treatments of 1 Cor 1:24. One fragment says:

> the apostle teaches that the Son is the Power of God and the Wisdom of God, not therefore that Power or Wisdom which is in the invisible God without beginning, but the one sitting at the right hand of God so that he might be by the Father, the Son receiving the love of God, who loves God.[13]

The second fragment is interesting for the way it connects the late Homoian understanding of the title "Power" to the Homoian emphasis on invisibility and

9. By *power* I mean the affective capacity or capacities of any given existent that is distinctive to the identity of that existent; I very specifically do not mean the Aristotelean sense of "potentiality." As will become clear, what distinguishes Nicenes from non- or anti-Nicenes is that Nicenes discuss the Son in terms of the Father's unique Power, while the others discuss the Son in terms of the Father's multiple powers. Eunomius is something of an exception to this generalization, since he seems not to use "power" in any ontological sense. See my *The Power of God,* which includes a history of the term's philosophical use as well as (in chapter 5) an examination of Eunomius's aetiology.

10. Athanasius, *First Oration Against the Arians* I,2.5, NPNF II/4, 309. Arius had made a similar argument, but he seems to have argued about the attribution of the titles "Wisdom" and "Word" to the Son: the Son is not the very Wisdom or very Word of God.

11. *Actes du Concile d'Aquiliée* 21, in Gryson, *Scolies Ariennes,* 344.

12. *The Arian Sermon* 22, in Teske, *Arianism and Other Heresies,* 135.

13. "Vnde apostolus d(e)i uirtutem et d(e)i sapientia(m) docet esse filium, no(n) illa igitur quae <in> inuisibile d(e)o est sine initio uirtute siue sapientia, sed sedentem in dextris d(e)i, ut esset a patre accipientem filium dilectionis d(e)i, quem diligit d(eu)s." *Fragmenta ariana*—codice Bobiensi rescripto Cl. 0705, fr. 22, pg. ms 209, line 35.

visibility as distinguishing features of true divinity versus equivocal divinity: "Hence the apostle preaches the image of this invisible God by showing God, his invisible Power or Wisdom, in the substance of the Son."[14] These examples give us the basis for recognizing Augustine's opponents, namely that they are Latin Homoians, and to place their exegesis of 1 Cor 1:24 within their theology overall, and in this way to understand what is at stake in Homoians denying the Son the title of true Power, and in insisting that the Son is but an image of the true God.

In the Latin Homoian exegesis of 1 Cor 1:24, then, the power and wisdom "*of God*" that Christ is identified with by Paul is not the power and wisdom as the terms are used unequivocally of true divinity. Paul calls Christ the power and wisdom *of God* to indicate the derivative and equivocal way in which the Son is given these titles at all. The Son is called after that which the Father already truly has—or *is*—His own power and wisdom. "Equality is entirely lacking between Father and Son." This kind of contrast is consistent throughout Homoian Trinitarian theology: there is the true God, who is true Good, true Life, true Eternal, true Wisdom, and true Power; and there is the Son, God for us, Good in obedience of the Good, Life by mediating true Life, Eternal because always made by the uncaused Eternal, Wisdom by revealing true Wisdom, and Power in service to the Power.

THE NICENE READINGS OF 1 COR 1:24

Interest in 1 Cor 1:24 on the side of those sympathetic to Nicaea goes back, according to Athanasius, to the Council in 325.[15] I have elsewhere documented and described the role of "one nature, one power" theology in anti-Arian and Nicene theology,[16] so I will not rehearse those details now. I will say simply that among both Latins and Greeks sympathetic to Nicaea there is an argument for the unity of nature between the Father and Son based on the doctrine that God has one power and the Son is that very power. This argument is supported by an appeal to 1 Cor 1:24. The Son is united to the Father as a power is united to any existent; that is, connaturally, as part of what it is. Gregory of Elvira, writing in Spain in the early 360s, provides a good example of this exegesis when he says that the Son is "called 'power' because he is truly from God and is with God and all the power of the Father is in him."[17] This statement by Gregory of Elvira serves as a good illustration of the exegesis that was authoritative for Augustine, and indeed it may have been Gregory's own work that brought this understanding of

14. "Vnde etiam imagine(m) d(e)i inuisibilis hunc apostolos praedicat, inuisibilem suam uirtutem siue sapientia(m) ostendentem d(eu)m in substantia fili." *Fragmenta ariana*—codice Bobiensi rescripto Cl. 0705, fr. 22, pg. ms 209, line 25.

15. See his *de Decretis* V.20 and *de Synodis* 18.

16. Barnes, "One Nature, One Power," 205–23.

17. "Virtus dicitur, quia uere de deo et semper cum deoest et omnis potestas patris in ipso consistit; sapientia apellatur, quia."

1 Cor 1:24 before Augustine since we know that Augustine read Gregory, as he quotes him in *Ep.* 148, although Augustine misidentifies Gregory as Gregory of Nazianzus.

Gregory of Elvira's exegesis of 1 Cor 1:24 offers, moreover, what can serve to us as a typical expression of one of the two understandings among Nicenes of the "power" named in 1 Cor 1:24. In this *first* understanding of power, which I call the *Neo-Nicene*, the Son is identified with the very power that God the Father has as an existent: the Son is *the* power of God. This understanding of the doctrine of God's one power may be found in the writings of Athanasius and in the sermon attributed to Liberius of Rome in Ambrose's *Concerning Virginity*, book III. It is the same understanding of 1 Cor 1:24 that Augustine displays twice in the 393 *de Fide et Symbolo*, and in his *Third Tractate on John*, usually dated to 404–6, where he invokes that scriptural passage in a clearly anti-Homoian argument. Augustine says: "The Wisdom of God cannot be seen by the eyes. Brothers, if Christ is the Wisdom of God and the Power of God, if Christ is the Word of God, [and if] the word of man is not seen by the eyes, can the Word of God be so seen?"[18] Here Augustine lays the three titles alongside each other as naming what Christ is of God's. As in the earlier *de Fide et Symbolo* "Word, Power and Wisdom" are "titles which commend the Lord Jesus to our faith as the Son of God, only-begotten of the Father."

A second understanding of the doctrine of "one power" based upon 1 Cor 1:24 by those sympathetic to Nicaea is that there is one divine power that the Father and Son both share, that is, the Father and the Son have the same power (and therefore have the same nature). I call this understanding the *Pro-Nicene* doctrine[19] of "one power": it is found, e.g., in the later books of Ambrose's *de Fide*, in Niceta of Remesiana's *De Ratione Fidei* and *De Spiritus Sancti Potentia*, as well as in the writings of Gregory of Nyssa and Gregory of Nazianzus. Augustine understands 1 Cor 1:24 precisely in this

---

18. *Tractate on John* 3.18.2, in Rettig, *Tractates on John 1–10*, 89. I have rendered the titles "Wisdom" and "Power" in uppercase, while Rettig gives them in lower case, giving only "Word" in uppercase. A similar use of 1 Cor 1:24 can be found in *Ep.* 137.

19. The reader should be aware that my use of the term "Pro-Nicene" is not the same as Lewis Ayres's in his article, "Giving Wings to Nicaea." For Ayres, the term encompasses both what I call "Neo-Nicene" and "Pro-Nicene." Simply put, the distinguishing doctrinal features of *Neo-Nicene* theology include: Son identified as the Power, Wisdom, Word of God; co-naturalness argued from "Father" and "Son" relationship; little interest in ontological language for Individual(s) of the Trinity; and no use of John 5:19. The distinguishing doctrinal features of *Pro-Nicene* theology include: Father, Son (and Holy Spirit) share the same Power, perform the same operations, and thus have one nature; substantial interest in ontological language for Individual(s) of the Trinity; and strong use of John 5:19 as support for "same power, same operation, same nature" argument. The beginning of Pro-Nicene theology is later than the beginning of Neo-Nicene theology, but Pro-Nicene theology is not to be understood simply as a succeeding development of Neo-Nicene theology that replaces the latter: the two theologies can co-exist chronologically. (Hilary of Poitiers' Trinitarian theology of the early 360s fits the Pro-Nicene model and keeps the relationship between the two forms of Nicene theologies from being treated simply as "developmental.") Eventually Pro-Nicene theology becomes normative, but never in the sense that Neo-Nicene doctrines are forbidden or condemned. Finally, neither Ayres's nor my distinctions owe anything to Theodore Zahn's and Adolf von Harnack's language of "Old Nicenes" and "Neo-Nicenes."

sense in *Sermon* 215, which Hill dates to 425, when he says, "There is one substance of Godhead in the Trinity, one power, one might, one majesty, one name of divinity."[20] The existence of these two Nicene readings of the term "power" in 1 Cor 1:24, and the differences between them, is important for understanding Augustine's argument in *de Trinitate* VI and VII.

THREE CONTEMPORARY ENGAGEMENTS WITH 1 COR. 1:24 AMONG LATIN NICENES

There are a few surviving Latin Trinitarian writings closely contemporary to Augustine's *de Trinitate* that enable us to place Augustine's concern with 1 Cor 1:24 in its immediate context. Three texts in particular show similar concerns with the exegesis of 1 Cor 1:24 and a power-based Trinitarian theology: Rufinius of Aquilaea's Latin translation of Origen's *Peri Archon*; Rufinius the Syrian's *de Fide*, and Consentius's unnamed work on the Trinity.

My interest in Rufinus of Aquileia's 398 translation of the *Peri Archon* is not for the purpose of suggesting that Augustine read the work and was influenced by it. Instead, I read Rufinus's *De Principiis* as a work revealing the interests and concerns of late-fourth- and early-fifth-century Latin Trinitarian theology of an openly Nicene sympathy, which is clearly where Rufinus's sympathies lay. Rufinus's updating of Origen's Trinitarian theology in his translation of the *De Principiis*[21] is well-documented: he even goes so far as to put the term omoousios into Origen's mouth.[22] Origen's *Peri Archon* was undoubtedly the authority for much Greek "power" theology; Rufinus-Origen's *De Principiis* is, I suggest, the voice of Latin interest in a variety of contemporary Trinitarian topics, including "power" Trinitarian theology.

De Principiis I.II.6–9 begins with the statement that the will of God is in itself sufficient as the cause of the Son's existence: nothing else is needed. This assertion is developed into the argument that the Son is not a material image of the Father, but an invisible image. The original assertion by Origen to this effect was probably the first time a doctrine of the Son as invisible image of God was articulated by a Christian author, and the development of this doctrine marks Greek Trinitarian theology off from Latin until the end of the fourth century, when Latin Nicenes finally develop a similar doctrine. Rufinius's translation of Origen's early insight is one the earliest clear articulations in Latin: Hilary probably believed it already in *de Trin.* VIII.48–49, but he never actually says, "The Son is the *invisible* image . . ."—he merely denies that the Son can be a *material* image.

---

20. *Sermon* 215.8, *Sermons* III/6, Hill, 164.

21. Quasten, *Patrology IV*, 250. Jean Gribomont gives the date for Rufinus's translation as 398.

22. On this point I follow the judgement of R. P. C. Hanson, "Did Origen Apply the Word ὁμοούσιος to the Son?" in *Epektasis*, Jacques Fontaine and Charles Kannengiesser, eds., Paris: Beauchesne, 1972, 293–303.

De Principiis I.II.9 is devoted to an exploration of "power" as describing divine generation.[23] The power of God itself proceeds as will proceeding from mind, and the will of God comes to be a power of God. There comes into existence another power, whose existence derives exclusively from the power of God. Since God's power always existed the power that follows from the original power must have always existed as well. This argument culminates in the statement that there never was a time when the Son did not exist. In other words, the Son's origin in the eternal power of God is proof of his own eternal existence, and this eternal existence is itself a proof of the Son's divinity. One finds similar arguments in Athanasius and, more to the point, in book One of Augustine's *de Trinitate*. What is distinctive to the account in *De Principiis* I.II.9 of production of *a power from a power* is that the account clearly supports the understanding that the Son comes from the nature of the Father. However, when in his *Commentary on John* Origen describes the production of the Son from the Father he treats the aetiology of *a power from a power* as an alternative to *production from the nature*.[24] The contrast in doctrine between the two works is this: in *De Principiis* I.II.9 power aetiology is understood to be a kind of natural production, while in the *Commentary on John* power aetiology is understood to be an alternative to natural production. Whatever Origen may have originally written in the *Peri Archon*, the power theology of *De Principiis* is more congenial to Nicene tendencies.

The second Latin writing showing concern with the exegesis of 1 Cor 1:24 and a power-based Trinitarian theology similar to what Augustine talks about in *de Trin.* VI and VII is found in the *De Fide* of Rufinus "the Syrian"—not to be confused with the Iberian translator of Origen. The work was written about 400, probably in Rome; in modern scholarship it has been the subject of attention because the majority of the work is given over to statements on theological anthropology.[25] The work is the earliest attack on the doctrine of nature and grace articulated by Augustine in works such as *To Simplicianus* and *Confessions*. Rufinus's own anthropology has earned him the scholarly title of "The father of Pelagianism." However, the first third of the *De Fide*[26] is concerned with articulating a theology of the Trinity that is clearly Nicene, and Rufinus's Trinitarian theology has—to my knowledge—never been studied.[27] Throughout

23. See Crouzel and Simonetti, SC 252, 128ff.

24. See my *Power of God*, 118–24.

25. For text and translation, I use *Rufini Presbyteri—Liber De Fide*, Mary William Miller, ed. and trans., Washington, D.C.: The Catholic University of America Press, 1964.) See also H. Rondet, "Rufin le Syrien et le Liber de Fide," *Augustiniana* 22 (1972): 531–539. Jean Gribomont, writing in *Patrology* IV, expresses what he understands to be the current scholarly consensus that this Rufinus is responsible for "the Vulgate revision of the Pauline Epistles, the Catholic Epistles, and probably the Acts of the Apostles and the Apocalypse." See p. 246. The only date Gribomont can give for *de Fide* is "before 411."

26. Unlike most Latin works "on the faith" from the second half of the fourth century, Rufinus's is not explicitly engaged with refuting "Arians." In the last few sections of the book the stock condemnations of Arius and Eunomius appear, but only after Rufinus has already laid out his own position.

27. Berthold Altaner has some remarks about the Trinitarian theology of *De Fide* in his "Augustinus und Gregor von Nazianz, Gregor von Nyssa," in *Kleine Patristische Schriften*, TU 83 (Berlin:

his *De Fide* Rufinus lays great emphasis on the title of "Power" for the Second Person: he repeatedly asserts statements such as

> both the substance and the power of the Father, the Son, and the Holy Spirit are one and the same.[28]

The "one and same"-ness of the "substance and power"—"substantia et virtus"— is Rufinus's constant and consistent articulation of the unity among the Father, Son, and Holy Spirit. In some places Rufinus will use the biblical term, *virtus*; in others he will use the more abstract term, *potentia*. The phrasing for "one and the same" is almost always "*eiusdem . . . atque . . .*": no form of "consubstantial" appears.[29] As I have shown elsewhere, this language is the common and standard articulation of Latin Nicene theology at the turn of the centuries.[30] That "*eiusdem substantia atque virtus*" functions as the fundamental expression of the unity of the Trinity is made clear by the way Rufinus exegetes John 10:30, "The Father and I are one," a key scriptural passage for Alexander, Athanasius, Hilary, and Ambrose, among others. Rufinus cites the Johannine passage to support the statement that the *substance and the power of the Father, the Son, and the Holy Spirit are one and the same.* Rufinus's power Trinitarian theology is what I call "pro-Nicene": he believes that the Father, Son, and Holy Spirit share one power as they share one nature, and he does not base the unity between Father and Son on identifying the Son with the one Power of God.

There is one further feature of Rufinus's argument that is directly relevant: Rufinus remarks at one point that while it is true that the power of the Father, the Son, and the Holy Spirit are one and the same, this is not what is meant by 1 Cor 1:24, "Christ, the Power and Wisdom of God."[31] Rufinus knows that some of those who teach the unity of the substance and power of the Trinity use 1 Cor 1:24 as a proof-text, and although he agrees with their teaching, he rejects their exegesis of the Corinthians passage in support of their doctrine.

The third Latin Nicene engagement with 1 Cor 1:24 contemporary with Augustine's is represented by a letter of Consentius, written to Augustine in 410, and included in Augustine's letters as *Ep. 119*. Consentius writes Augustine to ask him to critique Consentius's Trinitarian formula. Consentius says, "The Father is in the Son, the Son in the Father, the Holy Spirit in both, because the one individual God dwells in the Three, who are distinct in number, but not in rank; [distinct in] Person, but

---

Akademie-Verlag, 1967), 277–85. Altaner's interest in the text is limited, however, to determining whether it was Augustine's source for his knowledge of Gregory of Nazianzus's doctrine of relations that Altaner sees evidence of at *de Trinitate* XV.20.38 (and *only* there.) The question of whether Augustine might have read the *De Fide* is not touched. That Augustine would not have read this the first direct and elaborate attack on his doctrine of grace seems unlikely.

28. Miller, *Rufini Presbyteri—Liber De Fide* IX.16–17, 63.

29. See Teske, "Augustine's Use of 'Substantia,'" 147–63.

30. See my "Exegesis and Polemic," 43–59.

31. Miller, *Rufini Presbyteri—Liber De Fide* XI.5–7, 67.

not in power. There is one power which the triune power possesses, one substance in which these that are Three subsist."[32] Consentius's power Trinitarian theology is thus "pro-Nicene." On this point Consentius's Trinitarian theology is more sophisticated than Augustine's is at the beginning of book VI of *de Trinitate*.[33]

AUGUSTINE'S TWO CRITICISMS

I make this comparative judgment in Consentius's favor because at the beginning of *de Trinitate* VI we find Augustine knowledgeable of, but uncomfortable with, the *neo*-Nicene exegesis of 1 Cor 1:24 that identifies the Son with the very Power and Wisdom of God, an exegesis he has himself used regularly. However, Augustine has not yet recognized the pro-Nicene understanding of 1 Cor 1:24. He offers an alternative to the neo-Nicene , which by the end of book VII moves away from the neo-Nicene exegesis and toward the pro-Nicene exegesis, although Augustine does not arrive at the pro-Nicene position. Augustine has two critiques of the Nicene position that the Son is the very Power and Wisdom of God: the first of these critiques I call the "simple" criticism, the second is the "sophisticated" criticism; it is this second, "sophisticated" criticism that Augustine works the hardest to resolve.

Augustine's initial or "simple" criticism of the Neo-Nicene position is that if Nicenes are right that the Son is the very Power and Wisdom of God, then God the Father lacks wisdom and power until He begets the Son. We find this critique at *de Trin.* VI. 2: "This argument forces us to say that God is only wise by having the wisdom which he begot."[34] Augustine's second or "sophisticated" criticism is that if the Neo-Nicenes are right, then God the Father's being depends upon his begetting the Son, and Sonship is not *relation* but *being*. According to Augustine, if the Neo-Nicene exegesis of 1 Cor 1:24 is right, then Power and Wisdom are "christological"—or what is more commonly called "relational"—because they refer to who the Father generates or by whom the Father stands in relation to by generating. Augustine adds to this observation the fact of the ultimate identity of divine titles or properties, i.e., that *power* is the same as *wisdom* which is the same as *goodness* which is the same as *greatness* which is the same as *being* which is the same as "*light*" which is the same as *Spirit*, etc. If all these equivalent predications refer to the Son and are relational, Augustine argues, then these predications are not substantial, and we have thereby emptied the person of God the Father and the concept of divinity of any substantial predications, that is, of

32. Augustine of Hippo, *Letters 83–130*, FotC 18, 297.

33. In his *The Origin of the Soul in St. Augustine's Later Works* (New York: Fordham University Press, 1987), O'Connell has an interesting discussion of the place of *Ep.* 119 (and Augustine's reply in *Ep.* 120) in Augustine's developing Trinitarian theology and the writing of *de Trinitate*. See 93–98. For a recent treatment of Augustine's theology in *Ep.* 120, see Ayres, "Remember That You Are Catholic," 69–74.

34. Augustine, *The Trinity*, 206.

any content.[35] Such a conclusion is untenable, so therefore Power and Wisdom cannot be christological or relational, but must be substantial predicates. Power and Wisdom can no more refer exclusively to the Son than do *goodness, greatness, being,* "*light,*" and *Spirit.* Alternately, for Augustine neither power nor wisdom nor goodness nor being nor any of the rest are relational; they are all substantial, and therefore they are predicated of Father, Son and Holy Spirit equally inasmuch as each of them is God.[36]

Augustine's exegesis of 1 Cor 1:24 in *de Trin* VI and VII may thus be characterized in the following two ways. *First,* Augustine is declining the neo-Nicene exegesis with which, as he says quite explicitly, he now has logical problems but which he has himself affirmed earlier in his theological career. When, in 410, Augustine replies to Consentius in Epistle 120 he entirely avoids discussing Consentius's exegesis of 1 Cor 1:24. *Second,* Augustine has not yet articulated a fully pro-Nicene exegesis of "Wisdom" and "Power": he *has* identified the single power of God as a power that all three persons share, but he has not moved that understanding into doctrinal statements of "one nature, one power." Such articulations will appear in the last phase of Augustine's Trinitarian writings, such as in the *Twentieth Tractate on John, Sermon* 215, the *Sermo ad Catechumenos de symbolo,* and the *Answer to Maximinus,* all written 420 or later. Augustine's Trinitarian theology *develops,* and its most fully developed articulations are not in *de Trinitate* at all. The significance of these characterizations may be summarized as follows:

Latins of both Homoian and Nicene sympathies understood titles such as Power, Wisdom and Word to involve assertions of the Son's identity and the kind of union he has with the Father. Homoians and Neo-Nicenes both understand the genitive in 1 Cor 1:24 to indicate that Christ's identity as the Power and Wisdom of God follows from His production by the Father. Whether those titles are given equivocally or univocally is a decision made by both Homoians and Neo-Nicenes on the basis of a judgment on what kind of *image* the Father produces in the Son. In other words, for both Neo-Nicenes and Homoians the character of the so-called Father-Son relationship determines whether the Son is truly God or not. For Neo-Nicenes, titles such as Power, Wisdom, and Word indicate the Son's union with the Father while preserving the integrity of the Son's existence as such. Augustine recognizes that this production-based model of equality and union cannot be sustained. The alternative that Augustine articulates in *de Trin* VII parallels the solution developed by Pro-Nicenes, namely that

35. If "Word," "Wisdom," and "Power" (etc.) are all proper or univocal titles of the Son, then they all name that which is begotten. If this is true then these exist and are the Father's because they are begotten. And if God is simple, then "Word, Wisdom, Power" equal essence. If indeed the Son *is* literally the Wisdom, Power, et al. of God, then the Father has being in respect to the Son, the essence he begot, and by which essence He is whatever He is (Augustine, *The Trinity,* 220).

36. "So the Father is himself wisdom, and the Son is called the wisdom of the Father in the same way as he is called the light of the Father, that is, that as we talk of light from light, and both are one light, so we must understand wisdom from wisdom, and both one wisdom. And therefore also one being, because *to be* is the same as to be wise." *De Trin.* VII.2–3, in Augustine, *The Trinity,* 220–21.

a Trinitarian theology of the unity of nature is not anchored in titles of relation. What Augustine does not do at this time is to develop the Pro-Nicene argument that the unity of nature is anchored in the common power of the Father and Son.

CONCLUSION

The driving force behind *de Trinitate* VI and VII is not Aristotle's *Categories*. What drives Augustine's concern with 1 Cor 1:24 in these two books of *de Trinitate* is exactly what Augustine says it is at the beginning of *de Trin* VI: an awareness of the weakness of Nicene exegesis of 1 Cor 1:24 and the vulnerability of that exegesis to anti-Nicene claims on the Pauline passage.

One way of describing what I have tried to do in this paper is to recover an awareness of the theological "field" or conceptual idioms within which Augustine thought and wrote. Without an ability to recognize these idioms we are, I believe, unable to read with any understanding Augustine's writings—in this case, his great Trinitarian writing, *de Trinitate*. In some important ways it may be said that, faced with the task of reading Augustine, we are in fact "illiterate," in that we cannot read the language in which he communicates. We are now, as scholarly readers of Augustine, in the process of discovering what Augustine read and when. For example, thanks to the series on commentaries on Aristotle edited by Richard Sorabji we are now able to see the complexity of what it meant for someone in the late Graeco-Roman period to have "read" what we now recognize as Aristotle's *Categories*. The older, confident scholarly judgment that Augustine read Aristotle's book, the *Categories*, has to be regarded as provisional, even if it was not understood that way at the time. The driving force behind Augustine's concern for understanding what we mean when we say that Christ is the Power and Wisdom of God is not an impulse towards theological abstraction, but Augustine facing, for the first time, the full consequences of the contemporary Latin Homoian criticism of an important articulation of "Nicene" theology. Never one to shrug off a challenge, nor to seek half-heartedly for answers, Augustine saw the weakness of "Neo-Nicene" theology and began his search for the solution.

Chapter 12

Augustine's Last Pneumatology

WHILE *DE TRINITATE* CAN justifiably receive the greater share of scholarly attention as Augustine's statement of his Trinitarian theology, it is a mistake to regard that work either as his only significant treatment of the doctrine of the Trinity or as his last word on the subject. Augustine's reflections on the Trinity are spread across a wide variety of genres, including sermons, letters, and scriptural commentaries. Moreover, these reflections are often written with very specific purposes and audiences in mind. Perhaps most importantly, Augustine learned from his experiences and his engagements with others. Finally, it probably needs to be said that Augustine's Trinitarian theology was not a static thing that achieved its complete expression in *De Trinitate* and then froze in his mind, never to develop further—silently awaiting the birth of Thomas Aquinas in order to be finally and truly made perfect.

The purpose of this chapter is to examine Augustine's last treatments of the Holy Spirit. In this paper, I will examine two of the most important ones: the *Ninety-Ninth Tractate on John* and the collection of writings produced from Augustine's public debate with Maximinus, a Homoian bishop. These texts are read with a specific methodological judgment in mind; namely, that the *Ninety-Ninth Tractate on John* is examined outside the context of the progress of Augustine's argument in *De Trinitate*. The tractate obviously does not postdate the completion of *De Trinitate*, and cannot contain the developments in Augustine's thought achieved in that work. I will discuss the tractate as a polemical work arising within a tradition of pro-Nicene polemic on the status of the Holy Spirit. The importance of the works against Maximinus is sufficiently guaranteed by their being literally Augustine's "last words" on Trinitarian theology. He died less than two years later. Enough has been said in the previous chapter by way of context to allow me to move directly to the *Ninety-Ninth Tractate on John*.

Tractate 99 is an exegetical treatment of John 16:13, "The Spirit will not speak of himself, but whatsoever he will hear, he will speak." Augustine recognizes in this passage something similar to what John 5:30 reports from Jesus: "I cannot do anything of myself; as I hear, I judge." Both passages have to Augustine's ear a potentially subordinationist import. The subordinationism of John 5:30 Augustine resolved by judging that the passage applied to the humanity of Christ and not his divinity. That resolution is not possible regarding John 16:13 and the Holy Spirit because there is no union of natures—uncreated and created—in the Holy Spirit. None of the multiple appearances of the Holy Spirit—as dove, as fire, as cloud—involve the Spirit assuming a created nature. Neither did the Holy Spirit ever assume a human nature or an angelic nature.

Augustine argues that John 16:13 means that the Spirit speaks what he receives, and what the Spirit receives, in the fundamental sense of that word, is his existence or being.[1] The Spirit is not from himself, but from another. "The Father alone is not from another," Augustine says. The Spirit, then, must proceed from the Father. But, Augustine asks, does the Holy Spirit also proceed from the Son? At this point, Augustine marshals the New Testament passages already described in the previous paper—passages that describe the Spirit as of the Father and of the Son. Augustine rests in particular on John 20:22, the scene of Jesus breathing upon the apostles and saying, "Receive the Holy Spirit." With this one quotation, Augustine imports the entire pericope of the "Johannine Pentecost." The passage at 99.7.1 bears quoting in full:

> Why, therefore, should we not believe that the Holy Spirit also proceeds from the Son since He is also the Spirit of the Son? For if he did not proceed from him, [Jesus] after the resurrection, showing himself anew to the disciples, would not have breathed upon them, saying, "Receive the Holy Spirit." For what else did that insufflation signify except that the Holy Spirit also proceeds from him?[2]

The last sentence—the rhetorical question—is a question that hangs in the air. Christ breathing upon the apostles and saying, "Receive the Holy Spirit," means that the Holy Spirit proceeds from him—and in a literal way. At the Johannine Pentecost, the Holy Spirit comes from—even *out of*—the Son; this is the "insufflation" Augustine speaks of. John 20:22 provides a description of the Spirit not simply as the "Spirit of" the Son or Lord, but of the Spirit proceeding from him. What Augustine derives from the insufflation scene is an excellent example of a point made in the previous paper:

1. The relationship between the Son's and Holy Spirit's knowledge of the Father, and their respective generation/spiration from him, is a very important part of the "logical" foundation of Augustine's Trinitarian theology.

2. Rettig, trans., *Tractates*, FotC 90, 226, for which the Latin reads: "Cur ergo non credamus quod etiam de Filio procedat Spiritus sanctus, cum Filii quoque ipse sit Spiritus? Si enim non ab eo procederet, non post resurrectionem se repraesentans discipulis suis insuffl asset dicens: Accipite Spiritum sanctum (Joan. XX, 22). Quid enim aliud signifi cavit illa insuffl atio, nisi quod procedat Spiritus sanctus et de ipso?"

namely, that Augustine reads virtually all statements about the relations of Son and Spirit as also signifying aspects of their eternal relationship.[3]

At 99.7(2), Augustine follows the literal "the Holy Spirit comes from or out of the Son" with another set of descriptions of the Holy Spirit coming from or out of the Son. The insufflation described at John 20:22 is an important, especially significant, case of the Holy Spirit coming from[4] or out of the Son, but it is not the only case of the Spirit being described as coming from the Son. There is a Lucan model of "insufflation" which is "empowerment," in which the Holy Spirit is not spoken of in terms of breath, but in terms of power (in each case the Latin for power is *virtus*). Augustine brings forward a set of New Testament testimonies to the Holy Spirit coming from the Son: Power proceeding from the Son.[5] In every case from Luke–Acts that Augustine brings forward, the proper exegesis of the passage means that the appearance of *virtus* should be understood as *Virtus*. The subject of Augustine's theologizing is again that the Holy Spirit proceeds from both the Father and the Son (as at 99.6), the argument being intended to support particularly the "from the Son also" statement.

> To this that also pertains which he said about the woman who was suffering an issue of blood. "Someone has touched me; for I felt that power has gone out from me" [Luke 8:46]. For that the Holy Spirit is also called the name of Power is clear from the passage where to Mary who said, "How will this be done because I know not man," the angel answered, "The Holy Spirit will come upon you, and the power of the Most High will overshadow you" [Luke 1:35]. And the Lord himself, promising him [the Holy Spirit] to the disciples, said, "But stay you in the city until you are endued with power from on high" [Luke 24:49]. And again he says, "You will receive the power of the Holy Spirit coming upon you and you will be witnesses to me [Acts 1:8]. About this power we must believe, as the Evangelist says, "Power went out from him and healed all" [Luke 6:19].[6]

In each case, the word translated as "power" is *virtus*, which translates, in each case, the Greek *dunamis*.

---

3. Page 215.

4. "Coming from" means in all cases "Going out from."

5. For a discussion of Luke's Power pneumatology, see Bruce, "Holy Spirit in the Acts of the Apostles," esp. 169–71. Augustine's implicit list of "Power = Holy Spirit" passages complements Bruce's explicit list nicely.

6. Rettig, *Tractates*, 226. "Ad hoc pertinet etiam illud quod de muliere quae fl uxum sanguinis patiebatur, ait: Tetigit me aliquis; ego enim sensi de me virtutem exiisse (Luc. VIII, 46). Nam virtutis nomine appellari etiam Spiritum sanctum, et eo loco clarum est, ubi angelus dicenti Mariae, Quomodo fi et istud, quoniam virum non cognosco? respondit, Spiritus sanctus superveniet in te, et virtus Altissimi obumbrabit tibi (Id. I, 34, 35): et ipse Dominus promittenseum discipulis, ait, Vos autem sedete in civitate quousque induamini virtute ex alto (Id. XXIV, 49); et iterum, Accipietis, inquit, virtutem Spiritus sancti supervenientem in vos, et eritis mihi testes (Act. I,8). De hac virtute credendus est dicere evangelista, Virtus de illo exibat, et sanabat omnes (Luc.VI, 19)."

According to Augustine, then, when Jesus says, "The power has gone out from me" at Luke 8:46, the power he speaks of is the Holy Spirit, for we know that the Holy Spirit is sometimes called the Power from Luke 1:35. There are the other examples in Luke of the Power *coming from*[7] the Son: Luke 24:49, Acts 1:8, and Luke 6:19. In short, Luke 8:46 should be read as "The Holy Spirit has gone out from me." There is, so far as I can discover, no precedent in pro-Nicene writings for the constellation of these Lucan power texts. There *is* an early Christian tradition of "Power Pneumatology," although it is not so prevalent as angelomorphic pneumatology or Wisdom pneumatology. There is a strong Power Pneumatology trajectory in pro-Nicene theology, but it does not utilize or incorporate every one of these Lucan texts. No one before Augustine seems to have identified the power flowing out from Christ in the two healing episodes of Luke 6:19 and 8:46 as referring to the Holy Spirit.

The *repeated* character of the Spirit–Power going out from the Son—to heal this blind person, to heal that lame person—connects to reflections on the mission of the Holy Spirit explicit in Ambrose and implicit in Augustine: repetition is a distinctive characteristic of the Holy Spirit being sent, in contrast to the unique sending of the Son.[8] This repetitious character of the Spirit's *missio* is both revealed by and serves to explain the different manifestations of the Holy Spirit, the cloud in Exodus, the dove at the Jordan, and the tongues of fire at Pentecost being the paradigmatic cases. Repetition as a distinctive characteristic of the mission of the Holy Spirit helps to explain the difference between the manifestations of the Spirit and the Incarnation of the Word: the mission of the Word is unique, his relationship to his created manifestation is unique. The Word's relationship to created humanity in the Incarnation is hypostatic, while the Spirit never has a hypostatic unity with any of its created manifestations. If the Holy Spirit ever had a hypostatic union with any of its created manifestations, then that union could not be set aside, just as even now the Word remains in hypostatic union with its human nature, and that union will never be, and cannot be, set aside.

Lurking deep in the exegetical background is the conclusion of *De Trinitate* VI and VII on the proper understanding of 1 Corinthians 1:24: although the Son is sometimes called the Wisdom of God, he cannot be the very Wisdom of God the Father, for the Father is wise, too. Wisdom, properly understood, is an attribute of divinity shared equally by the Three. Still, Scripture does sometimes use Wisdom as a title for the Son. The latter fact, however, cannot be understood in any way which conflicts with the former fact (that Wisdom properly understood is an attribute of divinity). The appearance of the title "Power" in 1 Corinthians 1:24, as well its traditional attribution to the Son, is almost ignored in *De Trinitate* VI and VII, where the emphasis is on Wisdom as a Christological title. I think now that perhaps this is the case because Augustine

---

7. The verbs in each case are *exiisse* and *exibat*.

8. The unique sending of the Son versus the repeated sending of the Spirit is bedrock Catholic theology, and by Augustine's time was taken for granted (though not always articulated and developed for its significance as well as Augustine does).

shares a sensitivity with that Latin tradition exemplified by Niceta of Remesiana in which Power is associated with Holy Spirit.[9]

In *De Trinitate* VII, Augustine argues that although 1 Corinthians 1:24 refers to Christ as the Power and Wisdom of God, strictly speaking the traditional Christological title Wisdom belongs to the divine Trinity and not to any individual. However, there is a certain appropriateness to referring to the Son as Wisdom, particularly in light of the fact that Scripture consistently speaks of divine Wisdom as something generated. A similar line of thought seems to be behind Augustine's claims for "Power" as a title of the Holy Spirit, specifically. Certainly, power is one of those terms that belong to the divine Trinity and not to any individual, but just as certainly, the New Testament—Luke, in particular—seems to consistently refer to the Holy Spirit as "Power," especially in the context of speaking of the Spirit proceeding from the Son. (The fact that these descriptions of the Spirit as Power coming forth from Christ are all by Christ himself provides a unique authority for this language.)

I turn now to the last writings by Augustine on the Trinity, the *Debate with Maximinus* and the *Reply to Maximinus*.[10] Written in 427 or 428, the *Debate with Maximinus* (*Conlatio cum Maximino*) records an actual debate in Hippo between the Homoian bishop Maximinus and Augustine. While the debate moves back and forth between questions of the Son and of the Holy Spirit, the exegetical points that Augustine pushes Maximinus the hardest on are Pneumatological. The debate opens with comments on the fact that the Holy Spirit "enlightens" us, but Maximinus is not clear about who enlightens through whom: The Son through the Holy Spirit, or the Holy Spirit through the Son? He says both. Under pressure from Augustine, Maximinus says enlightenment is properly from its true author, the Father (the one true God). In saying this, Maximinus speaks of the Son being subject to the Father, and the Holy Spirit being subject to the Son. Augustine pounces. Where does Scripture say the Holy Spirit is subject to the Son? Where, in fact, does Scripture say the Holy Spirit is subject to the Father?

We see in the debate that both sides are interested in the meaning of the Pauline statement that the Holy Spirit "groans." Maximinus takes the statement to mean that the Holy Spirit *suffers*, and so cannot be God; Augustine takes it to mean that the Holy Spirit intercedes and mediates. Interestingly, Augustine's final criticism of Maximinus' understanding of "Spirit groans" is that Maximinus does not understand figures of speech in the Bible: "If you recognized these figures of speech like a man learned in the divine books, you would not ascribe unhappiness to the Holy Spirit on account of

---

9. It seems likely that this Latin "Power Pneumatology" owes a great deal to the theology of Cyril of Jerusalem; his writings are known to Ambrose, Nicetas, and Rufinus of Aquilea.

10. English quotations are from Roland Teske's translation in the volume *Arianism and Other Heresies*.

those groans with which he is said to plead."[11] One wonders if there are echoes of the old *tropici* debate here?

In the last quarter to fifth of the debate, Maximinus is on a roll: he has taken the debate over as a monologue. At one point (15.17) he remarks that while John 1:3 says that the Son created everything, nothing similar can be found in Scripture about the Holy Spirit. This remark by Maximinus is very important: he is not using John 1:3 to say that the Holy Spirit is among those "things" the Son created as Origen did—for by this time anti-Nicenes energetically avoid using "created" of the Son or Holy Spirit. Maximinus is using John 1:3 to claim the capacity of creator for the Son and to make the point that there is no scriptural warrant for saying that the Holy Spirit created.

Maximinus' statement that Scripture never speaks of the Holy Spirit requires our attention, in that there has recently been a strong representation in scholarship of Latin Homoianism as a Bible-based theology. R. P. C. Hanson goes so far as to deny any philosophical influence upon its theology.[12] One does, however, sometimes get the impression that modern judgments on the decisive role of scriptural exegesis as the basis of Homoian theology are because modern scholars and theologians explicitly link their own rejection of traditional Nicene Christology with their judgments about the poor credibility of Nicene exegetical practice: reading the Homoian rejection of traditional Nicene Christology may suggest that they, too, like modern scholars and theologians, were better readers of Scripture than Nicenes. Historically, the impression that Latin Homoians found their voice, as it were, in scriptural exegesis and not other genres of theological literature seems to be supported by the fact that most of the literature of Latin Homoianism that we possess is scriptural commentary.

Maximinus' comment that there are no scriptural testimonies to the Holy Spirit returns us to the exegetical transformation that passages like Psalm 33:6 underwent at the beginning of the third century, and brings us up short against the fact that from the early third century until the late-370s, Latin exegesis identified the "Spirit" of Psalm 33:6 with the pre-existent Son. (Greek exegesis is no different.) The exegesis of Psalm 33:6 does not differ among Nicenes, non-Nicenes, and anti-Nicenes. Phobaedius, for example, writing in 359 against the anti-Nicene manifesto of Sirmium (the "Blasphemy"), understands the Spirit of Psalm 33:6 to refer to the Son; he makes no mention of the Holy Spirit. In his *De Trinitate*, Hilary likewise never discovers the Holy Spirit as the subject of Psalm 33:6b. In short, Maximinus' remarks correspond to the unanimous exegesis of Latins from 210 until sometime in the second half of the fourth century.

Any judgment about who was the first Latin to identify the "Spirit of his mouth" with the Holy Spirit depends upon which chronology one accepts of the works of three authors: Ambrose of Milan, Faustinus, and Niceta of Remesciana. The first time Ambrose makes the exegetical identification is in *On the Holy Spirit* (381): this

---

11. Teske, *Arianism and Other Heresies*, 195.
12. See Hanson, *The Search*, 557ff.

exegesis is not in his earlier work, *On the Faith* (377–78 and 380). Faustinus, a priest in Rome with the "Luciferians," writes a work, *De Trinitate*, in 380 or 381. Finally, if Burns is right that Niceta's writings date from the mid- to late-370s,[13] then his short catechetical treatise, *Power of the Holy Spirit*, would be the first time a Latin author exegetes Psalm 33:6 as a reference to the Holy Spirit, and with this scriptural support, proclaims the Holy Spirit as co-creator.

When Maximinus says that he knows of no scriptural passage that says that the Holy Spirit is creator, he is saying in 428 what all Latin Trinitarians from 210 to the late 370s said. His repetition of the old doctrine is not a simple thing, as if he were just being "traditional." Maximinus does not speak of the Holy Spirit as co-creator, but he withholds this title without the allied-in-logic doctrines that formed the old understanding of what "spirit" meant: he lacks, most importantly, a spirit Christology. Almost as significant (and surely aligned with the lack of spirit Christology) is the fact that Maximinus' understanding of what "spirit" means when applied to all Three (usually in pairs, e.g., "the Son of one spirit with the Father") lacks substance: "the Son is of one spirit with the Father" means that the Son is one in will with the Father. ("[M]ay we fulfill it [God's will] with our actions so that we become one spirit with God when we want what God wants.")[14] Western Trinitarian tradition "saved" so special a term as "spirit" for the Son in order to guarantee his distinct existence (from the Father) and to identify his divine nature (in relation to the Incarnation). The two exegetical arguments have fallen out from Homoian theology, but the only scriptural spirit passages recognized as speaking of the Holy Spirit remain those of prophecy and sanctification: "We properly honor the Holy Spirit as teacher, as guide, as enlightener, as sanctifier. We worship Christ as creator."[15] I now turn to what was Augustine's "last Pneumatology," written two years before his death, in response to his debate with the Latin Homoian, Maximinus.

Augustine's full reply to Maximinus comes in the form of the *Answer to Maximinus*, a work in two parts. The starting point for Augustine's Pneumatology is again the question of where does Scripture say that the Holy Spirit adores the Father (see IX). John 14:28 says that the Father is greater than the Son, but no passage says that the Father is greater than the Holy Spirit. The "greater than the Son" passage Augustine elaborates in terms of the Son's Incarnation (Phil 2:5–7), and the fact that the Son's

---

13. There are two schools of thought about the dates of writings by Niceta of Remesciana: A.E. Burns has argued that his writings should be dated in the mid- to late-370s, because they show no awareness of the Apollinarianian controversy; W.A. Patin argued that Niceta's sophisticated Trinitarian theology, especially regarding the Holy Spirit, requires that his writings date from after Constantinople (381), perhaps well after 381. I find Patin's argument circular and side with Burns.

14. *Debate* 15, 20, Teske, *Arianism and Other Heresies*, 214.

15. *Debate* 15.5, Teske, *Arianism and Other Heresies*, 204. The Spirit is honored, Christ is worshipped: "Nos enim spiritum sanctum competenter honoramus ut doctorem, ut ducatorem, ut illuminatorem, ut sanctifi catorem: Christum colimus ut creatorem: patrem cum sincera deuotione adoramus ut auctorem."

relationship to his humanity is different than the Holy Spirit's relationship with the dove or tongues of fire. Augustine then addresses the sense of "one" in, e.g., Deuteronomy 6:4 (see X). Following closely is Augustine's argument from the Holy Spirit's "temple," citing several passages from First Corinthians (see XI).

Augustine's purpose in making the question of *Where, in fact, does Scripture say the Holy Spirit is subject to the Father?* central to his argument is to show that by the rules of Homoian exegesis, Scripture presents a hyper-Pneumatology, that is, a theology in which the Son is subordinated to the Holy Spirit.[16] If, as the Homoians insist, the silence of Scripture is adequate ground for a doctrinal conclusion, then the fact is that Scripture says that the Son obeys and glorifies the Father, but it says nothing about the Spirit obeying and glorifying the Son, or, for that matter, the Father. If taken seriously, the rules of Homoian exegesis actually produce a conclusion opposite to what the Homoians teach. Augustine raises the spectre of hyper-Pneumatology not simply to reduce Homoian doctrine to an absurdity, but also to show that only pro-Nicene theology can read the scriptural texts with the interpretation that corresponds to the doctrine and sense of the church—namely, that the Holy Spirit is not "above" or prior to the Son.

I come now to my last point, and the climax of Augustine's argument for the full divinity of the Holy Spirit; namely, that the Holy Spirit is creator.[17] I have noted that Maximinus refers to John 1:3 to make the point that while Scripture testifies to the Son as creator, it says nothing similar about the Holy Spirit, and from this silence, Maximinus argues, we can conclude that the Holy Spirit did not create. In *Conlatio Maximinus* II, Augustine replies to Maximinus' claim that Scripture nowhere speaks of the Holy Spirit by citing as proof to the contrary, Psalm 32:6 and Psalm 103:29–30:

> By the Word of the Lord the heavens were spread out,
> And by the Spirit of His mouth all their power.

and

> When you send forth thy Spirit, they are created;
> and you renew the face of the ground.

These two passages do, in fact, name the Holy Spirit as creator, Augustine asserts, and he then adds to these references an argument he made previously in *Tr Jo* 99: he cites Luke 1:35 and Matthew 1:18 to the effect that the One who overshadowed Mary was the Holy Spirit and thus Christ's "flesh, which was given for the life of the world, was made through the Holy Spirit."[18] Augustine's pro-Nicene theology—common opera-

---

16. The old concern of Origen echoes here.

17. *Answer to Maximinus* II.XVII.1ff., Teske, *Arianism and Other Heresies*, 294ff.

18. This statement by Augustine implicitly uses anti-Apollinarian exegesis.

tions, common power, common divinity—requires him to insist that the Holy Spirit does everything that Father and Son do.[19]

What adds more interest to Augustine's argument in *Against Maximinus* II that Psalm 33:6 testifies that the Holy Spirit is creator is that Augustine has never before made this argument: *Conlatio Maximio* II is the first (and, sadly, the last) time that Augustine says that Psalm 33:6 identifies the Holy Spirit as creator. There is no mention of Psalm 33 in *De Trinitate*. If one turns to *Sermon* 52, one finds a remarkably weak Pneumatology, for the Holy Spirit is not described as a participant when Augustine speaks of the inseparable operations of the Trinity: even in the account of the overshadowing of Mary there is no mention of the Holy Spirit (52.11).

In *En Ps* 33 (32 LXX) Augustine gives a running elucidation of the psalm.[20] Of 33:6 he says: "'By the Word of the Lord were the heavens made firm': for not by themselves, but 'By the Word of the Lord' were the righteous made strong. 'And all the strength of them by the Breath of His Mouth.' And all their faith by His Holy Spirit." Augustine does recognize that the passage is about the Word and the Holy Spirit, which is an important appreciation. Augustine reads the passage as an account of restoration and not one of creation: the Word makes the righteous strong; the Holy Spirit gives strength to the faith of the righteous. He does not yet recognize the full import of either the statement that the Holy Spirit is creator just as the Father and Son are, or of the testimony Psalm 33 offers in support of that doctrine. The significance of the doctrine that the Holy Spirit is creator too is not simply the commonplace notion that the Creator is God (and vice versa), but the integrity of the argument of "same operation(s) means same power means same nature." If the Holy Spirit does not act with the Father and the Son in creating, then the basic pro-Nicene understanding of (and argument for) "same in essence" is lost.[21]

While I suspect that Niceta was the first Latin pro-Nicene to recognize the significance of Psalm 33:6 for Pneumatology, I think that the source for Augustine's Trinitarian appreciation of the passage is Ambrose.[22] Since I say "source," I mean that I do not believe that Augustine himself discovered (or re-discovered) the importance of Psalm

19. One clear example of the pro-Nicene logic of "common works" supporting a doctrine of the Holy Spirit as creator can be found in *Against the Arian Sermon* XV. Augustine first states that the Father and Son do the same works, and that they do them with the same power. The Spirit of both of them cannot be excluded from their works, and thus the Holy Spirit does the same works with the same power

20. Unfortunately, this psalm was not amongst those Hilary commented upon in his *En. Ps.*

21. In his earlier work against Homoian theology, *Answer to the Arian Sermon*, Augustine strongly emphasizes the doctrine of the inseparable works of the Trinity. See *Answer to the Arian Sermon* I. Ambrose has a similar argument in *On the Holy Spirit* II.v.34: the work of the Holy Spirit is not a "later addition" to the creative work of the Father and Son

22. "For every creature exists both of the will, and through the operation and in the power of the Trinity, as it is written: 'Let Us make man after Our image and likeness;' and elsewhere: 'By the word of the Lord were the heavens established, and all their power by the Spirit of His mouth'" (Ambrose, *On the Holy Spirit* II.ix.100; NPNF II/10, 228)

33:6 for pro-Nicene theology and polemic against the Homoians. Augustine learned the full pneumatological application of Psalm 33:6 from Ambrose, but he only learned of it just before the debate.[23] (Or better, he only made it part of his own Trinitarian theology just before the debate.) For most of his writing career, Augustine did not know this pro-Nicene exegesis, he did not know how much Ambrose (or Niceta) had said about it, and he did not appreciate how important the doctrine of "creator" was for pro-Nicene (and anti-Homoian) Pneumatology. Many of the authorities he would have consulted—Hilary, Gregory of Elvira, not to mention any third-century authors—would have said nothing about this.

Finally, we should note one peculiarity about the presence in Augustine's writings of the doctrine that the Holy Spirit is creator. I have said that in *De Trinitate* and works contemporary to the process of the writing of that volume (e.g., *Sermon* 52, *Tr Jo.* XX, *Against the Arian Sermon*), Augustine does not speak of the Holy Spirit as creator, and then in the writings against Maximinus he does speak of the Holy Spirit as creator. What is peculiar is this: in Augustine's early, anti-Manichaean writings, he does call the Holy Spirit "creator." One of the best examples of Augustine's anti-Manichaean claims for the creator status of the Holy Spirit is in *On True Religion*:

> There is one God: Father, Son and Holy Spirit. When this Trinity is known as far as it can be in this life, it is perceived without the slightest doubt that every creature, intellectual, animal and corporeal, derives such existence as it has from that same creative Trinity, has its own form, and is subject to the most perfect order. It is not as if the Father were understood to have made one part of creation, the Son another, and the Holy Spirit another, but the Father through the Son in the gift of the Holy Spirit together made all things and every particular thing. For every thing, substance, essence or nature, or whatever better word there may be, possesses at once these three qualities: it is a particular thing; it is distinguished from other things by its own proper form; and it does not transgress the order of nature.[24]

Augustine understands, when facing the Manichees, the necessity and even the utility of arguing that the Holy Spirit is creator: the entire Trinity (according to catholic Christian doctrine) must be shown to be creator, and not just one or two Persons.[25]

---

23. As is clear from other of Augustine's writings, the influence of Ambrose was very strong in the last ten years of Augustine's life, stronger than it had ever been. (See, e.g., *Against the Arian Sermon* and *Against Julian*.) My proposal that here, in his last engagement with the Homoians, Augustine understood something new from reading Ambrose fits in with the general hypothesis of Ambrose's late influence. This hypothesis must be joined with the awareness that Augustine's reading of his authorities was not comprehensive or meticulous: he did not "get" all that they were saying, nor did he always desire all that was there as he read.

24. Augustine, *On True Religion*, 7.13 (*Earlier Writings*, 232).

25. Augustine does attend, in his early exegesis of Gen 1:2b, to the question of the Spirit being borne over the waters, but the consequences for his theology of the Holy Spirit are not clear. In *On Genesis Against the Manichees* I(6)12, Augustine says that the "Spirit of God was borne as the will of a

What Augustine evidently did not understand or appreciate, for most of his career, was the necessity and utility of arguing that the Holy Spirit is creator when he confronted the Homoians. Nor did he realize the place Psalm 33 played in pro-Nicene Pneumatology. These are lessons late learned.

---

craftsman is borne over things to be crafted." See I(5)8 for the beginning of this treatment. The difficulty is that Augustine says nothing that positively identifies this "Spirit if God" as the Holy Spirit, the Third Person of the Trinity. If Augustine is making points against the Manichees, they are very subtle points, indeed. In *Unfinished Literal Commentary on Genesis* 16–17, which treats Gen 1:2b, Augustine starts with the "will of a craftsman" language he had earlier used, but then he addresses the question directly: What does "spirit" mean here? It could mean "created vitality," a kind of Stoic *pneuma*. The last alternative Augustine considers is that spirit here means "air." Twice Augustine compares the hypothetical sense with the possibility that the Spirit over the water is the Holy Spirit, which is probably the means by which he tips his hand. Finally, in *Literal Meaning of Genesis* I (6)12 Augustine identifies the Spirit of Gen 1:2b with the Third Person of the Trinity, but in the discussion that follows (to I (8)14) "Spirit of God" seems to revert to meaning "God." If it does mean Holy Spirit after all, then once again Augustine has not made this identification strongly

Chapter 13

Ebion at the Barricades

Moral Narrative and Post-Christian Catholic Theology

The veiled goddess before which we on both sides bend our knees is the moral law in us in its invulnerable majesty. We certainly perceive its voice, and we understand very clearly its commandments.

—IMMANUEL KANT

The knowledge of good and evil seems to be the aim of all ethical reflection. The first task of Christian ethics is to invalidate this knowledge.

—DIETRICH BONHOEFFER

You can offer to the righteous all the good that you have won,

But down here among the unclean, all your good just comes undone, Your good just comes undone.

—LYLE LOVETT

INTRODUCTION: "YOU CANNOT BE NEUTRAL AND BE CHRISTIAN"

THERE ARE MANY POSSIBLE meanings intended in this statement on the lawn sign outside a church near my home. It can be intended to refer to prisons at Guantanamo Bay or to the war in Afghanistan; it can be an exhortation to be "for" something or to be "against" something. I am sure that this imperative is not intended to contradict another, more frequently posted statement: "Everyone is welcome." Or perhaps there is a contradiction, but unobserved and unacknowledged because the two statements never occupy the lawn sign at the same time, and memory is no longer a virtue that Christians cultivate. Some Catholic communities have, for example, gone effortlessly from saying, "'Catholic' means 'everyone,'" to saying, "Not him, not here." In the context of my own experience, I am brought to this theological judgment: the first task of any scripturally-based soteriology is to ask the question, How will our knowledge of good and evil be overcome? How is this, the first temptation to sin, and the first consequence of the fall, overcome in Christ?

When I first began teaching at a religiously-affiliated college, I occasionally would offer what I knew was a startling suggestion, the kind of comment an undergraduate teacher sometimes makes to prompt a discussion. I would suggest that given the failure of moral insight evidenced by the Church in the last two or so centuries (but especially in the twentieth century), perhaps the Church ought to call a moratorium on its moral claims, and back off to think things through and rework the basics. Perhaps for a decade, perhaps for a century, Christianity ought to quiet its collective moral voice, in embarrassed if not shameful recognition of the many failures of that voice. After one says enough wrong things, the time comes to be quiet. My suggestion arose far from any intention of a thought experiment that would lead to a tacit endorsement of relativism.[1]

The acts by "corporate" Christianity that my students thought de-legitimized the moral authority of any church were of the sort reported and discussed on CNN and "portrayed" in films. The flaw that I thought most greatly de-legitimized modern Christian theology was the intellectual and moral respect it continued to show modern atheism long after the twentieth century had revealed—and continued to reveal—the violence beating in the heart of programmatic atheism. Was there anything in programmatic atheism's creatures—National Socialism, Marxist Communism, and Scientificism—that had not revealed itself as tyrannical and vicious? And yet Christian theologians continued to treat atheism with intellectual respect, as if programmatic atheists were modern versions of freethinkers in French *salons* (like, e.g., Voltaire). The fact that modern atheism had clearly revealed itself to have more in common with Jean-Paul Marat than with Voltaire was ignored: judgment was never passed.[2] The myth of self-definition of atheist thinkers was taken at face value: each such intellectual was treated as *sui generis*—a philosophical freelancer,

1. Relativism among the young is genuine: it arises out of adolescent confusion, exacerbated by consumerism and by the de-ontologizing of the photographic image. (No one reads André Bazin anymore.) "Relativism" among the not-young is simply a rhetorical strategy, a cover story.

2. A recent, and egregious, example of an atheist (self-proclaimed, in this case) failing to recognize the post-twentieth century burden of programmatic atheism can be found in "Ethics of Being a Theologian," *Chronicle of Higher Education* (July 27, 2009), in which K.L. Noll proposes vivisection as a paradigm for "advancing knowledge." After the twentieth century, the only moral stance an atheist can have—and he or she must have it loudly—is to condemn any kind of methodological link between taking the organs out of a living creature until it dies and "advancing knowledge." The connection between programmatic atheism and this kind of "advancing knowledge" is too strong, and too recent, for atheists to think that they can get away with talking this way *again*.

with no history that needed to be acknowledged and repented of.[3] While even the most independent of any free church Christianity, traditionally anti-Catholic and thus rejecting the history of Christianity prior to the 1860s, was nonetheless regarded as implicated in century-old "crimes of Christianity" and denied any status of "freelancing," atheism was a moral blank slate that could be, and had to be, taken seriously and respected: any atheist had no history that needed to be accounted for. In my eyes, the credentialing of programmatic atheism was a deep moral and intellectual failure by modern theologians.[4]

It was "conservative" Christians who first objected to my hypothesis that the moral failure of the Church should lead it to be silent on moral questions. The Church had certain obligations to make judgments and to speak up about matters of sexuality, for example, and about the rights of the unborn in the face of their murder. However, as the discussion continued the outrage shifted its center: eventually, it was the leftist Christians, "progressives," that were most outraged with this suggested silencing of the Church's moral voice. The Church had an obligation (then) to speak against the deployment of medium-range nuclear-armed missiles in NATO; an obligation to speak against the continued existence of tyrannical regimes in Central America (and to denounce support for those regimes); and an obligation to support economic, racial, and sexual social justice, and to enact a "preferential option for the poor." A morally silent Christianity, a Christianity that did not, could not, judge (which meant *accuse*), was a contradiction in terms. Class discussions could become quite energetic.[5]

3. Because the programmatic atheism of Nazi Germany occurred in a country that was historically Christian, it seemed as though Germany had to apologize and atone for its violence. Russia, by then a self-declared "post-Christian" country, did not need to apologize or atone: it was sheltered by its ideological cloak of programmatic atheism. Japan could not be said to be culturally atheist, but it was culturally anti-Christian, and that sufficed. The non-Christian past of Japan removed expectation that it should apologize and atone for its violence—and so it never has.

4. The consistent historical result of programmatic atheism has been to raise the bar for what qualifies someone as a human person. Modern Christians still have problems facing the depth of their twentieth-century intellectual and emotional entanglement with programmatic atheism. One important reason for this is that during the 1930s, Christian theologians saw that they had common cause with National Socialism and Marxist–Leninism: like these two programmatically atheist ideologies, Christian theologians were anti-capitalist and anti-bourgeois; and like these two quintessentially Enlightenment ideologies, Christian theologians criticized Liberalism. The last fatal attraction these ideologies held for Christian theologians perhaps produced the deepest seduction in modern Christianity: *communio*. Christian intellectuals as varied as Tillich and Pieper, for example, admired Nazi ideology for the emphasis it placed on providing a true community: if the State was necessarily the basis for a new real community, then so be it. It is difficult to know just how far European Christian intellectuals would have gone with National Socialism if the Night of the Long Knives had not occurred and momentarily interrupted theology's co-dependency. Power, Henry Kissinger once said, is the strongest aphrodisiac, and after the war, when the bruises faded, churches forgave and came back. The thrill was not gone.

5. Obviously the list of left-wing sensitivities I've just paraded locates the time I am here remembering as that of the 1980s, but I would argue that the time and the list have a broader significance than just my own autobiographical history. These cases are still important because they represent the coming-of-age issues for a host of European (especially British) Anglican and Catholic liberal theologians; these constitute the defining milieu for a generation of Christian theologians who are now

What struck me during these discussions was not simply the shift in those Christians who felt the most attached to a morally proactive Church, the shift from right to left, but that many of those (of whatever political persuasion) were outraged by my proposal because it left them with a Christianity lacking any recognizable content. If Christianity was not a moral system embracing some actions and denouncing others, it was nothing. Whether the denunciation was of gays or nukes was not as striking as the fact that many Christians did not simply value the religious capacity to make moral judgments, they *identified* this capacity with what "religion" meant. The denouement of this revelation came in another undergraduate class at another university, in which I assigned the Russian classic of spirituality, *The Way of a Pilgrim*. A number of the students felt that the pilgrim could not be Christian at all because he wanted to live in solitude. When I responded that perhaps one might have a relationship with God that was not necessarily routed through people, that is, a personal relationship with God directly and not only through one's "neighbor," these students recognized such a possibly as "psychotic." Everyone on both sides of the political aisle seemed to assume that Christian attention belonged on the "practical" and on the narrative of Christ's *ministry,* and to view the idea that "contemplation of the divine was the goal and root of theology" as virtually anti-Christian.[6] This assumption and this view together constitute a fundamental judgment of modern Christianity (*qua* modern).[7]

My students' reactions can, in one sense, be easily explained: they were taught to have this understanding of Christianity—by the Church itself through its catechetical instruments. If the Church were herself ever vague on the priority of the ethical in Christian (specifically, Catholic) identity, then theologians, professors, teachers, and instructors filled that vagueness with their own content. Now we have perhaps two full generations of Catholics who have been taught that Christianity is a kind

---

active authors and parts of academic and ecclesiastical establishments, not to mention archbishops of Canterbury. There is much more to the relationship in theology between the 70s and the 90s than Lampe's 1977 *God as Spirit* and Haight's 1992 "Spirit Christology." The years between 1975 and 1985 (loosely speaking) were the years in which the now-reigning politico-moral narratives were institutionalized. During these years, the narratives were not first articulated, or even first rallied around. From 1975 to 1985, the now-reigning politico-religious narratives took concrete social forms so that they were no longer simply the content of a particular discourse; they were the shape within which discourse took place, either externally (in academia or church) or internally (as presumed metanarratives and "horizons" of thought). If my generation constantly relives the politico-moral dramas of the 60s (e.g., the Vietnam War) that is so not because of clergy, academics, and politicians who held their offices in 1968, but because of people who began to hold those offices between 1975 and 1985. The "institutionalized" character of such politico-moral narratives must never be underestimated, for they are, in this, every bit as reified as the stones, concrete, and bricks of the institutions they live in: they are thoughts and feelings frozen in time, each year made more dense by the hypothermia of *power*.

6. Ayres, "Against Hegel, Fire and Sword," in *Nicaea and Its Legacy*, 384–429.

7. It will become clear that I am using the word "modern" in two distinct senses: one sense is the chronological, and in that capacity names an era of time which while recognizable nonetheless has only vaguely determined boundaries; the second sense of "modern" is as a genre of thought which can be distinguished from other genres of thought which are somehow "non-modern" (e.g., pre-modern, postmodern, whatever).

of morality, or a kind of moral "openness" (to a secular closure).[8] The present article develops primarily out of a concern for the way modern Christian understandings of evil express and support this fundamental judgment; namely, that the cause of evil can be truly identified.[9] The narrative of why we ought to judge casts *moral judgment* as the expression of each individual's knowledge of good and evil, a knowledge revealed in conscience, spirit, reason, or sincerity. This narrative is thus the source of the problem of Christian moral judgment.[10] My secondary concern (which comes first in my exposition) is for the way modern Christian understandings of the *meaning* of pre-modern Christianity are taken as prolegomena to and justification for the fundamental judgment that Christian attention belongs on the "practical" and on the narrative of Christ's ministry, and rejects the idea that contemplation of the divine is the goal and root of theology.[11]

8. Just as the dog that did not bark is sometimes more significant than the dog that does, what failed to happen can sometimes be as provocative as what does. World War I ended, in American Protestantism, the social optimism that had reigned previously. After World War I, an eschatology of postmillenialism (in which Christians would present to the returning Christ a world that was the kingdom of God) lost all credibility, and was replaced by a premillenialism, in which the arrival of Christ was necessary for the reordering of this world. In a different way, some European Protestants experienced this same seismic shift: Barth may be understood as rejecting the old Liberal Protestant understanding of Divine Providence. Strangely, although Roman Catholicism, being so centered in Europe at the time, suffered more severely from the violence of the Great War than did American Protestantism, there was no Catholic stepping back from social optimism. We still sing "Building the City of God"—and without any sense of irony. The revelation that was the First World War, which was repeated, for the slow-minded, in the Second World War, was the botttomlessness of moral depravity that individual humans, and their social institutions, were capable of. Not only was "progress" revealed to be a fiction, it was revealed to be an evil lie, for it was the notion of "progress" that directed and fueled the worst atrocities of the European wars. It can be imagined that the war(s) could have provoked the return of invigorated Augustinianism, like, e.g., the kind shut down in the seventeenth century (see Kolakowski, *God Owes Us Nothing* [Chicago, IL: University of Chicago Press, 1995]). This did not happen. The self-satisfied optimism of scholasticism reigned without interruption, until it was replaced by an even stronger optimism with greater powers of self-satisfaction. ("Self-satisfied" means this: that the achievement of the "optimistic" goals is measured by the degree to which, within a closed circle of discourse, these goals can seem to be, or can be spoken about as if they are, fulfilled. This "self-satisfied" optimism seeks a social mirror in which it can see itself acknowledging the good.)

9. Whenever I speak of the idea that "the cause of evil can be truly identified" or "can be known" I mean this: the idea that by some form of rational analysis the cause of evil (however it is defined according to axioms of the analysis) can be known to the degree that the cause can be eliminated and evil (as defined) ceases to exist (or to be "practiced"). Some low church Protestants might call this idea "pre-dispensationalism": by doing so, they accurately identify the social environment that supports this idea as well as the events which destroyed its credibility for a great number of Christians.

10. The "problem" of Christian moral judgment is the problem of our knowledge of good and evil gained and maintained as an independence from God.

11. In *Ethics*, (New York, NY: Simon & Schuster, 1949; 1995), 81, Dietrich Bonhoeffer criticizes the moral claims by theologies of social or practical Christianity by pointing out that there is no evidence that this kind of Christianity is more effective than dogmatic Christianity in bringing about any desired cultural change. (It would be next to impossible to judge the "transformative" effects of dogmatic Christianity working from the perspective of modern theology, since all the dominant metanarratives in theology assume the inefficacy of dogmatic Christianity and the unique effectiveness of social Christianity.) Certainly one of the strongest and most widespread examples of Christianity having a

My task in this article is to explore the question of the "place" of moral questions—questions of good and evil—in Christian faith, "faith" here being considered particularly as the content or narrative of belief. The thesis I will argue is that Christianity offers no substantial account or explanation of the origin(s) and nature of evil, that in a fundamental way Christianity is not concerned with offering such accounts, and that when the task of supplying accounts of the origin(s) and nature of evil is made central to the content or narrative of Christian faith that faith is made false: it is misunderstood.[12] To use historical language to restate my thesis, I will argue that "catholic" or "orthodox" Christianity is distinguished precisely by a refusal to treat the questions of the origin and nature of evil as fundamental to the faith. I will argue that the way moderns read pre-modern texts excludes most of what could be regarded as "tradition"—especially that of doctrine. This exclusion has resulted in a misrepresentation of Christian faith by eliminating the full narrative which expresses the content of the faith and which provides the basis by which select components of—or *moments in*—Christian faith are correctly understood. The misrepresentation of Christian faith identifies moral judgment based upon an account of the nature and origin of evil as decisive for and fundamental to the faith. The modern hermeneutical conclusion that the only continuing content of pre-modern texts into the modern world is their moral content colludes with the modern abandonment of doctrine as a fundamental and enduring element in Christian faith.[13] By contrast, for the purposes of this article what

---

substantial and long-term "transformative" effect upon Western secular culture is the one that G.E.M. Anscombe describes in her influential essay, "Modern Moral Philosophy"; namely, a sense of moral *obligation*, a sense originally developed in Christian doctrine. Anscombe's point is that the Western sense of moral obligation is in fact an intellectual gift of Christianity, and she makes the provocative point that since the justifying intellectual superstructure of dogmatic Christianity no longer holds in the culture that prizes the concept of moral obligation, then it has to be set aside: "[T]he concepts of obligation, and duty—*moral* obligation and *moral* duty, that is to say—and of what is *morally* right and wrong, and of the *moral* sense of 'ought,' ought to be jettisoned if this is psychologically possible; because they are survivals, or derivatives from survivals, from an earlier conception of ethics which no longer survives, and is only harmful without it." The essay was originally published in *Philosophy* 33 (1958). I quote from the essay's publication in *Collected Philosophical Papersof G. E. M. Anscombe, Volume Three: Ethics, Religion and Politics* (Minneapolis, MN: University of Minnesota Press, 1981), 26–42; here 26. What Bonhoeffer and Anscombe, a devout Catholic, have in common as Christians reflecting upon moral thought is that they both critique the modern project of "ethics," a project in which post-dogmatic theology participates, and with which post-Christian Catholic theology identifies.

12. Something very similar to this thesis, but one which produces a very different judgment about the significance and credibility of Christianity, may be found in Bart D. Ehrman, *God's Problem: How the Bible Fails to Answer Our Most Important Question—Why We Suffer* (New York, NY: HarperOne, 2008). What Ehrman brings forward as his "discovery" (i.e., that the Bible does not explain suffering), I suggest has been in plain sight in Christian theology since the beginning. The presuppositions in a strong, or at least loud, narrative can hide the obvious, however.

13. Noll gives examples in his article of atheist presuppositions in religious studies methodology that he claims "theologians" are incapable of accepting. (These examples must be fantasies—from Noll's own perspective—because he offers them without any of the "scientific" proofs he advocates as necessary for the advancement of knowledge.) Noll is mistaken, because some "theologians" can and do accept the fundamental presuppositions that an atheist like Noll requires. Noll thinks that

I am calling the "full narrative" is identified with the *regula fidei*, the creed, and with doctrinal assertions.[14]

Christianity does indeed make judgments about practice, exhorting some and damning others; the primitive "two ways" catechisms of the *Didache* and the *Epistle of Barnabas* are obvious witnesses to this fact. But the justification for such exhortations and condemnations remains in terms of the relationship between each of these two ways (or types of practice) and God. To do good is to walk towards (or with) God; to do evil is to walk away from (or without) God. What makes some actions good or evil is comprehensible only by referring the object to God: to be with God is virtue, to be without God is evil. This reality can be understood only as a result of understanding how it is that humans understand God; for the Christian, this means recognizing the decisive revelatory moment of the Incarnation, and how that moment relates to our condition (*geworfenheit*, "life in the diastemic mode"). The technical term for this human understanding of God is "wisdom."

The problem, then, comes down to this: if indeed it is true that Christianity has no proper explanation for evil, then to make such a proper explanation to evil central to Christian self-consciousness and self-definition requires two moves: misrepresenting the content and character of Christianity; and subordinating the content of Christianity to some other narrative which does have a "proper explanation for evil," such that Christianity receives this proper explanation to fill its own lack. My first task, then, is to locate the place of moral concerns within modern theology and to show how the content of Christian belief has been subordinated to—identified with—identifying and solving the problem of evil in the world. Such a task is diagnostic in nature, for it seeks to explain the "symptoms" evidenced in my stories (above) of a popular understanding of Christianity and faith. After the statement of a diagnosis, I will turn to more remedial tasks, which include recounting the way(s) "full narrative" Christianity describes evil. The last section of this article turns to Augustine for his understanding of the way doctrine grounds (and must precede) Christian reflection

---

"theologians"—by virtue of being "theologians"—regard as "reductionistic" the thesis that the effects of rituals are limited to creating a sense of community, maintaining identity boundaries, and defeating inclinations to pursue heterodox behaviors. On the contrary, there are a number of theologians who think that this is precisely and exclusively what rituals do—which is why, for example, rituals can be changed simply to meet newly judged social needs. Noll also thinks that theologians ought to declare to congregations (it is Noll who links theologians to churches) that "the god described in this sacred text [the Bible] is fictional, and any resemblance to an actual god is purely coincidental." Again, Noll is ignorant of the fact that there are theologians who teach exactly this. If we change Noll's thesis to "the god described in this sacred text is fictional, and any resemblance to an actual god is that of the logic of ideas" the number of theologians who would agree increases exponentially. See K. L. Noll's article, "Ethics of Being a Theologian."

14. In several ways, my thesis has much in common with the judgment of Dietrich Bonhoeffer in *Creation and Fall—Temptation: Two Biblical Studies* (1959; New York, NY: MacMillan, 1967), 72–76, "The Fall," among other of his writings. What I call the "larger narrative" is, in Bonhoeffer's account, the "overcoming of evil on the Cross" (*Creation and Fall*, 76). The question of the origin of evil, its aetiology, is "not a theological question" at all, according to Bonhoeffer—I agree.

on the problem of evil. The reader must keep in mind that the modern theology I am concerned with here is principally modern Roman Catholic theology in its academic setting. To make such a statement does not mean I will have nothing to say about Protestant theology, for it is a feature of modern Catholic theology that formally it shapes its methods upon Protestant theology, and that materially it borrows heavily from Protestant theology.

A POSTMODERN CATHOLIC LOOKS AT OUTDATED LIBERALISM

The best way to define the fundamental rhetorical purpose of modern Catholic systematic theology is "The attempt to articulate Christianity in terms and concepts which non-believing intellectual elites can find reasonable." Or more practically, "To talk to the establishment of non-believing intelligentsia in terms which they can credit, understand, and find respectable." Speculative theology has rejected Scripture as an intellectual idiom due to both purposes: against the first purpose, Scripture is seen both as particularist ("triumphalist") and simple or anachronistic, and thus offensive and off-bounds for modern theology; against the second purpose, the "conception of . . . Scripture as intended to draw Christians towards contemplation" of God is held suspect by modern theology.[15]

In the twentieth century, a counter-argument was made by what we might call the trajectory of Henri de Lubac; namely that, as Thomas says, Scripture was theology and vice versa: no theology could speak or reflect without using biblical idioms. Rahner could hardly accept that argument, but his students developed a strategy that defanged the Lubac trajectory: speculative theology was indeed to be articulated in scriptural idiom, but it was a Scripture that was demythologized, in which the text was suggestive but not literally true. Properly demythologized, the scriptural idioms could be preserved and contemporary theology articulated in many familiar terms whose meaning had been transposed into a more modern—i.e., "reasonable"—field. Bultmann, for example, gave systematicians an understanding which allowed for the use of Scripture to articulate modern theology. By this understanding, the Christian story—the Gospel(s), especially—is a drama of Spirit seeking greater consciousness and revealing itself as what it is. The Gospel is about—and *only* truly about—Spirit. The "low" or "ascending" Christologies of the Synoptics are apt stories of the struggle of Geist's self-realization, while the "high" or "descending" Christology of John is the story of Geist's initiative in the process of self-realization. The "Resurrection" is a moment in Spirit's self-understanding, and has nothing to do with the body except insofar as the body leaves a trace memory upon spirit. Resurrection occurs not because one is saved but because one is spirit. The call to recognize change within spirit as the realm in which the Christian faith acts is well expressed in logion 50–51 of the

---

15. Ayres, *Nicaea and Its Legacy*, 389.

Gospel of Thomas: "His disciples said to him: 'When will the repose of the dead occur? And when will the new cosmos come?' He said to them: 'This thing which you expect has come, but you do not recognize it.'" This metaphysic leads us to a proper understanding of the tension between the "already—but not yet" eschatologies of the Gospels: transformation has already occurred in Spirit, but not all spirits recognize the realized transformation that occurs outside empirical history. Some Christians, like the mystified disciples in logion 50–51 still look to a historical, empirical eschatology. However, the things the disciples hope for (to stay with the logion a moment longer) have indeed already happened in the realm of spirit; they are anthropological realities. The foolish, unfortunately, still seek to find them among the bodies, that is, as a historical event. Those who cling to history are the dead burying the dead.

The theology of Geist metaphysic identifies the real as what happens in the realm of spirit (Spirit). Christianity cannot rest its claim upon any historical, "positivist," claims because—it is argued—everything from the Virgin Birth to the empty tomb lacks the possibility of empirical verification and, moreover, runs counter to our normal material expectations; thus we are left only with the possibility of logical verification. ("Logic" in a Hegelian sense of the word.) The argument runs like this: (1) empirical verification is a science with real rules and true judgments; (2) most religious events are not verifiable under those rules and in those judgments; and (3) this is not a bad thing, because we really want to talk about something Super-real, i.e., outside the realm of empirical history. The first two points can be used to stop any tendency among those who might want to take empirical history as fundamental (the new "fundamentalists"), for history is, as has already been noted, particularist and therefore triumphalist, and that is bad. The Super-real is neither: it is perfectly general and universal; it is transcendental. Looking forward to what I will say about the modern Catholic systematic tendency to reduce problems of epistemology to their social basis, it might seem as though an emphasis on Geist is antithetic to such materialism and that the two cannot coexist in the same school of thought. In fact, however, the coexistence of a Geist "metaphysics" and epistemological materialism is a profound feature of one influential form of philosophy in the twentieth century, left-wing Hegelianism. It is left-wing Hegelianism that has been, in the twentieth century, both the dominant form of Hegelianism and the most intellectually credible form of Marxism.[16]

One peculiar feature of modern theological statements about the limits imposed upon theologumena by the "rules of science" cannot be passed over and needs to be noted. The truth claims made for the rules and judgments of science allow the above argument(s) to be presented as though it were a statement made within the

16. The most important philosopher of left-wing Hegelianism was the Paris-based Jean Hippolyte, whose translated writings include: *Genesis and Structure of Hegel's Phenomenology of Spirit*, Samuel Cherniak and John Heckman, trans., (Evanston, IL: Northwestern University Press, 1974); *Logic and Existence*, Lawrence Taylor and Amit Sen, trans., (Albany, NY: State University of New York Press, 1997); *and Studies on Marx and Hegel*, John O'Neill, ed. and trans., (New York, NY: Harper Torchbooks, 1969).

realm of scholarly or academic discourse. But scholarly discourse is characterized by authentication, and by that I do not mean experimentation but credentialing. In an academic institution, a serious question about biochemistry is asked of a biochemist—not because one expects that the biochemist has performed some experimental verification, but because the biochemist has apprenticed to the body of knowledge called biochemistry: she or he has a PhD in biochemistry. For exactly the same reason, any statement by a biochemist on the historical fact of Shakespeare's Catholicism or the difference between Ionic and Attic aorist declensions would not be regarded as scholarly. Theologians with a PhD in theology can speak in a scholarly way about the field of theology, but any statement about the integrity of scientific method or about how much of what happens in the empirical world is verifiable by scientific means must necessarily be nothing more than amateur enthusiasm, even if those statements happen to travel within scholarly discourses on theology. The validity of this criticism is implicitly acknowledged in one important way: modern theology based upon Geist metaphysic proceeds from the presupposition that there is no credentialed discourse that has the specific authority to speak about spirit because spirit is experienced within the act of living and not through the means of any specialized method or technique. In contemporary theology, *being alive* is the authenticating criterion that allows a theologian to speak about Geist. Just as Kant's limitations on what religion can know are bracketed off, so are any claims by academic science: spirit is the precondition of consciousness, and reflecting upon our spirits, we are in truth seeing through to Spirit.

A final observation can be offered on Geist metaphysics and modern theology: the debt to Geist metaphysics is not always clear in modern theologies because systematicians interweave different narratives with no sense of the contradictions between these narratives and their different historical genealogies. Philosophies are treated as though their constitutive concepts are modular and parts can be mixed and matched freely at the initiative of the theologian. Moreover, the discipline as a whole has opted for a form of discourse that does not own up to its allegiances and feels no need or obligation to do so. Even where one might expect a clear choice to be made—Kant *or* Hegel?—the boundaries between the alternatives are dissolved in the vehicle of appropriation, for both Hegel and Kant are mediated to moderns via themes of German idealism. There are systematicians who demand metaphysics (e.g., Karl Rahner), and systematicians who declare themselves free of it (e.g., Jürgen Moltmann), but the difference between the two kinds lies primarily in the fact that the second group has given up acknowledging what it is doing.

THE ETHICAL FOUNDATIONS OF POST-
CHRISTIAN ROMAN CATHOLIC THEOLOGY[17]

In modern theology there is an understanding that some cultural event or moment has occurred which divides Western history into two unequal eras or epochs: these two eras or epochs may be called the pre-modern and the modern. This understanding belongs to more than just modern theology, and in modern theology itself this understanding is derived from a host of influences. The momentous event that divides history is, for modern theology, best articulated and explained in the language of modern philosophy (especially some hermeneutical theory) while at the same time the movement from one era to another is thought to be reflected best in "science." For such moderns, this epoch-making event is adequately captioned by the title "the Enlightenment." The result of this epoch-making event is that all pre-modern "texts" (including events, symbols, expressions of self-consciousness and self-definitions: so, "artifacts") no longer hold any intrinsic or self-evident significance for "readers" on the other side of that epoch-making moment, i.e., moderns. Pre-modern texts are now blank slates. (The "monuments" have been sand-blasted.) Whatever significance pre-modern texts may continue to occasion for modern consciousness results from the projection of modern meaning back onto these texts: the significance of pre-modern artifacts occurs exclusively insofar as they function as screens onto which modern meaning is projected. A modern judgment to preserve a pre-modern text-artifact is always utilitarian to the extent that preservation depends directly upon the text-artifact's suitability as a screen for modern meaning (and modern meaning-making). It is worth noting here, even if in passing, that a seemingly obvious question which does *not* get asked is "How do we distinguish this hypothetically *progressive* meaning-loss and the accompanying text-artifact destruction from *repression*, which, after all, manifests itself in precisely the same processes of epoch-centered meaning-loss and text-artifact destruction?"[18]

For such modern theologians who are Roman Catholic, even if only professionally or as a job description, the greatness of any given modern theologian is to be found in the programmatic skill with which that theologian handles pre-modern text-artifacts (e.g., Scripture, liturgy, the Creed of 381), projecting modern significance onto pre-modern screens without—as it were—"breaking" those artifacts. From this

17. To remove any ambiguity in terminology: "post-Christian" does not mean "in the context of Christianity"; it means "after Christianity is done" or "without Christianity."

18. I mean "repression" here in both its psychological and political senses. As an example, one thinks of the history of the monastery of Mt. St. Michel in northern France. As any tourist can see, the interior walls are bare, without any trace of murals or tapestries. This barrenness owes to the French Revolution, when the monastery was seized, all religious art and artifacts destroyed, and the building turned into a political prison to hold enemies of the Revolution. (A better metaphor for the French Revolution would be hard to invent.) For a working-through of the telling absence of the question—distinguishing repression from progress—in other aspects of modern culture, see the first two chapters of Russell Jacoby's *Social Amnesia* (Boston, MA: Beacon Press, 1975).

perspective, the master modern Catholic theologian is often thought to be Karl Rahner. However, the need to handle pre-modern text-artifacts among modern Catholic theologians is itself transitional for modern theology, and as the project of "enacting the modern" (i.e., declaring the limits of the continuity of meaning) progresses, Catholic theologians have lost the imperative to handle-without-breaking (or in Catholic systematic jargon, "preserve") the text-artifacts.[19] As this imperative fades away, modern Catholic theologians are seen to become more like modern (i.e., liberal or "progressive") Protestant theologians in the casuistry they employ to justify the loss of traditional Christian text-artifacts. However, it is important to say clearly that there are really two "moderns" or modernities in contemporary theology. The "First Modernity" of theology regards the cultural events of the last four hundred years as decisive for defining authentic content and method in theology and religion. The "Second Modernity" of theology regards the cultural events of the twentieth century as decisive for the same definitions.[20] The first of these eras or patterns of thought is largely identical with the cultural forms (here, particularly, forms of thought) associated with the Enlightenment. If the first moment of this era is not quite agreed upon (does it "begin" with, e.g., Bacon or Descartes?), the dissolution of this modernity may safely be said to have begun in the twentieth century, most clearly after the Second World War. It is in fact the pulling away of the second of these modernities from the first which makes the identity and limits of the "First Modern" clear, for while there is a fundamental commonality between the two moderns, there is also a distinction between them—a distinction which sometimes grows into a tension between the two.[21] First Modern Catholic theologians pride themselves on their ability to handle pre-modern text-artifacts; Second Modern Catholic theologians are clear that the status of such text-artifacts as screens for meaning-projection is entirely accidental.[22]

19. In this context, a "broken" text-artifact is one whose integrity is so degraded by circumstances that it can no longer act as a screen for the projection of modern significance.

20. I understand that my readers probably expect a description of these types of "modern" theologies by referring one or both to "postmodernism." However, I have observed in the humanities generally that the term "postmodern" is used as an ideological marker in myths of self-definition. Both theology and religious studies present strong examples of ideological identities being read onto the term. My terms "First" and "Second" Moderns step outside the burdens of myths of self-definition. The reader is free to link my use of "moderns" with their own understanding of "postmodern" as she or he pleases.

21. Second Moderns tend to think that the time of metaphysics is long passed—and here Kant counts as "metaphysics"—and that theology now has to be constructed upon this new "fact." Unfortunately, the theologians who most fervently announce the death of metaphysics are almost always people with no scholarly authority or credibility in the field of philosophy. It is one thing to build a theology on a hypothesis—e.g., "this theology will be articulated *as if* metaphysics were dead"—but it is something quite different to base one's theology upon one's own impersonation of a philosopher. The proper question to ask whenever judgments about philosophy are integral to a theology are mooted is, "Why should I value your opinion on the field of philosophy?"

22. The "accidental" character of text-artifacts in the theology of "Second Modern" Catholics corresponds to the attack on individuality that Dietrich Bonhoeffer attributes to what he calls "docetetic Christology" in *Christ the Center* (New York, NY: HarperCollins, 1966, 1978), 76–79. My category of "Ebionite" does not correspond with his, but I have no quarrel with his analysis.

For example, First Modern theology typically justifies Christian pluralism of doctrine and method by adopting a modern thesis like Walter Bauer's, that Christianity *originally* was pluralistic in its expression and content. This judgment appeals to a logic still theological in character. Second Modern theology typically justifies pluralism in doctrine and method by appealing to an understanding of anthropological realities, i.e., the manifest diversity of human nature. This line of thought is no longer based upon a theological logic.[23] Politically, these two modernities coexist as factions in a common "party," as it were, but the academic ascendancy of Second Modernity has seen the bracketing off of the history and content of First Modernity. The heart of First Modern theology, the years 1550 to 1950, has been relegated to what one scholar has called "The New Dark Ages."[24] This bracketing-off has occurred for what must be considered—from the perspective of the logic of Second Modern theology—a legitimate reason: First Modern theology, like the Enlightenment form of thought that supports it, is in fact too much like the pre-modern theology and general form of thought it ostensibly intended to replace. The commonality between pre-modern and First Modern theologies can be dramatized in the common existence of a "scholasticism" or manualism in both. In terms of affect, First Modern theology draws upon and projects "universal" feelings; Second Modern theology draws upon and projects "contextual" anger. The affect of pre-modern theology was (for lack of a better word) "worship," that is, an emotion combining delight and sadness in a variety of mixtures. Postmodern theology—not "spun" Second Modern theology—will, I think, draw heavily upon sadness, since both forms of modern theologies have worked so hard at expelling sadness from Christian self-consciousness.[25] (How many congregations singing "On Eagle's Wings" realize it is a Christological hymn and not a hymn about the believer? It is this latter common misunderstanding that makes it so popular for funerals.)

23. An *argument* for Christian pluralism based upon a Bauer-like understanding of early Christianity does not in itself indicate a First Modern theology at work, as the rhetoric of First Modern can be utilized to produce a Second Modern result.

24. The state of primary and secondary material on European Catholic theology and identity in the second half of the nineteenth century is now so poor that any attempt to give an account of this era runs a profound risk of simply being co-opted into the drama of Catholic systematics' hyper-sentimental attachment to the modernist crisis: it is still very much a part of Catholic systematics' melodrama that one wraps one's self in the flag of modernism and that one be on the "right side" of the modernist crisis. Christian systematians who are not Catholic can hardly imagine the passion that burns in the heart of those Catholics for whom the Vatican's failure in the "crisis" was a moral failure second only to its complicity with the Nazis.

25. I will say more about this in a forthcoming essay, "The End of 'Communio': Towards a Preferential Option for the Mortal." I will add this further point to what I have said above: just as the doctrines of Second Modern theology cannot coexist with those of patristic theology, so too the affect (anger) of Second Modern theology cannot coexist with the dominant affect in patristic theology. You cannot "do," think, or receive patristic theology (and its doctrines) from within Second Modern theology. This is why those with a Second Modern theology do the early church with socio-political or critical anthropological methodologies: the theology of the early church is, *qua* theology, not simply empty and meaningless: it is the butt of cleverness.

For what I am calling the Second Modern generation of Catholic systematicians, the delicate job performed by, e.g., Rahner is respected for its pivotal contribution to the continuing project of enacting the modern,[26] although for this second generation of Catholic systematicians[27] it is clear that the time for such a contribution has substantially passed. In the judgment of this second generation of Catholic theologians (among others), what properly answers to the title "postmodern" is that contemporary thought which begins with the assumption that the significance of pre-modern artifacts occurs exclusively insofar as they function as screens onto which meaning is projected. For Second Moderns, modern thought is understood to have resisted the teleological presuppositions characteristic of pre-modernity by taking on the notion of "objectivity"—just as, according to Harnack, early Christianity inoculated itself against *radical* hellenization by taking on *chronic* hellenization.[28] Second Modernism thus aims to finish the reform of modern consciousness by stripping away the no-longer-needed remedial attachment to the myth of objectivity—just as liberal Protestantism stripped chronic hellenization (i.e., "doctrine") from Christian self-consciousness.[29]

There is one exception to the "fact" of the discontinuity in significance between the pre-modern and the modern. The one and only meaning in the pre-modern that remains significant for the modern is *moral content*.[30] We moderns can still recognize

26. It is a peculiarity of the state of contemporary Catholic systematic theology that a high value is placed upon Second Modern theologians who can talk like First Moderns, and First Modern theologians who can talk like classical theologians.

27. I am not using "generation(s)" literally, as though with the advent of Second Moderns there would be no more First Moderns. I am using "modern" in the sense of genre and not era.

28. The classic modern critique of telelology is found in Part II of Immanuel Kant's *Critique of Judgment*. Teleology represents the most substantial and complex assertion of intrinsic meaning; it is, in fact, the paradigmatic ontologization of intrinsic meaning. While "objectivity" seems equally to presume intrinsic meaning, an examination of the character of the modern prescribed methods which might reveal intrinsic meaning—"science"—makes clear that any such meaning is approached as no more than the "limit" in calculus is approached: one never arrives.

29. The best way to understand the nature of the assertion of epoch-centered hermeneutical discontinuity and the two different kinds of reading is as a *theory*: it is not tested by being proved or disproved; rather, its credibility rests on how well it organizes and explains otherwise disparate Baconian facts. For First Moderns, the historicity of traditional text-artifacts renders them exemplary but only insofar as they can be read as shaping or contributing to a moral discourse whose fundamental conditions of possibility are Enlightenment assumptions about the structure of human subjectivity and the character of the basic rights, structure, and autonomy of the human community. For Second Moderns, the historicity of traditional text-artifacts renders them "accidental" statements of the content of Christianity, and as such they can function as no more than examples of moral exhortation, without any normative status. Where these examples fail to exhort us towards what we now know to be correct moral judgments and practice they simply cease to be employed heuristically (e.g., Paul on homosexuality). In First Modern theology is still an attempt at correlation or at rescuing the earlier texts, but on the implied premise that such rescuing is necessary because of the superior character of modern thought. Thus in Rahner the limitation of meaning in traditional text-artifacts is implied but never explicitly articulated. In *Second* Modern theology, the desire for correlation ceases.

30. This is true as a minimum insofar as pre-modern text-artifacts dramatize modern moral concerns.

the moral concerns of pre-moderns, even if we do not share those precise moral concerns. We do not, after all, share the same moral concerns with all of our contemporaries, as continuing ideological struggle teaches us. The exceptional continuity of moral significance across the epoch-making event indicates that moral concerns (i.e., theory and practice) constitute the single and exclusive distinguishing feature inherent to human consciousness continuously available in human history, however distorted that human consciousness (i.e., moral concern) may be at times. It remains a given that such moral concerns are to be found in their most substantial and sophisticated form in modern consciousness. Phenomenologically, the modern theology which thinks through other forms of theology by referring the ostensive content of those forms to moral concerns I call "ethical-impulse" theology. The end result of this referral is the dissolution of doctrine per se or doctrine as content in itself. An older, conspicuous example of such "ethical-impulse" theology dissolving doctrine would be the theology of John Hick. However, Hick's theology cannot be considered as mainstream, and a better illustration of such a referring of the ostensive content of doctrine (with its epistemological claims) to moral concerns can be seen in work of Moltmann, whose theology may be described as a re-mythologizing of the basic narrative for the sake of fortifying the moral imperatives revealed in the narrative.[31]

A third, slightly more ambiguous, example of the constraints of ethical-impulse theology may be seen in the continuing failure of many "Radical Orthodoxy" theologians to treat doctrine in any substantial way, to the point where even a sympathetic reader can wonder if what truly is being developed is simply a post-British Empire Anglican theology (occasionally re-articulated as the desire to develop a post-"American Empire" theology). Finally, in the case of Roman Catholic systematicians, it may be remarked that whatever Rahner may have meant when he said that Christian theology has no technical language of its own but must constantly appropriate such language from other sources, this judgment now represents a paradigmatic theoretical justification for the "appropriation" of political-moral accounts of reality.

I can illustrate the kind of judgment I am positing in modern theology by working through some text-artifacts. For modern theologians, certain words/ideas are archaic artifacts, really archeological artifacts, which must be recognized as such. These words/ideas have been passed on as though they still carried meaning, but in fact they do not. Such meaningless-but-not-recognized-as-such words/ideas include "miracle," "being," "heaven," "resurrection," etc. These words are unrecognized empty signifiers. What is most decisive about their character is not that they are "empty," but that they are not recognized as such. People use words such as "miracle," "being," "heaven," "resurrection" (etc.) without realizing that unless and until modern significance is

---

31. One can make further distinctions and say that Moltmann's theology re-mythologizes the basic narrative at its dramatic level, while Miroslav Volf's theology is directed to restoring the narrative insofar as it is considered as a technical construct, in order to keep the text-artifact from breaking down in the middle of the screening.

projected onto them, these words mean nothing beyond position-filling, or social-recognition totems (like tattoos). If one unpacks the word "miracle" (etc.), then one realizes there is no experience that corresponds to the literal meaning of the word. Moreover, the literal meaning runs afoul of, and thus contradicts, the world of experience that we *do* (assuredly) have. As a New Testament scholar once put it to me, when speaking of the impossibility of New Testatment miracles and thus the necessity of "other" readings of such passages: "We live in the same world they lived in, there are not two worlds, and there are no miracles in our world." Such a judgment reflects what Martin Hengel identified in these terms: "The fundamental axiom of '*the* historical critical method' is the postulate of 'one reality' which can be comprehended by men and is at their disposal; in history this presents itself as 'the similarity in principle of all historical events' (Troeltsch)."[32] For such theologians losing the word "miracle" (etc.) and replacing it with something else (e.g., "social transformation," an "empowering myth," "cynic pronouncement," or a "legitimizing of structure") constitutes not simply erasing a false word (like "unicorn"), but a moral growth through the recognition of that falsity. A similar case of moral growth arising out of the recognition of false terminology would be the rejection of racial or ethnic slurs or—more analogously—not using "Santa Claus."

There is one more point to be made here about the character of contemporary theology. Even while limits are being drawn on the confidence with which one can assent to the products of any given epistemology, there is an implicit assumption that one can nonetheless confidently assert facts about moral relationships in the world: we can know that "X is doing bad thing Y to Z now," or, "In the past X did bad thing Y to Z." In some quarters this "moral epistemology" qualifies not simply as a "science," but as *the sole science*.[33] Fuzzy articulations of this confident moral knowing can sound as if they derive from Aristotle's definition of politics as the art of what is possible to do, but more succinct assertions of this moral knowledge make clear that its certainty lies in the social character of its epistemological objects: to paraphrase Marx on Feuerbach, there is "a resolving of the epistemological world into its social basis."[34]

32. Martin Hengel, *Acts and the History of Earliest Christianity*, John Bowden, trans., (Philadelphia, PA: Fortress Press, 1979), 129; emphasis in the original. He continues: "Thus the present-day experience of reality—which in any case is a limited one—is made the decisive criterion for what can and what cannot have happened in the past".

33. The modern judgment of the fundamental character of moral concerns is—ironically—most clearly dramatized in theology's encounter with contemporary aesthetic-literary theories. When deconstruction was in vogue, it eventually became clear that as a reading strategy deconstruction could de-center *all* kinds of texts, including moral and political ones. Theological and ideological interest in deconstruction faded quickly. Newer postmodern reading strategies either have been governed by moral narratives, or, with unconscious humor, identified as a moral-political strategy.

34. A statement I develop from Kenneth Surin's assertion of Dorothee Soelle's continuity with Marx. See Surin, *Theology and the Problem of Evil* (Oxford: Blackwell, 1986), 122–23, especially where he refers to Marx's judgment that Feuerbach "was seeking a way of 'resolving the religious world into its secular basis.'" My paraphrase could be construed as a cheap insight describing the project(s) of Foucault and parts of the Frankfurt School.

This epistemological certainty may be said both to make possible and to derive from the exceptional continuity of moral significance across otherwise discontinuous history (as I described just above). Prior to any contemporary theological narrative that would centralize moral concerns generally, and the problem of evil specifically, is the hermeneutical presupposition that only such concerns can "carry" across time and culture, and that only such concerns can be known with certainty—or with enough certainty to make them actionable.[35] The most trivial but most common theological expression of this hermeneutical presupposition is the *a priori* judgment that "-isms" such as racism and sexism are real, significant, and actionable in a way in which such "-isms" as modalism, subordinationism, and atheism are not.[36] A more sophisticated but less common expression of this hermeneutical presupposition is that there is an epistemology distinct to moral anthropology, and that this epistemology does not operate under the same limitations as any other epistemology inherent in other anthropologies. In fact, this "moral epistemology" may be said to operate outside the realms of other anthropological epistemologies generally.[37] Theologians badly trained in philosophy think that Heidegger "proves" this.

35. Mark Lilla offers one account of the rise of this identification of religion with moral anthropology in *Stillborn God* (New York, NY: Alfred A. Knopf, 2007), 107–62. Lilla argues that the shift occurs in Rousseau after the deep criticisms by Hobbes of religious impulses. The content of religion is limited to simple truths discovered through self-reflection: that there is a God who is good; that our emotional reach always exceeds our intellectual grasp, so we must learn to securely locate religion within those limits; and that humans possess a free will. These are the fundamentals Kant learns from Rousseau and which Kant systematizes. Lilla summarizes Rousseau's analysis of religion in this way: "In *Emile* he [Rousseau] suggests that so long as men are social, religion will arise, though not for the reasons given by Hobbes. But their naive faith in God will be fragile, so long as it is tied to an external, objective, authoritative revelation and not tailored to their moral needs. The best way to protect that faith, and thus morality, is to reinterpret it in subjective terms and root it in our moral sentiments, or conscience. That exercise in reinterpretation is not an exercise in determining the true nature of the divine nexus; it is an exercise in determining what we can plausibly believe about such a nexus as an aid to cultivating our virtue. And since virtue depends upon independence and self-confidence, this theology must be one that reconciles us with our freedom, not with God" (Lilla, *Stillborn God*, 125). We may wonder, now, whether postmodernism in the sense of "after modernity" must require the giving up of both the Enlightenment critique of religious sensibility (Hobbes) as well as its Enlightenment rehabilitation in the face of that critique (Rousseau and Kant). In any case, "stopping with the subject" now seems a quintessentially Enlightenment project, whatever anti-"objective" claims that project might make for itself.

36. I acknowledge that Jacques Ellul has focused upon the advent of "-ism" as an ideological event, but he and I are not making the same point, nor do we diagnose the problem to the same end. See Ellul, *The Subversion of Christianity*, Geoffrey W. Bromiley, trans., (Grand Rapids, MI: Wm. B. Eerdmans Publishing Company, 1986).

37. Thus we see the central role confident intuitions or insights have played in John Milbank's thought.

THE MODERN UNDERSTANDING OF EVIL:
MORAL PURITY AND MAGIC THINKING

In modern moral theology, knowledge of the cause(s) of evil can be attained with our "normal equipment for knowing," and its appropriation is a "natural consequence of the facts."[38] Not everyone is prepared to know the truth of the cause(s) of evil; some are held back by their own wills (or the wills of others), but nothing beyond unfettered reason is necessary to understand the origins of evil. Not revelation (i.e., mythology) nor even experience is necessary. "Unfettered" reason is that reason free from states (both senses) of coercion, and reason that approaches the problem of evil seeking a solution, i.e., with a commitment to or for the existence of a solution. ("If you are not part of the solution, you are part of the problem.")

Even though modern moral theology maintains that the cause of and solution for moral evil can be identified rationally, in fact the people who—and institutions that—are judged evil are experienced and treated as stains or defilements.[39] In this sensibility, the products of evil are evil not only in their function, but by their very existence: they are contaminants. This kind of "unfettered reason" seeks purity in its mental and physical space, an ethical room of its own. The quest for interior purity is not new, but what distinguishes the modern moral quest is its rejection of previous quests for purity because of their irrationality and their lack of enduring meaning. The other feature of the modern moral quest is its inability to articulate a justification for the new moral purity that is not fascist.[40]

If one cannot separate the perception and sensation of an outside object from the feelings and thoughts created in oneself by the object then one has entered the moral realm of defilement and purity (in which the object *is* what I judge it to be) and the

38. A variant statement derived from Pannenberg, *Revelation as History*: "Nothing must mute the fact that all truth lies right before our eyes, and that its appropriation is a natural consequence of the facts. There is no need for any additional perfection of man as though he could not focus on the 'supernatural' truth with his normal equipment for knowing."

39. The apparent exceptions or contra-indicators are in fact not cases of evil, but of the victims of evil.

40. "Fascist" is a word used most often in stupidity, an everywo/man's political version of "Neo-platonism." I use the word in its proper sense, as scholars use it in scholarly discourse. Fascism is an ideology of revolt advocating a revolution of the spirit and the will, of manners and morals, promising not only new political and social structures, but also new relationships between man and society, between man and nature, based upon a theory of an organic or communitarian society, with a rejection of individualism and (above all) materialism in all its forms: the rejection of individualism, utilitarianism, and bourgeois values, of democracy and majority rule, of the principle of the absolute primacy of the individual in relation to society; and a condemnation of the notion of the equal rights of all, and of politics as a consultation of the will of the majority. This definition is based upon Zeev Sternhell, *Neither Right Nor Left: Fascist Ideology in France*, David Maisel, trans., (Princeton, NJ: Princeton University Press, 1986/1991). As Rene Albrecht-Carrie points out in *The Meaning of the First World War* (Englewood Cliffs, NJ: Prentice-Hall, 1965), the most visible distinguishing feature of fascism is its total unwillingness to abide any criticism of a democratic sort. See also *Society* 18 (1981) for nine essays on "Left-Wing Fascism." Sadly, Susan Sontag's essay on this subject (published in the *Village Voice*) has not been anthologized among her writings, and has thus been airbrushed from history.

precondition for magic thinking. When one believes that the strength of one's moral feelings and thoughts will command obedience from outside objects (not to mention people), then one enters the realm of magic thinking.[41] If you stand in the way of a tank or bulldozer expecting to die, that is realism; if you stand in the way of a tank or bulldozer expecting it to stop because you will it to stop, or because you are "special," that is magic thinking.[42] Empathy can quickly become magic thinking. "If I feel as they feel, [then] they can feel as I feel"[43] becomes, "If I feel as they feel, then that will cause them to feel as I feel." In this case, there is a psychological move from knowledge of others by analogy—as Augustine describes in *Confessions*, book I—to power over others by andualism. The role of power in this example is obvious—"By what I do I can make them feel as I feel"—but the role of insecurity is no less relevant: "If I feel what they feel, then they will feel what I feel and *not hurt me*."[44]

One significant effect of the belief that there is a reasonable cause for evil (and thus evil is subject to being changed by reason) is a willingness to value an attempt to change evil through reason over the life of individuals. The argument runs something like this: if evil can be changed through reason, then when faced with evil we are morally obliged to attempt to use reason to change evil—to "reason with evil." By this logic, then, any act which pre-empts the attempt to use reason to change evil is by this very fact irrational and immoral. Mass murder (to take the most dramatic case) counts as an evil, but the fact of this specific evil does not override the moral obligation to try to "reason with [this] evil." If someone continues their evil action (e.g., mass murder) amidst the attempt to reason, the guilt of that action is imputed to them (and only to them).

The modern "progressive" theologian's willingness to value an attempt to change evil through reason over the life of individuals is in fact especially illustrated by their responses to genocide. When recognized, genocide-in- progress provokes vocal condemnation and programmatic denunciation. Progressive sensibilities mobilize in the effort to stop the killing through negotiation and world public opinion. But nothing

41. Charles Odier, *Anxiety and Magic Thinking*, Marie-Louis Schoelly, M.D., and Mary Jane Sherfey, M.D., trans., (New York, NY: International Universities Press, Inc., 1956/1974), p. 8.

42. The idea that "war is over/obsolete" is magic thinking whether declared by John Lennon or Lewis Lapham. The only *non*-magical thinking repudiation of war is, "I will not fight. I will be killed or enslaved: everyone I love will be killed or enslaved. Those who kill and enslave will triumph in this world." The life of Franz Jagerstatter is a good example of moral choice completely free of magic thinking, as is Bonhoeffer's.

43. Odier, *Anxiety and Magic Thinking*, 11.

44. It is pagan (or clinically "infantile") and not Christian to believe that trust can buy off deceit: that trust can—and should—purchase security for the trustee against deceit. Nothing in the Gospels suggests this dynamic: nothing in the Gospels suggests that this is a proper motivation for Christians to be faithful or trusting or undefended, etc. This total incommensurateness between trust given and any presumed moral state in return is true for the Christian publicly as well as privately: if you trust someone in order to make them trustworthy, or to bind them to your expectations, you indulge in magic thinking and not Christian faith. Christianity does not turn trust into a spell.

is done to stop the killing *now*: to prevent the loss of life that will happen during the time when parties negotiate a dialogue that is only the prelude to negotiation over the killing. The deaths of multiple thousands while dialogue and the peace process "continues" is accepted as inevitable, a tragic consequence of a commitment to resolving conflict through reasoned discourse. Physical intervention to stop the deaths—through military action—is avoided as irrational: the inevitable morally-ambivalent effects of military action—innocent deaths—are grounds for rejecting intervention. The inevitable morally-ambivalent effects of rational discourse—innocent deaths—are not grounds for rejecting negotiation. There is hardly any recent history which escapes this model; Darfur is but the most contemporary case.[45] The willingness of Western theologians to countenance the deaths of thousands and thousands of people of color for the sake of a "peace process" is as undeniable as it is nauseating, but it is entirely rational by modern Enlightenment standards.[46] Reason first, human life second.[47] What must be made clear, however, is that the "reason" in question is the reason of magic thinking, the logic of defilement and purity. If I do not see it, I am not stained—like Noah's sons covering their naked father. Invisible people, those unseen in the imagination, literature, or video, are, in fact, no longer people *of any color*.

IS A MORAL MODERN THEOLOGY POSSIBLE?

I began this essay by referring to my heuristic proposal of a hypothetical response to a perceived moral failure on the part of the church. There is one other moral failure to be described before I turn to a pre-modern account of evil in which evil is not explained, but is understood to be out-narrated by the act of the Trinity in the Incarnation. This moral failure is not a failure of the Church as institution or hierarchy, but a failure within Catholic theology and among those who understand their academic office to function as an alternative magisterium for the Church.

Attention is regularly drawn to the question of Vatican complicity or self-interest in dealing with Nazi Germany. Motives for contemporary attention to this question vary from the apportionment of past guilt or moral failure to a general delegitimizing of papal authority in the post-World War II world, i.e., such a moral failure terminates the moral authority of Rome for Catholics. I cannot offer any judgments on whatever degrees of moral failure the hierarchy of the Catholic Church may have suffered in the

45. Some may object to military intervention in Darfur or Burma with "geopolitical" reasons, or whatever; my point here takes issue with the specific argument against the use of force.

46. We must be very clear that while Second Moderns define themselves out of the Enlightenment project, they are nonetheless its children even if they deny links to their parents.

47. Such a logic is so cherished that clear examples of genocide in the name of reason are forgotten and removed from modern consciousness: it is popular "knowledge" that many have been killed in the name of Christianity; it is *not* popular knowledge that in the twentieth century, millions were killed in the name of Reason or Science, for the Nazis identified their thought as true Reason and the Marxists identify their thought as Science.

late 1930s. The more important point, however, is that to whatever degree there was a problematic moral character of the relationship between the Roman Catholic hierarchy and the Third Reich, this problematic moral character is an important part of precisely what makes papal or curial theology "modern." My reading is this: it has been a distinctive feature of *modern theology* that it is characterized by an ambiguous or problematic moral or intellectual relationship with the culture of National Socialism. In fundamental ways, to be a *modern* theologian is to be a theologian entangled intellectually and thus morally with National Socialism. (This entanglement is not limited to Catholic theologians.) One can draw an arc of such entanglements which range at one end from the conscious and wholly engaged participation in National Socialism to be found in Martin Heidegger, to the other end with the seemingly pre-volitional participation in the Nazi war machine of Jürgen Moltmann. Within this arc one can map out a variety of degrees of complicity ranging from historical involvement and clear moral culpability to historical involvement with no apparent moral culpability.

Obviously, Heidegger represents a special and exceedingly troublesome case for established schools of modern theology because of the coincidence of two facts: (1) Heidegger's role in the construction of a specifically modern consciousness in theology is substantial and in many trajectories decisive; and (2) Heidegger's involvement in National Socialism was total, ranging from intellectual conceptualization to social action. Heidegger was no "accidental" Nazi; or if he was, then he was a fool.[48] (Heidegger was still paying his party dues in April of 1945.) In short, then, I am saying that post-World War II theology (which here equals "modern") is indebted at a fundamental conceptual level and at an articulation-of-doctrine level to figures whose status vis-à-vis Nazi ideology or the fact of the Third Reich ranges from wholly impugned to problematic. Moltmann may have offered a narrative of disclosure and discovery which maps his movement from problematic participation in the Third Reich to redemption—and we may even be inclined to take that narrative at face value—but most practitioners of modern theology have not worked through the question of the need for their own analogous intellectual movement and narrative. Why in this case do we find among theologians—and Scripture scholars—no worry about stain and contagion?

In every era, questions about the authenticity and reading of a theologian can include the problem of the moral status of the author, when the deviation of that author seems either excessive or contradictory to the message.[49] However, the problem of the ambiguous relationship with the Third Reich is historically specific to "modern"

48. See, e.g., Gunther Neske and Emil Kettering, *Martin Heidegger and National Socialism*, Lisa Harris, trans., (New York, NY: Paragon House, 1990); Hugo Ott, *Martin Heidegger—A Political Life*, Allan Blunden, trans., (New York, NY: Basic Books, 1993); *The Heidegger Controversy: A Critical Reader*, Richard Wolin, ed., (New York, NY: Columbia University Press, 1991); and Michael E. Zimmerman, *Heidegger's Confrontation With Modernity: Technology, Politics, Art* (Bloomington, IN: Indiana University Press, 1990).

49. An excellent treatment of such cases is Donald M. MacKinnon's "Tillich, Frege, Kittel: Some Reflections on a Dark Theme," *Explorations in Theology* 5 (London: SCM, 1979).

theology, and represents a particular problem with "modern" theology, whereas, e.g., the case of an out-of-control passion of a theologian reflects a problem not specific to modern theology. One cannot say that a moral discontinuity (or contradiction) is specifically indicative or a characteristic of modern theology, but one can say that the problem of physical and intellectual participation in the Third Reich is specifically indicative or a characteristic of modern theology (qua "modern"). The most specific visible effect of the "openness" that American Catholic systematic theology has to this intellectual heritage may be the progressive (in both senses of that word) "disinterest" in Judaism by such Catholics.

One lesson that modern theology may have learned from the Third Reich is the survival benefit of cultural collaboration and the inhibiting effect martyrdom has on the development and promulgation of one's own theology. *Opposition leading to death—"martyrdom"—is ineffective at every level except one: personal moral integrity or purity.*[50] There is a regularly expressed sentimental cliché that the effect of killing one's opponent is to turn her or him into a "martyr"—and so to give that opponent more presence and authority dead than when alive.[51] The truth, however, is that *the signifying value of an individual's death can always be contained and ultimately negated by surrounding that death with even more death.* How many Christians were martyred in Japan? What is the name of one of the fourteen million kulaks killed by Stalin?[52] The fact remains that the dead are silent and whatever voice they might have depends upon the memory, attentiveness, and will of the living.[53] If any of these three fail in

---

50. This is actually a lesson re-learned, for the rise of this understanding originally produced structural differences between *Christianity before* Islam and *Christianity after*. However, the present existence of a large religious body of believers who regard martyrdom to be effective on many levels provokes theological confusion (not to mention embarrassment and fear) among those who subscribe to the modern judgment that martyrdom is ineffective at every level except the personal. The strangely familiar character of the social effects of "self-initiated" martyrdom derives from the modern narrative that the theological content of early Christian martyrdom was social: Christians impressed pagans by their deaths and changed pagan minds. This understanding of early Christian martyrdom is a clear application of the root judgment that Christianity is about the "practical" and the narrative of Christ's ministry, *and* not about contemplation of the divine as the goal and root of theology.

51. I suspect this is a type of slogan developed by the weak as a defensive weapon to cause hesitation on the part of those who in reality can kill with impunity. Or it is another expression of magic thinking: "If they kill me then I will become *really* powerful."

52. Stalin famously said that one death is a tragedy; a million deaths is a statistic. He spoke as an expert.

53. Bonhoeffer's standing is a good illustration of the consumer-oriented character of the robe of martyrdom. In North America, Bonhoeffer has almost no presence as a Christian martyr, or even as a martyr for justice; Gandhi, by contrast, looms large even though he was not killed by those he protested against (i.e., the British). Part of Bonhoeffer's "problem" is that he endorsed and participated in *violent action* against a genocidal tyranny. (Gandhi's relationship in the early 1940s to the Japanese war machine more closely resembles the relationship of the Ukraine with the Nazi war machine at the same time.) Moreover, Bonhoeffer was not acting against "colonialism." Finally, Bonhoeffer's theology is so varied that no one ideo-theological group is comfortable claiming him.

us, the living, the dead—including martyrs and dead theologians—cease to connote.[54] But if one is alive, one can not only later repent, one can publish in the meantime. Even though one worked for the Vichy government, one can afterwards become a journalist and found an important newspaper, e.g., *Le Monde*, as Hubert Beuve-Mery did; or like another Petainist government bureaucrat, one can become a politician and go on to become Prime Minister of France, as did François Mitterand.

I turn now from the broad subject of the moral roots of post-Christian Catholic theology (though I did not mean to exclude the post-Christian theology of other denominations) to a pre-modern account of evil, and the example of a modern Christian living by a pre-modern account of evil. There are, of course, a variety of pre-modern accounts of evil, and I am concentrating on the one I think cuts straight to the modern (First and Second) understanding that the cause of evil can be known (and thus eliminated through *praxis*). I turn to the pre-modern account of evil that does not explain evil, but out-narrates it: that of Augustine.[55]

THE CONSCIENCE AS FALL

Despite their differences, most modern Catholic moral theologies have in common the important and central role they give to "conscience." The con- science figures as a kind of black box in moral theologies: mysterious in content and origin but integral to any account of moral acts.[56] The ubiquity of the assumption in Catholic moral theologies of the fundamental role con- science plays in moral decision-making owes—it

54. The day after Arafat died, Jeff Jacoby wrote in the *Boston Globe*: "In May 1974, three PLO terrorists slipped from Lebanon into the northern Israeli town of Ma'alot. They murdered two parents and a child whom they found at home, then seized a local school, taking more than 100 boys and girls hostage and threatening to kill them unless a number of imprisoned terrorists were released. When Israeli troops attempted a rescue, the terrorists exploded hand grenades and opened fire on the students. By the time the horror ended, 25 people were dead; 21 of them were children. Thirty years later, no one speaks of Ma'alot anymore. The dead children have been forgotten. Everyone knows Arafat's name, but who ever recalls the names of his victims? So let us recall them: Ilana Turgeman. Rachel Aputa. Yocheved Mazoz. Sarah Ben-Shim'on. Yona Sabag. Yafa Cohen. Shoshana Cohen. Michal Sitrok. Malka Amrosy. Aviva Saada. Yocheved Diyi. Yaakov Levi. Yaakov Kabla. Rina Cohen. Ilana Ne'eman. Sarah Madar. Tamar Dahan. Sarah Soper. Lili Morad. David Madar. Yehudit Madar."

55. Augustine's pre-modern account of evil is not to be identified with "Augustinian" accounts: Augustine's theology and Augustinianism are two very different things (like a grain of wheat and white bread). For different perspectives on "Augustinianism," see see Henri de Lubac, *Augustinianism and Modern Theology*, Lancelot Sheppard, trans., (London: G. Chapman, 1969); Leszek Kolakowski, *God Owes Us Nothing* (Chicago, IL: University of Chicago Press, 1995); Charles T. Mathewes, *Evil and the Augustinian Tradition* (Cambridge: Cambridge University Press, 2001), and J. D. Green, *"Augustinianism": Studies in the Process of Spiritual Transvaluation* (Leuven: Peeters, 2007). If the term "Augustinian" slips by me I mean nothing other than "what Augustine thought" or "like what Augustine thought," depending on the context. (Bonhoeffer is an "Augustinian" insofar as certain of his thoughts or judgments owe to Augustine and are very much like Augustine's.)

56. For an excellent description of the way in which conscience functions as the sufficient, exclusive moral arbiter in contemporary moral culture, see David B. Hart, "Christ and Nothing," *First Things* 136 (October 2003), pp. 47–57.

may reasonably be suggested—not to Thomas Aquinas and scholasticism, but to Alphonsus Liguori.[57] It is difficult for a modern, intelligent Catholic not to read St. Paul as though he were Alphonsus Liguori, busily separating conscience from the burden of law. For Augustine, Paul is separating virtue from intention, since for Augustine the law we are most burdened and enslaved by is that of our own will (*Conf.* VIII.v.10).[58] For most of the *Confessions*, Augustine's story is that of his attempt to become virtuous: to achieve beatitude. Augustine's unhappiness with his sexual distraction means he can measure his progress in virtue in a concrete manner: to the degree that he is free of the force of sexual desire, so has he reached virtue. The very concrete and specific identity—for Augustine—of a life without virtue simplifies the question, *What is virtue?* as well as, *Am I now virtuous?* Such simple measures of virtue are not without precedent in classical moral psychology or drama; the courses of tragedies are driven by some great single flaw in a protagonist (e.g., the lives of Medea or Oedipus). A life of virtue is equivalent to a life free from the control of tragic passion. Augustine seeks virtue from where he knows he ought to find it: in moral philosophy, the search for wisdom, and *paideia.*

The path to virtue that Augustine accepts and sets upon is the same path a modern would accept and set upon: education. Antique culture presumed that virtue could be taught—if the student possessed sufficient native intelligence and tuition. Philosophy was nothing else than the shaping of desire through the education of mind. Those bright enough to understand the truth would, through that knowledge, be able to harness their own passions and rescue themselves from their private tragedies. Augustine is a schoolman; he knows that the means of virtue are words, and he searches to hear the words that will silence his passion and seat virtue within him. Augustine initially hoped this course of words would be easy, as was learning Latin, but he comes to understand that learning the words that will teach him virtue is hard; the words are progressively stranger and more foreign, and despite his study the words remain ineffective. There is no virtue. Augustine has been taught to expect that he can be brought to virtue through education: the right lesson, the right habit, the right teacher, and then Augustine will be measured virtuous by the very standard he has set for himself, chastity. But this never happens; the culture (and cultivation) of virtue—*paideia*—fails. The word we have for the enculturing of virtue is *formation*, and neither the liberal nor the conservative Christian doubts that formation must be maintained sufficient for the desired outcome: virtue led by the right belief. Liberals and conservatives may disagree over whether the stories necessary for moral formation are the novels of the

57. See Theodule Rey-Mermet, *Moral Choices: The Moral Theology of Saint Alphonsus Liguori*, Paul Laverdure, trans., (Liguori, MO: Liguori Publications, 1998).

58. If it seems I am casting "saint against saint" in this article by suggesting a de-centering of the received notions of conscience and of conscience or moral formation, I am not—by this decentering—pitting Augustine against Thomas, but Augustine against Liguori.

marginalized or the lives of the saints, but they share the belief that the right culture of the correct words will *reduce*—as a besieged city is "reduced"—vice and seat virtue.

As Augustine finished writing *Confessions*, he also completed two letters to his mentor, the new bishop of Milan, Simplicianus. At the end of the second letter, Augustine draws Simplicianus' attention to the way virtue and vice are played out in the people around them, the way, in fact, they are played out in violation of the expectations of formation and *paideia*:

> Don't we see that many of our faithful people walking in the way of God suffer when compared in ability not just to the heretics but even with fools? Don't we see that there are some men and women who live blamelessly in a chaste marriage who are heretics or pagans or so lukewarm in the faith and the Church that we are amazed when we see them surpassed not only in patience and temperance but also in faith, hope and charity by prostitutes and charlatans who suddenly convert?[59]

In short, Augustine says, the appearance of virtue often comes as a surprise, for it appears in those who totally lacked prior formation. If C.S. Lewis was "surprised by joy," then Augustine is surprised by virtue. What Augustine observes in the untutored laity who were previously given over to sin is the same truth he discovered in his own life: it is not education or *paideia* that enables the will to turn to the good; it is God-given grace. This Spirit blows where it wills. I am not saying that, for Augustine, God never forms an individual for receiving grace, or that the gift of virtue always stands outside any personal—or world—history. To the contrary, *Confessions* is nothing less than Augustine's retrospective account of the ways God was shaping his life so that he would be able to respond to the gift of the grace of conversion; the way that God shaped Augustine's life was precisely through the quest for wisdom and virtue. But Augustine is clear that the actions God took to bring him to salvation consisted of reordering the products of Augustine's intentions (i.e., "grace"). For example, Augustine's reason for going to Milan was to gain imperial recognition of his oratory skills and thus to enter government. Augustine went to Milan as part of his project of moving up in the world. What actually happened to Augustine in Milan was his encounter with the circle of Platonic Christians represented by Simplicianus and Ambrose. (His reconciliation with his mother also occurs in Milan.) At this point, Augustine's career as a rhetor coasted to a stop even as he became a catechumen in the Catholic Church. The story in *Confessions* of Augustine's decisions and his conscious quest is revealed to be but a tremor in a tide pushing him to true faith. God's unfolding of Augustine's moral life "out-narrates" the story he was, literally, telling as his own. A proper account of Augustine's conversion requires a perspective far beyond that of the psychological or intentional, and indeed Augustine's last perspective on the story of his conversion is, in the last books of the *Confessions*, far beyond the drama of his own life. The cause

---

59. Augustine, *To Simplician*, 406.

of virtue in us is only slightly less mysterious than the cause of evil. The mystery of virtue is diminished only because we know its original and originating cause, God; the original or originating cause of evil, on the other hand, always remains unknown and unknowable, in significant part because ultimately it is ourselves.

There are three key doctrines in Augustine's theology that act to overturn the tyranny of the knowledge of good and evil. The first is Augustine's theology of grace; the second is his theology of God's providence. Both theological notions dislocate the yoke of the knowledge of good and evil; they render it, if not null and void, then of limited hermeneutical and anthropological significance. Grace performs an end-run around the knowledge of good and evil, removing it as necessary for acts of virtue, and, as well, providing an entirely new basis for virtue: virtue no longer begins with the will, and it no longer "merits" anything. Virtue now begins with grace. If we re-member that for Kant a human "person" is someone who can gain merit for her or his actions, then we can begin to glimpse just how radically grace decenters and then renders obsolete any "personal" (i.e., reasonable) claims to natural conscience, and the privileging of that conscience as a source for decision-making.[60]

The second key Augustinian doctrine that acts to overturn the tyranny of the knowledge of good and evil is his notion of divine providence. For any act to be evil, it would have to be able to resist its participation in the working out of God's ultimate goal, but nothing is capable of resisting the *telos* of God's will, therefore nothing can stand outside God's providence. What is in God's providence is not truly evil; it is only provisionally so. From our perspective something may seem evil, but we must understand that we can only call it that—know it as such—relatively and, as I said, provisionally. The true worth of anything is unknown to us, because the true role of any physical and psychological event in God's providence is unknown. The calculus of good versus evil turns out to be chaos theory; some deed in the rain forests of Brazil (a murder, or the rescue of a child from a jaguar) fits into a pattern of events which are unchartable to human knowledge. Our ability to actually see, recognize, and map out these consequences is not any less, and certainly not any more, than our ability to ac-tually see, recognize and map out the rippling effect upon the ecosphere of a butterfly flapping its wings in a Brazilian rainforest. In both cases, what makes the rippling effect plausible, even though we cannot directly observe the continuity of effects, is a faith that there exists a kind of closed system for causes and effects. God provides the unity to the chaos of actions by his providence; the system is closed because history will have an end. Just as "chaos theory" requires us to reconceive cause and effect as well as descriptive mathematics, a theology of providence requires us to reconceive intention and effect, while it also gives us a new perspective on history.[61]

---

60. See Susan Meld Shell, *Kant and the Limits of Autonomy* (Cambridge, MA: Harvard University Press, 2009).

61. Thus, *City of God*—and *Confessions*, all thirteen books, not just the first ten.

PRIVATION: OUT-NARRATING EVIL

The third key doctrine in Augustine's theology that acts to overturn the tyranny of the knowledge of good and evil is his doctrine of evil as privation. The theory of privation has two important "moments" that are related but distinct from one another. The first "moment" is the understanding that evil is the lack of some specific capacity or feature fundamental to the identity of an existent. An eye is supposed to see, and the loss of sight may properly be called an evil. It is not fundamental to the identity of skin or a head that it be covered with hair, so baldness cannot really be spoken of as an evil. Evil thus has no existence in itself, and may indeed be understood precisely as a specific lack of being: evil is an incompleteness, a disease or a flaw. Both Gregory of Nyssa and Augustine, for example, understood evil not as some *thing* that existed, that is, not as some substance, but as a lack of existence, a deprivation or brokenness in something. Thus Gregory says,

> For as sight is an activity of nature, and blindness a deprivation of that natural operation, such is the kind of opposition between virtue and vice. It is, in fact, not possible to form any other notion of the origin of vice than as the absence of virtue. For as when the light has been removed the darkness supervenes, but as long as it is present there is no darkness, so, as long as the good is present in the nature, vice is a thing that has no inherent existence; while the departure of the better state becomes the origin of its opposite.[62]

Obviously the point of departure for such an understanding of good and evil is the denial of any theory of radical dualism. Both Gregory and Augustine have the Manichees in mind as advocates of a radical dualism, in which evil has what can be called a "positive" existence.[63] However, the roots of the concern are not in the rebuttal of radical dualism, but in refuting the notion of co-eternal prime matter, that is, in the development of a Christian doctrine of creation *ex nihilo*.[64]

62. Gregory, *Cat. Or.* V.

63. Gregory also applies related arguments to refute what he takes to be his opponents' (i.e., the Eunomians) incorrect understanding of God; Augustine seems not to have an analogous Trinitarian application of privation theory.

64. Irenaeus is a good example of this: "But we shall not be wrong if we affirm the same thing also concerning the substance of matter, that God produced it. For we have learned from the Scriptures that God holds the supremacy over all things. But whence or in what way He produced it, neither has Scripture anywhere declared; nor does it become us to conjecture, so as, in accordance with our own opinions, to form endless conjectures concerning God, but we should leave such knowledge in the hands of God Himself. In like manner, also, we must leave the cause why, while all things were made by God, certain of His creatures sinned and revolted from a state of submission to God, and others, indeed the great majority, persevered, and do still persevere, in [willing] subjection to Him who formed them That eternal fire, [for instance,] is prepared for sinners, both the Lord has plainly declared, and the rest of the Scriptures demonstrate. And that God foreknew that this would happen, the Scriptures do in like manner demonstrate, since He prepared eternal fire from the beginning for those who were [afterwards] to transgress [His commandments]; but the cause itself of the nature of such transgressors neither has any Scripture informed us, nor has an apostle told us, nor has the Lord

The second "moment" in classical privation theory is a ranking of existents according to the relative fullness of their being. This produces a hierarchy of worth which begins with God and descends into rational creatures, then irrational creatures, then to lifeless creatures. This finds illustration in Augustine's famous (to those in the know) statement that a bad human still has more worth than a good ape, even Koko. Gregory of Nyssa will talk about such a hierarchy, but he never links this "second moment" in privation theory to the "first," as Augustine does.

There are, however, two applications of, or conclusions from, privation theory that are not generally recognized in accounts of the theory. The first such application or conclusion is that evil cannot be the proper subject of any narrative. Or to put this in a slightly different, more developed, form: what is usually understood as an ontological account of good and evil also brings forward a hermeneutical account of evil and a judgment on the narrative play of evil. If we understand "is" as "subject of speech" or "active agent," and "is not" as "not a subject of speech" or "not an active agent," then the impossibility of speaking of evil directly is clear. Evil can never be the subject of speech; it only can be spoken of insofar as one speaks of the good, that is, something that is, some subject. If we ask, "What is the narrative value or content of privation?" the answer is "none." The fact that privation theory prevents evil (as such) from being narrated (as it is in, e.g., the "mythologies" of radical dualism) has been taken by some critics to be a weakness or flaw in privation theory. That privation theory prevents any meaningful narration of evil (considered simply as evil) is rather the strength or virtue of the theory. Any narrative of "evil" reaches a limit at which point it becomes clear that any such narrative must become an account of intentionality. (Thus, from a Catholic Christian perspective, one cannot simply describe Satan as "evil personified": traditionally, the question of Satan's evilness becomes the question of "What did Satan want?" Early articulations—in Judaism and in Christianity—of Satan's identity and existence turn upon his intention: Satan possesses a *second desire* to God's.)

While it is obvious that the *Confessions* explore the experience and identity of evil, what has seemed less obvious is that Augustine's account of evil takes place within a larger narrated understanding of the experience and identity of good, the Good. It is worth pausing to note what might otherwise seem trivial: that in the *Confessions*, Augustine explains that while there is a "Good," there is no corresponding "Evil." There is really only one fundamental principle or cause, the Good, and whatever happens, whatever there is, *is* through the action of this Good. Evil neither causes nor explains anything. The wit and beauty of the *Confessions* is that Augustine can make such an assertion without falling prey to the blindness of sentimentality; indeed, Augustine can make such an assertion while at the same time offering one of the best descriptions that humans have produced of the experience of evil. In the *Confessions*, the recurring question of evil is always positioned within a narrative of salvation. For Augustine, there is no explanation of evil in itself; any account of evil exists only by virtue of a

---

taught us" (AH II.28.7 ANF 401).

real account of good. A privation account of evil is not refusing to talk about evil, it is an out-narrating of evil. This fact is expressed by Augustine in the famous passage from *City of God*:

> One should not try to find an efficient cause for a wrong choice. It is not a matter of efficiency but of deficiency; the evil will is not effective but defective. For to begin to have an evil will, is to defect from him who is the supreme existence to something of less reality. To try to discover the causes of such defections—deficient not efficient causes—is like trying to see darkness or hear silence.[65]

In the *City of God* Augustine offers us several case studies in which he takes the most extreme examples of social and individual evil and shows how each is to be truly understood as a miscarriage of a good intention. The social example of extreme evil is *war*; the individual example of extreme evil is a famous individual in the literature of the time named Cacus whose life contained every possible form of human depravity. War, Augustine says, is waged for the goal of peace, and peace is a good. This explanation does not excuse whatever occurs in a war, but it does mean that any general account of war that describes it as existing for its own sake—i.e., for the sake of violence in itself—is wrong.[66] Augustine's account of Cacus is more detailed. Cacus was a legendary character, described by Virgil and others, whose behavior drove him away from all positive human contact, and so he lived in a cave. Augustine's description of him is worth recalling:

> He had no wife with whom to give and receive caresses; no children to play with when little or to instruct when a little bigger; and no friends with whom to enjoy conversation, not even his father . . . He gave nothing to anyone; rather, he took what he wanted from anyone he could and whenever he could. Despite all this, however, in the solitude of his own cave, the floor of which, as Virgil describes it, ever reeked with the blood of recent butchery, he wished for nothing other than a peace in which no one should molest him, and rest which no man's violence, or the fear of it, should disturb. Also, he desired to be at peace with his own body . . . Thus, for all his monstrousness and savagery, his aim was peace; for he sought, by these monstrous and ferocious means, only to preserve the peace of his own life. Had he been willing to make with others the peace which he was ready enough to make in his cave and with himself, he would not have been called wicked, nor a monster, nor semi-human.[67]

65. Augustine, *City of God*, XII.7. Bk. XII, chs. 2–8, is devoted to the question of privation and volition.

66. I think it is fair to say that Augustine understood more clearly than most moderns that accurate accounts of a war would inevitably come upon good intentions; the "discovery" of these intentions was not a moment of surprise for him.

67. Augustine, *City of God*, XIX.12. In this description by Augustine, we can recognize the implicit similitude between the motives of an "evil" individual and the motives driving the evil of war.

The second generally unrecognized conclusion from privation theory is one I have already intimated: any narrative of "evil" reaches a limit at which point it becomes clear that any such narrative must become an account of intentionality. In all exemplary patristic articulations of "privation" theory—i.e., Gregory of Nyssa and Augustine—the "purely metaphysical" description of evil as privation *never* stands alone; it is *always* connected to an account of volition. This is true for Gregory, in, e.g., *Great Catechism* and *On Virginity*; and it is true for Augustine, in, e.g., *Confessions*, *On the Nature of the Good*, and *City of God*. Privation theory does not simply function to provide a correct orientation of creation (especially matter) to good and evil, but to provide a correct understanding of the role of the will in relation to good and evil.[68] Christians reflect upon the real or relative existence of evil in order to offer an account of the will that makes sense.[69] This is true from Origen to Augustine, and all points in between.[70] What is decisive for us today, then, is the realization that a patristic account of evil as privation never stands apart from an account of volition, and—almost just as important for the purposes of this article—we must realize that the connection between these two accounts has been lost to modern readers of classical privation theory.

Gregory provides us with several illustrations of how privation theory functions as a support for volition-psychologies. For example, in *Great Catechism* V, Gregory says,

> But the evil is, in some way or other, engendered from within, springing up in the will at that moment when there is a retrocession of the soul from the beautiful. For as sight is an activity of nature, and blindness a deprivation of that natural operation, such is the kind of opposition between virtue and vice. It is, in fact, not possible to form any other notion of the origin of vice than as the absence of virtue. For as when the light has been removed the darkness supervenes, but as long as it is present there is no darkness, so, as long as the good is present in the nature, vice is a thing that has no inherent existence; while the departure of the better state becomes the origin of its opposite. Since then, this is the peculiarity of the possession of a free will, that it chooses as it likes the thing that pleases it, you will find that it is not God Who is the author of the present evils, seeing that He has ordered your nature so as to be its own

---

68. Indeed, if we include Origen and Methodius (especially), we see that it is consistently true that cosmological (creation) accounts relating evil to being are related to accounts of volition.

69. A good example of this can be found at the beginning of *On the Nature of the Good*, where Augustine says, "To his most excellent creatures, that is to rational spirits, God has given the power not to be corrupted if they do not will to be; but remain obedient under the Lord their God and cleave to his incorruptible beauty" (Augustine, *Nature of the Good*, in *Augustine: Earlier Writings*, J. H. S Burleigh, trans., 328).

70. One might want to suggest that this fundamental feature of Catholic Christian thought is due to its engagement with varieties of radical dualism (Gnosticism and Manichaeism), but one could just as well say that catholic and dualist Christianity shared a categorical understanding of the link between metaphysical or cosmological accounts and volitional accounts.

master and free; but rather the recklessness that makes choice of the worse in preference to the better.

If we turn to Augustine, we see that in the *Confessions* the articulation of a privation theory of evil occurs within the larger context of a final meditation on whether the will is free. It is in book VII of *Confessions* that Augustine offers privation as a description of the character of evil; a careful reading of that book makes clear that the larger problematic is the character and nature of the will.

CAN ANY VIRTUE BE TAUGHT?

The theologies of grace and providence are illustrated in the novel *Brideshead Revisited*. At the end of the novel, when there has been so much personal failure, frustration, and loneliness, Charles recognizes the point of it all: to restore the Host to Brideshead chapel and relight the red lamp signaling God's presence. Augustine tells exactly the same kind of story in the *Confessions*. All that he does he does for personal, sometimes vain reasons: he leaves Thagaste for Carthage because a friend has died in Thagaste and he hopes to escape the painful memories; he leaves Carthage for Rome because his students in Carthage are rowdy and he has heard that such is not the case in Rome (and besides, he hopes to move up in life); he goes to Milan to compete in a contest of public oration so that he might gain the attention of a well-placed patron, and thus move into a career less taxing of his sick lungs (and besides, the students in Rome never pay their tuition on time); and while in Milan, Augustine goes to hear Ambrose in his church only to observe his style of public speaking. Not one of these decisions is made for the sake of moral improvement or greater faith, or even for a less disturbing sense of sexuality. But in retrospect, every decision moved him further along on the path to his "true Fatherland," and all the events shaped Augustine so that when the call came he would accept it (or, more accurately, he would come to the moment when he could recognize his own life as a call).[71] The stories of Augustine's chosen acts that constituted most of *Confessions* must be reread from a different perspective: Augustine discovers this about his life stories, and shares the discovery of the proper perspective with his reader. What was happening to Augustine was not what he thought, in his awareness of his life day by day. Augustine's story of his life has to be re-narrated; the meaning that Augustine set for that life was out-narrated by God.[72]

71. I agree with James Wetzel that Augustine's conversion occurs principally in his memory, and that this conversion is not a single moment which transforms everything like some kind of psychological philosopher's stone. It happens in the memory, over time. See Wetzel, *Limits of Virtue*, 187–215.

72. In his *Deconstructing Theodicy: Why Job has Nothing to Say to the Puzzle of Suffering* (Grand Rapids, MI: Brazos Press, 2008), pp. 126–133, David B. Burrell understands Augustine to be "deconstructing theodicy" in *Confessions* by moving the question of good and evil from one that speaks in terms of explaining (good and evil) to addressing God: more precisely, moving from a stand that asks—demands—an explanation because that is what is "needed" to one that speaks to God (knowing that that is what is needed). I do not disagree with Burrell's thesis: I simply have another one to offer that I think also describes how Augustine is "deconstructing theodicy."

Are all acts and intentions equal, then, because they all must figure in God's providence? By no means. The precise question we are dealing with is the overcoming of the knowledge of good and evil that was both the first temptation to sin and the first consequence of sin. We are talking about good and evil as objects of knowledge, and that knowledge as the basis for moral actions.[73] This "knowledge of good and evil" is based in human nature, expressed through the conscience, and accounted for by reason. This knowledge is, repeating myself, the consequence of sin, and its first product, the second sin, is to explain evil, to reduce it to a cause: "This woman, whom you gave me" (Gen 3:12). Christ overcomes this knowledge: he produces no account of the origin of evil (he taught no Gnostic gospel), and he overthrows all moral calculus. What is available to reason in his claim to be the Son of God? Nothing.[74] Standing in the epistemological field of the knowledge of good and evil, Jesus was, according to the Law and its interpreters (the scribes and Pharisees), a blasphemer. Standing in the modern epistemological field of the knowledge of good and evil, Jesus was, according to moral impulse theology and its proponents (both First and Second Moderns), "another holy person" or "of decisive historical significance."[75] Both epistemological fields deny his identity, and both produce clear consciences.

One important consequence of what I am saying is its implications for a proper understanding of "moral formation" in education. Augustine sought virtue through *paidea. Paidea* failed Augustine—and an entire civilization. Strangely, despite the failure of *paidea*, Augustine continued to value and extol education as moral formation. Why? For Augustine, the proper role of formation is to better prepare the mind

73. Leon Kass reads the significance of Genesis 1–2 in this way: "In short, Genesis 1 challenges the dignity of natural objects of thought and the ground of natural natural reverence; Genesis 2–3 challenges the human inclination to try to guide human life (solely) by our free will and our own human reason, exercised on the natural objects of thought. Ordinary human intelligence, eventually culminating in philosophy, seeks wisdom regarding how to live—that is, knowledge of good and bad—through contemplation of the nature of things. The Bible opposes, from the beginning, this intention and this possibility, first, in chapter one, by denying the dignity of the primary object of philosophy, the natural things, and second, in chapter two, by rebutting the primary intention of philosophy, guidance for life found by reason and rooted in nature. God, not nature, is divine; obedience to God, not the independent and rational pursuit of wisdom, is the true and righteous human way." See Leon Kass, "The Follies of Freedom and Reason: An Old Story," in *Freedom and the Human Person*, Richard Velkley, ed., Studies in Philosophy and the History of Philosophy Volume 48 (Washington, DC: The Catholic University of America Press, 2007), pp. 13–38; here, p. 14.

74. There are his miracles, which provide a kind of knowledge, a knowledge through sight and experience, a "knowledge" wholly unsusceptible to logic and over time standing outside reason. The knowledge of good and evil knows that experience and vision are irrational (because, although personal, they are not universal) and the voice of the knowledge of good and evil rejects the moral and theological significance of experience: see, e.g., Kant, Bultmann, Wiles, etc. What were once "proofs" of Jesus' divinity—when the miracles were seen—are now wholly outside the realm of proof.

75. The justification is this: propositions articulated through the knowledge of good and evil transition over time, and as such it is now clear to the modern conscience that no one can actually and truly blaspheme.

to think in terms of immaterial realities and to prepare the heart to love immaterial beauties.[76] Essential to expanding these capabilities is the acquisition of humility. Many of the liberal arts of the trivium and quadrivium lead the mind to think in terms of immaterial realities: geometry, astronomy, music. An ability for "thinking immaterially"—to use a "logic of immateriality"—is necessary for any advanced understanding of the doctrine of the Trinity.[77] Other forms of knowledge—geography, history, literature, medicine—enable us to better understand Scripture, which itself directs the mind and heart to immaterial realities, as well as giving us a sight of God's power and deity which have been revealed "in the things that have been made" (Rom 1:20). Literature and history reveal, through "analogy" (*Conf.* I), our own hearts to us (which should give us substantial cause for humility). The goal of this education is not to give us more facts about "the good" so that we can, statistically, make better judgments about what we recognize as the good. The goal of this education is to give our minds and hearts the "skills" necessary for knowing the invisible and immaterial Trinity, desiring that Trinity, and recognizing our need for the Trinity. Given that the goal of our life is to be with God, then our task in this life is to purify our hearts so that we might be able to see and know later what now we only understand through faith. If our goal is God as God truly exists—i.e., as the Trinity revealed through the Incarnation—then we can only be properly "formed" if we are formed towards the true God who is Trinity. Formation can never be separated from doctrine. This is what a pure "Augustinian" education would be like.[78]

There is also an unpredictable "providential" element to education that Augustine reveals in his autobiography. "Lessons" (broadly construed) can lead us with a strength and clarity beyond anything that could be expected of them in advance: the decisive role, for example, of Monica telling the young Augustine that the name of Jesus would be a part of true wisdom. There is no way to judge in advance what such sacramental facts will be for any individual, and no way to program them as such into

---

76. Again Bonhoeffer articulates this Augustinian perspective: "Just as we misunderstand the form of Christ if we take Him to be essentially the teacher of a pious and good life, so too we shall misunderstand the formation of man if we regard it as the way in which the pious life is to be attained" (Bonhoeffer, *Ethics*, 82).

77. The dogmatic logic of this is discussed in section 3 of Barnes, "Visible Christ and the Invisible Trinity," 329–55. For Augustine, real formation occurs within the life of the church: creed, Scripture, liturgy, sacraments, and the lives of the saints as exemplars.

78. It is at this moment that this essay's subtext of "Bonhoeffer as Augustinian Critic of 'Conscience'" cashes out, for while Bonhoeffer was a profound critic of the modern notion of an autonomous moral conscience, he truly had an alternative theological insight that made clear and made possible his own path as a Christian. Bonhoeffer was no quietist, no moral solipsist; he acted more wholeheartedly and decisively than many of the "prophets of conscience" among his peers. Bonhoeffer's life and death make it clear that rejecting the moral autonomy presumed in the modern notion of conscience does not reduce the Christian to passivity. Bonhoeffer's "post-moral" theology, based upon a living obedience to God, described a life for God enabled by God, and in Bonhoeffer's case, a life given up in witness to God.

formation.[79] This is the realm of God's ordering of our lives so that his call will be received efficaciously: providence and grace.

CONCLUSION: *DOMINE, NON SUM DIGNUS*

As an event within the trajectory of Second Temple theology of the messiah,[80] what is distinctive in Christian theology of the messiah is that the messiah dies as a sacrifice to redeem sinners. The sacrifice of Jesus—in both the objective and subjective genitive—saves. This sacrifice is not understood as a transitive act—as though the messiah sacrifices *something else* in a new way, except insofar as the new something that is sacrificed is himself. Jesus as new high priest is but the other side of the coin of Jesus as new oblation: the two identities are not separate realities. In the preaching of the "Christ crucified," the resurrection serves to reveal that Jesus was/is the Christ, and that his sacrifice was accepted by God. Faith means believing the testimony about the risen previously-dead Jesus, so that one knows these two facts of revelation (i.e., Jesus was/is the Christ, and that his sacrifice was accepted by God), and believing the promise that one day others will be resurrected, too. Jesus was not resurrected by God to undo his death as if that death was a sad accident that God could repair, but because of his death. If Jesus was not resurrected by God, then he was not the messiah, and his death did not affect the fundamental relationship between God and humans. That non-Christians would come to such conclusions is a tautology; that some "Christians" think that Jesus was not resurrected, that he was not the messiah, and that his death had no decisive and fundamental effect makes the continuity between such a "Christianity" and early Christianity of the same order as the continuity between modern "Druids" and the inhabitants of ancient Gaul.

Robert Daly has remarked that in the Old Testament how sacrifices worked was left to the individual to explain in his or her own mind;[81] the same seems to be true for the New Testament. Also common to both bodies of literature is the presumption that proper sacrifice "works"—it does something, somehow. Exactly what Jesus' sacrifice so efficiently works upon is not made clear, but what is clear is that it is of fundamental importance to recognize that Jesus' sacrifice did something decisive and unique. Why, exactly, dthe tenants in the parable of the landlord's son rebel against the landlord is not important—urban renewal or urban decay? What is important is that (1) the landlord's son is killed precisely because he is the landlord's son, and (2)

---

79. See Genevieve Lloyd, *Providence Lost* (Cambridge, MA: Harvard University Press, 2008).

80. I use the singular here—Second Temple *theology* of the messiah—not to say that there was only one theology of the messiah, but that a feature of Second Temple Judaism was reflection upon a messiah. Christianity is *prima facie* a theology of messiah—the Christ: identifying Jesus as the messiah is not a theology of the messiah, except insofar as the story of Jesus—the events in his life—tell us what the content of messiah is.

81. Robert Daly, *Christian Sacrifice: The Judaeo-Christian Background Before Origen* (Washington, DC: The Catholic University of America Press, 1978), p. 41.

the rebel tenants do not have the last word—they are punished. That Jesus' sacrifice did something decisive and unique is the last word: the story of that sacrifice out-narrates evil.

It was James Agee's judgment that Jesus' three hours on the cross was "but a noble and too trivial an emblem"[82] of how each human lives "crucified," and he was right in this way: any attempt to symbolize violence runs the risk of making violence banal. Agee said that rather than describe in words any real person in his or her wounded-ness, that "A piece of the body torn out by the roots might be more to the point,"[83] and I agree that violence is only properly perceived in its individuality. Attempts to make Jesus' suffering and death symbolic render that suffering and death banal; such attempts seek to control that violence and end up treating Jesus' suffering like a video game in which our score progresses as we move the content of that suffering through levels of meaning. This is modern Docetism and Gnosticism combined: to imagine Jesus' death as though its truest experience lay outside of the fact that it was *his* death, his unimaginably painful and deeply humiliating death.[84] The only legitimate way in which the individuality of Jesus' death may be pre-empted is insofar as we see it as a repetition of the fundamental fact of human existence: "after the first death there is no other"[85]—for, properly speaking, our grief should already be full.[86] But even so, to see Jesus' death as such a repetition is to see it only as a human event or experience, and thus not to see it precisely as Jesus' death. To see that death fully and individually is to recognize, as the centurion witness in Mark's Gospel did, that truly this was the Son of God, and so this death was different.

For some Christian theologians, there is no Incarnation, in the sense of a pre-existent being taking flesh and dwelling amongst us. Some of these theologians might say, as the Ebionites did, that Jesus was born only as human and nothing more, though

---

82. "[S]o situated in the universe that those three hours upon the cross are but a noble and too trivial an emblem how in each individual amongst the two billion now alive and in each successive instant of the existence of each existence is. generations upon generations unceasingly crucified and is bringing forth crucifixions into their necessities and each is in the most casual of his life so mea-surelessly discredited, harmed, insulted, poisoned, cheated, as all the wrath, compassion, intelligence, power of rectification in all the reach of the future shall in the least expiate or make one ounce more light" (James Agee and Walker Evans, *Let Us Now Praise Famous Men* [1941; reprint, Boston: Hough-ton Mifflin, 1988], 100).

83. Agee and Evans, *Let Us Now Praise Famous Men*, 13.

84. For an in-depth treatment of the theological significance in the New Testament of Jesus' pain-ful and humiliating death by crucifixion, see Morna D. Hooker, *Not Ashamed of the Gospel: New Testament Interpretations of the Death of Christ* (Carlisle: Paternoster Press, 1994).

85. Dylan Thomas, "A Refusal to Mourn the Death, by Fire, of a Child in London."

86. "All that each person is, and experiences, and shall never experience, in body and in mind, all these things are differing expressions of himself and of one root, and are identical: and not one of these things nor one of these persons is ever quite to be duplicated, nor replaced, nor has it ever quite had precedent: but each is a new and incommunicably tender life, wounded in every breath, and almost as hardly killed as easily wounded: sustaining, for a while, without defense, the enormous assaults of the universe" (Agee and Evans, *Let Us Now Praise Famous Men*, 56).

at some time in his life the Spirit came into him, his consciousness was raised, and he became a world-historical figure: the perfect prophet.[87] Death remains unchanged, our mortal ontological status is unaffected, except that we now understand that the death that really matters is the death of the will, and now in this life our volition can experience a "resurrection"—i.e., a reactivation, which enables us to act in this life. If there is any "life after death," it is because the substance of consciousness—"spirit"—endures in some condition or state after the death of the body. Christ came as teacher and prophet, as a catalyst for change: the change he caused has already occurred in consciousness if we but appropriate it for ourselves. At the beginning of this article, I quoted logion 50–51 of the Gospel of Thomas: "His disciples said to him: 'When will the repose of the dead occur?' He said to them: 'This thing which you expect has come, but you do not recognize it.'" It is time, some say, to recognize that the repose of the dead—even our death—has already occurred in the enspirited mind and resurrected will. The call to action is the call to come out of the tomb, and the call to come out of the tomb is nothing else but the call to action.

Either Christianity is an idiom or its claim is absolute. If Christianity is an idiom, then there exist only "hyphenated" Christians—Christian-Democrats, Christian-Liberals, Christian-Socialists, Christian-Communists, Christian-Marxists, Christian-Kantians, or Christian-Hegelians. If Christianity is not an idiom but a belief or faith that has its own identity, then Christianity does not take its authority from its congruity with any secular moral or ethical system. If Christianity is not an idiom, then its claim upon the believer cannot be explained in any other terms than its own: the "putting on" of Christ, the unity of the believer with Christ, and the reality of existence in the body of Christ. The content and reality of Christ cannot be seen or verified from anywhere but inside. Moreover, the message of the gospel announced in the Scriptures cannot properly be understood by anyone who is not in love with the beloved. Tertullian advised his fellow Christians not to dispute Scripture with those who failed to keep faith because the Scriptures were not theirs; non-believers grasping at the meaning of the Scriptures were no more than strangers grasping at uncovering what—or rather, who—they had no right to see. Only the pure of heart could see God, and purity—it has since been said—is to will one thing: to will Christ. The Christ of a hyphenated Christian is a hyphenated Christ. If Paul said that there is neither Jew nor Greek, neither male nor female, in Christ, then in the hyphenated Christ there is only this or that, she or he: the Christian's context. To will only one object of desire, Christ, is not only to have a single will, but to have a single object of that will: a seamless Christ, one who is not given over piecemeal to claims from many utilities. When it comes to our own virtue, I think we operate largely in ignorance, although, like Socrates' interlocutors, we are attached to thinking otherwise. The truth is more like trying to build a house in pitch black. We have so little idea of who we each are, what

---

87. "Thus, Ebion, assuming that the starting point of the Son of God is entirely from Mary, produces not a man from God, but a God from man" (Hilary, *Trin.* II.4).

the consequences of each action are, and how to accomplish what we think it is we want to accomplish. The great sin is in defining the value of one's thoughts and actions according to a standard that purchases clarity by removing God—in particular, removing God from Christ. I think that what really counts about God being omniscient is that he can see the depths of our ignorance and judge us according to the appropriate mercy or justice. I suspect that the greatest evils we face may be those we are least aware of and less consciously engaged with, and that our acts of greatest virtue are almost invisible to us.[88]

When I worked with the profoundly retarded, people would "ooh" and "ahh" over how kind and generous that was of me. I knew that there was no virtue involved on my part. These people could just as well have been praising my virtue because I was tall or had a beard. I saw no difference in the degree or character of choice involved in working with the retarded, drinking a coke, or watching a movie.[89] Each choice involves responding to a desire for these "goods"—being with and helping the profoundly retarded,[90] drinking a Coca-Cola, or watching a movie—and the fact that I have these desires to fulfill or not is through no choice or act of my own (or at least no conscious choice): there never was a day when I decided, "I should make myself enjoy being with the profoundly retarded," or "I should make myself enjoy Coca-Cola instead of Pepsi." There may be a higher good to "being with the profoundly retarded" over "drinking Coca-Cola," but the range is not something I decided had to happen.[91]

My faith is that God will be a good judge, and whatever he decides I deserve for this life, it will be the right decision. I trust him. I try to keep the number of things I might fry for to a minimum. Meanwhile, points of clarity are few. Everything now

88. This sensibility of mine turns out to be in intuitive agreement with Bonhoeffer's, who turns it into a positive statement about "overcoming the knowledge of good and evil" gained in (and coincident with) the fall. Bonhoeffer interprets Matt 6:3 (when giving alms, the left hand should not know what the right hand does) as meaning that Jesus "forbids the man who does good to know of this good" (Bonhoeffer, *Ethics*, 38). Moreover, "[t]he parable of the last judgment (Matt 25:31ff) completes and concludes what has so far been said. When Jesus sits in judgment His own will not know that they have given Him food and drink and clothing and comfort. They will not know their own goodness; Jesus will disclose it to them" (Bonhoeffer, *Ethics*, 39).

89. Originally, I would have said that if God knows why one of those three has to do with me being "good" while the other two don't, it cannot be because there was some discernable difference in my experience in the quality of my will in doing any one of the three. Even though "helping the retarded" is a kind of immaterial good, it is experienced as a material action. However, I now like to think that I have learned to distinguish, albeit weakly, differences in my experience of my will in doing any one of the three, but it remains true that discerning differences among types of will "for" a kind of good is much easier when the "*willing for*" involves a simultaneous rejection of another object.

90. It is more gentle to say "high functioning special needs" rather than "mildly retarded," but it is not more gentle to say "[very] low functioning special needs" rather than "profoundly retarded." Besides, I have never had much truck with Wolf Wolfsenberger, whose philosophy seemed to me to be about *using the retarded* for social ends.

91. There may be a "higher good" to drinking Coca-Cola and watching a movie: this pleasurable attachment to materialism rebuts fascisms of the left and right (see n40). (It constitutes a perspective. See Ayres, *Nicaea and Its Legacy*, vii.)

is tentative, through a glass darkly. We must try to be good, because to do otherwise would be a sin against hope. But we must also understand that the kingdom has not yet been handed over; it is being gathered. And we are a pitiful lot—which is why it is good that we receive pity.[92]

92. The essay is dedicated to the memory of Iris Chang, Michael Kelly, and Phil Hartmann.

Bibliography

Abramowski, Luise. "Marius Victorinus, Porphyrius und die römischcen Gnostiker." *ZNTW* 74 (1983) 108–28.

Agee, James, and Evans Walker. *Let Us Now Praise Famous Men*. Boston: Houghton Mifflin, 1988.

Albrecht-Carrie, Rene. *The Meaning of the First World War*. Englewood Cliffs: Prentice-Hall, 1965.

Alexander of Alexandria. "Letter to Alexander of Thessalonica." In *The Trinitarian Controversy*, edited and translated by William G. Rusch, 33–44. Sources of Early Christian Thought. Philadelphia: Fortress, 1980.

Altaner, Berthold. *Kleine Patristische Schriften*. Berlin: Akademie-Verlag, 1967.

Ambrose of Milan. *On the Holy Spirit*. CSEL 79; NPNF II/10 and FotC 44.

Anscombe, G.E.M. *The Collected Philosophical Papers of G.E.M. Anscombe*, vol. 3: *Ethics, Religion and Politics*. Minneapolis: University of Minnesota Press, 1981.

Arnold, Johannes. "Begriff und heilsökonomische Bedeutung der göttlichen Sendungen in Augustinus *De Trinitate*." *RecAug* 25 (1991) 3–69.

Augustine of Hippo. *Answer to Maximinus the Arian*. WSA I/18.

———. *The City of God against the Pagans*. Translated by R.W. Dyson. Cambridge: Cambridge University Press, 1998.

———. *Debate with Maximinus*. In *Arianism and Other Heresies*. WSA I/18.

———. *Eighty-Three Different Questions*. FotC 70.

———. *Letters*. FotC 20.

———. *Letters 83–130*. FotC 18.

———. *Against Faustus the Manichee*. NPNF I/4.

———. *The Nature of the Good* (*De Natura Boni*). In *Earlier Writings*, edited and translated by John H.S. Burleigh, 326–48. Philadelphia: Westminster John Knox Press, 1953.

———. *On Free Will* (*De Libro Arbitrio*). In *Earlier Writings*, edited and translated by John H.S. Burleigh, 113–217. Philadelphia: Westminster John Knox Press, 1953.

———. *On True Religion* (*De Vera Religione*). In *Earlier Writings*, edited and translated by John H.S. Burleigh, 225–283. Philadelphia: Westminster John Knox Press, 1953.

————. *Sermons*. WSA III/1-11.

————. *To Simplician—On Various Questions* (*De Diversis Quastionibus*). In *Earlier Writings*, edited and translated by John H.S. Burleigh, 376-406. Philadelphia: Westminster John Knox Press, 1953.

————. *Tractates on the Gospel of John 55–111*. CCSL 36; FotC 90.

————. *The Trinity*. CCSL 50/50A; WSA I/5.

Ayres, Lewis. *Augustine and The Trinity*. Cambridge: Cambridge University Press, 2010.

————. "The Christological Context of Augustine's *De trinitate* XIII: Toward Relocating Books VIII–XV." *AugStud* 29 (1998) 111–39.

————. "The Discipline of Self-Knowledge in Augustine's *De Trinitate* Book X." In *The Passionate Intellect: Essays on the Transformation of Classical Traditions Presented to I.G. Kidd*, 261–96. London: Transaction, 1995.

————. "The Grammar of Augustine's Trinitarian theology." In *Augustine and His Critics*, edited by Robert Dodaro and George Lawless, 56–71. London: Routledge, 1999.

————. *Nicaea and Its Legacy: An Approach to Fourth-Century Trinitarian Theology*. Oxford: Oxford University Press, 2004.

————. "'Remember That You Are Catholic' (*Serm.* 52.2): Augustine on the Unity of the Triune God." *JECS* 8 (2000) 39–82.

Babcock, William. "Sin and Punishment: The Early Augustine on Evil." In *Collectanea Augustiniana. Augustine: Presbyter Factus Sum*, edited by Joseph Lienhard et al., 235–48. New York: Peter Lang, 1993.

Balthasar, Hans Urs von. *Présence et pensée: Essai sur la philosophie religieuse de Grégoire de Nysse*. Paris: Beauchesne, 1942.

Bardy, Gustave. "L'occident et les documents de la controverse arienne." *Revue des sciences religieuses* 20 (1940) 28–63.

Barnes, Michel René. "The Arians of Book V, and the Genre of *de Trinitate*." *JThS* ns 44 (1993) 185–95.

————. "The Background and Use of Eunomius' Causal Language." In *Arianism after Arius: Essays on the Development of Fourth Century Trinitarian Conflicts*, edited by Michel R. Barnes and Daniel H. Williams, 217–36. Edinburgh: T&T Clark, 1993.

————. "The Beginning and End of Early Christian Pneumatology." *Augustinian Studies* 39 (2008) 169–86.

————. "De Régnon Reconsidered." *Augustinian Studies* 26 (1995) 51–79.

————. "Eunomius of Cyzicus and Gregory of Nyssa: Two Traditions of Transcendent Causality." *Vigiliae Christianae* 52 (1998) 59–87.

————. "Exegesis and Polemic in *de Trinitate I*." *Augustinian Studies* 30 (1999) 43–59.

————. "The Fourth Century as Trinitarian Canon." In *Christian Origins: Theology, Rhetoric and Community*, edited by L. Ayres and G. Jones, 47–67. London: Routledge, 1998.

————. "One Nature, One Power: Consensus Doctrine in Pro-Nicene Polemic." *Studia Patristica* 29 (1997) 205–23.

————. *The Power of God: Dunamis in Gregory of Nyssa's Trinitarian Theology*. Washington, DC: Catholic University of America Press, 2001.

————. "Rereading Augustine's Theology of the Trinity." In *The Trinity: An Interdisciplinary Symposium on the Trinity*, edited by Stephen T. Davis et al., 145–76. Oxford: Oxford University Press, 2000.

————. "The Visible Christ and the Invisible Trinity: Mt. 5:8 in Augustine's Trinitarian Theology of 400," *Modern Theology* 19 (2003) 329-355.

———. "The Use of Augustine in Contemporary Trinitarian Theology." *Theological Studies* 56 (1995) 237–51.

———. "*De Trinitate* VI and VII: Augustine and the Limits of Nicene Orthodoxy," Augustinian Studies 38 (2007) 189-202.

———. "Ebion at the Barricades: Moral Narrative and Post-Christian Catholic Theology," *Modern Theology* 26 (2010) 511–548.

———. "Snowden's Secret: Gregory of Nyssa on Passion and Death." In A Man of the Church. Honoring the Theology, Life, and Witness of Ralph Del Colle, edited by Michel René Barnes, 107–122. Eugene OR: Wipf & Stock, 2012.

Bell, David. "Esse, Vivere, Intelligere: The Noetic Triad and The Image of God." *Recherches de Theologie ancienne et Medievale* 50 (1985) 5–43.

Berrouard, Marie-François. "La date des *Tractatus I-LIV in Iohannis Evangelium* de sain Augustin." *RecAug* 7 (1971) 105–68.

Bettenson, Henry. *The Later Christian Fathers*. London: Oxford University Press, 1970.

Bonhoeffer, Dietrich. *Christ the Center*. New York: HarperCollins, 1978.

———. *Creation and Fall—Temptation: Two Biblical Studies*. New York: MacMillan, 1967.

———. *Ethics*. New York: Simon & Schuster, 1995.

Bourassa, F. "Théologie trinitaire chez saint Augustin." *Gregorianum* 58 (1977) 675–725.

Boyer, C. "L'image de la Trinité synthèse de la pensée augustienne." *Gregorianum* 27 (1946) 173–99; 333–52.

Brown, David. *The Divine Trinity*. La Salle: Open Court, 1985.

Bruce, F.F. "The Holy Spirit in the Acts of the Apostles." *Interpretation* 27 (1973) 166–83.

Buckley, Francis J. *Christ and the Church according to Gregory of Elvira*. Rome: Gregorian University Press, 1964.

Burrell, David B. *Deconstructing Theodicy: Why Job Has Nothing to Say to the Puzzle of Suffering*. Grand Rapids: Brazos, 2008.

Cavadini, John C. "The Darkest Enigma. Reconsidering the Self in Augustine's Thought," *Augustinian Studies* 38 (2007) 119–132.

———. "The Quest for Truth in Augustine's *De Trinitate*." *TS* 58 (1997) 429–40.

———. "The Structure and Intention of Augustine's *De Trinitate*." *AugStud* 23 (1992) 103–23.

Chevalier, Irenée. *S. Augustin et la Pensée Grecque: les relations trinitaires*. Fribourg en Suisse: Librairie de l'Université, 1940.

Cipriani, Nello. "La Fonti Christiane della Dottrina Trinitaria nei primi Dialoghi di S. Agostino." *Augustinianum* 34 (1994) 253–312.

Clement of Alexandria. *Stromateis* 5 and 7. SC 278 and 248. ANF 2 and F. J. A. Hort and J. B. Mayor. *Clement of Alexandria, Miscellanies Book VII. The Greek Text With Introduction, Translation, Notes, Dissertation and Indices*. Cambridge: Cambridge University Press, 1902/2010.

Colish, Marcia L. *The Stoic Tradition from Antiquity to the Early Middle Ages*. Leiden: Brill, 1985.

Congar, Yves. *I Believe in the Holy Spirit*, vol. 3. New York: Seabury, 1983.

Conti, Marco. *The Life and Works of Potamius of Lisbon*. Steenbrugis: Brepols, 1998.

Crowe, Frederick E. *The Doctrine of the Most Holy Trinity*. Willowdale: Regis College, 1965/66.

D'Ales, R.P. *Étude sur la théologie romaine au milieu du IIIe siècle*. Paris: Gabriel Beauchesne, 1925.

Daley, Brian. "The Giant's Twin Substances: Ambrose and the Christology of Augustine's *Contra sermonem Arianorum.*" In *Augustine: Presbyter Factus Sum*, edited by Joseph T. Lienhard et al., 477–95. New York: Peter Lang, 1993.

Daly, Robert. *Christian Sacrifice: The Judaeo-Christian Background before Origen.* Washington, DC: Catholic University of America Press, 1978.

Damasus of Rome. *Epistulae.* For details of editions, see *CPL* 1633.

Daniélou, Jean. *Gospel Message and Hellenistic Culture.* History of Early Christian Doctrine 2. Translated by John Austin Baker. London: Darton, Longman & Todd, 1973.

———. *The Origins of Latin Christianity.* History of Early Christian Doctrine 3.Translated by David Smith and John Austin Baker. London: Darton, Longman & Todd, 1977.

———. *Platonisme et théologie mystique.* Paris: Aubier, 1944.

DelCogliano, Mark. "Eusebian Theologies of the Son as the Image of God before 341." *JECS* 14 (2006) 459–84.

Di Berardino, A., and B. Studer, eds. *History of Theology I: The Patristic Period.* Translated by M.J. O'Connell. Collegeville: Liturgical, 1997.

Dillon, John. "'A Kind of Warmth': Some Reflections on the Concept of 'Grace' in the Neoplatonic Tradition." In *The Passionate Intellect: The Transformation of Classical Traditions*, edited by Lewis Ayres, 323–32. Piscataway: Transaction, 1995.

———. "Logos and Trinity: Patterns of Platonist Influence on Early Christianity." In *The Philosophy in Christianity*, edited by Godfrey Vesey, 1–14. Cambridge: Cambridge University Press, 1989.

———. *The Middle Platonists: 80 BC to 220 AD.* London: Duckworth, 1977.

Doignon, Jean. "Une exégèse d'Hilaire de Poitiers sur le désir de voir la face de Dieu (Hil., In Psalm 118, 8, 7/8." *Freiburge Zeitschrift fur Philosophie und Theologie* 41 (1994) 542–45.

Doull, James. "What Is Augustinian 'Sapientia'?" *Dionysius* 12 (1988) 61–67.

Drobner, Hubertus R. "Grammatical Exegesis and Christology in St. Augustine." *SP* 18 (1990) 49–63.

———. *Person-Exegese und Christologie bei Augustinus: zur Herkunft der Formel Una Persona.* Leiden: Brill, 1986.

Du Roy, Olivier. *L'Intelligence de la foi en la trinité selon saint Augustin.* Paris: Études Augustiniennes, 1966.

Edwards, Mark. *Aristotle and Early Christian Thought.* London: Routledge, 2020.

———. "Porphyry and the Intelligible Triad." *Journal of Hellenic Studies* 110 (1990) 14–25.

Ehrman, Bart D. *God's Problem: How the Bible Fails to Answer Our Most Important Question—Why We Suffer.* New York: Harper, 2008.

Ellul, Jacques. *The Subversion of Christianity.* Translated by Geoffrey W. Bromiley. Grand Rapids: Eerdmans, 1986.

Eunomius of Cyzicus. *The Extant Works.* Edited and translated by Richard P. Vaggione. Oxford: Clarendon, 1987.

Eusebius of Caesarea. *Against Marcellus and On Ecclesiastical Theology.* Translated by Kelly McCarthy Spoerl and Markus Vinzent. FotC 135. Washington DC: Catholic University of America Press, 2017.

Festugière, R.P. *La Révélation d'Hermès Trismégiste.* 4 vols. Paris: Societe d'Editions des Belles Lettres, 1944–45.

Field, Lester L. *On the Communion of Damasus and Meletius: Fourth-Century Synodal Formulae in the Codex Veronensis LX.* Toronto: Pontifical Institute of Mediaeval Studies, 2004.

Fossum, Jarl. "The Image of the Invisible God: 1 Col. 15–18a, Jewish Mysticism and Gnosticism." *New Testament Studies* 35 (1989) 183–201.

Gehrke, Jason. *From Power to Virtue: The Early Latin Theology of Lactantius.* Oxford: Oxford University Press, forthcoming.

———. "Lactantius's Power Theology." *Nova et Vetera* 17 (2019) 683–715.

Gersh, Stephen. *Middle Platonism and Neoplatonism: The Latin Tradition.* 2 vols. Notre Dame: University of Notre Dame Press, 1986.

Gillette, Gertrude. "Purity of Heart in St. Augustine." In *Purity of Heart in Early Ascetic and Monastic Literature*, edited by Harriet A. Luckman and Linda Kulzer, 161–95. Collegeville: Liturgical, 1999.

Ginoulhiac, J.M. *Histoire du dogme catholique.* 2nd ed. Paris: Auguste Durand Librarie, 1866.

Golitzin, A. "'The demons suggest an illusion of God's glory in a form': Controversy over the Divine Body and Vision of Glory in some late Fourth, early Fifth Century Monastic Literature." *Scrinium* 3 (2007) 49–82.

González, Severino. "La identidad de operación en las obras exteriores y la unidad de la naturaleza divina en la-teologia trinitaria de S. Gregoria de Nisa." *Gregorianum* 19 (1938) 280–301.

Green, J.D. *"Augustinianism": Studies in the Process of Spiritual Transvaluation.* Leuven: Peeters, 2007.

Gregg, Robert C., and Dennis E. Groh. *Early Arianism: A View of Salvation.* Philadelphia: Fortress, 1981.

Gregory of Elvira. *De fide,* CCSL 69.

Griffe, Elie. *La Gaule Chrétienne à l'époque romaine,* V. I *Des Origines Chrétiennes à la fin du IVe siècle.* Paris: Editions A. et J. Picard & Co., 1947.

Gruenwald, Ithamar. "Knowledge and Vision." *Israel Oriental Studies* 3 (1973) 63–107.

Gryson, Roger, ed. and trans. *Scolies Ariennes sur le Concile d'Aquilée.* Sources Chrétiennes 267. Paris: Les Editions du Cerf, 1980.

Gunton, Colin E. "Augustine, the Trinity and the Theological Crisis of the West." *Scottish Journal of Theology* 43 (1990) 33–58.

Hadot, Pierre. "Etre, Vie, Pensée chez Plotin et avant Plotin." In vol. 5, *Entretiens sur l'antiquité classique,* 107–57. Geneva-Vandeouvres: Fondation Hardt, 1960.

Halleux, André de. "Hypostase et personne dans la formation du dogme trinitaire (ca. 375–81)." *Revue d'Histoire Ecclesiastique* 79 (1984) 313–69, 625–70.

———. "Personnalisme ou essentialisme trinitaire chez les Pères cappadociens?" *Revue theologique de Louvain* 17 (1986) 129–55, 265–92.

Hankinson, Robert J. "Galen and the Ontology of Power." *British Journal for the History of Philosophy* 22 (2014) 951–73.

Hanson, R.P.C. "Did Origen Apply the Word ὁμοούσιος to the Son?" In *Epektasis,* edited by Jacques Fontaine and Charles Kannengiesser, 293–303. Paris: Beauchesne, 1972.

———. *The Search for the Christian Doctrine of God.* Edinburgh: T&T Clark, 1988.

Harnack, Adolph. *History of Dogma.* Translated by Neil Buchanan. 4 vols. New York: Dover, 1960.

Hart, David B. "Christ and Nothing." *First Things* 136 (October 2003) 47–57.

Heine, Ronald E. "The Christology of Callistus." *JThS* ns 49 (1998) 56–91.

———. *Perfection in the Virtuous Life.* Cambridge: Philadelphia Patristic Foundation, 1975.

Hengel, Martin. *Acts and the History of Earliest Christianity.* Translated by John Bowden. Philadelphia: Fortress, 1979.

Henry, Paul. "The 'Adversus Arium' of Marius Victorinus: the First Systematic Exposition of the Doctrine of the Trinity." *JThS* ns 1 (1950) 42–55.

———. *Plotin et l'Occident*. Louvain: Spicilegium Sacrum Lovaniense, 1934

Hilary of Poitiers. *In Matthaeum*. In *Sur Matthieu*, edited and translated by Jean Doignon, 126–27. Sources Chrétiennes 254. Paris: Editions du Cerf, 1978; FotC 125.

Hill, Edmund. "Karl Rahner's 'Remarks on the Dogmatic Treatise De Trinitate and St. Augustine." *AugStud* 2 (1971) 67–80.

———. *The Mystery of the Trinity*. London: Geoffrey Chapman, 1985.

———. "St. Augustine's *De Trinitate*: The Doctrinal Significance of its Structure." *Revue des Études Augustiniennes* 19 (1973) 277–86.

Hippolyte, Jean. *Genesis and Structure of Hegel's Phenomenology of Spirit*. Translated by Samuel Cherniak and John Heckman. Evanston: Northwestern University Press, 1974.

———. *Logic and Existence*. Translated by Lawrence Taylor and Amit Sen. Albany: State University of New York Press, 1997.

———. *Studies on Marx and Hegel*. Translated by John O'Neill. New York: Harper Torchbooks, 1969.

Hooker, Morna D. *Not Ashamed of the Gospel: New Testament Interpretations of the Death of Christ*. Carlisle: Paternoster, 1994.

Horst, Pieter W. van der. "'The Finger of God': Miscellaneous Notes on Luke 11:20 and its Umwelt." In *Sayings of Jesus: Canonical and Non-Canonical. Essays in Honour of Tjitze Baarda*, edited by W.L. Petersen et al., 89–104. Leiden: Brill, 1997.

Inwood, Brad. *Ethics and Human Action in Early Stoicism*. Oxford: Clarendon, 1985.

Jeanotte, Henri. *Le Psautier de saint Hilaire de Poitiers*. Paris: Gabalda, 1917.

Jenson, Robert W. *The Triune Identity*. Philadelphia: Fortress, 1982.

Jordan, Mark. D. "Words and Word: Incarnation and Signification in Augustine's *De Doctrina Christiana*." *AugStud* 11 (1980) 177–96.

Kass, Leon. "The Follies of Freedom and Reason: An Old Story." In *Freedom and the Human Person*, edited by Richard Velkley, 13–38. Washington, DC: Catholic University of America Press, 2007.

Kearsley, Roy. *Tertullian's Theology of Divine Power*. Milton Keynes: Paternoster, 1999.

Kelly, J.N.D. *Early Christian Creeds*. 3rd ed. London: Longman, 1986.

———. *Early Christian Doctrines*. 5th ed. London: Longman, 1977.

Kleinman, Arthur. "'Everything that Really Matters': Social Suffering, Subjectivity, and the Remaking of Human Experience in a Disordering World," *HTR* 90 (1997) 315–35.

Kolakowski, Leszek. *God Owes Us Nothing*. Chicago: University of Chicago Press, 1995.

Kopecek, Thomas A. *A History of Neo-Arianism*. 2 vols. Cambridge: Philadelphia Patristic Foundation, 1979.

Lactantius. *Diviniae institutiones*, CSEL 19; Lactantius, *Divine Institutes*, translated by Anthony Bowen and Peter Garnsey. Translated Texts for Historians. Liverpool: Liverpool University Press, 2004.

LaCugna, Catherine Mowry. *God for Us*. San Francisco: Harper, 1991.

Lafont, G. *Peut-on connaître Dieu en Jésus-Christ?* Paris: Cerf, 1969.

Larcher, Chrysostome. *Études sur le Livre de La Sagesse*. Paris: J. Gabalda, 1969.

Lavaud, Laurent. "Substance et movement: Marius Victorinus et l'héritage plotiinien." *Les Etudes Philosophiques* 101 (2012) 163–80.

Lebreton, Jules. "Saint Augustin théologien de la trinité. Son exégèse des théophanies." *Studi Agostiniani* 2 (1931) 821–36.

Legrand, Louis. *La Notion philosophique de la Trinité chez Saint Augustin*. Paris: Editions de l'Oeuvre d' auteuil, 1931.

Le Guillou, M.-J. "Réflexions sur la théologie trinitaire à propos de quelques livres anciens et récents." *Istina* 17 (1972) 457–64.

Lienhard, Joseph T. "The Arian Controversy: Some Categories Reconsidered." *TS* 48 (1987) 415–36.

———. *Contra Marcellum: Marcellus of Ancyra and Fourth-Century Theology*. Washington, DC: Catholic University of America Press, 1999.

———. "*Ousia* and *Hypostasis*: The Cappadocian Settlement and the Theology of 'One Hypostasis.'" *Trinity* (1999) 99–122.

Lilla, Mark. *The Stillborn God*. New York: Alfred A. Knopf, 2007.

Lloyd, Genevieve. *Providence Lost*. Cambridge: Harvard University Press, 2008.

Logan, A.H.B. "Marcellus of Ancyra and the Councils of AD 325: Antioch, Ancyra, and Nicaea." *JThS ns* 43 (1992) 428–46.

Lossky, Vladimir. *The Mystical Theology of the Eastern Church*. Cambridge and London: James Clark, 1973.

Louth, Andrew. "The Use of the Term 'idios' in Alexandrian Theology from Alexander to Cyril." *SP* 19 (1989) 198–202.

Lubac, Henri de. *Augustinianism and Modern Theology*. Translated by Lancelot Sheppard. London: G. Chapman, 1969.

Mackey, James P. *The Christian Experience of God as Trinity*. London: SCM, 1983.

MacKinnon, Donald M. "Tillich, Frege, Kittel: Some Reflections on a Dark Theme." In vol. 5, *Explorations in Theology*, 129–37. London: SCM, 1979.

Madec, Goulven. "Christus, scientia et sapientia nostra. Le principe de cohérence de la doctrine augustinienne." *RecAug* 10 (1975) 77–85.

Majercik, Ruth. *The Chaldean Oracles, Text, Translation and Commentary*. Leiden: Brill, 1989.

Malet, Andre. *Personne et Amour dans la theologie trinitaire de saint Thomas d'Aquin*. Paris: Vrin, 1956.

Mali, Franz. Das "*Opus imperfectum in Matthaeum*" *und sein Verhaltnis zu den Matthauskommentaren von Origenes und Hieronymus*. Insbruck: Tyrolia-Verlag, 1991.

Manchester, Peter. "The Noetic Triad in Plotinus, Marius Victorinus, and Augustine." In *Neoplatonism and Gnosticism*, edited by R. Wallis and J. Bregman, 207–22. Albany: State University of New York, 1992.

Margerie, Bertrand de. *La Trinité chrétienne dans l'histoire*. Paris: Beauchesne, 1975.

Marius Victorinus. *Adversus Arium*, etc. CSEL 83; FotC 69.

Markschies, Christoph. "Was ist latinischer 'Neunizanismus'?" *Zeitschrift fur Antikes Christentum* 1 (1997) 73–95.

Markus, Robert A. "Marius Victorinus and Augustine." In *Cambridge History of Later Greek and Early Medieval Philosophy*, edited by A.H. Armstrong, 327–419. Cambridge: Cambridge University Press, 1970.

———. "Trinitarian Theology and the Economy." *JThS ns* 9 (1958) 89–102.

Martland, T.R. "A Study of Cappadocian and Augustinian Trinitarian Methodology." *Anglican Theological Review* 47 (1965) 252–63.

Mathewes, Charles T. *Evil and the Augustinian Tradition*. Cambridge: Cambridge University Press, 2001.

McFadden, William. "The Exegesis of 1 Cor. 1:24, 'Christ the Power of God and the Wisdom of God until the Arian Controversy.'" Diss., Pontifical Gregorian University, 1963.

Meslin, Michel. *Les ariens d'Occident 335–430*. Paris: Éditions du Seuil, 1967.

Milbank, John. "Sacred Triads: Augustine and the Indo-European Soul." *Modern Theology* 13 (1997) 451–74.

Miller, Mary William, ed. and trans. *Rufini Presbyteri—Liber De Fide*. Washington, DC: The Catholic University of America Press, 1964.

Moltmann, Jürgen. *History and the Triune God*. London: SCM, 1991.

Muller, Earl C. *Trinity and Marriage in Paul*. New York: Peter Lang, 1990.

Nemesius of Emesa. *On the Nature of Man*. In *Cyril of Jerusalem and Nemesius of Emesa*, edited by William Telfer, 224–453. Library of Christian Classics 4. London: SCM, 1955.

Neske, Gunther, and Emil Kettering. *Martin Heidegger and National Socialism*. Translated by Lisa Harris. New York: Paragon, 1990.

Nicetas of Remesiana. *Competentibus ad baptismum instructionis*. A. E. Burn, *Nicetas of Remesiana*. Cambridge: Cambridge University Press, 1905; FotC 7.

Noll, Mark. "The Ethics of Being a Theologian." *Chronicle of Higher Education* (July 27, 2009).

Novatian. *De trinitate*. CCSL 4; FotC 67.

O'Connell, Robert. *The Origin of the Soul in St. Augustine's Later Works*. New York: Fordham University Press, 1987.

Odier, Charles. *Anxiety and Magic Thinking*. Translated by Marie-Louis Schoelly and Mary Jane Sherfey. New York: International Universities Press, 1974.

O'Donnell, James. *Augustine: The Confessions*. 3 vols. Oxford: Clarendon, 1992.

O'Donnell, John J. *Trinity and Temporality: The Christian Doctrine of God in the Light of Process Theology and the Theology of Hope*. Oxford: Oxford University, 1983.

O'Leary, Joseph. "Dieu-esprit et Dieu-Substance Chez Saint Augustin." *Recherches de Science Religieuse* 69 (1981) 357–90.

O'Meara, John J. "St. Augustine's View of Authority and Reason in A. D. 386." *Irish Theological Quarterly* 18 (1951) 338–46.

Origen of Alexandria. *Commentary on John*. SC 120, 157, 222, 290, 385; FotC 80.

———. *Dialogue with Heraclides*. SC 67.

———. *On First Principles*. SC 252, 253, 268, 269, & 312. Translated by Henry Butterworth. Gloucester: Peter Smith, 1973.

Ott, Hugo. *Martin Heidegger: A Political Life*. Translated by Allan Blunden. New York: Basic Books, 1993.

Paissac, Henri. *Théologie du Verbe: Saint Augustin et Saint Thomas*. Paris: Les Editions du Cerf, 1951.

Pannenberg, Wolfhart. *Revelation as History*. London: Sheed & Ward, 1969.

Parvis, Sara. *Marcellus of Ancyra and the Lost Years of the Arian Controversy 325–345*. Oxford: Oxford University Press, 2006.

Peck, A.L. "Anaxagoras: Predication as a Problem in Physics." *Classical Quarteiburly* 25 (1931) 27–37, 112–20.

Pelikan, Jaroslav. "'Canonica regula': the Trinitarian Hermeneutics of Augustine." In *Augustine: Second Founder of the Faith. Collectanea Augustiniana*, edited by J. Schnaubelt and F. van Fleteren, 329–43. New York: Peter Lang, 1990.

Peters, F.E. *Greek Philosophical Terms*. New York: New York University Press, 1967.

Petit, Alan. "Existence et manifestation: Le Johannine platonicien de Marius Victorinus." *Les Études Philosophiques* 101 (2012) 152–62.

Phoebadius of Agen. *Contra Arianos*. CCSL 65.

Potamius of Lisbon—See Conti, Marco

Quasten, Johannes. *Patrology*. Edited by Angelo Di Berardino. Translated by Placid Solari. 4 vols. Westminster: Christian Classics, 1991.

———. *Patrology: The Golden Age of Greek Patristic Literature*. 4th ed. Antwerp: Spectrum, 1975.

Quispel, Gilles. "Ezekiel 1:26 in Jewish Mysticism and Gnosis." *VigChr* 34 (1980) 1–13.

Régnon, Theodore de, SJ. *Banes et Molina: Histoire, Doctrines, Critique metaphysique*. Paris: V. Retaux, 1883

———. *Études de théologie positive sur la Sainte Trinité*, four volumes bound as three. Paris: Victor Retaux, 1892/1898.

———. *Métaphysique des causes, d'après Saint Thomas et Albert le Grand*. Paris: Retaux-Bray, 1886.

Remy, G. *Le Christ médiateur dans l'oeuvre de saint Augustin*. 2 vols. Paris: Librarie H. Champion, 1979.

Rettig, John, trans. *Tractates on John 1–10*. Fathers of the Church 88. Washington, DC: Catholic University of America Press, 1988.

Rey-Mermet, Theodule. *Moral Choices: The Moral Theology of Saint Alphonsus Liguori*. Translated by Paul Laverdure. Liguori: Liguori, 1998.

Ringgren, Helmer. *Word and Wisdom: Studies in the Hypostatization of Divine Qualities and Functions in the Ancient Middle East*. Lund: Hakan Ohlssons Boktryckeri, 1947.

Rist, John. *Augustine: Ancient Philosophy Baptized*. Cambridge: Cambridge University Press, 1994.

Robb, Fiona. "The Fourth Lateran Council's Definition of Trinitarian Orthodoxy." *Journal of Ecclesiastical History* 48 (1997) 22–43.

Rondet, H. "Rufin le Syrien et le Liber de Fide." *Augustiniana* 22 (1972) 531–39.

Rose, H.J. *A Handbook of Latin Literature from the Earliest Times to the Death of St Augustine*. London: Methuen, 1936.

Rufinus "the Syrian." *De fide*. Mary W. Miller, *Rufini presbyteri Liber de Fide: a Critical Text and Translation with Introduction and Commentary*. Washington DC: Catholic University of America Press, 1964.

Rusch, William. *The Trinitarian Controversy*. Philadelphia: Fortress, 1980.

Scheel, Otto. *Die Anschauung Augustins uber Christi Person und Werk*. Tubingen: Verlag von J.C.B. Mohr, 1901.

Schindler, Alfred. *Wort und Analogie in Augustins Trinitatslehre*. Tubingen: Mohr, 1965.

Schmaus, Michael. *Die psychologische Trinitatslehre des heiligen Augustinus*. Munster: Aschendorff, 1927.

Segal, Alan. *Two Powers in Heaven: Early Rabbinic Reports About Christianity and Gnosticism*. Leiden: Brill, 1977.

Shell, Susan Meld. *Kant and the Limits of Autonomy*. Cambridge: Harvard University Press, 2009.

Souilhe, Jean. *Étude sur le terme Dunamis dans les dialogues de platon*. Paris: Librairie Felix Alcan, 1919.

Spoerl, Kelley McCarthy. "Two Early Nicenes: Eutathius of Antioch and Marcellus of Ancyra." In *The Shadow of the Incarnation*, edited by Peter W. Martens, 121–48. Notre Dame: Notre Dame of University Press, 2008.

Stead, G. Christopher. *Divine Substance*. Oxford: Oxford University Press, 1977.

———. "The Platonism of Arius." *JThS ns* 15 (1964) 16–31.

Stepanich, M.F. *Christology of Zeno of Verona*. Washington DC: Catholic University of America Press, 1947.

Sternhell, Zeev. *Neither Right Nor Left: Fascist Ideology in France*. Translated by David Maisel. Princeton: Princeton University Press, 1986/1991.

Strange, Steven K. "Plotinus on the Articulation of Being." *Society for Ancient Greek Philosophy Newsletter* (1989) 155.

Studer, Basil. "Augustin et la foi de Nicée." *Recherches Augustiniennes* 19 (1984) 133–54.

———. *The Grace of Christ and the Grace of God in Augustine of Hippo: Christocentrism or Theocentrism?* Collegeville: Liturgical, 1997.

———. "History and Faith in Augustine's *de Trinitate*." *Augustinian Studies* 28 (1997) 7–50.

———. *Zur Theophanie-Exegese Augustins*. Roman: Liberia Herder, 1971.

Sullivan, John Edward. *The Image of God. The Doctrine of Saint Augustine and its Influence*. Dubuque IO: The priory Press, 1963.

Sumruld, William A. *Augustine and the Arians*. Selinsgrove: Susquehanna University Press, 1994.

Surin, Kenneth. *Theology and the Problem of Evil*. Oxford: Blackwell, 1986.

"The Synodal Letter of the Council of Antioch." In *The Trinitarian Controversy*, edited and translated by William G. Rusch, 45–48. Sources of Early Christian Thought. Philadelphia: Fortress, 1980.

Tavard, Georges. "The Christological Tradition of the Latin Fathers." *Dialog* 18 (1979) 265–70.

Tertullian of Carthage. *Treatise against Praxeas*. Translated and edited by Ernest Evans, with commentary. Bilingual ed. Eugene, OR: Wipf and Stock, 2011.

TeSelle, Eugene. *Augustine the Theologian*. New York: Herder & Herder, 1970.

———. "Rufinus the Syrian, Caelestius, and Pelagius." *AugStud* 3 (1972) 61–65.

Teske, Roland, trans. *Arianism and Other Heresies*. Brooklyn: New City Press, 1995.

———. "Augustine's Use of 'Substantia' in Speaking About God." *Modern Schoolman* 62 (1985) 147–63.

———. "St. Augustine and the Vision of God." In *Collectanea Augustiniana. Augustine: Mystic and Mystagogue*, edited by F. Van Fleteren et al., 287–308. New York: Peter Lang, 1994.

Thistlethwaite, Susan B. "On the Trinity." *Interpretation* 45 (1991) 159–71.

Ulrich, Jorg. Ed. Phoebadius. *Contra Arianos: Streitschift Gegen die Arianer*. Freiburg: Herder, 1999.

———. "Nicaea and the West." *Vigiliae Christianae* 51 (1997) 10–24.

Van Banning, J.H.A. "Gregory the Great and the Surviving Arianism of His Time: Did He Know the *Opus Imperfectum in Matthaeum*?" *Studia Patristica* 38 (2001) 481–95.

Van der Lof, L. J. "L'exégèse exacte et objective des théophanies de l'Ancien Testament dans le 'De Trinitate.'" *Augustiniana* 14 (1984) 485–99.

Vasiliu, Anca. "L'argument de l'image dans la défense de la consubstantialité par Marius Victorinus." *Les Etudes Philosophiques* 101 (2012) 191–216.

Voelker, J. "An Anomalous Trinitarian Formula in Marius Victorinus' *Against Arius*." *Studia Patristica* 43 (2006) 517–22.

Weedman, Mark. *The Trinitarian Theology of Hilary of Poitiers*. Leiden: Brill, 2007.

Wetzel, James. *The Limits of Virtue*. Cambridge: Cambridge University Press, 1992.

Wickham, L.R. "The Syntagmation of Aetius the Anomean." *JThS* ns 19 (1968) 532–69.

Williams, Daniel H. *Ambrose of Milan and the End of the Nicene-Arian Conflicts*. Oxford: Clarendon, 1995.

———. "Defining Orthodoxy in Hilary of Poitiers' *Commentarium in Matthaeum*." *JECS* 9 (2001) 7–22.

———. "Monarchianism and Photinus of Sirmium as the Persistent Heretical Face of the Fourth Century." *Harvard Theological Review* 99 (2006) 201–20.

———. "Polemics and Politics in Ambrose of Milan's *De Fide*." *JThS* ns 46 (1995) 519–31.

Williams, Rowan. *Arius: Heresy and Tradition*. London: Darton, Longman, and Todd, 1987.

———. "The Paradoxes of Self-Knowledge in the *De trinitate*." In *Collectanea Augustiniana. Augustine: Presbyter Factus Sum*, edited by Joseph Lienhard et al., 121–34. New York: Peter Lang, 1993.

———. "'Sapientia' and the Trinity: Reflections on 'de Trinitate.'" In *Collectanea Augustiniana: Mélanges T.J. Van Bavel*, edited by B. Bruning, 317–32. Leuven: Leuven University Press, 1990.

Winkler, Gabriele. "The Antiochene Synods and the Early Armenian Creeds Including the 'Rezeptionsgeschichte' of the Synod of Antioch 341 in the Armenian Versian of the Anaphora of Bail." *Bollettino della Badia Greca Grottaferrata* 3 (2006) 275–98.

Wolin, Richard, ed. *The Heidegger Controversy: A Critical Reader*. New York: Columbia University Press, 1991.

Yannaras, Christos. *Philosophie sans rupture*. Geneva: Labor et Fides, 1986.

Zeno of Verona. *Tractates*. CCSL 22. For translation see Stepanich.

Zimmerman, Michael E. *Heidegger's Confrontation with Modernity: Technology, Politics, Art*. Bloomington: Indiana University Press, 1990.

Name and Subject Index

Name and Subject Index

302

Name and Subject Index

Scripture Index

Printed in the USA
CPSIA information can be obtained
at www.ICGtesting.com
LVHW071008221123
764538LV00061B/414